Selected Works of
William T Ziemba
A Memorial Volume

World Scientific Series in Finance

(ISSN: 2010-1082)

Published:*

Vol. 21 *Selected Works of William T. Ziemba: A Memorial Volume*
edited by Leonard MacLean (Dalhousie University, Canada) &
Sébastien Lleo (NEOMA Business School, France)

Vol. 20 *Essays on Trading Strategy*
by Graham L. Giller (Giller Investments, USA)

Vol. 19 *Adventures in Financial Data Science: The Empirical Properties of Financial and Economic Data*
Second Edition
by Graham L. Giller (Giller Investments, USA)

Vol. 18 *Sports Analytics*
by Leonard C. Maclean (Dalhousie University, Canada) &
William T. Ziemba (University of British Columbia, Canada)

Vol. 17 *Investment in Startups and Small Business Financing*
edited by Farhad Taghizadeh-Hesary (Tokai University, Japan),
Naoyuki Yoshino (Keio University, Japan),
Chul Ju Kim (Asian Development Bank Institute, Japan),
Peter J. Morgan (Asian Development Bank Institute, Japan) &
Daehee Yoon (Korea Credit Guarantee Fund, South Korea)

Vol. 16 *Cultural Finance: A World Map of Risk, Time and Money*
by Thorsten Hens (University of Zurich, Switzerland),
Marc Oliver Rieger (University of Trier, Germany) &
Mei Wang (WHU – Otto Beisheim School of Management, Germany)

*To view the complete list of the published volumes in the series, please visit:
www.worldscientific.com/series/wssf

World Scientific Series in FINANCE vol. 21

Selected Works of William T Ziemba

A Memorial Volume

Editors

Leonard MacLean

Dalhousie University, Canada

Sébastien Lleo

NEOMA Business School, France

World Scientific

NEW JERSEY • LONDON • SINGAPORE • BEIJING • SHANGHAI • HONG KONG • TAIPEI • CHENNAI • TOKYO

Published by

World Scientific Publishing Co. Pte. Ltd.
5 Toh Tuck Link, Singapore 596224
USA office: 27 Warren Street, Suite 401-402, Hackensack, NJ 07601
UK office: 57 Shelton Street, Covent Garden, London WC2H 9HE

Library of Congress Cataloging-in-Publication Data
Names: MacLean, L. C. (Leonard C.), editor. | Lleo, Sébastien, editor.
Title: Selected works of William T. Ziemba : a memorial volume / editors, Leonard MacLean, Dalhousie University, Canada, Sébastien Lleo, NEOMA business School, France.
Description: New Jersey : World Scientific, [2024] | Series: World Scientific series in finance, 2010-1082 ; vol. 21 | Includes bibliographical references and index.
Identifiers: LCCN 2024000271 | ISBN 9789811285523 (hardcover) | ISBN 9789811285530 (ebook) | ISBN 9789811285547 (ebook other)
Subjects: LCSH: Finance. | Economics.
Classification: LCC HG173 .Z54 2024 | DDC 332--dc23/eng/20240111
LC record available at https://lccn.loc.gov/2024000271

British Library Cataloguing-in-Publication Data
A catalogue record for this book is available from the British Library.

For any available supplementary material, please visit
https://www.worldscientific.com/worldscibooks/10.1142/13656#t=suppl

Desk Editors: Soundararajan Raghuraman/Pui Yee Lum

Typeset by Stallion Press
Email: enquiries@stallionpress.com

Preface

On June 22, 2022, Dr. William Ziemba passed away. Although Bill had some health issues in recent years, his burning desire for research was undiminished. In common with many intellectuals, Bill Ziemba's mind was in overdrive, always contemplating challenging problems. He was in regular contact with colleagues, discussing projects and opportunities for collaboration.

Over more than 50 years, Bill Ziemba studied important problems in mathematical programming, finance, risk control, gambling, and sports. Bill's lengthy research career produced an amazing array of papers and books. Our intention in this memorial volume is to give a flavor of the diversity and quality of Bill Ziemba's work. With his output of hundreds of papers and forty books, we decided to focus on journal articles. One of Bill's unfinished projects was a set of volumes in the World Scientific Series on Finance, with each volume collecting his papers on a research topic. The organization of the volumes provided section topics for this memorial volume.

Bill Ziemba's collaborators somewhat align with his research topics. By organizing the memorial volume using topics, we include papers with some of Bill's traditional co-authors. Also, the collected papers cover the many decades of his career. This volume is a representative sample of Bill's work, but he did so much more. His full set of publications is listed in an appendix.

Leonard MacLean and Sébastien Lleo

Reflections on a Life of a Renaissance Academic

Sandra Lynn Schwartz and Rachel Elizabeth Schwartz Ziemba*

We are so honored at the collection of Bill's work and testimonials from his colleagues and glad to share some of our reflections as his wife and daughter respectively and intermittent academic collaborators. His work and approaches shaped our lives and brought many opportunities and insights. Bill's work focused on decision-making under uncertainty with recourse. His tools could and were applied to so many different areas of financial markets and life.

Bill's core approach of stochastic optimization and scenario modeling with recourse contrasts with the more static mean–variance models used by others. This approach allowed him (aka Dr. Z) to reassess the performance of an investment decision while in progress and, if needed, to hedge and adjust the bet accordingly as the situation evolved. This could include making several bets over the course of one football game or a long election. His preference for setting the scenario, monitoring the expected outcome, or changing one and adjusting the portfolio could be applied to sports betting (on platforms like Belfair), equity investing (via option contracts), and in portfolio allocation. It also could inform decisions like real estate purchases, haggling and beyond. As a result, his work was characterized by an interest in a wide variety of markets and investment strategies, always seeking to learn more and delving into new specialties.

He believed strongly in a few fundamental precepts:

- The best way to learn about a topic was to write about it, and he wrote many books and articles, some of which are collected in this book.

*The authors are respectively the wife and daughter of William Ziemba, both of whom wrote articles and did other work with him at various points in his career.

- The best research is informed by solving practical problems rather than oversimplified theories. Many of his key contributions were informed by situations, questions, or games in the real world. In particular, his investment work was informed by his time managing funds and testing these strategies live, something he thought made him stand out among his peers.
- Always be a student. Do your research, look into adjacent areas, and look for ways to improve the process.
- Writing about a variety of topics with a range of smart co-authors can keep you and the field smarter and bring in lessons from other adjoining fields. As his career progressed, he partnered with junior scholars, helping them bring their careers to a new stage. Partnering with a variety of co-authors also helped him bring together aligned fields and deepen understanding. It was also more fun and led to a lot of long friendships.

Bill was inspired by polymath masters like Leonardo da Vinci who made contributions in a variety of areas and pushed the boundaries of existing approaches. Such figures influenced Bill's scope of research and indeed his memoir, titled *Adventures of a Renaissance Academic*. He enjoyed exploring different areas, traveled widely, and enjoyed a good meal and meeting new people. These quests influenced and added to our lives, just as our work and interests influenced his. Sandra's work as an economist tracking the real economy and how businesses interact in society, including early social responsibility, brought new areas of research and learnings about industrial structure. Rachel's interests, first as a historian and international relations expert and then as a geo-economic expert, brought to the fore regulatory and political issues that could create edges and obstacles for some of the market work Bill did. While the collaborations weren't always easy, they helped us all see things in new ways.

Regular travel abroad for conferences and collaborations had perhaps the most important impact on our lives. Bill valued travel abroad, to gain new ideas, explore new places, collect beautiful things, and work with colleagues. From his graduate student days onward, Bill traveled, especially to Europe and also to Asia, often with us in tow. These trips included academic conferences, work placements, many visiting professorships as well as vacation sandwiched between such work events. Bill worked remotely long before it was in vogue and rarely was really "offline". We remember many times needing to stop to "call the market" and check prices on positions or to fax in orders. Thank goodness for the advent of cellphones, Wi-Fi, and mobile data. This frenetic activity was no doubt occasionally challenging for co-authors.

Research placements in graduate school included one to Norway where he acquired cross-country skis that he kept for many years, even if they were rarely useful in rainy Vancouver. He returned often to Italy, Greece, and Turkey, in part influenced by Sandra's love of the Mediterranean and his love of the sun. In the 1970s, they often took long trips from Europe to Iran or Afghanistan, taking advantage of those long academic summers. After Rachel was born, she was brought along, and the trips instilled in her a great love of travel. She also became interested in how regulations work in different countries, about which she and Bill occasionally wrote together, and also in her various professional capacities.

While based in Vancouver at UBC, his academic community was global. He connected with colleagues, mentored younger scholars, and helped support and develop financial programming and related schools that were developing in the 1970s, 1980s, and 1990s. He spent time in Italy as their programs were developing, relished years of presentations and lecturing in Turkey, and took pride in being invited to the launch of the Polish School of Economics in Krakow given his Polish roots.

He always took the opportunity to try local food and wine, finding places for good dinners and discussions. He even became friendly with the leaders of the American Association of Wine Economists, attending several of their conferences and helping edit a two-part volume on the economics of wine as part of his World Scientific series. Inspired by that and many visits to wine regions, Rachel has taken this interest to the next level, combining her love of wine, wine tourism, and economics to write about topics, such as trade disputes on wine as well as consolidation in the field. She learned at an early age that visiting wine regions was a wonderful way to see some beautiful countryside.

Adhering to his belief that the best way to learn about a topic in depth was to write a book, he deployed research skills in many different areas over his career. This even included *Turkish Flatweaves*, one of the first books in English on Turkish kilims. Bill and Sandra fell in love with these textiles in their many sojourns in Turkey, began collecting them, and eventually partnered with a rug dealer to write a book. Conversations with weavers in rural Turkey revealed some great examples and wonderful stories, at a time when such knowledge was at risk of dying out. Bill loved bright colors and clear designs, whether they were in textiles, Turkish tiles, or paintings, and brought many items back from his journeys. Sandra, a textile artist as well as an economist, continues to create beautiful textile art, and Rachel continues to enjoy time in rug stores whether in Turkey, Morocco, or Uzbekistan, to name a few locations where she sourced art that decorates her NY apartment. She, an expert in emerging market currency policy and politics, also gets a kick out of the fact that Bill and Sandra, faced with Turkish foreign currency controls, had to take some of their book royalties out in physical carpets. The stories about Turkish and Argentine currency volatility and barter trade influenced much of her work and research questions.

Following the energy crises of the 1970s, he and Sandra wrote about the Canadian and North American energy systems. They did early optimization work on the fossil fuel deposits that were eventually rebranded Canada's oil sands, advising oil companies about the economic and environmental costs of deploying them. At the time, it was hard to envision that geopolitics and revenue maximization approaches of the OPEC countries would bring prices high enough to make consistent money on these deposits.

Our year spent in Japan when Bill was Yamaichi Professor of Finance opened up many years of fruitful research for Bill and Sandra as well as great experiences for the family. The work included many writings on Japanese asset mispricing, arbitrage, and crashes. He wrote several books on Japanese financial markets, several with Sandra, and used relevant cases to identify arbitrage opportunities that he then tracked in other areas, such as China. Rachel, in elementary school at the time, learned to throw herself into new cultures, make friends, and see what she could learn. She also reveled in being an interpreter for the family, learning Japanese and experiencing Japanese school and culture and learning how to be different in a constructive way.

From the 1980s onward, Bill sought out the chance to write in a range of publications, including *Gambling Times*, seeking to bring the economics and finance of betting and investment to a wider audience. At its inception, Bill began writing for *Wilmott Magazine*, a quantitative finance journal with a broad audience of researchers and practitioners. He covered topics ranging from sports betting, investment themes, and even the issues of owning horses.

Dr. Z believed that his approach to decision-making with recourse could be applied to any market in which one could find an edge, including many that others would dismiss as "gambling". While he eschewed betting in games that were entirely based on luck, such as slot machines, he found edges in seemingly random markets, such as lotteries. While you can't get an edge in picking which number will come out of the hopper first, you can choose a number likely to give a higher return if you do win. This turned lotteries into a pari-mutuel situation, reducing the chance you would have to share your returns with as large a group. This work on lotteries led to consultancy work with several gaming regulators and the occasional implementation. One year he and colleagues discovered an edge in a game, leading to the group rushing around Vancouver to buy tickets to take advantage of this rare buyer advantage over the house. One needs to be alert to edges.

Sizing bets is key, something Rachel struggled to learn at the racetrack as a child and even as a young adult in her investment portfolios. She often under bet. Beyond obvious lessons like not betting what one cannot afford to lose or tying up more liquidity in illiquid assets that would be needed in the short term, Dr. Z preferred the Kelly criterion for many of his investment decisions. By taking a large bet on a high-likelihood outcome, an investor can maximize returns if the assumed (high) return is accurate. For horse racing, individual bets are seen as part of an infinite series of bets, so Kelly betting gave the best returns.

He did extensive work applying these techniques to traditional pari-mutuel betting on Thoroughbred horse racing. Bill grew up going to Saratoga Racetrack in NY state and long enjoyed racing. He argued that one could create factor models using information, such as dosage (lineage) of the horse, past performance of the trainers, jockeys, and the horse. His work with Don Hausch identified a Dr. Z system bet that leveraged the "wisdom of crowds", especially the late 'smart' money, and took advantage of under-betting on quality horses to place and show versus the sizeable win pools.

After a successful book, *Beat the Racetrack*, Dr. Z also developed a calculator that allowed bettors, including young Rachel, to easily follow this system, plugging in their budget for the day and data for each race. The market has somewhat changed, as betting syndicates reshape the odds, meaning it can be somewhat harder, if not impossible, to find these system bets today, but system bets can still be found. However, some of these structural changes provided opportunities for Bill and other medium-sized bettors to take advantage of "rebate" systems and receive returns on the volume, not just on the correctness of their bets. Not content to rest on his laurels, he turned his attention to complicated exotic bets like the Pick 6, always looking for the right combination of past performance, pedigree, and handicapper insight to plug into models. Sandra and colleagues spent many hours helping develop models.

He then applied some of these techniques to other markets. With horse racing, unlike other investments, you only have to make one decision: getting in and hoping your bet comes to fruition. With financial investments, you have the critical decisions and indeed opportunity to get out or put on alternate bets to hedge as the "race" keeps running.

Bill's focus on edges put him solidly in the camp of those who disagreed with the perfect market hypotheses. Instead, Dr. Z repeatedly pointed to anomalies in the markets in which investors could take advantage. In his view, anomalies can help make a great investor, both presenting inefficiencies of which one can take advantage and help avoid potential pitfalls. He wrote regularly about great investors, such as Warren Buffett and Ed Thorp, as well as presented a taxonomy of different investment strategies. He and Rachel wrote several articles on the role of university endowment strategies as well as investors that had blow-ups. They occasionally sparred over the role of sovereign wealth funds, which Bill typically saw as missing opportunities due to occasionally conservative positioning, while Rachel countered that some of the nimble investment strategies were either more difficult as the funds got bigger or political stresses intervened. The discussions sharpened both their views and work.

Bill wrote regularly about calendar anomalies, such as the turn of the month, "sell in May", and turn of the year which could present edges for investors. Other anomalies could have political triggers. Bill's work with Chris Hensel found that small-cap equities do better with Democratic presidents, while bonds and large caps do better with Republican presidents. Some of these trends have ebbed over time, especially given the increase in algorithmic trading, but they are still a fruitful area of research. These "edges" identified systematic mispricing among seemingly similar assets and could be combined with other factors, especially macro, liquidity, and market conditions.

On the portfolio side, Bill was particularly proud of his work on the Russell Yasuda model developed with the Frank Russell Company. This helped Yasuda Kasai better manage its pension assets and assess tradeoffs with stakeholders. It received recognition as a finalist in the Edelman Prize for Management Science, the top prize in the field. The area of retirement optimization was particularly important. He and Sandra joined forces to assess the macro and financial issues associated with insufficient and sometimes ineffective retirement investments.

He liked experimenting with new things and would go all in. For example, he fell in love with a B&B on Saltspring Island in the 1990s. While not wanting to move there, we ran the inn at a distance for many years and even had sheep, chickens, and llama. These animals provided farm-fresh eggs, the occasional lamb, and wool. Sandra learned to weave and spin, and Rachel learned that she wasn't a fan of working in hospitality, but we did have many wonderful weekends on the island. Occasionally, we hosted academics including a memorable weekend where a neighboring wild turkey got loose, and we learned that academics might not be the best game hunters.

Bill liked to hold equity and take a stake in projects believing that one could always sell or exit when needed. Some of those investments played out better than others. He got a lot of enjoyment out of owning race horses, setting up and investing in some syndicates, and enjoying the characters who frequented the tracks and the horse farms. The investment return was more mixed — there are too many human and animal factors to make it easy to spot an edge, at least in our view. But we all enjoyed watching the races.

He suggested that an investor determine in advance the bad scenarios that could occur and how much one might lose in each. The true size of an active bet constantly changes based on the hedge ratio, meaning risk assessment and control cannot be static. As the risk position of the portfolio is constantly changing, one needs a risk-control method that keeps up. Dr. Z's work studied other cases of blowups, including Amaranth and long-term capital management, to assess these risks and develop tools to avoid them. Even earlier, when in Japan, Bill tried to warn his Yamaichi bosses about financial vulnerabilities via a Japanese colleague. The Nikkei has only just regained its pre-crash valuation.

Knowing when to get out is as important as getting in. Ziemba's work included assessment of "crash signals" of unsustainable market trends. His work began with his adjustments of a bond stock equity yield model for Japan, inspired in part by the very stretched valuations we observed while in Japan. More recently, he studied the optimal investment strategy for Apple stock, assessing whether buying and holding through the cycles was the optimal strategy or whether one might better exit and re-enter.

We leave you with **Dr. Z's Philosophy**. We hope it will inspire you:

1. Only bet when you have an edge.
2. Those who win on every trade are losers or liars.
3. Know what you expect to gain from a trade before you enter.
4. Do your research.
5. Truly diversify.
6. Do not over-bet.
7. Evaluate the impact of all scenarios.
8. Have deep pockets.
9. Accept small losses.
10. Follow a risk-control system.

Testimonials

Bill Ziemba's research activities involved numerous collaborations, and we have invited some of his colleagues to contribute testimonials to Bill's legacy. We are including some of them in this piece.

[1] Giorgio Consigli
I first met Bill at the 6th International Conference of Stochastic Programming in Udine in 1992 and regularly in all subsequent triannual events of the Stochastic Programming Society. He organized the conference at UBC in 1998 and on that occasion, I had the opportunity to be introduced to Frank Russell's colleagues and Yasuda Kasai representatives who collaborated with him to develop and implement in practice a decision tool based on multistage stochastic programming techniques for a large insurance company in Japan during the previous years. At the same conference, Bill introduced me to Professor George Dantzig, which was a true honor. Going back to the Yasuda Kasai project, it focused on an asset-liability management (ALM) problem formulated as a long-term stochastic linear program. This had been indeed the subject of my PhD thesis under the supervision of Michael A.H. Dempster in the UK With the other nine scholars, both Bill and Michael were awarded in 2004 (SP conference in Tucson, Arizona) the prize of Pioneers of Stochastic Programming, in stochastic programming theory and applications. Since we met in Vancouver in 1998, the exchange on ALM developments and stochastic programming methods between me and Bill has been frequent and systematic. He was a tremendous source of news and contributions in the area. These interests happened to be further motivated and consolidated after I became Associate Professor at the University of Bergamo in 2005: Bill and Sandra were regular guests of my department thanks to their long-term friendship and relationship with Marida Bertocchi who for many years was the Director of the PhD program and Head of Department at the University of Bergamo. At the time, when visiting the department

and flying from abroad to Milan, Bill used to travel with a very heavy and large bag containing papers and books he was working on at the time together with plenty of printed references (he wasn't looking much after sustainability criteria). Primarily thanks to Sandra, not sure if inspired or motivated by a conversation we had, increasingly in the following years that heavy bag disappeared leaving space for an efficient and digital database. A turning point in Bill's traveling customs! To me, that full and heavy bag still witnesses a distinctive aspect of Bill's personality, incredibly full of life and experiences, good humor, and sensibility.

My interest in ALM and long-term modeling represented a relevant but not unique reason to stay closely in touch over the years: indeed, Bill has been deeply interested in financial economics and I had been working in Italy in a financial company in the 1980s and in 1998 at the time of the conference at UBC, after the PhD and a period in Cambridge, back in Italy I was Vice Director in the finance division of a large banking conglomerate. That very year, in the Fall of 1998, financial markets experienced relevant financial instability due first to the default on domestic debt but with a heavy impact on bonds in the Euromarket and the subsequent bankruptcy of the hedge fund Long-Term Capital Management (LTCM) leading to a dramatic increase in volatility in equity markets worldwide. This event came after the 1995 crisis in the banking system caused by the collapse of Barings Bank in the UK and after the dramatic US market instability in 1987. Bill's interest in and understanding of financial instability events globally was unique and fueled our relationship over the years as well.

Common interests in stochastic modeling and global financial instability phenomena were on the grounds of a research project that involved Professors Leonard C. MacLean, co-author of this important volume, and Yonggan Zhao who started in 2001 at a conference organized by Stan Uryasev at the University of Florida in Gainesville. Inspired by Alan Greenspan, then Governor of the US Federal Reserve, already after the 1987 crisis, Bill was advocating the role of irrational exuberance phenomena to motivate the crashes induced by speculative bubbles in the economy: Bill's proposal was to follow (from a practical and very much operational perspectives) the dynamic behavior of the bond-equity yield ratio, the bond yield being associated with the 30-year treasury bond, a liquid instrument in fixed-income markets, and the equity yield being represented by the SP500 market-wide yield. Over the following 5 years, Bill, Len, and I, along with Yonggan published several articles on this topic, proposing and developing to my knowledge the first stochastic model based on a Cox process in which the random shock intensity was driven by an underlying hidden bond-equity yield disequilibrium dynamic. This model was then enriched with the celebrated SP500 implied volatility index (VIX) as an early warning signal of forthcoming instability and applied to several equity markets with extremely interesting results. During this period, I would also like to mention that I invited Bill as a guest to the Finance Directorate of the UniCredit investment bank I was working for and I interviewed him on hedge funds' strategies and financial markets' behavior, starting with the interview of a research series of the investment bank that helped introduce not only advanced modeling approaches in the Italian banking community but also stochastic programming techniques in corporate decision processes.

Bill has been one of my references over the years and he was instrumental to my appointment in 2021 in the Department of Mathematics of Khalifa University of Science and Technology in the UAE, for which I will always be grateful to him. Thanks, Dr. Z, you are missed a lot!

Dr. Giorgio Consigli
Department of Mathematics,
Khalifa University,
Abu Dhabi

[2] Michael Dempster
Bill Ziemba's legacy is a wide range of contributions to the literature ranging from pure mathematics and theoretical physics to engineering, economics, politics, finance, and professional baseball.

Dr. Michael Dempster
Professor Emeritus,
Cambridge University,
Cambridge, UK

[3] Chanaka Edirisinghe

I received my PhD degree under the guidance of Professor Bill Ziemba in August 1991 from the University of British Columbia. Bill was the key figure and mentor behind my specialization in stochastic optimization and its applications in finance, which led to not only joint research publications in top-tier academic journals but also several consulting collaborations with Bill for the investment industry. Bill's passion in the early days was to develop theory and methodology for decision problems involving risk as many practical problems contain some element of uncertainty that critically impacts strategic decisions. He successfully applied this research in asset and liability management for banks, investment management at financial institutions, and sports betting and gambling. In the early 1990s, Bill and I collaborated in developing the Russell–Yasuda Kasai asset allocation stochastic programming model for the Frank Russell Company in Tacoma, known to be the largest model of its kind at the time. From then on, Bill and I developed a comprehensive theory and computational procedures for stochastic analysis and optimization of large-scale models for financial and other decision problems using approximations, particularly for those problems prescribed with a large number of future scenarios of uncertainty. My work with Bill continued for nearly three decades since the UBC days, which resulted in a close personal friendship that took us to Keeneland tracks, the most prominent Thoroughbred auction house, as well as consulting trips to Italy and the Bahamas. We had a chance to interact closely again when I moved to Albany and when Bill became involved in horse racing at Saratoga Springs, NY. Unfortunately, those opportunities were cut short by Bill's untimely departure in 2022. I will continue to cherish those memories.

Dr. Chanaka Edirisinghe
Kay and Jackson Tai '72 Chaired Professor in Quantitative Finance,
Lally School of Management and Technology,
Rensselaer Polytechnic Institute,
Troy, NY

[4] John Guerard
William T. (Bill) Ziemba was a man of great intelligence, and his breadth of knowledge was amazing. Bill was a long-term Finance Department editor at *Management Science*, a very respected peer-reviewed professional journal. To say that Bill was an interdisciplinary researcher was a vast understatement. Bill was a PhD from the University of California, Berkeley, and he served as the Alumni Professor (Emeritus) of Financial Modelling and Stochastic Optimization at the Saunder School of Business, the University of British Columbia. This work, the *Selected Works of William T Ziemba: A Memorial Volume*, by editors Leonard MacLean and Sébastien Lleo, offers a one-volume set of 19 of Professor Ziemba's highly cited peer-reviewed articles in stochastic programming, finance, and economics, asset and liability management, Kelly optimal growth, sports betting and efficient markets, and market anomalies and crashes. The volume papers were published in top-tier professional journals, including *Management Science*, *Operations Research*, *American Economic Review*, *The Journal of Finance*, *Mathematical Programming*, *JFQA*, *The Journal of Portfolio Management*, and the *International Journal of Forecasting*, but many offer insights into Bill's consulting engagements with hedge funds and asset management consultants. As a visiting Professor at Oxford, Cambridge, MIT, Berkeley, UCLA, and the Universities of Bergamo, Washington, Chicago, Tsukuba (Japan), and Zurich, Bill got around in many academic circles. The array of co-authors in this volume speaks of Bill's friendship, mentorship, and the great respect that his peers held him in. This volume is a must-read for graduate students and working professionals. *Selected Works of William T Ziemba: A Memorial Volume* becomes a welcome addition to Bill's World Scientific Handbooks in Financial Economics Series.

Dr. John Guerard
Chairman, Scientific Advisory Board McKinley Capital Management, LLC Anchorage, AK USA, GMT-9

[5] Don Hausch
I am honored and grateful to offer a testimonial for William T. Ziemba, my teacher, mentor, co-author, and friend for 47 years.

In December 1975, while trying to figure out what to do after completing my bachelor's degree in mathematics, I was encouraged to reach out to someone named William Ziemba, a Professor in the management science group at UBC's Business School. I appeared at Professor Ziemba's office door, introduced myself, we had a very brief conversation, and I left with instructions to register for his graduate nonlinear programming course starting a few weeks later. I was an undergrad and I had never heard of nonlinear programming, but it was a life-changing moment for me. Looking back, I realize that I experienced the first of what I now refer to as Dr. Z's Seven Principles of Academics.

Principle 1: Throw yourself into a subject. Embrace the challenge and don't worry about prerequisites and rules.

I soon became a research assistant for Bill, experiencing the following:

Principle 2: The best way to learn about a topic is to jump into research on that topic.

At this point, Bill also welcomed me into his life, which meant getting to know his creative and brilliant wife, Sandra Schwartz, and traveling to conferences, and ideas for other research. For Bill, life and research were so intertwined that his RAs and co-authors were naturally invited into his full life. Still, I understood and deeply valued the privilege of this wider and deeper relationship with Bill.

It took me a few more years to experience Bill's third principle of academics:

Principle 3: The best way to learn a subject is to write a book about it.

And write them he did: 40+ books and edited volumes on subjects as diverse as Turkish flat weaves, energy policy modeling, lotteries, varied applications of stochastic optimization, economics of wine, and, to my great fortune, several books and edited volumes on horserace gambling that established Bill as "Dr. Z."

Bill was a world-class researcher who collaborated with many top academics in operations research, finance, and economics, including two Nobel laureates. Bill also had high regard for the best practitioners, and he valued learning from them and engaging in joint research.

Principle 4: The best practitioners have deep insights and understandings of their fields that deserve much respect, and they can contribute to cutting-edge research that benefits from their knowledge and experience.

And Bill often took this principle further:

Principle 5: There is great value for academics to engage personally in practice.

Bill lived this principle in many ways, including creating and managing funds that relied on trading strategies related to market anomalies that he and other academics had studied; consulting with governments on the design of lotteries; writing a regular column in a trade publication about anomalies and betting strategies; and co-owning and racing Thoroughbreds, including being part of a syndicate that owned Honor Code, the dazzling Thoroughbred who won the 2015 Whitney Stakes at Saratoga Race Course. Research informed each of these activities and each activity informed research.

Bill was dedicated to his students and dedicated to research. So, he excelled at graduate-level courses where he could emphasize research and challenge students to develop and advance their own research ideas.

Principle 6: Inspire, prepare, guide, and support the next generation of researchers.

Bill worked with many students over his career. He was extremely generous with his time. He had an endless supply of important and challenging research ideas that interested and motivated students could work on, but he was also excited about supporting research efforts advanced by students. He was a great teacher and advisor, always helpful and encouraging. Bill would continue research programs with graduates if they were interested, and he would continue friendships even if joint research had ended. He offered sage guidance on research efforts and one's career. And his advice and recommendation letters for graduate programs and careers were highly influential for many students.

Bill's retirement from UBC in 2006 coincided with an increase in research productivity, based on a simple count of articles and books post-2006. Of course, this is not a surprise to those who knew him. Retirement simply afforded Bill more time for his beloved research with his dear research colleagues and friends.

Principle 7: A life of research is a life well lived. A life of research filled with good friends, colleagues, loved ones, wide interests, insatiable curiosity, and abundant energy is a life exceedingly well lived. Bill's life was exceedingly well lived.

Dr. Don Hausch
Emeritus Professor,
University of Wisconsin,
Madison, Wisconsin, United States

[6] Haim Levy
I was really sad to hear that Bill passed away. I met Bill personally only once, at an international conference, when we both were very young, but I still remember him very vividly. I was impressed by his energy, his wide interest in many topics, and his enthusiasm for conducting research. Indeed, decades of his research reveal that I was not wrong in my impression. Bill was a very prolific researcher and published many articles and books in portfolio theory, operation research, management science, finance, sport, and lottery investment and in many more research areas.

I had the pleasure of working with him for about ten years when he was the department of finance editor of *Management Science*, and I served as an associate editor. We will all miss him as a person and as a prolific colorful researcher.

Dr. Haim Levy
Professor,
Department of Economics,
Hebrew University,
Jerusalem, Israel

[7] Sébastien Lleo
I had the immense privilege and pride of knowing Bill and sharing his intellectual adventures for over a decade. I contacted Bill for the first time at a critical juncture in my career. I sought his advice about transitioning from the financial industry to pursue a PhD I was deeply touched and impressed by his thoughtful reply. Although Bill was retiring from the University of British Columbia and could not commit to a new PhD supervision, he took the time and care to reply. His message was detailed, supportive, open, and gently directive, with encouragement, numerous pieces of advice, and a list of potential supervisors.

As I continued to discover, Bill was incredibly supportive, generous with his time, willing to lend a hand, and invariably happy to connect with colleagues and friends. I can attest to, and greatly benefited from, his exceptional support to younger researchers.

Supportive, open, and gently directive, Bill was all that and some more! He was an absolute force of nature, an intellectual hurricane. He possessed unbridled energy and curiosity, a desire to try things out and see how they work, a focus on ensuring that his work was usable in practice, and an appetite for life. Bill was constantly reflecting, trying new ideas, planning projects, and traveling all over the world.

Bill's intellectual prowess was legendary, matched only by his encyclopedic knowledge of the literature and his own substantial contributions to it. He needed no introduction at conferences and lecture halls. He knew everyone in the finance and optimization communities. And everyone knew Bill. We all remember him as direct and entertaining. He would tell everyone exactly what he thought, as he thought it. He backed his arguments with data, stories, and thought-provoking anecdotes.

As I reflect on our time together, I am filled with gratitude for the profound impact Bill had on my life. Every moment shared with him remains a cherished memory, a testament to his enduring friendship and mentorship.

Dr. Sébastien Lleo
Professor,
NEOMA Business School,
Reims, France

[8] Leonard MacLean
I first met Bill Ziemba when I spent a sabbatical term at UBC in 1983. I traveled to Vancouver in the hope of collaborating with Bill since he had an established reputation for research in stochastic methods in finance and economics. Shortly after arriving at UBC, Bill arranged a meeting to discuss a topic of interest to him: the Kelly strategy for decisions in investment and gambling. I was familiar with the "golden rule" in economics but didn't know about the related growth concept in finance: "fortunes formula." Bill had great respect for Ed Thorp at UC Irvine and presented me with literature on the Kelly criterion, including Ed's work. My interest in collaborating with Bill on the Kelly topic was sparked and I got to work.

That was 1983 and my collaboration with Bill continued for 40 years until his death in 2022. We co-authored many papers and books and traveled to conferences across the world. Since Bill was so well known internationally, he was invited to speak in many interesting places. I traveled to many important conferences and met leading scholars through my association with Bill.

Of course, my collaboration with Bill was not founded on travel or networking opportunities. It was based on friendship and shared interests. For example, we both loved sports, especially NFL football. I could expect a phone call from Bill on Sunday during the NFL season. We would exchange opinions on the favorites in the scheduled games. Bill would invariably make a small wager on games where there appeared to be a risk arbitrage opportunity. For several years, Bill and I would write a column for *Wilmott* magazine on the most recent football season. That was a lot of fun.

Bill Ziemba was a force of nature. He continuously contemplated problems in business, politics, and sports. His mind didn't rest, and he challenged colleagues to contribute to a better understanding of complex systems.

Dr. Leonard MacLean
Professor Emeritus,
Dalhousie University,
Halifax, Canada

[9] John Mulvey
I first met Bill during my interview for a junior faculty position at UBC in 1974. His outsized personality was immediately evident as was his nature to encourage young researchers. Bill was always enthusiastic along multiple dimensions. He loved traveling with his wife Sandra throughout the world. He was a natural storyteller. And he was hooked on betting situations, from games of chance (blackjack) to athletic competitions (notably horse racing) to economic markets (the turn of the year pattern). He was an early observer that these situations share common opportunities. In particular, he wrote about and endeavored to take advantage of periods of positive performance (edges, anomalies, arbitrage, and regimes) across all these diverse domains. In this regard, Bill was a pioneer; his insights will only become more relevant as the world expands in areas, such as sports gaming and analytics, and as novel markets arise (take cryptocurrencies).

John Mulvey
Professor,
Operations Research and Financial Engineering,
Princeton University,
Princeton, NJ

[10] Stein Wallace
I remember Bill as a whirlwind of ideas, with an ability to see across disciplines. My PhD student (now professor) Stein-Erik Fleten spent time in

Vancouver, looking into what is now obvious (but was not at the time), namely the connections between financial portfolio theory, stochastic programming, and energy markets. Bill was also very concerned about the world being stochastic, so we needed to show how stochastic programming was applicable to many areas, and we ended up with an edited book on the subject. Always active, always questioning things, never time to waste — that's the Bill I knew.

Dr. Stein Wallace
Professor of Operational Research,
NHH Norwegian School of Economics,
Bergen, Norway

[11] Paul Wilmott
Bill Ziemba was my favorite polymath! He made important advances in many different fields, but my association with him was through the theory and practice of investing and gambling. The articles he wrote on these subjects for my magazine and the lectures he gave for the CQF were always among the most popular.

My fondest memory of Bill has to be the time he invited me and my family to Saratoga. I didn't strike it rich, but he made the occasion one that still makes me smile! And thanks to him, I can now add 'racehorse owner' to my CV!

Dr. Paul Wilmott
Founder,
CQF Institute,
London, UK

About the Editors

Leonard MacLean is a Professor Emeritus in the Faculty of Management at Dalhousie University in Halifax, Canada. Dr. MacLean has held visiting appointments at Cambridge University, University of Bergamo, University of British Columbia, Simon Fraser University, Royal Roads University, University of Zimbabwe, and University of Indonesia. From 1989 to 1995, he served as Director of the School of Business Administration at Dalhousie University. Professor MacLean's research focuses on stochastic models in finance, systems reliability in transportation, and sports analytics. He has authored more than 100 papers, appearing in journals, such as the *Journal of Economic Theory, Management Science, Quantitative Finance, Transportation Research,* the *Journal of Banking and Finance*, and the *Journal of Economic Dynamics and Control*. Professor MacLean has also co-authored six books. His work has been funded by grants from the Natural Sciences and Engineering Council of Canada and the Herbert Lamb Trust. Dr. MacLean teaches in the areas of statistics and operations management.

Sébastien Lleo is a Professor of Finance at NEOMA Business School (France) and was the 2020 Bruti-Liberati Fellow at the Quantitative Finance Research Center, University of Technology Sydney (Australia). He is also a tutor on the Certificate in Quantitative Finance at FitchLearning (UK). He joined NEOMA Business School in 2010 and served as the Director of the Doctoral School for five years, during which he developed the PhD in Management and a DBA in partnership with Shanghai Jiaotong University. Sébastien started his career at the Bank of Canada and Canada Mortgage and Housing Corporation. Sébastien co-authored books on risk-sensitive stochastic control and stock market crashes, authored a monograph on risk management commissioned by the CFA Institute, and published more than 20 articles in academic and professional journals. He earned a PhD in Mathematics from Imperial College London (UK), an HDR in Social Science from Conservatoire national des arts et métiers (France), an MBA from University of Ottawa (Canada), and an MSc in Management from NEOMA Business School (France). He is also a CFA Charter Holder, Certified Financial Risk Manager, Professional Risk Manager, and CQF alumnus.

Acknowledgments

We would like to thank the following publishers and journals for granting their permissions to reproduce the articles:

Publishers

Blackwell Publishing Inc.
Cambridge University Press
Pageant Media
Taylor & Francis
The Institute for Operations Research and the Management Sciences (INFORMS)
The University of Chicago Press

Journals

Journal of Business
Journal of Financial and Quantitative Analysis
Journal of Portfolio Management
Management Science
Mathematics of Operations Research
Operations Research
Quantitative Finance

Contents

Introduction

Chapter 1

An Overview of the Research of William T. Ziemba

Leonard MacLean and Sébastien Lleo

1 Academic Profile — William T. Ziemba, PhD

What is more important, the question or the answer? Questions are more important because they seek to frame problems while answers are temporary responses.

William Ziemba completed a PhD in Business Administration at the University of California, Berkeley, in 1969. His thesis was titled "Essays on Stochastic Programming and the Theory of Economic Policy". As is often the case with academics, Bill's thesis topics dominated his research over the following five decades. At the completion of doctoral studies, Bill accepted an academic appointment in the Faculty of Commerce and Business Administration, University of British Columbia. Commerce at UBC was in the early stages of significant growth and the setting was very good for an ambitious and talented professor. There are characteristics of Canadian universities which helped sustain Bill's long productive career. The Natural Sciences and Engineering Council of Canada (NSERC) provided annual funding for his research; a third of the academic year is non-teaching and travel to leading universities for research collaboration is encouraged.

Bill Ziemba thrived in the university environment. He traveled the globe and collaborated with numerous scholars. His creativity and relentless pursuit of excellence contributed to a large throve of research papers and books. In a limited way, this overview will attempt to give a sense of the volume and breath of William Ziemba's writings. We have classified his work under the following headings: Stochastic Programming, Economics and Finance, Asset and Liability Management, Kelly Optimal Growth Strategies, Sports Betting and Analytics, and Market Anomalies and Crashes. It is not possible to give a thorough review of Bill's contributions, but achievements from multiple papers and collaborators will be noted. A full listing of his publications is provided at the end of this book. The subsequent chapters contain a selection of papers covering the decades of activity and contributions to the variety of classifications.

2 Stochastic Programming

Operations Research (OR) is a discipline that deals with the development and application of analytical methods to improve decision-making. The term management science (MS) is used for the business use of operations research. In the 1960's, OR/MS was taking hold in universities. Bill was fortunate to study for his PhD at the University of California at Berkley. George Dantzig, a pioneer in mathematical programming, was a Professor and Roger J-B Wets, an early developer of stochastic programming, was his student. Bill's interest was stimulated, and stochastic programming became a theme of his thesis. At the 10th International Conference on Stochastic Programming, Tucson, Arizona, in October 2004, Bill Ziemba was honored as one of the ten pioneers who helped develop the field of stochastic programming. He was a member of the Committee on Stochastic Programming (COSP) and organized many sessions in their triennial conferences.

A stochastic program is an optimization problem where the objective function and/or constraint functions contain random variables. It is typically referred to as decision-making under uncertainty. The goal of stochastic programming is to find a decision which both optimizes some outcome criterion, typically an expected value, and also accounts for the uncertainty in the random inputs. Because many real-world decisions involve uncertainty, stochastic programming has found applications in a broad range of areas. Bill Ziemba is applications-oriented and from the outset recognized the applications of stochastic programming, particularly in finance.

Bill Ziemba hit the ground running when he moved to an academic appointment at the University of British Columbia. He quickly published papers in top journals. He contributed to the modeling and computational techniques in stochastic programming with a series of articles (SP1, SP2, SP3, SP4, SP5, SP13, SP14). Stochastic programming problems present difficult computational challenges, particularly for multistage processes. Except for special problems with probability assumptions (Gaussian), the approach is to solve an approximating problem with discrete scenarios. Bounds on the approximation error are important. Bill and his students made many contributions to obtaining bounds on stochastic programs (SP6, SP7, SP8, SP9, SP10, SP11, SP12).

Considering his interest in applications, Bill edited a series of books with contributions of stochastic programming to diverse fields (SP15, SP16, SP17, SP18, SP19).

SP Publications (Selected Papers in Bold)

SP1. Ziemba, W. T. (1970). Computational algorithms for convex stochastic programmes with simple recourse, *Operations Research* XVIII: 414–431.

SP2. Ziemba, W. T. (1970). Stochastic programming models of dynamic planning problems, *Economic Computation and Economic Cybernetics* (Studies and Research) 3: 67–85.

SP3. Ziemba, W. T. (1971). Transforming stochastic dynamic programming problems into nonlinear programmes, *Management Science* XVIII: 450–462.

SP4. Ziemba, W. T. (1971). Duality relations, certainty equivalents and bounds for convex stochastic programmes with simple recourse, *Cahiers du Centre d'Etudes de Recherche Operationnelle* XIII: 85–97.

SP5. Ziemba, W. T. (1972). Solving nonlinear programming problems with stochastic objective functions, *Journal of Financial and Quantitative Analysis* VII: 1809–1827.

SP6. Ziemba, W. T. and Butterworth, J. E. (1974). Bounds on the value of information in uncertain decision problems, *Stochastics* IV: 1–18.

SP7. Huang, C. C., Vertinsky, I. and Ziemba, W. T. (1977). Sharp bounds on the value of perfect information, *Operations Research* XXV: 128–139.

SP8. Huang, C. C., Ziemba, W. T. and Ben-Tal, A. (1977). Bounds on the expectation of a convex function of a random variable: With applications to stochastic programming, *Operations Research* XXV: 315–325.

SP9. Hausch, D. B. and Ziemba, W. T. (1983). Bounds on the value of information in uncertain decision problems, II, *Stochastics* X: 181–217.

SP10. Gassmann, H. and Ziemba, W. T. (1986). A tight upper bound for the expectation of a convex function of a multivariate random variable, *Mathematical Programming Study, Recent Advances in Stochastic Programming* XXVII: 39–53.

SP11. Edirishinghe, N. C. P. and Ziemba, W. T. (1992). Bounds for stochastic programmes with recourse, *Operations Research* 40, 660–677.

SP12. Edirishinghe, N. C. P. and Ziemba, W. T. (1994). Bounds for two-stage stochastic programs with fixed recourse, *Mathematics of Operations Research* 19: 292–313.

SP13. Ziemba, W. T. (2008). Use of stochastic and mathematical programming in portfolio theory and practice: Keynote address, *Annals of Operations Research* 166 (October): 5–22.

SP14. Edirisinghe, N. C. P. and Ziemba, W. T. (2018). A boundary-point LP method and its application to dense linear programs, *International Journal of Mathematics in Operational Research* 1–27.

SP15. Wets, R. J. B. and Ziemba, W. T. (Eds.) (1999). Stochastic programming — state of the art 1998, (main lectures *VIII International Conference on Stochastic Programming*), Baltzer Science Publishers BV (Special Issue *Annals of Operations Research*), March, 285 p.

SP16. Birge, J. B., Edirisinghe, N. C. P. and Ziemba, W. T. (Eds.) (2001). Research in stochastic programming (selected, refereed papers from the *VIII International Conference on Stochastic Programming*), Baltzer Science Publishers BV (Special Issue *Annals of Operations Research*), June, 306 p.

SP17. Ziemba, W. T. (2003). *The Stochastic Programming Approach to Asset Liability and Wealth Management*, AIMR, December, 192 p. + 72-p. appendix. [A review by Alan King is in Interfaces April 2006].

SP18. Wallace, S. W. and Ziemba, W. T. (Eds.) (2005). *Applications of Stochastic Programming*, SIAM — Mathematical Programming Society Series on Optimization, 707 p.

SP19. Gassman, H. I. and Ziemba, W. T. (Eds.) (2012). *Stochastic Programming Applications in Finance, Energy and Production*, World Scientific, 518 p.

3 Finance and Economics

A second theme of Bill Ziemba's PhD thesis was economic policy, and his supervisor Willard Zangwill was particularly interested in policy. Bill's first paper was on capital budgeting (FE1). He considered optimal investment portfolios for a variety of realistic problem formulations (FE3, FE4, FE5, FE6, FE7, FE10, FE11). The choice of utility, state dynamics, and planning horizon were explored. Bill had a particular interest in decision risk and contributed to the measurement of risk aversion (FE8, FE9, FE13, FE14, FE19, FE22, FE25, FE29, FE42). His paper on the effects of parameter estimation error continues to be cited (FE17). The use of shared covariance information in reducing the error in mean return estimates was developed (FE30).

Although Bill Ziemba was widely recognized for model building, he continued with theoretical work with an emphasis on risk control (FE64, FE65, FE66.) He promoted the bond-stock yield differential as a risk indicator and considered approaches to hedging the risk in investment decisions (FE33, FE34, FE35, FE36, FE40). It is worth noting that Bill managed a hedge fund where he used his many ideas to generate excess returns.

Bill traveled extensively. His time in Japan provided material for an analysis of Japanese markets (FE15, FE16, FE18). It was also the beginning of his work on the Russell–Yasuda Kasai Financial Planning Model.

F&E Publications (Selected Papers in Bold)

FE1. Ziemba, W. T. (1969). A myopic capital budgeting model, *Journal of Financial and Quantitative Analysis* IV: 305–328.

FE2. Ziemba, W. T. (1971). A note on economic policy under uncertainty, *Socio Economic Planning Sciences* V: 407–410.

FE3. Ziemba, W. T., Parkan, C. and Brooks-Hill, F. J. (1974). Calculation of investment portfolios with risk free borrowing and lending, *Management Science* XXI: 209–222.

FE4. Ziemba, W. T. and Vickson, R. G. (Eds.) (1975). *Stochastic Optimization Models in Finance*, Academic Press, July, 744 p. (388 p. reprinted and 356 p. new). 2nd edition with new preface, World Scientific, Singapore, 2006.

FE5. Ohlson, J. A., Ziemba, W. T. (1976). Optimal portfolio policies for an investor with a power utility function facing a log normal securities market, *Journal of Financial and Quantitative Analysis* XI: 57–71.

FE6. Huang, C. C., Wehrung, D. A. and Ziemba, W. T. (1976). A homogeneous distribution problem with applications to finance, *Management Science* XXIII: 297–304.

FE7. Ziemba, W. T. (1977). Multiperiod consumption-investment decisions: Further comments, *American Economic Review* LXVII: 766–767.

FE8. Kallberg, J. G. and Ziemba, W. T. (1979). On the robustness of the Arrow-Pratt risk aversion index, *Economic Letters* II: 21–26.

FE9. Kira, D. and Ziemba, W. T. (1980). The demand for a risky asset, *Management Science* XXVI: 1158–1165.

FE10. Kallberg, J. G., White, R. and Ziemba, W. T. (1982). Short term financial planning under uncertainty, *Management Science* XXVIII: 670–682.

FE11. Kallberg, J. G. and Ziemba, W. T. (1983). Comparison of alternative utility functions in portfolio selection problems, *Management Science* XXIX: 1257–1276.

FE12. Schaible, S. and Ziemba, W. T. (1986). On the concavity of the sum of lognormals in lognormal approximation in portfolio theory, *Zeitschriff fur Operations Research* XXIX: 161–186.

FE13. Li, Y. and Ziemba, W. T. (1989). Characterizations of optimal portfolios by univariate and multivariate risk aversion, *Management Science* XXXV: 259–269.

FE14. Li, Y. and Ziemba, W. T. (1990). Rules for diversification by all risk averters, *Journal of Economics and Business*, Fall (Special issue): 165–170. 5.

FE15. Ziemba, W. T. and Schwartz, S. L. (1991). The growth in the Japanese stock market, 1949-90 and prospects for the future, *Managerial and Decision Economics* 12: 183–195.

FE16. Ziemba, W.T (1991). Fundamental factors in Japanese stock returns, 1979 to 1989, *Investing* (Winter): 73–79.

FE17. Chopra, V. and Ziemba, W. T. (1993). The effect of errors in mean and co-variance estimates on optimal portfolio choice, *Journal of Portfolio Management* (Winter): 6–11.

FE18. Stone, D. and Ziemba, W. T. (1993). Land and stock prices in Japan, *Journal of Economic Perspectives* (Summer): 149–165.

FE19. Li, Y. and Ziemba, W. T. (1993). Univariate and multivariate measures of risk aversion and risk premiums, *Annals of Operations Research* (Financial Engineering, Special issue) 45: 265–296.

FE20. Ziemba, W. T. (1994). Worldwide security market regularities, *European Journal of Operational Research* 74: 198–229.

FE21. Zhao, Y. and Ziemba, W. T. (2000). A dynamic asset allocation model with downside risk control, *The Journal of Risk* 3 (Fall): 91–113.

FE22. Zhao, Y. and Ziemba, W. T. (2001). A stochastic programming model using an endogenously determined worst case risk measure in a risk-return framework for dynamic asset allocation, *Mathematical Programming, Series B* 89(2): 293–309.

FE23. Zhao, Y., Haussmann, U. and Ziemba, W. T. (2003). A dynamic investment model with a minimum attainable wealth requirement, *Mathematical Finance* 13 (October): 481–501.

FE24. Rudolf, M. and Ziemba, W. T. (2004). Intertemporal asset-liability management, *Journal of Economic Dynamics and Control* 28(4): 975–990.

FE25. Ziemba, W. T. (2005). The symmetric downside risk Sharpe ratio and the evaluation of great investors and speculators, *Journal of Portfolio Management* (Fall): 108–122.

FE26. Koivu, M., Pennanen, T. and Ziemba, W. T. (2005). Cointegration analysis of the FED model, *Finance Research Letters* 2: 248–259.

FE27. MacLean, L. C., Zhao, Y. and Ziemba, W. T. (2006). Dynamic portfolio selection with process control, *Journal of Banking and Finance* 30(2): 317–339.

FE28. Zhao, Y. and Ziemba, W. T. (2007). On Leland's option pricing and hedging strategy with transactions costs, *Finance Research Letters* 4: 49–58.

FE29. Kouwenberg, R. and Ziemba, W. T. (2007). Incentives and risk taking in hedge funds, *Journal of Banking and Finance* 31: 3291–3310.

FE30. MacLean, L. C., Foster, M. and Ziemba, W. T. (2007). Empirical Bayes estimation with dynamic portfolio models, *Journal of Banking and Finance* 31: 3503–3523.

FE31. Kallio, M. and Ziemba, W. T. (2007). Using Tucker's theorem of the alternative to simplify, review and expand discrete arbitrage theory, *Journal of Banking and Finance* 31: 2281–2302.

FE32. Zhao, Y. and Ziemba, W. T. (2008). Calculating risk neutral probabilities and optimal portfolio policy in a dynamic investment model with downside risk control, *European Journal of Operational Research* 185: 1525–1540. 7.

FE33. Berge, K., Consigli, G. and Ziemba, W. T. (2008). The predictive ability of the bond stock earnings yield differential, *Journal of Portfolio Management* (Spring): 63–80.

FE34. Rodriguez, J. and Ziemba, W. T. (2008). Duality relations of hedge fund managers' incentive fee optimization problems, *Mathematical Programming* 113: 95–131.

FE35. Consigli, G., MacLean, L. C., Zhao, Y. and Ziemba, W. T. (2009). The bond-stock yield differential as a risk indicator in financial markets. *Journal of Risk* 11(3): 3–24.

FE36. MacLean, L. C., Consigli, G., Zhao, Y. and Ziemba, W. T. (2011). Risk indicators in equity markets. *Mathematical Methods in Economics and Finance* 3(2): 101–118.

FE37. MacLean, L. C., Zhao, Y. and Ziemba, W. T. (2011). Intertemporal mean variance efficiency with Markovian state price density, *Journal of Banking and Finance* 27 p.

FE38. MacLean, L. C., Zhao, Y. and Ziemba, W. T. (2011). Mean-variance versus expected utility in dynamic investment analysis, *Computational Management Science* 8(1): 3–22.

FE39. MacLean, L. C., Zhao, Y. and Ziemba, W. T. (2012). Currency returns, market regimes and behavorial biases, *Annals of Finance* 9(2): 249–269.

FE40. MacLean, L. C., Zhao, Y. and Ziemba, W. T. (2013). Endogenous volatilities for hedging and pricing option with transaction costs, *Quantitative Finance* 13(5): 699–713.

FE41. Ziemba, W. T. (2013). Is the 60-40 stock-bond pension fund rule wise? *Journal of Portfolio Management* 39(2): 63–72.

FE42. Ziemba, W. T. (2013). The case for convex risk measures, *Quantitative Finance Letters* 1: 47–54.

4 Asset and Liability Management

As an academic, Bill Ziemba worked on theory and contributed many papers in leading journals. In addition to theoretical contributions to financial planning, Bill was greatly interested in the practical application of the theory in the finance industry. His approach was grounded in the stochastic programming models he studied at Berkeley. An asset and liability model (ALM) for banks (AL1) introduced stochastic programming to ALM. It was sort of a pioneering contribution since financial modeling became a major theme of stochastic programming conferences.

Bill subsequently collaborated with the Frank Russell Corporation in the development of a major financial planning model (AL2, AL3, AL4). With the successes of the ALM models, he became a guru for the practice of stochastic programming (AL6, AL7). Bill wrote a well-received book on the SP approach to ALM (AL5). He subsequently worked on the development of a pension planning model in Austria (AL9) and produced important works on pension planning (AL10, AL11, AL12).

ALM Publications (Selected Papers in Bold)

AL1. Kusy, M. I. and Ziemba, W. T. (1986). A bank asset and liability management model, *Operations Research* XXXIV: 356–376.

AL2. Cariño, D. *et al.* (1994). The Russell-Yasuda Kasai model: An asset/liability model for a Japanese insurance company using multistage stochastic programming, *Interfaces* (January–February, Edelman Prize issue): 29–49. (A story about this paper is in the March 31, 1991 issue of the New York Times.)

AL3. Cariño, D. and Ziemba, W. T. (1998). Formulation of the Russell–Yasuda Kasai financial planning model, *Operations Research* 46(4) (July/August): 433–449.

AL4. Cariño, D., Myers, D. and Ziemba, W. T. (1998). Concepts, technical issues and uses of the Russell–Yasuda Kasai financial planning model, *Operations Research* 46(4) (July/August): 450–462.

AL5. Ziemba, W. T. (2003). *The Stochastic Programming Approach to Asset Liability and Wealth Management*, AIMR, December, 192 p. + 72-p. appendix. [A review by Alan King is in Interfaces April 2006].

AL6. Board, J. L. C., Sutcliffe, C. M. S. and Ziemba, W. T. (2003). Applying operations research techniques to financial markets. *Interfaces* 32(2) (March–April): 12–34.

AL7. Rudolf, M. and Ziemba, W. T. (2004). Intertemporal asset-liability management, *Journal of Economic Dynamics and Control* 28(4): 975–990.

AL8. Douglass, J., Wu, O. and Ziemba, W. T. (2004). Stock ownership decisions in defined contribution pension plans, *Journal of Portfolio Management* (Summer): 92–100.

AL9. Geyer, A. and Ziemba, W. T. (2008). The innovest Austrian pension fund planning model InnoALM, *Operations Research* 56(4): 797–810.

AL10. Bertocchi, M., Schwartz, S. L. and Ziemba, W. T. (Eds.) (2010). *Optimizing the Aging, Retirement and Pensions Dilemma*, 2nd edition, Wiley, 411 p., February 2015.

AL11. Ziemba, W. T. (2013). Is the 60-40 stock-bond pension fund rule wise? *Journal of Portfolio Management* 39(2): 63–72.

AL12. Ziemba, W. T. (2016). An approach to financial planning of retirement pensions with scenario dependent correlation matrices and convex risk measures, *Journal of Retirement* (Summer): 1–13.

5 Kelly Optimal Growth

Bill Ziemba studied optimal growth as part of this PhD thesis and published early papers on the topic (K1, K2). His popular book "Stochastic Optimization Models in Finance" contained a section devoted to the optimal growth or Kelly strategy (K3). Bill's interest in gambling stimulated his work on the log-optimal or Kelly strategy. He had great admiration for Ed Thorp, who promoted the Kelly strategy in gambling and in investment.

The Kelly strategy is based on probabilities and returns (odds and edge) and remains outside mainstream finance. The strategy works in log-space and the implied log utility has its critics (K12). Bill Ziemba considered the performance of the Kelly strategy in a series of papers (K3, K5, K6, K7). In the fashion of two-fund analysis, he explored the fractional Kelly approach to risk control (K8, K11). Bill considered the log-optimal strategy with traditional risk criteria such as VaR and CVaR (K13). He documented the positive and negative aspects of log-optimal investment (K9). The MacLean, Thorp, and Ziemba book brought together many of the significant papers contributing to the theory and practice of log-optimal or Kelly investing (K10). Bill explained the use of the Kelly strategy by leading investors (K14).

Kelly Publications (Selected Papers in Bold)

K1. Ziemba, W. T. (1972). Note on 'optimal growth portfolios when returns are serially correlated', *Journal of Financial and Quantitative Analysis* VII: 1995–2000.

K2. Ohlson, J. A. and Ziemba, W. T. (1976). Optimal portfolio policies for an investor with a power utility function facing a log normal securities market, *Journal of Financial and Quantitative Analysis* XI: 57–71.

K3. MacLean, L. C. and Ziemba, W. T (1991). Growth-security profiles in capital accumulation under risk, *Annals of Operations Research* 31: 501–510.

K4. Markowitz, H. M., Schaible, S. and Ziemba, W. T. (1992). An algorithm for portfolio selection in a lognormal market, *International Journal of Financial Analysis* 1(2): 109–113.

K5. MacLean, L. C., Ziemba, W. T. and Blazenko, G. (1992). Growth versus security in dynamic investment analysis, *Management Science* 38: 1562–1585.

K6. MacLean, L. C. and Ziemba, W. T. (1999). Growth versus security tradeoffs in dynamic investment analysis, in Wets, R. J.- B. and Ziemba, W. T. (Eds.) Stochastic Programming: State of the Art 1998, *Annals of Operations Research*, Balzer Science Publishers, pp. 193–226.

K7. MacLean, L. C., Sanegre, R., Zhao, Y. and Ziemba, W. T. (2004). Capital growth with security, *Journal of Economic Dynamics and Control* 28(4): 937–954.

K8. MacLean, L., Ziemba, W. T. and Li, Y. (2005). Time to wealth goals in capital accumulation and the optimal trade-off of growth versus security, *Quantitative Finance* 5(4): 343–357.

K9. MacLean, L. C., Thorp, E. O. and Ziemba, W. T. (2010). Long term capital growth: The good and bad properties of the Kelly and fractional Kelly capital growth criterion, *Quantitative Finance* 681–687.

K10. MacLean, L. C., Thorp, E. O. and Ziemba, W. T. (Eds.) (2011). *The Kelly Capital Growth Criterion: Theory and Practice*, World Scientific, 853 p.

K11. MacLean, L. C., Thorp, E. O., Zhao, Y. and Ziemba, W. T. (2011). How does the Fortune's formula-Kelly capital growth model perform? *Journal of Portfolio Management* 37(4): 96–111.

K12. Ziemba, W. T. (2015). Response to Paul A Samuelson letters and papers on the Kelly capital growth investment strategy, *Journal of Portfolio Management* 41(1): 153–167. 8.

K13. MacLean, L. C., Zhao, Y. and Ziemba, W. T. (2016). Optimal capital growth with convex shortfall penalties, *Quantitative Finance* 16(1): 101–117.

K14. Ziemba, W. T. (2016). Understanding and using the Kelly capital growth, *Alternative Investment Analyst Review* 44–55.

6 Sports Betting and Analytics

Bill Ziemba had a lifelong interest in sports and sports betting. His love for horses and horseracing was evident in his ownership of thoroughbred horses, regular travel to leading tracks for top races, betting on races, and regular columns in the journal *Wilmott* dealing with featured races and horses. Bill was a sought-after expert on strategies for racetrack betting. His books on racetrack betting are classics (SA14, SA15, SA17, SA20). Bill had a special interest in the inefficiencies of racetrack betting and opportunities for risk arbitrage (SA1, SA3, SA4, SA6, SA7, SA9).

Lotteries are very popular in Western society and Bill studied their characteristics (SA5, SA7, SA12, SA13). He wrote a guidebook on lottery gambling (SA16) and a handbook on sports and lottery markets (SA18). Bill was an expert on gambling markets and provided design advice for Canadian lotteries.

Bill's interest in sports was broad. He was fascinated with the great players in sports (SA22). He was a devoted American football fan and followed his favorite teams (particularly the New England Patriots) religiously. He wrote a primer on the NFL (SA19). He wagered on games, with an eye on competitions where the in-game odds provided a risk arbitrage opportunity, understanding the mean reversion in scores. Bill contributed regular columns to *Wilmott* at the conclusion of NFL and NBA seasons. He combined many of his sports-themed papers in a Sports Analytics book (SA21).

Sports Publications (Selected Papers in Bold)

SA1. Hausch, D. G., Ziemba, W. T. and Rubinstein, M. E. (1981). Efficiency of the market for racetrack betting, *Management Science* XXVII: 1435–1452.

SA2. Judah, S., Ziemba, W. T. (1983). Three person Baccarat, *Operations Research Letters* II: 187–192.

SA3. Hausch, D. B. and Ziemba, W. T. (1985). Transactions costs, entries and extent of inefficiencies in a racetrack betting model, *Management Science* XXXI: 381–394.

SA4. Ziemba, W. T., Canfield, B. and Fauman, B. (1987). Efficient market adjustment of odds prices to reflect track biases, *Management Science* XXXIII: 1428–1439.

SA5. Thaler, R. H. and Ziemba, W. T. (1988). Parimutuel betting markets: Racetracks and lotteries, *Journal of Economic Perspectives* II: 161–174.

SA6. Hausch, D. B. and Ziemba, W. T. (1990). Arbitrage strategies for cross track betting on major horseraces, *Journal of Business* LXIII: 61–78.

SA7. Hausch, D. B. and Ziemba, W. T. (1990). Locks in racetrack minus pools, *Interfaces* (May–June): 41–48.

SA8. Lane, D. and Ziemba, W. T. (2004). Jai-Alai hedging strategies, *European Journal of Finance* 353–369.

SA9. Hausch, D. B., Bain, R. and Ziemba, W. T. (2006). An application of expert information to win betting on the Kentucky Derby, 1981–2001, *European Journal of Finance* 12: 283–301. (Featured on BCTV, May 1999 and in Louisville Times, June 2001).

SA10. MacLean, L. C., Ziemba, W. T. and Korgan, A. (2018). The expected utility of performance: Dominant batting seasons in baseball, *Wilmott* (November): 40–43.

SA11. MacLean, L. C. and Ziemba, W. T. (2019). Efficiency of NFL betting markets, *Wilmott* (January): 34–38.

SA12. Moffitt, S. and Ziemba, W. T. (2019). A risk arbitrage strategy for lotteries, *Wilmott* (March): 52–62.

SA13. Moffitt, S. and Ziemba, W. T. (2019). Does it pay to buy the pot in the Canadian 6/49 lotto? Implications for lottery design, *Wilmott* (May): 43–52.

SA14. Hausch, D. B. and Ziemba, W. T. (1984). *Beat the Racetrack*, Harcourt, Brace and Jovanovich (432 p.); revised and expanded 2nd edition titled Dr. Z's Beat the Racetrack, William Morrow, 1987, 524 p. Both re-issued in hardback and paperback in 2018, 2019 by Echo Books.

SA15. Ziemba, W. T. and Hausch, D. B. (1985). *Betting at the Racetrack*, Dr. Z Investments, Los Angeles, November, 176 p., 2nd edn., Norris Strauss, New York, November 1986, 140 p.

SA16. Ziemba, W. T., Brumelle, S. L., Gautier, A. and Schwartz, S.L. (1986). *Dr. Z's 6/49 Lotto Guidebook*, Dr. Z Investments, Los Angeles, June, 124 p.

SA17. Hausch, D. B., Lo, V., and Ziemba, W. T. (Eds.) (1994). *Efficiency of Racetrack Betting Markets*, Academic Press, 648 p., reprinted in 2008 by World Scientific with a new preface.

SA18. Hausch, D. B. and Ziemba, W. T. (Eds.) (2008). *Handbook of Sports and Lottery Markets*, North Holland Handbooks in Finance Series, September, 536 p.

SA19. Ziemba, W. T. and MacLean, L. C. (2018). *Dr. Z's NFL Guidebook*, World Scientific.

SA20. Ziemba, W. T. (2019). *Exotic Betting at the Racetrack*, World Scientific.

SA21. MacLean, L. C. and Ziemba, W. T. (2021). *Sports Analytics*, World Scientific.

SA22. MacLean, L. and Ziemba, W. (2021). Who are the most important players in team sports? *Journal of Prediction Markets* 15(3): 33–83.

7 Market Anomalies and Crashes

In common with most finance academics, Bill Ziemba believed in the long-term efficiency of financial markets. However, in the short term, there are investor decision biases which create inefficiencies, and a form of risk arbitrage exists. Mean reversion eventually removes the advantage, but for a time, the opportunity for excess returns is available. This effect was observable in horseracing. The favorite-longshot bias is the tendency of bettors to consistently over-bet longshots and under-bet favorites. The prospect of a large payout from a very unlikely result affects the decision (Prospect Theory). Bill wrote widely on racetrack betting and applied his theories at the track (AC1, AC6). He also considered anomalies in the financial market (AC9). Particular attention was focused on seasonal anomalies. The behavior of investors at certain calendar times creates risk arbitrage opportunities. Bill studied the turn-of-the-year effect in multiple papers (AC3, AC4, AC5, AC10, AC16). He also looked at weekend effects and end-of-month effects (AC7, AC8, AC13). Timing is crucial in these anomalies since the advantage is temporary.

In observations on the stock market, there is evidence that the market is not a random walk, but rather there are cycles of expansion and contraction. Bill Ziemba worked on models to anticipate market turns and thereby change the investment strategy. The change point was analyzed as an optimal stopping time in a series of papers (AC20, AC22, AC23, AC24). The bond-stock yield differential (BSEYD) was considered as an index to anticipate or predict a market turn or crash (AC17, AC21, AC25, AC26, AC27). Bill's final papers looked at the prediction of crashes worldwide, particularly in China (AC28, AC30, AC31).

Anomalies and Crashes Publications (Selected Papers in Bold)

AC1. Hausch, D. B. and Ziemba, W. T. (1985). Transactions costs, entries and extent of inefficiencies in a racetrack betting model, *Management Science* XXXI: 381–394.

AC2. Sick, G. and Ziemba, W. T. (1986). Review of "arbitrage theory: Introductory lectures on arbitrage based financial asset pricing by J. E. M. Wilhelm, *European Journal of Operations Research* XXVII: 255–256.

AC3. Ziemba, W. T. (1988). Synopsis of 'playing the turn of the year effect with index futures', *OR/MS Today* XV: 37–38.

AC4. Clark, R. and Ziemba, W. T. (1988). Playing the turn-of-the-year effect with index futures, *Operations Research* XXXV: 799–813.

AC5. Ziemba, W. T. (1988). Discussion of 'the buying and selling behavior of individual investors at the turn of the year' by Jay R. Ritter, *Journal of Finance* XLIII: 717–719.

AC6. Hausch, D. B. and Ziemba, W. T. (1990). Arbitrage strategies for cross track betting on major horseraces, *Journal of Business* LXIII: 61–78.

AC7. Ziemba, W. T. (1991). Japanese security market regularities: Monthly, turn of the month and year, holiday and golden week effects, *Japan and the World Economy* 3: 119–146.

AC8. Ziemba, W. T. (1993). Comment on 'why a weekend effect?' *Journal of Portfolio Management* (Winter): 93–99.

AC9. Ziemba, W. T. (1994). Worldwide security market regularities, *European Journal of Operational Research* 74: 198–229.

AC10. Ziemba, W. T. (1994). Investing in the turn-of-the-year effect in US futures markets, *Interfaces* 24(3): 46–61.

AC11. Hensel, C. R. and Ziemba, W. T. (1995). The January barometer: Swiss, European and global results, *Finanzmarket and Portfolio Management* 9(2): 187–196.

AC12. Shaw, J., Thorp, E. O. and Ziemba, W. T. (1995). Convergence to efficiency of the Nikkei put warrant market of 1989-90, *Applied Mathematical Finance* 2: 243–271.

AC13. Hensel, C. R., Sick, G. and Ziemba, W. T. (1996). Investment results from exploiting turn-of-the-month-effects, *Journal of Portfolio Management* (Spring): 17–23. (A story about this paper is in the November 7, *the Wall Street Journal*)

AC14. Rendon, J. and Ziemba, W. T. (2007). Is the January effect still alive in the futures markets? *Financial Markets and Portfolio Management* 21: 381–396.

AC15. Dzhabarov, C. and Ziemba, W. T. (2010). Do seasonal anomalies still work? *Journal of Portfolio Management*, 36(3): 93–104.

AC16. Ziemba, W. T. (2011). Investing in the turn-of-the-year effect, *Finanzmarket und Portfolio Management* 25(4): 455–472.

AC17. Lleo, S. and Ziemba, W. T. (2012). Stock market crashes in 2007–2009: Were we able to predict them? *Quantitative Finance* 12(8): 1161–1187.

AC18. Shiryaev, A. N., Zhitlukhin, M. V. and Ziemba, W. T. (2014). When to sell apple and the NASDAQ? Trading bubbles with a stochastic disorder model, *Journal of Portfolio Management* (Winter): 1–10.

AC19. Lleo, S. and Ziemba, W. T. (2014). How to lose money in financial markets: Examples from the recent financial crisis, *Alternative Investment Analyst Review* 3(3): 22–35.

AC20. Shiryaev, A. N., Zhitukhin, M. V. and Ziemba, W. T. (2015). Land and stock bubbles, crashes, entry and exit strategies in Japan, circa 1990 and in 2013, *Quantitative Finance*: 30 p.

AC21. Lleo, S. and Ziemba, W. T. (2015). Some historical perspectives on the bond-stock yield model for crash prediction around the world, *International Journal of Forecasting* 31: 399–425.

AC22. Lleo, S., Zhitlukhin, M. V. and Ziemba, W. T. (2016). Introduction to bubbles and crashes, *Quantitative Finance Letters*: 1–3.

AC23. Zhitlukhin, M. V. and Ziemba, W. T (2016). Exit strategies in bubble-like models using a change point model, *Quantitative Finance Letters* 4(1): 47–52.

AC24. Ziemba, W. T. (2016). Non-predictable stock market declines, *Quantitative Finance Letters* 4(1): 53–59.

AC25. Lleo, S. and Ziemba, W. T (2016). The BSEYD crash prediction model: The basic idea and early applications, *Quantitative Finance Letters* 4(1): 19–25.

AC26. Lleo, S. and Ziemba, W. T. (2016). The BSEYD crash prediction model: Additional applications and other models for stock market crash prediction, *Quantitative Finance Letters* 4(1): 26–34.

AC27. Lleo, S. and Ziemba, W. T. (2017). Does the bond stock earnings yield difference model predict equity market corrections better and high PE models? *Financial Markets, Institutions and Instruments* 26(2): 61–123.

AC28. Lleo, S. and Ziemba, W. T. (2018). Predicting stock market crashes in China, *Journal of Portfolio Management* 44(5): 25–135.

AC29. Dzhabarov, C., Ziegler, A. and Ziemba, W. T. (2018). Sell in May: Worldwide evidence, *Quantitative Finance* 18(2): 171–181.

AC30. Lleo, S. and Ziemba, W. T. (2019). Can Warren Buffett also predict equity market downturns? *European Journal of Finance* 25(4): 369–393.

AC31. Lleo, S., Zhitlukhin, M. and Ziemba, W. T. (2022). Using a mean-changing stochastic processes exit–entry model for stock market long–short prediction, *The Journal of Portfolio Management* 49(1) (November): 172–197.

AC32. Lleo, S. and Ziemba, W. T. (2023). Crash prediction using fundamental variables: Evidence from Mainland China, *The Journal of Prediction Markets* 17(1): 85–115.

8 Conclusion

Over a span of 52 years, Bill Ziemba worked tirelessly on important problems in finance and economics. In his work, he collaborated with academics and practitioners worldwide. To those of us who collaborated with Bill, we often struggled to keep up with his pace. In this overview, we are seeking to give a general perspective on the products of Bill's research.

Bill wrote for a variety of audiences. There are several research output measures for academics, primarily the h-index of citations of peer-reviewed journals. There are also practitioner metrics, such as books in the Library of Congress (LOC) and professional articles in *Portfolio Management Review (PMR)* journals. If one ranks practitioners from highest to lowest, one finds that in a group of applied financial researchers compiled by John Guerard, Bill was the highest-ranked composite (equally weighted) contributing author.

We have benefited greatly from interactions with Bill Ziemba. He has helped shape our careers and those of many other colleagues. We miss Bill and thank him for years of fun and inspiration.

Section I

Stochastic Programming

Chapter 2

SOLVING NONLINEAR PROGRAMMING PROBLEMS WITH STOCHASTIC OBJECTIVE FUNCTIONS#

*William T. Ziemba**

In many nonlinear programming applications the objective function has an inherent uncertainty that depends upon a set of random variables that have a known distribution. If one wishes to optimize the expectation of the objective, as suggested by the expected utility theorem, then as is shown here one can often solve such problems by modifying standard nonlinear programming algorithms. To illustrate what is involved, the details and justification for the application of the interior parametric sequential unconstrained maximization technique and the generalized programming method for the solution of such problems are given. Some related problems with stochastic constraints for which the solution method applies are mentioned and an example of a portfolio selection problem is given.

I. Introduction

In many nonlinear programming applications the numerical valuation of the objective function depends upon several random variables. If the joint distribution of these random variables is known or can be subjectively estimated, there are several ways of approaching such problems. One may wish to look at the distribution of the maximum overall possible occurrences of the random variables. This is the method utilized in stochastic linear programming as formalized by Tinter. See Bereanu [2 and 3] and Walkup and Wets [32] for recent research and references in this area. Alternatively, one may treat the problem as either an aspiration or fractile program, see [14, 17, and 25], if one wishes to maximize the probability that the return will be at least some given amount or if one wishes to maximize the return level which is attained with at least a given probability level. For a recent review of these and other approaches to problems involving Charnes's and Copper's idea of using chance constraints, see [18]. A third approach is to utilize the expected

**University of British Columbia.* *This research has been partially supported by the National Research Council and by the University of British Columbia Committee on Research. Without implicating them, I would like to thank S. L. Brumelle, L. G. Mitten, J. Ohlson, G. Pye, and a referee of this journal for helpful comments on this work.*

#This chapter was originally published in: Ziemba, W. T. (1972). Solving Nonlinear Programming Problems with Stochastic Objective Functions. *Journal of Financial and Quantitative Analysis*, 7(3), 1809–1827.

utility approach of Bernoulli, Ramsey, Von Neumann, and Morgenstern. If several rationality assumptions concerning the decision maker's behavior are satisfied, then the decision maker behaves so as to maximize the expectation of a continuous utility function; see Fishburn [10] for references and a comprehensive presentation of many such theories.

It is of interest to consider methods for calculating optimal decisions for expected utility problems in which the decision vector is constrained. Research in this area falls mainly into five categories. First there are cases in which the optimal solution may be explicitly determined, e.g., [28]. Secondly there are a number of special cases in which the optimization problem reduces to an explicit deterministic equivalent, e.g., when the nonseparable decision and random terms of the utility function are bilinear [21], when the utility function is exponential and the random variables have a joint normal distribution [12], when the random variables are discrete [4 and 26], and when the utility function is polynomial [27].

A third approach is to integrate out the random variables to obtain an explicit deterministic program whose solution may be sought via standard algorithms. This approach is usually difficult although for some special cases such expressions have been obtained [1, 34, and 39].

A fourth approach is to apprxoimate either the utility function or the random variables to reduce the problem to one of the preceding cases. Discrete approximations of the random variables and Taylor series approximations of the utility function (see e.g. [16, 29]) are leading examples of this approach.

A fifth approach with which this paper is concerned is to provide modifications that enable standard nonlinear programming algorithms to be utilized in the solution process. Examples of algorithms so modified are the Arrow-Hurwicz gradient procedure [7], the Dantzig-Wolfe generalized programming algorithm [25], the Frank-Wolfe Algorithm [34 and 38], and the convex simplex method [38]. Williams [35] has provided an additional algorithm that proceeds via a series of linear programming surrogate approximations. These algorithms were presented in the context of the linear or concave simple recourse problem (see Section III below for these definitions). The essential idea in each of these algorithmic modifications is that one can either: (a) evaluate the gradient of the objective at all feasible points; (b) evaluate the objective at all feasible points, or both. Hence, under such assumptions, essentially all nonlinear programming algorithms may be employed for the solution of these problems.

II. Basic Algorithmic Modifications

The problem is to find an x* that solves

(1) maximize $Z(x) \equiv E_\xi\,[f(x,\xi)]$,
subject to $g_i(x) \geqq 0,\ i=1,\ \ldots,\ m$,

where $x \varepsilon R^n$, ξ is a random s-vector defined on the probability space $(\Xi, \mathcal{F}, F)$ that is distributed independently of x; E_ξ denotes mathematical expectation with respect to ξ; $f, g_1, \ldots, g_m$ and Z are real valued scalar functions; and $K \equiv \{x \mid g_1(x) \geqq 0, \ldots, g_m(x) \geqq 0\}$ is the feasible region. Recall that the object is to solve (1) without explicitly calculating Z or ∇Z, the gradient of Z.

Feasible direction algorithms (see e.g. [37, 42, and 43] for details) proceed via the following procedure:

0. Initialization. Find an $x^1 \varepsilon K$. Set k=1.
1. Find an n dimensional direction vector d^k that is:
   a. Feasible. $\exists \lambda^\circ > 0: \forall\, 0 \leqq \lambda \leqq \lambda^\circ \quad (x^k + \lambda d^k)\ \varepsilon\ K$; and
   b. Usable. $\nabla Z(x^k)' d^k > 0$.
2. Find a step length λ^k:

$$Z(x^k + \lambda^k d^k) = \max_{\lambda \geqq 0} \{Z(x^k + \lambda d^k) \mid (x^k + \lambda d^k)\ \varepsilon\ K\}.$$

   Set $x^{k+1} = x^k + \lambda^k d^k$.
3. Terminate if the stopping criteria is satisfied. Otherwise go to (1) with k=k+1.

The initialization step may proceed, e.g., by a repeated application of a standard algorithm [9] or by a Phase I procedure (if the g_i are linear). Feasible direction vectors d^k have the property that they do not point out of K, i.e., $\nabla g_i(x^k)' d \geqq \varepsilon$ $(\varepsilon > 0)$ for constraints that are active at x^k, i.e., $g_i(x^k)=0$. The direction-finding subproblem can take a number of forms such as a simplex pivot (in the convex simplex method), or a linear or quadratic program (in various first- and second-order gradient methods, respectively). These calculations may require that Z, ∇Z, and the Hessian matrix $\nabla\nabla Z$ be evaluated at x^k. The step-length calculation, of which that suggested in (2) is one of several possibilities, usually proceeds via a search procedure or an explicit calculation. In either case, evaluations of Z and ∇Z may be required at a number of points. Clearly then, such procedures may be applied to (1) if the appropriate function evaluations can be performed.

Topkis and Veinott [31, Theorem 2] and Zangwill [37, p. 281] have proven general convergence theorems for feasible direction methods. Under appropriate assumptions, convergence is guaranteed to a stationary point which will be an optimal point if f is pseudoconcave and the g_i are quasiconcave. The essential conditions these authors utilize in their convergence proofs that are relevant here (since K corresponds to a "standard" feasible region) are that Z must be continuously differentiable. A set of sufficient conditions implying that ∇Z is continuous and can be easily calculated is contained in

Theorem 1 [38]: Suppose that $f(x,\varepsilon)$ defined on an open subset of R^{n+s} is integrable and continuously differentiable in x and that there exist n integrable functions G_i on Ξ such that

$$|\partial f(x,\xi)/\partial x_i| \leq G_i(\xi), \quad i=1, \ldots, n.$$

Then $Z(x) \equiv E_\xi[f(x,\xi)]$ is continuously differentiable and $\partial Z(x)/\partial x_i = E_\xi[\partial f(x,\xi)/\partial x_i], \quad i=1, \ldots, n.$

A number of algorithms such as various penalty function methods, some cutting plane algorithms, and various methods of centers, do not utilize direction vectors and converge to an optimal point even if Z (and the g_i) are not continuously differentiable -- concavity is required only for the cutting plane methods.[1] These algorithms proceed by solving a sequence of problems that approximate either K or Z.

The convergence proofs given in [37] assume in particular that Z and the g_i are continuous (and that K satisfies certain regularity assumptions). The following theorem presents sufficient conditions for Z to be continuous on K.

Theorem 2: Suppose that for any $x^\circ \varepsilon K$ and $\varepsilon>0$, $\exists \delta>0$: $|x-x^\circ|<\delta$ for $x\varepsilon K$ implies $|f(x,\xi) - f(x^\circ,\xi)|>\varepsilon$, for almost all $\xi\varepsilon\Xi$, where $Z(x) \equiv \int \ldots \int f(x,\xi)dF(\xi)$ exists and is finite at x° and exists at all x in any neighborhood of x°.

Proof:

$$\begin{aligned} |Z(x) - Z(x^\circ)| &\equiv \left| \int \ldots \int f(x,\xi)dF(\xi) - \int \ldots \int f(x^\circ,\xi)dF(\xi) \right| \\ &\leq \int \ldots \int |f(x,\xi) - f(x^\circ,\xi)|dF(\xi) \\ &< \int \ldots \int \varepsilon dF(\xi) = \varepsilon. \end{aligned}$$

Hence under this convergence assumption and the assumption that Z can be evaluated for all $x\varepsilon K$, one can apply any of these algorithms to solve (1) (as long as K satisfies the required regularity conditions).

III. Related Simple Recourse Problems

Many two-stage stochastic programs with recourse may be formulated as

[1]The generalized programming algorithm considered below in Section VI is dual to a cutting plane algorithm.

(2) $\quad \text{maximize } \ell_1(x) + E_\xi[\max_y\{\ell_2(y,\xi)\}],$

$\quad\quad \text{subject to } \ell_3(x,y,\xi) = 0,$

$\quad\quad\quad x\varepsilon K, \quad y\varepsilon Y,$

where $K\subset R^n$, $Y\subset R^q$, $\xi\varepsilon\Xi\ R^s$, ℓ_1 and ℓ_2 are real valued scalar functions, and ℓ_3 is a real valued vector function. The program (2) depicts the following decision situation: choose the decision x in such a way that, after the random vector ξ is observed, a recourse action y may be chosen and the sum of the preferences for x and the recourse and random vectors is maximized. The formulation (2) is very similar to that considered by Mangasarian and Rosen [23] in a paper where bounds on the optimal solution were presented as well as two examples.

Let $U(x,\xi) \equiv \{y|y\varepsilon Y, \ell_3(x,y,\xi) = 0\}$. Now if U has at most one element for each $(x,\xi)\ \varepsilon\ (K\times\Xi)$, the maximization over y is ficticious and (2) is equivalent to

(3) $\quad \text{maximize } \ell_1(x) + E_\xi[\ell_2(y,\xi)|\ell_3(x,y,\xi) = 0\ ],$

$\quad\quad \text{subject to } x\varepsilon K.$

In some cases, e.g. [13], there exists a unique q-dimensional inverse function $\tilde{\ell}_3$ such that $y = \tilde{\ell}_3(x,\xi)$ and (3) simplifies to

(4) $\quad \text{maximize } \ell_1(x) + E_\xi\ \{\ell_2[\tilde{\ell}_3\ (x,\xi),\xi]\},$

$\quad\quad \text{subject to } x\varepsilon K,$

which is a special case of (1) with $f(x,\xi) = \ell_1(x) + \ell_2[\tilde{\ell}_3\ (x,\xi),\xi]$.

Often (4) will satisfy the hypotheses needed for the application of various algorithms because $\ell_2[\tilde{\ell}_3(x,\xi),\xi]$ is: (a) a concave function of x if $\tilde{\ell}_3$ is concave in x (see [33] for some conditions on ℓ_3 that guarantee this) and ℓ_2 is concave and monotone nondecreasing in y; and (b) a continuously differentiable function of x if ℓ_2 and ℓ_3 are both continuously differentiable functions of their first argument.

Two special cases of (4) are of special interest and are termed: (i) the linear simple recourse model [34] if ℓ_1 and ℓ_3 are linear, ℓ_2 is a piecewise linear function about the origin, and K is a convex polytope; and (ii) the concave simple recourse model [38] if ℓ_1 and ℓ_2 are concave, ℓ_3 is linear, and K is a closed convex set.

Note that a number of important special cases, such as the "linear everything random" case, i.e., $\ell_3(x,y,\xi) = A(\xi)x + B(\xi)y-b(\xi)$, where the matrix $B(\xi)$ is nonsingular for all $\xi\varepsilon\Xi$, may be put into the form of (4).

IV. Solution Method via SUMT

A number of interesting and useful penalty function methods have been discussed by a number of authors and particularly by Fiacco and McCormick. The various methods differ in several ways, the most important of which is whether or not the method works in the interior or exterior of the feasible region. Interior, exterior, and interior-exterior methods have been proposed and general convergence theorems for interior and exterior methods have been given by Fiacco and McCormick [9] and Zangwill [37]. Convergence to an optimal solution x* is proved under rather mild assumptions. Zangwill's proofs, for example, assume for exterior methods that the problem's functions are continuous and that x* and the sequence of unconstrained optima $\{x^k\}$ exist and belong to a compact set, and they assume for interior methods that the problem's functions are continuous, x* exists and is not isolated, and the compact feasible region has an interior point.

For our purpose it suffices to consider the less general interior method conjectured by Carroll that Fiacco and McCormick [8, 9] have justified. For problem (1) let $K^\circ \equiv \{x|g_1(x)>0, \ldots, g_m(x)>0\}$ be the interior of the feasible region K and assume

A1. The functions $g_1, \ldots, g_m$ are concave as is the function f for every fixed $\xi\varepsilon\Xi$.

A2. The functions $g_1, \ldots, g_m$ are twice continuously differentiable as is the function f for every fixed $\xi\varepsilon\Xi$.

A3. $K^\circ \neq \phi$.

A4. $f(x,\xi), \partial f(x,\xi)/\partial x_i$ and $\partial^2 f(x,\xi)/\partial x_i\partial x_j$ are integrable functions of ξ for all $x\varepsilon K$, i, j=1, ..., n.

A5. For every finite L, $\{x|Z(x)\leqq L, x\varepsilon K\}$ is a bounded set.

A6. The function $P(x,r) \equiv Z(x) - r\sum_{i=1}^{m} 1/g_i(x)$ is, for each r>0, strictly concave for all $x\varepsilon K^\circ$.

A7. Given any $x\varepsilon K^\circ$, it is possible to numerically evaluate $E_\xi[\partial f(x,\xi)/\partial x_i]$ and $E_\xi[\partial^2 f(x,\xi)/\partial x_i\partial x_j]$, i, j=1, ..., m.

The following theorem will prove useful.

Theorem 3: Suppose $f(x,\xi)$ and $\partial f(x,\xi)/\partial x_i$, i=1, ..., n defined on open subsets of R^{n+s} are integrable and twice $(f(x,\xi))$ is continuously different-in x and there exist nxn integrable functions G_{ij} on Ξ such that

$$|\partial^2 f(x,\xi)/\partial x_i \partial x_j| \leqq G_{ij}(\xi),\ i,\ j=1,\ \ldots,\ n.$$

Then $Z(x) \equiv E_\xi[f(x,\xi)]$ is twice continuously differentiable and

$$\partial^2 Z(x)/\partial x_i \partial x_j = E_\xi[\partial^2 f(x,\xi)/\partial x_i \partial x_j],\ i,\ j=1,\ \ldots,\ n.$$

Proof i: Differentiability.

Since $\partial f(x,\xi)/\partial x_i$, i=1, ..., n, is integrable, $\partial^2 f(x,\xi)/\partial x_i \partial x_j$ is measurable, and $E_\xi\ \{\partial^2 f(x,\xi)/\partial x_i \partial x_j$ exists, i, j=1, ..., n. By the mean value theorem for given vectors x and x^1, there exists an $\hat{x}$ such that

$$\frac{\partial f(x^1,\xi)}{\partial x_i} - \frac{\partial f(x,\xi)}{\partial x_i} = (x_j^{\ 1} - x_j)\ \frac{\partial^2 f(\hat{x},\xi)}{\partial x_i \partial x_j},\quad i,\ j=1,\ \ldots,\ n$$

Thus

$$\left|\frac{\partial f(x^1,\xi)}{\partial x_i}\right| = \left|\frac{\partial f(x,\xi)}{\partial x_i}\right| + \left|x_j^{\ 1} - x_j\right|\ G_{ij}(\xi),$$

and

$$\frac{\ell_1(x^1) - \ell_1(x)}{x_j^1 - x_j} = E_\xi\left[\frac{\partial f(x^1,\xi)/\partial x_i - \partial f(x,\xi)/\partial x_i}{x_j^1 - x_j}\right]$$

where $\ell_i(x) \equiv E_\xi[f(x,\xi)/\ x_i]$, i, j=1, ..., n.
Since the integrand is bounded by $G_{ij}\ (\xi)$, we may apply the Lebesgue dominated convergence theorem [20] to verify that

$$\frac{\partial^2 Z(x)}{\partial x_i \partial x_j} = E_\xi\left[\frac{\partial^2 f(x,\xi)}{\partial x_i \partial x_j}\right],\ i,\ j=1,\ \ldots,\ n.$$

Proof ii: Continuous differentiability.

Again by the dominated convergence theorem, if $\partial^2 f(x,\xi)/\partial x_i \partial x_j$ is continuous in x for all $\xi \varepsilon \Xi$, $\partial^2 Z(x)/\partial x_i \partial x_j$ is continuous for all $x \varepsilon R^n$, i, j=1, ..., n.

For the penalty function $P(x,r) \equiv Z(x) - r \sum_{i=1}^{m} 1/g_i(x)$, it may be observed as in [8] that:

1. A2-A5 imply existence of finite number v_o, where

$$v_o = \sup_{x\varepsilon K} Z(x) = \max_{x\varepsilon K} Z(x).$$

2. A1 implies that (1) is a concave program.
3. A1 implies that $P(x,r)$ is concave, for all $x\varepsilon K°$, for each fixed $r>0$. Strict concavity is satisfied if:
   (i) for some subset Ξ_1 of Ξ having positive measure, $f(x,\xi)$ is strictly concave for every fixed $\xi\varepsilon\Xi_1$; or
   (ii) any g_i is strictly concave; or
   (iii) there exists n independent linear constraints to the problem such as $x_i \geqq 0$, $i=1, \ldots, n$.

Using P, one chooses an initial value of r, say r_1, and maximizes $P(x,r_1)$ over R^n. If the starting point of the unconstrained optimization method is in K°, the boundary repulsion term $(-r_1 \sum_{i=1}^{m} {}^1/g_i(x))$ which $\to -\infty$ as $x\to$ (the boundary of K) forces all points in the unconstrained maximization sequence, including the maximizer, to belong to K°. One then reduces r to $r_2<r_1$ and repeats. Fiacco and McCormick proved under hypotheses analogous to A1-A7 that the sequence of $x^k \to x^*$.

Specifically they proved:

Theorem 4 [8]: If conditions A1-A7 obtain:

(a) each function $P(x,r_k)$ is maximized over K° at a unique $x^k\varepsilon K°$ where $\nabla_x P(x^k,r_k) = 0$;

(b) $\lim_{k\to\infty} P(x^k,r_k) = \max_{x\varepsilon K} Z(x) = v_o$; and

(c) $\lim_{k\to\infty} Z(x^k) = v_o$, $\lim_{k\to\infty} r_k \sum_{i=1}^{m} {}^1/g_i(x^k) = 0$.

They also observed the important fact that the method yielded dual feasible points (x^k, u^k) to the Wolfe dual [36] of (1) namely

$$\text{minimize } W(x, u) \equiv Z(x) + \sum_{i=1}^{m} u_i g_i(x),$$

$$\text{subject to } \nabla_x W(x, u) = 0,$$

$$u_i \geqq 0, \; i=1, \ldots, m.$$

where $u_i^k \equiv r_k/g_i^2(x^k)$, $i=1, \ldots, m$, and hence:

Theorem 5[8]: If conditions A1-A7 obtain:

(a) $\lim_{k\to\infty} W(x^k, u^k) = v_o$; and

(b) $W(x^k, u^k) \geqq v_o \geqq Z(x^k)$.

The algorithmic procedure is

0. Initialization. Set $r_1 = r_1°$.
1. Set $r_k = \phi_k(r_{k-1})$.

Solve $\max_{x \in R^n} P(x,r_k)$ for x^k.

2. If $r_k \sum_{i=1}^{m} {}^1/g_i(x^k) \leqq \varepsilon$,

terminate with ε-optimal solution x^k. If not go to Step 1 with k = k+1.

The major computation effort is in the maximization of the $P(x,r_k)$. Under the assumptions, P is twice continuously differentiable, hence first- and second-order gradient methods are used to maximize P utilizing the gradient vector

$$\nabla P(x,r) = E_\xi[\nabla h(x,\xi)] + r \sum_{i=1}^{m} \nabla g_i(x) \ [g_i(x)]^2,$$

and the Hessian matrix

$$\nabla\nabla P(x,r) = E_\xi[\nabla\nabla h(x,\xi)] - r \sum_{i=1}^{m} \nabla\nabla g_i(x)/[g_i(x)]^3.$$

V. Example: Portfolio Selection

Consider an investor faced with the task of allocating his budget B among n possible investment opportunities $I_1, \ldots, I_n$. Each investment of x_j dollars in I_j returns ξ_j dollars per dollar invested at the end of the investment period, with $F(\xi_1, \ldots, \xi_n)$ being the joint distribution of returns. If the investor is a risk averter, in that he prefers not to take fair gambles, his utility function u is concave. Assume that the investor is rational in that he behaves as if he wishes to choose a portfolio that maximizes the expectation of u. The investment choices x_j must satisfy certain size-purchase constraints, related to minimum and maximum investment in particular opportunities, as well as the budget constraint. If the investor wishes to include the possibility of short sales, in which he sells x_j dollars ($x_j<0$) of investment I_j and must buy (repay) at ξ_j, then α_j the lower bound on x_j will be negative.[2] The

[2] In practice one usually has the further complication that the investor must put up ϕ dollars security for each dollar invested in I_i sold short and x_i is received at the end, not the beginning, of the investment period. For convenience we will assume that there are sufficient funds invested to provide the necessary security for the short sales and hence formulation 5 need not be altered. If such funds are not available, one may accommodate this short-sale regulation by letting

$$x_j = x_j^+ + x_j^-, \text{ where } x_j^+ \geqq 0 \text{ and } x_j^- \leqq 0$$

represent investment and short selling in investment i, respectively. The essential changes in formulation B are that the budget constraint becomes

$\sum_{j=1}^{n} \{x_j^+ - (1+\phi)x_j^-\} \leqq B(1+y)$, and the objective's argument becomes

borrowing of margin funds yB at cost c(yB) is also accommodated in the formulation

$$\text{(5)}\quad \text{maximize } E_{\xi_1,\ldots,\xi_n}\, u\{\sum_{j=1}^{n} \xi_j\cdot x_j - c(yB)\},$$

$$\text{subject to } \sum_{j=1}^{n} x_j \leqq B(1+y),$$

$$\alpha_j \leqq x_j \leqq B_j,$$

$$x_j/B \leqq \gamma, \qquad j=1,\ldots,n,$$

$$0 \leqq y \leqq \delta.$$

Since u is a utility function over wealth, it is monotone nondecreasing and hence the objective of (5) will be concave in y if c is convex in y, that is, if the marginal cost of the margin funds is nondecreasing.

The investor's problem can be further complicated by supposing that he wants to guard against ruination and hence he would like $P_r\{\sum_{j=1}^{n} \xi_j x_j \geqq 0\}$ to be at least ϕ, where ϕ is a number strictly below but close to 1. Suppose that $\xi \equiv (\xi_1 \ldots \xi_n)$ has a multivariate normal distribution with mean vector $\bar{\xi}$ and variance-covariance matrix V. Let F be the cumulative distribution of a normally distributed random variable with zero mean and unit variance, i.e., $F(z) = \int_{-\infty}^{z} \frac{1}{\sqrt{2\pi}} \exp\{-t^2/2\}dt$, and D_ϕ is the ϕ-fractile of F, thus $F(D_\phi) = \phi$. Then it is well known in the chance constrained programming literature, see [25], that:

(i) $P\{\sum_{j=1}^{n} \xi_j x_j \geqq 0\} \geqq \phi$ if and only if $h(x) \equiv \sum_{j=1}^{n} \bar{\xi}_j x_j - D_\phi (x'Vx)^{1}/2 \geqq 0$;

(ii) h is concave if $\phi \geqq .5$; and

(iii) $\ell(x) \equiv (x'Vx)^{1}/_2$ is subdifferentiable with

$$\nabla\ell(x) = \begin{cases} \dfrac{Vx}{\ell(x)} & \text{if } \ell(x) > 0 \\ 0 & \text{if } \ell(x) = 0. \end{cases}$$

Now $\ell(x)$ and hence $h(x)$ are continuously differentiable in the interior of $\{x|h(x)\geqq 0\}$, if V is positive definite and $x \neq 0$. These assumptions are required

---

$$[\sum_{j=1}^{n} \{\xi_j x_j^{+} - (2+\phi-\xi_j)x_j^{-}\} \quad -c(yB)].$$

if a first-order method is used to maximize the penalty function, otherwise the SUMT method may fail if $\nabla\ell(x)$ is not continuous. If a second-order method is used to maximize the penalty function, it must also be assumed that V is positive definite and $x\neq 0$ to guarantee that the Hessian of ℓ, namely, $[\ell(x)V-\nabla\ell(x)'Vx]/[\ell(x)]^2$ is continuous. Under this specification, the problem is to solve (5) with the additional nonlinear restriction that

$$\sum_{j=1}^{n} \bar{\xi}_j x_j - c(yB) - D_{\phi} (x'Vx)^{1/2} \geqq 0.$$

VI. Solution Method of the Portfolio Problem via Generalized Programming

In the portfolio selection example, although the optimization problem is to choose the investment allocations, the utility function depends only upon the single random variable wealth. It is clear that in the use of SUMT and all other first- and second-order methods, one will need to evaluate multivariate integrals (if the ξ_j do not have discrete distributions). However, if one considers methods that only utilize function evaluations, only univariate integrations are required. One such method that appears to be particularly well suited for such problems is the Dantzig-Wolfe generalized programming algorithm [5]. Let us suppose that the problem has form (5). If $c(\cdot)$ is linear, that problem has the form of

$$(6)\qquad v_o = \text{maximum } Z(x) \equiv E_{\xi}\, u(\xi'x),$$
$$\text{subject to } Ax \leqq b,\ x \geqq 0,$$

where u is a concave utility function over returns $R = \xi'x$; x is an nx1 decision vector; A is an mxn matrix of constants; and b is a mx1 vector of constants. Assume that Z(x) is finite for finite x, that (6) has an optimal solution, and that at each iteration the linear program (8) (see below) has at least one non-degenerate basic feasible solution.

Theorem 6: (i) Z is concave and continuous in x if u is concave and continuous in R; (ii) Z is strictly concave in x if u is strictly concave in R, and $\xi'x^1 = \xi'x^2$ for all $\xi\in\Xi$ implies $x^1 = x^2$.

Proof: By the concavity of u

$$(7)\qquad u\{\xi'[\lambda x^1+(1-\lambda)x^2]\} \geqq \lambda u(\xi'x^1) + (1-\lambda)u(\xi'x^2)$$

for $0 \leqq \lambda \leqq 1$, fixed ξ and all $x^1, x^2 \in K$. Taking the expectation of both sides of (7) gives

$$Z\{\lambda x^1+(1-\lambda)x^2\} \geqq Z(x^1) + (1-\lambda)Z(x^2);$$

hence Z is concave. The same argument applies for strict concavity with $x^1 \neq x^2$ and strict inequalities replacing inequalities, under the assumptions.

The continuity assumption implies that for any $\varepsilon>0$ and fixed ξ, there exists a $\delta>0$ such that

$$||x^1-x^2|| < \delta \qquad \text{implies} \qquad |u(\xi'x^1) - u(\xi'x^2)|<\varepsilon.$$

Hence

$$\begin{aligned} |Z(x^1)-Z(x^2)| &\equiv |\int\cdots\int u(\xi'x^1)dF(\xi)- \int\cdots\int u(\xi'x^2)\, dF(\xi)| \\ &\leqq \int\cdots\int|u(\xi'x^1) - u(\xi'x^2)|dF(\xi) \\ &< \int\cdots\int\varepsilon dF(\xi) = \varepsilon. \end{aligned}$$

Thus Z is continuous in x.

Thus under reasonable assumptions, Z is continuous and hence (6) has a maximum if $\{x|Z(x)\geqq\alpha\}$ is nonempty and bounded for all scalars α [41]. If Z is concave, local maxima to (6) will be global maxima and the Kuhn-Tucker saddle-point conditions are necessary and sufficient for a global maxima. The maximizing point will be unique in the strict concavity case.

It is our purpose to solve (6) without explicitly calculating Z(x) when Z is concave and continuous (but not necessarily continuously differentiable) and Z(x) can be numerically evaluated for any feasible x. The generalized programming algorithm utilizes the simplex method to solve a sequence of linear programs. At each step the linear program adds an additional column which is chosen from a convex set. The determination of this column involves an unconstrained maximization, and the discussion here utilizes the cyclic coordinate ascent method (see, e.g., [37]) for this purpose.[3]

A generalized linear program that is equivalent to (6) is

$$\begin{aligned} &\text{maximize} \quad \theta\lambda, \\ &\text{subject to} \quad Ax \leqq b,\ x \geqq 0, \\ &\qquad\qquad\quad \lambda = 1, \end{aligned}$$

[3] In practice one would normally combine the cyclic coordinate ascent method with other methods such as that of conjugate directions or Stewart's modification of Davidson's method to improve the rate of convergence. See Fletcher [11] and Zangwill [37] for more discussion.

where the column $\begin{pmatrix}\theta \\ x\end{pmatrix}$ is to be chosen from the convex set

$$T \equiv \{(\theta,x) \mid Z(x) \geqq \theta\}.$$

Let (θ^1,x^1), ..., (θ^L,x^L) be L points in T. Then in the Lth iteration one solves the linear program

$$\text{(8)} \quad \begin{aligned} &\text{maximize } W = \theta^1\lambda^1 + \cdots + \theta^L\lambda^L, \\ &\text{Subject to } A(\lambda^1x^1 + \cdots + \lambda^Lx^L) \geqq b \qquad : \alpha^L, \\ &\qquad \lambda^1 + \cdots + \lambda^L = 1 \qquad : \beta^L, \\ &\qquad \lambda^1 \geqq 0, \ldots, \lambda^L \geqq 0 . \end{aligned}$$

For any value of x^ℓ, $\ell=1$, ..., L, $Z(x^\ell)$ is the largest value θ^ℓ can take in the set T, and it is clear that θ^ℓ does achieve this value.

Let (α^L,β^L) be an optimal dual solution to (6) having solution value W^L. By duality

$$W^L = b'\alpha^L + \beta^L.$$

To test for the optimality of the solution $(x^*)^L = \lambda^1x^1 + \cdots + \lambda^Lx^L$, one solves the subproblem

$$\text{(9)} \quad \begin{aligned} &\text{maximize } \theta - \alpha^LAx + \beta^L, \\ &\text{Subject to} \quad (\theta,x)\varepsilon T. \end{aligned}$$

Since β^L is a constant and since θ can achieve its largest value Z(x), (9) is equivalent to

$$\text{(10)} \quad S^L = \text{maximize } S(x) = Z(x) - \alpha^LAx.$$

If $S^L \leqq 0$ then $(x^*)^L$ is optimal. Otherwise any x^{L+1}, such that $S(x^{L+1}) > 0$ with corresponding $\theta^{L+1} = Z(x^{L+1})$ represents a column to be entered into the master program (8) for iteration L+1.

The calculation of an x^{L+1} may proceed via the cyclic coordinate ascent method as follows. Let e_i, i=1, ..., n be unit n-vectors having all coordinates zero except the ith coordinate which is unity. Given a point x^1 set $x^{10} = x^1$.

Determine x^{11} by maximizing $S(x)$ in the positive and negative direction e_1 from x^1. Then determine x^{12} by maximizing $S(x)$ in the positive and negative direction e_2 from x^{11}. Continuing in this manner, after determining x^{12}, one determines x^{21}, etc.

The x^{ij} may be determined via a one-dimensional Fibonnacci search. Under the assumptions, it can be shown [5] that the method converges to an optimal solution to (6) and that at each iteration the following bounds obtain

$$(11)\quad W^L \leqq Z\,[(x^*)^L] \leqq Z \leqq S^L + W^L.$$

Hence one may stop at an ε-optimal solution when $S^L \leqq \varepsilon$.

A flow chart of the procedure appears in Figure I. A similar procedure may be developed for cases in which the constraints are nonlinear. See [5].

VII. Some Remarks

A. The use of SUMT or the generalized programming or any other algorithm for the solution indicated of the expected utility problem involves the numerical evaluation of single or multivariate integrals (unless the random variables have discrete distributions). The development of approximation schemes for evaluating such integrals as those encountered in the problems considered here is a standard problem in numerical analysis. A number of these methods are presented in [6] and [15]. The multivariate calculations are usually difficult and computationally time-consuming if one demands high accuracy. The level of difficulty rises much more than linearly with the number of dimensions. Univariate calculations are relatively easy, and only univariate calculations are required in the following two leading cases. If $f(x,\xi)$ is separable into $\sum_{j=1}^{n} f_j(x_j,\xi_j)$ with $n=s$, then only the univariate integrals $E_{\xi_j}[f_j(x_j,\xi_j)]$, $E_{\xi_j}\left[\frac{\partial^k f_j(x_j,\xi_j)}{\partial x_j^k}\right]$, $k=1,2$ must be evaluated for fixed x_j using the marginal distributions of the ξ_j even if the ξ_j are correlated. The other leading case, which is illustrated in the portfolio example, obtains when the functional depends upon a single random variable W which in turn is the linear sum, $\sum_{j=1}^{n} \xi_j x_j$, and the x_j are the decision variables. Given the distribution function of the ξ_j, $F(\xi_1, \ldots, \xi_n)$ and a given vector x, one may generate the distribution function of W, say $G(W|x)$, and the numerical evaluations may utilize G. In general G will not have a simple parametric form unless F is multivariate normal or stable.

FIGURE 1

GENERALIZED PROGRAMMING ALGORITHM FLOWCHART

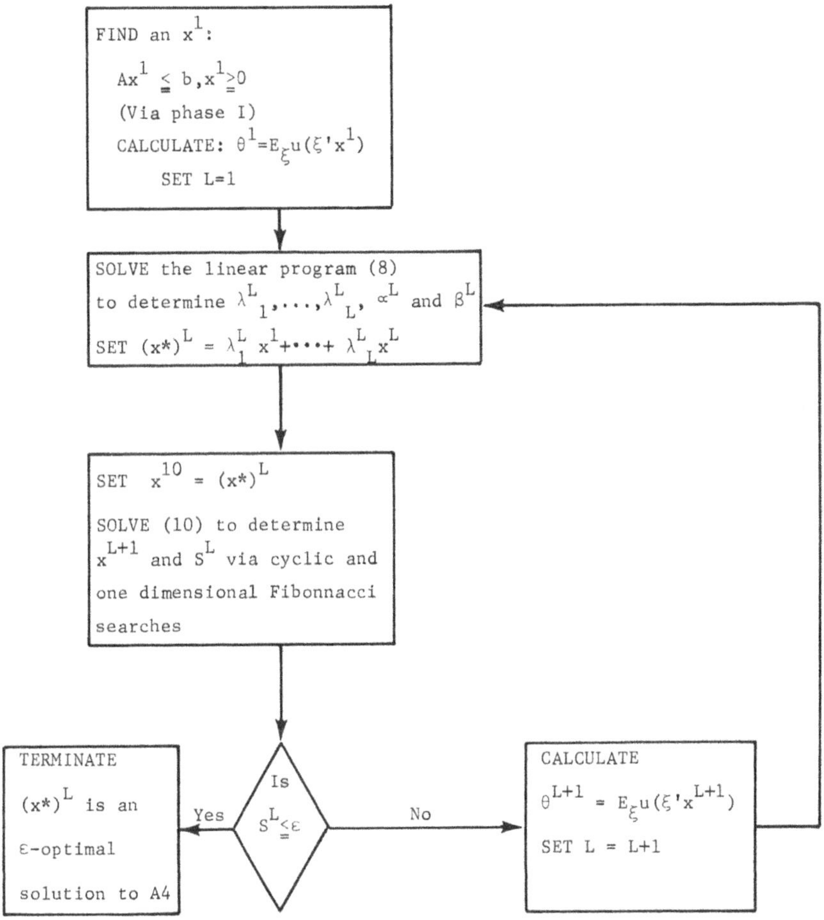

B. The case when F is multivariate normal simplifies dramatically when one recalls that, under the assumption that the investor can borrow or lend any given quantity x_o at a pure interest rate r_o, the Tobin separation theorem [30] guarantees that all the x_j^*/x_i^* except that corresponding to x_o are constant independent of the utility function as long as that function is concave. One may compute the optimal proportions $x_1^*, \ldots, x_n^*$ by solving a single fractional program as Lintner has shown [19]. One then chooses the best weights α and $(1-\alpha)$ between the risky asset $r_1 = \sum_{j=1}^{n} \xi_j x_j^*$ and the pure interest asset x_o having return r_o. One solves, $\max \{h(\alpha) \equiv \max E_{r_1} [\alpha r_o + (1-\alpha)r_1]\}$ using either a bisecting or a Fibonnacci search [37] for the best $\alpha\epsilon[\alpha_\ell,\alpha_u]$. Strictly speaking, α_ℓ may be < 0 and $\alpha_u > 1$; however, one may check to see if the interval [0,1] may be used by evaluating the partial derivatives of h at 1 and 0. If these derivatives are nonpositive and nonnegative, respectively, the interval [0,1] will suffice as h is concave in α. Otherwise one must consider larger intervals that have end points having these respective signs. See [41] for more detail on this and for some numerical results utilizing several common utility function classes. A similar theory is available for certain classes of stable investments; see [40].

C. The numerical evaluation of the various functions involved provides one source of error in the calculation. To minimize such errors one would, of course, utilize finer tolerances in the approximate calculations in the later iterations of the particular algorithm used.

Regarding the SUMT method, there is another source of error involved because the P-function often becomes ill-conditioned particularly as r gets very small. This is particularly true when Newton's method is used to maximize P. In this case Murray [24] showed that the ratio of the largest to smallest eigenvalues of $\nabla\nabla P$ tends to ∞ as $r \to 0$ if there are an unequal number of constraints and variables. Hence the determination of the search directions by solving $(\nabla\nabla P)\, d = -\nabla P$ as is done in Newton's method becomes more and more ill-conditioned. However if one uses Davidson's method which approximates the inverse of $\nabla\nabla P$ without actually calculating $\nabla\nabla P$, this cannot happen. See the article by Fletcher and McCann in [11] for a discussion of this and also for some improved search procedures. In the same volume [11] McCormick and Pearson discuss the use of Davidson's method for this purpose.

D. The uniqueness property in (ii) of Theorem 6 is satisfied by most distributions. If the random variables have a joint normal distribution, the uniqueness property requires that the variance-covariance matrix of the random variables be nonsingular.

E. Theorems 1 and 2 state that under mild convergence hypotheses Z will have continuous first and second partial derivatives, if f has these respective properties. As is well known, the expectation operator tends to smooth functions and hence there are cases in which Z will have these smoothness properties even though f does not. For example, if f is piecewise continuously differentiable (e.g., f is asymmetric about certain axes) and ξ has an absolutely continuous density, then Z will often be continuously differentiable. One can show that this will always happen in the separable case by application of Leibniz's rule [20]. An analogous result is probably true in the multivariate case.

F. Theorem 5b and equation (11) give upper and lower bounds on the value of the optimal solution v_o. Alternative bounds have been given by Mangasarian [22].

REFERENCES

[1] Beale, E.M.L. "The Use of Quadratic Programming in Stochastic Linear Programming." Santa Monica: The RAND Corporation, August 1961, p. 2404.

[2] Bereanu, B. "On Stochastic Linear Programming: The Laplace Transform of the Distribution of the Optimum and Applications." *Journal of Mathematical Analysis and Applications*, XV, 1966, pp. 280-290.

[3] _________. "Numerical Methods in Stochastic Linear Programming: the Convergence of the Cartesian Integration Method." Paper presented at the 7th Mathematical Programming Symposium, the Hague, 1970.

[4] Dantzig, G.B. "Linear Programming under Uncertainty." *Management Science*, I, 1955, pp. 197-206.

[5] _________. *Linear Programming and Extensions*. Princeton, N.J.: Princeton University Press, 1963.

[6] Davis, P.J. and P. Rabinowitz. *Numerical Integration*. Waltham, Mass: Blaisdell Publishing Co., 1967.

[7] Elmaghraby, S.E. "Allocation under Uncertainty When the Demand has Continuous D.F." *Management Science*, X, 1960, pp. 270-294.

[8] Fiacco, A.V., and G.P. McCormick. "The Sequential Unconstrained Minimization Technique for Non-linear Programming: A Primal-Dual Method." *Management Science*, X, 1964, pp. 360-366.

[9] _________. *Non-linear Programming: Sequential Unconstrained Minimization Techniques*. New York: John Wiley and Sons, Inc., 1968.

[10] Fishburn, P.C. *Utility Theory for Decision Making*. New York: John Wiley and Sons, Inc., 1970.

[11] Fletcher, R. *Optimization*. New York: Academic Press Inc., 1969.

[12] Freund, R.J. "The Introduction of Risk into a Programming Model." *Econometrica*, XXIV, 1956, pp. 253-263.

[13] Gale, D., and H. Nikaidô. "The Jacobian Matrix and Global Univalence of Mappings." *Mathematische Annalen*, CLIX, 1965, pp. 81-93.

[14] Geoffrion, A.M. "Stochastic Programming with Aspiration or Fractile Criteria." *Management Science*, XIII, 1967, pp. 672-679.

[15] Haber, S. "Numerical Evaluation of Multiple Integrals." *SIAM Review*, XII, 1970, pp. 481-526.

[16] Hillier, F.S. *The Evaluation of Risky Interrelated Investments*. Amsterdam: North-Holland Publishing Co., 1969.

[17] Katoaka, S. "A Stochastic Programming Model." *Econometrica*, XXXI, 1963, pp. 181-196.

[18] Kirby, M.J.L. "The Current State of Chance-Constrained Programming." In *Proceedings of the Princeton Symposium on Mathematical Programming*, edited by H. W. Kuhn, 1970.

[19] Lintner, J. "The Valuation of Risk Assets and the Selection of Risky Investments in Stock Portfolios and Capital Budgets." *Review of Economics and Statistics*, XLVII, 1965, pp. 13-37.

[20] Loeve, M. *Probability Theory*, 3rd ed., Princeton: D. Van Nostrand and Co., 1963.

[21] Madansky, A. "Inequalities for Stochastic Linear Programming Problems." *Management Science*, VI, 1960, pp. 197-204.

[22] Mangasarian, O.L. "Nonlinear Programming Problems with Stochastic Objective Functions." *Management Science*, X, 1964, pp. 353-359.

[23] Mangasarian, O.L., and J. B. Rosen. "Inequalities for Stochastic Nonlinear Programming Problems." *Operations Research*, XII, 1964, pp. 143-154.

[24] Murray, W. "Ill-conditioning in Barrier and Penalty Functions Arising in Constrained Nonlinear Programs." Paper presented at the Princeton Symposium on Mathematical Programming, 1967.

[25] Parikh, S.C. "Notes on Stochastic Programming." Unpublished, Department of Industrial Engineering and Operations Research, University of California, Berkeley, 1968.

[26] Pye, G. "Portfolio Selection and Security Prices." *Review of Economics and Statistics*, XLIX, 1967, pp. 111-115.

[27] Richter, M.K. "Cardinal Utility, Portfolio Selection and Taxation." *Review of Economic Studies*, XXVII, 1959, pp. 152-166.

[28] Samuelson, P.A. "General Proof that Diversification Pays." *Journal of Financial and Quantitative Analysis*, II, 1967, pp. 1-13.

[29] ________. "The Fundamental Approximation Theorem of Mean-Variance Analysis in Terms of Means, Variance, and Higher Moments." *Review of Economic Studies*, XXXVII, 1970, pp. 537-542.

[30] Tobin, J. "Liquidity Preference as Behavior Towards Risk." *Review of Economics Studies*, XXVI, 1958, pp. 65-86.

[31] Topkis, D.M., and A.F. Veinott, Jr. "On the Convergence of Some Feasible Direction Algorithms for Nonlinear Programming." *J. SIAM Control*, V, 1967, pp. 268-279.

[32] Walkup, D.W., and R.J.B. Wets. "Stochastic Programs with Recourse: Special Forms." In *Proceedings of the Princeton Symposium on Mathematical Programming*, edited by H.W. Kuhn, 1970.

[33] Warburton, A., and W.T. Ziemba. "Convex Inversion." *Journal of Mathematical Analysis and Applications*, XXXV, 1971, pp. 58-66.

[34] Wets, R. "Programming under Uncertainty: The Complete Problem." *Z. Wahrscheinlichkeitstheorie und Verw. Gebite*, IV, 1966, pp. 316-339.

[35] Williams, A.C. "Approximation Formulas for Stochastic Linear Programming." *J. SIAM Appl. Math.*, XIV, 1966, pp. 668-677.

[36] Wolfe, P. "A Duality Theorem for Nonlinear Programming." *Quart. Appl. Math.*, XIX, 1961, pp. 239-244.

[37] Zangwill, W.I. *Nonlinear Programming: A Unified Approach*. Englewood Cliffs, N.J.: Prentice-Hall, Inc., 1969.

[38] Ziemba, W.T. "Computational Algorithms for Convex Stochastic Programs with Simple Recourse." *Operations Research*, XVIII, 1970, pp. 414-431.

[39] __________. "Essays on Stochastic Programming and the Theory of Economic Policy." Ph.D. diss. Berkeley: University of California, 1969.

[40] __________. "Calculating Investment Portfolios when the Returns have Stable Distributions, Part I: Theory." University of British Columbia Faculty of Commerce, Working Paper No. 133, February 1972.

[41] Ziemba, W.T.; F.J. Brooks-Hill; and C. Parkan. "Calculating Investment Portfolios when the Returns are Normally Distributed." University of British Columbia Faculty of Commerce, Working Paper No. 118, November 1971.

[42] Zoutendijk, G. *Methods of Feasible Directions*. Amsterdam: Elsevier Publishing Co., 1960.

[43] __________. "Nonlinear Programming Computation Methods." In *Integer and Nonlinear Programming*, edited by J. Abadie. Amsterdam: North-Holland Publishing Co., 1970.

Chapter 3

Bounds on the Expectation of a Convex Function of a Random Variable: With Applications to Stochastic Programming*

C. C. HUANG

Memorial University of Newfoundland, St. Johns, Newfoundland

W. T. ZIEMBA

University of British Columbia, Vancouver, British Columbia

A. BEN-TAL

Technion, Haifa, Israel

(Received original December 1974; final, July 1976)

This paper is concerned with the determination of tight lower and upper bounds on the expectation of a convex function of a random variable. The classic bounds are those of Jensen and Edmundson-Madansky and were recently generalized by Ben-Tal and Hochman. This paper indicates how still sharper bounds may be generated based on the simple idea of sequentially applying the classic bounds to smaller and smaller subintervals of the range of the random variable. The bounds are applicable in the multivariate case if the random variables are independent. In the dependent case bounds based on the Edmundson-Madansky inequality are not available; however, bounds may be developed using the conditional form of Jensen's inequality. We give some examples to illustrate the geometrical interpretation and the calculations involved in the numerical determination of the new bounds. Special attention is given to the problem of maximizing a nonlinear program that has a stochastic objective function.

IN THIS PAPER we determine sharp lower and upper bounds on the expectation of a convex (or concave with reversed bounds) function ϕ of a random variable t. The problem of evaluating such expectations arises in a number of stochastic optimization problems (see, e.g., Bereanu [5] and Ziemba [13]) as well as in numerical integration. The classic lower bound, Jensen's inequality [11], is based on bounding the expectation of ϕ by the expectation of its linear support at its mean. Similarly, the classic upper bound, the Edmundson-Madansky (E-M) inequality [8] uses the expected value of a linear function that overestimates ϕ. The sharpness of

*This chapter was originally published in: Huang, C. C., Ziemba, W. T. & Ben-Tal, A. (1977). Bounds on the Expectation of a Convex Function of a Random Variable: With Applications to Stochastic Programming. *Operations Research*, 25(2), 315–325.

both of these bounds depends crucially upon how close ϕ is to being linear. We indicate how sharper bounds may be generated by applying the classic bounds on subintervals of the range of t. This is equivalent to using the expectation of piecewise linear bounding functions that more closely approximate ϕ; hence the bounds are sharper. The subintervals may be defined sequentially using iterated partial means or may be chosen arbitrarily. The bounds are monotone as long as the partitions become finer.

We give two examples that illustrate how quickly the bounds become quite sharp and how much they improve over the classic bounds. We show that, as the number of subintervals increases without limit while each subinterval becomes arbitrarily small, the generalized bounds converge to the expected value of ϕ. The generalized Jensen bounds apply equally well for unbounded ranges and when there are several random variables. When the random variables are dependent, the bounds use the conditional form of Jensen's inequality. The E-M bounds exist over unbounded ranges if a linear homogeneous growth condition is met. In the multivariate case the generalized E-M bounds exist but cannot be determined for general ϕ. We present the expressions for these bounds when there are several independent random variables.

The results are useful in the solution of a number of difficult stochastic optimization problems. In particular, we discuss how one may obtain good approximate solutions to the distribution and simple recourse stochastic programming problems. The bounds yield monotone bounds on the optimal objective value for both of these problems. We show that for the simple recourse problem the optimal decision vectors for the bounding problems also converge to an optimal solution of the original stochastic program. The bounds also provide an apparently new method for the numerical integration of convex and some nonconvex, nonconcave functions. The monotone property of the bounds provide tolerance bounds on the value of the integral. A companion paper [6] discusses how these bounds can be used to sharpen the available bounds on the value of perfect information for static and dynamic decision problems.

1. JENSEN'S LOWER BOUND AND ITS GENERALIZATION

Let $t \in (a, b) \subset R$ be an integrable random variable having distribution function F and finite mean μ_0. Suppose $\phi(t): (a, b) \to R$ is an integrable convex function. Then Jensen's inequality $\phi(\mu_0) \leq \int_a^b \phi(t)\, dF(t) \equiv \bar{\phi}$ provides a lower bound to the expected value of ϕ. The bound $J_0 \equiv \phi(\mu_0)$ is an equality if ϕ is linear on a set of measure one. The tightness of the bound depends crucially upon how close ϕ is to being linear. Hence if we decompose the interval (a, b) into $(a, \mu_0]$ and $[\mu_0, b)$ and apply Jensen's inequality on each subinterval, the combined lower bound generates a piecewise linear function whose expectation will be closer to $\bar{\phi}$. (Any positive mass at μ_0 is allocated arbitrarily between the two intervals so that they both have nonzero probability.) This yields $J_0 \leqq J_1 \equiv c_{11}\phi(\mu_{11}) + c_{12}\phi(\mu_{12}) \leqq \bar{\phi}$, where

$$c_{11} \equiv \int_a^{\mu_0} dF(t) > 0, \qquad c_{12} \equiv 1 - c_{11} > 0,$$

$$\mu_{11} \equiv \int_a^{\mu_0} t\, dF(t)/c_{11} \quad \text{and} \quad \mu_{12} \equiv \int_{\mu_0}^{b} t\, dF(t)/c_{12}.$$

This result is much more general.

THEOREM 1. *Let $\phi(t)$ be an integrable convex function defined on the convex set $C \subset R^n$ and t be an integrable random vector such that $P[t \in C] = 1$. Then $Et \in C$ and*

$$\underset{(b)}{\phi(Et) \leqq} P_A\phi(E(t \mid t \in A)) + P_{C/A}\phi(E(t \mid t \in C/A) \underset{(a)}{\leqq E\phi(t)},$$

for all measurable sets $A \subset C$, such that A and C/A are convex.

Proof. (a) The conditional form of Jensen's inequality [11, 12] states that $\phi[E(t \mid t \in A)] \leqq E(\phi(t) \mid t \in A)$, and $\phi[E(t \mid t \in C/A)] \leqq E(\phi(t) \mid t \in C/A)$. Multiplying by P_A and $P_{C/A}$, respectively, and adding yield the result.

(b) Since $Et = P_A E(t \mid t \in A) + P_{C/A} E(t \mid t \in C/A)$, the result follows by the convexity of ϕ.

Theorem 1 can be used to prove that $J_0 \leqq J_1 \leqq \bar{\phi}$ by letting $A = (a, \mu_0]$. J_1 is the best lower bound M_4 given in Ben-Tal and Hochman [3].

The interval $(a, b) \subset R$ may be further subdivided as many times as desired to provide sharper and sharper lower bounds to $\bar{\phi}$.

THEOREM 2. (a) *Suppose (a, b) is subdivided at arbitrary points $d_0, \cdots, d_m$, where $a = d_0 < \cdots < d_m = b$. Let $J^m \equiv \sum_{i=1}^{i=m} \alpha_i\phi(\beta_i)$, denote the m-fold generalized Jensen bound, where $\alpha_i \equiv \int_{d_{i-1}}^{d_i} dF(t) > 0$, $\beta_i \equiv \alpha_i^{-1} \int_{d_{i-1}}^{d_i} t\, dF(t)$, $i = 1, \cdots, m$. Then, assuming that the partition corresponding to $k+1$ is at least as fine as that corresponding to k for $k = 1, \cdots, m-1$, we obtain $J_0 \equiv J^1 \leqq \cdots \leqq J^m \leqq \bar{\phi}$.*

(b) *Suppose (a, b) is subdivided n times on the basis of the partial means of the previous subintervals. Let $J_k \equiv \sum_{i=1}^{i=2^k} c_{ki}\phi(\mu_{ki})$, $k = 0, 1, \cdots, n$, denote the generalized Jensen bound obtained from the kth subdivision. Then $J_0 \leqq J_1 \leqq \cdots \leqq J_n \leqq \bar{\phi}$, where $c_{01} = 1$, $\mu_{01} = \mu_0$ and the ith interval of the kth subdivision is denoted by $[a_{ki}, b_{ki}]$, $c_{ki} \equiv \int_{a_{ki}}^{b_{ki}} dF(t) > 0$, $\mu_{ki} \equiv \int_{a_{ki}}^{b_{ki}} t\, dF(t)/c_{ki}$,* where $c_{k+1,2i-1} \equiv \int_{a_{ki}}^{\mu_{ki}} dF(t) > 0$ and $c_{k+1,2i} \equiv \int_{\mu_{ki}}^{b_{ki}} dF(t) > 0$.

Proof. Repeatedly apply Theorem 1. A simple direct proof appears in [4].

Remark 1. For a given $m = 2^k$ the bound J_k will generally be sharper than J^m because it considers the global shape of F in the determination of the subintervals. However, the calculation of J^m is simpler because the d_i may be chosen arbitrarily, while the μ_{ki} must be calculated.

2. THE EDMUNDSON-MADANSKY UPPER BOUND AND ITS GENERALIZATION

Let $t \in [a, b] \subset R$ have distribution function F and finite mean μ_0. Suppose ϕ is a bounded convex function of $t \in [a, b]$. The classic upper bound is the *Edmundson-Madansky inequality* $M_0 \equiv [(b - \mu_0)/(b - a)]\phi(a) + [(\mu_0 - a)/(b - a)]\phi(b) \geqq \bar{\phi}$.

Proof. Since ϕ is convex and $[a(b - t) + (t - a)b]/(b - a) \equiv t$, for all $t \in [a, b]$, we have $[(b - t)/(b - a)]\phi(a) + [(t - a)/(b - a)]\phi(b) \geqq \phi(t)$. Integrating gives the result.

Remark 2. Madansky [8] attributes this bound to Edmundson, who suggested it in a 1957 RAND report. We refer to it as the Edmundson-Madansky (E-M) bound because it was Madansky who pioneered the use of moment inequalities to derive bounds on the expectation of a convex function. Madansky's analysis yields the existence of bounds for a convex function of a vector argument. This simple proof, which was suggested by a referee, illustrates the geometric construction that yields the bound in one dimension. Clearly, $M_0 = \bar{\phi}$ if ϕ is linear on a set of measure one.

We may obtain a sharper upper bound by applying the E-M inequality on the subintervals $[a, \mu_0]$ and $[\mu_0, b]$. This yields the first generalized upper bound

$$\bar{\phi} \leqq M_1 \equiv [c_{11}\{[(\mu_0 - \mu_{11})/(\mu_0 - a)]\phi(a) + [(\mu_{11} - a)/(\mu_0 - a)]\phi(\mu_0)\}$$
$$+ c_{12}\{[(b - \mu_{12})/(b - \mu_0)]\phi(\mu_0) + [(\mu_{12} - \mu_0)/(b - \mu_0)]\phi(b)\}] \leqq M_0,$$

where the c_{1i} and μ_{1i} are defined in *Section* 1. M_1 is the best upper bound $\bar{M}_4$ given in Ben-Tal and Hochman [3]. A direct proof of these inequalities appears in [4].

The interval $[a, b]$ may be further subdivided as many times as desired to generate sharper and sharper upper bounds to $\bar{\phi}$.

THEOREM 3. (*a*) *Suppose* $[a, b]$ *is subdivided at arbitrary points* $d_0, \cdots, d_m$, *where* $a = d_0 < \cdots < d_m = b$. *Let* $M^m \equiv \sum_{i=0}^{i=m} \delta_i \phi(d_i)$ *denote the m-fold generalized E-M bound, where* $\delta_i \equiv \alpha_i[(\beta_i - d_{i-1})/(d_i - d_{i-1})] + \alpha_{i+1}[(d_{i+1} - \beta_{i+1})/(d_{i+1} - d_i)]$, $i = 0, 1, \cdots, m$, $\alpha_i \equiv \int_{d_{i-1}}^{d_i} dF(t) > 0$, $\beta_i \equiv \alpha_i^{-1} \int_{d_{i-1}}^{d_i} t\, dF(t)$, $i = 1, \cdots, m$, $\alpha_0 = \alpha_{m+1} \equiv 0$. *Then* $M_0 \equiv M^1 \geqq \cdots \geqq M^m \geqq \bar{\phi}$, *assuming that the partition corresponding to* $k + 1$ *is at least as fine as that corresponding to* k *for* $k = 1, \cdots, m - 1$.

(*b*) *Suppose* $[a, b]$ *is subdivided n times on the basis of the partial means of the previous subintervals. Let*

$$M_k \equiv \sum_{i=1}^{i=2^k} c_{ki}[((b_{ki} - \mu_{ki})/(b_{ki} - a_{ki}))\phi(a_{ki}) + ((\mu_{ki} - a_{ki})/(b_{ki} - a_{ki}))\phi(b_{ki})], \qquad k = 0, 1, \cdots, n,$$

denote the generalized E-M bound obtained from the kth *subdivision. Then* $M_0 \geqq M_1 \geqq \cdots \geqq M_n \geqq \bar{\phi}$, *where the* c_{ki}, μ_{ki}, a_{ki} *and* b_{ki} *are defined in Theorem 2.*

Proof. The bound $M^k \equiv \sum_{i=1}^{i=k} \alpha_i[((\beta_i - d_{i-1})/(d_i - d_{i-1}))\phi(d_i) + ((d_i - \beta_i)/(d_i - d_{i-1}))\phi(d_{i-1})] \equiv \sum_{i=0}^{i=k} \delta_i\phi(d_i)$, by reindexing. Let the partitions corresponding to M^k and M^{k+1} be $P^k \equiv (d_0^k, \cdots, d_k^k)$ and $P^{k+1} \equiv (d_0^{k+1}, \cdots, d_{k+1}^{k+1})$, respectively. Since $P^k \subset P^{k+1}$, there is an interval in P^k, $[d_{i-1}^k, d_i^k]$ that is subdivided in P^{k+1} into the two intervals $[d_{i-1}^{k+1}, d_i^{k+1}]$ and $[d_i^{k+1}, d_{i+1}^{k+1}]$. By the E-M inequality it follows that $\delta_{i-1}^k\phi(d_{i-1}^k) + \delta_i^k\phi(d_i^k) \geqq \delta_{i-1}^{k+1}\phi(d_{i-1}^{k+1}) + \delta_i^{k+1}\phi(d_{i+1}^{k+1})$, where $\alpha_{i-1}^k = \alpha_{i+1}^k = \alpha_{i-1}^{k+1} = \alpha_{i+2}^{k+1} = 0$.

Since the other intervals in P^k and P^{k+1} are identical, it follows that $M^k \geqq M^{k+1}$. Since $M^1 \equiv M_0 \geqq \bar{\phi}$, the induction argument is complete if $M^k \geqq \bar{\phi}$. By the E-M inequality $\delta_{i-1}^k\phi(d_{i-1}^k) + \delta_i^k\phi(d_i^k) \geqq \int_{d_{i-1}^k}^{d_i^k} \phi(t)\, dF(t)$, for $i = 1, \cdots, k$, where $\alpha_{i-1}^k = \alpha_{i+1}^k = 0$. Summing yields the result.

The results in (b) follow by applying the partitioning procedure k times (where $m = 2^k$).

For any n, $J_n \leqq \bar{\phi} \leqq M_n$ and $J^n \leqq \bar{\phi} \leqq M^n$. We now establish that the lower and upper bounds converge to $\bar{\phi}$.

THEOREM 4. Suppose $\phi(t)$ is a continuous convex function on $[a, b]$, and Et is finite. Then $\bar{\phi}$ is finite, $J^n \to \bar{\phi} \leftarrow M^n$, assuming that each subinterval becomes arbitrary small as $n \to \infty$, and $J_n \to \bar{\phi} \leftarrow M_n$.

Proof. Since ϕ is continuous and F is nondecreasing and hence of bounded variation, $\bar{\phi}$ exists (see Apostol [1, pp. 168, 211]). Let $U_k \equiv \sum_{i=1}^{i=2^k} c_{ki}M_{ki}$ and $L_k \equiv \sum_{i=1}^{i=2^k} c_{ki}m_{ki}$, where $M_{ki} \equiv \sup\{\phi(t) \mid t \in [a_{ki}, b_{ki}]\}$ and $m_{ki} \equiv \inf\{\phi(t) \mid t \in [a_{ki}, b_{ki}]\}$. By construction $L_n \leqq J^n \leqq \bar{\phi} \leqq M^n \leqq U_n$ and $L_n \leqq J_n \leqq \bar{\phi} \leqq M_n \leqq U_n$. Since F is nondecreasing on $[a, b]$, existence of $\bar{\phi}$ implies that $L_n \to \bar{\phi} \to U_n$ (see Apostol [1, p. 206]). Hence the result.

3. GENERALIZATIONS AND DISCUSSION

The results regarding the E-M bounds in section 2 are presented for the case when t is a bounded random variable. If either $a = -\infty$, $b = +\infty$ or both, then, as noted by Ben-Tal and Hochman [3], all the bounds exist (except for M_0 in the case $(-\infty, \infty)$) if one assumes that for:

$(-\infty, b]$ $\lim_{t\to-\infty} \phi(t)/t \equiv \alpha$, exists and is finite;

$[a, \infty)$ $\lim_{t\to\infty} \phi(t)/t \equiv \beta$, exists and is finite; and

$(-\infty, \infty)$ $\lim_{t\to\pm\infty} \phi(t)/t$ exists and is finite.

Expressions for M_0, M_1, and M_2 appear in reference 4.

The E-M bound and its generalizations cannot be used when there are several dependent random variables; the bounds exist (see Madansky [8]) but cannot be explicitly determined for general ϕ. (See, however, Marshall and Olkin [10] for the explicit determination of some related upper bounds in the dependent case when $\phi(t_1, \cdots, t_m) = \sum_{i=1}^{i=m} \psi(t_i)$, where ψ is convex on $[0, 1]$, $\psi(0) \geqq 0$ and $\psi(1) \geqq 0$.) However, if there are several independent random variables, one may apply any of the bounds $M_0, \cdots, M_n$ in a sequential fashion, one random variable at a time. Ben-Tal and Hochman [3] have developed the expressions for M_1 based on Madansky's [8] expression for M_0. We now develop the expression for J^n and M^n. Suppose $t_1, \cdots, t_m$ are independent random variables, where each t_k is distributed on $[a_k, b_k]$ with distribution function F_k and finite mean μ_k. Let $\{d_i^k\}$, $i = 0, \cdots, n_k$ be a partition of $[a_k, b_k]$ such that $a_k = d_0^k < d_1^k < \cdots < d_{n_k-1}^k < d_{n_k}^k = b^k$,

$$\alpha_i^k \equiv \int_{d_{i-1}^k}^{d_i^k} dF_k(t) > 0, \beta_i^k \equiv (1/\alpha_i^k) \int_{d_{i-1}^k}^{d_i^k} t\, dF(t), \qquad i = 1, \cdots, n_k,$$

$$\delta_i^k \equiv \alpha_i^k [(\beta_i^k - d_{i-1}^k)/(d_i^k - d_{i-1}^k)] + \alpha_{i+1}^k [(d_{i+1}^k - \beta_{i+1}^k)/(d_{i+1}^k - d_i^k)], \qquad i = 0, \cdots, n_k,$$

where $\alpha_0^k = \alpha_{n_k+1}^k \equiv 0$. Suppose $\phi(t_1, \cdots, t_m)$ is bounded and convex on $\prod_{k=1}^{k=m} [a_k, b_k]$. A conditioning argument yields

$$\sum_{i_1=1}^{i_1=n_1} \cdots \sum_{i_m=1}^{i_m=n_m} \left(\prod_{k=1}^{k=m} \alpha_{i_k}^k\right)\phi(\beta_{i_1}^1, \cdots, \beta_{i_m}^m) \leqq E\phi(t_1, \cdots, t_m) \leqq \sum_{i_1=0}^{i_1=n_1} \cdots \sum_{i_m=0}^{i_m=n_m} \left(\prod_{k=1}^{k=m} \delta_{i_k}^k\right)\phi(d_{i_1}^1, \cdots, d_{i_m}^m).$$

In the dependent multivariate case lower bounds are available using the conditional form of Jensen's inequality. For example, suppose $\bigcup_{k=1}^{k=K} B_k = C$ is a partition of C, where each B_k is convex and $\neq \phi$ and $B_k \cap B_l = \phi$ if $k \neq l$. For $t \in B_k$ we have

$$p(B_k)\phi\left(\int_{B_k} (t/p(B_k))\, dF(t)\right) \leqq \int_{B_k} \phi(t)\, dF(t), \quad p(B_k) > 0.$$

Then the conditional form of Jensen's inequality may be written as

$$\sum_{k=1}^{k=K} p(B_k)\phi\left(\int_{B_k} (t/p(B_k))\, dF(t)\right) \leqq \sum_{k=1}^{k=K} \int_{B_k} \phi(t)\, dF(t).$$

One then develops a bound by determing K, the B_k, $p(B_k)$, $\phi\left(\int_{B_k} (t/p(B_k))\, dF(t)\right)$, and adding.

4. APPLICATIONS

The Distribution Problem

In many applications (see Bereanu [5] and Huang, Wehrung, and Ziemba [7] for detailed discussion and additional references) it is of interest to study the distribution properties of the random mathematical program $\phi(c) \equiv \max_x \{\psi(c, x) \mid x \in K\}$, where ϕ and ψ are scalar functions, $K \subset R^q$, c is a random vector having distribution function G, and x is a decision vector. In the simplest case one is only interested in the mean of ϕ, namely,

$$\int \cdots \int \max_x \{\psi(c, x) \mid x \in K\} \, dG(c). \tag{1}$$

In general, the solution of (1) requires the solution of a large number of mathematical programs of the form

$$\max_x \{\psi(\hat{c}, x) \mid x \in K\}, \tag{2}$$

where $\hat{c}$ is a fixed value of c. If G is continuous, then one must in principle solve an infinite number of these programs. One is thus led to consider special cases in which the solution of a finite number of programs of form (2) will suffice to generate the entire infinite class (see references 5 and 7 for examples).

Alternatively, one may seek approximations to the solution of (1). Mangasarian [9] has considered this problem and has applied the bounds J_0 and J_1 to its solution. He showed that ϕ is convex whenever c belongs to a closed convex region C and ψ is convex in c for every feasible x. Then under the assumption that the components of the random vector c are independent, one has the bounds

$$J_0 \leqq \int \psi(c, \bar{x}(\bar{c})) \, dG(c) \leqq \bar{\phi} \leqq M_0, \tag{3}$$

where $\bar{x}(\bar{c})$ solves $\max_x \{\psi(\bar{c}, x) \mid x \in K\}$, and J_0 and M_0 are the Jensen and E-M bounds of ϕ, respectively. As an example, he considers

$$\phi(c) \equiv \max_x \{c_1 x_1^2 + c_2^2 x_2^2 \mid 0 \leqq x_1 \leqq 10, 0 \leqq x_2 \leqq 5\},$$

where c_1 and c_2 have independent uniform distributions on $[-\frac{1}{2}, \frac{1}{2}]$ and $[0, 1]$, respectively. Now

$$\phi(c) = \begin{cases} 100c_1 + 25c_2^2 & \text{if} \quad c_1 \geqq 0 \\ 25c_2^2 & \text{otherwise} \end{cases} \quad \text{and} \quad \bar{\phi} = 20.833.$$

The bounds in (3) are then $6.25 < 8.33 < 20.833 < 37.5$, respectively. Ben-Tal and Hochman [3] applied the generalized bounds J_1 and M_1 to obtain the sharper bounds $J_1 = 20.312 < 20.833 < 21.875 = M_1$, respectively. (Please note that their equation (27) and the definition of $\bar{x}(Ec)$ are in error; $\equiv$ should be replaced by $\geqq$; see Theorem 2 in reference 9 for proof.) The next two generalized bounds yield the still sharper bounds $J_2 = 20.70313 < \underset{(J_3)}{20.80078} < 20.833 < \underset{(M_3)}{20.89844} < 21.09375 = M_2$, respectively.

The results in Theorems 1–4 may be used, when they are applicable, to sharpen the available bounds on the value of information; see Huang, Vertinsky and Ziemba [6] for details and further references.

Stochastic Programs with Simple Recourse

The bounds may also be used to generate approximate solutions to certain stochastic mathematical programs that are difficult to solve. Let

$$Z \equiv \max_x \{\int \psi(c, x)\, dG(c) \mid x \in K\}, \tag{4}$$

where the notation and assumptions follow those above. (See Ziemba [13] for a survey of results and solution methods for problems that may be put into the form of (4).) Suppose $c \in [a, b]$; then the bounds $\{J_n\}$ (or $\{J^n\}$) and $\{M_n\}$ (or $\{M^n\}$) may be used to bound the optimal value of (4). For J_1 and M_1 one obtains

$$\max_x [c_{11}\psi(\mu_{11}, x) + c_{12}\psi(\mu_{12}, x) \mid x \in K] \leqq Z \leqq \tag{5}$$

$$\max_x [c_{11}\{((\mu_0-\mu_{11})/(\mu_0-a))\psi(a, x)+((\mu_{11}-a)/(\mu_0-a))\psi(\mu_0, x)\}$$

$$+ c_{12}\{((b - \mu_{12})/(b - \mu_0))\psi(\mu_0, x) + ((\mu_{12} - \mu_0)/(b-\mu_0))\psi(b, x)\}$$

$$\mid x \in K].$$

Solutions to the left and right side of (5) are approximate solutions to (4). Indeed, under proper regularity assumptions optimal solutions using the bounds $\{J^n\}$ and $\{M^n\}$ (and hence $\{J_n\}$ and $\{M_n\}$) converge to optimal solutions of (4).

THEOREM 5. *Suppose K is a nonempty compact convex set, ψ is a continuous concave function of x possessing uniformly bounded subgradients for each $c \in [a, b]$, and ψ is a continuous convex (or concave with reversed bounds) function of c for each $x \in K$. Assume that $[a, b]$ is subdivided at points $P_n \equiv \{d_0, \cdots, d_n\}$, where $a = d_0 < \cdots < d_n = b$. Let $J^n(x) \equiv \sum_{i=1}^{i=n} \alpha_i\psi(\beta_i, x)$, where $\alpha_i \equiv \int_{d_{i-1}}^{d_i} dF(c) > 0$, $\beta_i \equiv \alpha_i^{-1} \int_{d_{i-1}}^{d_i} c\, dF(c)$, $i = 1, \cdots, n$, $\delta_i \equiv \alpha_i[(\beta_i - d_{i-1})/(d_i - d_{i-1})] + \alpha_{i+1}[(d_{i+1} - \beta_{i+1})/(d_{i+1} - d_i)]$, $i = 0, \cdots, n$, $\alpha_0 = \alpha_{n+1} = 0$, and it is assumed that $P_{n-1} \subset P_n$ and every subinterval becomes infinitely small as $n \to \infty$. Let $J^n(x_n) = \max\{J^n(x) \mid x \in K\}$, $M^n(z_n) = \max\{M^n(x) \mid x \in K\}$, $\bar\phi(x) = \int \psi(c, x)\, dG(c)$, and $\bar\phi(x^*) = \max\{\bar\phi(x) \mid x \in K\}$.*

Then if $x_n \to x_\infty$ and $z_n \to z_\infty$,

(a) (i) $J^n(x_n) \to \bar\phi(x_\infty)$ *and* (ii) $M^n(z_n) \to \bar\phi(z_\infty)$.

(b) $\bar\phi(x_\infty) = Z \equiv \bar\phi(x^*) = \bar\phi(z_\infty)$.

Proof. (a–i) (Grinold) $|J^n(x_n) - \bar{\phi}(x_\infty)| \leqq |J^n(x_n) - J^n(x_\infty)| + |J^n(x_\infty) - \bar{\phi}(x_\infty)|$. Now $J^n(x_\infty) \leqq J^n(x_n)$ since x_n is optimal and $x_\infty \in K$. Further, J^n, being a finite non-negative linear combination of concave functions, is concave. Hence by the concavity of J^n, $0 \leqq J^n(x_n) - J^n(x_\infty) \leqq d_n(x_\infty)(x_n - x_\infty)$, where d_n is a subgradient of J^n at x_∞. Thus

$$|J^n(x_n) - \bar{\phi}(x_\infty)| \leqq \underbrace{|d_n(x_\infty)(x_n - x_\infty)|}_{\substack{\downarrow \\ 0}} + \underbrace{|J^n(x_\infty) - \bar{\phi}(x_\infty)|}_{\substack{\downarrow \\ 0}}.$$

The proof of (a–ii) is analogous.

(b) Under the assumptions $\bar{\phi}(x)$ is a continuous concave function of x. For any $x \in K$ we have that $J^1(x) \leqq \cdots \leqq J^n(x) \leqq \cdots \leqq \bar{\phi}(x) \leqq \cdots \leqq M^n(x) \leqq \cdots \leqq M^1(x)$.

By Theorem 4, $J^n(x) \to \bar{\phi}(x) \leftarrow M^n(x)$ pointwise. Then if x^* solves $\{\max \bar{\phi}(x) \mid x \in K\}$, it follows that $J^n(x^*) \to \bar{\phi}(x^*) \leftarrow M^n(x^*)$. Thus $J^n(x_n) \to Z \leftarrow M^n(z_n)$ follows as long as x^* solves $\lim \max_x J^n(x)$ and $\lim \max_x M^n(x)$. The sequences on the left and right of $\bar{\phi}(x)$ are monotone; hence $\lim J^n(x^*) = \bar{\phi}(x^*) \geqq \lim J^n(x)\ \forall x \in K$ and $\lim M^n(x) \leqq \lim M^n(z_\infty) = \bar{\phi}(z_\infty) \leqq \bar{\phi}(x^*) = \lim M^n(x^*)\ \forall\, x \in K$. Since $J^n(x_n) \to Z \leftarrow M^n(z_n)$, it follows by (a) that $\bar{\phi}(x_\infty) = Z = \bar{\phi}(x^*) = \bar{\phi}(z_\infty)$.

Remark 3. It should be noted that x_∞, x^* and z_∞ need not be equal unless $\bar{\phi}$ is strictly concave. The generalizations to the multivariate and unbounded cases discussed in section 2 apply here as well.

Numerical Integration

For a given n, $J_n \leqq J_{n+1} \leqq \bar{\phi} \leqq M_{n+1} \leqq M_n$ (similar statements may be made using J^n and M^n). Since ϕ is convex, $M_{n+1} = M_n$ and $J_{n+1} = J_n$ if and only if (assuming F is continuous) $\phi(t)$ is linear on each of the subintervals generated by the nth decomposition, in which case $J_{n+1} = \bar{\phi} = M_{n+1}$. If $M_{n+1} \neq M_n$ and $J_{n+1} \neq J_n$, then $J_n < J_{n+1} \leqq \bar{\phi} \leqq M_{n+1} < M_n$. Hence for a given tolerance level $\epsilon > 0$ there always exists an n such that $M_n - J_n < \epsilon$ so that both J_n and M_n are within ϵ of $\bar{\phi}$ and the estimate $\frac{1}{2}(J_n + M_n)$ is within $\frac{1}{2}(M_n - J_n)$ of $\bar{\phi}$. Thus the bounds may be used to calculate the expected value of a given convex function of a random variable. For example, if $\phi(t) = t^2$ and t has a uniform distribution on $[-10, 10]$, the first five bounds are: $J_0 = 0.0000$, $M_0 = 100.0000$; $J_1 = 25.0000$, $M_1 = 50.0000$; $J_2 = 31.2500$, $M_2 = 37.5000$; $J_3 = 32.8125$, $M_3 = 34.3750$; $J_4 = 33.2031$, $M_4 = 33.5938$, while $\bar{\phi} = 100/3$.

It is not easy to determine the class of functions ϕ and F for which this approach will be competitive or superior to standard numerical quadrature schemes. However, it does seem to have an advantage in cases where one wishes to perform calculations for several ϕ with a given F.

Remark 4. Ben-Tal [2] indicates how the bounding results may be used to approximate the integrals of certain nonconvex, nonconcave functions. The bounding scheme is applicable if the integrand is a product of a convex or concave function and a positive "density-like" function whose mass and mean are finite and can be calculated analytically. When using J^n and M^n one can devise an optimal partitioning of the domain of t by solving a simple nonlinear programming problem and apply the scheme over an infinite integration range (assuming $\lim_{t\to\pm\infty}\phi(t)/t$ is finite).

ACKNOWLEDGMENTS

This research was partially supported by the National Research Council of Canada. The authors would like to thank A. Amershi, S. L. Brumelle, E. U. Choo, R. C. Grinold, M. Kusy, S. Larsson, M. Puterman, R. Wets, and the referees for some helpful discussions and comments on earlier versions of this paper. In particular, R. Wets provided us with many detailed comments that have improved the exposition and strengthened the results.

REFERENCES

1. T. M. Apostol, *Mathematical Analysis*, Addison-Wesley, Reading, Mass., 1967.
2. A. Ben-Tal, "Approximation Methods to the Expectation of a Convex Function of a Random Variable with Applications to Stochastic Programming," unpublished M.A. Thesis, Department of Statistics, University of Tel-Aviv, 1971.
3. A. Ben-Tal and E. Hochman, "More Bounds on the Expectation of a Convex Function of a Random Variable," *J. Appl. Probability* **9,** 803–812 (1972).
4. A. Ben-Tal, C. C. Huang, and W. T. Ziemba, "Bounds on the Expectation of a Random Variable: with Applications to Stochastic Programming," Faculty of Commerce, The University of British Columbia, W. P. No. 280, revised August, 1975.
5. B. Bereanu, "The Cartesian Integration Method in Stochastic Linear Programming" in *Numerische Methoden bei Optimierungsaufgaben*, L. Collatz and W. Wetterling, (eds.), Springer-Verling Publishing Co., Basle, 1973.
6. C. C. Huang, I. Vertinsky, and W. T. Ziemba, "Sharp Bounds on the Value of Perfect Information," *Opns. Res.* **25,** 128–139 (1977).
7. C. C. Huang, D. A. Wehrung, and W. T. Ziemba, "A Homogeneous Distribution Problem with Applications to Finance," *Management Sci.*, **23,** 297–304 (1976).
8. A. Madansky, "Bounds on the Expectation of a Convex Function of a Multivariate Random Variable," *Ann. Math. Stat.* **30,** 743–746 (1959).

9. O. L. Mangasarian, "Nonlinear Programming Problems with Stochastic Objective Functions," *Management Sci.* **10,** 353–359 (1964).
10. A. W. Marshall and I. Olkin, "Reversal of the Lyapunov, Holder and Minkowski Inequalities and other Extensions of the Kantorovich Inequality," *J. Math. Anal. Appl.* **8,** 503–514 (1964).
11. M. D. Perlman, "Jensen's Inequality for a Convex Vector-Valued Function on an Infinite Dimensional Space," *J. Multivariate Anal.* **4,** 52–65 (1974).
12. J. Pfanzagl, "Convexity and Conditional Expectations," *Ann. Probability* **2,** 490–494 (1974).
13. W. T. Ziemba, "Stochastic Programs with Simple Recourse," pp. 213–273, in *Mathematical Programming in Theory and Practice*, P. L. Hammer and G. Zoutendijk, (Eds.), North Holland Publishing Co., Amsterdam, 1974.

Chapter 4

BOUNDS FOR TWO-STAGE STOCHASTIC PROGRAMS WITH FIXED RECOURSE*

N. C. P. EDIRISINGHE AND W. T. ZIEMBA

This paper develops upper and lower bounds on two-stage stochastic linear programs using limited moment information. The case considered is when both the right-hand side as well as the objective coefficients of the second stage problem are random. Random variables are allowed to have arbitrary multivariate probability distributions with bounded support. First, upper and lower bounds are obtained using first and cross moments, from which we develop bounds using only first moments. The bounds are shown to solve the respective general moment problems.

1. Introduction. A stochastic program arises when some or all of the problem parameters of a deterministic mathematical program are subject to random variation. These problems often involve optimizing an expectation functional of multivariate random variables which may be stochastically dependent. Multidimensional numerical integration as a computational strategy is prohibitively expensive. This is not only because it is at the outer limits of computer technology, but also because it may become necessary to evaluate the expectation functional as many times as would be necessary in an iterative search of an optimal set of decisions for the problem at hand. Inevitably, therefore, one is forced to look for approximations, such as upper and lower bounds to the stochastic program. A possible solution strategy is to compute bounds for the expectation functional which can eliminate the need for multidimensional numerical integration and then to use these bounding functions in the inner optimization. This paper is a contribution in this direction.

We are concerned with the two-stage stochastic linear programming problem with fixed recourse, see, for instance, Kall (1976) and Wets (1982). The model is

$$(1) \qquad Z^* := \min_x \{c'x + E_\omega[\phi(x,\xi,\eta)]: Ax = b,\ x \geqslant 0\}$$

where

$$(2) \qquad \phi(x,\xi,\eta) := \min_y \{q(\eta)'y: Wy = h(\xi) - T(\xi)x,\ y \geqslant 0\},$$

with primes (′) denoting transposition of vectors and E_ω denoting mathematical expectation with respect to the joint random vector $\omega := (\xi, \eta)$. The domain of the random vector ξ is denoted by $\Xi \subset \Re^K$ and that of η by $\Theta \subset \Re^L$. The joint domain of the random $(K + L)$-vector ω is denoted by Ω. The recourse problem (2) has fixed recourse because the $(m_2 \times n_2)$-matrix W is deterministic. A is a fixed $(m_1 \times n_1)$-matrix and c is a fixed vector in $\Re^{n_1}$. T is a $(m_2 \times n_1)$-dimensional stochastic matrix

Received March 30, 1990; revised May 25, 1992.
AMS 1980 subject classification. Primary: 90C42.
IAOR 1973 subject classification. Main: Programming, probabilistic.
OR/MS Index 1978 subject classification. Primary: 663 Programming/Stochastic.
Key words. Stochastic programs with recourse, generalized moment problems, bounds on expectation.

*This chapter was originally published in: Edirisinghe, N. C. P. & Ziemba, W. T. (1994). Bounds for Two-Stage Stochastic Programs with Fixed Recourse. *Mathematics of Operations Research*, 19(2), 292–313.

and q is a n_2-dimensional random vector. Define the set

(3) $$X^1 := \{x \in \Re^{n_1}: Ax = b, x \geqslant 0\}.$$

Let the first stage decisions x induced by the second stage recourse problem (2) (for almost sure satisfaction of its constraints) be

(4) $$X^2 := \{x \in \Re^{n_1}: \exists y \geqslant 0 \text{ s.t. } Wy = h(\xi) - T(\xi)x, \quad \forall \xi \in \Xi\}.$$

The set of feasible solutions of the stochastic program (1)–(2) is

(5) $$X := X^1 \cap X^2.$$

Assume that:
(A1) $X \neq \emptyset$,
(A2) $\{\pi \in \Re^{m_2}: \pi' W \leqslant q(\eta), \eta \in \Theta\} \neq \emptyset$,
(A3) $q(\eta) \equiv q_0 + Q\eta$,
$h(\xi) \equiv h_0 + H\xi$,
$T(\xi) \equiv T_0 + \Sigma_{k=1}^K T_k \xi_k$,
where the vectors q_0, h_0 and matrices Q, H, T_k are all fixed and defined with appropriate dimensions,
(A4) $\Omega = \Xi \times \Theta$, and
(A5) Ξ and Θ are convex, compact subsets of $\Re^K$ and $\Re^L$, respectively.

Assumption (A1) ensures that the stochastic program (1)–(2) is feasible with probability one while (A2) ensures that the recourse problem (2) is never unbounded. Furthermore, due to (A3), the recourse function $\phi(x, \xi, \eta)$ is a convex-concave saddle function in (ξ, η) for fixed $x \in X$. Moreover, from the linear programming theory, $\phi(x, \xi, \eta)$ is polyhedral in (ξ, η) for fixed $x \in X$, thus ensuring continuity of ϕ for fixed $x \in X$. The convexity assumption in (A5) is not restrictive for, if not, one could work with the convex hulls of the domains. In particular, consider these convex hulls as being generated by a finite set of extreme points, which we shall follow subsequently in order to make the exposition easy.

Properties of the program (1)–(2) are well known, see Wets (1974). For example, the set X is convex. Moreover, since integration with respect to a probability measure preserves order, convexity of ϕ in x implies that the deterministic equivalent program of (1)–(2) is a convex program. However, direct application of convex programming algorithms is difficult (except, for example, when W has special structure such as simple recourse) due to the multidimensional integration required for evaluating (1), of which the integrand is the optimization in (2). Such procedures become even more prohibitive computationally as one would need to evaluate gradients as well. A standard approach to alleviate this difficulty is to develop approximations.

This paper is concerned with determining tight upper and lower approximations to (1)–(2) using limited moment information on the random vector ω. This is accomplished by developing upper and lower bounds on the expectation of the recourse function $\phi(x, \xi, \eta)$ for a fixed first stage decision $x \in X$. The literature on bounds for such problems is extremely sparse. Frauendorfer (1988b, c, d, 1989) obtained upper and lower bounds for the expectation of the convex-concave recourse function. These bounds have been derived when domains are either multidimensional rectangles or simplices. In the former case, approximating extremal discrete distributions are determined on vertices of the domains, and thus, is exponential in the dimensions of the random vectors, while in the latter case, bounding computations can be afforded within a quadratic amount of function evaluations. In §2, we extend the ideas to determine tight upper and lower bounds using only first and cross moments of the random vector ω, with no independence assumption and requiring only that the random vectors have bounded domains, more precisely, polytopes.

Using these bounds, in §3, we obtain tight upper and lower bounds using only first moments and without any independence assumption. These bounds may be viewed as a generalization of the known bounds in the pure convex case, that is, the special case when randomness is only present in h and T of (2). Bounding techniques for this special case has been developed by, for example, Birge and Wets (1986), Dula (1992), Frauendorfer (1988a), and Gassmann and Ziemba (1986), using limited moment information.

In §4, we apply these bounding strategies to the stochastic linear program (1)–(2) to obtain finite mathematical programming formulations to compute the bounds. In particular, we obtain upper and lower bounds which are convex polyhedral in the first stage decisions x so that the bounding computations do not require any more sophistication than solving linear programs.

Tightness of bounds is discussed in the context of generalized moment problems. Specifically, we investigate if the bounds solve the dual of the moment problem. For this purpose, the required duality relationships are summarized in the remainder of this section. Notation is introduced as it becomes necessary.

1.1. Bounds using moment problems. We define the generalized moment problem without any reference to a stochastic program and subsequently duality relationships are specified.

Consider a set of finite measurable functions $f_i(\omega)$: $\Re^n \to \Re$, for $i = 1, \ldots, m + 1$, with ω being a random vector mapping the measurable space $(\Omega, \mathscr{B})$ to $\Re^n$ and $\mathscr{B}$ the Borel-sigma field of the events in Ω. Suppose the (*generalized*) moments $E_\omega[f_i(\omega)]$ for $i = 1, \ldots, m$ are given, where $E_\omega[\cdot]$ denotes mathematical expectation with respect to the true probability measure on $(\Omega, \mathscr{B})$. For simplicity, $E_\omega[f_i(\omega)]$ is written as Ef_i. We are concerned with upper bounds on Ef_{m+1}. Given the generalized moments $Ef_1, \ldots, Ef_m$, we say, a *tight* upper bound is determined for Ef_{m+1} when one solves the following moment problem (GMP), see Kemperman (1968):

$$(6)\qquad \begin{aligned} Ef_{m+1} \leqslant V(\text{GMP}) := \sup_{P \in \mathscr{P}} \; & \int_\Omega f_{m+1}(\omega)\, P(d\omega) \\ \text{s.t.} \; & \int_\Omega f_i(\omega)\, P(d\omega) = Ef_i, \qquad i = 1, \ldots, m, \end{aligned}$$

where $\mathscr{P}$ is the set of all probability measures on Ω. The dual formulation of (6) is the semi-infinite linear program (SIP):

$$(7)\qquad \begin{aligned} V(\text{SIP}) := \inf_y \; & y_0 + \sum_{i=1}^m (Ef_i) y_i \\ \text{s.t.} \; & y_0 + \sum_{i=1}^m f_i(\omega) y_i \geqslant f_{m+1}(\omega), \quad \forall \omega \in \Omega. \end{aligned}$$

While the weak duality for (6) and (7) is immediate, i.e., $V(\text{GMP}) \leqslant V(\text{SIP})$, to ensure strong duality, certain mild conditions are required, in general.

THEOREM 1.1. *If*
(i) f_i, $i = 1, \ldots, m$, *are continuous*,
(ii) Ω *is compact, and*
(iii) *there exists a probability measure which achieves the given moments* Ef_i*s on* Ω, *then* (*GMP*) *is solvable and* $V(GMP) = V(SIP)$.

For a proof of the above results, see Kall (1987) or Kemperman (1968). The issue of strong duality for semi-infinite linear programs and the associated dual problems has been addressed in a general sense by Glashoff and Gustafson (1983) who also develop this theory from first principles.

It is assumed that the information on limited moments of the random vector ω is such that there exists a true probability measure that achieves these. Moreover, for the stochastic program defined before, together with the assumptions listed therein, the sufficient conditions in Theorem 1.1 are satisfied. Consequently, we use strong duality for the underlying moment problem and its semi-infinite dual, without any ambiguity.

2. Bounds for the expectation of the recourse function. Consider the stochastic program (1)–(2) under Assumptions (A1)–(A5). The recourse function $\phi(x, \xi, \eta)$ is a convex-concave saddle function in $(\xi, \eta) := \omega$, for fixed $x \in X$. Let us fix the following notation with regard to domains of the random vectors: Ξ is a polytope with extreme points $u^1, \ldots, u^I$ and Θ is a polytope with extreme points $v^1, \ldots, v^J$. The first moments of ξ and η, respectively, denoted by $\bar{\xi}$ and $\bar{\eta}$, as well as the cross moments $E[\xi_k \eta_l]$ (for $k = 1, \ldots, K$; $l = 1, \ldots, L$), denoted by m_{kl}, are all assumed to exist and be finite. The expectation of the recourse function $\phi(x, \xi, \eta)$, for fixed $x \in X$, is denoted by $\bar{\phi}(x)$.

We are concerned with developing upper and lower bounds to $\bar{\phi}(x)$ using limited moment information of the random vector ω and without making any independence assumption with regard to the random vector ω. We take an approach similar to that used by Birge and Wets (1986, §5) in their work in the pure convex case. The basic idea is to consider each realization of the random vector as a convex combination of the extreme points of the domain. Thus, by the convexity of Ξ, for given $\xi \in \Xi$ there exist scalars $\lambda(\xi)$ that satisfy

$$(8) \qquad \sum_{i=1}^{I} u^i \lambda_i(\xi) = \xi, \qquad \sum_{i=1}^{I} \lambda_i(\xi) = 1, \qquad \lambda_i(\xi) \geqslant 0, \quad i = 1, \ldots, I.$$

Similarly, by the convexity of Θ, for given $\eta \in \Theta$ there exist scalars $\mu(\eta)$ satisfying

$$(9) \qquad \sum_{j=1}^{J} v^j \mu_j(\eta) = \eta, \qquad \sum_{j=1}^{J} \mu_j(\eta) = 1, \qquad \mu_j(\eta) \geqslant 0, \quad j = 1, \ldots, J.$$

Then by the saddle property of $\phi(x, \cdot, \cdot)$,

$$(10) \qquad \sum_{j=1}^{J} \mu_j(\eta) \phi(x, \xi, v^j) \leqslant \phi(\xi, \eta) \leqslant \sum_{i=1}^{I} \lambda_i(\xi) \phi(x, u^i, \eta)$$

$$\text{for all } (\xi, \eta) \in \Xi \times \Theta =: \Omega.$$

Upon integration of (10), with respect to the true probability measure, bounding inequalities for $\bar{\phi}(x)$ are

$$(11) \qquad \sum_{j=1}^{J} E\left[\mu_j(\eta)\phi(x,\xi,v^j)\right] \leqslant \bar{\phi}(x) \leqslant \sum_{i=1}^{I} E\left[\lambda_i(\xi)\phi(x,u^i,\eta)\right].$$

The lower and upper bounds in (11) are difficult to compute since the scalars λ and μ are to be determined according to (8) and (9), respectively, and moreover, product terms involving these scalars and nonlinear functional forms of ϕ need to be integrated with respect to the true probability measure. To alleviate this difficulty, we use a two-step procedure in the next section. First, each of the functions $\phi(x,\xi,v^j)$ and $\phi(x,u^i,\eta)$ are linearized at some arbitrary points in the respective domains, similar in spirit to what was done in Frauendorfer (1988c). Bounds are then determined by considering the resulting inequalities in expectation, an idea originally due to Birge and Wets (1986). Since the bounds from this procedure would depend on the chosen linearizations, in the second step, we optimize over all possible linearizations to tighten the bounds. Finally, we will show that these bounds solve the respective generalized moment problems, hence, the bounds are tight.

2.1. Tight bounds using first and cross moments. In the ensuing development, the first stage decision x ($\in X$) is fixed. First, considering the lower bounding inequality in (11), linearize each of the convex functions $\phi(x,\xi,v^j)$, being convex in $\xi \in \Xi$, at some known point $\hat{\xi}^j \in \Xi$, i.e., consider the supporting hyperplane $\langle \pi^j, \xi \rangle + \sigma^j$, for fixed coefficients $\pi^j \in \Re^K$ and $\sigma^j \in \Re$, to the epigraph of $\phi(x,\xi,v^j)$ at $(\hat{\xi}^j, \phi(x,\hat{\xi}^j,v^j))$. Dependence of the latter coefficients on x is suppressed for simplicity. The coefficient vector π^j is a subgradient of the recourse function at $\xi = \hat{\xi}^j$ and may be interpreted as an optimal dual solution of the linear program:

$$(12) \qquad \phi(x,\hat{\xi}^j,v^j) = \min_y \left\{q(v^j)'y : Wy = h(\hat{\xi}^j) - T(\hat{\xi}^j)x,\ y \geqslant 0\right\}.$$

Similarly, linearize each of the concave functions $\phi(x,u^i,\eta)$ in the upper bounding inequality in (11), being concave in $\eta \in \Theta$, at some known point $\hat{\eta}^i \in \Theta$ to obtain the linear support $\langle \alpha^i, \eta \rangle + \beta^i$. $\alpha^i \in \Re^L$ is a subgradient of $\phi(x,u^i,\eta)$ at $\eta = \hat{\eta}^i$ and is interpreted as a primal solution of the linear program:

$$(13) \qquad \phi(x,u^i,\hat{\eta}^i) = \min_y \left\{q(\hat{\eta}^i)'y : Wy = h(u^i) - T(u^i)x,\ y \geqslant 0\right\}.$$

Therefore,

$$(14) \qquad \langle \alpha^i, \eta \rangle + \beta^i \geqslant \phi(x,u^i,\eta), \qquad \forall \eta \in \Theta \text{ and } i = 1,\ldots,I,$$

$$(15) \qquad \langle \pi^j, \xi \rangle + \sigma^j \leqslant \phi(x,\xi,v^j), \qquad \forall \xi \in \Xi \text{ and } j = 1,\ldots,J.$$

Substituting (14)–(15) in (11), the resulting lower and upper bounds to the expectation functional are

$$(16) \quad \sum_{j=1}^{J} E\left[\mu_j(\eta)\langle \pi^j,\xi \rangle + \mu_j(\eta)\sigma^j\right] \leqslant \bar{\phi}(x) \leqslant \sum_{i=1}^{I} E\left[\lambda_i(\xi)\langle \alpha^i,\eta \rangle + \lambda_i(\xi)\beta^i\right]$$

where λ's and μ's satisfy (8) and (9), respectively.

Denote the kth element of the K-vector u^i by u^i_k and that of π^j by π^j_k. Also, the lth element of the L-vector v^j is denoted by v^j_l and that of α^i by α^i_l. Since Ξ is compact, for each component random variable ξ_k, $k = 1, \ldots, K$, there exist (finite) lower and upper bounds denoted by $\hat{a}_{k0}$ and $\hat{a}_{k1}$, respectively. Similarly, those for components η_l, $l = 1, \ldots, L$, are denoted by $\tilde{a}_{l0}$ and $\tilde{a}_{l1}$, respectively.

PROPOSITION 2.1.

$$
\begin{aligned}
\bar{\phi}(x) \leqslant \max_{t,p} \quad & \sum_{i=1}^{I} \langle \alpha^i, t^i \rangle + \beta^i p_i \\
\text{s.t.} \quad & \sum_{i=1}^{I} u^i_k t^i_l = m_{kl}, \quad \forall k = 1, \ldots, K; \quad \forall l = 1, \ldots, L, \\
& \sum_{i=1}^{I} t^i_l = \bar{\eta}_l, \quad \forall l, \\
& \sum_{i=1}^{I} u^i_k p_i = \bar{\xi}_k, \quad \forall k, \\
& \sum_{i=1}^{I} p_i = 1, \quad p_i \geqslant 0, \\
& \tilde{a}_{l0} p_i \leqslant t^i_l \leqslant \tilde{a}_{l1} p_i, \quad \forall l, i.
\end{aligned} \tag{17}
$$

PROOF. From every feasible solution $\lambda(\xi)$ of (8), a feasible solution of (17) can be constructed by setting

$$p_i := E[\lambda_i(\xi)] \quad \text{and} \quad t^i_l := E[\lambda_i(\xi)\eta_l]$$

for all $i = 1, \ldots, I$ and $l = 1, \ldots, L$. Moreover, under this construction, the upper bound in (16) develops to be the objective function in (17). Hence, the right-hand side upper bound in (16) is obtained as a feasible point lower bound to the maximization in (17). □

In an analogous manner, the following lower bound is derived.

PROPOSITION 2.2.

$$
\begin{aligned}
\bar{\phi}(x) \geqslant \min_{t,p} \quad & \sum_{j=1}^{J} \langle \pi^j, t^j \rangle + \sigma^j p_j \\
\text{s.t.} \quad & \sum_{j=1}^{J} v^j_l t^j_k = m_{kl}, \quad \forall k = 1, \ldots, K; \quad \forall l = 1, \ldots, L, \\
& \sum_{j=1}^{J} t^j_k = \bar{\xi}_k, \quad \forall k, \\
& \sum_{j=1}^{J} v^j_l p_j = \bar{\eta}_l, \quad \forall l, \\
& \sum_{j=1}^{J} p_j = 1, \quad p_j \geqslant 0, \\
& \hat{a}_{k0} p_j \leqslant t^j_k \leqslant \hat{a}_{k1} p_j, \quad \forall k, j.
\end{aligned} \tag{18}
$$

The bounds in (17) and (18) require solution of linear programs. Although these are valid upper and lower bounds to $\bar{\phi}(x)$ using only first and cross moments and without any independence assumption, even tighter bounds may be obtained as follows. Moreover, these tightened bounds also serve to develop the *best* possible upper and lower bounds under the *linearization* procedure.

PROPOSITION 2.3.

$$\bar{\phi}(x) \leqslant \max_{p \in \mathscr{C}} \sum_{i,j} (\langle \alpha^i, v^j \rangle + \beta^i) p_{ij} \tag{19}$$

and

$$\bar{\phi}(x) \geqslant \min_{p \in \mathscr{C}} \sum_{i,j} (\langle \pi^j, u^i \rangle + \sigma^j) p_{ij} \tag{20}$$

where the feasible set $\mathscr{C}$ is the polytope defined by

$$\mathscr{C} := \left\{ p \in \Re^{I \times J} \colon \sum_{i,j} (u^i, v^j) p_{ij} = (\bar{\xi}, \bar{\eta}),\ \sum_{i,j} u_k^i v_l^j p_{ij} = m_{kl},\right.$$
$$\left. \forall k = 1, \ldots, K;\ l = 1, \ldots, L,\ \sum_{i,j} p_{ij} = 1,\quad p_{ij} \geqslant 0 \right\}. \tag{21}$$

PROOF. For any feasible solution $\lambda(\xi)$ of (8) and $\mu(\eta)$ of (9), define

$$p_{ij} := E\big[\lambda_i(\xi)\mu_j(\eta)\big].$$

For this $\lambda(\xi)$ and $\mu(\eta)$, defining p_i and t_l^i, $i = 1, \ldots, I$ and $l = 1, \ldots, L$, as in the proof of Proposition 2.1, observe that $\sum_j v^j p_{ij} = t^i$, $\sum_j p_{ij} = p_i$, and $p_{ij} \geqslant 0$ hold. Substituting these in the upper bound in (17), the upper bound in (19) follows. Similarly, one obtains the lower bound in (20). □

COROLLARY 2.4. *If the domains Ξ and Θ are multidimensional rectangles of the form $\Xi := \times_{k=1}^{K} [\hat{a}_{k0}, \hat{a}_{k1}]$ and $\Theta := \times_{l=1}^{L} [\tilde{a}_{l0}, \tilde{a}_{l1}]$, then the upper and lower bounds in* (17) *and* (18) *coincide with those in* (19) *and* (20), *respectively.*

PROOF. Considering the upper bound in (19), from any of its feasible solutions, a feasible solution for the linear program in (17) may be constructed having the same objective value, i.e., the bound in (19) is never worse than that in (17). Consider a feasible solution (t^i, p_i), $\forall i$, of (17). Since Θ is a multidimensional interval, $t^i/p_i \in \Theta$ for $p_i \neq 0$. Thus, for each i, there exist convex combinations θ_{ij} such that $t^i = (\sum_j v^j \theta_{ij}) p_i$. The construction $p_{ij} := p_i \theta_{ij}$ results in a feasible solution to (19), implying that the upper bound in (17) is as good as that in (19), hence the result. The lower bounding result follows analogously. □

If the supports are multidimensional intervals, due to Corollary 2.4, we may continue the ensuing discussion with the bounds in (17) and (18). However, we shall keep the discussion general by requiring only that the supports Ξ and Θ be convex polyhedral sets. Consequently, we shall be concerned with the bounds given in (19) and (20). The latter upper and lower bounds, respectively, depend on the *linearizing* points which determine the supporting hyperplanes in (14) and (15). Therefore, it is of interest to determine those $\hat{\eta}^{*i}$, $i = 1, \ldots, I$, that lead to the *best* linearization upper bound. That is, one needs to determine that linearization of $\phi(x, u^i, \eta)$ for each i such that the upper bound in (19) becomes the smallest of all possible linearizations. Likewise, we obtain that linearization of $\phi(x, \xi, v^j)$ for each j such that the lower bound in (20) becomes the largest of all possible linearizations. For this development, first note the following result.

LEMMA 2.5. *Let $\rho \in \mathscr{C}$ where $\mathscr{C}$ is as defined in* (21). *Then,*

(i) $\forall i = 1, \ldots, I$: $\quad \sum_j \rho_{ij} = 0$ *implies* $\sum_j v^j \rho_{ij} = 0$,

$$\sum_j \rho_{ij} > 0 \quad \textit{implies} \quad \frac{\sum_j v^j \rho_{ij}}{\sum_j \rho_{ij}} \in \Theta.$$

(ii) $\forall j = 1, \ldots, J$: $\quad \sum_i \rho_{ij} = 0$ *implies* $\sum_i u^i \rho_{ij} = 0$,

$$\sum_i \rho_{ij} > 0 \quad \textit{implies} \quad \frac{\sum_i u^i \rho_{ij}}{\sum_i \rho_{ij}} \in \Xi.$$

PROOF. For $\rho \in \mathscr{C}$, since ρ_{ij} is nonnegative, $\sum_j \rho_{ij} = 0$ (for some i) implies $\rho_{ij} = 0$ for all j, and thus, $\sum_j v^j \rho_{ij} = 0$ for such i. If $\sum_j \rho_{ij} \neq 0$ for some i, then

$$\frac{\sum_j v^j \rho_{ij}}{\sum_j \rho_{ij}} = \sum_j v^j \left(\frac{\rho_{ij}}{\sum_j \rho_{ij}} \right) = \sum_j v^j \nu_j$$

where $\nu_j := \rho_{ij} / \sum_j \rho_{ij}$. Since $\sum_j \nu_j = 1$ and $\nu_j \geqslant 0$ for all j, $\sum_j v^j \nu_j \in \Theta$ proving the first assertion. The second assertion follows similarly. □

THEOREM 2.5. *The best-linearization upper bound from* (19) *is*

$$(22)\qquad \begin{aligned} \phi_U(x) := \max_{\rho \in \mathscr{C}} \quad & \sum_{i,j} \rho_{ij} \phi(x, u^i, \hat{\eta}^i(\rho)) \\ \text{s.t.} \quad & \sum_j v^j \rho_{ij} = \hat{\eta}^i(\rho) \sum_j \rho_{ij}, \qquad i = 1, \ldots, I, \end{aligned}$$

where $\mathscr{C}$ is defined in (21).

PROOF. The best-linearization upper bound from (19) is obtained from

$$(23)\qquad \inf_{\alpha, \beta} \left[\sup_{\rho \in \mathscr{C}} \left\{ \sum_{i,j} (\alpha^i v^j + \beta^i) \rho_{ij} : \alpha^i \eta + \beta^i \geqslant \phi(x, u^i, \eta), \ \eta \in \Theta, \ \ \forall i \right\} \right].$$

In (23), transposes have been removed for simplicity. Observe that (23) is equivalent to:

$$(24)\qquad \sup_{\rho \in \mathscr{C}} \left[\inf_{\alpha, \beta} \left\{ \sum_{i,j} (\alpha^i v^j + \beta^i) \rho_{ij} : \alpha^i \eta + \beta^i \geqslant \phi(x, u^i, \eta), \ \eta \in \Theta, \ \ \forall i \right\} \right].$$

For a given feasible solution $\rho \in \mathscr{C}$, consider the inner infimum in (24), the value of which is denoted by $Z(\rho)$. This problem decomposes to I subproblems of the form

$$(25)\quad Z^i(\rho) := \inf_{\alpha^i,\beta^i}\left\{\alpha^i\sum_j v^j\rho_{ij} + \beta^i\sum_j\rho_{ij} : \alpha^i\eta + \beta^i \geqslant \phi(x,u^i,\eta),\ \eta\in\Theta\right\}$$

and $Z(\rho) = \Sigma_i Z^i(\rho)$. First consider the case when $\Sigma_j\rho_{ij} \neq 0$. Let (α^i,β^i) be a feasible pair to (25), the existence of such being ensured by the concavity of $\phi(x,u^i,\eta)$ in η. Then multiplying the constraints in (25) by $\Sigma_j\rho_{ij}$, since

$$\hat{\eta}^i(\rho) := \frac{\Sigma_j v^j\rho_{ij}}{\Sigma_j\rho_{ij}} \in \Theta$$

(by Lemma 2.5), it follows that $Z^i(\rho) \geqslant \Sigma_j\rho_{ij}(x,u^i,\hat{\eta}^i(\rho))$ holds. Furthermore, the continuity and concavity of $\phi(x,u^i,\cdot)$ is sufficient to guarantee that $Z^i(\rho) = \Sigma_j\rho_{ij}\phi(x,u^i,\hat{\eta}^i(\rho))$ is attained; i.e., choose the coefficients (α^i,β^i) corresponding to the supporting hyperplane at the boundary point $(\hat{\eta}^i(\rho),\phi(x,u^i,\hat{\eta}^i(\rho)))$ of the closed convex set $\{(\eta,\nu): \nu \leqslant \phi(x,u^i,\eta),\ \eta\in\Theta,\ \nu\in\mathfrak{R}\}$. On the other hand, if $\Sigma_j\rho_{ij} = 0$, by Lemma 2.5, $\Sigma_j v^j\rho_{ij} = 0$ and (one may choose any $\hat{\eta}^i \in \Theta$) thus $Z^i(\rho) = 0$ (hence it is not necessary to linearize $\phi(x,u^i,\eta)$). Noting that $\mathscr{C}$ is a closed set and replacing the outer "sup" by "max" completes the proof. □

THEOREM 2.7. *The best-linearization lower bound from* (20) *is*

$$(26)\quad \begin{aligned} \phi_L(x) := \min_{\rho\in\mathscr{C}}\ & \sum_{i,j}\rho_{ij}\phi(x,\hat{\xi}^j(\rho),v^j) \\ \text{s.t.}\ & \sum_i u^i\rho_{ij} = \hat{\xi}^j(\rho)\sum_i\rho_{ij}, \qquad j = 1,\ldots,J, \end{aligned}$$

where $\mathscr{C}$ *is defined in* (21).

PROOF. The proof is similar to that of Theorem 2.6. □

It is clear from (22) and (26) that one needs to solve nonlinear programs to obtain the best-linearized upper and lower bounds. However, as follows from Lemma 2.8, these are in fact convex programs.

LEMMA 2.8. *Let* $g\colon \mathfrak{R}^n \to \mathfrak{R}$ *be convex and define* $f\colon \mathfrak{R}^n \times (0,\infty) \to \mathfrak{R}$ *by* $f(t,p) = pg(t/p)$. *Then* f *is (jointly) convex.*

PROOF. We show that epi f is a convex cone.

$$\begin{aligned} \text{epi } f &= \left\{(t,p,\theta): \theta \geqslant pg\left(\frac{t}{p}\right),\ p > 0\right\} \\ &= \{(t,p,\theta): \exists\nu > 0 \text{ with } \nu\theta \geqslant g(\nu t),\ \nu p = 1\} \\ &= \{(t,p,\theta): \exists\nu > 0 \text{ with } \nu(t,p,\theta) \in \mathscr{E}\} \end{aligned}$$

where $\mathscr{E} := \{(t,p,\theta): p = 1,\ \theta \geqslant g(t)\}$. Since $g(\cdot)$ is convex, $\mathscr{E}$ is a convex set. Next observe that epi f = rc $\mathscr{E}$, the recession cone of $\mathscr{E}$, and is thus convex. □

Although the bounding expressions $\phi_U(x)$ and $\phi_L(x)$ are convex programming problems, for fixed first stage decisions x, our intent here is not to suggest solution schemes for computing these bounds in the present form. We will use these bounds to derive finite linear programming formulations by using the properties of the recourse function $\phi(x,\xi,\eta)$, being defined by (2), which is the discussion in §4.

2.2. Convexity of the bounds. Observe that the upper and lower bounds are obtained through approximating the true probability distribution by discrete probability distributions defined on the boundary of the joint domain Ω. Moreover, these approximating probability measures have the same first moments and cross moments as the given true measure. However, these approximating measures may depend on the functional form of ϕ, and more importantly, on the first stage decisions x. Nevertheless, as shown next, the upper bounding measure preserves convexity of the bound in the first stage decisions x.

THEOREM 2.9. *The upper bound $\phi_U(x)$ in (22) is convex in the first stage decisions $x \in X$.*

PROOF. For $x^1, x^2 \in \Re^{n_1}$, such that $x^1 \neq x^2$, and scalar $\nu \in (0,1)$, defining $x^\nu := \nu x^1 + (1-\nu)x^2$,

$$\begin{aligned}
\phi_U(x^\nu) = \max_{\rho\in\mathscr{C}} \quad & \sum_{i,j} \rho_{ij}\phi(x^\nu, u^i, \hat{\eta}^i(\rho)) \\
\text{s.t.} \quad & \sum_j v^j\rho_{ij} = \hat{\eta}^i(\rho)\sum_j \rho_{ij} \\
\leqslant \max_{\rho\in\mathscr{C}} \quad & \sum_{i,j} \rho_{ij}\left[\nu\phi(x^1, u^i, \hat{\eta}^i(\rho)) + (1-\nu)\phi(x^2, u^i, \hat{\eta}^i(\rho))\right] \\
\text{s.t.} \quad & \sum_j v^j\rho_{ij} = \hat{\eta}^i(\rho)\sum_j \rho_{ij} \\
\leqslant \max_{\rho^1,\rho^2\in\mathscr{C}} \quad & \sum_{i,j} \rho^1_{ij}\left[\nu\phi(x^1, u^i, \hat{\eta}^i(\rho^1))\right] + \sum_{i,j} \rho^2_{ij}\left[(1-\nu)\phi(x^2, u^i, \hat{\eta}^i(\rho^2))\right] \\
\text{s.t.} \quad & \sum_j v^j\rho^k_{ij} = \hat{\eta}^i(\rho^k)\sum_j \rho^k_{ij}, \qquad k = 1,2, \\
= \nu\phi_U(x^1) + (1-\nu)\phi_U(x^2),
\end{aligned}$$

i.e., $\phi_U(x)$ is convex in x. □

In §4, when the bounds are formulated explicitly for the stochastic program (1)–(2), it will be shown that $\phi_U(x)$ is in fact polyhedral convex in x. The lower bound $\phi_L(x)$ in (26) may fail to be convex in x. In §4, we use $\phi_L(x)$ to derive a weaker lower bound which is convex in the first stage decisions x, still using first and cross moments.

Nonetheless, in certain special cases, when the domains Ξ and Θ are restricted to be of a certain shape, the bounds $\phi_U(x)$ and $\phi_L(x)$ are obtained with unique (i.e., independent of x or ϕ) discrete measures on the boundary of Ω, i.e., the optimizations in (22) and (26) are trivial, and consequently, convexity of $\phi_L(x)$ is guaranteed. This indeed is the case when Ξ and Θ are multidimensional simplices since every point in a simplex can be represented as a unique convex combination of the extreme points of the simplex, the barycentric coordinates. Consequently, the feasible set $\mathscr{C}$ in (21) implies that the values of $\Sigma_j\rho_{ij}$, $\Sigma_i\rho_{ij}$, for any i, and $\Sigma_j v^j\rho_{ij}$, $\Sigma_i u^i\rho_{ij}$, for any j, are uniquely determined. That is, the upper and lower bounding discrete probability measures are being determined independently of the function ϕ or the decisions x. This special case is discussed in Frauendorfer (1989).

When ξ and η are *univariate* random variables, hence the domains are one-dimensional simplices, the bounds $\phi_U(x)$ and $\phi_L(x)$ are simplified as follows:

THEOREM 2.10. *If ξ and η are both univariate (with interval domains $\Xi := [\hat{a}_0, \hat{a}_1]$, $\Theta := [\tilde{a}_0, \tilde{a}_1]$ such that $\hat{a}_0 < \hat{a}_1$ and $\tilde{a}_0 < \tilde{a}_1$), then denoting the cross moment $C := E[\xi\eta]$, the upper bound $\phi_U(x)$ simplifies to*

$$(27)\quad \phi_U(x) = \left(\frac{\hat{a}_1 - \bar{\xi}}{\hat{a}_1 - \hat{a}_0}\right)\phi\left(x, \hat{a}_0, \frac{\hat{a}_1\bar{\eta} - C}{\hat{a}_1 - \bar{\xi}}\right) + \left(\frac{\bar{\xi} - \hat{a}_0}{\hat{a}_1 - \hat{a}_0}\right)\phi\left(x, \hat{a}_1, \frac{C - \hat{a}_0\bar{\eta}}{\bar{\xi} - \hat{a}_0}\right)$$

and the lower bound $\phi_L(x)$ simplifies to

$$(28)\quad \phi_L(x) = \left(\frac{\tilde{a}_1 - \bar{\eta}}{\tilde{a}_1 - \tilde{a}_0}\right)\phi\left(x, \frac{\tilde{a}_1\bar{\xi} - C}{\tilde{a}_1 - \bar{\eta}}, \tilde{a}_0\right) + \left(\frac{\bar{\eta} - \tilde{a}_0}{\tilde{a}_1 - \tilde{a}_0}\right)\phi\left(x, \frac{C - \tilde{a}_0\bar{\xi}}{\bar{\eta} - \tilde{a}_0}, \tilde{a}_1\right).$$

PROOF. Let us consider the upper bound when ξ and η are univariate. Setting $u^1 = \hat{a}_0$, $u^2 = \hat{a}_1$, $v^1 = \tilde{a}_0$, and $v^2 = \tilde{a}_1$, from the corresponding feasible region $\mathscr{C}$ for ρ_{11}, ρ_{12}, ρ_{21}, and ρ_{22}, one can show that $(\rho_{i1} + \rho_{i2})$ and $(\tilde{a}_0\rho_{i1} + \tilde{a}_1\rho_{i2})$ are uniquely determined for each $i = 1, 2$ as follows:

$$\rho_{11} + \rho_{12} = \frac{\hat{a}_1 - \bar{\xi}}{\hat{a}_1 - \hat{a}_0} \quad \text{and} \quad \rho_{21} + \rho_{22} = \frac{\bar{\xi} - \hat{a}_0}{\hat{a}_1 - \hat{a}_0},$$

$$\tilde{a}_0\rho_{11} + \tilde{a}_1\rho_{12} = \frac{\hat{a}_1\bar{\eta} - C}{\hat{a}_1 - \bar{\xi}} \quad \text{and} \quad \tilde{a}_0\rho_{21} + \tilde{a}_1\rho_{22} = \frac{C - \hat{a}_0\bar{\eta}}{\bar{\xi} - \hat{a}_0}.$$

Moreover, since

$$\frac{\hat{a}_1 - \bar{\xi}}{\hat{a}_1 - \hat{a}_0} > 0 \quad \text{and} \quad \frac{\bar{\xi} - \hat{a}_0}{\hat{a}_1 - \hat{a}_0} > 0,$$

$$\hat{\eta}^1 = \frac{\hat{a}_1\bar{\eta} - C}{\hat{a}_1 - \bar{\xi}} \in \Theta \quad \text{and} \quad \hat{\eta}^2 = \frac{C - \hat{a}_0\bar{\eta}}{\bar{\xi} - \hat{a}_0} \in \Theta.$$

Substituting these in the upper bound $\phi_U(x) = \Sigma_{i=1}^2\Sigma_{j=1}^2\rho_{ij}\phi(x, u^i, \hat{\eta}^i)$ gives (27). Similarly, one can obtain the lower bound in (28). □

The bounds in (27) and (28) for a saddle function in 3-dimensions are depicted in Figure 1.

REMARK. Frauendorfer (1988c) derived bounds for the expectation of a convex-concave function using the following moments (for the case when Ξ and Θ are multidimensional rectangles):

$$(29)\quad \begin{cases} m_{\Lambda,1} := \int_\Theta \left(\prod_{l\in\Lambda}\eta_l\right)P(d\eta) & \text{for all } \Lambda \in B_2, \\ m^l_{\Lambda,2} := \int_\Omega \eta_l\left(\prod_{k\in\Lambda}\xi_k\right)P(d\xi, d\eta) & \text{for all } l = 1,\dots,L \text{ and } \Lambda \in B_1, \\ m_{\Lambda,3} := \int_\Xi \left(\prod_{k\in\Lambda}\xi_k\right)P(d\xi) & \text{for all } \Lambda \in B_1, \\ m^k_{\Lambda,4} := \int_\Omega \xi_k\left(\prod_{l\in\Lambda}\eta_l\right)P(d\xi, d\eta) & \text{for all } k = 1,\dots,K \text{ and } \Lambda \subset B_2, \end{cases}$$

where B_1 is the set of all subsets of $\{1,\ldots,K\}$ and B_2 is the set of all subsets of $\{1,\ldots,L\}$. The moment information in (29) allows one to determine upper and lower bounding extremal (discrete) distributions uniquely. For the special case of univariate ξ and η, the upper and lower bounds due to Frauendorfer (1988c) can be shown to coincide with those given in (27) and (28), respectively.

2.3. Relation to generalized moment problems. An immediate concern would be whether or not the bounds $\phi_U(x)$ and $\phi_L(x)$ derived in the previous section are tight, in the sense of the corresponding generalized moment problems. We will show that this indeed is the case. First, observe that it is possible to attain these bounds as the exact expectation in certain cases, i.e.,

THEOREM 2.11. *If the convex-concave recourse function $\phi(x,\xi,\eta)$ is bilinear in ξ and η, for fixed x, then $\phi_L(x)=\bar{\phi}(x)=\phi_U(x)$ holds where $\phi_U(x)$ and $\phi_L(x)$ are defined in* (22) *and* (26), *respectively.*

PROOF. Bilinearity allows one to simplify the upper bounding formulation in (22) so that the constraints defining the set $\mathscr{C}$ imply that $\phi_U(x)=\bar{\phi}(x)$. The lower bounding result also follows trivially. □

To show that the bounds $\phi_U(x)$ and $\phi_L(x)$ are the *best* using first and cross moments, consider upper and lower bounds on $\bar{\phi}(x)$ by formulating the corresponding moment problems as follows, where the set of all probability measures on Ω is denoted by $\mathscr{P}$:

$$(30)\qquad \begin{aligned} \bar{\phi}(x)\leqslant V_U(x):=\sup_{P\in\mathscr{P}}\ &\int_\Omega \phi(x,\xi,\eta)P(d\xi,d\eta)\\ \text{s.t.}\ &\int_\Omega \xi P(d\xi,d\eta)=\bar{\xi},\\ &\int_\Omega \eta P(d\xi,d\eta)=\bar{\eta},\\ &\int_\Omega \xi_k\eta_l P(d\xi,d\eta)=m_{kl},\\ &\qquad k=1,\ldots,K;\ l=1,\ldots,L, \end{aligned}$$

and

$$(31)\qquad \begin{aligned} \bar{\phi}(x)\geqslant V_L(x):=\inf_{P\in\mathscr{P}}\ &\int_\Omega \phi(x,\xi,\eta)P(d\xi,d\eta)\\ \text{s.t.}\ &\int_\Omega \xi P(d\xi,d\eta)=\bar{\xi},\\ &\int_\Omega \eta P(d\xi,d\eta)=\bar{\eta},\\ &\int_\Omega \xi_k\eta_l P(d\xi,d\eta)=m_{kl},\\ &\qquad k=1,\ldots,K;\ l=1,\ldots,L. \end{aligned}$$

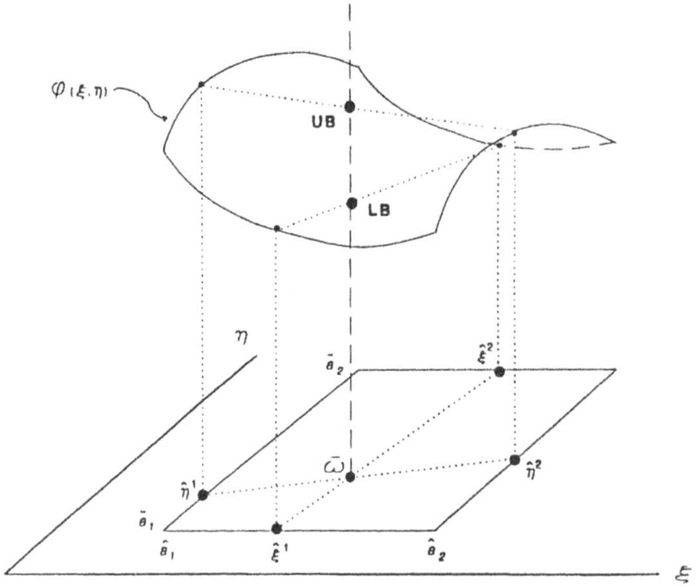

FIGURE 1. Upper and lower bounds using first and cross moments in the univariate case.

THEOREM 2.12. *Assuming that* (30) *and* (31) *are feasible*, $V_U(x) = \phi_U(x)$ *and* $V_L(x) = \phi_L(x)$ *hold, where* $\phi_U(x)$, $\phi_L(x)$, $V_U(x)$, *and* $V_L(x)$ *are defined in* (22), (26), (30), *and* (31), *respectively*.

PROOF. We shall prove the result for the upper bound. The proof for the lower bound is analogous.

Consider the symmetric dual problem of the upper bounding moment problem in (30), which is a semi-infinite linear program. By feasibility of (30), compactness of Ω, and continuity of $\phi(x, \cdot, \cdot)$, it follows by Theorem 1.1 that strong duality holds and thus,

$$
\begin{aligned}
V_U(x) = \inf_{\theta} \quad & \theta_0 + \sum_{k=1}^{K} \theta_k^1 \bar{\xi}_k + \sum_{l=1}^{L} \theta_l^2 \bar{\eta}_l + \sum_{k,l} \theta_{kl} m_{kl} \\
\text{s.t.} \quad & \theta_0 + \sum_{k=1}^{K} \theta_k^1 \xi_k + \sum_{l=1}^{L} \theta_l^2 \eta_l + \sum_{k,l} \theta_{kl} \xi_k \eta_l \geqslant \phi(x, \xi, \eta), \\
& \qquad \forall (\xi, \eta) \in \Omega, \\
= \inf_{\theta} \quad & \theta_0 + \sum_{k=1}^{K} \theta_k^1 \bar{\xi}_k + \sum_{l=1}^{L} \theta_l^2 \bar{\eta}_l + \sum_{k,l} \theta_{kl} m_{kl} \\
\text{s.t.} \quad & \theta_0 + \sum_{k=1}^{K} \theta_k^1 u_k^i + \sum_{l=1}^{L} \theta_l^2 \eta_l + \sum_{k,l} \theta_{kl} u_k^i \eta_l \geqslant \phi(x, u^i, \eta) \\
& \qquad \forall i = 1, \ldots, I;\ \eta \in \Theta.
\end{aligned} \tag{32}
$$

The equality in (32) is due to convexity of $\phi(x, \cdot, \eta)$ and the Assumption (A4) that $\Omega = \Xi \times \Theta$. Consider any feasible solution $\rho \in \mathscr{C}$. Due to Lemma 2.5, $\Sigma_j \rho_{ij} > 0$ implies

$$\frac{\Sigma_j v^j \rho_{ij}}{\Sigma_j \rho_{ij}} =: \hat{\eta}^i(\rho) \in \Theta.$$

If $\Sigma_j \rho_{ij} = 0$, pick any arbitrary $\hat{\eta}^i(\rho)$ from the domain Θ. It is easy to verify that the pairs $(\Sigma_j \rho_{ij}, \hat{\eta}^i(\rho))$, $i = 1, \ldots, I$, are dual feasible to (32)[1], hence $V_U(x) \geqslant \Sigma_{i,j} \rho_{ij} \phi(x, u^i, \hat{\eta}^i(\rho))$ for any such feasible solution $\rho \in \mathscr{C}$. That is, $V_U(x) \geqslant \phi_U(x)$.

To claim that $V_U(x) \leqslant \phi_U(x)$ holds, note that, by Theorem 1.1, (30) is solvable. Let P^* be a maximizing measure in (30). Now, applying the upper bounding technique in the previous section, with the underlying probability measure being replaced by P^*, yields

$$\int_\Omega \phi(x, \xi, \eta) P^*(d\xi, d\eta) \leqslant \phi_U(x), \tag{33}$$

since P^* has the same first and cross moments as the *true* probability measure. Therefore, $V_U(x) \leqslant \phi_U(x)$ holds and the proof is completed. □

3. First moment bounds—dependent case. If the random vectors ξ and η are stochastically independent of each other, then Jensen's inequality and the Gassmann-Ziemba (1986) inequality can be utilized simultaneously to obtain upper and lower bounding functions for $\bar{\phi}(x)$, using only first moments, as follows.

$$\begin{aligned} \bar{\phi}(x) &= E_\eta\left[E_\xi[\phi(x, \xi, \eta)]\right] \quad \text{(due to independence)} \\ &\geqslant E_\eta\left[\phi(x, \bar{\xi}, \eta)\right] \quad \text{(due to Jensen's inequality)} \\ &\geqslant \min_{\mu \geqslant 0}\left\{\sum_{j=1}^{J} \phi(x, \bar{\xi}, v^j)\mu_j : \sum_{j=1}^{J} v^j \mu_j = \bar{\eta}, \sum_{j=1}^{J} \mu_j = 1\right\}. \end{aligned} \tag{34}$$

The last inequality follows from the Gassmann-Ziemba inequality being applied on the concave function $\phi(x, \bar{\xi}, \cdot)$. Similarly, one obtains

$$\bar{\phi}(x) \leqslant \max_{\lambda \geqslant 0}\left\{\sum_{i=1}^{I} \phi(x, u^i, \bar{\eta})\lambda_i : \sum_{i=1}^{I} u^i \lambda_i = \bar{\xi}, \sum_{i=1}^{I} \lambda_i = 1\right\}. \tag{35}$$

However, under dependence between ξ and η, the above derivation is no longer valid and thus one has to proceed differently. In this section, we show that the approach in §2 can be used to obtain tight lower and upper bounds for $\bar{\phi}(x)$, in the dependent case, under the first moment information. These bounds could also be viewed as generalizations of Jensen's and the Gassmann-Ziemba bounds, from the pure convex case to the convex-concave case. Most results follow trivially from those in the

[1] We thankfully acknowledge the referee who pointed out the dual feasibility here, thus shortening the proof.

preceding sections. Define the bounded convex polyhedron $\overline{\mathscr{C}}$ by

$$\overline{\mathscr{C}} := \left\{ \rho \in \Re^{I \times J} : \sum_{i,j} (u^i, v^j) \rho_{ij} = (\bar{\xi}, \bar{\eta}), \sum_{i,j} \rho_{ij} = 1, \rho_{ij} \geq 0 \right\}. \tag{36}$$

Then,

THEOREM 3.1. *An upper bound to $\overline{\phi}(x)$ using only first moments is*

$$\begin{aligned} \hat{\phi}_U(x) := \max_{\rho \in \overline{\mathscr{C}}} \quad & \sum_{i,j} \rho_{ij} \phi(x, u^i, \hat{\eta}^i(\rho)) \\ \text{s.t.} \quad & \sum_j v^j \rho_{ij} = \hat{\eta}^i(\rho) \sum_j \rho_{ij}, \qquad i = 1, \ldots, I. \end{aligned} \tag{37}$$

A lower bound to $\overline{\phi}(x)$ using only first moments is

$$\begin{aligned} \hat{\phi}_L(x) := \min_{\rho \in \overline{\mathscr{C}}} \quad & \sum_{i,j} \rho_{ij} \phi(x, \hat{\xi}^j(\rho), v^j) \\ \text{s.t.} \quad & \sum_i u^i \rho_{ij} = \hat{\xi}^j(\rho) \sum_i \rho_{ij}, \qquad j = 1, \ldots, J, \end{aligned} \tag{38}$$

where $\overline{\mathscr{C}}$ is defined in (36).

PROOF. $\phi_U(x) \leq \hat{\phi}_U(x)$ and $\phi_L(x) \geq \hat{\phi}_L(x)$ trivially hold since $\mathscr{C} \subseteq \overline{\mathscr{C}}$, where $\phi_U(x)$ and $\phi_L(x)$ are defined in (22) and (26), respectively, hence the result. □

To see that the bounds $\hat{\phi}_U(x)$ and $\hat{\phi}_L(x)$ are tight, formulate the upper and lower bounding problems as generalized moment problems. One obtains

THEOREM 3.2. *Defining $\mathscr{P}$ as the set of all probability measures on the domain Ω,*

$$\hat{\phi}_U(x) = \sup_{P \in \mathscr{P}} \left\{ \int_\Omega \phi(x, \xi, \eta) P(d\xi, d\eta) : \int_\Omega \xi P(d\xi, d\eta) = \bar{\xi}, \int_U \eta P(d\xi, \eta) = \bar{\eta} \right\} \tag{39}$$

and

$$\hat{\phi}_L(x) = \inf_{P \in \mathscr{P}} \left\{ \int_\Omega \phi(x, \xi, \eta) P(d\xi, d\eta) : \int_\Omega \xi P(d\xi, d\eta) = \bar{\xi}, \int_\Omega \eta P(d\xi, \eta) = \bar{\eta} \right\} \tag{40}$$

hold where $\hat{\phi}_U(x)$ and $\hat{\phi}_L(x)$ are defined in (37) *and* (38), *respectively*.

PROOF. Noting that (39) and (40) are always feasible, the proof is similar to that in Theorem 2.12. □

These first moment bounds inherit the following properties:

THEOREM 3.3. (1) *$\hat{\phi}_U(x)$ is convex in x.*

(2) *If $\phi(x, \xi, \eta)$ is jointly linear in ξ and η, then $\hat{\phi}_U(x) = \overline{\phi}(x) = \hat{\phi}_L(x)$.*

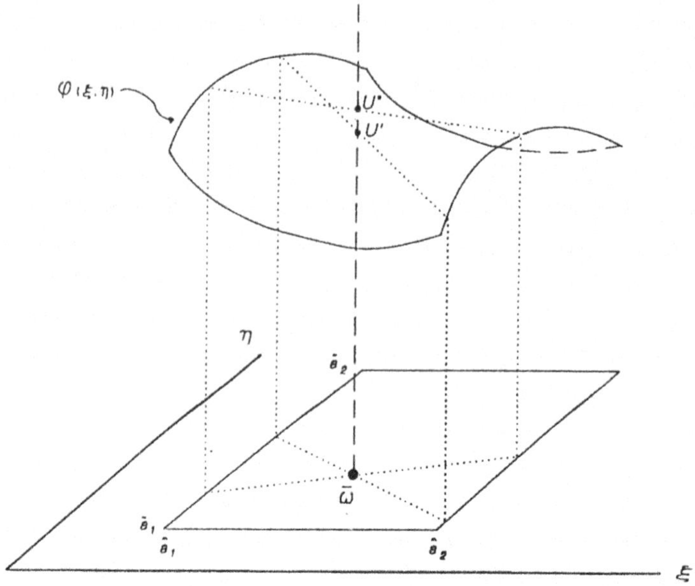

FIGURE 2. First moment bounds in the univariate case. To determine the upper bound, pick the plane through first moments, which gives the maximum height of U', U'', etc.

(3) *If the function ϕ is convex (in random vector ξ), for fixed x, then*
 (i) *$\hat{\phi}_L(x)$ simplifies to Jensen's lower bound, and*
 (ii) *$\hat{\phi}_U(x)$ simplifies to the Gassmann-Ziemba upper bound.*

PROOF. Straightforward. □

As pointed out in the previous section, when first and cross moments are used, the resulting bounds are trivially determined for the case when domains are multidimensional simplices. However, with the first moment bounds $\hat{\phi}_U(x)$ and $\hat{\phi}_L(x)$, such is not possible. As illustrated in Figure 2, when ξ and η are univariate, the upper bound is determined by choosing a "vertical" cross section of the saddle surface through the point of first moments ($\bar{\omega}$) such that the line joining the points of intersection of the saddle surface has a maximum height at $\bar{\omega}$.

When ξ and η are known to be stochastically independent, the bounds in (35) and (34) are generally tighter than those in (37) and (38), respectively.

4. Application to stochastic programming. In this section, the bounds derived using first and cross moments are applied to the stochastic program (1)–(2) to obtain finite mathematical programming formulations. The intent here is to develop upper and lower bounding formulations which are amenable to efficient solution techniques, such as linear programming.

Consider the upper and lower bounds $\phi_U(x)$ and $\phi_L(x)$ in (22) and (26), respectively, on the expectation $\bar{\phi}(x)$, using first and cross moments of the random vector. With Z^* being defined by (1), the resulting upper and lower bounding approximations for Z^* are

$$Z^* \leqslant Z_U^* := \min_{x \in X}\{c'x + \phi_U(x)\} \tag{41}$$

and

(42) $$Z^* \geqslant Z_L^* := \min_{x \in X} \{c'x + \phi_L(x)\}.$$

PROPOSITION 4.1. *For the stochastic program in (1)–(2), under the Assumptions (A1)–(A5), $\phi_U(x)$ is convex polyhedral in $x \in X$, where $\phi_U(x)$ is defined by (22).*

PROOF. That $\phi_U(x)$ is convex in x was shown in Theorem 2.9. Here we show that it is convex polyhedral, when applied to the recourse function definition in (2).

For any $i = 1, \ldots, I$,

(43) $$\phi(x, u^i, \hat{\eta}^i(\rho)) := \min_{y^i} \{q(\hat{\eta}^i(\rho))' y^i : Wy^i = h(u^i) - T(u^i)x,\ y^i \geqslant 0\}.$$

Denote the feasible set on y^i, $i = 1, \ldots, I$ (simply referred to as y), for any given x, by $\mathscr{Y}(x)$. Thus,

(44) $$\phi_U(x) = \max_{\rho \in \mathscr{C}} \min_{y \in \mathscr{Y}(x)} G(y, \rho) := \sum_{i,j} \rho_{ij} q(\hat{\eta}^i(\rho))' y^i.$$

By Assumption (A3) in §1, $G(y, \rho) = \sum_{i,j} q(v^j)' y^i \rho_{ij}$, i.e., $G(y, \rho)$ is bilinear in y and ρ. Moreover, since $\mathscr{C}$ and $\mathscr{Y}(x)$ are polyhedral sets, interchanging maximization and minimization in (44),

(45) $$\phi_U(x) = \min_{y \in \mathscr{Y}(x)} \max_{\rho \in \mathscr{C}} G(y, \rho).$$

Using linear programming strong duality for the inner maximization in (45),

$$\max_{\rho \in \mathscr{C}} G(y, \rho) = \min_{w} \quad w^0 + w^1 \bar{\xi} + w^2 \bar{\eta} + \sum_{k,l} m_{kl} w_{kl}^3$$

$$\text{s.t.} \quad w^0 + w^1 u^i + w^2 v^j + \sum_{k,l} u_k^i v_l^j w_{kl}^3 \geqslant q(v^j)' y^i, \quad \forall i, j.$$

Therefore,

(46) $$\begin{aligned} \phi_U(x) = \min_{y, w} \quad & w^0 + w^1 \bar{\xi} + w^2 \bar{\eta} + \sum_{k,l} m_{kl} w_{kl}^3 \\ \text{s.t.} \quad & Wy^i = h(u^i) - T(u^i)x, \quad \forall i, \\ & w^0 + w^1 u^i + w^2 v^j + \sum_{k,l} u_k^i v_l^j w_{kl}^3 - q(v^j)' y^i \geqslant 0, \quad \forall i, j, \\ & y^i \geqslant 0, \quad \forall i, \end{aligned}$$

and thus is convex polyhedral in x. □

Since $\phi_U(x)$ is convex polyhedral, as follows from the above proof, the upper bounding approximation Z_U^* in (41) can be solved as a linear program. On the contrary, the lower bounding approximation $\phi_L(x)$ may fail to be convex. To see this, rewrite $\phi_L(x)$ using the recourse function definition in (2) as

(47)

$$\phi_L(x) = \min_{\rho \in \mathscr{C},\, y \geqslant 0} \left\{ \sum_{i,j} \rho_{ij} q(v^j)' y^j \colon Wy^j + T(\hat{\xi}^j(\rho))x - h(\hat{\xi}^j(\rho)) = 0, \quad \forall j \right\}.$$

Due to our Assumptions (A2) and (A3):

$$\phi_L(x) = \min_{\rho \in \mathscr{C},\, y \geqslant 0} \sum_{j=1}^{J} q(v^j)' y^j$$

$$\text{(48)} \qquad \text{s.t.} \quad Wy^j + (T_0 x - h_0) \sum_i \rho_{ij} + \sum_{k=1}^{K} (T_k x - h_k) \left(\sum_i u_k^i \rho_{ij} \right) = 0, \quad \forall j.$$

Although for any given $x \in X$, $\phi_L(x)$ could be evaluated by solving a linear program, observe that it cannot be concluded from (48) that $\phi_L(x)$ is convex in x. Therefore, in general, the lower bounding approximation Z_L^* in (42) involves nonconvex optimization. To overcome this computational difficulty, we derive below an alternative convex polyhedral lower bound $\bar{\phi}_L(x)$, using first and cross moments, which is generally weaker than $\phi_L(x)$.

Construct the $(K \times L)$-dimensional matrix M of cross moments, with the entry at the kth row and the lth column being m_{kl}.

PROPOSITION 4.2.

$$\text{(49)} \qquad \bar{\phi}(x) \geqslant \phi_L(x) \geqslant \bar{\phi}_L(x)$$

where

$$\text{(50)} \qquad \bar{\phi}_L(x) := \min_y \sum_j q(v^j)' y^j$$

$$\text{s.t.} \sum_j Wy^j = h(\bar{\xi}) - T(\bar{\xi})x,$$

$$\sum_j v_l^j W y^j = h(M_{(l)}) - T(M_{(l)})x + (h_0 - T_0 x)(\bar{\eta}_l - 1),$$

$$l = 1, \ldots, L, \phi y^j \geqslant 0, \qquad j = 1, \ldots, J,$$

and $M_{(l)}$ is the lth column of the cross moment matrix M. Moreover, $\bar{\phi}_L(x)$ is convex polyhedral in x.

PROOF. Summing the constraints (involving variables y^j) of (48) for all $j = 1, \ldots, J$,

$$\text{(51)} \qquad \sum_j Wy^j = h(\bar{\xi}) - T(\bar{\xi})x$$

follows since $\rho \in \mathscr{C}$. Multiplying the constraints (involving variables y^j) of (48) by v_l^j (for some $l = 1, \dots, L$) and summing the resulting equalities together for all $j = 1, \dots, J$,

$$\text{(52)} \qquad \sum_j v_l^j W y^j = (h_0 - T_0 x)\overline{\eta}_l + \sum_{k=1}^{K} (h_k - T_k x) m_{kl}$$

$$= h(M_l) - T(M_l)x + (h_0 - T_0 x)(\overline{\eta}_l - 1).$$

Since the constraints are aggregated, (51)–(52) provide a relaxation to the feasible set of (48), hence a lower bound which is convex polyhedral in x. □

The constraint aggregation procedure above should be viewed as a rather natural way to obtain a convex polyhedral lower bound from the generally nonconvex bound in (48), as evident from the next proposition.

PROPOSITION 4.3. *If Θ, the domain of the random vector η, is an L-dimensional simplex, then $\phi_L(x) = \overline{\phi}_L(x)$ for all $x \in X$.*

PROOF. Since $\phi_L(x) \geqslant \overline{\phi}_L(x)$ holds trivially from (49), we only need to show that $\phi_L(x) \leqslant \overline{\phi}_L(x)$ holds when Θ is a simplex.

For every feasible $(L+1)$-tuple $(\Sigma_j y_n^j, \Sigma_j v_l^j y_n^j,\ l = 1, \dots, L)$ of (50), where $n = 1, \dots, n_2$, observe that Θ being a simplex implies that y_n^j, $\forall j$, $\forall n$ are completely and uniquely determined. It is easy to verify that this unique solution y^j, for the chosen feasible $(L+1)$-tuple, is feasible in (48) since $\Sigma_i \rho_{ij}$ and $\Sigma_i u^i \rho_{ij}$ are uniquely determined for Θ being a simplex. □

Therefore, not only is the lower bound $\overline{\phi}_L(x)$ in (50) tight in the sense of Proposition 4.3, but it also allows one to solve the resulting lower bounding approximation

$$\text{(53)} \qquad Z_{LL}^* := \min_{x \in X} \{c'x + \overline{\phi}_L(x)\}$$

as a linear program. We illustrate these bounds on a simple numerical example below.

EXAMPLE 4.4. Consider the following two-stage stochastic programming (complete recourse) problem with random right-hand side, technology matrix, and cost coefficients:

$$Z^* = \min_{x \geqslant 0} 2x_1 + 2x_2 + E_{\xi,\eta}\left[\min_{y \geqslant 0} \quad 2\eta_1 y_1 + 3\eta_2 y_2 + y_3\right]$$

$$\text{s.t. } 2x_1 - x_2 \leqslant 1, \quad \text{s.t.} \quad 2y_1 + y_2 - 3y_3 = 2 + 3\xi_1 - 3(\xi_1 + \xi_2)x_1 + 4\xi_1 x_2,$$

$$x_1 + x_2 \leqslant 1, \qquad -y_1 + 3y_2 + y_3 = 4 + 2\xi_2 - x_1 - 3\xi_2 x_2,$$

where $\Xi = [0, 1] \times [0, 1] = \Theta$ and the joint distribution of $(\xi_1, \xi_2, \eta_1, \eta_2)$ is given by

$$f_k(\xi_k, \eta_k) = \begin{cases} \dfrac{2\eta_k}{\xi_k} & \text{if } \eta_k \leqslant \xi_k, \\[2ex] \dfrac{2(1-\eta_k)}{1-\xi_k} & \text{if } \eta_k \geqslant \xi_k, \end{cases}$$

for $k = 1, 2$ with (ξ_1, η_1) being independent of (ξ_2, η_2). One obtains $\bar{\xi}_k = \bar{\eta}_k = 0.5$ for $k = 1, 2$ and the cross moments $m_{11} = m_{22} = \frac{5}{18}$ and $m_{12} = m_{21} = 0.25$.

Using the lower bounding approximation in (53), solving only a linear program, yields $Z^*_{LL} = 3.6369$ and the approximate solution $x_L = (0.5, 0)$. Using the upper bounding approximation in (41) and solving only a linear program, one obtains $Z^*_U = 3.7977$ and the approximate solution $x_U = (0, 0)$. Thus, the relative error of the bounds is

$$\frac{3.7977 - 3.6369}{3.6369} < 5\%.$$

Moreover, from the dual solution of the upper bounding linear program, one obtains that the true distribution is approximated by a discrete probability measure on the boundary of the joint domain as $\omega^1 = (0, 0, 0.4580, 0.5420)$, $p(\omega^1) = 0.3306$; $\omega^2 = (1, 0, 0.5821, 0.2538)$, $p(\omega^2) = 0.1694$; $\omega^3 = (1, 1, 0.5420, 0.6261)$, $p(\omega^3) = 0.3306$; and $\omega^4 = (0, 1, 0.4180, 0.4180)$, $p(\omega^4) = 0.1694$; where $p(\omega)$ denotes the probability assigned to the point $\omega = (\xi_1, \xi_2, \eta_1, \eta_2)$.

Since the stochastic program above has complete recourse, using the lower bounding solution x_L in the upper bounding function $\phi_U(x)$ in (46), one obtains a less tight upper bound to Z^* as 4.1226.

Since (ξ_1, η_1) is independent of (ξ_2, η_2), the univariate bounding inequalities (27) and (28) may be used successively to determine tighter bounds than above. Under this pairwise independence, one obtains the bounds $3.6369 \leqslant Z^* \leqslant 3.7973$. Using the lower bounding solution, one computes a slightly weaker upper bound (under pairwise independence) as 3.8874.

5. Concluding remarks. This paper presents a general approach for bounding the expectation of a saddle function using limited moment information when random vectors have compact domains. The procedure formalizes concepts from Birge and Wets (1986) and Frauendorfer (1988d) in an attempt to formulate bounds as finite mathematical programs. Solutions of these mathematical programs provide discrete probability measures on the boundary of the joint domain of the random vectors to determine upper and lower approximations for the given stochastic program. Furthermore, these measures are shown to solve the respective moment problems, thus in the sense of Kemperman (1968), the derived bounds are tight. In fact, it follows that with using first and cross moment conditions, the *linearization* strategy is *optimal*, in the sense of the specific moment problem. This is also the case with the bounds due to Frauendorfer (1988b, c, d, 1989). However, if other joint moment conditions such as $E[\xi_j \xi_k]$ are used, then linearization may not be an optimal strategy and one needs to use higher order, such as quadratic, function approximations which is due to the nature of the moment problem of concern. In the latter case, even with a linearization strategy, our approach can be shown to yield valid bounds, although they may not generally solve the moment problem of interest.

It is easy to prove that the bounds $\phi_U(x)$ and $\phi_L(x)$ behave monotonously under partitioning the domain, an approach generally used to solve stochastic programs to ϵ-optimality, see Birge and Wallace (1986). In fact, these bounds converge to the optimal value of the stochastic program as long as the diameters of the partitioning cells (the cells being polytopes themselves) are sufficiently small, and furthermore, one can even claim convergence of approximate solutions to a true optimal solution, relying on epi-convergence arguments, see Birge and Wets (1986). Nevertheless, such assertions do not hold, in general, regarding the *relaxed* lower bound $\bar{\phi}_L(x)$, an exception being when Θ is a simplex. Despite this shortcoming, the convex polyhedral lower bound $\bar{\phi}_L(x)$ is numerically attractive because even with larger dimensions, the number of constraints grows only linearly in the dimension L of η since the linear program defining $\bar{\phi}_L(x)$ has only $L + 1$ blocks of constraints. The number of variables, however, depends on the chosen shape for domain Θ.

Towards solving stochastic programs to ϵ-optimality, what remains to be addressed is the choice of such partitioning schemes so that the computational burden does not become excessive; for instance, how to refine partitions based on information gained from previous partitions. Frauendorfer (1988c) addressed the issues when domains are rectangles. More recently, simplicial domains have been investigated by Frauendorfer (1991).

An extension of the results in this paper to the case when domains are possibly unbounded sets appears in Edirisinghe and Ziemba (1994).

Acknowledgements. The authors wish to thank the anonymous referees for their useful comments on earlier versions of the paper, which have improved the presentation of the paper significantly. This research was partially supported by the Natural Sciences and Engineering Research Council of Canada and the National Science Foundation. An earlier version of this paper was presented at the ORSA/TIMS meeting in Vancouver, May 1989 and at the Fifth International Conference on Stochastic Programming, University of Michigan, Ann Arbor, Michigan, August 1989.

References

Birge, J. R. and Wallace, S. W. (1986). Refining Bounds for Stochastic Linear Programs with Linearly Transformed Independent Random Variables. *Oper. Res. Lett.* **5** 73–77.

______ and Wets, R. J-B. (1986). Designing Approximation Schemes for Stochastic Optimization Problems, in Particular for Stochastic Programs with Recourse. *Math. Programming Stud.* **27** 54–102.

Dula, J. H. (1991). An Upper Bound on the Expectation of Simplicial Functions of Multivariate Random Variables. *Math. Programming*. **55** 69–80.

Edirisinghe, N. C. P. and Ziemba, W. T. (1994). Bounding the Expectation of a Saddle Function with Application to Stochastic Programming. *Math. Oper. Res.* **19** 314–340.

Frauendorfer, K. (1988a). SLP Recourse Problems with Arbitrary Multivariate Distributions—the Dependent Case. *Math. Oper. Res.* **13** 377–394.

______ (1988b). SLP Problems: Objective and Right-Hand Side being Stochastically Dependent—Part I. Proceedings of the 12th IMACS World Congress in Paris. (to appear).

______ (1988c). SLP Problems: Objective and Right-Hand Side being Stochastically Dependent—Part II. Manuscript. IOR, University of Zurich.

______ (1988d). Solving SLP Recourse Problems: The Case of Stochastic Technology Matrix, RHS and Objective. *Proceedings of the 13th IFIP Conference on System Modelling and Optimization*. Springer-Verlag, (to appear).

______ (1989). A Simplicial Approximation Scheme for Convex Two-Stage Stochastic Programming Problems. Presented at the *Fifth International Conference on Stochastic Programming*. University of Michigan, Ann Arbor, Michigan.

______ (1991). A Barycentric Approximation Scheme for Convex Stochastic Optimization Problems (Algorithmic Design and Computational Results). Presentation at *ORSA Applied Probability Conference*, Monterey, CA, January 9–11.

Gassmann, H. and Ziemba, W. T. (1986). A Tight Upper Bound for the Expectation of a Convex Function of a Multivariate Random Variable. *Math. Programming Stud.* **27** 39–53.

Glashoff, K. and Gustafson, S.-A. (1983). *Linear Optimization and Approximation*. Springer-Verlag, NY.

Kall, P. (1976). *Stochastic Linear Programming*. Springer-Verlag, Berlin.

______ (1987). Stochastic Programming with Recourse: Upper Bounds and Moment Problems—A Review. In *Advances in Mathematical Optimization and Related Topics* (J. Guddat, P. Kall, K. Lommatzsch, M. Vlach, and K. Zimmermann, Eds.), Akademie-Verlag, Belrin.

Kemperman, J. (1968). The General Moment Problem. A Geometric Approach. *Ann. Math. Statist.* **39** 93–112.

Wets, R. J.-B. (1974). Stochastic Programs with Fixed Recourse: The Equivalent Deterministic Problem. *SIAM Rev*. **16** 309–339.

______ (1982). Stochastic Programming: Solution Techniques and Approximation Schemes. In *Mathematical Programming: State-of-the-Art* (A. Bachem, M. Groetschel, B. Korte, Eds.) Springer-Verlag, Berlin, pp. 566–603.

N. C. P. Edirisinghe: Management Science Program, College of Business Administration, University of Tennessee, Knoxville, Tennessee 37996; e-mail: pa144918@utkvm1.bitnet

W. T. Ziemba: Faculty of Commerce and Business Administration, University of British Columbia, Vancouver, British Columbia, Canada V6T 1Y8

Section II

Finance and Economics

Chapter 5

PORTFOLIO SELECTION IN A LOGNORMAL MARKET WHEN THE INVESTOR HAS A POWER UTILITY FUNCTION#

*J. A. Ohlson and W. T. Ziemba**

I. Introduction and Summary

Multiasset portfolio selection models stated in terms of the expected utility criterion generally require the evaluation of multiple integrals. This reality has severely hindered attempts towards the development of computation methods to determine optimal portfolio allocations when there are a large number of assets. Aside from special cases, expected utility is not convergent into a simple closed form; the complexity from the point of view of computation is then perhaps most easily appreciated if one realizes that *every* iteration in a non-linear program demands the estimation of several integrals (see Ziemba [23] for details). Such calculations are extremely costly when the number of assets is large. It is, consequently, of interest to approximate the expected utility function by a function which is easier to optimize over the set of feasible portfolios.

Two basic approaches suggest themselves when one wishes to approximate the objective function: (i) the utility function is approximated; (ii) the assumed distributions of the asset returns and/or portfolio returns are approximated. In the literature of portfolio selection, method (i) has often been employed by approximating utility of wealth by a quadratic function. This, of course, leads to a simple quadratic program provided the expected returns and the variances-covariances are furnished or easy to calculate. Moreover, such problems are not difficult to solve even when the number of assets is large. The second approach is rarely used. Notable exceptions are cases when it is assumed *a priori* that the returns have a distribution which is convenient from an analytical point of view; e.g., the distribution is assumed to be approximately normal, or discrete.

In this paper approach (ii) will be exploited for purposes of developing a surrogate objective function, which can be solved using a standard nonlinear

---

**University of California, Berkeley, and University of British Columbia.*
This research was partially supported by the National Research Council of Canada. The authors would like to thank C. E. Lemke, D. Murdoch, S. J. Press, and an anonymous referee for valuable comments on an earlier version of this paper.

#This chapter was originally published in: Ohlson, J. A. & Ziemba, W. T. (1976). Portfolio Selection in a Lognormal Market When the Investor has a Power Utility Function. *Journal of Financial and Quantitative Analysis*, 11(1), 57–71.

programming algorithm. The specific class of problems to be analyzed is one where the investor's utility is a (positive or negative) power or logarithmic function of wealth, and the return process is assumed to be multivariate lognormal. Both of these specifications are of considerable relevance in portfolio theory. Hakansson [5,6], among others, has pointed out many important properties of power utility (e.g., it exhibits constant relative risk-aversion, and optimal strategies are myopic in some multiperiod models). Specifically, in [6] it is shown that in certain multiperiod models the induced (one-period) utility function is of the power class. Hence, while the formal setting of this paper is single period, the general problem will be applicable in these multiperiod models as well. The lognormal assumption is also significant. Several authors (e.g., Lintner [8], Rosenberg [18], Blattberg and Gonedes [1]) have found that actual security price data are well approximated by the lognormal distribution.

The basic approximation utilized in this paper is that sums of lognormal variables are also lognormal; that is, it is assumed that every portfolio has a lognormal distribution. The appropriateness of this approximation is difficult to evaluate in precise terms. To do so would generally require knowledge of the true optimal solution, and the original problem would have to be solved. In addition, any measure of the efficiency (goodness) of the approximation will, in all likelihood, be dependent upon the specific problem under consideration, i.e., the parameters determining the lognormal distribution, and the specification of the utility function.[1] Some observations, however, can be made in support of the above approximation. First Lintner [8] has analyzed security-price data extensively and concluded that:

> ...on the basis of these simulations that the approximation to lognormally distributed *portfolio* outcomes of lognormally distributed stock is sufficiently good that theoretical models based on these twin premises should be useful in a wide range of applications and empirical investigations.

Secondly, and perhaps more important, the goodness of any approximation method should be compared with alternative methods of the same order of

---

[1] Some numerical tests along these lines are given in Dexter, Yu, and Ziemba [2]. They used data from the Center for Research in Security Prices Monthly Price Information Tape for the 200 months between February 1926 and July 1942, and parametrized values of the power coefficient. They found that "... for n = 2, 3, and 4 the optimal portfolio allocations for the true and approximate problems are close (generally within ten percent). However, the difference in the value of the true objective function using the true and approximately optimal portfolio allocations is virtually negligible. The ratio of the computing times is (approximately) exponential in n. Hence, in this case, the loss in accuracy due to the approximation is more than recovered from the economics of computations."

computational complexity. An obvious alternative to the lognormal approximation is the quadratic program obtained by a Taylor's expansion of the utility function. Such optimization problems are relatively easy to solve for a surrogate-optimal portfolio on the mean-variance efficient frontier. However, the surrogate problem developed in this paper is no more difficult to solve utilizing the Frank-Wolfe algorithm, and the optimal portfolio is also mean-variance efficient. The preceding would therefore indicate that the quadratic utility approach does not necessarily have characteristics which are superior to the lognormal approximation. In fact, the quadratic approximation is in some qualitative respects inferior. It will be shown that the original problem is invariant with respect to certain changes of the parameters of the lognormal distribution, and these properties are *not* preserved in the quadratic program. The surrogate problem suggested in this paper, however, preserves these important properties of the original problem.

A weighty defense for the quadratic utility surrogate occurs when probabilities are "small risk" in a sense analyzed by Samuelson [19], Merton [12-14], and Ohlson [15]. In the lognormal case "small risk" probabilities may be constructed by assuming expectations and variance-covariances of the logarithm of returns are linear in time. That is, the return process is determined by a stationary "geometric" Wiener process. As the investor's trading interval approaches zero, the probabilities become "small risk" and the optimal solution of the original problem is asymtotically equal to the solution of a quadratic utility problem. However, it will be shown that this is true also for the surrogate problems suggested in this paper, and the two approaches are identical in a limiting sense. Thus, there appears to be no apparent reason to presume that quadratic utility is the preferable approximation even when the context is one of power utility and "small risk" lognormal returns.

II. The Portfolio and Surrogate Problems

The following notation and assumptions are used:[2] $X \equiv (X_1,\ldots,X_m)' =$ the vector of random returns or asset price-relatives. The vector X is assumed to have a multivariate lognormal distribution; that is, $(\log X_1,\ldots,\log X_m)'$ has a multivariate normal distribution with mean $(E \log X_1,\ldots,E \log X_m)' \equiv (\mu_1,\ldots,\mu_m)' \equiv \mu$ and variance-covariance matrix Σ having typical element $\operatorname{covar}(\log X_i, \log X_j) \equiv \sigma_{ij}$. We will write $X \sim ML_m(\mu,\Sigma)$ to denote that X follows a probability

[2]Primes denote transposition and all unprimed vectors are columns.

law, ML_m, determined by a multivariate lognormal distribution with parameters μ and Σ. The matrix Σ is assumed to have rank m, implying that all assets are risky. However, the introduction of a riskfree asset in the analysis that follows does not introduce any complications.

Let $\lambda \equiv (\lambda_1,\ldots,\lambda_m)'$ and $D \equiv \{\lambda|\Sigma\lambda_i=1, \lambda_i \geq 0\}$ denote the decision variables and the set of feasible portfolios, respectively. For simplicity and without loss of generality it is assumed that the asset returns have been scaled so the amount of capital to be invested is 1. If portfolio allocations λ are made, then the return is $W = \Sigma\lambda_i X_i$. The investor's utility function is $U(W) = s(\gamma)W^\gamma$, where $\gamma \neq 0$, $s(\gamma) = 1$ (-1) if $\gamma > 0$ (<0). It is assumed that $\gamma < 1$ so that U is strictly increasing, strictly concave, and its Arrow-Pratt absolute risk-aversion index is strictly decreasing.

The portfolio problem is

$$\text{(P)} \qquad \max_{\lambda\in D} E\, s(\gamma)(\Sigma\lambda_i X_i)^\gamma \equiv \max_{\lambda\in D} V(\lambda,\mu,\Sigma),$$

Where E represents mathematical expectation and $X \sim ML_m(\mu,\Sigma)$.

There is no known closed form analytical expression for the objective function $V(\lambda,\mu,\Sigma)$. However, the following result shows that any problem in the set P has a unique optimal solution.

Theorem I: Any problem in the set P has a unique optimal solution.

Proof: Since D is compact, it suffices to show that V is (i) finite, (ii) strictly concave on D, and (iii) continuous.

i) Observe that

$$\min_i\{X_i\} \leq \Sigma\lambda_i X_i \leq \max_i\{X_i\}\ .$$

Further, X_i^γ is a one-to-one mapping in X_i implying

$$(\Sigma\lambda_i X_i)^\gamma \leq (\max_i\{X_i\})^\gamma \leq \Sigma X_i^\gamma \quad \text{if } 0 < \gamma < 1, \text{ and}$$

$$(\Sigma\lambda_i X_i)^\gamma \leq (\min_i\{X_i\})^\gamma \leq \Sigma X_i^\gamma \quad \text{if } \gamma < 0.$$

The random variables X_i^γ are all lognormal with finite means. Consequently,

$$E(\Sigma\lambda_i X_i)^\gamma \leq E\ \Sigma X_i^\gamma < \infty.$$

ii) $s(\gamma)(\Sigma\lambda_i X_i)^{\gamma}$ is strictly concave on D with probability one. Hence, V is also strictly concave on D.

iii) Let $\lambda^{(1)}$, $\lambda^{(2)}$,...be a sequence of points in D such that $\lambda^{(n)} \to \lambda\varepsilon D$, λ fixed, as $n \to \infty$. Lebesque's dominated convergence theorem (Loeve [9]) then implies that $\lim_{n\to\infty} V(\lambda^{(n)},.,.)=V(\lambda,.,.)$ since $|V(\lambda^{(n)},.,.)| \leq E\ \Sigma X_i^{\gamma} < \infty$ for every n.

Next we derive a closed analytical expression of $s(\gamma)E(\Sigma\lambda_i X_i)^{\gamma} \equiv s(\gamma)\ EW^{\gamma}$ assuming that W is lognormal. If W is lognormal, then W^{γ} is also lognormal, and $EW^{\gamma} = \exp\{\gamma\ E \log W + \frac{1}{2}\gamma^2 \text{ Var Log } W\}$. To find E Log W and Var Log W as functions of λ, μ, and $\ddagger$, we use the following relations:

(1) $$EW = \exp\{E \text{ Log } W + \frac{1}{2} \text{ Var Log } W\}$$

(2) $$EW^2 = \exp\{2\ E \text{ Log } W + 2 \text{ Var Log } W\}$$

and

(3) $$EW = \Sigma\lambda_i \exp\{\mu_i + \frac{1}{2}\sigma_{ii}\}$$

(4) $$EW^2 = \Sigma\Sigma\lambda_i\lambda_j \exp\{\mu_i+\mu_j + \frac{1}{2}(\sigma_{ii}+\sigma_{jj}+2\sigma_{ij})\}.$$

Taking the logs of both sides of the equality sign in (1) and (2), and solving for E Log W and Var Log W as a function of EW and EW^2, one obtains:

(5) $$E \text{ Log } W = 2 \text{ Log } EW - \frac{1}{2} \text{ Log } EW^2, \text{ and}$$

(6) $$\text{Var Log } W = -2 \text{ Log } EW + \text{Log } EW^2.$$

Maximizing $s(\gamma) \exp\{\gamma\ E \text{ Log } W + \frac{1}{2}\gamma^2 \text{ Var Log } W\}$ is equivalent to maximizing $E \text{ Log } W + \frac{1}{2}\gamma \text{ Var Log } W$. Substituting (5) and (6) into the last expression and simplifying we have:

(7) $$E \text{ Log } W + \frac{1}{2}\gamma \text{ Var Log } W = (2-\gamma) \text{ Log } EW + \frac{1}{2}(\gamma-1) \text{ Log } EW^2.$$

Substituting (3) and (4) into (7) then implies that the class of surrogate problems, S, can be stated as

$$\max_{\lambda\varepsilon D}(2-\gamma)\log \Sigma\lambda_i \exp\{\mu_i + \frac{1}{2}\sigma_{ii}\} - \frac{1}{2}(1-\gamma)\ \text{Log}\ \Sigma\Sigma\lambda_i\lambda_j \exp\{\mu_i + \mu_j + \frac{1}{2}(\sigma_{ii} + \sigma_{jj} + 2\sigma_{ij})\}$$

or, for simplicity, as

$$\text{(S)}\ \max_{\lambda\varepsilon D}(2-\gamma)\ \text{Log}\ \Sigma\lambda_i a_i - \frac{1}{2}(1-\gamma)\ \text{Log}\ \Sigma\Sigma\lambda_i\lambda_j c_{ij} \equiv \max_{\lambda\varepsilon D} g(\gamma,\mu,\ddagger)$$

where $a_i \equiv \exp\{\mu_i + \frac{1}{2}\sigma_{ii}\}$ and

$$c_{ij} \equiv \exp\{\mu_i + \mu_j + \frac{1}{2}(\sigma_{ii}+\sigma_{jj} + 2\sigma_{ij})\}\ .$$

Since g will serve as a surrogate objective function to V, it is worthwhile to observe that a number of qualitative properties of P are preserved when V is replaced by g. This is of importance not only in support for the appropriateness of the chosen approximation, but also in the consideration of alternative approximations. Three properties of the optimal solutions to P and S are given in

<u>Theorem II:</u> Let $\lambda^*(\mu,\ddagger) \equiv (\lambda_1^*(\mu,\ddagger),\ldots,\lambda_m^*(\mu,\ddagger))'$ be the solution to max V, and let $\lambda^{**}(\mu,\ddagger)$ be the solution to max g. For both λ^* and λ^{**} we have the following properties:

(i) For all j, $\lambda_j^*(.,.)|\sum_k \lambda_k(.,.)$ is independent of the amount of capital invested; i.e., $\lambda_j^*(.,.)$/cap. is a constant.

(ii) For any scalar $k > 0$, $\lambda^*(.,[\sigma_{ij}]) = \lambda^*(.,[\sigma_{ij} + k])$.

(iii) For any scalar q, $\lambda^*(\mu,.) = \lambda^*(\mu + qe.,)$,

where $e = (1,\ldots,1)'$.

<u>Proof:</u> (i) Pye [17] has shown that P always satisfies the proposition. That S also satisfies the proposition is immediately seen because

$$g(\lambda k,.,.) = g(\lambda,.,.) + (2-\lambda)\ \text{Log}\ k + (1-\gamma)\text{Log}\ k = g(\lambda,.,.) + \text{Log}\ k$$

for any scalar $k > 0$; essentially a change of wealth is simply a rescaling which adds a constant to the objective function.

(ii) The problem P is equivalent to $\max_{\lambda \varepsilon D} s(\gamma)\, EY^{\gamma} E(\Sigma\lambda_i X_i)^{\gamma}$, for any random variable Y satisfying $0 < EY^{\gamma} < \infty$. Let $Y \sim ML_1(0, k)$, $k > 0$, and covar(Log Y, Log X_i) = 0 for all i. Then X and Y are independent so $EY^{\gamma}\, E(\Sigma\lambda_i X_i)^{\gamma} = E(\Sigma\lambda_i (X_i Y))^{\gamma}$. $X_i Y$ is lognormal with parameters E Log X_i + Log Y = μ_i and covar(Log X_i + Log Y, Log X_j + Log Y) = $\sigma_{ij} + k$, so the assertion $\lambda^*(.,\ddagger) = \lambda^*(.,[\sigma_{ij} + k])$ clearly follows.

For the surrogate problem, S, it is straightforward to show that

$$g(.,.,[\sigma_{ij} + k]) = g(.,.,[\sigma_{ij}]) + \frac{1}{2}(2-\gamma)k - (1-\gamma)k$$

$$= g(.,.,[\sigma_{ij}]) + \frac{\gamma k}{2}\,.$$

The constant k, therefore, will not affect the optimal solution and $\lambda^{**}(.,[\sigma_{ij}]) = \lambda^{**}(.,[\sigma_{ij} + k])$.

(iii) Consider first P. Let $Z \sim ML_m(0, [\sigma_{ij}])$, then $((\exp\{\mu_i\} Z_1,\ldots,\exp\{\mu_m\}Z_m)') \sim X \sim ML_m(\mu,[\sigma_{ij}])$. Hence, let q be any scalar, and we have that

$$V(.,\mu + qe,.) \equiv s(\gamma)E(\Sigma\lambda_i \;\exp\{\mu_i + q\}Z_i)^{\gamma} = s(\gamma)\;\exp\{\gamma q\}E(\Sigma\lambda_i X_i)^{\gamma}$$

$$\equiv V(.,\mu,.)\;\exp\{\gamma q\}\,.$$

Accordingly, adding an arbitrary constant to the μ_i's will not affect the optimal solution of P and $\lambda^*(\mu,.) = \lambda^*(\mu + qe,.)$.

Similarly for S we have that

$$g(.,\mu + qe,.) = g(.,\mu,.) + (2-\gamma)q - \frac{1}{2}\,(1-\gamma)2q\;,$$

and this also implies that $\lambda^{**}(\mu,.) = \lambda^{**}(\mu + qe,.)$.

III. Comparing S with Quadratic Approximations

It is easy to show that $\partial g/\partial EW > 0$ and $\partial g/\partial \mathrm{Var}\, W < 0$ for all $\lambda \varepsilon D$ and $\gamma < 1$; the optimal solution to a problem in S is, therefore, always meanvariance efficient. Thus it might appear that the traditional quadratic programming approach to portfolio selection would be as adequate as S to solve for optimal portfolios. That is, the surrogate problems, say Q, of the types

$$\max_{\lambda \varepsilon D} EW - \varphi_1 EW^2 \qquad \varphi_1 > 0$$

or

$$\max_{\lambda \varepsilon D} EW - \varphi_2 \,\mathrm{Var}\, W \qquad \varphi_2 > 0$$

should also provide approximate solutions of P. In general, however, several circumstances tend to mitigate against the efficiency of this approach. The risk-aversion parameter φ_1 (or φ_2) must be expressed as a function of γ, and it is not clear how such a function should be determined. A Taylor's series expansion of $s(\gamma)W^\gamma$ provides one method, but this method will not produce a unique $\varphi_1(\gamma)$, since W^γ can be expanded around any selected constant. More severe, however, is the fact that neither of the qualitative properties (ii) and (iii) of P stated in Theorem II is satisfied for the quadratic programming surrogate problems. This is in contrast to the surrogate problems S; accordingly, if a problem in S is just as easy to solve from a computational point of view as a problem in Q, then there is little *a priori* reason to presume that a quadratic programming approach is preferable to solving S.

One case when we do know how to find φ_1--and there is a problem in Q which will be a good approximation--occurs when probabilities have "small risk." Such small risk probabilities are closely related to a decision context in which the trading interval becomes increasingly short, and the limiting case is one in which the trading horizon is instantaneous. In showing that quadratic utility is valid in this time-asymptotic sense, we follow Merton [13] and assume $X \sim ML_m(t\mu, t\ddagger)$, where $t > 0$ is conveniently interpreted as time. We first derive the quadratic program which is equivalent to a problem in Q as $t \to 0$, and then show that this is equivalent to $\lim \frac{1}{t} g(\lambda, t\mu, t\ddagger)$; i.e., there are problems in S, P, and Q that all have identical solutions as $t \to 0$.

Expanding $s(\gamma)W^\gamma$ around W=1, it follows that

$$s(\gamma)W^\gamma = \text{const.} + s(\gamma)\gamma(W-1) + \frac{1}{2}\gamma(\gamma-1)\, s(\gamma)\, (W-1)^2 + R(W)$$

where R(W) is the remainder term. Now, it can be shown that

$$\lim_{t\to 0} \frac{ER(W)}{E(W-1)^n} = 0 \quad \text{for } n = 1, 2, \text{ and}$$

$$\lim_{t\to 0} \frac{E(W-1)}{E(W-1)^2} = \text{constant} \neq 0 \; .$$

It follows that ER(W) can be neglected from $\max_{\lambda\varepsilon D} s(\lambda)EW^{\gamma}$ provided t is small, and in an asymptotic sense the solution of

$$s(\gamma)\,[\gamma E(W-1) + \frac{1}{2}\gamma(\gamma-1)E(W-1)^2\,]$$

is identical to the solution of the original problem as $t \to 0$. Maximizing the last expression is equivalent to maximizing

$$\frac{1}{t}\left[EW - \frac{1-\gamma}{2(2-\gamma)} EW^2\right], \qquad t > 0 \; .$$

Note that $EW = \Sigma\lambda_i \exp\{t[\mu_i + \frac{1}{2}\sigma_{ii}]\}$ and $EW^2 = \Sigma\Sigma\lambda_i\lambda_j \exp\{t[\mu_i + \mu_j + \frac{1}{2}(\sigma_{ii}+\sigma_{jj} + 2\sigma_{ij}]\}$, and if t is small and the exponential function is expanded around zero, then all terms of order t^2 may be deleted. This yields the quadratic program

$$\Sigma\lambda_i(\mu_i + \frac{1}{2}\sigma_{ii}) - \frac{1-\gamma}{2(2-\gamma)} \Sigma\Sigma\lambda_i\lambda_j(\mu_i + \mu_j + \frac{1}{2}(\sigma_{ii} + \sigma_{jj} + 2\sigma_{ij}))$$

for which the solution is asymptotically valid as $t \to 0$.

Interestingly enough, the same quadratic program is the limiting function of the surrogate objective function

$$\frac{1}{t}\Big[\text{Log}\, \Sigma\lambda_i \exp\{t[\mu_i + \frac{1}{2}\sigma_{ii}]\} - \frac{1-\gamma}{2(2-\gamma)} \text{Log}\, \Sigma\Sigma\lambda_i\lambda_j \exp\{t[\mu_i + \mu_j + \frac{1}{2}(\sigma_{ii} + \sigma_{jj} + \sigma_{ij})]\}\Big]$$

as $t \to 0$. This follows immediately from straightforward but lengthy expansions of the logarithmic and exponential functions; the exponential function is expanded around zero, and the logarithmic function around 1. Thus, one may conclude that in the "small risk" limiting sense considered here, the two approaches as approximations of the original problem are identical.

IV. Solving the Surrogate Problem

The problem S is to

$$\max_{\lambda\varepsilon D} \; (2-\gamma) \text{ Log } \Sigma\lambda_i a_i - \frac{1}{2}(1-\gamma) \text{ Log } \Sigma\Sigma\lambda_i\lambda_j c_{ij} \;, \text{ or to}$$

$$\max_{\lambda\varepsilon D} \; f(\lambda) \equiv \text{Log } \Sigma\lambda_i a_i - \psi \text{ Log } \Sigma\Sigma\lambda_i\lambda_j c_{ij} \;,$$

where $\psi \equiv \frac{1-\gamma}{2(2-\gamma)}$. Since $\gamma\varepsilon\ (-\infty, 1)$, it follows that

$\psi\varepsilon\ (0, \frac{1}{2})$.

Theorem III:

(i) The function f is concave.

(ii) S has a unique optimal solution λ^* .

(iii) The Kuhn-Tucker conditions are necessary and sufficient for optimality.

Proof: (i) The function Log $\Sigma\lambda_i a_i$ is concave because it is the composition of a nondecreasing concave function and a linear function (see Mangasarian [10]).

Let $e(\lambda) \equiv \frac{1}{2} \text{ Log } \Sigma\Sigma\lambda_i\lambda_j c_{ij}$. Then the gradient vector $\nabla e \equiv$

$\equiv (\partial e/\partial\lambda_i, \ldots, \partial e/\partial\lambda_m)' = \frac{C\lambda}{\lambda' C\lambda}$ and the Hessian matrix $H(\lambda)$, having typical element $\partial^2 e(\lambda)/\partial\lambda_i\partial\lambda_j$, is $\frac{C}{\lambda' C\lambda} - \frac{(C\lambda)(C\lambda)'}{(\lambda\ C\lambda)^2}$.

Now $e(\lambda)$ is a convex function of λ if and only if $s'H(\lambda)s \geqq 0$ for all $s\varepsilon R^m$ and $\lambda\varepsilon D$. This expression is

$$s' \; [(\lambda' C\lambda)^{-2} \{(\lambda' C\lambda)C \; - \; (C\lambda)(C\lambda)'\}] \; s,$$

which has the same sign as

$$s' \; [(\lambda' C\lambda) \; C \; - \; (C\lambda)(C\lambda)']s$$

$$= \; (\lambda' C\lambda)(s' Cs) - (s' C\lambda)(\lambda' Cs).$$

Since C is positive definite[3] there exists a matrix D such that $D'D = C$. Let $u \equiv Ds$ and $v \equiv D\lambda$. Then the above expression is equal to

$$(u'u)(v'v) - (v'u)^2$$

which is nonnegative by the Cauchy-Schwartz inequality.[4]
Since $\text{Log}\ \Sigma\lambda_i a_i$ is concave and $e(\lambda)$ is convex it follows that $f(\lambda)$ is concave.

(ii) Since $\partial f/\partial EW > 0$ and $\partial f/\partial\ \text{Var}\ W < 0$ any point λ^* that maximizes f must be mean-variance efficient. One may generate the entire mean-variance frontier by solving $h(\alpha) \equiv \max_{\lambda \varepsilon D} \lambda'a - \alpha\lambda'C\lambda$ for all $\alpha \geq 0$. Since C is positive definite, the optimal solution $\tilde{\lambda}(\alpha)$ is unique for any $\alpha > 0$; moreover h is strictly concave in $\alpha > 0$. Thus, there exists a unique $\tilde{\alpha}$ such that $\tilde{\lambda}(\tilde{\alpha}) = \lambda^*$. Now $\tilde{\alpha} > 0$ because all assets are risky; hence λ^* is unique.

(iii) Since the constraints are linear and the objective concave it follows (see Zangwill [22]) that the Kuhn-Tucker conditions are necessary and sufficient for optimality.

---

[3]The typical element of C is $c_{ij} = \exp\{\mu_i+\mu_j+\frac{1}{2}(\sigma_{ii}+\sigma_{jj}+2\sigma_{ij})\}$. Let D be the diagonal matrix $\begin{pmatrix} \exp(\mu_1+\frac{1}{2}\sigma_{11}) & & 0 \\ & \ddots & \\ 0 & & \exp(\mu_m+\frac{1}{2}\sigma_{mm}) \end{pmatrix}$ and L be a matrix whose typical element is $\exp(\sigma_{ij})$. Then $C = D^tLD$. Since D is nonsingular, C is positive definite if L is positive definite.

A series expansion of H yields

$$L=\{1\}+\{\sigma_{ij}\} + \{\frac{\sigma_{ij}^2}{2!}\} + \{\frac{\sigma_{ij}^3}{3!}\} + \ldots.$$

where $\{a_{ij}\}$ refers to the matrix whose typical element is a_{ij}. It is known that the series on the right hand converges for positive definite ‡ (see Marcus and Ming [11, p. 72]. Since ‡ is positive definite and a matrix of ones is positive semidefinite, L will be positive definite as long as $\{\sigma_{ij}^2\}$, $\{\sigma_{ij}^3\}$,... are all positive semidefinite. That this is indeed the case follows directly because $\{\sigma_{ij}^2\}$ is the Hadamard product of ‡ and ‡ , and $\{\sigma_{ij}^3\}$ is the Hadamard product of ‡ and $\{\sigma_{ij}^2\}$, etc., and it is known, see [11, p. 121] that the Hadamard product of two positive semidefinite matrices is positive semidefinite. This proof is due to D. Murdoch.

[4]Thanks are due to C. E. Lemke for the idea of this proof.

There are a number of algorithms[5] that one might utilize to solve the problem S. The algorithm devised by Frank and Wolfe [4] is particularly simple to implement and leads to a very simple iterative scheme when applied to S. The algorithm is based on the fact that λ^* solves $\max_{\lambda \varepsilon D} f(\lambda)$ if and only if it solves the linear program $\max_{\lambda \varepsilon D} \Sigma \frac{\partial f(\lambda^*)}{\partial \lambda_i} \lambda_i$. Given any feasible solution vector λ^k, the program $\max_{\lambda \varepsilon D} \Sigma \frac{\partial f(\lambda^k)}{\partial \lambda_i} \lambda_i$ has an optimal solution vector y^k. If $\lambda^k = y^k$, then λ^k is an optimal solution[6] for S. If not, there always exists a vector λ^{k+1} on the line segment between λ^k and y^k that is strictly preferred to λ^k. Hence one starts with a $\lambda^o \varepsilon D$ and iterates until a λ^k equal to y^k is found or a tolerance bound is satisfied. The beauty of the method for problem S is that the direction-finding problem to find y^k is trivial[7] since $y^k_j = 1$ if $\max_i \partial f(\lambda^k) \partial \lambda_i = \partial f(\lambda^k)/\partial \lambda_j$, and all other $y^k_i = 0$.

The algorithm has the following steps (ties are broken arbitrarily):

0. Initialization: Let $a_j = \max_i a_i$.

   Set $\lambda^0_j = 1$, and $\lambda^0_i = 0$ if $i \neq j$. Go to step 1 with $k = 0$.

1. Direction Finding Problem:

   Let $\partial f(\lambda^k)/\partial \lambda_j = \max_i \partial f(\lambda^k)/\partial \lambda_i$.

   Set $y^k_j = 1$ and $y^k_i = 0$ if $i \neq j$.

2. Optimality Test:

   If $\lambda^k = y^k$. Stop y^k solves problem S.

   If $||\lambda^k - y^k|| < \varepsilon_1$ and $||f(\lambda^k) - f(\lambda^{k-1})|| < \varepsilon_2$

   for given positive tolerance levels ε_1 and ε_2[8].

---

[5]See Fletcher [3] or Zangwill [22] for the presentation of many such algorithms and for further references.

[6]It may be noted, and easily proved using the Kuhn-Tucker conditions, that all variables that enter positively in the optimal solution have equal $\partial f(\lambda^*)/\partial \lambda_i$.

[7]See Hogan and Warren [7] for an analysis of a different portfolio problem that has the same simplification when the Frank-Wolfe algorithm is utilized in its solution.

[8]Although any metric may be used, it is customary to utilize $||z|| = \{\Sigma z_i^2\}^{1/2}$.

Stop λ^k is an approximate solution to S.

Otherwise go to Step 3.

3. Search Problem:

$$\text{Solve } \max_{0 \le \alpha \le 1} \phi^k(\alpha) \equiv f[\alpha\lambda^k + (1-\alpha)\, y^k]$$

for α^k. Set $\lambda^{k+1} = \alpha^k\lambda^k + (1-\alpha^k)\, y^k$.

Go to Step 1 with $k = k+1$.

A proof that the algorithm converges in the sense that $\lim_{k\to\infty} f(\lambda^k) = \max_{\lambda\varepsilon D} f(\lambda)$ may be found in Zangwill [22]. Since f is concave, the following bounds are available in each iteration: $f(\lambda^k) \leqslant f(\lambda^*) \le \min_{\ell\leqslant k} \{f(\lambda^\ell) + \nabla f(x^\ell)'\, (y^\ell-\lambda^\ell)\}$, see e.g., Wagner [20].

It may be noted that the expression inside the braces is not monotone nondecreasing in k, implying that the least upper bound is the minimum of all of these expressions. This suggests that one may utilize the following additional stopping rule in step 2: Stop λ^k is an approximate solution to S if

$$\left[\min_{\ell\leqslant k} \{f(\lambda^\ell) + \nabla f(\lambda^\ell)'\, (y^\ell-\lambda^\ell)\} - f(\lambda^k)\right] < \varepsilon_3 \text{ for some } \varepsilon_3 > 0 .$$

The only substantive work involved in the algorithm is in step 3 because the direction-finding problem is trivial. Since $\partial\phi^k/\partial\alpha$ is much more difficult to evaluate than ϕ^k, it is advisable to utilize a search technique that requires only function values such as the method of golden sections (see Zangwill [22]) to find α^k. It is known that the Frank-Wolfe method converges even if the search problems are not solved exactly as long as succeeding search problems are solved with greater and greater accuracy. One is led to an extremely simple algorithm if a quadratic or cubic approximation to ϕ is utilized to obtain a good (i.e., one such that $f(\lambda^{k+1}) > f(\lambda^k)$) value of α^k, see Wagner [20]. Such an approximation yields an explicit analytic expression for α^k. Since each iteration may be performed so easily, the algorithm should be very efficient despite its poor rate of convergence per iteration, see Wolfe [21]. Further improvement in the efficiency may be obtained by utilizing the linearly convergent modification of the Frank-Wolfe method described in Wolfe [21].

REFERENCES

[1] Blattberg, R. C., and N. J. Gonedes. "A Comparison of the Stable-Paretian and Student Distributions as Statistical Models for Stock Prices." *Journal of Business*, Vol. 47 (1974), pp. 244-280.

[2] Dexter, A. S.; J. N. W. Yu; and W. T. Ziemba. "Portfolio Selection in a Lognormal Market when the Investor Has a Power Utility Function: Computational Results." In *Proceedings of the International Conference on Stochastic Programming*, edited by M. A. H. Dempster. New York: Academic Press (1975), forthcoming.

[3] Fletcher, R., ed. *Optimization.* New York: Academic Press, Inc. (1969).

[4] Frank, M., and P. Wolfe. "An Algorithm for Quadratic Programming." *Naval Research Logistics Quarterly*, Vol. 3 (1956), pp. 95-110.

[5] Hakansson, N. H. "Multi-Period Mean Variance Analysis: Toward a General Theory of Portfolio Choice." *Journal of Finance*,Vol. 26 (1971), pp. 857-884.

[6] __________. "On Optimal Myopic Portfolio Policies, with and without Serial Correlation of Yields." *Journal of Business* (1972), pp. 324-334.

[7] Hogan, W. W., and J. M. Warren. "Computation of the Efficient Boundary in the E-S Portfolio Selection Model." *Journal of Financial and Quantitative Analysis*, Vol. 7 (1972), pp. 1881-1896.

[8] Lintner, J. "Equilibrium in a Random Walk and Lognormal Securities Market." Discussion Paper Number 235 (July 1972). Harvard Institute of Economic Research, Harvard University.

[9] Loeve, M. *Probability Theory.* Princeton: D. Van Nostrand and Co. (1963).

[10] Mangasarian, O. L. "Convexity, Pseudo-Convexity and Quasi-Convexity of Composite Functions." *Cahiers du Centre d'Etudes de Recherche Operationelle*, Vol. 12 (1970), pp. 114-122.

[11] Marcus, M., and H. Ming. *A Survey of Matrix Theory and Matrix Inequalities.* Boston: Allyn and Bacon Publishing Co., Inc. (1964).

[12] Merton, R. C. "Lifetime Portfolio Selection under Uncertainty: the Continuous-Time Case." *Review of Economics and Statistics*, Vol. 51 (1969), pp. 247-257.

[13] __________. "Optimum Consumption and Portfolio Rules in a Continuous-Time Model." *Journal of Economic Theory*, Vol. 3 (1971), pp. 373-413.

[14] __________. "An Intertemporal Capital Asset Pricing Model." *Econometrica*, Vol. 41 (1973).

[15] Ohlson, J. A. "Optimal Portfolio Selection in a Lognormal Market When the Investor's Utility Function is Logarithmic." Research Paper No. 117, Graduate School of Business,Stanford University (September 1972).

[16] __________. "The Asymptotic Validity of Quadratic Utility as the Period-Spacing Approaches Zero." In *Stochastic Optimization Models in Finance*, edited by W. T. Ziemba and R. G. Vickson. New York: Academic Press (1975).

[17] Pye, G. "Portfolio Selection and Security Prices." *Review of Economics and Statistics*, Vol. 49 (1967), pp. 111-115.

[18] Rosenberg, B. "The Behavior of Random Variables with Non-Stationary Variance and the Distribution of Security Prices." Unpublished Paper. University of California, Berkeley (1973).

[19] Samuelson, P. A. "The Fundamental Approximation Theorem of Portfolio Analysis in Terms of Means, Variances and Higher Moments." *Review of Economic Studies*, Vol. 37 (1970), pp. 537-542.

[20] Wagner, H. M. *Fundamentals of Operations Research*. Englewood Cliffs, N. J.: Prentice-Hall, Inc. (1969).

[21] Wolfe, P. "Convergence Theory in Non-Linear Programming." In *Integer and Non-Linear Programming*, edited by J. Abadie. Amsterdam: North-Holland Publishing Co., Inc. (1971).

[22] Zangwill, W. I. *Nonlinear Programming: A Unified Approach*. Englewood Cliffs, N. J.: Prentice-Hall, Inc. (1969).

[23] Ziemba, W. T. "Solving Nonlinear Programming Problems with Stochastic Objective Functions." *Journal of Financial and Quantitative Analysis*, Vol. 7 (1972), pp. 1809-1827.

Chapter 6

COMPARISON OF ALTERNATIVE UTILITY FUNCTIONS IN PORTFOLIO SELECTION PROBLEMS*,#

J. G. KALLBERG† AND W. T. ZIEMBA‡

This paper examines the effect of alternative utility functions and parameter values on the optimal composition of a risky investment portfolio. Normally distributed assets are the setting for the theoretical and empirical analyses. The results agree well with the available theory and imply utility functions and parameter values that are appropriate for investors with particular risk-bearing attitudes. The results give strong empirical support to the proposition that utility functions having different functional forms and parameter values but "similar" absolute risk aversion indices have "similar" optimal portfolios. These results suggest that over horizons up to one year one can safely substitute "convenient" surrogate utility functions for other utility functions, for reasons of tractability or otherwise. The results also provide guidance regarding the significance of the magnitude and change of particular numerical values of the risk aversion index. Moreover, theoretical ("exact") results are obtained using Rubinstein's measure of global risk aversion.

(PORTFOLIO SELECTION; RISK AVERSION MEASURES; UTILITY FUNCTIONS; MODEL APPROXIMATIONS)

1. Introduction

One of the basic concepts in financial theory has been the Arrow [1]–Pratt [18] measures of absolute and relative risk aversion, respectively,

$$R_A(w) = -u''(w)/u'(w) \quad \text{and} \quad R_R(w) = -wu''(w)/u'(w),$$

where u is a von Neumann–Morgenstern utility function. The risk premium Π for a (fair) gamble $\tilde{z}$ encountered at wealth level w is defined by

$$u(w - \Pi) = E\{u(w + \tilde{z})\}.$$

Pratt has shown (under suitable regularity conditions) that

$$\Pi \cong \tfrac{1}{2}\sigma^2 R_A(w) \tag{1}$$

where $\sigma^2 = \text{var}(\tilde{z})$. This and related results suggest that R_A is a local characterization of an investor's risk attitudes.

A related, key aspect of the theory of portfolio selection is concerned with the robustness of optimal portfolio choice with respect to changes in return distributions and wealth levels. There has been an extensive study of the case where there is a choice between a risky and a safe asset in an expected utility setting, see e.g. Arrow [1], Cass and Stiglitz [2], Fishburn and Porter [6], and Kira and Ziemba [14]. These results generally hinge on the magnitude or the direction of change of the absolute or relative risk aversion indices. Levy [15], Merton [17], Tobin [24], and others have extended these types of results to an n-asset, mean-variance setting.

However, a rather neglected area of research has been the empirical analysis of portfolio selection problems. Indeed, Gordon, Paradis, and Rorke [8] state " . . . there

*Accepted by Martin J. Gruber, former Departmental Editor; received August 6, 1977. This paper has been with the authors 12 months for 2 revisions.

†New York University.

‡University of British Columbia.

#This chapter was originally published in: Kallberg, J. G. & Ziemba, W. T. (1983). Comparison of Alternative Utility Functions in Portfolio Selection Problems. *Management Science*, 29(11), 1257–1276.

has been no empirical research into optimal portfolio policy". These authors utilize portfolio games to obtain insight into the relationship between risk preference and wealth. The other existing research includes: Ziemba, Parkan, and Brooks-Hill [25] on portfolio choice when there is a riskless asset and several joint normally distributed assets; Stuck [23] in the safe versus (log stable distributed) risky asset case when the investor has a negative power or logarithmic utility function; and Lintner [16] and Dexter, Yu, and Ziemba [4] on empirical results to support the approximation of a sum of lognormally distributed assets by a lognormal distribution.

This paper can be viewed as addressing generalizations of (1). In Pratt's case of a simple lottery, specification of R_A was enough to characterize the investor's risk attitudes; see also Samuelson [21] for proof that in the choice between a safe asset and a risky asset, the optimal amount to invest in the risky asset is inversely proportional to R_A asymptotically as the variance becomes infinitesimal. Here our context is a portfolio selection problem and we determine the extent to which generalizations of the Arrow–Pratt measure characterize and approximate optimal investment behavior when the variances are not infinitesimal. §2 formulates the portfolio problem. In §3 we develop optimality properties of the portfolio problem using Rubinstein's global risk aversion measure. The fundamental result is that investors with the same Rubinstein measure have the same optimal portfolios. In §4 we empirically examine the extent to which investors with "similar" Arrow–Pratt measures have "similar" optimal portfolios. Our results suggest that even over horizons of one year the average Arrow–Pratt measure is accurate enough (i.e., less than data estimation errors) to characterize portfolio behavior.

2. The Portfolio Problem

An investor wishes to allocate his wealth among assets[1] $i = 1, \ldots, n$. Let ξ_i denote the gross rate of return on investment i, where $\xi = (\xi_1, \ldots, \xi_n)^T$ is normally distributed with mean vector $\bar{\xi}$ and positive definite covariance matrix Σ; notationally, $\xi \sim N(\bar{\xi}, \Sigma)$. ($T$ denotes transposition.) The investor chooses the x_i to maximize the expected utility of final wealth $w = w_0 \xi^T x$, where $x = (x_1, \ldots, x_n)^T$. It is assumed that the utility function u is in the class of nondecreasing, continuously differentiable, concave utility functions, such that the expected utility and expected marginal utility are bounded.[2]

The investor's problem is

$$\text{maximize} \quad E_\xi\{u(w_0 \xi^T x)\} \quad \text{s.t.} \quad e^T x = 1, \qquad x \geqslant 0, \tag{2}$$

where w_0 is the initial wealth level, E_ξ represents expectation with respect to ξ and $e = (1, \ldots, 1)^T$.

[1] For many utility functions, a simple transformation of the parameter β_i allows one to obtain results for general $w_0 > 0$ using the results for $w_0 = 1$. For example the quadratic utility function

$$u_1(w) = w - \beta_1 w^2 = (\xi^T x w_0) - \beta_1 (\xi^T x w_0)^2 = w_0\left(\xi^T x - (\beta_1 w_0)(\xi^T x)^2\right)$$

is equivalent to the utility function

$$\hat{u}_1(w) = \xi^T x - \hat{\beta}_1 (\xi^T x)^2$$

where $\hat{\beta}_1 \equiv \beta_1 w_0$. Hence one may obtain results with initial wealth w_0 and parameter β_1 using the previously calculated results for $w_0 = 1$ with parameter $\hat{\beta}_1$. Except for the arctan, which does allow factorization of w_0, such a procedure is applicable to all other utility functions studied here.

[2] More specifically assume that there exist constants $m_0, \ldots, m_n$ such that $|E_\xi u(\xi^T x)| < m_0$ and $|E_\xi[du(\xi^T x)/dw \cdot \xi_i]| < m_i$, $i = 1, \ldots, n$. Then $Z(x) \equiv E_\xi u(\xi^T x)$ is continuously differentiable and one may differentiate under the integral sign to calculate the partial derivatives via $\partial Z(x)/\partial x_i = E_\xi[du(\xi^T x)/dw \cdot \xi_i]$. When ξ is joint normally distributed a sufficient condition for the m_i to exist is that there exist positive constants A and B such that $|u(w)| \leqslant Ae^{Bw^2}$, and the convergence applies whenever the variance of w, namely $x^T \Sigma x \in (0, (2B)^{-1/2})$.

In the empirical study in §4 we utilize utility functions and parameter values with widely differing risk attitudes (decreasing, constant, and increasing absolute and relative risk aversion) and varying degrees of tractability. The seven chosen functions (each dependent upon a single parameter) are listed in Table 3.

3. Rubinstein's Risk Aversion Measure and Characterization of Optimal Portfolios

Rubinstein [19] developed a measure of global risk aversion in the context of a parameter-preference equilibrium relationship:

$$R(w_0) = \frac{-w_0 E_\xi\{u''(w)\}}{E_\xi\{u'(w)\}},$$

where w_0 is the initial wealth level and primes denote differentiation. (Some properties of this measure in the context of risk aversion with changing initial wealth levels appear in Kallberg and Ziemba [12].)

This measure is less tractable and less familiar than the Arrow–Pratt measure. Note that in contrast to the Arrow–Pratt measure which is a function of wealth w, R is a constant. Except for a few special cases, R does not have a simple form. For exponential utility, $R(1) = \beta_2 = R_A(w)$ and for quadratic utility, $R(1) = R_A(\bar{w})$; thus the Rubinstein measure is the Arrow–Pratt measure evaluated at the expected final wealth level. Within the context of (2) it has some very important properties.[3]

With ξ as defined above, assume that u is twice continuously differentiable with $u' > 0$ and that the relevant expectations are finite. Computing the partial derivatives of the objective of (2) with respect to the portfolio proportions yields

$$\begin{aligned}\partial Z(x)/\partial x_i &= E_\xi\{u'(w_0\xi^T x) w_0 \xi_i\} \\ &= \operatorname{cov}(w_0\xi_i, u'(w_0\xi^T x)) + w_0\bar{\xi}_i E_\xi\{u'(w_0\xi^T x)\}. \end{aligned} \tag{3}$$

Rubinstein [20] and Stein [22] have independently proven the useful result that

$$\operatorname{cov}(x, g(y)) = E(g'(y))\operatorname{cov}(x, y)$$

if g is continuously differentiable, all expectations are finite and (x, y) is bivariate normal. Hence

$$\partial Z(x)/\partial x_i = w_0\bar{\xi} E_\xi\{u'(w_0\xi^T x)\} + w_0^2 E_\xi\{u''(w_0\xi^T x)\} \sum_j \operatorname{cov}(\xi_i, \xi_j) x_j .$$

Dividing by the (positive) expression $w_0 E_\xi\{u'(w_0\xi^T x)\}$ yields

$$(\partial Z(x)/\partial x_i)\big(w_0 E_\xi\{u'(w_0\xi^T x)\}\big)^{-1} = \bar{\xi}_i + \frac{w_0 E_\xi\{u''(w_0\xi^T x)\}}{E_\xi\{u'(w_0\xi^T x)\}} \sum_j \operatorname{cov}(\xi_i, \xi_j) x_j . \tag{4}$$

Equation (4) yields the following comparative statics result: if investors 1 and 2 have the same x and R (but possibly different w_0 and u), then the sign of $\partial Z(x)/\partial x_i$ is the same for both investors. In particular (as proven in the appendix) we have the following powerful result.

Optimality of Rubinstein's Risk Aversion Measure. Investors with the same R have the same optimal portfolios, i.e., if x^* solves (2) for investor 1 then it also solves the corresponding portfolio problem for investor 2.

[3] R is also related to Tobin's [24] notion that an investor is risk averse if $d\mu/d\sigma > 0$ and $d^2\mu/d\sigma^2 > 0$, i.e., the indifference curves of portfolio mean and variance are convex to the σ-axis. It can be shown, see e.g., Rubinstein [19], under usual two parameter capital market equilibrium assumptions that $\partial\mu/\partial\sigma = \sigma R$.

4. Empirical Results

A major conclusion of this study is that "similar" R_A values yield "similar" optimal portfolios, regardless of the functional forms of the utility functions concerned. The empirical results are outlined after defining these measures of similarity.

An appropriate measure of the proximity of portfolios x^1 and x^2 is the percentage cash equivalent difference; see Dexter, Yu, and Ziemba [4]:

$$\frac{u^{-1}\{Z(x^1)\} - u^{-1}\{Z(x^2)\}}{u^{-1}\{Z(x^1)\}} \times 100 \tag{5}$$

where $Z(x^i) = E\{u(\xi^T x^i)\}$, $i = 1, 2$. Recall that $u^{-1}\{Z(x^i)\}$ is the cash equivalent value of the random return $\xi^T x^i$ generated by portfolio x^i.

To formalize the concept of similar R_A, let u be the base utility function to which comparisons of the other u_i will be made. If $\beta = \hat{\beta}$ and x^* solves (2), the average risk aversion of u is

$$\int R_A(\hat{\beta}, w)\, dN(w), \tag{6}$$

where $w \sim N(\bar{\xi}^T x^*, x^{*T}\Sigma x^*)$. We say u_i has the same risk aversion as u if its average risk aversion is the same as u's over the distribution of (u-optimal) final wealth, i.e.,

$$\int R_A^i(\beta_i, w)\, dN(w) = \int R_A(\beta, w)\, dN(w). \tag{7}$$

The solution of (7) is the appropriate value of β_i to compare u_i with u. To simplify the solution[4] of (7), we let exponential utility (u_2) be the base utility function (since with constant absolute risk aversion, the right-hand side of (7) is simply β_2, the parameter of the exponential utility function). This choice also simplifies the calculation of the percentage error because

$$Z(x) = E_\xi\{1 - \exp(-\beta \xi^T x)\} = 1 - \exp\left(-\beta \bar{\xi}^T x + \tfrac{1}{2}\beta^2 x^T \Sigma x\right),$$

see Freund [7]. The expected utility[5] may now be computed explicitly using only the

[4]Equation (7) was solved using a hybrid bisection-secant algorithm. Difficulties in solving this equation motivated the exponential extension described in footnote 5. In all cases we used a tolerance of 10^{-6} so that the β_i chosen were within $\pm 10^{-6}$ of the true β_i. See [11] for further details.

[5]Of the seven utility functions used in this study only the exponential is well behaved over the whole real line as required for normally distributed final wealth. The other utility functions for certain values of w may be undefined (e.g., log, special exponential, power and negative power), may have decreasing marginal utility (e.g., quadratic) or may be convex (e.g., arctan). A common method of modifying the domain utilizes a linear segment near the boundary of the problem area, see [25] for technique. For the data and utility functions used here this method (usually) leads to a jump discontinuity in the $R_A(w)$ function. This may lead to either instability of the optimal portfolio weights and/or difficulties in solving (7). Since $R_A = 0$ at $w = 0$ for the arctan function the linear segment suffices since it also has $R_A = 0$ at $w = 0$. For the log, special exponential, power and negative power we appended an exponential segment at the points $w_0 = 0.01$, 0.25, 0.8, and 0.6, respectively, to yield the extended function

$$\hat{u}(w) \equiv \begin{cases} u(w) & \text{if } w \geqslant w_0, \\ u(w_0) + K\left(1 - e^{-R_A^0(w - w_0)}\right) & \text{if } w \leqslant w_0, \end{cases}$$

where

$$R_A^0 \equiv \frac{-u''(w_0)}{u'(w_0)} \quad \text{and} \quad K \equiv \frac{u'(w_0)}{R_A^0}.$$

Using this $\hat{u}(w)$ guarantees that u, u', u'' and hence R_A are continuous. We did not append any segment onto the quadratic utility since $u' < 0$ only above $\beta_1 \simeq 0.5$. However, the $u' \simeq 0$ behavior near 0.5 yields flat behavior in this region, see e.g., Figure 1a.

TABLE 1

Security Means and Variances

	Monthly		Yearly	
	Mean	Variance	Mean	Variance
1. Cunningham Drug Stores	1.0194	0.0105	1.2852	0.3276
2. National Cash Register	1.0173	0.0050	1.2549	0.2152
3. Metro-Goldwyn-Mayer	1.0162	0.0148	1.1819	0.1711
4. Gillette Co.	1.0137	0.0044	1.1694	0.0666
5. Household Finance Corp.	1.0128	0.0052	1.1484	0.0517
6. H. J. Heinz Co.	1.0112	0.0049	1.1608	0.1413
7. Anaconda Co.	1.0111	0.0081	1.1711	0.1865
8. Kaiser Al. & Chem.	1.0095	0.0073	1.0861	0.0324
9. Maytag Co.	1.0084	0.0048	1.1292	0.1676
10. Firestone Tire and Rubber	1.0064	0.0036	1.0626	0.0155

TABLE 2

Monthly Security Correlation Matrix

	Security Number									
	1	2	3	4	5	6	7	8	9	10
1	1.000	0.2843	0.1313	0.3049	0.1739	0.3457	0.4556	0.3033	0.4229	0.2822
2		1.0000	0.1333	0.3859	− 0.0101	0.2334	0.1880	0.4155	0.2680	0.1332
3			1.0000	0.2882	0.1251	0.3243	0.2974	0.2010	0.1762	0.1272
4				1.0000	0.2063	0.2750	0.4110	0.3557	0.2088	0.2616
5					1.0000	0.2847	0.2757	0.2670	0.2528	0.3167
6						1.0000	0.3031	0.1259	0.3178	0.2501
7							1.0000	0.4546	0.3445	0.3020
8								1.0000	0.3315	0.1968
9									1.0000	0.1898
10										1.0000

given means and variances. Furthermore, since

$$u^{-1}\{Z(x)\} = -\beta^{-1}\log\{1 - Z(x)\},$$

the calculation of the cash equivalent is simplified.

The data were obtained from the CRSP tape and consisted of monthly observations of ten well-known U.S. securities. These were selected from a group of 60 to form a sample that provided ample diversification and smooth transitions in means and variances (so that no securities were obviously dominant or dominated). Ten was chosen as the number of securities because it appears to be the optimum number when one balances the criteria of ease of exposition, interpretation of results, computational considerations, and diversification properties. (Evans and Archer [5] found that about 10–12 securities provide ample diversification for individual investors.) The relatively stable period January 1965–December 1969 was used in an attempt to satisfy the stationarity assumption made. The price relatives were adjusted to reflect investment of dividends, stock splits, etc. The 60 observations were used to obtain maximum likelihood estimates of the means and covariances of monthly returns. Tables 1 and 2 summarize these statistics.[6]

[6]Quarterly and yearly means and variances estimates were obtained in the usual way after computing the corresponding compound rates of return. The variances were then combined with the monthly correlation coefficients to generate the quarterly and yearly covariances using the formula $\sigma_{ij}(k) = \rho_{ij}\sigma_i(k)\sigma_j(k)$, where k = quarterly and yearly, and $i, j = 1, \ldots, 10$ with $i \neq j$. Note that these are no longer MLE. See [10] for more details.

TABLE 3

Monthly Empirical Test Data

Utility Function	$u(w)$	Absolute Risk Aversion, R_A	Theoretical Parameter Range	Parameter Range Used	Theoretical Range of R_A with fixed $w = 1$	Corresponding Range of R_A with fixed $w = 1$ with Parameter Range Used	Remarks
Quadratic	$w - \beta w^2$	$\frac{2\beta_1}{(1 - 2\beta_1 w)}$	$0 \to w/2$	$0 \to 0.50$	$0 \to \infty$	$0 \to \infty$	u_1 begins with the highest mean return portfolio which is also a high variance portfolio. Then as $\beta_1 \to 0.50$, $R_A \to \infty$ which yields the minimum variance portfolio. This is consistent with the theory that increasing R_A yields more risk averse behavior, see Theorem 1 in Pratt [18].
Exponential	$1 - e^{-\beta_2 w}$	β_2	$0 \to \infty$	$0 \to 10$	$0 \to \infty$	$0 \to 10$	u_2 is quite similar to u_1 except that the final portfolio (when $\beta_2 = 10$) has a low variance but is not a minimum variance portfolio. There is a gradual shift for increasing β_2 out of the risky security 1 into the safer securities 2–5. The largest change occurs in the $0 < \beta_2 = R_A < 3$ range. When $\beta_2 = R_A > 3$ and there is little change in behavior.
Logarithmic	$\log(\beta_3 + w)$	$\frac{1}{(\beta_3 + w)}$	$-w \to \infty$	$-0.80 \to 1.2$	$\infty \to 0$	$5.0 \to 0.45$	As u_3 ranges from -0.60 to 1.2 there is relatively little change in the optimal portfolio composition except for a gradual switch out of the safer securities 3, 5 into the riskier security 1. Security 2 with its high mean and low variance always forms about half of the portfolio.

TABLE 3 (*continued*)

Monthly Empirical Test Data

Utility Function	$u(w)$	Absolute Risk Aversion, R_A	Theoretical Parameter Range	Parameter Range Used	Theoretical Range of R_A with fixed $w = 1$	Corresponding Range of R_A with fixed $w = 1$ with Parameter Range Used	Remarks
Special Exponential	$e^{\beta_4/w}$	$\frac{2w + \beta_4}{w^2}$	$\max(0, 2w)$ $0 \to \infty$	$0.10 \to 4.1$	$2 \to \infty$	$2.1 \to 6.1$	There is relatively little variation in the optimal portfolio composition because R_A ranges from 2.1 to 6.1 and hence never has low values. There is a gradual shift into the lower variance securities 4, 5 at the expense of the higher variance security 1 and security 2 (because of the diversification effects, in particular 2 and 5 are negatively correlated).
Power	$(w - w_0)^{\beta_5}$ $w_0 = 0.75$	$\frac{(1 - \beta_5)}{(w - w_0)}$	$0 \to 1.0$	$0.05 \to 1.0$	$4 \to 0$	$3.8 \to 0$	u_5 initially yields low variance portfolios when $\beta_5 = 0.05$ and $R_A = 3.8$. However, as $\beta_5 \to 1.0$, R_A drops sharply to 0 and the corresponding optimal portfolios have high variances. There is a gradual shift out of the safer securities 5, 7, 9 into the high return (and also high variance) Security 1.
Negative Power	$-(w - w_0)^{-\beta_6}$ $w_0 = 0.50$	$\frac{1 + \beta_6}{(w - w_0)}$	$0 \to \infty$	$0.10 \to 2.1$	$2 \to \infty$	$2.2 \to 6.2$	u_6 has an R_A range of $2.2 \to 6.2$ which is nearly identical to that of u_4 and indeed the optimal portfolio proportions are also nearly identical.
Arctan	$\tan^{-1}(w + \beta_7)$	$\frac{2(w + \beta_7)}{1 + (w + \beta_7)^2}$	$-w \to \infty$	$0.10 \to 4.1$	$0 \to 0$ max $= 1.0$ at $\beta_7 = 0$	$1.0 \to 0.38$	u_7 has low risk aversion for all $\beta_7 \in [0.10, 4.1]$ and always yields high variance portfolios. As β_7 increases the portfolios become more and more risky since R_A is decreasing.

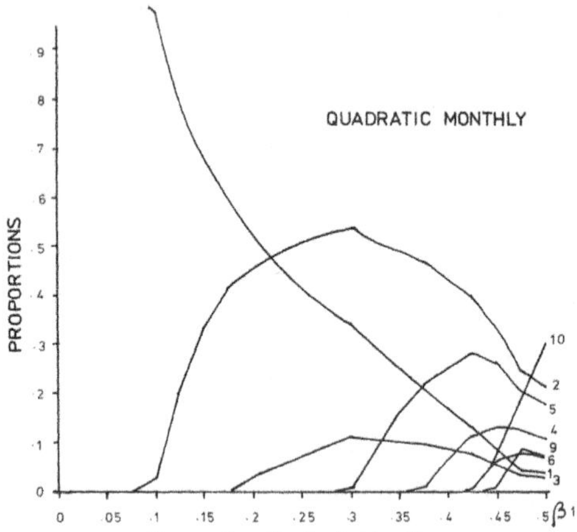

FIGURE 1a. Quadratic Monthly.

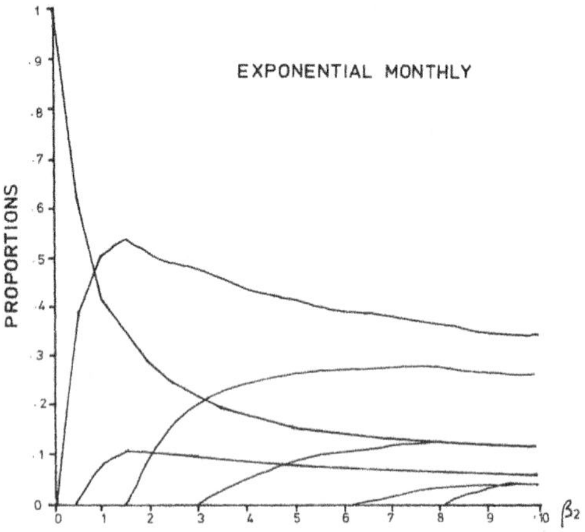

FIGURE 1b. Exponential Monthly.

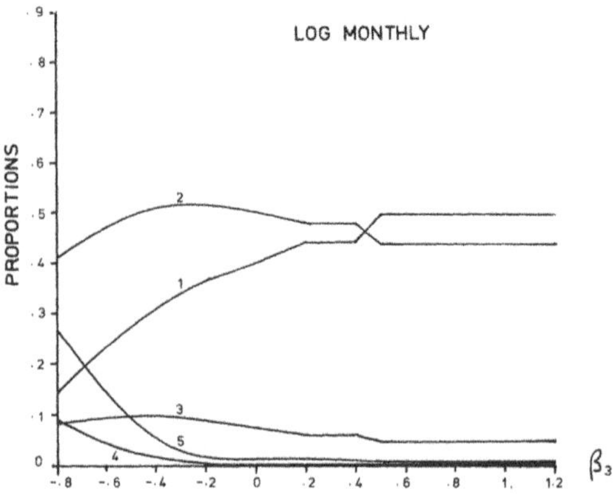

FIGURE 1c. Log Monthly.

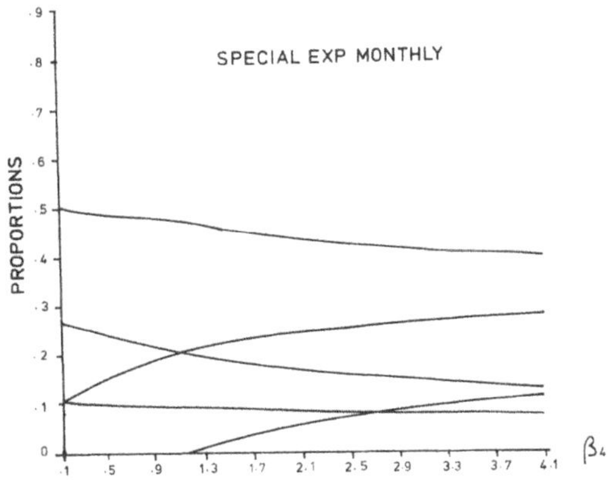

FIGURE 1d. Special Exponential Monthly.

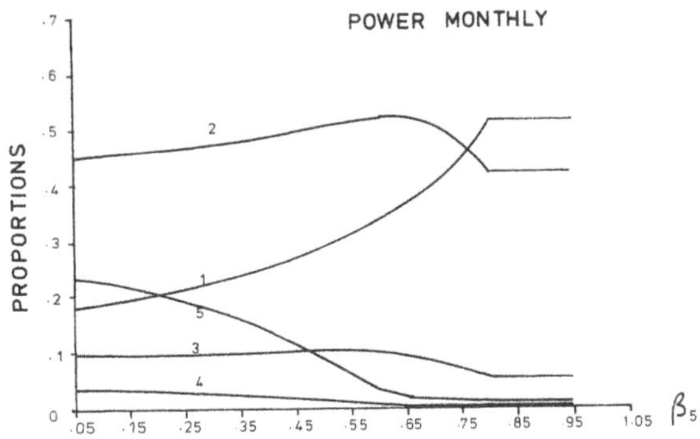

FIGURE 1e. Power Monthly.

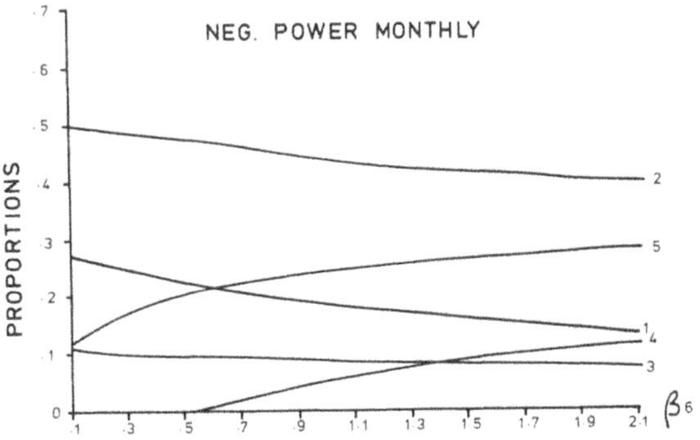

FIGURE 1f. Negative Power Monthly.

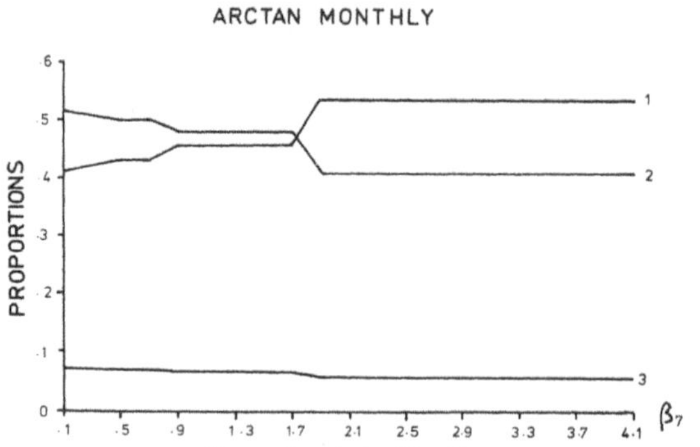

FIGURE 1g. Arctan Monthly.

The seven utility functions used in this study along with the ranges of the various parameter values are described in Table 3. This table also gives the corresponding ranges of the absolute risk aversion and describes the qualitative behavior of the portfolio composition for changing parameter values. For comparison, the theoretically largest ranges of the parameters and corresponding risk aversion are also given. Plots of the optimal proportions of the investor's initial wealth to be invested in each security over various parameter values using monthly data appear in Figures 1a–1g. (Quarterly and yearly plots, omitted here because of space considerations, may be found in [9].) The optimal portfolio weights were calculated at 21 discrete values and the plots were drawn accordingly. Note the similarity between Figures 1d (special exponential) and 1f (negative power); this occurs because the R_A ranges are virtually identical $2.1 \rightarrow 6.1$ and $2.2 \rightarrow 6.2$, respectively. Table 4 summarizes the solutions to the portfolio problems[7] classified by $\overline{R}_A = 0.5$, 1, 2, 4, and 10. For each value of $\overline{R}_A$ the portfolio weights across various utility functions are very close and in all cases the percentage error is less than $10^{-4}\%$ (recorded as zero). Table 5 provides portfolio weights using yearly data for the various utility functions and $\overline{R}_A$. The portfolio weights for different utility functions while not as close as with the monthly data are still reasonably close. They tend in the yearly as well as monthly data to be closer for smaller values of R_A because at the higher level of risk aversion the resulting utility function equivalents have more "curvature" hence approximations are less accurate. The percentage error with the yearly data is still quite small and is always less than 1%. Similar tables for quarterly data appear in [9], [10] and give results intermediate to the monthly and yearly values; the maximum percentage error is less than 0.2%.

Of importance is the significance of particular R_A values for the composition of the optimal portfolio. The results in Figures 1a–1g, and Tables 4 and 5, provide guidance regarding the significance of the (changes in) the magnitude of R_A. For example, R_A values greater than about 4 always yield very risk averse portfolios with low variance, and there is little change in the optimal composition even for large changes in R_A. The range $2 \leqslant R_A \leqslant 4$ yields moderately risk averse portfolios with a modest degree of change in the optimal portfolio composition when R_A changes. The range $0 \leqslant R_A \leqslant 2$ yields risky portfolios and there are dramatic changes in the optimal portfolio composition for even small changes in R_A.

[7] Additional calculations for different $\overline{R}_A$ values, omitted here because of space considerations, appear in Kallberg [9].

TABLE 4

Optimal Portfolio Weights for Alternative Utility Functions and $\overline{R}_A$ Values: Monthly Data

Utility Function		Exponential	Quadratic	Log	Power	Arctan	Exponential	Quadratic	Log	Power
Parameter		0.5	0.165483	0.984259	0.879183	2.714659	1.0	0.247237	−0.013835	0.750988
	1	0.618500	0.618500	0.621151	0.611083	0.626174	0.414406	0.418291	0.418190	0.410246
	2	0.381500	0.381500	0.378849	0.388917	0.373826	0.506770	0.508365	0.508198	0.507673
	3						0.078824	0.073344	0.073612	0.082082
	4									
Security	5									
	6									
	7									
	8									
	9									
	10									
Mean		1.018596	1.018596	1.018602	1.018581	1.018512	1.018094	1.018108	1.018108	1.018082
Variance		0.005704	0.005704	0.005725	0.005644	0.005767	0.004241	0.004269	0.004268	0.004218
Expected Utility		0.398654	0.398654	0.398654	0.398654	0.398654	0.637950	0.637950	0.637950	0.637950
% Error		—	0	0	0	0	—	0	0	0

TABLE 4 (*continued*)

Optimal Portfolio Weights for Alternative Unity Functions and $\overline{R}_A$ Values: Monthly Data

Utility Function		Exponential	Quadratic	Log	Special Exponential	Power	Negative Power
Parameter		2.0	0.328093	− 0.510706	0.048556	0.492853	0.021701
	1	0.282218	0.285479	0.279667	0.283320	0.283888	0.298170
	2	0.512462	0.513005	0.510997	0.513247	0.501787	0.510228
	3	0.103576	0.103887	0.103271	0.108219	0.103719	0.101422
	4						
Security	5	0.101745	0.097629		0.095213	0.110606	0.090181
	6						
	7						
	8						
	9						
	10						
Mean		1.017332	1.017357	1.017307	1.017359	1.017295	1.017420
Variance		0.003268	0.003294	0.003244	0.003296	0.003232	0.003360
Expected Utility		0.868418	0.868418	0.868418	0.868418	0.868418	0.868417
% Error		—	0	0	0	0	0

TABLE 4 (*continued*)

Optimal Portfolio Weights for Alternative Unity Functions and $\overline{R}_A$ Values: Monthly Data

Utility Function		Exponential	Quadratic	Special Exponential	Negative Power	Exponential	Quadratic	Special Exponential	Negative Power
Parameter		4.0	0.391591	2.061483	1.045389	10.0	0.440442	8.156772	4.109086
	1	0.179684	0.177566	0.169275	0.177531	0.118851	0.095302	0.079358	0.080020
	2	0.438363	0.447755	0.440878	0.436866	0.342845	0.364688	0.336837	0.333334
	3	0.086301	0.088783	0.089433	0.085550	0.062053	0.068848	0.053716	0.053053
	4	0.051708	0.045061	0.054509	0.054076	0.120721	0.129129	0.129992	0.130616
Security	5	0.243944	0.240835	0.245978	0.245978	0.264604	0.278670	0.259364	0.260044
	6					0.044528	0.043953	0.062782	0.062214
	7								
	8								
	9							0.008197	0.009482
	10					0.646398	0.019411	0.069754	0.071237
Mean		1.016303	1.016335	1.016260	1.016282	1.015080	1.015229	1.014559	1.014531
Variance		0.002509	0.002525	0.002487	0.002498	0.002113	0.002141	0.001994	0.001989
Expected Utility		0.982493	0.982493	0.942493	0.982493	0.999957	0.999957	0.999957	0.999957
% Error		—	0	0	0	—	0	0	0

[1]Only those utility functions for which (7) has a solution (i.e., such that $\overline{R}_A$ is attainable) are included for each value of $\overline{R}_A$. Zeros and blanks indicate values less than 10^{-6}.

[2]For comparison the riskiest portfolio (i.e. highest variance) has mean and variance of (1.016216, 0.014840) and the equal investment portfolio $x = (0.1, \ldots, 0.1)$ has mean and variance of (1.012607, 0.002232).

TABLE 5

Optimal Portfolio Weights for Alternative Utility Functions and $\overline{R}_A$ Values: Yearly Data

Utility Function		Exponential	Quadratic	Log	Power	Arctan	Exponential	Quadratic	Log	Power
Parameter		0.5	0.148687	0.821859	0.907691	2.498551	1.0	0.210483	− 0.112980	0.765732
	1	0.511442	0.518551	0.502147	0.480496	0.509709	0.342082	0.381592	0.287004	0.245520
	2	0.488558	0.481449	0.497853	0.509913	0.490291	0.421457	0.454136	0.373936	0.339830
	3				0.009590		0.146545	0.146148	0.163999	0.141238
	4									0.006089
Security	5						0.089916	0.018123	0.175061	0.267322
	6									
	7									
	8									
	9									
	10									
Mean		1.270399	1.270614	1.270117	1.268761	1.270345	1.244992	1.253864	1.232981	1.223041
Variance		0.174774	0.175657	0.173680	0.169126	0.174565	0.110314	0.129135	0.088336	0.073005
Expected Utility		0.458468	0.458466	0.458465	0.458407	0.458468	0.695729	0.695565	0.695417	0.694724
% Error		—	0.0006	0.0008	0.0185	0	—	0.0454	0.0861	0.2772

TABLE 5 (*continued*)

Optimal Portfolio Weights for Alternative Utility Functions and $\overline{R}_A$ Values: Yearly Data

Utility Function		Exponential	Quadratic	Log	Exponential	Special Power	Negative Power
Parameter		2.0	0.275157	− 0.587446	0.350128	0.413450	0.213501
	1	0.174457	0.208418	0.116236	0.149547	0.081275	0.120428
	2	0.262884	0.300979	0.202592	0.240565	0.167586	0.205169
	3	0.126734	0.133008	0.115598	0.129158	0.099687	0.113806
	4	0.094320	0.048109	0.159015	0.116267	0.184367	0.157239
Security	5	0.341605	0.309487	0.406559	0.364464	0.417025	0.403389
	6						
	7						
	8						
	9						
	10					0.050061	
Mean		1.206489	1.214433	1.193087	1.201245	1.180277	1.193834
Variance		0.053081	0.061813	0.041833	0.048167	0.035125	0.042347
Expected Utility		0.900422	0.900265	0.899992	0.900356	0.898764	0.900039
% Error		—	0.0684	0.1868	0.0286	0.7158	0.1665

TABLE 5 (*continued*)

Optimal Portfolio Weights for Alternative Utility Functions and $\bar{R}_A$ Values: Yearly Data

Utility Function		Exponential	Quadratic	Log	Special Exponential	Negative Power	Exponential	Quadratic	Negative Power
Parameter		4.0	0.351447	− 0.832954	2.884400	1.443557	10.0	0.423749	4.935791
	1	0.088239	0.082991	0.046975	0.021224	0.047611	0.031553		0.017099
	2	0.169455	0.165982	0.11622	0.185274	0.112794	0.075474	0.050898	0.044526
	3	0.106894	0.106663	0.080160	0.104064	0.079600	0.056237	0.050898	0.041265
	4	0.194026	0.198830	0.161247	0.048522	0.154474	0.111908	0.094011	0.054966
Security	5	0.441385	0.445533	0.343318	0.441182	0.328958	0.237341	0.190958	0.135844
	6								
	7								
	8						0.087302	0.143023	0.184158
	9								
	10			0.252077	0.199733	0.258232	0.400185	0.470213	0.522144
Mean		1.186170	1.185175	1.151634	1.158397	1.149527	1.125199	1.108230	1.101730
Variance		0.037743	0.037247	0.024382	0.027802	0.023756	0.017605	0.014485	0.013892
Expected Utility		0.988236	0.988236	0.987863	0.987589	0.987821	0.999969	0.999968	0.999967
% Error		—	0	0.7030	0.7099	0.7827	—	0.2261	0.4728

[1]Only those utility functions for which (7) has a solution (i.e., such that $\bar{R}_A$ is attainable) are included for each value of $\bar{R}_A$. Zeros and blanks indicate values less than 10^{-6}.

[2]For comparison the riskiest portfolio (i.e. highest variance) has mean and variance of (1.285196, 0.327557) and the equal investment portfolio $x = (0.1, \ldots, 0.1)$ has mean and variance of (1.164958, 0.042719).

To illustrate the relative "riskiness" of the various optimal portfolios, consider the monthly data with an exponential utility function. Then the variances at $R_A = (0.5, 1, 2, 4, 10)$ are $(0.55, 0.41, 0.31, 0.24, 0.20)$ times the variance at $R_A = 0$ (i.e., the highest return portfolio). This is further illustrated in Figure 2 which shows the percentage of maximum variance as a function of R_A for monthly, quarterly, and yearly data.

The results also yield the following conclusions:

1. The special exponential and negative power utility functions yield very risk averse portfolios. This is in contrast with the positive power utility function which yields highly risky portfolios and moderately risk averse portfolios for different values of β_5.

2. The arctangent utility function usually yields highly risky portfolios and has risk aversion equal to one or less.

3. The quadratic, exponential and logarithmic utility functions yield the largest range in variation of R_A and yield the safest and riskiest portfolios for extreme values of β. Extremely low values of R_A are easily implementable for all three utility functions. However, extremely high values of R_A are not implementable for the exponential or logarithmic functions because one must either have $\beta_2 \to \infty$ or $\beta_3 \to -w$ (which causes domain problems). Thus the quadratic utility function despite its two well-known limitations ($u' < 0$ for large w and $R_A' > 0$) may well play a useful role as a computational surrogate for more plausible utility functions when the number of possible investment securities is large, say $n \geqslant 50$.

4. With horizons of a year or less one can substitute easily derived surrogate utility functions that are mathematically convenient for more plausible but mathematically more complicated utility functions and feel confident that the errors produced in the calculation of the optimal portfolios are at most of the order of magnitude of the errors in the data. Moreover there is a fairly well-defined tradeoff of computational accuracy versus computing costs. For rough calculations one can use the measure $w_0 R_A(\bar{w})$ and obtain reasonable results for small variance problems (e.g., monthly data). For the most accurate results one uses Rubinstein's measure in (7). The most cost effective measure is $w_0 \bar{R}_A$.

5. An implication of the results for econometric research is that based only on observed portfolio data it will be extremely difficult to discriminate amongst alternative models since these models will be observationally practically equivalent with different parameter values.

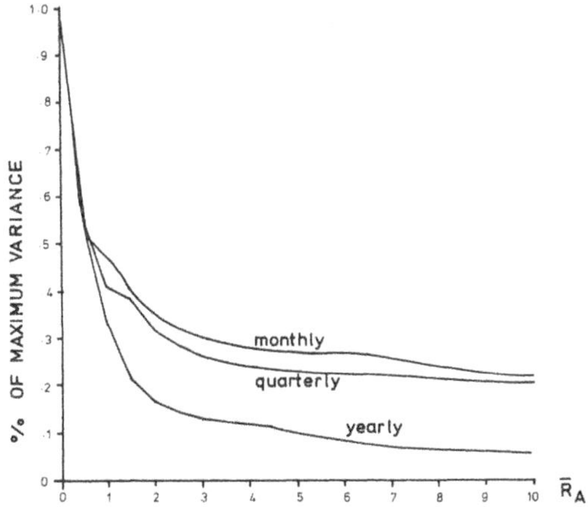

FIGURE 2. Percentage of Maximum Variance vs. R_A.

6. The results suggest that one can derive an analytically tractable utility function whose use will generate portfolio allocations nearly indistinguishable from those of a given risk averse utility function given a known distribution of returns. However if we substitute $\hat{u}$ for u when the distribution is $F(\xi)$ are the results robust if the distribution is really $\tilde{F}(\xi)$? Calculations in Kallberg and Ziemba [10] indicate that the maximum expected utility and optimal portfolio composition are relatively insensitive to errors in estimation of the variance-covariance matrix. However, errors in estimating the mean return vector do significantly change these quantities.[8]

Appendix: Optimality of Rubinstein's Risk Aversion Measure

THEOREM 1. *Suppose $\xi \in R^n$ has a multivariate normal distribution with finite means and variances and that u_i is twice continuously differentiable with $u_i' > 0$ and $u_i'' < 0$ for $i = 1, 2$. Consider the following two portfolio problems*

$$\text{(P1)} \qquad \left\{\max E_\xi u_1\left(w_1 \xi^T x\right) \mid e'x = 1,\ x \geqslant 0\right\}, \quad \textit{and}$$

$$\text{(P2)} \qquad \left\{\max E_\xi u_2\left(w_2 \xi^T x\right) \mid e'x = 1,\ x \geqslant 0\right\},$$

where w_i refers to investor i's initial wealth. Suppose that x^* is an optimal solution to (P1) *and that*

$$\frac{w_1 E_\xi u_1''\left(w_1 \xi^T x^*\right)}{E_\xi u_1'\left(w_1 \xi^T x^*\right)} = \frac{w_2 E_\xi u_2''\left(w_2 \xi^T x^*\right)}{E_\xi u_2'\left(w_2 \xi^T x^*\right)}. \tag{8}$$

Then x^* is an optimal solution to (P2).

PROOF. The necessary and sufficient Kuhn–Tucker conditions for (P1) are:

$$\text{(A1)} \qquad E_\xi\left\{u_1'\left(w_1 \xi^T x\right) w_1 \xi_i\right\} - \lambda - \mu_i = 0,$$

$$\text{(B1)} \qquad \mu_i x_i = 0,$$

$$\text{(C1)} \qquad \mu_i \geqslant 0, \quad \text{and}$$

$$\text{(D1)} \qquad e^T x = 1, \qquad x \geqslant 0, \qquad \text{where} \quad i = 1, \ldots, n.$$

As $\operatorname{cov}(u, v) = E(uv) - \bar{u}\bar{v}$, we have

$$E_\xi\left\{u_1'\left(w_1 \xi^T x\right) w_1 \xi_i\right\} = \operatorname{cov}\left(w_1 \xi_i, u_1'\left(w_1 \xi^T x\right)\right) + w_1 \bar{\xi}_i u_1'\left(w_1 \xi^T x\right). \tag{9}$$

Now

$$\operatorname{cov}(x, g, (y)) = E(g'(y)) \operatorname{cov}(x, y),$$

whenever g is continuously differentiable, all expectations are finite and x and y have

[8]This research was partially supported by National Research Council Grant No. 67-7147 and Canada Council Grant No. S75-1307-R1. Without implicating them, we wish to thank M. J. Brennan, S. Ginsburg, R. C. Grinold, M. J. Gruber, D. Hausch, A. Kraus, M. Kusy, M. E. Rubinstein, G. Sick, and the referees for helpful discussions and comments on earlier drafts of this paper. Special thanks go to M. E. Rubinstein for formulating Theorem 1 for us and allowing us to publish this joint result here. Rubinstein devised a proof for the case when nonnegativity constraints are absent. The proof given here applies for the nonnegativity case. Cases when some or all of the assets may be sold short or long follow directly from this result.

a bivariate normal distribution. Thus

$$\begin{aligned}\operatorname{cov}\big(w_1\xi_i, u_1'(w_1\xi^Tx)\big) &= E_\xi\big(u_1''(w_1\xi^Tx)\big)\operatorname{cov}\big(w_1\xi_i, w_1\xi^Tx\big)\\ &= w_1^2E_\xi\big(u_1''(w_1\xi^Tx)\big)\sum_j \operatorname{cov}(\xi_i,\xi_j)x_j, \end{aligned} \tag{10}$$

since $\operatorname{cov}(u, \Sigma v_i) = \Sigma \operatorname{cov}(u, v_i)$. Using (9) and (10) in (A1) yields

$$\lambda + \mu_i = w_1\bar{\xi}_i E_\xi\big(u_1'(w_1\xi^Tx)\big) + w_1^2E_\xi\big(u_1''(w_1\xi^Tx)\big)\sum_j \operatorname{cov}(\xi_i,\xi_j)x_j.$$

The Kuhn–Tucker conditions for (P2) are then

$$\text{(A2)} \qquad \hat{\lambda} + \hat{\mu}_i = w_2\bar{\xi}_i E_\xi\big(u_2'(w_2\xi^Tx)\big) + w_2^2E_\xi\big(u_2''(w_2\xi^Tx)\big)\sum_j \operatorname{cov}(\xi_i,\xi_j)x_j,$$

$$\text{(B2)} \qquad \hat{\mu}_i x_i = 0,$$

$$\text{(C2)} \qquad \hat{\mu}_i \geqslant 0, \quad \text{and}$$

$$\text{(D2)} \qquad e^Tx = 1, \qquad x \geqslant 0, \qquad \text{where} \quad i = 1, \ldots, n.$$

Now (A1) and (A2) are equivalent to:

$$(\lambda + \mu_i)/\Big(w_1E_\xi\big(u_1'(w_1\xi^Tx)\big)\Big) = \bar{\xi}_i + R_1\sum_j \operatorname{cov}(\xi_i,\xi_j)x_j \quad \text{and} \tag{11}$$

$$(\hat{\lambda} + \hat{\mu}_i)/\Big(w_2E_\xi\big(u_2'(w_2\xi^Tx)\big)\Big) = \bar{\xi}_i + R_2\sum_j \operatorname{cov}(\xi_i,\xi_j)x_j, \quad \text{respectively,} \tag{12}$$

where

$$R_i \equiv \frac{w_iE_\xi u_i''(w_i\xi^Tx)}{E_\xi u_i'(w_i\xi^Tx)}.$$

Now if x^* satisfies (A1)–(D1) with corresponding optimal multipliers λ^* and μ_i^*, $i = 1, \ldots, n$, and (8) holds, (11) and (12) have equal right-hand sides. It then follows that x^* solves (A2)–(D2) with corresponding optimal multipliers $\hat{\lambda}^* = k\lambda^*$ and $\hat{\mu}_i^* = k\mu_i^*$, $i = 1, \ldots, n$ where the positive constant

$$k \equiv \frac{w_2E_\xi\big(u_2'(w_2\xi^Tx^*)\big)}{w_1E_\xi\big(u_1'(w_1\xi^Tx^*)\big)}.$$

REMARK. It is straightforward to extend this result to more general portfolio problems i.e.,

$$\big\{\max E_\xi u_i(w_i\xi^Tx) \,|\, g(x) = 0, h(x) \geqslant 0\big\}$$

where $g: R^n \to R^{m_1}$ is quasilinear, $h: R^n \to R^{m_2}$ is quasiconcave, and a constraint qualification holds.

References

1. ARROW, K. J., *Essays on the Theory of Risk Bearing*, Markham, Chicago, 1971.
2. CASS, D. AND STIGLITZ, J. E., "Risk Aversion and Wealth Effects on Portfolios with Many Assets," *Rev. Econom. Studies*, Vol. 39 (1972), pp. 331–354.
3. CHIPMAN, J., "The Ordering of Portfolios in Terms of Mean and Variance," *Rev. Econom. Studies*, Vol. 40 (1973), pp. 167–190.

4. Dexter, A. S., Yu, J. N. W. and Ziemba, W. T., "Portfolio Selection in a Lognormal Market When the Investor Has a Power Utility Function: Computational Results," in *Stochastic Programming*, M. A. H. Dempster (Ed.), Academic Press, New York, 1980, pp. 507–523.
5. Evans, J. L. and Archer, S. H., "Diversification and the Reduction of Dispersion: An Empirical Analysis," *J. Finance*, Vol. 23 (1968), pp. 761–767.
6. Fishburn, P. C. and Porter, R. B., "Optimal Portfolios with One Safe and One Risky Asset: Effects of Changes in the Rate of Return and Risk," *Management Sci.*, Vol. 22 (1976), pp. 1064–1073.
7. Freund, J., "The Introduction of Risk into a Programming Model," *Econometrica*, Vol. 14 (1956), pp. 253–263.
8. Gordon, M. J., Paradis, G. E. and Rorke, C. H., "Experimental Evidence on Alternative Portfolio Decision Rules," *Amer. Econom. Rev.*, Vol. 52 (1972), pp. 107–118.
9. Kallberg, J. G., "Computational Algorithms for Stochastic Nonlinear Programs with Application to Portfolio Selection and Revision," unpublished Ph.D. dissertation, University of British Columbia, 1979.
10. ——— and Ziemba, W. T., "Comparison of Alternative Utility Functions in Portfolio Selection Problems," mimeo, University of British Columbia, 1978.
11. ——— and ———, "An Extended Frank–Wolfe Algorithm for Portfolio Selection Problems," *Recent Results in Stochastic Programming*, P. Kall and A. Prékopa (Eds.), Springer-Verlag, Berlin and New York, 1980, pp. 139–159.
12. ——— and ———, "Remarks on Random Wealth Level Risk Aversion Measures," working paper, New York University, 1982.
13. Keeney, R. L. and Raiffa, H., *Decisions with Multiple Objectives: Preferences and Value Tradeoffs*, Wiley, New York, 1976.
14. Kira, D. and Ziemba, W. T., "The Demand for a Risky Asset," *Management Sci.*, Vol. 26, No. 11 (November 1980), pp. 1158–1165.
15. Levy, H., "The Demand for Assets Under Conditions of Risk," *J. Finance*, Vol. 28 (1973), pp. 79–96.
16. Lintner, J., "Equilibrium in a Random Walk and Lognormal Securities Market," Discussion Paper, No. 235, Harvard Institute of Economic Research, 1972.
17. Merton, R. C., "An Analytic Derivation of the Efficient Portfolio Frontier," *J. Financial Quantitative Anal.*, Vol. 7 (1972), pp. 1851–1872.
18. Pratt, J. W., "Risk Aversion in the Small and in the Large," *Econometrica*, Vol. 32 (1964), pp. 122–136.
19. Rubinstein, M. E., "The Fundamental Theorem of Parameter-Preference Security Valuation," *J. Financial Quantitative Anal.*, Vol. 8 (1973), pp. 61–70.
20. ———, "A Comparative Statics Analysis of Risk Premiums," *J. Business*, Vol. 46 (1973), pp. 605–615.
21. Samuelson, P. A., "The Fundamental Approximation Theorem of Portfolio Analysis in Terms of Means, Variances and Higher Moments," *Rev. Econom. Studies*, Vol. 37 (1970), pp. 537–542.
22. Stein, C., "Estimation of the Mean of a Multivariate Normal Distribution," *Proceedings of the Prague Symposium on Asymptotic Statistics*, 1973.
23. Stuck, B. W., "Explicit Solutions to Some Single Period Investment Problems for Risky Log-Stable Stocks," *J. Financial Econom.*, Vol. 3 (1976), pp. 277–294.
24. Tobin, J., "Liquidity Preference as Behavior Towards Risk," *Rev. Econom. Studies*, Vol. 25 (1958), pp. 65–86.
25. Ziemba, W. T., Parkan, C. and Brooks-Hill, R., "Calculation of Investment Portfolios with Risk Free Borrowing and Lending," *Management Sci.*, Vol. 21 (1974), pp. 209–222.

Chapter 7

The Effect of Errors in Means, Variances, and Covariances on Optimal Portfolio Choice*

Good mean forecasts are critical to the mean-variance framework.

Vijay K. Chopra and William T. Ziemba

There is considerable literature on the strengths and limitations of mean-variance analysis. The basic theory and extensions of MV analysis are discussed in Markowitz [1987] and Ziemba and Vickson [1975]. Bawa, Brown, and Klein [1979] and Michaud [1989] review some of its problems.

MV optimization is very sensitive to errors in the estimates of the inputs. Chopra [1993] shows that small changes in the input parameters can result in large changes in composition of the optimal portfolio. Best and Grauer [1991] present some empirical and theoretical results on the sensitivity of optimal portfolios to changes in means. This article examines the relative impact of estimation errors in means, variances, and covariances.

Kallberg and Ziemba [1984] examine the question of misspecification in normally distributed portfolio selection problems. They discuss three areas of misspecification: the investor's utility function, the mean vector, and the covariance matrix of the return distribution.

They find that utility functions with similar levels of Arrow-Pratt absolute risk aversion result in similar optimal portfolios, irrespective of the functional form of the utility.[1] Thus, misspecification of the utility function is not a major concern because several different utility functions (quadratic, negative exponential, logarithmic, power) result in similar portfolio allocations for similar levels of risk aversion.

VIJAY K. CHOPRA is Senior Research Analyst at the Frank Russell Company in Tacoma (WA 98401).

WILLIAM T. ZIEMBA is the Alumni Professor of Management Science at the University of British Columbia in Vancouver (B.C., Canada V6T 1Y8).

*This chapter was originally published in: Chopra, V. K. & Ziemba, W. T. (1993). The Effect of Errors in Means, Variances, and Covariances on Optimal Portfolio Choice. *Journal of Portfolio Management*, 19(Winter), 6–11.

Misspecification of the parameters of the return distribution, however, does make a significant difference. Specifically, errors in means are about ten times as important as errors in variances and covariances.

We show that it is important to distinguish between errors in variances and covariances. The relative impact of errors in means, variances, and covariances also depends on the investor's risk tolerance. For a risk tolerance of 50, errors in means are about eleven times as important as errors in variances, a result similar to that of Kallberg and Ziemba.[2] Errors in variances are about twice as important as errors in covariances.

At higher risk tolerances, errors in means are even more important relative to errors in variances and covariances. At lower risk tolerances, the relative impact of errors in means, variances, and covariances is closer. Even though errors in means are more important than those in variances and covariances, the difference in importance diminishes with a decline in risk tolerance.

These results have an implication for allocation of resources according to the MV framework. The primary emphasis should be on obtaining superior estimates of means, followed by good estimates of variances. Estimates of covariances are the least important in terms of their influence on the optimal portfolio.

THEORY

For a utility function U and gross returns r_i (or return relatives) for assets i = 1, 2, ..., N, an investor's optimal portfolio is the solution to:

$$\text{maximize} \quad Z(x) = E[U(W_0 \textstyle\sum_{i=1}^{N} (r_i) x_i)]$$

$$\text{such that} \quad x_i \geq 0, \textstyle\sum_{i=1}^{N} x_i = 1,$$

EXHIBIT 1
List of Ten Randomly Chosen DJIA Securities

1. Aluminum Co. of America
2. American Express Co.
3. Boeing Co.
4. Chevron Co.
5. Coca Cola Co.
6. E.I. Du Pont De Nemours & Co.
7. Minnesota Mining and Manufacturing Co.
8. Procter & Gamble Co.
9. Sears, Roebuck & Co.
10. United Technologies Co.

where Z(x) is the investor's expected utility of wealth, W_0 is the investor's initial wealth, the returns r_i have a distribution F(r), and x_i are the portfolio weights that sum to one.

Assuming a negative exponential utility function U(W) = -exp(-aW) and a joint normal distribution of returns, the expected utility maximization problem is equivalent to the MV-optimization problem:

$$\text{maximize} \quad Z(x) = \textstyle\sum_{i=1}^{N} E[r_i] x_i - \frac{1}{t} \sum_{i=1}^{N} \sum_{j=1}^{N} x_i x_j E[\sigma_{ij}]$$

$$\text{such that} \quad x_i \geq 0, \textstyle\sum_{i=1}^{N} x_i = 1,$$

where $E[r_i]$ is the expected return for asset i, t is the risk tolerance of the investor, and $E[\sigma_{ij}]$ is the covariance between the returns on asset i and asset j.[3]

A natural question arises: How much worse off is the investor if the distribution of returns is estimated with an error? This is an important consideration because the future distribution of returns is unknown. Investors rely on limited data to estimate the parameters of the distribution, and estimation errors are unavoidable. Our investigation assumes that the distribution of returns is stationary over the sample period. If it is time-varying or non-stationary, the estimated parameters will be erroneous.

To measure how close one portfolio is to another, we compare the cash equivalent (CE) values of the two portfolios. The cash equivalent of a risky portfolio is the certain amount of cash that provides the same utility as the risky portfolio, that is, U(CE) = Z(x) or CE = $U^{-1}[Z(x)]$ where, as defined before, Z(x) is the expected utility of the risky portfolio.[4] The cash equivalent is an appropriate measure because it takes into account the investor's risk tolerance and the inherent uncertainty in returns, and it is independent of utility units. For a risk-free portfolio, the cash equivalent is equal to the certain return.

Given a set of asset parameters and the investor's risk tolerance, a MV-optimal portfolio has the largest CE value of any portfolio of those assets. The percentage cash equivalent loss (CEL) from holding an arbitrary portfolio x instead of an optimal portfolio o is

$$CEL = \frac{CE_o - CE_x}{CE_o}$$

where CE_o and CE_x are the cash equivalents of portfolio o and portfolio x, respectively.

DATA AND METHODOLOGY

The data consist of monthly observations from January 1980 through December 1989 on ten randomly selected Dow Jones Industrial Average (DJIA) securities. We use the Center for Research in Security Prices (CRSP) data base, having deleted one security (Allied-Signal, Inc.) because of lack of data prior to 1985. Each of the remaining twenty-nine securities had an equal probability of being chosen. The securities are listed in Exhibit 1.

MV optimization requires as inputs forecasts for: mean returns, variances, and covariances. We computed historical means ($\bar{r}_i$), variances (σ_{ii}), and covariances (σ_{ij}), and assumed that these are the "true" values of these parameters. Thus, we assumed that $E[r_i] = \bar{r}_i$, $E[\sigma_{ii}] = \sigma_{ii}$, and $E[\sigma_{ij}] = \sigma_{ij}$. A base optimal portfolio allocation was computed on the basis of these parameters for a risk tolerance of 50 (equivalent to the parameter $a = 0.04$).

Our results are independent of the source of the inputs. Whether we use historical inputs or those based on a complex forecasting scheme, the results continue to hold as long as the inputs have errors.

Exhibit 2 gives the input parameters and the optimal base portfolio resulting from these inputs. To examine the influence of errors in parameter estimates, we change the true parameters slightly and compute the resulting optimal portfolio. This portfolio will be suboptimal for the investor because it is not based on the true input parameters.

Next we compute the cash equivalent values of the base portfolio and the new optimal portfolio. The percentage cash equivalent loss from holding the suboptimal portfolio instead of the true optimal portfolio measures the impact of errors in input parameters on investor utility.

To evaluate the impact of errors in means, we replaced the assumed true mean $\bar{r}_i$ for asset i by the approximation $\bar{r}_i(1 + kz_i)$ where z_i has a standard normal distribution. The parameter k is varied from 0.05 through 0.20 in steps of 0.05 to examine the impact of errors of different sizes. Larger values of k represent larger errors in the estimates. The variances and covariances are left unchanged in this case to isolate the influence of errors in means.

The percentage cash equivalent loss from holding a portfolio that is optimal for approximate means $\bar{r}_i(1 + kz_i)$ but is suboptimal for the true means r_i then

EXHIBIT 2
Inputs to the Optimization and the Resulting Optimal Portfolio for a Risk Tolerance of 50 (January 1980–December 1989)

	Alcoa	Amex	Boeing	Chev.	Coke	Du Pont	MMM	P&G	Sears	U Tech
Means (% per month)	1.5617	1.9477	1.907	1.5801	2.1643	1.6010	1.4892	1.6248	1.4075	1.4537
Std. Dev. (% per month)	8.8308	8.4585	10.040	8.6215	5.9886	6.8767	5.8162	5.6385	8.0047	8.2125
Correlations										
Alcoa	1.0000									
Amex	0.3660	1.0000								
Boeing	0.3457	0.5379	1.0000							
Chev.	0.1606	0.2165	0.2218	1.0000						
Coke	0.2279	0.4986	0.4283	0.0569	1.0000					
Du Pont	0.5133	0.5823	0.4051	0.3609	0.3619	1.0000				
MMM	0.5203	0.5569	0.4492	0.2325	0.4811	0.6167	1.0000			
P&G	0.2176	0.4760	0.3867	0.2289	0.5952	0.4996	0.6037	1.0000		
Sears	0.3267	0.6517	0.4883	0.1726	0.4378	0.5811	0.5671	0.5012	1.0000	
U Tech	0.5101	0.5853	0.6569	0.3814	0.4368	0.5644	0.6032	0.4772	0.6039	1.0000
Optimal Port. Weights	0.0350	0.0082	0.0	0.1626	0.7940	0.0	0.0	0.0	0.00	0.00

is computed. This procedure is repeated with a new set of z values for a total of 100 iterations for each value of k.

To investigate the impact of errors in variances, each variance forecast σ_{ii} was replaced by $\sigma_{ii}(1 + kz_i)$. To isolate the influence of variance errors, the means and covariances are left unchanged.

Finally, the influence of errors in covariances is examined by replacing each covariance σ_{ij} (with i not equal to j) by $\sigma_{ij}(1 + kz_{ij})$, where z_{ij} has a standard normal distribution, while retaining the original means and variances. The procedure is repeated 100 times for each value of k, each time with a new set of z values, and the cash equivalent loss computed. The entire procedure is repeated for risk tolerances of 25 and 75 to examine how the results vary with investors' risk tolerance.

EXHIBIT 3

Cash Equivalent Loss (CEL) for Errors of Different Sizes

k (size of error)	Parameter with Error	Mean CEL	Min. CEL	Max. CEL
0.05	Means	0.66	0.01	5.05
0.05	Variances	0.05	0.00	0.34
0.05	Covariances	0.02	0.00	0.25
0.10	Means	2.45	0.01	15.61
0.10	Variances	0.22	0.00	1.39
0.10	Covariances	0.11	0.00	0.66
0.15	Means	5.12	0.15	24.35
0.15	Variances	0.55	0.00	3.35
0.15	Covariances	0.27	0.00	1.11
0.20	Means	10.16	0.17	36.09
0.20	Variances	0.90	0.01	4.16
0.20	Covariances	0.47	0.00	1.94

RESULTS

Exhibit 3 shows the mean, minimum, and maximum cash equivalent loss over the 100 iterations for a risk tolerance of 50. Exhibit 4 plots the average CEL as a function of k. The CEL for errors in means is approximately eleven times that for errors in variances and over twenty times that for errors in covariances. Thus, it is important to distinguish between errors in variances and errors in covariances.[5] For example, for k = 0.10, the CEL is 2.45 for errors in means, 0.22 for errors in variances, and 0.11 for errors in covariances.

Our results on the relative importance of errors in means and variances are similar to those of Kallberg and Ziemba [1984]. They find that errors in means are approximately ten times as important as errors in variances and covariances considered together (they do not distinguish between variances and covariances).

Our results show that for a risk tolerance of 50 the importance of errors in covariances is only half as much as previously believed. Furthermore, the relative importance of errors in means, variances, and covariances depends upon the investor's risk tolerance.

Exhibit 5 shows the average ratio (averaged over errors of different sizes, k) of the CELs for errors in means, variances, and covariances. An investor with a high risk tolerance focuses on raising the expected return of the portfolio and discounts the variance more relative to the expected return. To this investor, errors in expected returns are considerably more important than errors in variances and covariances. For an investor with a risk tolerance of 75, the average CEL for errors in means is over twenty-one times that for errors in variances and over fifty-six times that for errors in covariances.

Minimizing the variance of the portfolio is more important to an investor with a low risk tolerance than raising the expected return. To this investor, errors in means are somewhat less important than

EXHIBIT 4
MEAN PERCENTAGE CASH EQUIVALENT LOSS DUE TO ERRORS IN INPUTS

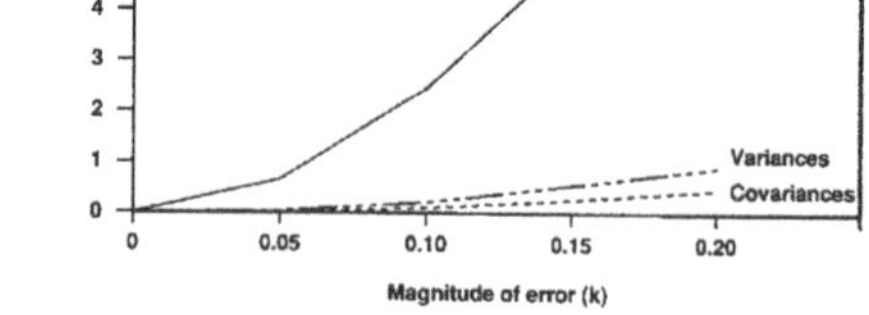

EXHIBIT 5
Average Ratio of CELs for Errors in Means, Variances, and Covariances

Risk Tolerance	Errors in Means versus Variances	Errors in Means versus Covariances	Errors in Variances versus Covariances
25	3.22	5.38	1.67
50	10.98	22.50	2.05
75	21.42	56.84	2.68

errors in variances and covariances. For an investor with a risk tolerance of 25, the average CEL for errors in expected returns is about three times that for errors in variances and about five times that for errors in covariances.

Most large institutional investors have a risk tolerance in the 40 to 60 range. Over that range, there is considerable difference in the relative importance of errors in means, variances, and covariances. Irrespective of the level of risk tolerance, errors in means are the most important, followed by errors in variances. Errors in covariances are the least important in terms of their influence on portfolio optimality.

IMPLICATIONS AND CONCLUSIONS

Investors have limited resources available to spend on obtaining estimates of necessarily unknowable future parameters of risk and reward. This analysis indicates that the bulk of these resources should be spent on obtaining the best estimates of expected returns of the asset classes under consideration.

Sometimes, investors using the MV framework to allocate wealth among individual stocks set all the expected returns to zero (or a non-zero constant). This can lead to a better portfolio allocation because it is often very difficult to obtain good forecasts for expected returns. Using forecasts that do not accurately reflect the relative expected returns of different securities can substantially degrade MV performance.

In some cases it may be preferable to set all forecasts equal.[6] The optimization then focuses on minimizing portfolio variance and does not suffer from the error-in-means problem. In such cases it is important to have good estimates of variances and covariances for the securities, as MV optimizes with respect to these characteristics only.

Of course, if investors truly believe that they have superior estimates of the means, they should use them. In this case it may be acceptable to use historical values for variances and covariances.

For investors with moderate to high risk tolerance, the cash equivalent loss for errors in means is an order of magnitude greater than that for errors in variances or covariances. As variances and covariances do not influence the optimal MV allocation much (relative to the means), investors with moderate to high risk tolerance need not expend considerable resources to obtain better estimates of these parameters.

ENDNOTES

[1]For an investor with utility function U and wealth W, the Arrow-Pratt absolute risk aversion is $ARA = -U''(W)/U'(W)$. Friend and Blume [1975] show that investor behavior is consistent with decreasing ARA; that is, as investors' wealth increases, their aversion to a given risk decreases.

[2]The risk tolerance reflects the investor's desired trade-off between extra return and extra risk (variance). It is the inverse slope of the investor's indifference curve in mean-variance space. The greater the risk tolerance, the more risk an investor is willing to take for a little extra return. Under fairly general input assumptions, a risk tolerance of 50 describes the typical portfolio allocations of large U.S. pension funds and other institutional investors. Risk tolerances of 25 and 75 characterize extremely conservative and aggressive investors, respectively.

[3]Although the exponential utility function is convenient for deriving the MV problem with normally distributed returns, the MV framework is consistent with expected utility maximization for any concave utility function, assuming normality.

[4]For negative exponential utility, Freund [1956] shows that the expected utility of portfolio x is $Z(x) = 1 - \exp(-aE[x] + (a^2/2)\mathrm{Var}[x])$, where E[x] and Var[x] are the expected return and variance of the portfolio. The cash equivalent is $CE_x = (-1/a)\log(1 - Z(x))$. If returns are assumed to have a multivariate normal distribution, this is also the cash equivalent of a MV-optimal portfolio. See Dexter, Yu, and Ziemba [1980] for more details.

[5]The result for covariances also applies to correlation coefficients, as the correlations differ from the covariances only by a scale factor equal to the product of two standard deviations.

[6]This approach is in the spirit of Stein estimation and is discussed in Chopra, Hensel, and Turner [1993]. As a practical matter, it should be used for assets that belong to the same asset class, e.g., equity indexes of different countries or stocks within a country. It would be inappropriate to apply it to financial instruments with very different characteristics, stocks and T-bills, for example.

REFERENCES

Bawa, Vijay S., Stephen J. Brown, and Roger W. Klein. "Estimation Risk and Optimal Portfolio Choice." *Studies in Bayesian Econometrics*, Bell Laboratories Series. New York: North Holland, 1979.

Best, Michael J., and Robert R. Grauer. "On the Sensitivity of Mean-Variance-Efficient Portfolios to Changes in Asset Means: Some

Analytical and Computational Results." *Review of Financial Studies*, 4, No. 2 (1991), pp. 315-342.

Chopra, Vijay K. "Mean-Variance Revisited: Near-Optimal Portfolios and Sensitivity to Input Variations." *Russell Research Commentary*, 1991.

Chopra, Vijay K., Chris R. Hensel, and Andrew L. Turner. "Massaging Mean-Variance Inputs: Returns from Alternative Global Investment Strategies in the 1980s." Forthcoming in *Management Science*, 1993.

Dexter, Albert S., Johnny N.W. Yu, and William T. Ziemba. "Portfolio Selection in a Lognormal Market When the Investor Has a Power Utility Function: Computational Results." In M.A.H. Dempster, ed., *Proceedings of the International Conference on Stochastic Programming*. New York: Academic Press, 1980, pp. 507-523.

Freund, Robert A. "The Introduction of Risk into a Programming Model." *Econometrica*, 24 (1956), pp. 253-263.

Friend, I., and M. Blume. "The Demand for Risky Assets." *The American Economic Review*, December 1975, pp. 900-922.

Kallberg, Jarl G., and William T. Ziemba. "Mis-specification in Portfolio Selection Problems." In G. Bamberg and K. Spremann, eds., *Risk and Capital: Lecture Notes in Economics and Mathematical Systems*. New York: Springer-Verlag, 1984.

Klein, Roger W., and Vijay S. Bawa. "The Effect of Estimation Risk on Optimal Portfolio Choice." *Journal of Financial Economics*, 3 (June 1976), pp. 215-231.

Markowitz, Harry M. *Mean-Variance Analysis in Portfolio Choice and Capital Markets*. New York: Basil Blackwell, 1987.

Michaud, Richard O. "The Markowitz Optimization Enigma: Is 'Optimized' Optimal?" *Financial Analysts Journal*, 45 (January-February 1989), pp. 31-42.

Ziemba, William T., and Raymond G. Vickson, eds. *Stochastic Optimization Models in Finance*. New York: Academic Press, 1975.

Chapter 8

A DYNAMIC INVESTMENT MODEL WITH CONTROL ON THE PORTFOLIO'S WORST CASE OUTCOME*

YONGGAN ZHAO

Nanyang Business School, Nanyang Technological University, Singapore

ULRICH HAUSSMANN

Department of Mathematics, University of British Columbia

WILLIAM T. ZIEMBA

Sauder School of Business, University of British Columbia

This paper considers a portfolio problem with control on downside losses. Incorporating the worst-case portfolio outcome in the objective function, the optimal policy is equivalent to the hedging portfolio of a European option on a dynamic mutual fund that can be replicated by market primary assets. Applying the Black-Scholes formula, a closed-form solution is obtained when the utility function is HARA and asset prices follow a multivariate geometric Brownian motion. The analysis provides a useful method of converting an investment problem to an option pricing model.

KEY WORDS: portfolio selection, martingale, option, worst case outcome, downside risk control

1. INTRODUCTION

Intertemporal investment policies in continuous time under uncertainty have been characterized by stochastic dynamic programming and martingale analysis. Merton (1969, 1971) is the pioneering work in using stochastic dynamic programming theory for investment. The stochastic control methodology often reduces the problem to an intractable partial differential equation for which explicit solutions can only be obtained for the simplest cases. Karatzas et al. (1986) discussed the solution to a general consumption/investment model. For a more detailed discussion of the stochastic control approach in the theory of continuous trading, see Karatzas (1989). However, this approach becomes very difficult when either the control variables or the state variables are constrained. Harrison and Pliska (1981), Pliska (1986), and Cox and Huang (1989) have applied martingale analysis to this problem. The existence of risk neutral probability facilitates the martingale approach for investment modeling. One solves this problem by separating the problem into two parts: first identifying the subspace of attainable wealth, then choosing the best wealth level that satisfies the constraints (if any). In these models downside control was

Without implicating them we would like to thank Hong Chen and Lorenzo Garlappi for helpful comments on an earlier draft of this paper. This research was partially supported by NSERC.

Manuscript received June 2001; final revision received August 2002.

Address correspondence to Prof. William T. Ziemba, Sauder School of Business, University of British Columbia, Vancouver, Canada V6T 1Z2; e-mail: ziemba@interchange.ubc.ca.

*This chapter was originally published in: Zhao, Y., Haussmann, U. & Ziemba, W. T. (2003). A Dynamic Investment Model with Control on the Portfolio's Worst Case Outcome. *Mathematical Finance*, 13(4), 481–501.

not explicitly considered in constructing the model. Maximizing expected utility of wealth can be used by investors to trade off profits in good future states against losses incurred in bad states. However, explicit downside risk control approaches seem preferable for investors with a liability stream.

Basak (1995) examined the effects of portfolio insurance on market and asset price dynamics in a general equilibrium continuous-time model. Grossman and Zhou (1996) analyzed a similar problem but allowed insurers and uninsurers to have different utility functions. However, in these models, the "floor" or the worst-case outcome of the portfolio insurance is exogenously given. It is possible that, if the worst outcome of the porfolio were incorporated in the insurer's objective function as a variable, the equilibrium asset price and the optimal portfolio would be affected. The feasible region of the admissible strategies for the optimization model would be enlarged and the equilibrium asset price and the optimal portfolio would only depend on the choice of the utility functions for both insurers and uninsurers. Unlike Basak (1995) and Grossman and Zhou, this paper focuses on determining the dynamic optimal portfolio with control on downside losses, specifically the worst possible loss.

To incorporate downside risk control, we assume the investor's objective function is decided not only by the end-of-horizon wealth but also by the worst wealth outcome. Increasing expected terminal wealth will usually reduce the worst outcome of the wealth. How do we compromise between these two competing aspects to develop a dynamic investment portfolio? The revised utility function reflects investor's risk aversion and is a weighted sum of the expected wealth and the worst wealth outcome. Zhao and Ziemba (2001) used a similar risk measure to develop a multiperiod stochastic programming model for asset allocation.

We prove that the investor's optimal portfolio is equivalent to a call option on a mutual fund that can be replicated by market primary assets. The strike price of the call will be the worst outcome that might have occurred. If this mutual fund exists in the market and options with different strike prices can be written on it, a two-fund separation theory applies, in which case all investors will only invest in a call option and the riskless asset. With HARA utility and geometric Brownian motion for prices, a closed-form solution is given. The optimal investment policies will be a leveraged growth optimal portfolio, but with contingent leverages as time goes along.

In Section 2, we discuss the asset price process and the wealth evolution for given admissible strategies. Section 3 presents the model formulation and its solution. Section 4 shows the equivalence of the option strategy and the economic interpretation of the model. Section 5 deals with the setting of HARA utility and geometric Brownian motion for prices and gives an analytic solution to the model. Section 6 concludes.

2. ASSET PRICE MODEL AND WEALTH PROCESS

Assume a complete probability space $(\Omega, \mathcal{F}, P)$ and a time horizon $[0, T]$, where T is a strictly positive real number. Let $z(t) = (z_1(t), \ldots, z_n(t))^\top$ denote an n-dimensional standard Brownian motion, which generates a filtration $\mathbf{F} = \{\mathcal{F}_t \subseteq \mathcal{F}; t \in [0, T]\}$ completed by the null set of $\mathcal{F}$. A stochastic process $X(t)$ is called adapted to $\mathbf{F}$ if $X(t)$ is measurable with respect to $\mathcal{F}_t$. Consider a frictionless securities market with $n + 1$ long-lived securities traded. Security B is a locally riskless asset and securities S_i, $i = 1, \ldots, n$, are risky assets. $(B, S_1, \ldots, S_n)$ are called the primary assets for the market. The stochastic processes for the prices of these securities are

$$(2.1)\qquad \begin{cases} dB(t) = r(t)B(t)\,dt, & B(0) = 1, \\ dS_i(t) = b_i(t)\,dt + \sum_{j=1}^{n} \sigma_{ij}(t)\,dz_j(t), & \forall i = 1, 2, \ldots, n. \end{cases}$$

To make the problem a general Markovian diffusion process, $r(t)$, $b_i(t)$, and $\sigma_{ij}(t)$ are allowed to be functions (nonrandom) of $B(t)$ and $\{S_i(t)\}$. For simplicity, we suppress $B(t)$ and $S_i(t)$ whenever the expression is clear. Let $b(t) = (b_1(t), \ldots, b_n(t))^\top$ and $\sigma(t) = (\sigma_{ij}(t))_{n\times n}$ be an $n \times n$ matrix process. Assume that b and σ are Borel measurable and satisfy the Itô conditions and $\sigma(t)$ is a nonsingular matrix.

A trading strategy is the $n+1$ vector process

$$\{\alpha(t), \theta(t) \equiv (\theta_1(t), \ldots, \theta_n(t))^\top; t \in [0, T]\},$$

where $\alpha(t)$ and $\theta_i(t)$ are the number of shares of the riskless asset and of the ith risky asset, respectively, and they are $\mathcal{F}_t$-predictable processes. A self-financing strategy can be characterized by

$$(2.2)\qquad \alpha(t)B(t) + \theta(t)^\top S(t) = \alpha(0)B(0) + \theta(0)S(0) + \int_0^t \alpha(s)\,dB(s) + \int_0^t \theta(s)^\top\,dS(s),$$

which ensures that the instantaneous portfolio return is a weighted sum of the asset returns. The interpretation is that the current portfolio value, given by the left-hand side of (2.2), equals the initial investment plus capital gains to date. We allow $(\alpha(t), \theta(t))$ to take negative as well as positive values. Let $W(t)$ be the portfolio value at time t, then

$$(2.3)\qquad dW(t) = \alpha(t)\,dB(t) + \theta(t)^\top\,dS(t).$$

The portfolio value process is

$$(2.4)\qquad \begin{aligned} dW(t) &= r(t)W(t)\,dt + \theta(t)^\top[(b(t) - r(t)S(t))\,dt + \sigma(t)\,dz(t)] \\ &= r(t)W(t)\,dt + \theta(t)^\top\sigma(t)\,dz^Q(t), \end{aligned}$$

where $dz^Q(t) = \sigma(t)^{-1}(b(t) - r(t)S(t))\,dt + dz(t)$. To make the above stochastic differential equation well defined, we assume that an admissible trading strategy must satisfy the following conditions:

$$(2.5)\qquad \begin{cases} \text{(i)} & E\int_0^T |\theta^\top(t)(b(t) - r(t)S(t))|\,dt < \infty, \\ \text{(ii)} & E\int_0^T \|\theta(t)^\top\sigma(t)\|^2\,dt < \infty. \end{cases}$$

We need that $\int_0^T |r(t)|\,dt < K_0$, $\int_0^T |b_i|\,dt < \infty$, $\int_0^T |\sigma_{ij}|^2\,dt < \infty$, P-a.s., and that the Novikov condition holds: $E[\exp\{\frac{1}{2}\int_0^T \|\sigma(t)^{-1}(b(t) - r(t)S(t))\|^2\,dt\}] < \infty$. A typical example is $b_i(t) = \bar{b}_i(t)S(t)$, $\sigma_{ij} = S_i\bar{\sigma}_{ij}$, where $\bar{b}_i, \bar{\sigma}_{ij}$ are bounded functions of t and $\bar{\sigma}^{-1}(t)$ is bounded. This implies that $\kappa = \sigma(t)^{-1}(b(t) - r(t)S(t)) = \bar{\sigma}(t)^{-1}(\bar{b}(t) - r(t)\mathbf{1})$ is bounded; therefore, the Novikov condition holds.

With the setting of model (2.1), there exists a unique equivalent martingale measure which has the explicit form

$$\frac{dQ}{dP} = \exp\left\{-\int_0^T \kappa(s)^\top\,dz(s) - \frac{1}{2}\int_0^T \|\kappa(s)\|^2\,ds\right\},$$

where $\kappa(t) \equiv \sigma(t)^{-1}(b(t) - r(t)S(t))$, called the market price of risk. κ satisfies the Novikov condition, $E[\exp\{\frac{1}{2}\int_0^T \|\kappa(s)\|^2\,ds\}] < \infty$, hence $E^Q[\mathbf{1}_\Omega] = 1$, which implies there is no arbitrage and Q is a probability measure. The exponential P-martingale generated by $\kappa(t)$ is

$$\eta(t) \equiv \exp\left\{-\int_0^t \kappa(s)^\top dz(s) - \frac{1}{2}\int_0^t \|\kappa(s)\|^2 ds\right\}.$$

It is known that

$$z^Q(t) \equiv z(t) + \int_0^t \kappa(s)\, ds$$

is a standard Brownian motion under the probability measure Q.

Under the Brownian motion $z^Q(t)$, the asset prices and the portfolio value are

$$dS_i(t) = r(t)S_i(t)\,dt + \sum_{j=1}^{n} \sigma_{ij}(t)\,dz_j^Q(t) \tag{2.6}$$

$$dW(t) = r(t)W(t)\,dt + \theta(t)^\top \sigma(t)\,dz^Q(t),$$

which implies that all self-financed portfolio processes (including the primary assets) have the same drift rate $r(t)$ under the Q-Brownian motion. We will use the following well-known result (cf. Karatzas and Shreve 1998), which connects a stochastic dynamic programming problem to a martingale analysis.

THEOREM 2.1. *Let Y be $\mathcal{F}_T$ measurable such that $E^Q[B(T)^{-1}|Y|] < \infty$. Then there exists a self-financing strategy $(\alpha(t), \theta(t))$ such that $W(T) = Y$ and $B(t)^{-1}W(t)$ is a martingale.*

3. MODEL FORMULATION AND SOLUTION

3.1. Model Formulation

In standard utility maximization models, portfolio values are allowed to take zero or even negative values if the utility function of wealth is defined on the whole real line. This is not acceptable for some investors who have a liability stream to pay.

Consider the following two possible ways to efficiently control such downside losses: choosing a better risk-averse utility function or changing the probability weights in forming the objective function. The first approach is the traditional expected utility maximization with the objective probability measure; the second approach is an expected utility maximization problem but with a different probability measure. The reassignment of probability to each possible outcome draws the investor's attention to the bad outcome states.

Our focus is on the worst possible outcome of terminal wealth. By assumption, the wealth W at the end of the horizon is a random variable under probability measure P and its probability support Ξ might be bounded or unbounded. Let

$$W^L = \begin{cases} \sup\{K; \Pr[W \geq K] = 1\}, & \text{if } \Xi \text{ is bounded} \\ -\infty & \text{if } \Xi \text{ is unbounded} \end{cases} \tag{3.1}$$

be the *worst outcome of wealth* with respect to a given portfolio strategy. Investors develop optimal strategies to measure the overall performance (expected utility) while controlling the level of W^L. Since the market admits of no arbitrage, increasing the level of W^L would generally decrease the expected wealth at the same time (see Zhao and Ziemba 2001).

There is a trade-off between the overall wealth and the worst outcome. A natural way to balance these two competing aspects is to maximize a convex combination of "utilities" received from both the actual outcome and the worst outcome of wealth. The investor's objective function is

$$V(x, y) = \rho U(x) + (1 - \rho)U(y), \tag{3.2}$$

where x is the actual wealth outcome, y is the worst possible outcome, and $U(\cdot)$ is the investor's utility function. This is equivalent to maximizing expected utility with a different probability measure—that is, reducing the probabilities (density) of all states by the ratio ρ and adding the total reduced probability weights to that of the worst case outcome. The control intensity of downside losses increases as ρ decreases.

EXAMPLE 3.1. With the log utility function, an investor with initial wealth \$100 is to decide whether to play a gamble that pays \$1 with probability 0.8 and −\$2 with probability 0.2. If the gamble is taken, terminal wealth is

$$\begin{cases} \$101 & \text{with probability } 0.8 \\ \$98 & \text{with probability } 0.2. \end{cases}$$

Without the downside control variable, the expected utility is

$$0.8\ln(101) + 0.2\ln(98) = 4.6091 > \ln(100),$$

which implies that the investor would take the gamble. With downside control variable, the expected "utility" becomes

$$0.8\rho\ln(101) + 0.2\rho\ln(98) + (1 - \rho)\ln(98) = 0.8\rho[\ln(101) - \ln(98)] + \ln(98). \tag{3.3}$$

Hence, setting equation (3.3) to be greater than or equal to ln(100) implies that the investor takes the gamble only if $\rho > 0.8375$.

In general, a downside-control investor will not maximize the expected utility with the objective probability measure but with an adjusted one. To achieve this purpose, one needs only to shift a portion of the probability mass at higher outcomes to that at lower outcomes. To illustrate, consider a simple situation where each experiment produces one of two possible outcomes of wealth (good or bad) denoted by W_g and W_b. Let $\mathcal{W}$ be the set of possible outcomes which is assumed to be convex. The occurrence of the good outcome is at probability p. The problem for an ordinary investor with utility function of wealth $U(W)$ is

$$\max_{(W_g, W_b)\in\mathcal{W}} pU(W_g) + (1 - p)U(W_b).$$

But a downside risk control type investor will maximize the expected utility with a shifted probability measure Q. If the investor weighs the "good" state with probability $q = \rho \cdot p$, his investment problem is

$$\max_{(W_g, W_b)\in\mathcal{W}} qU(W_g) + (1 - q)U(W_b).$$

Since the marginal rate of substitution between these two approaches is changed, the optimal strategy is changed correspondingly. Figure 3.1 depicts the change of the optimal portfolio policy from point A to point B if downside risk control is considered.

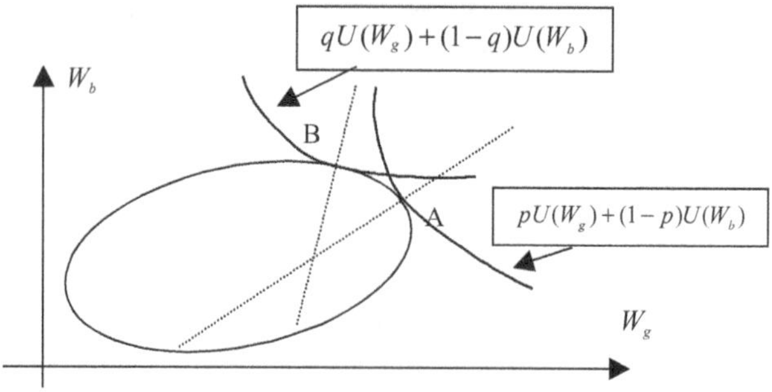

FIGURE 3.1. The change of the optimal policy with risk control.

Let $\mathcal{A}$ be the set of all admissible strategies defined by condition (2.5). Let $W(t)$ denote a possible wealth process generated by an admissible strategy. The investor's dynamic optimization problem is

$$(3.4) \qquad \max_{(\alpha(\cdot),\theta(\cdot))\in\mathcal{A}} E[\rho U(W(T)) + (1-\rho)U(W^L(T))]$$

$$\text{s.t.} \quad dW(t) = (\alpha(t)r(t)B(t) + \theta(t)^\top b(t))\,dt + \theta(t)^\top \sigma(t)\,dz(t).$$

If $U(\cdot)$ is an increasing function, investors prefer more wealth to less. Hence, an equivalent representation of model (3.4) is

$$(3.5) \qquad \sup_{K,(\alpha(\cdot),\theta(\cdot))} E[\rho U(W(T)) + (1-\rho)U(K)]$$

$$\text{s.t.} \quad dW(t) = (\alpha(t)r(t)B(t) + \theta(t)^\top b(t))\,dt + \theta(t)^\top \sigma(t)\,dz(t),$$

$$W(T) \geq K, \qquad P\text{-a.s.},$$

where K is constant through time and $(\alpha(\cdot), \theta(\cdot)) \in \mathcal{A}$ is an admissible strategy. By Theorem 2.1, (3.5) can be divided into two problems, an optimization problem identifying the optimal terminal wealth and a replication problem deriving the optimal portfolio strategy. The optimization problem is

$$(3.6) \qquad \sup_{W,K} E[\rho U(W) + (1-\rho)U(K)]$$

$$\text{s.t.} \quad E^Q\left[\frac{W}{B(T)}\right] = W_0$$

$$W \geq K, \qquad P\text{-a.s.},$$

where W is $\mathcal{F}_T$ measurable. We assume that $U(x)$ is strictly concave and increasing with a continuous first-order derivative. We write *Dom U* for $\{x : U(x) > -\infty\}$, hence *Dom* $U = (a_0, \infty)$ for some $a_0 > -\infty$. Since (2.5) implies that $W(T) \in L^1(P)$ and since the equality constraint in (3.6) implies that $W \in L^1(Q)$, the supremum in (3.6) should be sought in $L^1(P) \cap L^1(Q) \times$ *Dom U*.

REMARK 3.1. Obviously, if $\rho = 1$ the problem reduces to the traditional utility maximization problem. If $\rho = 0$ the investor will not make any investment under uncertainty (will put the money in the bank).

3.2. Model Solution

To solve model (3.6), we provide the following Extended Kuhn-Tucker Criterion.

THEOREM 3.1 (Extended Kuhn-Tucker Criterion). *The pair* (W, K) *is an optimal solution to model (3.6) if and only if the following conditions hold:*

(i) $\rho U_x(W) - \lambda_0 \frac{\eta(T)}{B(T)} + \lambda = 0$, P-a.s.
(ii) $(1-\rho)U_x(K) - E[\lambda] = 0$
(iii) $E[\frac{W\eta(T)}{B(T)}] - W_0 = 0$
(iv) $\lambda(W - K) = 0$, P-*a.s.*
(v) $\lambda \geq 0$, $W \geq K > a_0$ *for some constant* a_0, P-*a.s.*,

where $U_x(\cdot)$ *is the first-order derivative,* $\lambda_0 \in \Re$ *is the Lagrange multiplier on the martingale constraint, and* λ*, a random variable, is the multiplier on the wealth level constraints.*

Proof. See Appendix A. □

Conditions (i), (iv), and (v) yield

$$\lambda = \left(\frac{\lambda_0 \eta(T)}{B(T)} - \rho U_x(K)\right)^+. \tag{3.7}$$

If $W > K$, then $\lambda = 0$ and $W = U_x^{-1}(\frac{\lambda_0 \eta(T)}{\rho B(T)})$. Here $U_x^{-1}(\cdot)$ is the inverse of the marginal utility $U_x(\cdot)$. Hence, the investor's optimal terminal portfolio value is

$$W = K + \left(U_x^{-1}\left(\frac{\lambda_0 \eta(T)}{\rho B(T)}\right) - K\right)^+. \tag{3.8}$$

Since the portfolio value at any time $t \in [0, T]$ is the cost for hedging the terminal portfolio, by Theorem 2.1 its value at time t must be

$$\begin{aligned} W(t) &\equiv B(t)E^Q\left[\frac{W}{B(T)}\,\middle|\,\mathcal{F}_t\right] \\ &= B(t)E^Q\left[\left(\left(U_x^{-1}\left(\frac{\lambda_0 \eta(T)}{\rho B(T)}\right) - K\right)^+ + K\right) B(T)^{-1}\,\middle|\,\mathcal{F}_t\right], \end{aligned} \tag{3.9}$$

which establishes the following proposition.

PROPOSITION 3.1. *The investor's optimal wealth at time* t *is*

$$W(t) = B(t)E^Q[KB(T)^{-1} \mid \mathcal{F}_t] + B(t)E^Q\left[\left(U_x^{-1}\left(\frac{\lambda_0 \eta(T)}{\rho B(T)}\right) - K\right)^+ B(T)^{-1}\,\middle|\,\mathcal{F}_t\right]. \tag{3.10}$$

The following equations, which are used for calculating the optimal λ_0 and K, can be derived from the Extended Kuhn-Tucker Criterion since U_x is decreasing.

$$\begin{cases} (1-\rho)U_x(K) - \rho E\left[\left(\frac{\lambda_0 \eta(T)}{\rho B(T)} - U_x(K)\right)^+\right] = 0 \\ E^Q[KB(T)^{-1}] + E^Q\left[\left(U_x^{-1}\left(\frac{\lambda_0 \eta(T)}{\rho B(T)}\right) - K\right)^+ B(T)^{-1}\right] = W_0. \end{cases} \tag{3.11}$$

For a given utility function $U(x)$, the value of the portfolio can be calculated directly through the calculation of a conditional expectation (3.9), after solving equation (3.11) for λ_0 and K. The expectation term is similar to a standard expression for the valuation of contingent claims. If there is a way of transforming a stochastic process to a martingale, then methods for valuation of contingent claims can be applied to solve this problem. The second expression in equation (3.11) can be interpreted to mean that investors allocate wealth to only two assets: the riskless asset and a call option on a mutual fund. For an optimal λ_0 and K, taking $U_x^{-1}\left(\frac{\lambda_0\eta(T)}{\rho B(T)}\right)$ as the terminal value of a mutual fund which can be generated by the primary assets, the investor "invests" some amount in the option on the mutual fund with strike price K and the balance in the riskless asset that will guarantee the amount K needed for exercising these options. We discuss this issue in the next section.

Since

$$\frac{\lambda_0\eta(T)}{\rho B(T)} = U_x\left(U_x^{-1}\left(\frac{\lambda_0\eta(T)}{\rho B(T)}\right)\right) \quad \text{and} \quad U_x^{-1}\left(\frac{\lambda_0\eta(T)}{\rho B(T)}\right)$$

is the terminal wealth when there is no requirement on the worst possible outcome wealth, the first equation in (3.11) implies that, at optimality, the marginal utility at K is equal to the proportion of the decrement of the marginal utility induced by increasing the worst outcome to the level K; that is,

$$U_x(K) = \rho E\left[U_x(L)\right], \tag{3.12}$$

where $L = \min\{U_x^{-1}(\frac{\lambda_0\eta(T)}{\rho B(T)}), K\}$ is a random variable. This relation represents a trade-off between the expected wealth and the worst possible outcome of wealth. The marginal utility at K is a proportion of the expected decrement of the marginal utility induced by increasing wealth to the level K; see Figure 3.2. The economic interpretation is that investors can only increase the expected value of wealth by reducing the worst possible outcome wealth, which characterizes the potential losses.

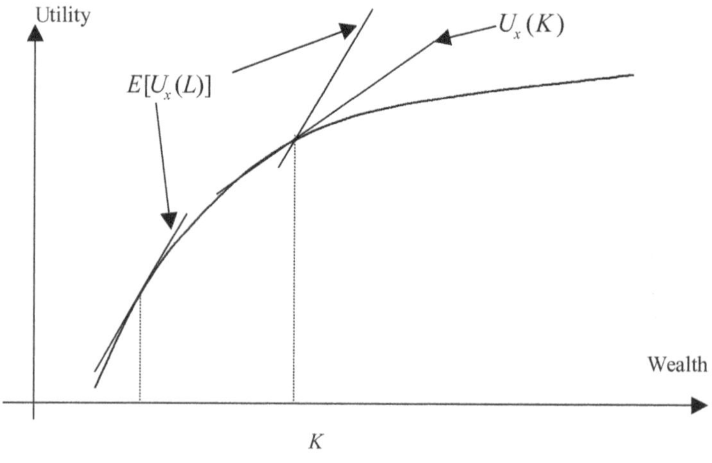

FIGURE 3.2. Marginal utility trade-off.

Having established the diffusion process for the wealth, we next derive the optimal trading strategy, which is equivalent to calculating the conditional expectation (3.10) for any t. This is usually a difficult task if parameters for asset prices are state-dependent because in such cases it is generally impossible to analytically compute the conditional density function under the risk-neutral probability. However, the problem can be transformed to the solution of a partial differential equation with boundary conditions to which numerical methods might apply.

If we can construct a stochastic process $v(t)$ that is a discounted martingale and has a terminal value equal to $U_x^{-1}\left(\frac{\lambda_0\eta(T)}{\rho B(T)}\right)$, then a partial differential equation can be derived. We can apply Theorem 2.1 with $Y = U_x^{-1}\left(\frac{\lambda_0\eta(T)}{\rho B(T)}\right)$ and $E^Q[B(T)^{-1}Y] = W_0 < \infty$. Let

$$v(t) = B(t)E^Q\left[U_x^{-1}\left(\frac{\lambda_0\eta(T)}{\rho B(T)}\right)B(T)^{-1} \mid \mathcal{F}_t\right].$$

Then $v(t)$ is a discounted martingale. By Theorem 2.1, the replicating portfolio value is given by the differential equation

$$dv(t) = r(t)v(t)\,dt + \tilde{\theta}(t)^\top\sigma(t)\,dz^Q(t),$$

where $\tilde{\theta}(t)$ is the solution of the utility maximization without the constraint $W \geq K$. $\tilde{\theta}$ may depend not only on the current asset prices but also on past observations. If $\tilde{\theta}(t)$ is a function of $(t, B(t), S(t), v(t))$ which means the optimal strategy is Markovian, then $(B(t), S(t), v(t))$ are jointly Markovian. The portfolio value can be represented as a function of $(t, B(t), S(t), v(t))$.

Denote $\xi(t) = \begin{pmatrix} S(t) \\ v(t) \end{pmatrix}$ and $\hat{\sigma}(t) = \begin{pmatrix} \mathbf{I} \\ \tilde{\theta}(t)^\top \end{pmatrix}\sigma(t)$. $\xi(t)$ is an $(n+1)$-vector and $\hat{\sigma}(t)$ is an $(n+1) \times n$ matrix.

$$d\xi(t) = \begin{pmatrix} dS(t) \\ dv(t) \end{pmatrix} = r(t)\xi(t)\,dt + \hat{\sigma}(t)\,dz^Q(t).$$

Let $W(t) = F(t, B(t), \xi(t))$ be the portfolio value at time t, where $F(t, x, y)$ is a real-valued function on $\Re^+ \times \Re \times \Re^{n+1}$. By Ito's formula, the optimal strategy is characterized as in Proposition 3.2.

PROPOSITION 3.2. *Assume that the optimal portfolio value $W(t) = F(t, B(t), \xi(t))$ where F has continuous partial derivatives. Then F satisfies the following partial differential equation with associated boundary conditions:*

$$(3.13) \qquad \begin{cases} -r(t)F + F_t + r(t)F_x x + r(t)F_y^\top y + \frac{1}{2}\mathrm{tr}\left(F_{yy}\hat{\sigma}(t)\hat{\sigma}(t)^\top\right) = 0 \\ F(0, 1, y) = W_0 \\ F(T, x, y) = K + (v - K)^+ \end{cases}$$

where tr( ) *stands for the trace function of a matrix and $y = (S, v)^\top$. The optimal strategy is*

$$(3.14) \qquad \begin{cases} \theta(t) = F_S + F_v\tilde{\theta}(t) \\ \alpha(t) = (W(t) - \theta(t)^\top S(t))/B(t). \end{cases}$$

The boundary condition for the above partial differential equation follows from (3.9).

Finding the optimal strategy for the original problem has been divided into two steps: (i) calculate the optimal strategy $\tilde{\theta}$ when there is no wealth level constraints, and (ii) find the optimal wealth as a solution to a partial differential equation and derive the optimal strategy thereafter. This approach is similar to the method used in Cox and Huang (1989) where an auxiliary process is used for deriving the optimal strategy. Since directly observable processes are the primary assets and the portfolio process, all other processes that are related to the derivation of the optimal trading strategies must be replicable using primary assets. To implement the dynamic optimal strategy one has to synthesize these processes on the side as if they were market-derived assets. This is especially important when we interpret the option investment strategy. Since the underlying asset of a call option is replicable using primary assets, we have to choose a suitable auxiliary process such that we can easily derive the optimal strategy.

4. OPTION STRATEGY INTERPRETATION

One approach to deal with downside risk is an option strategy. An option strategy for investment is usually used for the purpose of hedging. Before making decisions, investors have to think about how much to invest in different projects while simultaneously achieving the risk control. Exchange-traded options might not be suitable for specific investors. Not only might the strike price (the target) but also the investment horizon be different from the investor's concern. A more dynamic way is needed for creating such strategies. For an application of this idea, see Zhao and Ziemba (2001), which considers how to create synthetic option strategies with transaction cost in a discrete time and discrete state space model.

An alternative, possibly more insightful, interpretation of the optimal solution to the problem matches the view stated above. Using a martingale approach, the portfolio value at each time is a discounted Q-martingale given by (3.10), which can be interpreted as a strategy of investing in the call option on the mutual fund. In light of the option pricing methods, we may be able to construct an optimal strategy using the following four steps:

1. Find the optimal λ_0 and K.
2. Create the dynamic mutual fund using the $n+1$ available primary assets.
3. Calculate the hedging portfolio for a call option with strike price K on the mutual fund.
4. Transform the hedging portfolio into the portfolio of the primary assets.

REMARK 4.1. The first step can be obtained by solving (3.11). The second step is difficult to solve because finding the mutual fund

$$v(t) = B(t)E^Q\left[B(T)^{-1}U_x^{-1}\left(\frac{\lambda_0\eta(T)}{\rho B(T)}\right)\middle| \mathcal{F}_t\right]$$

is an intractable problem if market's parameters and the investor's utility function are arbitrarily chosen. The third step is to apply option pricing methodologies and the derivation of the hedging strategies. The last step is to combine the two decomposed methods together to obtain the optimal portfolio of the primary assets.

Two ways of obtaining the mutual fund $v(t)$ are calculating directly the conditional expectation and solving a boundary problem. These general approaches are valid for broad settings of market parameters and the utility function. Since a martingale is uniquely determined by the terminal value of the martingale and the filtration, we might want to look for a process that has the same terminal value as $U_x^{-1}\left(\frac{\lambda_0\eta(T)}{\rho B(T)}\right)$. Instead of going through a general approach, we might want to examine how the process $m(t) = U_x^{-1}\left(\frac{\lambda_0\eta(t)}{\rho B(t)}\right)$ will move with respect to the uncertainty and to derive the process that we need. Applying Itô's formula and assuming as much smoothness as required yields

$$
\begin{aligned}
(4.1)\qquad dm(t) &= \frac{1}{U_{xx}} d\left(\frac{\lambda_0 \eta(t)}{\rho B(t)}\right) - \frac{U_{xxx}}{2U_{xx}^3}\left(d\left(\frac{\lambda_0\eta(t)}{\rho B(t)}\right)\right)^2 \\
&= \frac{1}{U_{xx}}\left(-U_x\kappa(t)^\top dz(t) - U_x r(t)\,dt\right) - \frac{U_{xxx}U_x^2\|\kappa(t)\|^2}{2U_{xx}^3}\,dt \\
&= \frac{-U_x\left(2r(t)U_{xx}^2 + \|\kappa(t)\|^2 U_x U_{xxx}\right)}{2U_{xx}^3}\,dt + \frac{-U_x}{U_{xx}}\kappa(t)^\top dz(t).
\end{aligned}
$$

From (4.1), one can observe that the mutual fund chosen by investors depends only on the risk aversion and the skewness but not the specific form of the utility function. This implies that all investors with the same risk aversion and skewness of the utility function will choose the same mutual fund to invest, but this does not necessarily show that all investors with such a utility function will adopt the same investment strategy.

If the drift term in (4.1) is $rm(t)$, then $m(t)$ is a discounted martingale and option valuation models can be used. However, $m(t)$ is not a martingale in general, but if we can transform $m(t)$ to a martingale process that has the same terminal value as $v(T)$, then the problem has been reduced to an option valuation problem. The following proposition deals with this issue.

PROPOSITION 4.1 (Drift killing). *If a stochastic process $X(t)$ follows the diffusion*

$$dX(t) = \mu(t)X(t)\,dt + \gamma(t)^\top dz^Q(t)$$

then $\exp\{-\int_0^t \mu(s)\,ds\}X(t)$ will be a local Q-martingale. Furthermore, if $\mu(t)$ is deterministic, then $\exp\{\int_t^T \mu(s)\,ds\}X(t)$ is a local Q-martingale that has the same terminal value as $X(T)$ almost surely.

Proof. Since $\mu(t)$ is adapted, $\exp\{-\int_0^t \mu(s)\,ds\}$ is also $\mathcal{F}_t$ adapted and

$$d\exp\left\{-\int_0^t \mu(s)\,ds\right\}X(t) = \exp\left\{-\int_0^t \mu(s)\,ds\right\}\gamma(t)\,dz^Q(s).$$

Hence, $\exp\{-\int_0^t \mu(s)\,ds\}X(t)$ is a local Q-martingale.

If $\mu(t)$ is deterministic, then $\exp\{\int_t^T \mu(s)\,ds\}$ is also $\mathcal{F}_t$ adapted and

$$d\exp\left\{\int_t^T \mu(s)\,ds\right\}X(t) = \exp\left\{\int_t^T \mu(s)\,ds\right\}\gamma(t)\,dz^Q(s).$$

So, $\exp\{\int_t^T \mu(s)\,ds\}X(t)$ is a local Q-martingale with terminal value $X(t)$. □

It would be convenient if the drift rate in (4.1), $\frac{U_x(-2r(t)U_{xx}^2 - \|\kappa(t)\|^2 U_x U_{xxx})}{2U_{xx}^3}$, were a deterministic function of t, for in such cases we can apply Proposition 4.1 to transform $m(t)$ to a martingale. For some types of utility functions (e.g., the HARA family) with the assumption of geometric Brownian motion, we can verify that the drift rate of $v(t)$ is a deterministic function of t. However, in more general settings, this will not be the case and other approaches must be found.

We have discussed how to generate the mutual fund for a given utility function using the market's primary assets. The partial differential equation approach and the direct calculation of the conditional expectation are considered as general approaches. The optimal investment strategy is equivalent to investing in the riskless asset and in a call option on the synthetic mutual fund which has the same terminal value as $U_x^{-1}\left(\frac{\lambda_0 \eta(T)}{\rho B(T)}\right)$. The option valuation method can be used to generate the optimal investment portfolio. Having established the mutual fund, we now find the generating portfolio using primary assets. The existence and computation of this generating portfolio is given by Theorem 2.1. For future use, we state this result in the following proposition.

PROPOSITION 4.2. *If the stochastic process* $\frac{X(t)}{B(t)}$ *is a Q-martingale, that is,*

$$dX(t) = r(t)X(t)\,dt + \gamma(t)^\top dz^Q(t),$$

then the self-financing strategy $(\alpha(t), \theta(t))$ *generates* $X(t)$, *where*

$$\begin{cases} \alpha(t)B(t) + \theta(t)^\top S(t) = X(t) \\ \theta(t)^\top \sigma(t) = \gamma(t)^\top. \end{cases} \tag{4.2}$$

The next step is to compute the hedging portfolio of the call option on the auxiliary mutual fund. This is the most difficult task in the whole process if the instantaneous mean vector and the volatility matrix are specified as general diffusion coefficients. The call option can be hedged by the mutual fund $v(t)$ and the market's primary assets. Let $C(t, B(t), S(t), v(t))$ be the value of the option at time t. By Itô's formula, let $\xi(t)$ and $\hat{\sigma}(t)$ be as defined in Proposition 3.2,

$$\begin{aligned} dC(t, B(t), \xi(t)) = (C_t + r(t)B(t)C_B + r(t)C_\xi \xi(t) \\ + \frac{1}{2}\operatorname{tr}\big(C_{\xi\xi}\hat{\sigma}(t)\hat{\sigma}(t)^\top\big)\,dt + C_\xi^\top \hat{\sigma}(t)\,dz^Q(t). \end{aligned} \tag{4.3}$$

Since $C(t)$ should be also replicable by using $(B(t), S(t), v(t))$, let $(\alpha^v(t), \theta^S(t), \theta^v(t))$ be the hedging portfolio of the call option. Then

$$d(C(t, B(t), S(t), v(t)) = r(t)C(t, B(t), v(t))\,dt + (\theta^S(t)^\top + \theta^v(t)\tilde{\theta}(t)^\top)\sigma(t)\,dz^Q(t). \tag{4.4}$$

Equating (4.3) and (4.4) yields the following proposition.

PROPOSITION 4.3. *Let* $dv(t) = r(t)v(t)\,dt + \tilde{\theta}(t)^\top \sigma(t)\,dz^Q(t)$, *where* $\tilde{\theta}(t)$ *is a non-random function of* $(t, B(t), S(t), v(t))$. *The value of the call option is the solution to the boundary problem*

$$\begin{cases} C_t + r(t)BC_B + r(t)C_\xi \xi(t) + \frac{1}{2}\operatorname{tr}\big(C_{\xi\xi}\hat{\sigma}(t)\hat{\sigma}(t)^\top\big) - r(t)C = 0 \\ C(T, B, S, v) = (v - K)^+. \end{cases} \tag{4.5}$$

The number of shares of the mutual fund $\theta^v(t)$ *and the number of units of risky assets* $\theta^S(t)$ *needed for the hedging portfolio are given by the following linear relation*

$$\theta^S(t)^\top + \theta^v(t)\tilde{\theta}(t) = C_S^\top + C_v \tilde{\theta}(t)^\top.$$

For general settings of the market asset price model, we must apply numerical methods to solve the partial differential equation. However, in some cases, a closed-form solution can be obtained. We discuss this in the next section. The following theorem, which is implied by Propositions (4.2) and (4.3), summarizes how to convert an option hedging portfolio to the optimal investment portfolio of the primary assets.

THEOREM 4.1. *Let the mutual fund prices $v(t)$ follow the stochastic process*

$$dv(t) = r(t)v(t)\,dt + \tilde{\theta}(t)^\top \sigma(t)\,dz^Q(t)$$

and $(\alpha^v(t), \theta^S(t), \theta^v(t))$ is the hedging portfolio for the call option on $v(t)$ with strike price K, then the optimal investment portfolio $(\alpha(t), \theta(t))$ is given by

$$\begin{cases} \theta(t) = \theta^S(t) + \theta^v(t)\tilde{\theta}(t) \\ \alpha(t) = (W(t) - \theta(t)^\top S(t))\,B(t)^{-1}, \end{cases}$$

where $W(t)$ is the wealth at time t.

5. HARA UTILITY AND GBM PRICES

In this section, we consider a specialization of the model in which investors have a HARA utility function satisfying

$$-\frac{U_x}{U_{xx}} = \alpha x + \beta,$$

where $\alpha > 0$ is assumed. The case $\alpha = 0$ is trivial. The assumption of geometric Brownian motion for prices implies that

$$r(t) = r, \qquad \sigma(t) = \begin{pmatrix} S_1(t) & & & \\ & S_2(t) & & \\ & & \ddots & \\ & & & S_n(t) \end{pmatrix} \sigma, \qquad b(t) = \begin{pmatrix} b_1 S_1(t) \\ b_2 S_2(t) \\ \vdots \\ b_n S_n(t) \end{pmatrix},$$

where r, σ, b are constant matrices. By (4.1),

$$\begin{aligned} dm(t) &= \frac{-U_x\left(2r\,U_{xx}^2 + \|\kappa\|^2 U_x U_{xxx}\right)}{2U_{xx}^3} dt + \frac{-U_x}{U_{xx}} \kappa^\top dz(t) \\ &= (\alpha m(t) + \beta)\left[\left(r + \frac{1}{2}(\alpha - 1)\|\kappa\|^2\right) dt + \kappa^\top dz^Q(t)\right]. \end{aligned}$$

Let $v(t) = \left(m(t) + \frac{\beta}{\alpha}\right) \cdot \exp\left\{(\alpha - 1)(r + \frac{1}{2}\alpha\|\kappa\|^2)(T - t)\right\}$. By Proposition 4.1, $\frac{v(t)}{B(t)}$ is a Q-martingale, and

(5.1) $$dv(t) = r\,v(t)\,dt + \alpha v(t)\kappa^\top dz^Q(t).$$

It is well known that $v(t)$ is the standard optimal portfolio value for the utility function $U(x)$ that has a constant relative risk aversion index $1/\alpha$. Since $v(T) = m(T) + \frac{\beta}{\alpha}$, $E^Q[(m(T) - K)^+ B(T)^{-1}]$ is equal to the price of the call option on $v(t)$ with strike price $K + \frac{\beta}{\alpha}$. Hence, by the Black-Scholes formula

$$E^Q[(m(T)-K)^+B(T)^{-1}] = E^Q\left[\left(v(T)-\left(K+\frac{\beta}{\alpha}\right)\right)^+ B(T)^{-1}\right]$$
$$= \left(m(0)+\frac{\beta}{\alpha}\right)e^{(\alpha-1)(r+\frac{1}{2}\alpha\|\kappa\|^2)T}\cdot\Phi(\epsilon_1)$$
$$-\left(K+\frac{\beta}{\alpha}\right)e^{-rT}\cdot\Phi(\epsilon_2),$$

where

$$\begin{cases} \epsilon_1 = \dfrac{\ln\frac{\alpha m(0)+\beta}{\alpha K+\beta}+\left(\alpha r+\frac{1}{2}(2\alpha^2-\alpha)\|\kappa\|^2\right)T}{\alpha\|\kappa\|\sqrt{T}} \\ \epsilon_2 = \epsilon_1 - \alpha\|\kappa\|\sqrt{T} \\ m(0) = U_x^{-1}\left(\frac{\lambda_0}{\rho}\right) \end{cases}$$

and $\Phi(x)$ is the standard normal cumulative distribution function.

Similarly, $E[(\frac{\lambda_0\eta(T)}{\rho B(T)}-U_x(K))^+] = \frac{\lambda_0}{\rho}U_x(K)E^Q[(\frac{1}{U_x(K)}-\frac{\rho B(T)}{\lambda_0\eta(T)})^+B(T)^{-1}]$ can be calculated using the price formula of the put option on the "asset," $\frac{\rho B(t)}{\lambda_0\eta(t)}$, with strike price $\frac{1}{U_x(K)}$. Since

$$d\left(\frac{\rho B(t)}{\lambda_0\eta(t)}\right) = \frac{\rho B(t)}{\lambda_0\eta(t)}(r\,dt+\kappa^\top dz^Q(t)),$$

$\frac{\rho B(t)}{\lambda_0\eta(t)}$ is a discounted martingale, by the Black-Scholes formula,

$$E^Q\left[\left(\frac{1}{U_x(K)}-\frac{\rho B(T)}{\lambda_0\eta(T)}\right)^+ B(T)^{-1}\right] = \frac{1}{U_x(K)}\cdot e^{-rT}\cdot\Phi(-\epsilon_2') - \frac{\rho}{\lambda_0}\cdot\Phi(-\epsilon_1'), \tag{5.2}$$

where

$$\begin{cases} \epsilon_1' = \dfrac{\ln\frac{\rho U_x(K)}{\lambda_0}+(r+\frac{1}{2}\|\kappa\|^2)T}{\|\kappa\|T} \\ \epsilon_2' = \epsilon_1' - \|\kappa\|\sqrt{T}. \end{cases}$$

We are now able to calculate the optimal λ_0 and K. Equation (3.11) becomes

$$\begin{cases} (1-\rho) - \frac{\lambda_0 e^{-rT}}{U_x(K)}\Phi(-\epsilon_2') + \rho\cdot\Phi(-\epsilon_1') = 0 \\ K\cdot e^{-rT} + (m(0)+\frac{\beta}{\alpha})e^{(\alpha-1)(r+\frac{1}{2}\alpha\|\kappa\|^2)T}\cdot\Phi(\epsilon_1) - (K+\frac{\beta}{\alpha})e^{-rT}\cdot\Phi(\epsilon_2) = W_0. \end{cases} \tag{5.3}$$

The optimal λ_0 and K are the solutions to the transcendental equation system(5.3).

The investor's wealth at time t is

$$W(t) = B(t)E^Q[W_T B(T)^{-1}\,|\,\mathcal{F}_t]$$
$$= B(t)KE^Q[B(T)^{-1}\,|\,\mathcal{F}_t] + B(t)E^Q\left[\left(v(T)-\left(K+\frac{\beta}{\alpha}\right)\right)^+ B(T)^{-1}\,\middle|\,\mathcal{F}_t\right]$$
$$= K\cdot e^{r(t-T)} + C(t, B(t), v(t)),$$

which is equivalent to holding a call option on the mutual fund and investing the balance in the riskless asset. Hence, the investor's optimal strategy is to replicate this call option.

THEOREM 5.1. *Let $\tilde{\theta}(t) = (\tilde{\theta}_1(t), \ldots, \tilde{\theta}_n(t))^\top$ be the replicating portfolio of the mutual fund, where $\tilde{\theta}_i^m(t)$ is the number of shares of the ith risky asset. Then*

$$\tilde{\theta}(t) = \alpha v(t) I_S^{-1}(\sigma\sigma^\top)^{-1}(b - r\mathbf{1}),$$

where I_S is the diagonal matrix with risky asset prices as the entries, and the optimal investment portfolio of the primary assets is

$$\theta(t) = \Phi(\epsilon(t)) \cdot \tilde{\theta}(t), \tag{5.4}$$

where

$$\epsilon(t) = \frac{\ln \frac{v(t)}{\alpha K + \beta} + \left(r + \frac{1}{2}\alpha(b - r\mathbf{1})^\top(\sigma\sigma^\top)^{-1}(b - r\mathbf{1})\right)(T - t)}{\sqrt{(b - r\mathbf{1})^\top(\sigma\sigma^\top)^{-1}(b - r\mathbf{1})(T - t)}},$$

where λ_0 and K are given by (5.3).

Proof. By Theorem 2.1, v is replicable, so if $\tilde{\theta}(t)$ is the replicating portfolio, then

$$dv(t) = rv(t)\,dt + \tilde{\theta}(t)^\top I_S\sigma\, dz^Q(t).$$

Hence, cf. (5.1),

$$\tilde{\theta}(t)^\top I_S\sigma = \alpha v(t)\kappa^\top,$$

which yields

$$\begin{aligned} \tilde{\theta}(t) &= \alpha I_S^{-1}(\sigma^\top)^{-1}\kappa \\ &= \alpha I_S^{-1}(\sigma\sigma^\top)^{-1}(b - r\mathbf{1}). \end{aligned} \tag{5.5}$$

The number of units of the mutual fund needed to hedge this call option is equal to $\Phi(\epsilon(t))$ by the Black-Scholes formula. Hence, (5.4) is obtained. It is straightforward to show that θ is admissible; that is, it satisfies (2.5). □

Theorem 5.1 indicates that an investor will implement the optimal portfolio by first synthesizing the optimal portfolio in which the worst possible outcome wealth is not included (creating a mutual fund or an index), and then calculating the hedging portfolio for a call option on this mutual fund. This two-step procedure constructs the optimal investment strategy.

Notice that $v(t)$ of (5.1) does not depend on the risk control intensity ρ. Hence, if investors are identified by the risk control intensity ρ, the mutual fund separation theory applies. The following two results are implied by the previous discussion.

COROLLARY 5.1. *For investors with a HARA utility function, there exists a mutual fund such that the optimal investment strategy is equivalent to buying a call option on this mutual fund.*

COROLLARY 5.2. *For an investor with a HARA utility function, the optimal strategy is to invest in a mutual fund and the riskless asset. Furthermore, if all risky assets jointly follow a multivariate geometric Brownian motion, then this mutual fund must have used a fixed mix strategy as in Merton (1969).*

By equation (4.1), we observe that, if investors have same risk aversion and same risk skewness, their investment strategy should be identical.

EXAMPLE 5.1. We now examine the sensitivity of the investment strategy as the downside risk control intensity changes. Consider a two-asset market, one riskless and one risky asset. The riskless asset evolves with an annual continuously compound rate $r = 0.05$, and the risky asset has an instantaneous mean rate $b = 0.10$ and instantaneous volatility $\sigma = 0.3$. The market price for risk is

$$\eta(t) = e^{-0.167z(t)-0.014t}.$$

Suppose an investment horizon of $T = 1$. We use a logarithmic utility function as the investor's objective function. However the theory and the computational method apply to general concave utility functions. Then, the investor's objective function for the optimization model is

$$\rho \ln W(T) + (1-\rho)\ln K.$$

Hence the process $m(t) = \frac{\rho B(t)}{\lambda_0 \eta(t)}$ is a discounted Q-martingale as proved in (4.1). The optimal λ_0 and K satisfy

$$\begin{cases} 1-\rho-\lambda_0\left[Ke^{-rT}\Phi(-\epsilon_2)-\frac{\rho}{\lambda_0}\Phi(-\epsilon_1)\right]=0 \\ Ke^{-rT}+\frac{\rho}{\lambda_0}\Phi(\epsilon_1)-Ke^{-rT}\Phi(\epsilon_2)=W_0, \end{cases}$$

which implies that

$$\lambda_0 = \frac{1}{W_0},$$

and K satisfies that

$$K = W_0 e^{rT}\left(\frac{1-\rho\Phi(\epsilon_1)}{1-\Phi(\epsilon_2)}\right).$$

Note that ϵ_1 and ϵ_1' are identical when $\alpha \to 1$ and are dependent on K.

An investor may be interested in examining the expected return for the choice of different downside control intensities. So, the problem arises of how to choose an optimal ρ that will maximize one's performance under some risk measure accommodating the control of downside losses.

Value at risk is a popular measure that has been used in risk management practice. It is the minimum loss with respect to the expected return for a small tolerance p in probability where p is usually chosen between 0.01 or 0.05. Hence, the VaR of W is

$$\text{VaR}(W) := E[W] - K_W,$$

where K_W is the maximum such that

$$\Pr[W \le K_W] \le p.$$

Table 5.1 describes the performances with varying downside control intensities and the tolerance in probability is chosen to be 0.05. As ρ is increasing, the worst case outcome

TABLE 5.1
The Optimal K, $E[W(T)]$, and VaR

ρ	K	$E[W(T)]$	VaR
0.8	1.0441	1.0543	0.0102
0.81	1.0428	1.0548	0.0121
0.82	1.0411	1.0553	0.0142
0.83	1.0393	1.0570	0.0178
0.84	1.0371	1.0565	0.0193
0.85	1.0346	1.0563	0.0217
0.86	1.0317	1.0593	0.0276
0.87	1.0283	1.0582	0.0299
0.88	1.0245	1.0614	0.0369
0.89	1.0200	1.0601	0.0401
0.9	1.0148	1.0633	0.0485
0.91	1.0088	1.0633	0.0545
0.92	1.0017	1.0647	0.0629
0.93	0.9934	1.0642	0.0708
0.94	0.9834	1.0690	0.0856
0.95	0.9712	1.0695	0.0983
0.96	0.9560	1.0709	0.1149
0.97	0.9363	1.0737	0.1374
0.98	0.9088	1.0744	0.1659
0.99	0.8643	1.0765	0.2122
1	0.4884	1.0826	0.2707

decreases and the overall wealth represented by the expected value of the terminal wealth increases. This shows how investors trade off risk and return. For example, if VaR $< 5\%$ is required, one can implement the optimal strategy with $\rho = 0.9$.

The Sharpe ratio, as a measure of performance, is the ratio of excess expected return over the standard deviation. However, this measure considers both overperformance and underperformance as risk. Here we use a new performance measure that uses VaR and quantifies only the downside losses as risk:

$$\tau := \frac{E[W(T)] - W_0 e^{rT}}{\mathrm{VaR}[W(T)]}$$

For some results, see Zhao and Ziemba (2000). This measure of performance describes the return rate over a unit of pure losses against the market. By observation, the optimal ρ which maximizes τ is about 0.83 for this example.

6. CONCLUDING REMARKS

In this paper, we have incorporated a portfolio's worst outcome into the investment objective function. This characterizes the trade-off between the realized wealth and the possible downside losses. One of the main results of this paper shows that the investor's optimized portfolio is equivalent to holding a call option on a mutual fund which can be generated with the market's primary assets and the investor's utility function. After creating the mutual fund, investors will allocate the available wealth to the risky assets and the riskless asset in a way that is equivalent to the hedging portfolio of a call option on this mutual fund. Hence, finding the investors' optimal portfolio is equivalent to pricing a call option and deriving its hedging portfolio from there.

Another result is that the expected marginal utility at the worst outcome is equal to the expected marginal utility at the wealth below the worst outcome times the downside control intensity. This presents a criterion for investors to make decisions. Increasing the level of expected wealth will automatically lower the portfolio worst outcome which also represents the potential loss.

Finally, we give an analytical solution when the utility function is HARA and the asset prices follow a multivariate geometric Brownian motion. Merton (1971) showed that the optimal portfolio is a leveraged growth optimal portfolio for HARA utility functions, and Cox and Huang (1989) showed that the optimal portfolio weights are no longer linear in wealth if bankruptcy is considered. This paper confirms this result and it has a two-step interpretation as well. An issue for further study is the extension of the methods developed in this paper to the case in which transaction costs are incorporated.

APPENDIX

Proof of Theorem 3.1. We wish to apply Theorem II.1.4 of Neustadt (1976) to (3.6). If we let $\bar{U}(x) = -U(x)$, a convex function, then (3.6) is equivalent to

$$\text{(A.1)}\qquad \begin{aligned} &\inf_{W\in L^1(P)\cap L^1(Q),\, K\in Dom\, U} && E[\rho \bar{U}(W) + (1-\rho)\bar{U}(K)] \\ &\text{s.t.} && E^Q\left[\frac{W}{B(T)}\right] = W_0 \\ & && W \geq K, \qquad P\text{-a.s.} \end{aligned}$$

Let $\mathcal{Y} = L^1(P)\bigcap L^1(Q) \times \Re$, a linear vector space, and

$$\mathcal{C} = \{(y_1, y_2) \in \mathcal{Y} : y_1(\omega) \geq y_2 > a_0, \text{ a.s.}\}.$$

(i) $\mathcal{C}$ is finitely open in itself. In fact, if $y^0 \in \mathcal{C}$, $y^i \in \mathcal{C}$, then

$$z(\lambda) \equiv y^0 + \sum_{i=1}^{n} \lambda_i (y^i - y^0) = \left(1 - \sum_1^n \lambda_i\right) y^0 + \sum_1^n \lambda_i y^i, \qquad (\lambda_i \geq 0),$$

hence $z_2(\lambda) > a_0$ and $z_1(\lambda) \geq z_2(\lambda)$ provided $\sum_1^n \lambda_i \leq 1$. In that case $z(\lambda) \in \mathcal{C}$ (i.e., $\mathcal{C}$ is finitely open in itself).

(ii) Let $\varphi^1(y) \equiv E^Q[B(T)^{-1} y_1]$: $\mathcal{C} \to \Re$ and

$$\begin{aligned} D\varphi^1(y; v) &= \lim_{\varepsilon \downarrow 0} \frac{\varphi^1(y + \varepsilon v) - \varphi^1(y)}{\varepsilon} \\ &= \lim_{\varepsilon\downarrow 0} E^Q\left[B(T)^{-1} v_1\right] \\ &= E^Q\left[B(T)^{-1} v_1\right]. \end{aligned}$$

So φ is finitely differentiable.

(iii) Let $\varphi^0(y) \equiv \rho E\bar{U}(y_1) + (1-\rho)\bar{U}(y_2)$ for $y \in \mathcal{C}$. Since $\bar{U}$ is decreasing, then $\bar{U}(y_1(\omega)) \leq \bar{U}(y_2)$. Since $\bar{U}$ is convex, then $\bar{U}(y_1(\omega)) \geq \bar{U}(y_2) + \rho \bar{U}_x(y_2)(y_1(\omega) - y_2)$. It follows that

$$\bar{U}(y_2) + \rho \bar{U}_x(y_2)(Ey_1 - y_2) \leq \varphi^0(y) \leq \bar{U}(y_2),$$

so $\varphi^0 : \mathcal{C} \to \Re$.

Moreover, φ^0 is finitely semi-differentiable, that is, $\exists\, D\varphi^0(y; v)$, convex in v, and $D\varphi^0(y; 0) = 0$, such that

$$\limsup_{\varepsilon \downarrow 0} \frac{\varphi^0(y + \varepsilon v) - \varphi^0(y)}{\varepsilon} \leq D\varphi^0(y; v), \qquad \forall v \in \text{cone}(\mathcal{C} - y)$$

uniformly in v in any convex polyhedron. (Note that $v \in \text{cone}(\mathcal{C} - y)$ means $v = k(z - y)$ for some $k \geq 0$ and some $z \in \mathcal{C}$.) This follows since

$$\limsup_{\varepsilon \downarrow 0} \frac{\rho E[\bar{U}(y_1 + \varepsilon v_1) - \bar{U}(y_1)] + (1-\rho)[\bar{U}(y_2 + \varepsilon v_2) - \bar{U}(y_2)]}{\varepsilon}$$
$$\leq \limsup_{\varepsilon \downarrow 0} \rho E[\bar{U}_x(y_1 + \varepsilon v_1) v_1] + (1-\rho)[\bar{U}_x(y_2 + \varepsilon v_2) v_2]$$
$$= \rho E[\bar{U}_x(y_1) v_1] + (1-\rho) \bar{U}_x(y_2) v_2$$

and the last limit is uniform in $v \in$ convex hull $\{v^1, \ldots, v^n\} \equiv V$. The inequality above follows from convexity of $\bar{U}$. For the equality we observe that the decreasing nature of U_x implies

$$\bar{U}_x\Big(u_2 + \varepsilon \min_j v_2^j\Big) \leq \bar{U}_x(u_2 + \varepsilon v_2) \leq \bar{U}_x\Big(u_2 + \varepsilon \max_j v_2^j\Big),$$

and then the the continuity of U_x implies

$$\limsup_{\varepsilon \downarrow 0} \sup_{v \in V} |[\bar{U}_x(y_2 + \varepsilon v_2) - \bar{U}_x(y_2)] v_2| = 0.$$

Similarly,

$$\limsup_{\varepsilon \downarrow 0} \sup_{v \in V} |[\bar{U}_x(y_1 + \varepsilon v_1) - \bar{U}_x(y_1)] v_1| = 0, \qquad \forall \omega \in \Omega.$$

Since

$$0 \geq \bar{U}_x(y_1 + \varepsilon v_1) \geq \bar{U}_x(y_2 + \varepsilon v_2) \geq \bar{U}_x\Big(y_2 + \varepsilon \min_j v_2^j\Big) \equiv k_0 > -\infty$$

for sufficiently small $\varepsilon > 0$ (because $v_2^j > a_0$, $1 \leq j \leq n$), then

$$\sup_{v \in V} |[\bar{U}_x(y_1 + \varepsilon v_1) - \bar{U}_x(y_1)] v_1| \leq \sup_{v \in V} |\bar{U}_x(y_1 + \varepsilon v_1) - \bar{U}_x(y_1)| \sup_j |v_1^j|$$
$$\leq 2k_0 \sum_j |v_1^j| \in L^1(P).$$

By the dominated convergence theorem

$$\lim_{\varepsilon \downarrow 0} E[\bar{U}_x(y_1 + \varepsilon v_1) v_1] = E[\bar{U}_x(y_1) v_1]$$

uniformly in $v \in V$. It follows that $D\varphi^0(y; v) = \rho E\big[\bar{U}_x(y_1) v_1\big] + (1-\rho)\bar{U}_x(y_2) v_2$.

Now we prove the conditions of Theorem 3.1 are necessary. Theorem II.1.4 of Neustadt (1976) implies that if (W, K) solves (A.1) then there exist Lagrange multipliers $\phi \leq 0, \lambda_0$, not both zero, such that

$$\text{(A.2)} \qquad \phi E[\rho \bar{U}_x(W)v_1 + (1-\rho)\bar{U}_x(K)v_2] - \lambda_0 E^Q\left[B(T)^{-1}v_1\right] \leq 0$$

and

$$E^Q[B(T)^{-1}W] = W_0, \quad W \geq K > a_0, \quad \text{a.s.}$$

for all $v \in [\mathcal{C} - (W, K)$—that is, $v = (z_1 - W, z_2 - K)$ and $z = (z_1, z_2) \in \mathcal{C}$.

First, $\phi \neq 0$, for if $\phi = 0$, then (A.2) implies $\lambda_0 E^Q[\frac{v_1}{B(T)}] \geq 0$ and $\lambda_0 \neq 0$. Choose $p \in (-1, K - a_0)$ and set $z = (W - p, K - p)$. Then $z \in \mathcal{C}$ and

$$0 \leq \lambda_0 E^Q\left[\frac{v_1}{B(T)}\right] = \lambda_0 E^Q\left[\frac{z_1 - W}{B(T)}\right] = -\lambda_0 p E^Q[B(T)^{-1}].$$

Since p can be both positive and negative, this yields a contradiction.

Hence ϕ can be normalized to -1 and (A.2) becomes

$$\text{(A.3)} \qquad E[\rho U_x(W)v_1 + (1-\rho)U_x(K)v_2] - \lambda_0 E^Q\left[B(T)^{-1}v_1\right] \leq 0.$$

With $v_2 = 0$ and $\lambda \equiv -\rho U_x(W) + \lambda_0 \frac{\eta(T)}{B(T)}$, (A.3) reduces to $E[\lambda v_1] \geq 0, \forall (v_1, 0) \in [\mathcal{C} - (W, K)]$. This implies that $\lambda \geq 0$, P-a.s. and Theorem 3.1 (i), (iii), and (v) are proved.

If we set $v_1 = v_2$, then from (A.3)

$$[(1-\rho)U_x(K) - E(\lambda)]\, v_2 \leq 0 \qquad \forall\, v_2 > a_0 - K.$$

Since $a_0 - K < 0$, it follows that

$$[(1-\rho)U_x(K) - E(\lambda)] = 0.$$

Finally, if we take $z \equiv (K + \varepsilon(W - K), K) \in \mathcal{C}$ for arbitrary $\varepsilon > 0$, then $v_2 = 0$ and $v_1 = z_1 - W = (1-\varepsilon)(K - W)$. Hence, (A.3) reduces to

$$(\varepsilon - 1)E[\lambda(W - K)] \geq 0,$$

which implies $\lambda(W - K) = 0$ a.s. since both λ and $W - K$ are nonnegative almost surely.

To show that the conditions are sufficient, let

$$f(y_1, y_2) = \rho EU(y_1) + (1-\rho)U(y_2) - \lambda_0 E\left[\frac{\eta(T)y_1}{B(T)} - W_0\right].$$

Then $f(\cdot, \cdot)$ is concave on $\mathcal{C}$. The directional derivative of f is

$$\begin{aligned} \mathcal{D}f(y; v) &= \rho E[U_x(y_1)v_1] + (1-\rho)U_x(y_2)v_2 - \lambda_0 E\left[\frac{\eta(T)v_1}{B(T)}\right] \\ &= E\left[\left(\rho U_x(y_1) - \lambda_0 \frac{\eta(T)}{B(T)}\right) v_1\right] + (1-\rho)U_x(y_2)v_2. \end{aligned}$$

Setting $y = (W, K)$, (i) and (ii) imply

$$\begin{aligned} \mathcal{D}f(W, K; v) &= E[\lambda(v_2 - v_1)] \\ &= E[\lambda(z_2 - z_1)] + E[\lambda(W - K)] \\ &= E[\lambda(z_2 - z_1)] \quad \text{by } (iv) \\ &\leq 0 \quad \text{by } (v). \end{aligned}$$

Hence (W, K) solves (A.1).

REFERENCES

BASAK, S. (1995): A General Equilibrium Model of Portfolio Insurance, *Rev. Financial Stud.* 8, 1059–1090.

BLACK, F., and M. SCHOLES (1973): The Pricing of Options and Corporate Liabilities, *J. Polit. Econ.* 81, 637–654.

COX, J., and C.-F. HUANG (1989): Optimal Consumption and Portfolio Polices When Asset Prices Follow a Diffusion Process, *J. Econ. Theory* 49, 33–83.

GROSSMAN, S., and Z. ZHOU (1996): Equilibrium Analysis of Portfolio Insurance, *J. Finance* 51, 1379–1403.

HARRISON, M., and D. KREPS (1979): Martingale and Multiperiod Securities Markets, *J. Econ. Theory* 20, 382–408.

HARRISON, M., and S. PLISKA (1981): Martingales and Stochastic Integrals in the Theory of Continuous Trading, *Stoch. Process Appl.* 11, 215–260.

KARATZAS, I. (1989): Optimization Problems: The Theory of Continuous Trading, *J. Cont. Optim.* 27, 1221–1259.

KARATZAS, I., J. LEHOCZKY, S. SETHI, and S. SHREVE (1986): Explicit Solution of a General Consumption/Investment Problem, *Math. Oper. Res.* 11, 613–636.

KARATZAS, I., and S. SHREVE (1998): *Methods of Mathematical Finance*. New York: Springer.

MERTON, R. (1969): Lifetime Portfolio Selection Under Uncertainty: The Continuous Time Case, *Rev. Econ. Stat.* 51, 247–257.

MERTON, R. (1971): Optimal Consumption and Portfolio Rules in a Continuous-Time Model, *J. Econ. Theory* 3, 373–413.

NEUSTADT, L. (1976): *Optimization*. Princeton, NJ: Princeton University Press.

PLISKA, S. (1986): A Stochastic Calculus Model of Continuous Trading: Optimal Portfolio, *Math. Oper. Res.* 11, 371–382.

ZHAO, Y., and W. ZIEMBA (2000): A Dynamic Asset Allocation Model with Downside Risk Control, *J. Risk* 3, 91–113.

ZHAO, Y., and W. ZIEMBA (2001): A Stochastic Programming Model Using an Endogenously Determined Worst Case Risk Measure for Dynamic Asset Allocation, *Math. Programming* 89, 293–309.

Section III

Asset and Liability Management

Chapter 9

A BANK ASSET AND LIABILITY MANAGEMENT MODEL*

M. I. KUSY
Concordia University, Montreal, Quebec

W. T. ZIEMBA
International Institute for Applied Systems Analysis, Laxenburg, Austria, and University of British Columbia, Vancouver, British Columbia

(Received December 1983; revisions received August 1984, February 1985; accepted March 1985)

In managing its assets and liabilities in light of uncertainties in cash flows, cost of funds and return on investments, a bank must determine its optimal trade-off between risk, return and liquidity. In this paper we develop a multiperiod stochastic linear programming model (ALM) that includes the essential institutional, legal, financial, and bank-related policy considerations, and their uncertainties, yet is computationally tractable for realistically sized problems. A version of the model was developed for the Vancouver City Savings Credit Union for a 5-year planning period. The results indicate that ALM is theoretically and operationally superior to a corresponding deterministic linear programming model, and that the effort required for the implementation of ALM, and its computational requirements, are comparable to those of the deterministic model. Moreover, the qualitative and quantitative characteristics of the solutions are sensitive to the model's stochastic elements, such as the asymmetry of cash flow distributions. We also compare ALM with the stochastic decision tree (SDT) model developed by S. P. Bradley and D. B. Crane. ALM is computationally more tractable on realistically sized problems than SDT, and simulation results indicate that ALM generates superior policies.

The inherent uncertainty of their cash flows, cost of funds and return on investments has prompted banks to seek out greater efficiency in the management of their assets and liabilities. This need has led to studies concerned with how to structure a bank's assets and liabilities to make optimal trade-offs among risk, return and liquidity. These studies focus on determining how funds should be used in various economic scenarios. Important factors in these decisions include: balancing of anticipated sources and uses of funds to meet liquidity and capital adequacy constraints while concurrently maximizing profitability (Chambers and Charnes 1961, Cohen and Hammer 1967, 1972); allocating funds among assets based on risk and liquidity classification, maturity and rate of return (Bradley and Crane 1972, 1973, 1976); and adjusting a bank's financial structure in terms of liquidity, capital adequacy and leverage (Chambers and Charnes 1961, Cohen and Hammer 1967). See also Beazer (1975), Brodt (1979) and Spellman (1982).

Current research has stressed two approaches. The first, based on Markowitz's (1959) theory of portfolio selection, assumes that returns are normally distributed and that bank managers utilize risk-averse utility functions. The value of an asset then depends not only on the expectation and variance of its return but also on the covariance of its return with the returns of all other existing and potential investments. The second approach assumes that a bank seeks to maximize its future stream of profits (or expected profits) subject to portfolio mix constraints.

A general example of the use of the first approach is Pyle (1971), who developed a static model in which the financial intermediary (bank) can select the asset and liability levels it wishes to maintain throughout the period. He considers only the risk of the portfolio and not other possible uncertainties. The model omits trading activity, matching assets and liabilities, transaction costs, and other similar features. It is possible to develop dynamic models using constructs along these lines (see, e.g., Kallberg and Ziemba 1981). However, given the severe computational difficulties due to the complexity of algorithms for these problems, it is not at present possible to develop useful operational models for large organizations such as banks.

*This chapter was originally published in: Kusy, M. I. & Ziemba, W. T. (1986). A Bank Asset and Liability Management Model. *Operations Research*, 34(3), 356–376.

Since our interest is in operational models, we concentrate on the second approach, which has theoretical and empirical support. Myers (1968) attempted to determine which criteria are most suitable for the asset and liability management problem by showing that: a necessary condition for the existence of security market equilibrium is risk independence; security market equilibrium implies risk independence of securities; and risk independence of investment opportunities implies that the maximization of the expected net present value is the appropriate objective criterion.

Thus, if, as is widely believed, the securities held by financial institutions are in a state of equilibrium, and securities purchased do not have synergistic effect (implying the risk independence of securities), then the appropriate objective function for a financial institution is the maximization of the expected net present value (ENPV). Hester and Pierce (1975) used cross-sectional data to analyze the validity of a number of portfolio selection models in bank fund management. They concluded that banks can be well managed using models as a decision aid and that the best objective functions are either ENPV or the maximization of a two-variable function for which ENPV is dominant.

Asset and liability management models using an ENPV criteria can be deterministic or stochastic. Deterministic models use linear programming, assume particular realizations for random events, and are computationally tractable for large problems. The banking industry has accepted these models as useful normative tools (Cohen and Hammer 1967). Stochastic models, however, including the use of chance-constrained programming, dynamic programming, sequential decision theory, and linear programming under uncertainty, have achieved little success. This failure is due to inherent computational difficulties, the oversimplifications needed to achieve computational tractability, and practitioners' unfamiliarity with these models' potential.

Essentially all of the deterministic models, and many of the stochastic models, follow the approach of Chambers and Charnes' linear programming model. They maximize net discounted returns, subject to budget and liquidity constraints, using the Federal Reserve Board's (FRB) capital adequacy formulas (see Section 3). Examples of successful applications of this model are Cohen and Hammer (1967), Komar (1971), and Lifson and Blackman (1973). These models continue to be criticized largely because they omit uncertainty (Bradley and Crane 1976, Cohen and Thore 1970, and Eppen and Fama 1968). Probability distributions can be obtained for different economic scenarios and a linear programming formulation can be applied to each scenario to determine optimal solutions. However, this approach will not generate an optimal solution to the total problem, but rather acts as a deterministic simulation to observe portfolio behavior under various economic conditions. One must use care in defining such models, since it is possible that no scenario leads to an optimal solution (see Birge 1982).

Charnes and Kirby (1965), Charnes and Littlechild (1968), Charnes and Thore (1966), and others developed chance-constrained models that express future deposits and loan repayments as joint, normally distributed random variables, and that replace the capital adequacy formula by chance-constraints on meeting withdrawal claims. These approaches lead to a computationally feasible scheme for realistic situations (see, e.g., Charnes, Gallegos and Yao 1982). However, the chance-constrained procedure cannot handle a differential penalty for either varying magnitudes of constraint violations or different types of constraints. Moreover, multiperiod models raise conceptual difficulties, as yet unresolved in the literature, dealing with the treatment of infeasibility in periods $2, \ldots, n$ (see, e.g., Eisner, Kaplan and Soden 1971).

The second approach to stochastic modeling is dynamic programming. Eppen and Fama (1968, 1969, 1971) modeled two- and three-asset problems. Daellenbach and Archer (1969) extended their work to include one liability. For a survey of this literature, see Ziemba and Vickson (1975). These models are dynamic and account for the inherent uncertainty of the problem. However, given the small number of financial instruments that can be analyzed simultaneously, they are of limited use in practice. See Daellenbach (1974) for estimates of possible gain using these models. For a recent survey of related applications in banking, see Cohen, Maier and Van Der Weide (1981).

The third alternative in considering stochastic models, proposed by Wolf (1969), is a sequential decision theoretic approach that employs sequential decision analysis to find an optimal solution through the use of implicit enumeration. This technique does not find an explicit optimal solution to problems with a time horizon beyond one period, because it is necessary to enumerate all possible portfolio strategies for periods preceding the present decision point in order to guarantee optimality. To explain away this drawback, Wolf makes the dubious assertion that the solution to a one-period model would be equivalent to a solution provided by solving an n-period model. This approach ignores, among other things, the problem of synchronizing the maturities of assets and liabilities. Bradley and Crane (1972, 1973, 1976) have developed a stochastic decision tree model that has many of the desirable features essential to an operational bank portfolio model. Their model is conceptually similar to Wolf's model. To overcome computational difficulties, they reformulated the asset and liability problem and developed a general programming decomposition algorithm that minimizes the computational difficulties. This model is discussed in Section 5.

The fourth approach is stochastic linear programming with simple recourse (SLPSR), which is also called linear programming under uncertainty (LPUU). This technique explicitly characterizes each realization of the random variables by a constraint and leads to large problems in realistic situations. This method greatly handicaps modelers; in fact, Cohen and Thore viewed their model more as a tool for sensitivity analysis (in the aggregate) than a normative decision tool. The computational intractability and the perceptions of the formulation precluded consideration of problems other than those that were limited both in terms of time periods (Cohen and Thore used one, and Crane 1971 used two) and in the number of variables and realizations. Booth (1972) applied this formulation by limiting the number of possible realizations and the number of variables considered, in order to incorporate two time periods. Although relatively efficient solution algorithms are available for solving SLPSR's (Wets 1966), analysts have solved these models using an "extensive representation."

With the possible exception of the Bradley-Crane model, none of the cited models gives an adequate treatment of the essential features necessary for an adequate operational bank asset and liability management model that is computationally tractable. An ideal operational model should contain the following features:

1. multiperiodicity that incorporates: changing yield spreads across time, transaction costs associated with selling assets prior to maturity, and the synchronization of cash flows across time by matching maturity of assets with expected cash outflows;
2. simultaneous considerations of assets and liabilities to satisfy basic accounting principles and match the liquidity of assets and liabilities;
3. transaction costs that incorporate brokerage fees and other expenses incurred in buying and selling securities;
4. uncertainty of cash flows that incorporates the uncertainty inherent in the depositors' withdrawal claims and deposits (to ensure that the structure of the asset portfolio gives the bank the capacity to meet these claims);
5. the incorporation of uncertain interest rates into the decision-making process to avoid lending and borrowing decisions that may ultimately be detrimental to the financial well-being of the bank; and
6. legal and policy constraints appropriate to the bank's operating environment.

In this paper, we develop an SLPSR model that essentially captures these features of asset and liability management while maintaining computational feasibility. Section 2 contains background concerning SLPSR models and the solution algorithm. The asset and liability management (ALM) model is described and formulated in Section 3. In Section 4 we apply ALM to the operations of the Vancouver City Savings Credit Union. Section 5 compares ALM to Bradley and Crane's model. Final remarks and conclusions appear in Section 6.

2. Stochastic Linear Programs with Simple Recourse

The basic (SLPSR) model is

$$\underset{x\geq 0}{\text{minimize}}\ Z(x) \equiv c'x + E_\xi\left[\min_{y^+,y^-\geq 0}(q^{+\prime}y^+ + q^{-\prime}y^-)\right]$$

$$\text{subject to } Ax = b \qquad (1)$$

$$Tx + Iy^+ - Iy^- = \xi$$

where $c, x \in R^n$, $y^+, y^-, q^+, q^- \in R^{m_2}$, A is $m_1 \times n$, T is $m_2 \times n$, I is a m_2 = dimensional identity matrix and ξ is a m_2-dimensional random variable distributed independently of x on the probability space (Ξ, F, F). The SLPSR model is the two-stage process: choose a decision vector x, observe the random vector ξ, then take the corrective action (y^+, y^-). The model is said to have simple recourse because the second stage minimization is fictitious since (y^+, y^-) are effectively unique functions of (x, ξ).

Beale (1955) and Dantzig (1955) independently proposed the SLPSR model as a special case of the general linear recourse model that replaces $Iy^+ - Iy^-$ by Wy for a general matrix W. Detailed presentations of the theory of this model appear in Kall (1976), Parikh (1968), and Ziemba (1974). If we assume that $Ax = b, x \geq 0$ has a solution x^0 and $q^+ + q^- \geq 0$, then (1) has an optimal solution and is a separable convex program. If ξ is absolutely continuous, then Z is differentiable and (1) may be solved using modifications of standard feasible direction algorithms (see, e.g., Wets 1966 and Ziemba 1974). If ξ has a finite distribution, then Z is piecewise linear and (1) is equivalent to a large linear program. Wets (1974) noted that the deterministic equivalent linear program can be written in the form

$$\text{minimize } c'x - \sum_{i=1}^{m_2} \sum_{l=1}^{k_i+1} (q_i^- - F_{il}q_i)y_{il} + \sum_{i=1}^{m_2} q_i^+ \bar{\xi}_i$$

$$\text{subject to } Ax = b, \quad x \geqslant 0 \tag{2}$$

$$\sum_{j=1}^{n} t_{ij}x_j - \sum_{l=1}^{k_i} y_{il} = \alpha_i$$

$$y_{i1} \leqslant d_{i1}, \quad 0 \leqslant y_{il} \leqslant d_{il}, \quad 0 \leqslant y_{i,k_i+1}$$

where $i = 1, \ldots, m_2$, $l = 2, \ldots, k_i$, $d_{i1} = \xi_{i1}$, $d_{il} = \xi_{il} - \xi_{i,l-1}$, $q_i = q_i^+ + q_i^-$, $\xi_{i1} < \ldots < \xi_{ik_i}$ are the possible values of each ξ_i, the ith component of ξ, with probabilities $f_{i1}, \ldots, f_{ik_i}$ and $F_{is} = \Pr(\xi_i < \xi_{is}) = \sum_{l=1}^{s-1} f_{i1}$.

It is possible to develop an algorithm using generalized upper bounding constructs that will solve (2) in a number of pivots that is of the same order of magnitude as the number of pivots required to solve the mean linear programming approximation problem, i.e., (1) with $\bar{\xi}$ replacing ξ. The linear program (2) has the same number of working basis elements, $(m_1 + m_2)$, as the mean problem. Wets (1974, 1984) has developed an algorithm that has been coded by Collins (1975), Kallberg and Kusy (1976). The code was written to solve problems with up to 70 stochastic constraints, 220 total constraints and 8 realizations per random element. The code can be expanded to solve much larger problems. The International Institute of Applied Systems Analysis, Laxenberg, Austria (IIASA) is currently developing more sophisticated codes to handle larger problems. See Wets (1983) for extension of his algorithm to the convex case.

Formulation (1) is essentially static, while the asset and liability management problem is dynamic. We utilize model (2) and its efficient computational scheme, while at the same time retaining as many of the dynamic aspects of the model as possible. To do so, we utilize the approximation described below. The general n-stage SLPSR problem is

$$\underset{\substack{x^1 \geqslant 0 \\ Ax = b^1}}{\text{minimize}}\; c^{1\prime}x^1$$

$$+ E_{\xi^1}\left\{ \min_{y^{1+}, y^{1-} \geqslant 0} \left[q^{1+\prime}y^{1+} + q^{1-\prime}y^{1-} + \ldots + \right.\right.$$

$$+ \underset{\substack{x^n \geqslant 0 \\ A^n x^n = b^n}}{\text{minimize}} \left[c^{n\prime}x^n + E_{\xi^n|\xi^{n-1},\ldots,\xi^1} \right. \tag{3}$$

$$\left.\left.\left\{ \min_{y^{n+}, y^{n-} \geqslant 0} [q^{n+\prime}y^{n+} + q^{n-\prime}y^{n-}] \right\} \right] \ldots \right] \Big\}$$

$$\text{subject to } \sum_{j=1}^{i} T_{ij}x^i + Iy^{i+} - Iy^{i-} = \xi^i, \quad i = 1, \ldots, n.$$

The approximation procedure aggregates $x^2, \ldots, x^n$ with x^1 and $\xi^2, \ldots, \xi^n$ with ξ^1. Thus in (1), one chooses $x \equiv (x^1, \ldots, x^n)'$ in stage one, observes $\xi \equiv (\xi^1, \ldots, \xi^n)'$ at the end of stage one, and these steps together determine $(y^+, y^-) \equiv [(y^{1+}, y^{1-}), \ldots, (y^{n+}, y^{n-})]$ in stage two. This approach yields a feasible procedure for the true dynamic model (3) that is computationally feasible for large problems and incorporates partial dynamic aspects, since penalty costs for periods $2, \ldots, n$ are considered in the choice of $x^1, \ldots, x^n$. Aggregating all future period decision variables into x^1 would make the first period decision function as if all future period decisions were the same regardless of the scenario. The decision maker is primarily interested in the immediate revision of the bank's assets and liabilities. The ALM model incorporates immediate revision by setting apart by an arbitrarily small time period, times 0 and 1. Point 0 is the bank's initial position and point 1 is the bank's position immediately after running the model. In practice, the model is rolled over continuously. To partially overcome the drawbacks of a static solution technique, the decision variables are defined so that a security can be purchased in one time period and sold in one or more subsequent periods.

The feasibility of the SLPSR approximation provides an upper bound on the true optimal solution to (3). A lower bound on (3) is provided by Mandansky's (1960) linear programming mean model, that is, (3) with $\bar{\xi}^i$ replacing ξ^i for all i. Hence one can bound the true optimal solution with two easily computable programs. Specific numerical details of such bounds appear in Kallberg, White and Ziemba (1982) and Kusy (1978).

The recourse aspect of the model gives it a dynamic flavor. The model is two-stage: initially the decision variables are chosen, next the stochastic variables are observed, and these two steps determine the recourse variables (to recover feasibility) and their corresponding penalties. The penalty is a function of both the constraint violated and the magnitude of violation. The recourse cost has the effect of restraining "aggressive" choices of decision variables if the costs involved with regaining feasibility outweigh the benefits. The ALM model's dynamic features are embodied in its continuous rollover, the definition of variables that permits flexibility, and the recourse aspect of SLPSR.

A problem that arises in most deterministic as well as stochastic dynamic planning models is the handling of the end effects. In the formulation of ALM, we have assumed that the model runs for n periods; in the application, n is 5 years. This approach works well for our situation and our goal of obtaining a good first period decision. The most satisfactory theoretical approach to end effects is Grinold's (1977, 1983) dual equilibrium formulation. With this procedure, the dual variables for periods $n + 1, \ldots$ increase in value with the appropriate interest rate. This result yields an equivalent one-period constraint set for the infinite horizon-periods $n + 1, \ldots$. It is possible to extend Grinold's (1977, 1983) deterministic theoretical results and applications to energy planning models (Grinold 1980) to the stochastic case, although this has not appeared in the literature thus far. For ALM, applying Grinold's approach would yield one more set of constraints for a period "6." We did not make this further refinement because its added accuracy did not seem to outweigh the additional computational costs. However, developers of SLPSR models should keep this approach in mind in their choice of model formulation.

3. Formulation of the ALM Model

The ALM model is an intertemporal decision making optimization tool to determine a bank's portfolio of assets and liabilities given deterministic rates of returns and cost (interest rates), and random cash flows (deposits). Although the asset and liability management problem is a continuous decision problem, with portfolios constantly being revised over time, the computations and analysis involved with a continuous time process are infeasible for a practical model. Therefore, the ALM model is developed as a multiperiod decision problem in which portfolios are determined at discrete points in time (e.g., the end of each accounting period).

The ALM model has the following features:

1. Objective function: Maximize the net present value of bank profits minus the expected penalty costs for infeasibility.
2. Constraints:
   a. legal, being a function of the bank's jurisdiction;
   b. budget: initial conditions and the sources and uses of funds;
   c. liquidity and leverage, to satisfy deposit withdrawals on demand;
   d. policy and termination; constraints unique to the bank, and conditions to ensure the bank's continuing existence after the termination of the model; and
   e. deposit flows.

Constraints (a) and (b) are deterministic, (c) consists of both deterministic and stochastic constraints, (d) can consist of either deterministic or stochastic constraints, and (e) contains only stochastic constraints.

Chambers and Charnes, and Cohen and Hammer (1967) have justified the use of linear functions to model a bank's asset and liability management problem. Thus from the point of view of linearity, their analysis establishes the appropriateness of SLPSR. The recourse aspect is justified with the following argument. In the banking business, constraint violations do not imply that the intermediary is put into receivership. Rather, the bank is allowed to restructure its portfolio of assets to regain feasibility at some cost (penalties). With the inherent uncertainties, the asset and liability management problem is well modeled as a stochastic linear program with simple recourse.

3.1. Notation for the ALM Model

x_{ij}^k = amount of asset k purchased in period i sold in period j; $k = 1, \ldots, K$; $i = 0, \ldots, n - 1$; $j = i + 1, \ldots, n$

x_{00}^k = initial holdings of security k

$x_{i\infty}^k$ = amount of security k purchased in period i to be held beyond the horizon of the model

y_i^d = new deposits of type d in period i; $d = 1, \ldots, D$

y_0^d = initial holdings of deposit type d

b_i = funds borrowed in period i

y_{js}^+ = shortage in period j in stochastic constraint s

y_{js}^- = surplus in period j in stochastic constraint s

p_{js}^+ = proportional penalty cost associated with y_{js}^+

p_{js}^- = proportional penalty cost associated with y_{js}^-

β_{ij}^k = parameter for shrinkage, under normal economic conditions, in period j of asset type k purchased in period i

α_{ij}^k = parameter for shrinkage, under severe economic conditions, in period j of asset type k purchased in period i

t_i^k = proportional transaction cost on asset k, which is either purchased or sold in period i

r_i^k = return on asset k purchased in period i

T_j = tax rate on capital gains (losses) in period j

τ_j = marginal tax rate on income in period j

z_{ij}^k = proportional capital gain (loss) on security k purchased in period i and sold in period j

γ_d = the anticipated fraction of deposits of type d withdrawn under adverse economic conditions

c_i^d = rate paid on deposits of type d

p_i = discount rate from period i to period 0

K_0 = set of possible current assets as specified by the British Columbia Credit Union Act

K_1 = set of primary and secondary assets as defined in the capital adequacy formula (caf)

K_2 = set of minimum risk assets as defined in the caf

K_3 = set of intermediate risk assets as defined in the caf

q_i = penalty rate for the potential withdrawal of funds, in period i, that are not covered by assets in $K_1 \cup \ldots \cup K_3$

P_i = liquidity reserves for the potential withdrawal of funds, in period i, not covered by assets in $K_1 \cup \ldots U K_3$

k_{mi} = m_ith mortgage

ξ_{js} = discrete random variable in period j for stochastic constraint type s, $s \in S$ where S is the set of stochastic constraints.

3.2. The ALM Model

$$\underset{x,y,b}{\text{maximize}} \sum_{k=1}^{K} \Bigg[\sum_{j=2}^{n} x_{0j}^k \Big\{ \sum_{l=2}^{j} r_0^k(1-\tau_l)p_l + z_{0j}^k(1-T_j)p_j \Big\} + x_{01}^k z_{01}(1-T_j) + \sum_{i=1}^{n-1} \sum_{j=i+1}^{n} x_{ij}^k \Big\{ \sum_{l=i+1}^{j} r_i^k(1+\tau_l)p_l + z_{ij}^k(1-T_j)p_j \Big\} + x_{0\infty}^k \sum_{l=2}^{n} r_0^k(1-T_l)p_j \Bigg] + \sum_{j=\tau_l}^{n} \sum_{l=i+1}^{n} x_{i\infty}^k r_i^k(1-\tau_l)p_l$$

discounted returns and capital gains (net of taxes) on assets

$$-\sum_{d=1}^{i=1} \Bigg[\sum_{j=1} y_0^d(1-\gamma_d/2)(1-\gamma_d)^{j-1} c_j^d p_j + \sum_{j=1}^{n} 1/2 y_j^d c_j^d p_j + \sum_{i=1}^{n-1} \sum_{j=1}^{n-1} y_i^d(1-\gamma_d/2)(1-\gamma_d)^{j-i} c_j^d p_j \Bigg]$$

net discounted cost of deposits (demand and time)

$$-b_0 c_0^b p_1 - \sum_{j=1}^{n} b_j c_j^b p_{j+1}$$

cost of direct borrowing from other banks and a central bank

$$-E_\xi \min_{y^+,y^-} \sum_{j=1}^{n} \sum_{s \in S} p_{js}^+ y_{js}^+ + p_{js}^- y_{js}^-$$

expected penalty costs for constraint violations

subject to

(a) Legal constraints

$$\sum_{k \in K_0} \sum_{i=0}^{1} \Big\{ \sum_{l=2}^{n} x_{il}^k + x_{i\infty}^k \Big\} - 0.1 \Bigg[\sum_{d=1}^{D} y_0^d + (1-\gamma_d) y_0^d/2 + y_1^d/2 + b_0 + b_1 \Bigg] \geq 0, \qquad j = 1.$$

$$\sum_{k \in K_0} \sum_{i=0}^{j} \Big\{ \sum_{l=j+1}^{n} x_{il}^k + x_{i\infty}^k \Big\} - 0.1 \Bigg[\sum_{d=1}^{D} \Big\{ \sum_{i=0}^{j-1} y_i^d + (1-\gamma_d) y_0^d/2(1-\gamma_d)^{j-i-1} + y_1^d/2 \Big\} + b_j \Bigg] \geq 0, \qquad j = 2, \ldots, n.$$

(b) Budget constraints

i. Initial holdings

$$\sum_{j=1}^{n} x_{0j}^k + x_{0\infty}^k = x_{00}^k, \qquad k = 1, \ldots K.$$

$$y_0^d = y_{00}^d, \qquad d = 1, \ldots, D.$$

ii. Sources and uses

$$\sum_{k=1}^{K} \Bigg[\sum_{l=2}^{n} \{x_{1l}^k + x_{1\infty}^k\}\{1 + t_1^k - x_{01}^k\{1 + z_{01}^k(1-T_1) - t_1^k(1+z_{01}^k)\} \Bigg] + \sum_{d=1}^{D} [\gamma_d y_{0/2}^d - y_1^d/2] - b_1 = 0, \qquad j = 1.$$

$$\sum_{k=1}^{K} \Big\{ \sum_{l=j+1}^{n} x_{jl}^k + x_{j\infty}^k \Big\}\{1 + t_j^k\} - \sum_{i=0}^{j-1} \Bigg[\Big\{ \sum_{l=j}^{n} x_{il}^k + x_{i\infty}^k \Big\}\{r_i^k(1-\gamma_j)\} + x_{ij}^k\{1 + z_{ij}^k(1-T_j) - t_j^k(1+z_{ij}^k)\} \Bigg]$$

$$-\sum_{d=1}^{D} \Bigg[\sum_{i=0}^{j-2} y_i^d(1-\gamma_d)^{j-i-2}\{(-\gamma_d)(1-\gamma_d/2)\} + (1-\gamma_d) y_{j-1}^d/2 + y_j^d/2 - (1-\gamma_d/2)c_{j-1}^d - y_{j-1}^d c_{j-1}^d/2 \Bigg]$$

$$+ b_{j-1}(1 + c_{j-1}^b) - b_j = 0, \qquad j = 2, \ldots, n.$$

(c) Liquidity constraints

$$\text{i.}\quad -\sum_{k\in K}\sum_{i=0}^{j}\left[\sum_{l=j+1}^{n} x_{il}^{k}\alpha_{ij}^{k} + x_{i\infty}^{k}\alpha_{ij}^{k}\right] + b_j + \sum_{d=1}^{D}\gamma_d\left[\sum_{i=0}^{j-1} y_i^d(1-\gamma_d)^{j-i-1}(1-\gamma_d/2) + y_j^d/2\right] \leqslant P_{1j}/q_{ij}.$$

$$\text{ii.}\quad -\sum_{k\in K_1 U K_2}\sum_{i=0}^{j}\left[\sum_{l=j+1}^{n} x_{il}^{k}\alpha_{ij}^{k} + x_{i\infty}^{k}\alpha_{ij}^{l}\right] + b_j + \sum_{d=1}^{D}\gamma_d\left[\sum_{i=0}^{j-1} y_i^d(1-\gamma_d)^{j-i-1}(1-\gamma_d/2) + y_j^d/2\right] \leqslant P_{2j}/q_{ij}.$$

$$\text{iii.}\quad -\sum_{k\in K_1 U K_2 U K_3}\sum_{i=0}^{j}\left[\sum_{l=j+1}^{n} x_{il}^{k}\alpha_{ij}^{k} + x_{i\infty}^{k}\alpha_{ij}^{k}\right] + b_j + \sum_{d=1}^{D}\gamma_d\left[\sum_{i=0}^{j-1} y_i^d(1-\gamma_d)^{j-i-1}(1-\gamma_d/2) + y_j^d/2\right] \leqslant P_{3j}/q_{ij}$$

$$\text{iv.}\quad -\sum_{k=1}^{K}\sum_{i=0}^{j}\left[\sum_{l=j+1}^{n} (1-\beta_{ij}^{k})x_{il}^{k} + (1-\beta_{ij}^{k})x_{i\infty}^{k}\right] + y_{js}^{+} - y_{js}^{-} \geqslant P_{1j} + P_{2j} + P_{3j} + b_j$$

$$+\sum_{d=1}^{D}\left[\sum_{i=0}^{j-1} y_i^d(1-\gamma_d)^{j-i-1}(1-\gamma_d/2) + y_j^d/2\right] + \xi_{js}, \qquad j=1,\ldots,n,\quad s\in S.$$

(d) Policy constraints

$$-0.1\sum_{i=0}^{j}\left[\sum_{l=j+1}^{n} x_{il}^{k_{m1}} + x_{i\infty}^{k_{m1}}\right] + \sum_{i=0}^{j}\left[\sum_{l=j+1}^{n} x_{il}^{k_{m2}} + x_{i\infty}^{k_{m2}}\right] + y_{js}^{+} - y_{js}^{-} \leqslant \xi_{js}, \qquad j=1,\ldots,n,\quad s\in S.$$

(e) Deposit flows

$$y_j^d + \sum_{i=0}^{j-1} y_i^d(1-\gamma_d)^{j-i} + y_{js}^{+} + y_{js}^{-} = \gamma_{js}, \qquad j=1,\ldots,n;\quad d=1,\ldots,D,\quad s\in S.$$

(f) Nonnegativity

$$x_{ij}^{k},\ b_i,\ y_i^d,\ y_{js}^{+},\ y_{js}^{-} \geqslant 0 \quad \text{for all}\quad i, j, k, d.$$

There are no discount factors in the constraints since each constraint refers to conditions in one period. The ALM model treats the first two types of constraints, legal and budget, as deterministic. The legal constraint states that the current assets cannot be less than 10% of the total liabilities (as defined by the Credit Union Act, (British Columbia Government, Section 106, 1982a). The legal constraints are peculiar to the locale of the institution being studied. The budget constraints include the initial conditions and the accounting identity—uses and sources of funds are equal. See also Credit Union Regulations (British Columbia Government 1982b and Barr 1984).

The liquidity constraints follow from liquidity calculations in the Federal Reserve Board's capital adequacy formula (caf). The requirement that the market value of a bank's assets is adequate to meet depositor's withdrawal claims during adverse economic conditions is the principal constraint in the caf. The market value of the bank's assets should be not less than the liquidity reserves for disintermediation under severe economic conditions plus liabilities. This constraint is the final liquidity constraint in ALM. Although this constraint is not stochastic, a bank portfolio manager may violate it because the caf is merely a suggested guideline rather than a strict regulation. The penalty for a violation of this constraint is $\sum_{i=1}^{3} q_i$. This *elastic* treatment allows the constraint to be violated when the benefits of violation exceed the costs. In this manner, the criticism, levelled at modellers using FRB's conservative constraints, can be resolved in a systematic manner. See Section 4.1.3 for more discussion concerning these constraints.

The FRB's caf has been used as a suggested disintermediation liquidity guideline for U.S. banks but is not a legal requirement. Because it is quite conservative and tends to reflect depression style financial conditions, its formulas are not currently used by U.S banks. This policy may change in the future, however, given the extreme threat to the world banking system by the many nonperforming loans to countries such as Argentina, Brazil, Chile and Mexico. In British Columbia, however, where the Vancouver City Savings Credit Union operates, the banking establishment is quite conservative and has continued to use the caf's liquidity guidelines. Hence we have used them in ALM. Besides ALM, the caf is also used in British Columbia's Credit Union Reserve Board's credit union solvency model. Ellis (1984), the Board's manager of research services, who operates the solvency model as a regulatory tool, feels that "... the caf reflects the limited experience of the credit union movement in British Columbia when liquidating credit unions." In other environments where models such as ALM may be appropriate, alternative liquidity constraints are easily handled in the SLPWR formulation, assuming that such constraints are linear or can be linearized.

The fourth set of constraints is also elastic. These constraints are introduced to capture the internal policy of the institution modeled. In reality, minor constraint violations of bank policies are usually tolerable, while more severe violations are increasingly less tolerable. The introduction of a piece-wise linear convex penalty function (via additional constraints) can capture the dependency between the penalty costs and the extent of the policy violations. This result is accomplished by the addition of supplementary constraints to reflect the increased seriousness of the magnitude of constraint violations.

The final set of constraints, deposit flows, is stochastic. Since deposit flows are continually turned over and bear various rates of interest, the model must reflect the gross (and not net) flows during an accounting period. This property of the problem was incorporated in the model by establishing a proportional outflow (statistically calculated by the FRB and corroborated for use in British Columbia by White and Dobrzanshi 1976) of old funds during each period.

We now develop the three types of liability expressions in the ALM formulation. The deposit flow constraints represent the total amount of new deposits in the jth period. The total amount of new deposits of type d generated in period j yields the equation

$$y_j^d + \sum_{i=0}^{j-i} y_i^d(1-\gamma_d)^{j-i} = BS_j^d,$$

where y_j^d is the total amount of new type d deposits in period j, γ_d is the annual rate of withdrawal of type d deposits, and BS_j^d is the discrete random variable representing the balance sheet figure of type d deposits at the end of the jth period.

The second type of liability expression represents the total amount of deposits outstanding during a period. Since the model is discrete, an approximation to the continuous flow is made by assuming that half of a period's net flows arrive at the beginning of the period and the other half arrive at the beginning of the next period. During the first period, the funds available are

$$[y_0^d + (1-\gamma_d)y_0^d]/2 + y_1^d/2,$$

and for period j, they are

$$\sum_{i=0}^{j-1} [(1-\gamma)^{j-i-1}y_i^d + (1-\gamma)^{j-i}y_i^d]/2 + y_j^d/2,$$

or

$$\sum_{i=0}^{j-1} y_i^d(1-\gamma_d/2)(1-\gamma_d)^{j-i-1} + y_j^d/2.$$

This expression is used in the objective function and in the legal and liquidity constraints. The third liability expression is the incremental increase (decrease) of deposits from one period to the next. We use this incremental difference in the sources and uses constraint. For period j the incremental difference is

$$\left[\sum_{i=0}^{j-1} y_i^d(1-\gamma_d/2)(1-\gamma_d)^{j-i-1} + y_j^d/2\right] - \left[\sum_{i=0}^{j-2} y_i^d(1-\gamma_d/2)(1-\gamma_d)^{j-i-2} + y_{j-1}^d/2\right]$$

$$= \sum_{i=0}^{j-2} y_i^d(1-\gamma_d)^{j-i-2}[-\gamma_d(1-\gamma_d/2)] + (1-\gamma_d)y_{j-1}^d/2 + y_j^d/2.$$

3.3. Data Required to Implement the ALM Model

To implement the ALM model requires the following data:

1. the identification of assets in which the bank can potentially invest;
2. point estimates of the returns on these assets;
3. point estimates of capital gains (losses) as a function of the time the bank holds the assets;
4. identification of the liabilities that the bank can potentially sell;
5. point estimates of the costs of these liabilities;
6. the rate at which deposits are withdrawn;
7. an estimated weighted cost of funds to determine the discount rate;
8. pertinent legal constraints;
9. parameters used in the development of liquidity constraints;
10. policy constraints used by the bank;
11. estimates of the marginal distributions of the stochastic resources; and
12. unit penalties incurred for shortage or surplus in the stochastic constraints.

Remarks. a. Since the ALM model has a separable objective, only the marginal distributions of the components of the resource vector are needed to find the optimal solution.

b. The shortage (y^+) and surplus (y^-) variables have specific meanings in the ALM formulation. Consider a realization $\xi_{js}^{d\prime}$ of the random deposit ξ_{js}^d. If

$$y_j^d + \sum_{i=0}^{j-i} y_i^d(1-\gamma_d)^{j-i} < \xi_{js}^{d\prime},$$

then $y^+ > 0$ and $y^- = 0$, assuming $p^+ + p^- > 0$; y^+ is the amount of funds that could have been used for investment purposes in the ALM. Since the cost of deposits is usually lower than the returns on assets, the bank would want to utilize all available funds. A penalty $p^+ > 0$ for the opportunity cost can be determined by assuming that the funds not used can be invested in earning assets. The y^+ dollars would be available at rate c and invested in some asset at a rate r. The penalty, p^+, equals $(r - c)$ discounted to point 0 plus the net discounted returns on $y^+(r - c)$ to the horizon of the model (the profits that could have been generated).

If

$$y_j^d + \sum_{i=0}^{j-i} y_i^d(1 - \gamma_d)^{j-i} > \xi_{js}^{d\prime},$$

then $y^- > 0$ and $y^+ = 0$, and a surplus occurs. The bank would then have to divest itself of some earning assets. The cost, p^-, of this action is $(r - c)$ discounted to point 0 plus the net discounted returns on $y^-(r - c)$ to the horizon of the model (that is, the profits that would have been generated with unavailable funds). Both p^+ and p^- are positive, and profit is lowered if either too little or too much is invested.

4. Application of ALM to the Vancouver City Savings Credit Union

This section considers an application of the ALM model to the asset and liability portfolio problem of Vancouver City Savings Credit Union (VCS). We also discuss procedural aspects of implementing the model for this and related institutions. This study was prompted by the VCS's continual liquidity problem, and focuses on the five year planning period 1970–1974.

During this period, the firm's assets grew at a compound rate of 57%/year from \$26 million to \$160 million, and it developed an aggressive policy of investing in high yielding assets, predominantly mortgages. In 1974, VCS realized that the combination of their aggressive investment policy and changing market conditions was creating serious liquidity problems. Investors were trading low yield term deposits for higher yield deposits. Meanwhile, outstanding mortgage loans were still earning returns on the basis of lower fixed rates. At that point, this study was initiated.

4.1. Model Details

We now describe the input necessary to implement the ALM model at VCS. This discussion focuses on general concepts concerning methods of data collection, choice of decision variables, constraints and objective function. The actual data, a 92 × 257 input matrix, appear in Kusy.

The first-stage variables are assets (x_{ij}^k) and liabilities (y_i^d and b_i). There are eleven asset types:

1. cash;
2. British Columbia Central Credit Union shares;
3–6. federal government bonds maturing in $i = 1, \ldots, 4$ years;
7. federal government bonds maturing in 5–10 years;
8. provincial government bonds maturing in more than 10 years;
9–10. first and second mortgages with a 3-year term; and
11. personal loans.

Six types of liabilities are considered:

1. demand deposits;
2. share capital of VCS;
3. borrowing from banks; and
4–6. term deposits maturing in $i = 1, 3, 5$ years.

These asset and liability types generate 132 and 36 variables, respectively, including initial positions. For example, a 4-year federal government bond purchased at the beginning of the third time period generates decision variables x_{34}^6, x_{35}^6, and $x_{3\infty}^6$, where x_{34}^6 and x_{35}^6 are the amounts of the initial investment to be sold in period four and five, respectively, and $x_{3\infty}^6$ is the amount to be held at the horizon. The choice of assets and liabilities was based on VCS's historical portfolios (1968–1975), so that comparison between actual portfolios and ALM generated portfolios could be easily made. Although cash flows are continuous over time, the model assumes that all transactions occur at the beginning of periods. Cash flows during any period are modeled by assuming that half the flow occurs at the beginning of the present period and the other half at the beginning of the next period. The model has the following constraints.

4.1.1. Legal Constraints

The source for legal constraints is the Credit Union Act of British Columbia (British Columbia Government 1982a), which places three operational restrictions on the composition of the portfolio of assets and liabilities. The first constraint requires that credit unions maintain at least 10% of the total of nonequity shares, deposits and borrowings (denoted by the set I) in high liquid assets (denoted by the set I_L):

$$\sum_{i \in I_L} x_{it} \geq 0.1 \sum_{i \in I_L} x_{it}.$$

The second requirement states that credit unions must maintain at least 1% of their nonequity shares, deposits and borrowings in cash and term deposits:

$$x_{1t} + x_{2t} \geqslant 0.01 \sum_{i \in D} y_{it}.$$

The final constraint restricts the credit union's borrowing from opportunities denoted by the set B, to one half of the nonequity shares, deposits and statutory reserve account:

$$\sum_{b \in B} y_{bt} \leqslant 0.5 \sum_{i \in D} y_{it}.$$

Since the planning horizon has 5 periods, the legal requirements account for 15 constraints.

4.1.2. Budget Constraints

There are 22 budget constraints: 17 establish the initial positions of the 11 asset and 6 liability types, and 5 require the sources and uses of funds to be equal in each period.

4.1.3. Liquidity Constraints

The liquidity constraints ensure that the firm has sufficient capital reserves to meet severe withdrawal claims under adverse economic conditions. The application of the FRB's capital adequacy formula to British Columbia's credit unions is described in the 1973 Credit Union Reserve Board report.

The first three constraints establish capital reserves based upon the structure of the portfolio of assets and liabilities:

$$P_i \geqslant q_i\left(W - \sum_{k \in K_1 U \ldots UK_i} \alpha_k\right) \qquad i = 1, 2, 3,$$

where P_i is the required reserve necessary to meet the excess withdrawal claims, q_i measures the reserves required for potential withdrawal claims that exceed the realizable portion of the assets contained in $K_1U \ldots UK_i$, α_k is a parameter that measures the realizable portion of the value of asset k if the asset is to be liquidated quickly under adverse economic conditions, and $W = \sum_{i=1}^{m} \gamma_i y_i$ is the dollar value of the expected withdrawal claims under adverse conditions, where γ_i measures the contraction of liability y_i under adverse economic conditions. The γ's used were 0.47 for demand deposits, 0.36 for term deposits and 1.0 for borrowing; see White and Dobrzanshi for justification.

The assets are classified as follows:

1. "Primary and Secondary Reserves": (K_1), which include cash, treasury bills, and government bonds of less than 5 years' maturity;
2. "Minimum Risk Assets" (K_2), which include government bonds with more than 5 years' maturity, and municipal bonds; and
3. "Intermediate Assets," which include mortgage and personal loans. The principal constraint is

$$\sum_{i=1}^{K} (1 - \beta_i)x_i \geqslant \sum_{i=1}^{3} P_i + \left\{ \begin{array}{l} \text{total right-surplus-} \\ \text{equity-hand side} \\ \text{of balance sheet} \end{array} \right.$$

where β_i is a parameter to measure the shrinkage of asset i, when the asset is to be liquidated quickly. The values used for α_k, q_i, and β_i are those suggested by the FRB (Crosse and Hempel 1973). Since our purpose is not to develop an operational model for VCS, but rather to demonstrate the applicability of the ALM model, the parameter values used provide an adequate proxy. In the development of an operational model, it would be necessary to estimate the parameters. Since these constraints hold for all 5 periods, there are 20 liquidity constraints.

4.1.4. Policy Constraints

Two types of policy constraints are included:

1. personal loans should not exceed 20% of the first mortgage loans in any period t, $x_{tL} \leqslant 0.2x_{tm}$; and
2. second mortgages should not exceed 12.5% of first mortgages, $x_{tp} \leqslant 0.125\, x_{tm}$.

The rationale is that, since returns on first mortgages are less risky than second mortgages or personal loans, some first mortgages are desirable (even though they may have lower returns) to respond to management's preference for a less risky portfolio. These constraints may be violated without legal implications and are modeled by treating the constraints as stochastic using $(p^+, p^-) = (0, 1)$. There are 10 such constraints over the 5 periods.

4.1.5. Deposit Flows

The variable y_j^d represents new deposits of type $d = 1, \ldots, 5$ generated in period $j = 1, \ldots, 5$, and ξ_{jd} is a discrete random variable representing the balance sheet of deposit type d at the end of period j. The deposit flow constraints are

$$y_j^d + \sum_{i=0}^{j-i} y_i^d(1 - \gamma_d)^{j-i} + y_{jd}^+ - y_{jd}^- = \xi_{jd},$$

where the γ's (1.0 for demand deposits and 0.36 for term deposits) are included to relfect the gross flow of deposit funds. We estimated the distribution of ξ_{jd}

Table I
Discount Rate Factors

	1970	1971	1972	1973	1974
Average yearly yield	0.0559	0.0356	0.0356	0.0547	0.0782
Multiperiod discount factor $\pi(1/(1 + AYY_i))$	0.9435	0.9110	0.8797	0.8341	0.7736

Table II
Returns on Assets

Type of Asset	Returns on Asset by Year					
	1969	1970	1971	1972	1973	1974
1-year federal government bond (fgb)	0.0725	0.0620	0.0450	0.0510	0.0610	0.0800
2-year fgb	0.0749	0.0657	0.0490	0.0550	0.0654	0.0803
3-year fgb	0.0758	0.0684	0.0525	0.0590	0.0680	0.0807
4-year fgb	0.0767	0.0710	0.0555	0.0626	0.0698	0.0810
5-year fgb	0.0776	0.0758	0.0615	0.0674	0.0717	0.0827
10-year provincial government bond	0.0840	0.0904	0.0803	0.0813	0.0836	0.0991
First mortgage	0.0938	0.1040	0.0943	0.0921	0.0959	0.1124
Second mortgage	0.1050	0.1220	0.1108	0.1083	0.1123	0.1321
Personal loans	0.1040	0.1170	0.1075	0.1050	0.1075	0.1275
BCCU shares	0.0600	0.0600	0.0600	0.0600	0.0700	0.0700

using the balance sheet figures of VCS for 1970–1974; see Kusy for specific estimates.

The penalties for shortages associated with these constraints are:

1. for demand deposits and share capital, p^+ is the total discounted return on a 1-year term deposit minus the discounted cost of the funds calculated to the horizon of the model;
2. for term deposits maturing in 1 or 3 years, p^+ is the total discounted return on a 5-year term deposit minus the discounted cost of the funds over the model's horizon; and
3. for term deposits maturing in 5 years, p^+ is the total discounted return on a 10-year provincial government bond minus the discounted cost of the funds over the horizon.

The penalties p^- for surpluses associated with the deposit flow constraints are the total discounted returns on first mortgages minus the discounted costs of funds over the horizon. The penalty approach attempts to model a conservative management strategy with surplus funds when realized sources exceed uses and when there are shortages.

4.1.6. *Objective Function*

The objective is to maximize the expected discounted revenues minus expected discounted costs, including penalty costs. The source for data on the returns on the federal and provincial government bonds is the Bank of Canada (1975). The source for the returns on BCCU shares, demand deposits and share capital is Vancouver City and Savings Credit Union (1968–1975).

The discount rate used was the time value of money.

Table III
Returns on 5-Year Bonds

Decision Variable X_{ij}	Return r_{ij}^7
X_{12}^7	(0.0758)(0.9435) = 0.0720
X_{13}^7	(0.0758)(0.9435 + 0.9110) = 0.1410
X_{14}^7	(0.0758)(0.9435 + 0.9110 + 0.8797) = 0.2070
X_{15}^7	(0.0758)(0.9435 + 0.9110 + 0.8797 + 0.8341) = 0.2700
$X_{1\infty}^7$	(0.0758)(0.9435 + 0.9110 + 0.8797 + 0.8341 + 0.7736) = 0.3290

Table IV
Cost and Liabilities of Credit Union

Type of Liability	Cost of Liability by Year					
	1969	1970	1971	1972	1973	1974
1-year term deposit	0.0712	0.0780	0.0720	0.0680	0.0780	0.0990
3-year term deposit	0.0750	0.0820	0.0760	0.0690	0.0820	0.0980
5-year term deposit	0.0785	0.0850	0.0800	0.0800	0.0850	0.0975
Demand deposit	0.0400	0.0460	0.0410	0.0420	0.0560	0.0770
Share capital	0.0500	0.0500	0.0500	0.0550	0.0575	0.0800

The risk-free rate (the average yield on 3-month treasury bills) (Bank of Canada 1975) is given in Table I.

The returns on the assets (Bank of Canada 1975, Vancouver City Savings Credit Union 1968–1975) are given in Table II.

Purchase of a 5-year federal government bond in 1970 would generate decision variables X^7_{12}, X^7_{13}, X^7_{14}, X^7_{15}, and $X^7_{1\infty}$. The returns are the interest earned each year, discounted to the beginning of the planning horizon, and are given in Table III.

The costs of the liabilities (Vancouver City Savings Credit Union) are given in Table IV.

The cost of a 5-year term deposit (y^3_1) sold during 1970 is shown in Table V.

4.2. Results of the VCS Application

This application demonstrates applicability of the ALM model and tests the sensitivity of the solution generated. To accomplish these goals, we ran the basic model along with several variants that used modified penalty costs and probability distributions, as well as a deterministic model with all random variables replaced by their means.

The basic model has symmetric, 3-point probability distributions (0.2, 0.6, 0.2) for the deposit flow constraints and degenerate probability distributions for the liquidity and policy constraints. The penalties for all stochastic constraints are asymmetric. The optimal value of the basic model is $2,520,316.01 ($8,288,941.53 in expected profits minus $6,282,885 in expected penalties). As shown by Madansky (1960) the mean model provides an upper bound on the optimal value of a stochastic linear program; in this instance, the bound is 8.3% above the optimal value of the basic model, or $2,729,502.24. The solution to the mean model, when used as a feasible point in the basic model, provides the lower bound of $2,278,187, some 9.6% less than the optimal value. The structure of the two portfolios is similar in the initial period; however, the investment patterns differ in later periods. In particular, the basic model invests less heavily in less liquid assets (namely mortgages). See Kusy for specifics.

Table V
Cost of 5-Year Term Deposit

Year	Cost
1970	$(0.5)(0.0850)(0.9435) = 0.0401$
1971	$(0.82)(0.0850)(0.9110) = 0.0635$
1972	$(0.82)(0.64)(0.0850)(0.8797) = 0.0392$
1973	$(0.82)(0.64)^2(0.0850)(0.8341) = 0.0238$
1974	$(0.82)(0.64)^3(0.0850)(0.7736) = 0.0141$
Total Cost	0.1807

The mean model was initially infeasible, since the initial portfolio held by VCS violated the liquidity constraints (a situation known to management). To secure feasibility, we added variables to the liquidity constraints. The objective coefficients of these variables were the same as the penalties associated with violating the stochastic liquidity constraints in the basic model. To develop further insight into the operations of VCS, we could set the penalties arbitrarily high so that the model would vioalte the liquidity constraints only to attain feasibility. The amount by which the constraints are violated will be the amount of liquid reserves that the firm needs to meet the FRB's suggested liquidity requirements.

Variants of the basic model were run in order to ascertain the effects of different probability distributions, penalty costs and parameter values. The initial change was the alteration of the first legal constraint from the requirement that current assets be at least 10% of the liabilities to at least 1% of the liabilities. This change increases the optimal value of $2,906,773.53 ($8,657,619.24 in expected profits minus $5,750,845.71 in expected penalties). For the initial two periods, the investment pattern deviated substantially from that of the basic model in that more of the incremental funds were allocated to longer term assets. After the first two periods, there was no generalizable behavior in the investment patterns of the two models.

The basic model was then further altered to include a change in the probability distributions (0.05, 0.50,

0.45) of the cash flows. The optimal value increases to \$3,256,500.65 (\$8,872,911.53 in expected profits minus \$5,661,410.80 in expected penalties). The expected net profit rises compared with the basic model and the model with the parameter change, while the expected penalty costs decrease in both cases because:

1. all the violations of the stochastic constraints are now feasible only with a probability 0.05 instead of 0.2 (decreased penalties); and
2. constraints that were not violated in the basic model because of excessive penalties are now violated in the modified model by 15%, resulting in more profits.

Although it is not possible to make definitive generalizations from these runs of the ALM model, some conclusions may be inferred. First, the asymmetry of the probability distibutions may have a substantial effect on the optimal solutions and values. Of particular importance is the sensitivity of the estimate of the probability distribution around the value on the left-hand side of the stochastic constraints. Second, the solutions are sensitive to changing penalty costs. Third, the various stochastic models have substantially different solutions than the mean model. This result indicates that reliance on the deterministic models as normative tools can lead to erroneous solutions. Fourth, the implementation of this model is no more difficult than the implementation of a similar deterministic model. Finally, solving the ALM formulation requires the same order of computations necessary for the mean or related deterministic models. (Kallberg, White, and Ziemba found similar conclusions on a SLPSR model of short-term financial planning.) The runs were made on the University of British Columbia's IBM 370/168. The ALM model is 92 variables and 257 constraints, with 40 stochastic constraints. Using the SLPSR code (Kallberg and Kusy), the ALM model's solution took 37 seconds of CPU time. To solve an equivalent sized deterministic problem took 30 seconds using the SLPSR code and 17 seconds on the standard linear programming code UBC LIP. Experience in solving SLPSR models and related deterministic problems indicates that the CPU times are in a ratio of about 1.5–2 to 1. Detailed output appears in Kusy.

5. Comparison of the ALM and SDT Approaches

The asset and liability management problem is a continuous decision problem in which actions (e.g., portfolio revisions) are made continuously on the basis of new information (e.g., differing forecasts of future interest rates, and the like). The ideal way to model the ALM problem would be via a continuous, time-adaptive stochastic dynamic program. At present such a formulation is computationally intractable for the types of problems we are considering. ALM, and Bradley and Crane's stochastic decision tree model (SDT), which is described in this section, constitute two types of operational models that discretize time and probability distributions. In this section, we simulate a large number of economic scenarios to compare these two models.

5.1. The Bradley–Crane Stochastic Decision Tree Model (SDT)

The Bradley–Crane (1972, 1973, 1976) model depends upon the development of economic scenarios that are intended to include the set of all possible outcomes. The scenarios may be viewed as a tree diagram for which each element (economic conditions) in each path has a set of cash flows and interest rates. The problem is formulated as a linear program whose objective is the maximization of expected terminal wealth of the firm. There are four types of constraints:

A. cash flow—the firm cannot purchase more assets than it has funds available;
B. inventory balancing, which ensures that the firm cannot sell and/or hold more of an asset at the end of a period than it held at the beginning;
C. capital loss, which does not allow the net realized capital losses in a period to exceed some prespecified upper bound; and
D. class composition, which limits the holding of a particular asset.

The basic formulation is

$$\text{maximize} \sum_{e_N \in E_N} p(e_N) \sum_{k=1}^{K} \left\{ \sum_{m=0}^{N-1} [y_m^k(e_m) + v_{m,N}^k(e_N)] h_{mN}^k(e_N) + [y_N^k(e_N) + v_{NN}^k(e_N)] b_N^k(e_N) \right\}$$

subject to

$$\text{A)} \quad \sum_{k=1}^{K} b_n^k(e_n) - \sum_{k=1}^{K} \left[\sum_{m=0}^{n-2} y_m^k(e_m) h_{m,n-1}^k(e_{n-1}) + y_{n-1}^k(e_{n-1}) b_{n-1}^k(e_{n-1}) \right]$$

$$- \sum_{k=1}^{K} \sum_{m=0}^{n-1} [1 + g_{m,n}^k(e_n)] s_{m,n}^k(e_n) = f_n(e_n) \quad \text{(Cash flows)}$$

$$\text{B)}\quad -h^k_{m,n-1}(e_n-1)+s^k_{m,n}(e_n)+h^k_{m,n}(e_n)=0,\qquad m=0,\ldots,n-2$$

$$-b^k_{n-1}(e_{n-1})+s^k_{n-1,n}(e_n)+h^k_{n-1,n}(e_n)=0,$$

$$h^k_{0,0}(e_0)=h^k_0 \qquad \text{(Inventory Balance)}$$

$$\text{C)}\quad -\sum_{k=1}^{K}\sum_{m=0}^{n-1} g^k_{m,n}(e_n)s^k_{m,n}(e_n)\leqslant L_n(e_n) \qquad \text{(Capital Losses)}$$

$$\text{D)}\quad \sum_{k\in K^i}\left[b^k_n(e_n)+\sum_{m=0}^{n-1}h^k_{m,n}(e_n)\right](\lesseqgtr)C^i_n(e_n),\qquad i=1,\ldots I$$

$$\text{(Category Limits)}$$

$$b^k_{m,n}(e_n)\geqslant 0,\quad s^k_{m,n}(e_n)\geqslant 0,\quad h^k_{m,n}(e_n)\leqslant 0,\qquad m=1,\ldots,n-1$$

$$\text{(Nonnegativity)}$$

where

$e_n \in E_n$; $n = 1, \ldots, N$;
$k = 1, \ldots, K$;
e_n is an economic scenario from period 1 to n having probability $p(e_n)$;
E_n is the set of possible economic scenarios from period 1 to n;
K_i is the number of assets of type i, and K is the total number of assets;
N is the number of time periods;
$y^k_m(e_m)$ is the income yield per dollar of purchase price in period m of asset k, conditional on e_m;
$v^k_{m,N}(e_N)$ is the expected terminal value per dollar of purchase price in period m of asset k held at the horizon (period N), conditional on e_N;
$b^k_n(e_n)$ is the dollar amount of asset k purchased in period n, conditional on e_n;
$h^k_{m,n}(e_n)$ is the dollar amount of asset k purchased in period m and held in period n, conditional on e_n;
$s^k_{m,n}(e_n)$ is the dollar amount of asset k purchased in period m and sold in period n, conditional on e_n;
$g^k_{m,n}(e_n)$ is the capital gain (loss) per dollar of purchase price in period m of asset k sold in period n;
$f_n(e_n)$ is the incremental increase (decrease) of funds available for period n;
$L_n(e_n)$ is the dollar amount of maximum allowable net realized capital losses in period n; and
$C^i_n(e_n)$ is the upper (lower) bound in dollars on the amount of funds invested in asset type i in period n.

The SDT formulation is a true dynamic model. The first decision (immediate revision, $h^k_{01}(e_1)$, $b^k(e_1)$, $s^k_{01}(e_1)$) has as its feasible set the intersection of all possible realizations. That is, the current solution must be feasible for the set E_N. This decision is conditional on the realization of economic events in the first period. Similarly, in each succeeding period to the end of the planning horizon, the decisions generated are all conditional on the states of nature that have occurred up to the current decision point.

The model has a number of attractive features, including its dynamic nature and associated clever solution using decomposition. However, the formulation has features that detract from its practicability. The capital loss and category limit constraints have as upper (or lower) bounds amounts (resources) generated arbitrarily by portfolio managers rather than through a systematic procedure. For example, no consideration is given to the portfolio mix in the development of bounds, except in the sense that upper (or lower) bounds are placed on asset categories. At some point, this situation may imply that the bank has invested a disproportionate amount of its available funds in long-term bonds compared to the amount of short-term liabilities held. Also, the formulation does not have any liquidity constraints. Since the capital loss and category limit constraints actually determine the composition of the solution, the arbitrary nature of the choice may bias the solution.

One feature of the SDT model is that first period feasibility is assured for every possible scenario. Such fat formulations (see, e.g., Madansky 1962) shrink the feasible set and give substantial importance to scenarios with low probabilities of occurrence. For example, consider the two-period problem for which an investor:

1. has \$100 in period 1 to invest in asset x_{11} with return $r_{11} = 0.1$ maturing after one period, or x_{12} with return $r_{12} = 0.2$ per period maturing after two periods;
2. receives in period 2 either an additional \$50 to invest with probability 0.9 or loses \$50 with probability 0.1;
3. has, in period 2, the opportunity to invest in a one-period asset x_{21} with return $r_{21} = 0.1$ or can sell off his holdings in x_{12} at a 20% discount; and
4. stipulates that his realized capital losses cannot exceed 10% of the outstanding funds in any period.

The linear programming optimal solution is $b^1_1(l_1) = 11.11$, $b^2_1(l_1) = 88.89$, $b^1_2(l_{21}) = 80.00$, $h^1_2(l_{22}) = 0$, $h^2_{12}(l_{21}) = 88.89$, $h^2_1(l_{12}) = 63.89$, $S^1_{12}(l_{21}) = 11.11$, $S^1_{12}(l_{22}) = 11.11$, $S^2_{12}(l_{21}) = 0$, $S^2_{12}(l_{22}) = 25.00$, with optimal value \$42.87, where "*b*" means buy, "*h*" hold, and "*s*" sell and the *l*'s denote the possible scenario of events. The bound on realized capital losses is binding. If a maximal loss of 15% were allowed, it would be optimal to purchase \$100 of asset x_{12} and sell \$37.50

Table VI
Size of Bradley-Crane Model

Model	Number of: Assets	Asset Classes	Time Periods	Possible Realizations Per Period	Variables	Constraints
(1)	8	1	3	3	656	319
(2)	30	5	3	3	2,460	1,141
(3)	30	5	3	5	6,120	2,827
(4)	30	5	5	5	246,120	116,827

of x_{12} at the end of period 1, if the \$50 is lost. This modification yields an optimal value of \$44.11. Thus consideration of this low probability event significantly alters the optimal solution. By contrast, in the simple recourse ALM formulation, the right-hand sides are not binding; recourse at a penalty cost is allowed to compensate for decision infeasibility. The recourse formulation has more first-period decision flexibility than the decision tree formulation.

To gain computational tractability, the SDT model considers only bonds. If D is the number of possible realizations per period, n is the number of time periods, I is the number of asset claims, and K is the number of assets, then the number of variables is $(3 + 5D + 7D^2 + \ldots + (2n + 1)D^{n-1})$. The number of constraints equals the sum of the cash flow constraints: $(1 + D + D^2 + \ldots + D^{n-1})$, the capital loss constraints $(1 + D + D^2 + \ldots + D^{n-1})$, the category limit constraints $(I)(1 + D + D^2 + \ldots + D^{n-1})$, the inventory balance constraints $(K)(I + 2D + 3D^2 + \ldots + nD^{n-1})$, and the initial conditions K. Table VI shows the effect of differing numbers of assets, possible realizations per period, and number of periods on problem size.

Bradley and Crane (1976) solved model (1) in 68 seconds on an IBM 360/65. The subsequent models add more realism and are much larger. In the case of (4), the basis of the master problem, if one uses decomposition, has 5467 rows and the problem has about 850,000 nonzero elements. The computational and data-handling difficulties of (2) and (3) are less striking but remain formidable. Bradley and Crane (1976, p. 112) are aware of these computational difficulties:

> Unfortunately, taking uncertainty explicitly into account will make an asset and liability management model for the entire bank computationally intractable, unless it is an extremely aggregated model. The complexities of the general dynamic balance sheet management problem are such that the number of constraints and variables needed to accurately model the environment would be very large.

Our aim has been to develop a computationally tractable model that still has some dynamic and other desirable features and represents a practical approach to bank asset and liability management. We now compare the ALM and SDT models via simulation.

5.2. The Economic Scenarios

To maintain computational feasibility for the SDT model, we considered only three assets and one liability over three periods. The assets are a one-period treasury bill, a term deposit maturing beyond the horizon of the model and a long-term mortgage. The liability is a demand deposit. The returns and costs of these financial instruments were generated from 26 consecutive observations using data from the Bank of Canada. To obtain a reasonable correlation of interest rates, the returns and costs were made a function of the prime rate using the following distribution of the prime rate (R):

$\Pr(R = r)$	6/26	3/26	1/26	2/26	1/26	2/26	4/26
r	0.06	0.065	0.0675	0.075	0.0775	0.08	0.085

$\Pr(R = r)$	2/26	2/26	2/26	1/26
r	0.09	0.095	0.11	0.115

The distributions in Table VII were derived for the difference between the prime rate and the rate of return of each of the four financial instruments, where the random variables, M, D, T, and L are defined to be the difference between the prime rate and the

Table VII
Distributions Derived from Difference between the Prime Rate and Rate of Return of Financial Instruments

m	$P(M \leq m)$	d	$P(D \leq d)$	t	$P(T \leq t)$	l	$P(L \leq l)$
0.0037	0.0	−0.0104	0.0	−0.0388	0.0	−0.0275	0.0
0.0088	0.2	−0.0072	0.2	−0.306	0.2	−0.025	0.2
0.0198	0.42	+0.0008	0.44	−0.0253	0.5	−0.0225	0.31
0.0235	0.62	+0.004	0.5	−0.0225	0.77	−0.2	0.92
0.0297	0.81	+0.118	0.78	−0.0174	0.81	−0.175	1.00
0.0338	1.00	+0.0195	1.00	−0.0051	1.00		

mortgage rate, term deposit rate, treasury bill rate and liability rate, respectively. At time zero the investor has \$100,000 in demand deposits invested equally in the three assets. The demand deposits are assumed to increase (decrease) uniformly from one period to the next on [−20,000, 20,000]. If the demand deposits decrease so that assets must be liquidated, then the FRB's parameters for quick liquidation are used. The discounts for treasury bills, term deposits, and mortgages are 0.5%, 4%, and 6%, respectively. The constraints on the investor are of the BC type and include 1) cash flows, 2) capital losses, 3) class composition, and 4) terminal conditions. The capital loss constraints assume that the investor does not want to realize net losses of more than 3% of the outstanding demand deposits in periods 1 and 2, and 4% in period 3. The class composition constraints limit the investor from having more than \$50,000 in total investments in any asset in periods 1 and 2, and \$60,000 in period 3. The terminal constraints include a discount on the assets in the current portfolio so that all funds are not simply invested in the highest yielding assets and held to the horizon of the model. These discounts are one-half of the normal discounts. The objective of the model is to maximize the net expected returns.

5.3. Formulations of the Stochastic Dynamic Programming Model

Formulating the SDP requires the establishment of an economic scenario over the three-period horizon. This scenario includes a representative distribution for cash flows and the rate of return for the various financial instruments. Since for computational tractability SDP requires crude approximations of probability distributions, we limited to two the number of possible realizations of the random variables during each time period. With initial demand deposits of \$100,000 and an incremental difference in the interval [−20,000, 20,000], a natural 2-point distribution is \$90,000 and \$110,000 with equal probabilities. Using this distribution, we maintained the mean of the underlying distribution, although the variance was smaller (1.0×10^5 versus 1.33×10^5). The distribution was constructed similarly at the third decision point. The cash flows have the distribution shown in Figure 1.

Using the same approach gives the first period rate of return for a particular financial instrument (assume mortgage rate) as the median prime rate ($\bar{R}$) plus the median of the difference between the prime rate and the rate of return of the mortgages ($\bar{M}$). The two-point estimate in the second period is $\bar{R}$ plus m, where $P(M \leq m) = 0.25$. The four rates of return in the third period are $\bar{R} + m$ where $P(M \leq m)$ is 0.875, 0.625, 0.375, and 0.125, respectively.

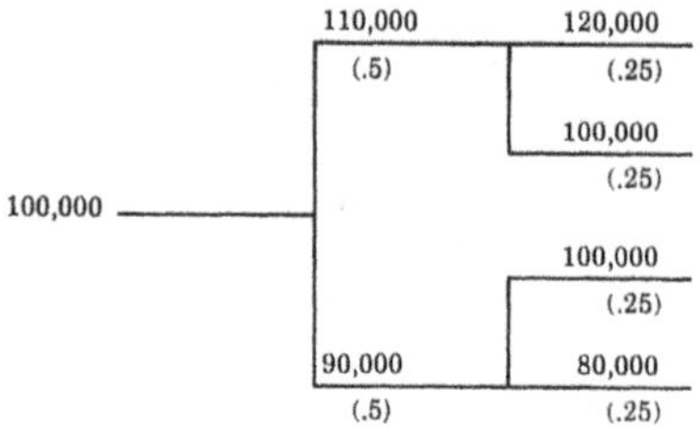

Figure 1. Cash flow distribution.

Figure 2 specifies the distribution of the rates of return used in this example.

For the simulation, we used 70% of the nonchecking rate as the demand deposit rate since the nonchecking rate dominates the treasury bill rate, a situation that would have precluded investment in treasury bills a priori. This ad hoc derivation of the demand deposit rate does not impinge on the usefulness of the simulation because the objective is to demonstrate that one solution technique may be operationally superior.

Treasury bills mature after one period, hence 18 variables define all potential investment opportunities. Since the term deposits and mortgages mature beyond the horizon of the model, 42 variables are required to describe all investment opportunities in each of these categories. The variables necessary to define the demand deposits include the initial position, the demand deposit flows in period 1, two demand deposit flows in period 2, and the 4 demand deposit flows in period 3. In all, 110 variables define the investment opportunities in the problem.

There are 4 types of constraints. Constraints 1 to 7 are the cash flow requirements for each period under each economic scenario; namely, uses of funds equal sources of funds. Constraints 8 to 14 require realized capital losses to be less than 3% of the outstanding demand deposits in period 1 and 2, and 4% in period 3. Constraints 15–35 limit the funds invested in each asset, as prescribed in the problem. Constraints 36–89 (inventory balancing) consist of the initial holdings of each of the four financial instruments and record the transactions in each economic scenario.

The demand deposit flow constraint for period 1 places an upper bound on the funds potentially available for investment. The capital loss constraints and the composition constraints add another 28 slack variables to the formulation. The SDT formulation has 89 constraints and 139 variables.

The objective is to maximize the expected value of the net returns from the portfolio over the horizon of

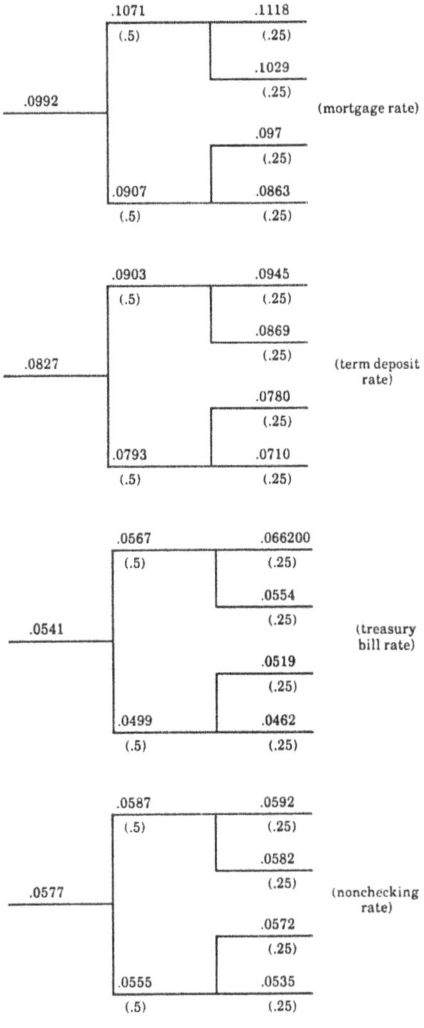

Figure 2. Distribution of rates of return.

the model. The coefficient of each variable is the product of the net return and its probability of occurrence.

5.4. Formulations of the ALM Model

The ALM uses the same information as the SDT model although it has fewer constraints because of its different treatment of uncertainty. The investment opportunities for treasury bills, term deposits, mortgages, and demand deposits are defined by 6, 11, 11 and 4 variables, respectively. There are 25 constraints, of which 5 are stochastic. The key constraints are:

(i) 3 constraints to balance the initial holding of an asset with the future buying and selling of the asset;

(ii) 3 constraints that equate the cash flows for the 3 periods;

(iii) 3 constraints for each of the 3 assets for composition requirements;

(iv) 4 constraints to describe the initial position of the 3 assets and 1 liability;

(v) 3 capital loss constraints of which the first period's is deterministic as constraints (i) to (iv) listed above, and the others are stochastic; and

(vi) 3 stochastic constraints that describe the flow of demand deposits.

When we add 9 slack variables for the class composition constraints and 1 for the deterministic capital loss constraint, the SLPR formulation has 25 constraints and 42 variables, plus the recourse variables.

The right-hand sides of the stochastic demand deposit constraints are representative points from the uniform distribution used in the SDT model. However, because of the ability of the Wets algorithm to handle many realizations without creating computational difficulties, the number of points chosen is larger than in the SDT model. The penalty for violations of any of these constraints is the net return to the horizon of the model, generated by a portfolio consisting of 50% mortgages and 50% term deposits, since their portfolio is considered, a priori, to be potentially the highest yielding portfolio. This penalty is

$$0.5[(1+\bar{r}_m)^{4-n}-1]+0.5[(1+\bar{r}_t)^{4-n}-1]-[(1+\bar{r}_d)^{4-n}-1],$$

where $n = 1, 2, 3$ is the period; $\bar{r}_m$ is the median return on mortgages; $\bar{r}_t$ is the median return on term deposits; and $\bar{r}_d$ is the median cost of demand deposits.

The right-hand sides of the stochastic capital loss constraints are the representative points used in the SDT formulation. A penalty of 4.1% is used for violations of these constraints.

The objective is to maximize the net returns minus the expected penalties for constraint violations. The coefficient of each variable is the net return for the first-stage variables and the penalty for the second-stage variables.

5.5. Results of the Simulation

In normative financial planning models, the objective is generally to determine which portfolio changes should be effected immediately. The multiperiodicity of financial models compensates for the shifting economic scenarios across time. However, the purpose of the model is to determine the changes to be implemented immediately. Hence the simulation is intended to determine which model produces the best first-period solution. In reality, decisions may be made at any point in a period; however, a discrete time model will aggregate information to consider all decisions to be made at the start of each period—facing random rates of return. Again, the incremental cash flows are aggregated so that one-half is available at the beginning of the current period. In both formulations the same initial security holdings are given and the cash flows for the next period are random.

The process starts with an initial portfolio. Both the ALM and SDT models determine an optimal solution for the first period. A random cash flow is then generated. If the amount of funds spent during the first period exeeds the random cash flow, then an amount equal to excess spending is divested from the present portfolio, which consists of 45% of mortgages, 45% term deposits and 10% treasury bills. If random cash flows exceed spending during the first period, then the incremental amount is invested in treasury bills. After this reconciliation, revenues are the sum of the known returns of the assets held since the start of the period and the random returns of the assets bought at the start of the period. The costs are the sum of the random cost of demand deposits and the discount for selling securities prior to maturity. The reconciled portfolio serves as the new initial portfolio, which is then used to generate new solutions for both models. This cycle is repeated 8 times. The process is repeated 50 times, for a total of 400 scenarios. See Kusy for the simulation flowchart, computer program and details of the results.

The simulation results for the ALM and SDT formulations are used to test two hypotheses. The first hypothesis

$$H_1\colon \mu_d = \mu^1_{\mathrm{SDP}} - \mu^1_{\mathrm{ALM}} \geqslant 0$$

is used to test whether or not the initial period profit for ALM is superior to that for SDT. We test this hypothesis by examining the paired differences of the profits for the initial run of the 50 cycles for both models. The specific information used is:

1. the mean of the paired difference ($251.37 in favor of ALM); and
2. the standard deviation of the paired differences ($150.43).

The correlation between the ALM and SDT profits is 0.958. Given the large sample, the significance of the paired differences is tested using the t statistic

$$\frac{-251.37}{1.50.43/\sqrt{50}} = -11.81.$$

The test statistic is significant at the 0.001 level, hence the null hypothesis is rejected. Thus, ALM yields a statistically significant better initial solution than SDT.

The second hypothesis

$$H_2\colon \mu_d = \mu_{\mathrm{SDP}} - \mu_{\mathrm{ALM}} \geqslant 0$$

is used to test whether the mean profit for ALM is superior to that for SDT.

We test this hypothesis by examining the paired differences of the mean profits of the 8 runs of 50 cycles for both models. The specific information used is:

1. the mean of the paired differences ($297.26 in favor of ALM); and
2. the standard deviation of the paired differences ($308.74).

The correlation between the ALM and SDT mean profits is 0.785. The t statistic is

$$\frac{-297.26}{308.74\sqrt{50}} = -6.81.$$

Since this statistic is significant at the 0.001 level, the null hypothesis is rejected. Thus the ALM formulation yields a statistically significant better solution than the SDT formulation.

To test the stability of these summary statistics, we ran a second simulation, using ALM. The results of this simulation are analyzed similarly: 1) a test of the initial solution of the 50 cycles, and 2) a test of the mean profits for the 8 runs of the 50 cycles. The information necessary to test the first hypothesis is 1) the mean profits for the first and second ALM runs ($4645.85 and $4672.23, respectively), and 2) the standard deviations for the 2 runs ($421.11 and $482.15, respectively). We first test the hypothesis that both samples have the same mean

$$H_3\colon \mu_{\mathrm{ALM}_1} = \mu_{\mathrm{ALM}_2}.$$

The standard deviation used for the test statistic is the root of the pooled variance. The test statistic is

$$\frac{4672.23 - 4645.85}{90.53} = 0.291.$$

The test statistic for the final hypothesis is established similarly and is

$$\frac{4783.13 - 4720.15}{86.84} = 0.730.$$

Since the test statistics for H_3 and H_4 are not significant at the 0.10 level, there is no evidence that the mean is not stable.

We used a CDC 6400 at the University of British Columbia to perform the computations. The total CPU time to perform the 400 iterations for ALM was 0.240 hours, and for SDP, 6.385 hours. This difference in computation time explains why only a limited number of financial instruments, time periods and realizations were used in the simulations, and highlights the gap in tractability between the ALM and SDT techniques. Details of the codes used to perform the simulations appear in Kusy.

6. Final Remarks

The existing literature on bank asset and liability management is based on two approaches: the mean variance portfolio selection model, and models that utilize an objective of maximizing expected net returns. Section 1 reviews deterministic and stochastic models that are based on these constraints. In an attempt to determine which of these two approaches is most suitable for asset and liability management problems, Myers (1968) showed that existence of security market equilibrium implies that net present value is the appropriate objective function. The most comprehensive model of this type is the Bradley–Crane stochastic decision tree model (1972, 1973, 1976). They attempted to overcome the crucial obstacle to asset and liability management of incorporating uncertainty while maintining computational tractability. Their model is a useful one and offers many important insights. However, it does not really maintain computational tractability for realistically sized bank asset and liability management problems. It also possesses some undesirable features, notably arbitrary constraints on capital losses, an absence of portfolio mix constraints and an immediate revision that must satisfy all possible forecasted economic constraints.

The ALM model is an attempt to remedy some of these deficiencies and, as shown in Sections 3 and 4, is an implementable model of bank asset and liability management. The results of the application to the Vancouver City Savings Credit Union indicate that the ALM model is superior to related deterministic models, and the simulations in Section 5 indicate that ALM generates better first-period decisions than does the Bradley–Crane SDT model. An additional advantage of ALM over SDT is that the results of small changes in parameter values and previous realizations can easily be determined by calculating penalties, while SDT may become infeasible. The CPU time to solve ALM is 1.5–2 times that of a related deterministic model and much less than that required for the Bradley–Crane model (0.24 hour versus 6.39 hours for simulation, as shown in Section 5). Hence ALM is a feasible option for implementation in large banks. To apply ALM, one must determine essentially the same information as with a deterministic model: 1) deposit flow estimates, 2) estimates fo the term structure of interest rates, 3) estimates of withdrawal rates of deposits under various economic conditions, 4) legal constraints governing the behavior of the financial institution, 5) policy constraints, 6) recommended reserves for maintaining a liquid position, and 7) the initial position of the firm plus discrete probability distributions for random elements and penalty costs. The model is capable of handling useful policy constraints. The major drawback of ALM is that it is not a true dynamic model. Simulations such as those in Section 5 provide confidence in the approach taken in ALM. Birge (1983) delineates bounds on the error associated with aggregation schemes (such as the one used in this paper) in the context of general recourse models. The general problem of the accuracy of various approximations in multiperiod stochastic programs is currently being studied by Ziemba in collaboration with J. Birge, M. A. H. Dempster, H. Gassman, P. Kall and R. Wets. The results of their work will, we hope, provide general guidance regarding solution technique trade-offs in dynamic stochastic modeling. See Birge and Wets (1986) and Kall, Frauendorfer and Ruszczyński (1984) for surveys of the current theory in this area.

Acknowledgment

Without implicating them, we would like to thank J. Birge, W. Bühler, D. T. Ellis, H. Gassmann, J. G. Kallberg, C. E. Sarndal, R. W. White and the referees for their helpful discussions and comments on an earlier draft, and Messrs. Bentley and Hook of the Vancouver City Savings Credit Union for providing data used in this study. This research was supported by the International Institute for Applied Systems Analysis, Laxenburg, Austria; the Canada Council; and the Natural Sciences and Engineering Research Council of Canada.

References

Bank of Canada Review. 1975. (various issues).

BARR, J. A. et al. 1984 *Financial Reporting for Credit Unions*, Canadian Institute of Chartered Accountants.

BEALE, E. M. L. 1955. On Minimizing a Convex Function Subject to Linear Inequalities. *J. Roy. Stat. Soc. Ser. B* **17**, 173–184.

BEAZER, W. F. 1975. *Optimization of Bank Portfolios*, D. C. Health, Lexington, Mass.

BIRGE, J. R. 1982. The Value of the Stochastic Solution in Stochastic Linear Programs with Fixed Recourse. *Math. Program.* **24**, 314–325.

BIRGE, J. R. 1983. Aggregation Bounds in Stochastic Linear Programming. Department of Industrial and Operations Engineering, University of Michigan, Technical Report 83-1.

BIRGE, J. R., AND R. J.-B. WETS. 1986. Designing Approximation Schemes for Stochastic Optimization Problems, in Particular for Stochastic Programs with Recourse. *Math. Program. Study* **27**, 54–102.

BOOTH, G. G. 1972. Programming Bank Portfolios Under Uncertainty: An Extension. *J. Bank Res.* **2**, 28–40.

BRADLEY, S. P., AND D. B. CRANE. 1972. A Dynamic Model for Bond Portfolio Management. *Mgmt. Sci.* **19**, 139–151.

BRADLEY, S. P., AND D. B. CRANE. 1973. Management of Commercial Bank Government Security Portfolios: An Optimization Approach Under Uncertainty. *J. Bank Res.* **4**, 18–30.

BRADLEY, S. P., AND D. B. CRANE. 1976. *Management of Bank Portfolios*. John Wiley & Sons, New York.

BRITISH COLUMBIA GOVERNMENT. 1982a. *Credit Union Act*.

BRITISH COLUMBIA GOVERNMENT. 1982b. *Credit Union Regulation*.

BRODT, A. I. 1979. A Multi-Period Portfolio Theory Model for Commercial Bank Management. In *Portfolio Theory: 25 Years After*, E. J. Elton and M. J. Gruber (eds.). TIMS Studies in the Management Sciences, pp. 191–213. North Holland, Amsterdam.

CENTRAL MORTGAGE AND HOUSING CORPORATION. 1975. Canadian Housing Statistics.

CHAMBERS, D., AND A. CHARNES. 1961. Inter-Temporal Analysis and Optimization of Bank Portfolios. *Mgmt. Sci.* **7**, 393–410.

CHARNES, A., GALLEGOS AND S. YAO. 1982. A Chance-Constrained Approach to Bank Dynamic Balance Sheet Management. Centre for Cybernetic Studies CCS 428, University of Texas, Austin.

CHARNES, A., AND M. J. L. KIRBY. 1965. Application of Chance-Constrained Programming to the Solution of the So-Called "Savings and Loan" Association Type of Problem. Research Analysis Corporation, McLean, Va.

CHARNES, A., AND S. C. LITTLECHILD. 1968. Intertemporal Bank Asset Choice with Stochastic Dependence. Systems Research Memorandum No. 188. The Technological Institute, Northwestern University.

CHARNES, A., AND S. THORE. 1966. Planning for Liquidity in Financial Institutions: The Chance-Constrained Method. *J. Finan.* **21**, 649–674.

COHEN, K. J., AND F. S. HAMMER. 1967. Linear Programming and Optimal Bank Asset Management Decision. *J. Finan.* **22**, 42–61.

COHEN, K. J., AND F. S. HAMMER. 1972. Linear Programming Models for Optimal Bank Dynamic Balance Sheet Management. In *Mathematical Methods in Investments and Finance*, G. P. Szego and K. Shell (eds.). North Holland, Amsterdam.

COHEN, K. J., AND S. THORE. 1970. Programming Bank Portfolios under Uncertainty. *J. Bank Res.* **1**, 42–61.

COHEN, K. J., S. F. MAISER AND J. H. VAN DER WEIDE. 1981. Recent Development in Management Science in Banking. *Mgmt. Sci.* **27**, 1097–1119.

COLLINS, H. 1975. A Code for Stochastic Linear Programs with Simple Recourse. Department of Mathematics, University of Kentucky.

CRANE, D. B. 1971. A Stochastic Programming Model for Commercial Bank Bond Portfolio Management. *J. Finan. Quant. Anal.* **6**, 955–976.

CREDIT UNION RESERVE BOARD. 1973. A Report on the Adequacy of the Financial Capacity of the Credit Union Reserve Board.

CROSSE, H. D., AND G. H. HEMPEL. 1973. *Management Policies for Commercial Banks*, Ed. 2. Prentice-Hall, Englewood Cliffs, N.J.

DAELLENBACH, H. G. 1974. Are Cash Management Optimization Models Worthwhile? *J. Finan. Quant. Anal.* **9**, 608–626.

DAELLENBACH, H. G., AND S. A. ARCHER. 1969. The Optimal Bank Liquidity: A Multi-Period Stochastic Model. *J. Finan. Quant. Anal.* **4**, 329–343.

DANTZIG, G. B. 1955. Linear Programming under Uncertainty. *Mgmt. Sci.* **1**, 197–206.

EISNER, M. J., R. S. KAPLAN, AND J. V. SODEN. 1971. Admissible Decision Rules for the E-Model of Chance-Constrained Programming. *Mgmt. Sci.* **17**, 337–353.

ELLIS, D. 1984. Personal Communication, July 20, 1984.

EPPEN, G. D., AND E. F. FAMA. 1968. Solutions for Cash Balance and Simple Dynamic Portfolio Problems. *J. Business* **41**, 94–112.

EPPEN, G. D., AND E. F. FAMA. 1969. Optimal Policies for Cash Balance and Simple Dynamic Portfolio Models with Proportional Costs. *Int. Econ. Rev.* **10**, 119–133.

EPPEN, G. D., AND E. F. FAMA. 1971. Three Asset Cash Balance and Dynamic Portfolio Problems. *Mgmt. Sci.* **17**, 311–319.

GRINOLD, R. 1977. Finite Horizon Approximations of Infinite Horizon Linear Programs. *Mathematical Programming*.

GRINOLD, R. 1980. Time Horizons in Energy Planning Models. In *Energy Policy Modeling: United States and Canadian Experiences*, Vol. II, pp. 216–237. W. T. Ziemba and S. L. Schwartz (eds.). Martinus Nijhoff, Boston.

GRINOLD, R. C. 1983. Model Building Techniques for the Correction of End Effects in Multistage Convex Programs. *Opns. Res.* **31,** 407–431.

HEMPEL, G. H. 1972. Basic Ingredients of Commercial Banks' Investment Policies. *Bankers Magazine* **155,** 59.

HESTER, D. D., AND J. L. PIERCE. 1975. *Bank Management and Portfolio Behavior.* Yale University Press, New Haven, Conn.

KALL, P. 1976. *Stochastic Programming.* Springer-Verlag, Berlin.

KALL, P., K. FRAUENDORFER AND A. RUSZCYŃSKI. 1984. Approximation Techniques in Stochastic Programming. Institut für Operations Research der Universität Zurich, Switzerland.

KALLBERG, J. G., AND M. I. KUSY. 1976. A Stochastic Linear Program with Simple Recourse. Faculty of Commerce, the University of British Columbia.

KALLBERG, J. G., R. W. WHITE, AND W. T. ZIEMBA. 1982. Short Term Financial Planning under Uncertainty. *Mgmt. Sci.* **28,** 670–682.

KALLBERG, J. G., AND W. T. ZIEMBA. 1981. An Algorithm for Portfolio Revision: Theory, Computational Algorithm and Empirical Results. In *Applications of Management Science*, R. L. Schultz (ed.). JAI Press, Greenwich, Conn.

KOMAR, R. I. 1971. Developing a Liquidity Management Model. *J. Bank Res.* **2,** 38–52.

KUSY, M. I. 1978. An Asset and Liability Management Model. Ph.D. dissertation, Faculty of Commerce, University of British Columbia.

LIFSON, K. A., AND B. R. BLACKMAN. 1973. Simulation and Optimization Models for Asset Deployment and Funds Sources, Balancing Profit, Liquidity and Growth. *J. Bank Res.* **4,** 239–255.

MADANSKY, A. 1960. Inequalities for Stochastic Linear Programming Problems. *Mgmt. Sci.* **6,** 197–204.

MADANSKY, A. 1962. Methods of Solutions of Linear Programs under Uncertainty. *Opns. Res.* **10,** 165–176.

MARKOWITZ, H. M. 1959. *Portfolio Selection, Efficient Diversification of Investments.* John Wiley & Sons, New York.

MYERS, S. C. 1968. Procedures for Capital Budgeting under Uncertainty. *Indust. Mgmt. Rev.* **9,** 1–20.

PARIKH, S. C. 1968. Notes on Stochastic Programming (unpublished), I.E.O.R. Department, University of California, Berkeley.

PYLE, D. H. 1971. On the Theory of Financial Intermediation. *J. Finan.* **26,** 737–746.

SPELLMAN, L. J. 1982. *The Depository Firm and Industry: Theory, History and Regulation.* Academic Press, New York.

VANCOUVER CITY SAVINGS CREDIT UNION. 1968–1975. Financial Statements.

WETS, R. J.-B. 1966. Programming under Uncertainty: the Complete Problem. *Z. Wahrscheinlichk. Verw. Gebiete* **4,** 316–339.

WETS, R. J.-B. 1974. Solving Stochastic Programs with Simple Recourse I, mimeo, University of Kentucky.

WETS, R. J.-B. 1983. A Statistical Approach to the Solution of Stochastic Programs with (Convex) Simple Recourse. In *Generalized Lagrangians in Systems and Economic Theory*, A. Wierzbicki (ed.). I.I.A.S.A. Proceedings Series, Pergamon Press, Oxford.

WETS, R. J.-B. 1984. Solving Stochastic Programs with Simple Recourse. *Stochastics* **10,** 219–242.

WHITE, R. W., AND C. DOBRZANSHI. 1976. A Financial Planning Model for the Credit Union Reserve Board, Credit Union Reserve Board, Vancouver, B.C.

WOLF, C. R. 1969. A Model for Selecting Commercial Bank Government Security Portfolios. *Rev. Econ. Stat.* **1,** 40–52.

ZIEMBA, W. T. 1974. Stochastic Programs with Simple Recourse. In *Mathematical Programming: Theory and Practice*, pp. 213–273, P. L. Hammer and G. Zoutendijk (eds.). North Holland, Amsterdam.

ZIEMBA, W. T., AND R. G. VICKSON (eds.). 1975. *Stochastic Optimization Models in Finance.* Academic Press, New York.

Chapter 10

FORMULATION OF THE RUSSELL-YASUDA KASAI FINANCIAL PLANNING MODEL*

DAVID R. CARIÑO

Frank Russell Australia, Sydney, Australia

WILLIAM T. ZIEMBA

University of British Columbia, Vancouver, British Columbia, Canada

(Received July 1995; revisions received January 1997, September 1997, December 1997; accepted January 1998)

This paper describes the formulation of the Russell-Yasuda Kasai financial planning model, including the motivation for the model. The presentation complements the discussion of the technical details of the financial modeling process and the managerial impact of its use to help allocate the firm's assets over time discussed in Cariño et al. (1994, 1998, respectively). The multistage stochastic linear program incorporates Yasuda Kasai's asset and liability mix over a five-year horizon followed by an infinite horizon steady-state end-effects period. The objective is to maximize expected long-run profits less expected penalty costs from constraint violations over the infinite horizon. Scenarios are used to represent the uncertain parameter distributions. The constraints represent the institutional, cash flow, legal, tax, and other limitations on the asset and liability mix over time.

The Yasuda Fire and Marine Insurance Co., Ltd. (Yasuda *Kasai*, or "fire," to distinguish it from the life insurer), based in Tokyo, commenced operations in 1888. It is the second largest Japanese property and casualty insurer and the seventh largest property and casualty insurer in the world by revenue. It has 685 branch offices in Japan and 31 overseas representative offices in 22 countries. The principal lines of business underwritten measured by premium volumes are voluntary automobile (43.0 percent), personal accident (14.4 percent), compulsory automobile (13.7 percent), fire and allied (14.4 percent), marine (3.3 percent), and other (11.2 percent). The firm's assets totaled 3.47 trillion yen ($26.2 billion) at the end of fiscal 1991 (March 31, 1992).

"The liability structure of the property and casualty insurance business has become very complex, and the insurance industry has various restrictions in terms of asset management."

"... we concluded that the existing models, such as Markowitz' mean-variance, would not function well and that we needed to develop a new asset-liability management model."

These words of Mr. Kunihiko Sasamoto, Director and Deputy President of Yasuda Kasai provide the motivation for the model developed in this paper. Yasuda Kasai sought the advice of a management consulting firm who recommended the Frank Russell Company (Russell) to develop and implement such a model.

Yasuda Kasai and Russell had discussions in 1988 and 1989 that led to an agreement for Russell to develop and implement a dynamic stochastic asset allocation model beginning in September 1989 for implementation by April 1, 1991. The goal was to implement a model of Yasuda Kasai's financial planning process to improve their investment and liability payment decisions and their overall risk management. The development by the Russell staff and consultants in Tacoma and Tokyo was made with collaboration with Yasuda Kasai staff in Tokyo. Yasuda Kasai's business goals were to (1) maximize long-run expected wealth, (2) pay enough interest on the insurance policies to be competitive in terms of both current yield and future reserves while at the same time they must (3) maintain adequate reserve and cash levels, and (4) meet regulatory requirements. Yasuda Kasai was faced with an increasing number of savings-oriented policies being sold which were generating new types of liabilities. Section 1 discusses the problem setting and provides an overview of the entire modeling and implementation effort.

The regulatory guidelines impose many restrictions through insurance law that lead to complex constraints. The approach should be superior to static Markowitz-style portfolio analysis which, although it is the industry standard for asset allocation, has several limitations for asset-liability management over time. In particular, it should have more realistic definitions of operating risks and business constraints than return variance, as well as a more explicit description of business goals, a greater expression

Subject classifications: Finance, management: asset and liability. Financial institutions, insurance: Japanese, property and casualty. Programming, stochastic: multiperiod, linear.
Area of review: OR PRACTICE.

*This chapter was originally published in: Cariño, D. R. & Ziemba, W. T. (1998). Formulation of the Russell–Yasuda Kasai Financial Planning Model. *Operations Research*, 46(4), 433–449.

of uncertainty, and a multistage as opposed to a single period analysis.

Yasuda Kasai wanted a model that would be solvable for runs with new data in several hours on a single workstation that could be operated by Yasuda Kasai staff independently of the Russell development team. They wanted all significant input to be parameterized and the model developed as a set of interlocking modules. It was desired that the risks be defined in operational terms such as the difference between actual and targeted income, cash flow shortages, and capital losses.

As model output it was essential to have the expected balance and income statements. This includes the optimal asset allocation for the initial period and the expected allocation for future periods, as well as the objective function values, shortfall costs, wealth accumulation over time, probability distribution of shortfalls by type and period, and information on various regulatory constraints, taxes, and foreign subsidiaries.

The modeling approach was multistage stochastic linear programming. The objective function maximizes the long run expected wealth net of penalty costs, subject to period-by-period constraints that model the asset allocation process, the liability commitments such as the policies with essentially guaranteed returns, the complex regulatory environment imposed by the regulatory guidelines, the effects of foreign subsidiaries, taxes, and other important considerations. The use of a linear (rather than nonlinear) formulation is not a significant simplification. The linear aspects of accounting relationships among variables in balance sheets and income statements lead to a linear formulation. Many financial problems have a natural linear constraint structure. The effects of the decision horizon were modeled using an end-effects steady-state period that adds one more set of constraints with one more set of variables for the steady-state period.

Section 2 provides background on multistage stochastic programming with recourse models and the application of such approaches to financial planning. The Russell-Yasuda Kasai (RY) model is developed in Section 3. It follows the Kallberg et al. (1982), Kusy (1978), and Kusy and Ziemba (1986) models, which considered liability balances as well as cash flows. KWZ showed how a two-stage model made improvements in short-term financial planning to match cash inflows and outflows over deterministic models with means inserted for the random variables. They learned how to set penalty costs and evaluated their effects on the problem's solution. Although the theory was developed, KWZ was not implemented. The Kusy-Ziemba model was an application to the Vancouver City Credit Union. They showed by simulation that the stochastic programming approach was superior to the decision tree dynamic programming approach developed by Bradley and Crane (1972, 1980). The latter model approach had a model size that escalated even more dramatically with additional periods and scenario realizations than the stochastic programming model. Also, the constraint structure was such that exact feasibility in later periods for all possible random return outcomes led to very few feasible first-period actions. Kusy and Ziemba implemented only a two-period model with rolling horizons. Even for that, they had to use many tricks to simplify and make feasible the computations including not using an end-effects period and using three point (high, low, and mean) distributions for the scenarios.

The RY model developed in Sections 3–7 has many more desirable features and is a much more sophisticated model of the complexity of Yasuda Kasai's business. The model is a true dynamic stochastic model with five decision periods (initialization, first quarter, rest of first year, second year, and third to fifth years) plus the end-effects periods. The discussion covers the model's constraints, including the regulatory guidelines' restrictions and the objective function.

Section 3 begins the formulation of the Russell-Yasuda model. The allocation constraints are discussed in Section 4. The loan model is presented in Section 5. The liability model is discussed in Section 6. The flow of funds model is presented in Section 7. Final remarks appear in Section 8. The companion paper, Cariño et al. (1998), presents technical aspects of the model, including the scenario generation process, the procedure for dealing with end effects, and a comparison of the multistage stochastic linear programming Russell-Yasuda model with static mean-variance analysis the previous technology used at Yasuda Kasai. Managerial and implementation aspects of the model are discussed in Cariño et al. (1994).

1. OVERVIEW OF YASUDA KASAI'S PROBLEM

The Russell-Yasuda Kasai (RY) model's software system discussed in Cariño et al. (1998) assists the firm in deciding how available funds should be allocated among potential investments to provide returns to cover liabilities and provide for long-term growth of the firm's wealth.

Yasuda Kasai's liabilities are multiperiod in character. At any given date there is a schedule of promised payouts to insurance policy holders and other creditors over time. Such obligations are accounted for in the books as liability balances. Liability balances change over time as scheduled payments are made, as reserves are set aside for existing obligations, or as new obligations are taken on. There is a multiperiod character to allocation decisions to be made. Although an allocation of assets is made today, similar decisions must be made in principle at every opportunity in the future. Given the influence of each allocation decision on future wealth, an asset/liability model should be a multiple-period decision model. Another fundamental aspect of the asset/liability problem is the random character of future asset returns. The asset/liability management problem of Yasuda Kasai is modeled as a multistage stochastic program over a finite horizon with a steady-state end-effects period.

We now discuss the setting of Yasuda Kasai's problem, review stochastic programming models, and formulate the model in detail. Yasuda Kasai's general problem is that of a financial institution that offers term deposit accounts with specified interest rates to individuals. Funds deposited by individuals are invested by the institution, and interest payments to individuals are made from the investment gains. The institution's problem is to choose amounts of the deposited funds to put into various investment asset classes to ensure that there will be sufficient funds available to pay the promised payments to depositors over time while maximizing long-run expected wealth net of penalty costs. Regulations restrict the amount and type of investments possible and affect the accounting of investment flows. There are substantial penalties if certain accounting flows are not achieved.

Term deposit accounts are offered in connection with insurance policies. For a specified premium an individual receives insurance coverage over a specified term plus a payment at the maturity of the policy. The payment consists of the deposit portion of the premium plus interest. Hence, part of a policy premium pays for simple insurance, while the remainder is a term deposit. Interest paid to policyholders consists of a guaranteed rate, stated in the policy, plus an extra dividend that is declared yearly, the amount depending on prevailing business conditions. A typical policy has a term of five years.

The firm offers several types of savings policies and nonsavings-type policies. The various savings-type products are similar from the point of view of policyholders but differ in terms of the regulations governing the investment of deposits by the institution. To facilitate meeting those regulations, incoming policy premiums are divided among various accounts: deposit portions of savings-type policy premiums are put into *savings accounts* by product line, and insurance portions of all policy premiums are put into a *general account*. Differing regulations govern the investment of the various accounts. Most of the regulations stipulate restrictions on asset classes in which the accounts may be invested. Some restrictions apply to each account separately, while others apply across all accounts.

Each of the accounts may invest in securities or assets either directly or indirectly. Indirect investments may be made either through special money trust funds, called *tokkin*, or through foreign subsidiaries. Furthermore, funds may be given to foreign subsidiaries either as capital ownership of the foreign subsidiary or as a loan to the foreign subsidiary. Thus, there are four means of investing in each asset class. Regulations stipulate the accounting treatment of capital gains from each type of investment. In the general account and in one type of savings account, capital gains that are realized from sales of securities and assets are *not* treated as investment income under accounting rules. The capital gain realized in a given accounting period must be added to a liability account called *Reserve under Article 86—Insurance Business Law*. Investment income received in a given period may either be added to other liability accounts or to shareholders' equity.

At the end of each fiscal year, market values of assets are appraised. For assets whose market values have dropped below book value, those book values are adjusted downward to reflect the lower of cost or market value. For assets whose market values have risen above book value, those book values are not adjusted upwards. Such revaluation losses are treated like realized capital losses. Both revaluation losses and realized capital losses may be deducted from Reserve under Article 86. As long as there is adequate Reserve under Article 86, it is preferable to deduct such losses from that account than from shareholders' equity.

There are special savings-type products whose investments are not subject to Article 86. In the special savings accounts, realized capital gains may be added to liability accounts or to shareholders' equity. Capital losses, either realized or resulting from revaluation, may be deducted from Reserve under Article 86. However, if such losses are deducted, any subsequent capital gains must be applied first toward Article 86 Reserve, until the amount of the accumulated losses have been recovered. Further capital gains may then be treated like income.

A *tokkin* fund is a trust fund, administered by a trust bank, that pays dividends to the owner of the trust. The trust may invest in any asset class and use either investment income or capital gains to pay the dividends. The owner may treat the dividends received as investment income. Thus, tokkin funds are vehicles for converting capital gains into investment income. Because of the possibility of circumvention of Article 86 through tokkin funds, there exists a regulatory restriction that tokkin funds may not exceed a percentage, currently five percent, of the total book value of the institution. From the standpoint of the institution, a tokkin fund is an investment that pays dividends and cannot appreciate in capital value above the initial investment. The trust may, however, suffer a capital loss. In fact, the trust's capital value may decrease in the same year as a dividend is paid. However, if the trust's capital value has decreased below its initial value, investment income and capital gains in subsequent years must be used first for restoring the capital value of the trust to its initial value, before providing for dividends. The accounting treatment of capital gains of indirect investments in assets through tokkin funds is similar to the accounting treatment of capital gains in the special savings accounts: capital losses are deducted from Article 86 Reserve; subsequent capital gains together with income must first restore the accumulated capital losses before being treated like income.

Foreign subsidiaries are investment companies that are created for much the same purpose as tokkin funds. Funds are given to a foreign subsidiary to invest; investment gains are received by the parent as income. Funds given to foreign subsidiaries may be structured either as capital ownership of the subsidiary or as a loan to the subsidiary. From the parent's standpoint, capital ownership represents ownership of an asset denominated in a foreign currency. A loan to the subsidiary is considered a loan in the parent's domestic currency. There is a regulatory restriction on the total value of foreign currency-denominated assets: such assets must not exceed a percentage, currently 30 percent, of the book value of the General and Savings Accounts. Capital ownership of foreign subsidiaries is included in this restriction, while loans to foreign subsidiaries are not.

As with tokkin funds, capital gains realized by the foreign subsidiary may be paid as dividends to the parent. However, unlike tokkin funds or direct investments, the parent need not account for limited revaluation losses of the subsidiary. Unless the total capitalization of the subsidiary (liability plus owner's equity or total asset value) decreases to 50 percent of the initial capitalization, the parent may keep the foreign subsidiary on its books at initial cost. If the total asset value drops below 50 percent, then the parent must account for a revaluation loss of the appropriate amount.

Since there is no regulatory restriction on loans, a loan to a foreign subsidiary is an unrestricted method of investing in assets that offer large potential capital gains and converting those gains to income. Hence, the institution follows regulatory guidance in making loans to foreign subsidiaries.

Under accounting rules, the institution is required to maintain underwriting reserves, which are liability accounts for underwriting activities. Underwriting reserves consist of *premium reserve* (a reserve for insurance claims) and *reserve for maturity refunds* (the reserve for policyholder deposits). Since the promised interest rates are declared each year, it is possible to calculate an accrued interest liability on deposits in the savings product accounts. Reserve for maturity refunds consists of the deposit portion of premiums plus the accrued interest called *reserve for maturity refund interest*. It is the institution's practice to compare the amount of investment gain received for the year with the increase in reserve for maturity refund interest. Any excess at a fiscal year-end is put into the general account. The amount that is transferred is called *overflow*. Conversely, if there is a shortfall, the shortfall amount is transferred from the general account to the savings product account. Such transfers are termed *replenishment*.

Accounting values of assets in the savings account are stated at the lower of cost or market value. Book values of assets reflect unrealized capital losses but not unrealized capital gains. The intended result of overflow/replenishment combined with lower-of-cost-or-market-value accounting is that the book balance in the savings account at a fiscal year-end should equal the net deposit premiums to date plus accrued interest at the declared interest rates. However, situations can arise, for certain configurations of capital losses and income gains, in which this equality does not hold. In such contingencies, other transfers from the general account must be made. Funds in the general account are used primarily to cover insurance claims. However, they are also used for paying taxes, dividends and other expenses.

The purpose of investing is to obtain sufficient funds to meet the cash flows of the business and maximize long run wealth. Cash flows include those associated with deposit liabilities (principal and interest payments), insurance claims, taxes, and shareholder dividends. The institution uses the accounting practices described above to identify situations that are not favorable to this purpose. For example, any replenishment from the general account is undesirable, as are any special transfers that must be made from the general account. Thus, the institutional investor can be thought of as having preferences over outcomes of certain accounting flows. In the case of transfers from the general account, these preferences result from two types of costs. First, there are direct costs associated with certain types of transfers since, for example, permission from the regulators must be sought for some types of transfers. Second, there are indirect costs since accounting statements are public knowledge; hence, adverse flows may result in the loss of business for the institution.

Apart from the desire to avoid adverse accounting flows, the institutional investor expresses no particular attitude toward risk in the customary sense. That is, if no adverse accounting flows were possible, then the investor would act as a risk-neutral expected-wealth maximizer.

2. BACKGROUND ON MULTISTAGE STOCHASTIC LINEAR PROGRAMMING AND FINANCIAL PLANNING MODELS

A typical two-stage stochastic linear program with recourse is to select the decision (vector) x, observe the random elements of the problem ξ and then select the corrective action $y(\xi)$:

$$\begin{aligned} \text{minimize } Z &= c'x + E\psi(x, \xi), \\ \text{s.t. } Ax &= b, \\ x &\geq 0, \end{aligned}$$

where the second stage function is

$$\begin{aligned} \psi(x, \xi) &= \min q'y(\xi) \\ \text{s.t. } Wy(\xi) &= \xi - Tx, \\ y(\xi) &\geq 0. \end{aligned}$$

The vectors c, q, and b, and the matrices A, W, and T are fixed and known and primes denote transposition. If the ξ have possible outcomes $r^1, \ldots, r^I$ with discrete probabilities $p^i = \Pr(\xi = r^i) > 0$, $i = 1, \ldots, I$ that sum to 1, the two-stage stochastic linear program with recourse is equivalent to the linear program

$$\text{minimize } Z = c'x + \sum_{i=1}^{I} p^i q' y^i,$$

$$\begin{array}{llll} \text{s.t.} & Ax & & = b \\ & Tx + Wy^1 & & = r^1 \\ & \vdots & & \vdots \\ & Tx & + Wy^I & = r^I \\ & x \geq 0, y^1, \ldots, y^I \geq 0. & & \end{array}$$

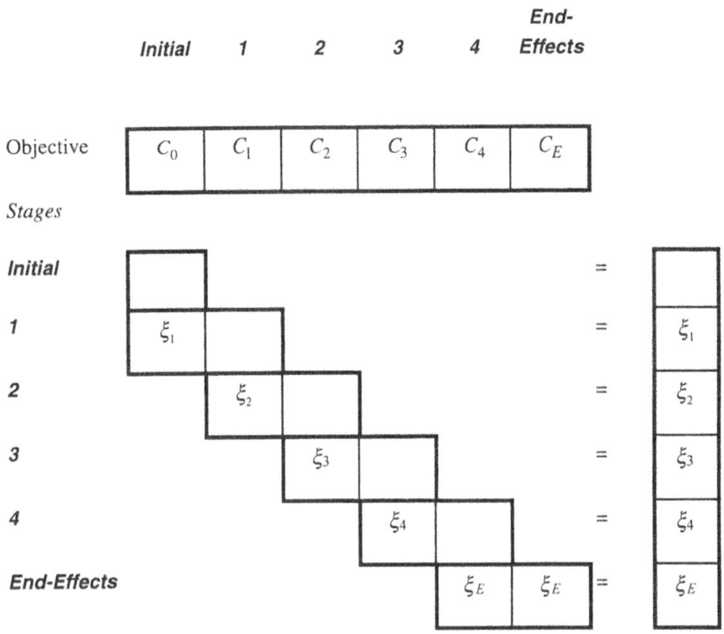

Figure 1. Multistage stochastic linear programming structure of the RY model.

In many applications other coefficients are uncertain. However, if the random elements have discrete probabilities (i.e., scenarios), there is always a deterministic equivalent that is a large special structured linear program. Such is also the case with multistage models with discrete scenarios. These models in linear and nonlinear formulations have been studied by authors such as Birge and Wets (1986), Edirisinghe and Ziemba (1992), Frauendorfer (1992), Gassmann (1990), Higle and Sen (1991), Huang et al. (1977), Infanger (1994), Wallace (1986), Wets (1966, 1974), and Ziemba (1970).

The RY model has the multistage stochastic linear program structure shown in Figure 1. There is an initialization stage with no uncertainty. Then follow four decision periods with linkage constraints in block diagonal structure. Uncertainty appears in the previous period linking constraints and the right-hand side. The steady end-effects stage (see Section 2 of Cariño et al. 1998) appears as one more period in the constraints and objective function. The RY model has this form with the decision periods being the first quarter, the rest of the first year, the second year, and years two to five.

There have been numerous applications of stochastic programming with recourse models in various areas (see e.g., Dempster 1980, Ermoliev and Wets 1988, Kall and Wallace 1994, and Birge 1997 for surveys). Actual and potential applications in finance are particularly rich. Some of the latter are surveyed in Dupacová (1991), Mulvey and Ziemba (1995), and Ziemba and Mulvey (1998).

This paper concerns asset and liability management over time. This problem is faced by all business firms and many other industrial, public, academic, and governmental agencies. Indeed the problem is crucial for economic survival of such organizations. The literature is rich in studies of various models of certain aspects of those problems for specific organizations. The model builds upon and improves this previous research in several ways by presenting a true dynamic stochastic model with end effects. The basic problem is to match asset returns and liability commitments, both of which occur over time and with considerable uncertainty to produce a superior outcome measured by a well-defined criterion subject to legal, policy, and other constraints. Early models were based on linear programming and include those by Chambers and Charnes (1961), Cohen and Hammer (1967), Beazer (1975), Brodt (1979), Komar (1971), and Lifson and Blackman (1973). These models attempted to balance anticipated sources and uses of funds to meet liquidity and capital adequacy constraints while maximizing profitability. Stochastic models have been of several types. Pyle (1971) developed a static mean-variance type model of a financial intermediary (bank) to select the asset and liability levels it wishes to maintain throughout the period. He considered only the risk of the portfolio and not other possible uncertainties. The model omitted trading activity, matching assets and liabilities, transaction costs, and other similar features. Such Markowitz (1952, 1987) models as shown in Section 4 of Cariño et al. (1998) are inadequate for decision problems that are inherently dynamic and are progressively worse with increasing time horizons.

A second approach assumes that the bank or other financial institution seeks to maximize its future stream of profits (or expected profits) subject to portfolio mix constraints.

Myers (1968) provides theoretical support for a linear objective function. He showed that a necessary condition for the existence of security market equilibrium is risk independence. Security market equilibrium implies risk independence of securities which implies that the maximization of the expected net present value is the appropriate objective criterion. The banking industry has long accepted deterministic models based on such a criterion (see, e.g., Cohen and Hammer 1967 and Hester and Pierce 1975). These models assume particular realizations for random variables to make them computationally tractable.

Uncertainties abound, however, and deterministic models cannot be good approximations of reality. Calculations in Kallberg et al. (1982) showed that there is considerable error in this approximation. Bradley and Crane (1972), Cohen and Thore (1970), and Eppen and Fama (1968) also criticized these models because they did not consider uncertainty. Charnes and his colleagues (see e.g., Charnes and Kirby 1965, Charnes and Littlechild 1968, and Charnes and Thore 1966), developed chance-constrained models (assuming that future deposits and loan repayments were joint, normally distributed random variables). These approaches led to computationally feasible schemes for realistic situations that replaced the capital adequacy formula with chance-constraints on meeting withdrawal claims (see, e.g., Charnes et al. 1982). However, the chance-constrained procedure cannot handle realistic penalties for either varying magnitudes of constraint violations or different types of constraints. Moreover, multiperiod models raise unresolved conceptual difficulties, dealing with the treatment of infeasibility in periods $2, \ldots, n$ as discussed by Eisner et al. (1971). Hence these models cannot really represent a realistic dynamic stochastic model of an actual business.

Dynamic programming deals well with uncertainty; however, the problem size escalates dramatically even for very small numbers of financial assets, periods, and possible return outcome values and liability levels it wishes to maintain throughout the period. Wolf (1969) constructed such a model. He only considered portfolio risk and not other possible uncertainties. The model omitted trading activity, matching assets and liabilities, transaction costs, and other similar features. Such models are inadequate for decision problems that are inherently dynamic and typically become progressively worse with increasing time horizons.

Other research along these lines includes Eppen and Fama (1968, 1971), who modeled two- and three-asset problems; and Daellenbach and Archer (1969), who extended their work to include one liability. Ziemba and Vickson (1975) survey this literature. These models consider uncertainty of return and are dynamic, but only problems with a very small number of financial instruments can be analyzed simultaneously; hence they, too, are of limited practice.

Wolf (1969), Bradley and Crane (1972, 1976, 1980), and Lane and Hutchinson (1980) used stochastic decision tree models. Bradley and Crane applied their dynamic stochastic model to bond portfolio management. Their model, while useful for small problems, becomes computationally very unwieldy with even a few periods and possible outcomes. Kusy and Ziemba (1986) discuss a stochastic linear program under uncertainty approach and compare it with Bradley and Crane's models via simulation. The stochastic decision tree approach has the drawback that few decisions in period one are feasible for all possible futures. The simulations lead to significantly higher risk-adjusted returns for the stochastic linear program under uncertainty model. The Kusy-Ziemba model allows constraint violations via penalty costs in the objective.

Buhler and Gehring (1978), Cohen and Thore (1970), Crane (1971), and Booth (1972) built very small models along these lines. Later, with better algorithms, Kallberg et al. (1982) developed a model for a business firm.

Kusy and Ziemba (1986) was an application to the Vancouver City Savings Credit Union. This model had: (1) multiperiodicity incorporating changing yield spreads across time, transaction costs associated with selling assets prior to maturity, and the synchronization of cash flows across time by matching maturity of assets with expected cash outflows; (2) simultaneous considerations of assets and liabilities to satisfy accounting principles and match the liquidity of assets and liabilities; (3) transaction costs incorporating brokerage fees and other expenses incurred in buying and selling securities; (4) uncertainty of cash flows incorporating the uncertainty inherent in the depositors' withdrawal claims and deposits that ensures that the asset portfolio gives the bank the capacity to meet these claims; (5) the incorporation of uncertain interest rates into the decision-making process to avoid lending and borrowing decisions that may ultimately be detrimental to the financial well-being of the bank; and (6) legal and policy constraints appropriate to the bank's operating environment.

To implement the model, Kusy and Ziemba made various simplications. Their model did not contain end effects, nor was it truly dynamic since it was solved two periods at a time in rolling fashion. The scenarios were high, low, and average returns that were independent over time.

Table I
Typical Period Structure Beginning at a Fiscal Year-End

t	Name	Length (Quarters)	Description
0	INI	—	Initialization
1	Q01	1	End of quarter 1
2	Y01	3	End of fiscal year 1
3	Y02	4	End of fiscal year 2
4	Y05	12	End of fiscal year 5
5	YFF	4	End-effects period

The RY model builds on this previous research to make a large scale dynamic model with possibly dependent scenarios, end effects, and all the relevant institutional and policy constraints of Yasuda Kasai's business enterprise. The model is formulated in Sections 3 through 7. The advent of modern workstations and other high-performance computers has aided others to make models as well. Dempster and Ireland (1988), Gassmann and Ireland (1990), Shapiro (1988), Hiller and Shapiro (1989), Mulvey and Vladimirou (1989, 1992), Hiller and Eckstein (1993), and Zenios (1991) have also made stochastic financial models. These models differ from the RY model because they focus on specific types of investments such as bonds or fixed income instruments or have a special network structure. The RY model developed the entire dynamic asset-liability management problem for Yasuda Kasai. For a survey of modern ALM models see Ziemba and Mulvey (1998).

3. FORMULATING THE RUSSELL-YASUDA KASAI MODEL AS A MULTISTAGE STOCHASTIC LINEAR PROGRAM

The basic unit of time in the model is a calendar quarter since the users run the model quarterly. The software system accommodates periods of varying lengths, as shown in Table I.

This period structure is for a model run at the end of a fiscal year. Hence, the lengths of the two periods Q01 and Y01 together comprise four quarters of the first fiscal year. Some model constraints apply only to periods that end at a fiscal year-end. The subscript t is used as an index for stages, with $t = 0$ denoting the initial stage and $t = T$ denoting the planning horizon stage. Different periods may be of different calendar lengths.

All variables in the model are *balance* or *flow* variables. Balance variables are analogous to normal accounting balance sheet variables; when subscripted with t they represent balances *after transactions* at the end of the indicated period. Flow variables are analogous to normal accounting income statement variables. They represent net flows occurring between dates. Flow variables subscripted by $t+1$ represent flows occurring after the end of period t and before the end of period $t+1$.

Table II
Accounts

Identifier	Description
S	Savings product
O	Other savings products
G	General
E	Exogenous

There are several types of accounts, as shown in Table II.

The savings product accounts contain deposit premiums and accumulated income that is earmarked for maturity refunds; thus we have savings accounts 1 and 2. Liability balances associated with these accounts are reserves for maturity refunds. All other assets are held in a single general account for insurance claims and operating expenses. However, some general account assets are not allocatable for various reasons. In the model the general account is split into two accounts, General G and Exogenous E, with the exogenous account containing the nonallocatable assets.

The objective is to maximize expected net wealth at the horizon net of penalty costs:

$$\text{Minimize } E[-\text{market value at planning horizon } T + \text{accumulated shortfall costs} + \text{shortfall costs in end-effects period}],$$

where

$$\text{market value at horizon} = \text{General Account market value} + \text{Exogenous market value} + \text{Savings Product Accounts market values.}$$

The accumulated shortfall costs are

$$\sum_i \sum_{t=1}^{T} (1+\gamma)^{N(t,T)} (\text{cost}_{it})(\text{shortfall}_{it}),$$

where

$N(t, T)$ = number of years from stage t to the horizon stage T,

γ = annual discount rate,

cost_{it} = cost efficient for shortfall type i at stage t, and

shortfall_{it} = amount of shortfall type i at stage t.

The shortfall costs in the end-effects period equal

$$\sum_i \alpha(\text{cost}_{if})(\text{shortfall}_{if}),$$

where

α = discount factor for end-effects period,

cost_{if} = cost coefficient for shortfall type i in end-effects period, and shortfall_{if} = amount of shortfall type i in the end-effects period.

The shortfalls and costs are defined to create piecewise-linear convex cost functions (as in Cariño and Fan 1993).

Table III
Typical Asset Class List

Identifier	Description	Identifier	Description
CJ	Cash	BF	Bonds—Foreign
LL	Loans—Floating rate	EU	Equity—U.S.
LF	Loans—Fixed rate	EN	Equity—Non-U.S. foreign
LO	Loans	EF	Equity—Foreign
BJ	Bonds—Domestic	FO	Foreign assets
EJ	Equity—Domestic	RE	Real Estate
BU	Bonds—U.S. and Canada	OT	Other
BA	Bonds—U.K. and Australia	GE	Generic assets
BE	Bonds—E.C (European Continent)		

The number of segments, the breakpoints, and the additional marginal costs are parameters that can be specified by the user.

To divide the universe of available investments into a manageable number of asset classes involves a tradeoff between detail and complexity. A large number of asset classes would increase detail and therefore be desirable. However, the number of asset classes is a key determinant of a model's size. Therefore, the model allows the number and definition of asset classes to be specified by the user. There can be different asset classes in different periods. For example, asset classes in earlier periods can be collapsed into aggregate classes in later periods (see Table III).

Investment in asset classes may be done either directly or indirectly through tokkin funds, capital ownership of foreign subsidiaries, or loans to foreign subsidiaries. The regulatory rules that apply to indirect investments yield the investment types in Table IV:

The model chooses an allocation of assets among asset classes. Variables represent the market values chosen for each class. Given the regulatory considerations, the number of allocation variables could potentially equal the product of the number of asset classes, the number of investment types, and the number of accounts. However, some asset class/investment type/account combinations are disallowed either by regulations or by company policy. An input table controls the available allocation classes of the model by specifying available allocation classes by period. Allocation class names identify the account, the investment type, and the asset class. This feature enables the user to specify fewer available allocation classes in later periods, thereby reducing the model's size (see Table V).

Allocation variables are denoted by X_{nt} where n denotes an allocation class available at stage t. Sets of allocation classes are by account and by whether the investment is

Table IV
Investment Types

Identifier	Description
D	Direct
T	Tokkin
C	Capital to foreign subsidiaries
L	Loans to foreign subsidiaries

direct or indirect. The sets of allocation classes use the account identifier (S, O, G, or E) and D (Direct) or I (Indirect). Thus, SD is the set of available allocation classes in the Savings Account for Direct investment; SI denotes the set of all Indirect (Tokkin, Foreign Capital, Foreign Loan) allocation classes in the Savings Account. The stage-dependence of the sets of allocation classes is implicit. For example,

$$\sum_{n \in GI} X_{nt+1},$$

is the sum of market value allocations over all available allocation classes of types T, C, and L in the General Account at stage $t+1$. Since the accounting treatment of capital gains differs from that of income, the formulation distinguishes price from income return: total return of an asset equals price plus income return. For each allocation class n, denote by RP_{nt+1} and RI_{nt+1} the price return and income return, respectively, for period $t+1$. The returns depend only on the asset class, not on account type or investment type.

4. ALLOCATION CONSTRAINTS

There are various restrictions on investment in certain asset classes that either regulatory guidelines or internal company policies impose. Because of the four possible ways to invest in a given asset class—directly, indirectly through tokkin funds, foreign subsidiary capital ownership, or loans to foreign subsidiaries—the precise specification of these restrictions is complex.

A further complication arises because allocation classes are specified by period and may differ across periods. A typical example of an allocation restriction is: "Total investment in domestic equities must not be greater than 30 percent of total book value of assets."

Allocation classes included in this constraint are domestic equities held directly, indirectly through tokkin funds, and indirectly through loans to foreign subsidiaries. However, investment in domestic equities through capital to foreign subsidiaries is not covered by this restriction.

Investments in any of the asset classes using capital to foreign subsidiaries are considered foreign investments. Another typical restriction is: "Total foreign investments must not be greater than 30 percent of total book value of

Table V
Typical Number of Allocation Variables by Stage

t	Stage name	S	1	Account 2	G	E	Total
0	INI	15	13	15	15	1	59
1	Q01	15	13	15	15	1	59
2	Y01	15	13	15	15	1	59
3	Y02	7	7	7	7	1	29
4	Y05	7	7	7	7	1	29
5	YFF	5	5	5	5	1	21

assets." Included in this constraint are foreign assets held directly and held indirectly through loans to foreign subsidiaries; further, any asset class (foreign or domestic) held by foreign subsidiary capital is included in this restriction.

Another complication is that, depending on the account, restrictions like these might apply to the assets of only one account. Other restrictions apply across the firm's total assets. Because of the complex nature of these restrictions, the model software includes a flexible tabular input mechanism for specifying the precise constraints. About 10 such allocation group constraints are typically applied.

The regulatory restrictions use book values. Allocation variables are in market-value units. The transformation between market and book values is nonlinear and complex. As an approximation, constant book-to-market-value ratios convert market values to book values. Those ratios are unity for most asset classes.

5. THE LOAN MODEL

The loan asset classes differ from other asset classes because the market for these assets is private. Loans are not listed on an exchange nor regularly traded through established brokers from which data on market size and returns could be obtained. Consequently, there is no index representing loan market performance.

Yasuda Kasai's own portfolio of loans is "the market." This entails assessing the characteristics of Yasuda Kasai's loans, valuing loans as of a specific date, and determining the return distribution by revaluing the loans under different scenarios. Given the illiquidity of loan assets, the user may constrain the allocations to loans.

The basic inputs for the loan model (see Table VI) are book values for both fixed- and floating-rate loans by account, accrued income for fixed-rate loans through the first four quarters (to the end of the first fiscal year), and the current short and long term interest rates.

In addition to the basic loan inputs, the model requires monthly cash flows (expected principal and interest payments) for fixed rate loans by account as shown in Table VII.

The market value of the fixed rate loans is found by discounting the dated cash flows at the appropriate spot yields given by an estimated term structure of interest rates. The term structure model is anchored to a short-term cash rate and to a long-term benchmark bond yield. Short- and long-term interest rate scenarios are developed together with the bond return scenarios that are generated as part of the asset return scenario generation procedure.

Given the interest rate scenarios, the model calculates the fixed rate loan market values at the beginning and at the end of each period under each scenario. The model then calculates the total return for fixed rate loans RLF_{t+1} from the market values and the cash flows during the period. The total return RLF_{t+1} is split into income return $RILF_{t+1}$ and price return $RPLF_{t+1}$. Income return $RILF_{t+1}$ is derived from the term structure in the scenario generation procedure. For a given income return $RILF_{t+1}$, the price return is

$$RPLF_{t+1} = RLF_{t+1} - RILF_{t+1}.$$

The returns do not depend on the account since the aggregate of fixed rate loan cash flows over all accounts is used in the valuations. The assumption that loan returns are independent of the account is analogous to the situation of other account-independent asset classes.

Table VI
Typical Loan Data File

	General	Savings	1	2
Fixed BV	64,178	198,611	396,502	0
AccInc Q01	925	3,100	5,500	0
AccInc Q02	895	2,900	5,400	0
AccInc Q03	800	2,500	5,200	0
AccInc Q04	800	2,200	5,100	0
Floating BV	23,641	68,265	348,377	12,150
Long rate r_L	0.071			
Short rate r_S	0.076			

Table VII
Typical Loan Cash Flow File

Month	Principal	Interest
1	3,312	1,084
2	3,006	886
3	2,796	937
4	5,300	1,090

Since the existing loan portfolio has cash flows in the first year that represent lower yields than current market yields, the income gap IG_{t+1} is computed and included in any flow of funds equations that include fixed rate loan income apart from total return. The income gap is calculated by account from the accrued income data (see Table VI).

For floating rate loans, the model assumes that market values are equal to book values and that price return $RPLL_{t+1}$ is zero. Income return $RILL_{t+1}$ for floating rate loans is derived from the term structure in the scenario generation procedure.

To model the illiquidity of loans, the loan allocation variables are constrained to lie within certain bounds specified by the user. By assumption, there is a natural amount of replacement of loans that mature and expire. The bounds are set to percentages around the natural replacement value. If X_{nt} is the allocation in period t to loan allocation class n, the allocation X_{nt+1} is constrained by

$$lb(1 + RI_{nt+1} + RP_{nt+1})X_{nt}$$
$$\leq X_{nt+1} \leq ub(1 + RI_{nt+1} + RP_{nt+1})X_{nt},$$

where lb and ub are bounds expressed as fractions of the loan amounts. Values of 1 for lb and ub represent natural replacement of maturing loans. The bounds are specified by account and by period. Bounds for initial period loan allocations are with respect to initial market values computed in the initial valuation.

6. THE LIABILITY MODEL

The flow of funds model described in Section 7 utilizes projected cash flows associated with liabilities. The liabilities of the savings product accounts arise because of the promised maturity refunds to policyholders. The inputs for the liability model consist of existing liability balances and future cash inflows due to existing quarterly policies and new policies. For each account, existing liability balances are disaggregated by maturity date. The amounts of existing liability balances that represent accrued interest is also required. Table VIII shows a sample set of inputs.

The value 43,575 is the liability balance, as of the initial stage, of deposits maturing at the end of one quarter; 61,150 is the liability balance of deposits maturing at the end of the second quarter, etc. The planning horizon is five years. Inputs are required quarterly through five quarters beyond the planning horizon. One year beyond the planning horizon is used for calculations in the end-effects period. The additional quarter is used to lump together all balances for that quarter and beyond to the longest maturity. Hence, quarter 24 is one year beyond the horizon of five years, and quarter 25 contains the total balance of all maturities of 25 quarters or longer.

The accrued interest part of total liabilities is required by maturity. If the model is set up for an initial stage representing the beginning of a fiscal year, then there is no effect on the model if accrued interest is specified as zero since accumulated asset income must be set equal to accrued interest liability. For a nonyear-end model, however, accrued interest liability may differ from accumulated income assets, and the full maturity schedule should be provided.

Future cash inflows are assumed to come from two sources: existing policies, and new policies to be sold in the future. For each of these sources (and for each account), a table of projected inflows by quarter is required. Projected inflows must be further disaggregated by the maturity quarter of the liability that the inflow will create, as shown in Table IX.

The value 466 is the amount of deposits expected in quarter one that are expected to mature in quarter one. The value 883 is the amount of deposits expected in quarter one that will mature in quarter two. As in the existing liability balances input table, the maturity schedule must extend five quarters beyond the planning horizon, with the last quarter representing all flows from the last quarter on. Input like Table IX is required for existing policies for each account and for new policies for each account. Although the projections for new policies are forecasts of expected values, the framework here could be adapted for scenario-dependent projections, with a corresponding increase in input data and complexity of calculations. Such an approach could capture the correlation of new deposits with interest rates. The model computes projected cash flows and liability balances for future periods from these inputs for each savings product account.

For the general account such computations are not done. Instead, projected inflows to and payouts from the general account are required inputs. The projected data

Table VIII
Example of Existing Liability Balance Inputs

	Maturity Quarter					
	1	2	3	...	24	25
Total liability	43,575	61,150	61,302	...	3,000	14,366
Accrued interest	0	0	0	...	0	0

Table IX
Example of Liability Inflow Projections

Deposit Quarter	Maturity Quarter 1	2	3	. . .	24	25
1	466	883	828	. . .	400	192
2	0	603	828	. . .	400	192
3	0	0	577	. . .	400	192
⋮	⋮	⋮	⋮	. . .	⋮	⋮
24	0	0	0	. . .	400	192

are quarterly through the planning horizon plus four quarters. The inflow projections represent insurance premiums received. The payout projections represent the sum of expected claim payments, other operating expenses, and projected payouts for investment in exogenous equity and exogenous real estate.

The liability generator aggregates the input tables by period lengths. Flows from existing and new policies are aggregated as are the flows from quarters comprising periods of the model. An aggregate input table is created in the form of Table X.

The symbol $F_t(i)$ denotes the deposit inflow in period t that creates a promised refund at period $t + i$. A vector $(F_t(0), F_t(1), F_t(2), \ldots)$ of promised maturity refunds is created at each period t. The total inflow F_t in period t is

$$F_t = \sum_i F_t(i).$$

The vector $(L_0(1), L_0(2), L_0(3), \ldots)$ represents the maturity schedule of the existing total reserve liability. This vector is split into two parts—principal reserve $(M_0(1), M_0(2), M_0(3), \ldots)$ and interest reserve $(N_0(1), N_0(2), N_0(3), \ldots)$—such that $L_0(i) = M_0(i) + N_0(i)$ for all i. The total reserve amounts are

$$M_0 = \sum_i M_0(i),$$

$$N_0 = \sum_i N_0(i),$$

$$L_0 = \sum_i L_0(i).$$

The outputs of the liability calculations are projections of principal and interest payouts and projections of liability reserve balances for all periods. Projections of interest payouts and interest reserve balances depend on the promised interest rates to be declared in future periods. The promised interest rates have two components: a guaranteed rate that is specified in the policy and an extra dividend, declared each year, that depends on prevailing business conditions. The sum of these is the rate at which interest accrues on the maturity refund reserve in a given year. Both the future guaranteed rates and the extra dividends are random variables. The sum of the two components is g_{t+1}, the liability growth rate. It is a random variable of the model that is generated by account along with asset returns in the scenario generator. For a given scenario, the growth rates g_{t+1} are fixed for each period. The liability calculations then proceed recursively. For period t, there are liability vectors and $(L_t(1), L_t(2), L_t(3), \ldots)$, $(M_t(1), M_t(2), M_t(3), \ldots)$ and $(N_t(1), N_t(2), N_t(3), \ldots)$ (analogous to those at $t = 0$). For all t and i, the identity $L_t(i) = M_t(i) + N_t(i)$ holds. P_{t+1} and I_{t+1} are the principal and interest payments, respectively. The following calculations are done recursively for $t = 0, 1, 2, \ldots$:

$$M_{t+1}(i) = M_t(i + 1) + F_{t+1}(i), \; i = 1, 2, \ldots,$$

$$N_{t+1}(i) = N_t(i + 1) + g_{t+1}L_t(i + 1), \; i = 1, 2, \ldots,$$

$$L_{t+1}(i) = (1 + g_{t+1})L_t(i + 1) + F_{t+1}(i), \; i = 1, 2, \ldots,$$

$$M_{t+1} = \sum_i M_{t+1}(i),$$

$$N_{t+1} = \sum_i N_{t+1}(i),$$

$$L_{t+1} = \sum_i L_{t+1}(i),$$

$$F_{t+1} = \sum_i F_{t+1}(i),$$

Table X
Aggregated Inputs

Deposit Period		Maturity Period 1	2	3	4	5	6
1	F_1	$F_1(0)$	$F_1(1)$	$F_1(2)$	$F_1(3)$	$F_1(4)$	$F_1(5)$
2	F_2	0	$F_2(0)$	$F_2(1)$	$F_2(2)$	$F_2(3)$	$F_2(4)$
3	F_3	0	0	$F_3(0)$	$F_3(1)$	$F_3(2)$	$F_3(3)$
4	F_4	0	0	0	$F_4(0)$	$F_4(1)$	$F_4(2)$
5	F_5	0	0	0	0	$F_5(0)$	$F_5(1)$
Principal reserve	M_0	$M_0(1)$	$M_0(2)$	$M_0(3)$	$M_0(4)$	$M_0(5)$	$M_0(6)$
Interest reserve	N_0	$N_0(1)$	$N_0(2)$	$N_0(3)$	$N_0(4)$	$N_0(5)$	$N_0(6)$
Total liability	L_0	$L_0(1)$	$L_0(2)$	$L_0(3)$	$L_0(4)$	$L_0(5)$	$L_0(6)$

$$P_{t+1} = M_t(1) + F_{t+1}(0),$$
$$I_{t+1} = N_t(1) + g_{t+1}L_t(1).$$

The liability balances are internally consistent with the cash flows. An example illustrates these calculations using the aggregated input table:

Deposit Period	F_t	Maturity period 1	2	3	4	5
1	200	0	50	50	100	0
2	200	0	0	50	50	100
M_0	1000	500	300	200	0	0
N_0	100	50	30	20	0	0
L_0	1100	550	330	220	0	0

If the growth rate g_1 is 0.05, then at the end of period 1,

		1	2	3	4	5	
F_1	200	0	50	50	100	0	In
M_1	700	500	350	250	100	0	
N_1	77.5	77.5	46.5	31	0	0	
L_1	777.5	577.5	396.5	281	100	0	

$$\begin{aligned}
M_1 &= (300+50)+(200+50)+(0+100)+(0+0)= 700,\\
N_1 &= (30+(.05\times 330))+(20+(.05)\times 220))=77.5,\\
L_1 &= (1.05\times 330+50)+(1.05\times 220+50)\\
&\quad +(1.05\times\ 0+100)=777.5,\\
F_1 &= 0+50+50+100+0=200,\\
P_1 &= 500+0=500,\\
I_1 &= 50+.05\times 550=77.5
\end{aligned}$$

If the growth rate g_2 is 0.06 then at the end of period 2,

		2	3	4	5	
F_2	200	0	50	50	100	In
M_2	550	350	300	150	100	
N_2	53.9	70.3	47.9	31	0	
L_2	420.3	577.5	396.5	281	100	

$$\begin{aligned}
M_2 &= (250+50)+(100+50)+(0+100)=550,\\
N_2 &= (31+(.06)\times 281))+(0+(.06\times 100))=53.9,\\
L_2 &= (1.06\times 281+50)+(1.06\times 100+50)\\
&\quad +(1.06\times\ 0+100) = 603.9,\\
F_2 &= 0+50+50+100=200,\\
P_2 &= 350+0=350,\\
I_2 &= 46.5+.06\times 396.5=70.3.
\end{aligned}$$

7. THE FLOW OF FUNDS MODEL

The flow of funds model accounts for the transfer of assets among accounts. The firm's accounting practice is to state the book values of assets at the lower of cost or market value. Both book and market values are important elements of the problem. Some variables are stated in book value terms, while others are measured using market values. The model utilizes transformations of balance sheet variables from one stage to the next. Tables XI to XIII define variables for the balance sheets and income statements. Equations describing the transformations of assets comprise constraints in the stochastic program formulation. Consider first the liability side of the balance sheet of the savings account. As described in Section 6, the total reserve for maturity refunds L_t^S grows from stage t to stage $t+1$ at the rate of interest g_{t+1}^S declared for the period.

Table XI
Balance Sheet at Stage t: Assets

Savings Account:	
Book value of assets:	
Total less accumulated income	A_t^S
Accumulated income	B_t^S
Total book value of savings account	T_t^S
Unrealized market value	U_t^S
Total market value of savings account	$\Sigma_{n\in S} X_{nt} = V_t^S$
Other Savings Product Accounts:	$\vdots$
General Account:	
Book value of allocatable assets:	
Total less accumulated income	A_t^G
Accumulated income	B_t^G
Total book value of allocatable general account	T_t^G
Unrealized market value	U_t^G
Total market value of allocatable general account	$\Sigma_{n\in G} X_{nt} = V_t^G$
Book value of exogenous assets	T_t^E
Unrealized market value of exogenous assets	U_t^E
Market value of exogenous assets	$\Sigma_{n\in E} X_{nt} = V_t^E$
Total market value of assets	$V_t^S + \cdots + V_t^G + V_t^E$

The liability generator uses the growth rates to project the liability reserves so that they are consistent with projected deposit premiums F_{t+1}^S and maturity refunds of principal P_{t+1}^S and interest I_{t+1}^S. The total reserve L_t^S has two components: M_{t+1}^S, represents accumulated net deposits, and N_t^S represents accrued interest. Accounting for inflows and outflows, the relations describing accumulation of liability reserves from stage t to $t+1$ are

$$\begin{aligned}
M_{t+1}^S &= M_t^S + F_{t+1}^S - P_{t+1}^S,\\
N_{t+1}^S &= N_t^S + g_{t+1}^S L_t^S - I_{t+1}^S, \qquad (1)\\
L_{t+1}^S &= (1+g_{t+1}^S)L_t^S + F_{t+1}^S - P_{t+1}^S - I_{t+1}^S.
\end{aligned}$$

These liability-related quantities, which are scenario-dependent, appear in the right-hand side of the stochastic program formulation.

Consider now the asset side of the balance sheet. For the savings account, define investment income D_{t+1}^S and capital gain G_{t+1}^S as

$$D_{t+1}^S = \sum_{n\in SD} RI_{nt+1}X_{nt} + \sum_{n\in SI} (RI_{nt+1} + RP_{nt+1})X_{nt} - IG_{t+1}^S, \qquad (2)$$

$$G_{t+1}^S = \sum_{n\in SD} RP_{nt+1}X_{nt}, \qquad (3)$$

where $\Sigma_{n\in SD} RI_{nt+1}X_{nt}$ is the income from direct investment, $\Sigma_{n\in SI} (RI_{nt+1} + RP_{nt+1})X_{nt}$ is income from indirect investment as described in Section 3, and IG_{t+1}^S is the income gap of fixed-rate loans as described in Section 5.

Table XII

Balance Sheet at Stage t: Liabilities and Shareholders' Equity

Savings Account:	
Reserve for maturity refunds:	
Principal	M_t^S
Interest	N_t^S
Total reserve for maturity refunds	L_t^S
Other Savings Product Accounts:	⋮
General Account:	
Reserve for insurance claims and other liabilities	L_t^G
Reserve under Article 86—Insurance Business Law	S_t
Shareholders' equity, book value	K_t
Total book value of liabilities and shareholders' equity	$T_t^S + \cdots + T_t^G + T_t^E$
Unrealized market value	$U_t^S + \cdots + U_t^G + U_t^E$
Total market value of assets	$V_t^S + \cdots + V_t^G + V_t^E$

If there were no transfers of funds between the savings and general accounts, then the relations describing accumulation of assets would be similar to those describing accumulation of liabilities in Equation (1):

$$A_{t+1}^S = A_t^S + H_{t+1}^S + F_{t+1}^S - P_{t+1}^S,$$

$$B_{t+1}^S = B_t^S + D_{t+1}^S - I_{t+1}^S,$$

$$T_{t+1}^S = T_t^S + H_{t+1}^S + D_{t+1}^S + F_{t+1}^S - P_{t+1}^S - I_{t+1}^S, \quad (4)$$

Table XIII

Income Statement for Period From t to $t + 1$

Savings Account:	
Deposit premiums by policyholders	F_{t+1}^S
Maturity refunds:	
Principal	$-P_{t+1}^S$
Interest	$-I_{t+1}^S$
Increase of reserves for maturity refunds	see text
Investment income	D_{t+1}^S
Net realized capital gains	H_{t+1}^S
Provision for reserves under Article 86	$-H_{t+1}^S$
Income before taxes from the savings account	v_{t+1}^S
Other Savings Product Accounts:	⋮
General Account:	
Insurance premiums received	F_{t+1}^G
Insurance claims paid and other expenses	$-P_{t+1}^G$
Increase of reserves for claims and other liabilities	see text
Investment income	D_{t+1}^G
Net realized capital gains	H_{t+1}^G
Provision for reserves under Article 86	see text
Income before taxes from the general account	see text
Income before taxes	Y_{t+1}
Income taxes	see text
Net income	see text
Shareholders' dividends	$-Q_{t+1}$

$$U_{t+1}^S = U_t^S + G_{t+1}^S - H_{t+1}^S,$$

$$V_{t+1}^S = V_t^S + G_{t+1}^S + D_{t+1}^S + F_{t+1}^S - P_{t+1}^S - I_{t+1}^S.$$

The market value V_{t+1}^S at stage $t + 1$ equals the prior market value V_t^S plus investment return $G_{t+1}^S + D_{t+1}^S$ and net flows $F_{t+1}^S - P_{t+1}^S - I_{t+1}^S$. Book value T_{t+1}^S follows a similar relation, except that capital gain G_{t+1}^S is replaced by *realized* capital gain H_{t+1}^S. The difference $U_t^S \equiv V_t^S - T_t^S$ between market value and book value is accumulated unrealized capital gain.

Of the total book value T_t^S of assets, an amount B_t^S is accumulated as the result of income received and is therefore eligible for use as interest payments. The remainder, $A_t^S \equiv T_t^S - B_t^S$, represents the book value of accumulated deposit premiums.

Transfers of funds between the savings accounts and the general account occur under certain circumstances. We model these situations with "soft" constraints in which both slack and surplus variables are included in the constraint definition; a cost in the objective function is assigned to one of the variables. The cost provides an incentive to satisfy the constraint, but the model allows a violation of the constraint (albeit at a cost). Slack or surplus variables model transfers of funds between accounts.

The first type of soft constraint is an *income constraint*. The desired investment outcome is to keep accumulated income B_{t+1}^S greater than accrued interest N_{t+1}^S, since any excess contributes to income before taxes. Since income D_{t+1}^S is random, B_{t+1}^S is therefore random and the desired outcome may not be achieved. Nonnegative complementary slack variables measure the shortfall w_{t+1}^S and excess v_{t+1}^S through the constraints

$$B_t^S + D_{t+1}^S + w_{t+1}^S - v_{t+1}^S = N_t^S + g_{t+1}^S L_t^S, \quad (5)$$

$$w_{t+1}^S \geq 0, \quad v_{t+1}^S \geq 0. \quad (6)$$

The firm transfers excess income, or overflow, to the general account at a fiscal year-end. The firm transfers, or replenishes, an income shortfall from the general account to the savings account. We include the income constraint at stages representing fiscal year-end dates, and the variables w_{t+1}^S and v_{t+1}^S are transfers of funds between the two accounts. These actions have *simple recourse* since they are uniquely determined once the random income is realized.

The second type of soft constraint is a *reserve constraint*. Whereas the income constraint focuses on income booked within a given fiscal year, the reserve constraint measures total reserve shortfall z_{t+1}^S and reserve surplus q_{t+1}^S through the constraints

$$V_t^S + G_{t+1}^S + D_{t+1}^S + z_{t+1}^S - q_{t+1}^S = (1 + g_{t+1}^S) L_t^S, \quad (7)$$

$$z_{t+1}^S \geq 0, \quad q_{t+1}^S \geq 0. \quad (8)$$

The reserve shortfall z_{t+1}^S does not represent a fund transfer, since no transfer need be made; the savings account may show a deficit as long as the totals for the firm show a positive net worth. We measure the reserve shortfall so that the objective function can assign a cost to the shortfall. The reserve excess q^S_{t+1} is a slack variable.

In addition to income and reserve constraints, one might want the total book value T^S_{t+1} to be greater than total reserve for maturity refunds L^S_{t+1}. To implement such a constraint would require a model of the firm's capital gain realization policy. However, due to the accounting treatment of capital gains, which are added to or subtracted from Article 86 reserve, such gains do not affect taxable income. Therefore, the total market value V^S_{t+1} is of greater importance than total book value T^S_{t+1} and we do not model a book value reserve constraint. As long as total market value V^S_{t+1} exceeds L^S_{t+1}, there will be realizable capital gains. Since such a book value reserve constraint is unnecessary, it simplifies the problem substantially to not keep track of total book value T^S_{t+1} in the model. Asset class restrictions that are stated as percentages of book value are treated in the approximate manner described in Section 4.

The third type of soft constraint is a *cash flow constraint*. The assets of the savings account are intended to be used for payouts of maturity refunds. Although the net payouts $P^S_{t+1} + I^S_{t+1} - F^S_{t+1}$ in any given period represent only a portion of total liability, it is possible in principle for there to be such a severe capital loss that the current period payouts cannot be met. This situation would be very undesirable; recourse in this contingency would be a transfer of assets from the general account. We measure payment shortfall y^S_{t+1} and payment surplus u^S_{t+1} through the constraints

$$V^S_t + G^S_{t+1} + D^S_{t+1} + w^S_{t+1} - v^S_{t+1} + y^S_{t+1} - u^S_{t+1} = -F^S_{t+1} + P^S_{t+1} + I^S_{t+1}, \tag{9}$$

$$y^S_{t+1} \geq 0, \quad u^S_{t+1} \geq 0. \tag{10}$$

A payment shortfall y^S_{t+1} represents a transfer from the general account, while a payment excess u^S_{t+1} is simply a slack variable that does not represent a transfer. Comparing the cash flow constraint with the reserve constraint, both payment shortfalls and reserve shortfalls arise from events in which total return $G^S_{t+1} + D^S_{t+1}$ is less than some desired amount. A payment shortfall is a more severe form of a reserve shortfall; since $(1 + g_{t+1})L^S_t \geq -F^S_{t+1} + P^S_{t+1} + I^S_{t+1} - w^S_{t+1} + v^S_{t+1}$, a payment shortfall occurs only if a reserve shortfall also occurs. The converse is not true. Thus, by defining two types of shortfalls we measure the severity of a single phenomenon.

Given the funds transfers defined by the income and cash flow constraints, the accumulation equations (4) are modified to reflect the transfers. Since it is unnecessary to keep track of M^S_t, A^S_t, T^S_t, and U^S_t, the relevant accumulation equations for the savings account are

$$B^S_{t+1} = B^S_t + D^S_{t+1} - I^S_{t+1} + w^S_{t+1} - v^S_{t+1}, \tag{11}$$

$$V^S_{t+1} = V^S_t + G^S_{t+1} + D^S_{t+1} + F^S_{t+1} - P^S_{t+1} - I^S_{t+1} + w^S_{t+1} - v^S_{t+1} + y^S_{t+1}. \tag{12}$$

Constraints (2), (3), and (5) through (12) model the savings account.

The modeling of other savings product accounts is similar to that of the savings account. Variations of the above constraints represent particular distinctions between income and capital gains that exist in the various product accounts. Modeling of the general account differs from that of the savings product accounts. Totals for the institution, taxes, and shareholders' dividends are modeled here.

Investment income D^G_{t+1} and capital gain return G^G_{t+1} are

$$D^G_{t+1} = \sum_{n \in \mathrm{GD}} RI_{nt+1} X_{nt} + \sum_{n \in \mathrm{GI}} (RI_{nt+1} + RP_{nt+1}) X_{nt} - IG^G_{t+1}, \tag{13}$$

$$G^G_{t+1} = \sum_{n \in \mathrm{GD}} RP_{nt+1} X_{nt}. \tag{14}$$

The reserve L^G_t for insurance claims and other liabilities accumulates through

$$L^G_{t+1} = L^G_t + F^G_{t+1} - P^G_{t+1}.$$

Income before taxes Y_{t+1} is calculated from the excess income from the general account plus the net overflow/replenishment from the savings product accounts:

$$Y_{t+1} - s_{t+1} = B^G_t + D^G_{t+1} + v^S_{t+1} - w^S_{t+1} + (\text{income from other product accounts}), \tag{15}$$

$$Y_{t+1} \geq 0, \quad s_{t+1} \geq 0, \tag{16}$$

where s_{t+1} is a slack variable; we assume that negative taxes are not possible. The model makes this calculation only at fiscal year-end stages. In the general account, B^G_t represents income accumulated since the beginning of the current fiscal year.

To model the preference for sufficient income to pay taxes and shareholders' dividends, let Γ_{t+1} be a required income target. Income taxes are modeled using a constant tax rate τ times taxable income; shareholders' dividends are included in the general account payouts P^G_{t+1}. The general account income constraint, adjusted to reflect replenishment of the savings product accounts, includes this required income:

$$Y_{t+1} - s_{t+1} - (\text{other outflows}) + w^G_{t+1} - v^G_{t+1} = \Gamma_{t+1}, \tag{17}$$

$$w^G_{t+1} \geq 0, \quad v^G_{t+1} \geq 0. \tag{18}$$

The variable v^G_{t+1} is income in excess of required income; it contributes directly to net worth. If there is a shortfall in this constraint, the shortfall amount w^G_{t+1} represents a reduction in economic net worth of the firm. The firm may account for this reduction in economic net worth by a reduction of Article 86 reserve, permissible if regulatory approval is sought and granted, or by a reduction in book value of shareholders' equity, or by a realization of unrealized capital gain while not increasing reserve under Article 86. Any of these recourses are undesirable and are therefore penalized as shortfalls in the objective function.

The reserve constraint for the general account similarly applies to the total balances of all the accounts together

$$V_t^E + V_t^G + G_{t+1}^G + D_{t+1}^G + q_{t+1}^S - z_{t+1}^S$$
$$+ \text{(net worth of other accounts)}$$
$$+ z_{t+1}^G - q_{t+1}^G = L_t^G, \tag{19}$$

$$z_{t+1}^G \geqslant 0, \quad q_{t+1}^G \geqslant 0. \tag{20}$$

The exogenous assets are included in this constraint, since their value must be included in the total value of the firm. The variable q_{t+1}^G represents economic net worth before taxes and shareholders' dividends. Economic net worth is the sum of book value of shareholders' equity plus reserve under Article 86 plus unrealized capital gains. A shortfall z_{t+1}^G would represent a negative economic net worth, a very undesirable situation.

The cash flow constraint for the general account is

$$V_t^G + G_{t+1}^G + D_{t+1}^G - \tau Y_{t+1} + v_{t+1}^S - w_{t+1}^S - y_{t+1}^S$$
$$+ \text{(transfers from other product accounts)}$$
$$+ w_{t+1}^G + y_{t+1}^G - u_{t+1}^G = -F_{t+1}^G + P_{t+1}^G, \tag{21}$$

$$y_{t+1}^G \geqslant 0, \quad u_{t+1}^G \geqslant 0. \tag{22}$$

A shortfall in this constraint would represent a very dire situation: cash flow in the General Account cannot be met even by liquidation of all allocatable assets. The payment shortfall y_{t+1}^G would have to be transferred from exogenous assets.

The accumulation relations for the General Account include outflows for taxes. Taxes are calculated as a tax rate τ times income before taxes Y_{t+1}. Increases k_{t+1}^E in the exogenous account are projected assumptions. The General Account accumulation constraints are

$$B_{t+1}^G = \begin{cases} 0 & \text{if } t+1 \text{ is a year-end stage,} \\ B_t^G + D_{t+1}^G & \text{otherwise,} \end{cases} \tag{23}$$

$$V_{t+1}^G = V_t^G + G_{t+1}^G + D_{t+1}^G + F_{t+1}^G - P_{t+1}^G - \tau Y_{t+1}$$
$$+ v_{t+1}^S - w_{t+1}^S - y_{t+1}^S + w_{t+1}^G + y_{t+1}^G$$
$$- \text{(other transfers out of the General Account)}, \tag{24}$$

$$V_{t+1}^E = V_t^E - w_{t+1}^G - y_{t+1}^G + k_{t+1}^E. \tag{25}$$

The constraints (13) through (25) represent the general account. The formal stochastic program specification consists of the objective function of Section 3, allocation constraints of Section 4, and funds-flow constraints for each account (savings, general, etc.) described in this section.

8. FINAL REMARKS

This paper presents the formulation of the RY model as a multistage stochastic linear program. Technical details of the model and its use appear in Cariño et al. (1998). A summary of the modeling effort and its managerial impact by Yasuda Kasai are discussed in Cariño et al. (1994). Various versions of the model as formulated here have been used in an integral way in the management of Yasuda Kasai's assets since April 1991.

ACKNOWLEDGMENTS

Research on the Russell Yasuda-Kasai model was supported by The Yasuda Fire and Marine Insurance Company and by the Frank Russell Company. Some basic research related to this work by William Ziemba was partially supported by the Natural Sciences and Engineering Research Council of Canada and the U.S. National Science Foundation. This paper was presented at the Sixth International Conference on Stochastic Programming in Udine, Italy, and at the Universities of Abo Academy (Finland), Bergamo, British Columbia, Cyprus, Erasmus, Hong Kong University of Science and Technology, National University of Singapore, Pennsylvania, Princeton, and Stanford. Without implicating them, we would like to thank the project team members, T. Eguchi, T. Kent, D. Myers, C. Stacy, M. Sylvanus, and A. Turner of Russell, T. Amaki, I. Harada, M. Harima, T. Morozumi, Y. Ohtani, K. Sasamoto, Y. Tayama, N. Ueda, K. Watanabe, and Y. Yazawa of Yasuda Kasai, and consultants C. Edirisinghe, A. King, K. Sawaki, and R. Wets for technical assistance. The results of this research were awarded second prize in the 1993 Franz Edelman Award for Management Science Achievement competition. Cariño et al. (1994), which focuses on the implementation and impact aspects of this research, was written for that competition. This paper and Cariño et al. (1998), which discusses the technical aspects of the model and its use, are intended to be a full treatment of the model's construction and implementation.

REFERENCES

BEAZER, W. F. 1975. *Optimization of Bank Portfolios*. D. C. Health, Lexington, MA.

BENDERS, J. F. 1962. Partitioning Procedures for Solving Mixed-Variable Programming Problems. *Numerische Mathematic* **4,** 238–252.

BIRGE, J. R. 1997. Stochastic Programming Computation and Applications. *Informs J. Comput.* **9,** 111–133.

BIRGE, J. R. AND J. B. WETS. 1986. Designing Approximation Schemes for Stochastic Optimization Problems, in Particular for Stochastic Programs with Recourse. *Math. Program. Study* **27,** 54–102.

BOOTH, G. G. 1972. Programming Bank Portfolios Under Uncertainty: An Extension. *J. Banking Res.* **2,** 28–40.

BRADLEY, S. P. AND D. B. CRANE. 1972. A Dynamic Model for Bond Portfolio Management. *Mgmt. Sci.* **19,** 139–151.

BRADLEY, S. P. AND D. B. CRANE. 1980. Managing a Bank Bond Portfolio Over Time. In *Stochastic Programming*. M. A. H. Dempster (ed.), Academic Press, London, 449–471.

BRODT, A. I. 1979. A Multi-Period Portfolio Theory Model for Commercial Bank Management. In *Portfolio Theory: 25 Years After*. E. J. Elton and M. J. Gruber (eds.), TIMS Studies in the Management Sciences, North Holland, Amsterdam, 191–213.

BUHLER, W. AND H. GEHRING. 1978. Short-term Financial Planning with Uncertain Receipts and Disbursements. *Eur. J. Opl. Res.* **2,** 313–326.

CARIÑO, D. R. AND Y. FAN. 1993. Alternative Risk Measures for Asset Allocation. *Gestion Collective International* **2,** 47–51.

CARIÑO, D. R., T. KENT, D. H. MYERS, C. STACY, M. SYLVANUS, A. L. TURNER, K. WATANABE, AND W. T. ZIEMBA. 1994. The Russell-Yasuda Kasai Model: An Asset/Liability Model for a Japanese Insurance Company Using Multistage Stochastic Programming. *Interfaces* **24,** 29–49.

CARIÑO, D. R., D. H. MYERS, AND W. T. ZIEMBA. 1998. Concepts, Technical Issues, and Uses of the Russell-Yasuda Kasai Financial Planning Model. *Opns. Res.* **46,** 450–462.

CHAMBERS, D. AND A. CHARNES. 1961. Inter-Temporal Analysis and Optimization of Bank Portfolios. *Mgmt. Sci.* **7,** 393–410.

CHARNES, A. AND M. J. L. KIRBY. 1965. Application of Chance-Constrained Programming to the Solution of the So-Called Savings and Loan Association Type of Problem. Research Analysis Corporation, McLean, VA.

CHARNES, A. AND S. THORE. 1966. Planning for Liquidity in Financial Institutions: The Chance Constrained Method. *J. Finan.* **21,** 649–674.

CHARNES, A. AND S. C. LITTLECHILD. 1968. Intertemporal Bank Asset Choice with Stochastic Dependence. Systems Research Memorandum No. 188. The Technological Institute, Northwestern University.

CHARNES, A., GALLEGOS, AND S. YAO. 1982. A Chance-Constrained Approach to Bank Dynamic Balance Sheet Management. Centre for Cybernetic Studies CCS 428, University of Texas, Austin.

COHEN, K. J. AND F. S. HAMMER. 1967. Linear Programming and Optimal Bank Asset Management Decision. *J. Finan.* **22,** 42–61.

COHEN, K. J. AND S. THORE. 1970. Programming Bank Portfolios under Uncertainty. *J. Bank Res.* **1,** 42–61.

CRANE, D. B. 1971. A Stochastic Programming Model for Commercial Bank Bond Portfolio Management. *J. Financial Quantitative Analysis* **6,** 955–976.

DAELLENBACH, H. G. AND S. A. ARCHER. 1969. The Optimal Bank Liquidity: A Multi-Period Stochastic Model. *J. Financial Quantative Analysis*, **4,** 329–343.

DEMPSTER, M. A. H. (ED.). 1980. *Stochastic Programming: Proceedings of the 1st International Conference on Stochastic Programming*, Academic Press, Oxford.

DEMPSTER, M. A. H. AND A. M. IRELAND. 1988. A Financial Expert Decision Support System. In *Mathematical Models for Decision Support*. B. Mitra (ed.), NATO ASI Series, **F48.** Springer-Verlag, Berlin, 415–440.

DUPACOVÁ, J. 1991. Stochastic Optimization Models in Banking (in Czech). *EMO 27* (1991) 201–234. (See *Stochastic Programming Models in Banking*, IIASA Laxenburg.)

EDIRISINGHE, N. C. P. AND W. T. ZIEMBA. 1992. Tight Bounds for Stochastic Convex Programs. *Opns. Res.* **40,** 660–677.

EISNER, M. J., R. S. KAPLAN, AND J. V. SODEN. 1971. Admissible Decision Rules for the E-Model of Chance-Constrained Programming. *Mgmt. Sci.* **17,** 337–353.

EPPEN, G. D. AND E. F. FAMA. 1968. Solutions for Cash Balance and Simple Dynamic Portfolio Problems. *J. Business* **41,** 94–112.

EPPEN, G. D. AND E. F. FAMA. 1971. Three Asset Cash Balance and Dynamic Portfolio Problems. *Mgmt. Sci.* **17,** 311–319.

ERMOLIEV, Y. AND R. J.-B. WETS (EDS.). 1988. *Numerical Techniques for Stochastic Optimization Problems*. Springer, Berlin.

FRAUENDORFER, K. 1992. *Stochastic Two-Stage Programming*. Springer-Verlag, New York.

GASSMANN, H. I. 1990. MSLiP: A Computer Code for the Multi-Stage Stochastic Linear Programming Problem. *Math. Programming* **47,** 407–423.

HESTER, D. D. AND J. L. PIERCE. 1975. *Bank Management and Portfolio Behavior*. Yale University Press, New Haven, CT.

HIGLE, J. L. AND S. SEN. 1991. Stochastic Decomposition: An Algorithm for Two-Stage Linear Programs with Recourse. *Math. OR.* **16,** 650–669.

HILLER, R. S. AND J. ECKSTEIN. 1993. Stochastic Dedication: Designing Fixed Income Portfolios Using Massively Parallel Benders Decomposition. *Mgmt. Sci.* **39,** 1422–1438.

HILLER, R. S. AND J. F. SHAPIRO. 1989. Stochastic Programming Models for Asset/Liability Management Problems. IFSRC Discussion Paper 105-89, Sloan School of Management, M.I.T., Cambridge, MA.

HUANG, C. C., W. T. ZIEMBA, AND A. BEN-TAL. 1977. Bounds on the Expectation of a Convex Function of a Random Variable: With Applications to Stochastic Programming. *Opns. Res.* **25,** 315–325.

HUTCHINSON, J. M. AND S. A. ZENIOS. 1991. Financial Simulations on a Massively Parallel Connection Machine. *Intntl. J. Supercomputer Appl.* **5,** 27–45.

INFANGER, G. 1994. *Planning Under Uncertainty: Solving Large-Scale Stochastic Linear Programs*. The Scientific Press, Danvers, Massachusetts.

KALL, P. AND S. W. WALLACE. 1994. *Stochastic Programming*. Wiley, New York.

KALLBERG, J. G., R. W. WHITE, AND W. T. ZIEMBA. 1982. Short Term Financial Planning Under Uncertainty. *Mgmt. Sci.* **28,** 670–682.

KOMAR, R. I. 1971. Developing a Liquidity Management Model. *J. Bank. Res.* **2,** 38–52.

KUSY, M. I. 1978. An Asset and Liability Management Model. Ph.D. Dissertation, Faculty of Commerce, University of British Columbia.

KUSY, M. I. AND W. T. ZIEMBA. 1986. A Bank Asset and Liability Management Model. *Opns. Res.* **34,** 356–376.

LANE, M. AND P. HUTCHINSON. 1980. A Model for Managing a Certificate of Deposit Portfolio Under Uncertainty. In *Stochastic Programming: Proceedings of the First International Conference on Stochastic Programming*. Academic Press, Oxford.

LIFSON, K. A. AND B. R. BLACKMAN. 1973. Simulation and Optimization Models for Asset Deployment and Funds Sources, Balancing Profit, Liquidity and Growth. *J. Bank Res.* **4,** 239–255.

MARKOWITZ, H. M. 1952. Portfolio Selection. *J. Finance* **7,** 77–91.

MARKOWITZ, H. M. 1987. *Mean-Variance Analysis in Portfolio Choice and Capital Markets*. Basil Blackwell Ltd., Oxford.

MULVEY, J. M. AND H. VLADIMIROU. 1989. Stochastic Network Optimization Models for Investment Planning. *Ann. O. R.* **20,** 187–217.

MULVEY, J. M. AND H. VLADIMIROU. 1992. Stochastic Network Programming for Financial Planning Problems. *Mgmt. Sci.* **38,** 1642–1664.

MULVEY, J. M. AND W. T. ZIEMBA. 1995. Asset and Liability Allocation in a Global Environment. In *Finance*. R. Jarrow, V. Maksimovic and W. T. Ziemba (eds.), North Holland, Amsterdam, 435–463.

MYERS, S. C. 1968. Procedures for Capital Budgeting under Uncertainty. *Indust. Mgmt. Rev.* **9,** 1–20.

PYLE, D. H. 1971. On the Theory of Financial Intermediation. *J. Finan.* **26,** 737–746.

SHAPIRO, J. F. 1988. Stochastic Programming Models for Dedicated Portfolio Selection. In *Mathematical Models for Decision Support*. B. Mitra (ed.), NATO ASI Series, **F48,** Springer-Verlag, Berlin, 587–611.

WALLACE, S. W. 1986. Solving Stochastic Programs with Network Recourse. *Networks* **16,** 295–317.

WETS, R. J.-B. 1966. Programming Under Uncertainty: the Complete Problem. *Z. Wahrscheinlichk. Verw. Gebiete* **4,** 316–339.

WETS, R. J.-B. 1974. Solving Stochastic Programs with Simple Recourse I. Mimeo, University of Kentucky.

WOLF, C. R. 1969. A Model for Selecting Commercial Bank Government Security Portfolios. *Rev. Economics and Statistics* **1,** 40–52.

ZENIOS, S. A. 1991. Massively Parallel Computations for Financial Planning Under Uncertainty. In *Very Large Scale Computation in the 21st Century*. J. Mesirov (ed.), SIAM, Philadelphia, 273–294.

ZIEMBA, W. T. 1970. Computational Algorithms for Convex Stochastic Programs With Simple Recourse. *Opns. Res.* **18,** 414–431.

ZIEMBA, W. T. AND R. G. VICKSON (EDS.). 1975. *Stochastic Optimization Models in Finance*. Academic Press, New York.

ZIEMBA, W. T. AND J. M. MULVEY (EDS.). 1998. *Worldwide Asset and Liability Modeling*. Cambridge University Press.

Chapter 11

CONCEPTS, TECHNICAL ISSUES, AND USES OF THE RUSSELL-YASUDA KASAI FINANCIAL PLANNING MODEL*

DAVID R. CARIÑO

Frank Russell Australia, Sydney, Australia

DAVID H. MYERS

University of Washington, Seattle, Washington

WILLIAM T. ZIEMBA

The University of British Columbia, Vancouver, British Columbia, Canada

(Received July 1995; revisions received January 1997, September 1997, December 1997; accepted January 1998)

This paper discusses technical aspects of the Russell-Yasuda Kasai financial planning model. These include the models for the discrete distribution scenario generation processes for the uncertain parameters of the model, the mathematical approach used to develop the infinite-horizon end-effects part of the model, a comparison of algorithms used in the model's solution, and a comparison of the multistage stochastic linear programming model with the previous technology, static mean-variance analysis. Experience and benefits of the model in Yasuda-Kasai's financial planning process is also discussed.

This paper discusses the concepts, technical issues, and use of the Russell-Yasuda Kasai model. The software model incorporates the firm's asset and liability mix, along with institutional (regulatory guidelines and other) constraints as well as uncertain cash flows, disbursements, and taxes. A major part of the firm's business is the issuance of insurance policies that are largely an investment vehicle for purchasers. Complex rules regarding the use of funds to pay dividends complicate the decision problem. Multistage stochastic linear programming with steady-state end effects was used as the modeling approach. The objective is to maximize long-run profits less penalty costs from constraint violations. Uncertainty in returns, interest rates, and other variables was modeled through scenarios using discrete probability distributions.

Several versions of the model were formulated and tested. The model implemented had an initialization period plus four decision periods, and an infinite-horizon end-effects period. The implementation was developed on an IBM RS/6000 workstation using the IBM OSL linear programming system at Russell in Tacoma and duplicated on site for Yasuda Kasai in Tokyo. Formulation aspects of the model appear in Cariño and Ziemba (1998).

The model has been used by Yasuda Kasai to aid in their overall financial planning process since April 1991; see Figure 5 for a schema of the overall financial planning process and the role of the Russell-Yasuda model in this process. Ex ante and ex post comparisons with the current planning process and static mean variance analysis (see Section 4) demonstrate the superiority of the approach both in terms of return characteristics and general understanding of the company's business and the effect of various policies and constraints.

The scenario generation process for the random parameters of the model is discussed in Section 1. The scenarios used are discrete. They can be independent period by period, dependent through a factor model, or general. In the implementation, various econometric models from Yasuda's economic planning department were used.

Grinold's (1977, 1980, 1983) dual-equilibrium approach for end effects is discussed in Section 2. The approach assumes that the technology matrices are constant beyond the horizon and that the resource costs and returns have values that increase with the rate of interest. The approach leads to an additional set of constraints and variables. Hence, the model that has four periods is then a five-period model, plus initialization.

Computations are discussed that adjust for nonsteady-state behavior at the horizon T, which in the RY model is after the fifth year. The RY model has many constraints such as those imposed by the regulatory guidelines that destroy or seriously limit the possibility of formulating or solving the model as a generalized network. The computations are feasible for a sophisticated application on a single IBM RS/6000 workstation. A comparison of computational times with various stochastic programming algorithms such as Rockafellar and Wets' progressive hedging (Rockafellar and Wets 1991), Benders decomposition (Van Slyke and Wets 1969, Wets 1988, Infanger 1994) and direct solve using IBM's interior point and simplex methods implemented in their OSL software on IBM RS/6000 workstations appears in Section 3. Problem size is dependent on

Subject classifications: Finance, Management, asset and liability, Financial Institutions, insurance: Japanese property and casualty. Programming, stochastic: multiperiod, linear.
Area of review: OR PRACTICE.

*This chapter was originally published in: Cariño, D. R., Myers, D. & Ziemba, W. T. (1998). Concepts, Technical Issues, and Uses of the Russell–Yasuda Kasai Financial Planning Model. *Operations Research*, 46(4), 450–462.

Table I
Example of an Independent Scenario Input Table

Period of Measurement (qtrs): 4
Lower Bounds (per qtr): g 0.0125 RIB 0.005 RIL 0.005 RIC 0.005

Prob	RICJ	RPCJ	RIBJ	RPBJ	...	RPEF	gS	g1	g2
0.0160	0.0798	0	0.0859	−0.0668	...	0.3002	0.0779	0.0779	0.0779
0.0230	0.0798	0	0.0859	−0.0668	...	−0.1498	0.0779	0.0779	0.0779
⋮	⋮	⋮	⋮	⋮	...	⋮	⋮	⋮	⋮
0.1410	0.0448	0	0.0579	0.0492	...	−0.1498	0.0541	0.0541	0.0541

the number of constraints and variables, but especially on the number of scenarios. For small problems with few scenarios, direct solve with an interior point algorithm finishing with the simplex method and progressive hedging are the preferred solution approaches. Direct solve with the interior point method finishing with the simplex is preferred for medium-size problems. As problem size increases, Benders decomposition is increasingly the preferred solution approach.

Sections 4 and 5 discuss the results of the model and its comparison to the previous technology used by Yasuda Kasai: static mean-variance analysis recomputed in each period with a rolling one-period horizon. The model has a modular structure with a matrix generator that creates the base linear program plus a set of random coefficient specifications for each period, a scenario generator that builds the decision tree structure and generates the random returns for each asset class, a liability generator that projects the random liabilities for each decision node, a coefficient generator that combines the random coefficient specifications with the random variables to generate random coefficients, and a solver that generates the optimal solution using a series of optimization codes. Reports produced by the system include allocations for the initial stage, expected allocations for each modeled stage, expected income statements for each modeled period, expected balance sheets for each modeled stage, probability distributions of shortfalls, and the status of each regulatory constraint row activity. A comparison of the RY model with a mean-variance model implemented through RAAM (the Russell Asset Allocation Model) is made in Section 4. The two models are compared using common data generated from the implemented scenarios from a realistic future. Using several test cases with varying horizons, the results show that the RY model solutions are close to mean-variance efficient. Meanwhile, the mean-variance solutions produce considerable penalty losses, and the larger the investment horizon the larger are the losses. The model was delivered by Russell to Yasuda Kasai and implemented in the 1991 fiscal year (April 1, 1991 to March 31, 1992). The results of the model were used on a test comparison basis for fiscal 1991 and were fully implemented in fiscal 1992. The results were very successful in both years. The actual return outperformed the constant mix (of the previous) strategy by 42 basis points in income return and 5 basis points in total return over the 2 years; these were ¥8.7 billion ($79 million) and ¥1.0 billion ($9 million), respectively. The model has also been used successfully in fiscal years 1993–1997. Since the objective is to maximize the total return target at the five-year horizon and the intermediate goal is income return, Yasuda Kasai expects even greater returns in the future. The model also has helped Yasuda Kasai in the general understanding of their insurance business and the approach that considers various possible scenarios will serve to protect the firm from future possible severe adverse events. For example, during the 1990 to 1992 stock market decline in Japan, the model suggested a higher exposure in bonds and less to stocks in a declining interest rate environment. As mentioned in Henriques (1991), this approach may well usher in a new way of looking at asset allocation as well as asset and liability management problems.

1. SCENARIO GENERATION

The model's software allows the user to utilize intertemporally independent, dependent (through factor modeling), and general scenarios. The scenarios are assumed to have known discrete probability distributions. The number and form of the scenarios are the most crucial factors in the size and complexity of the model. Their careful selection is crucial for a successful application. Various related models are obtained with modifications and aggregations of a basic set of scenarios.

The strongest assumption is that the scenarios are independent across periods. This substantially reduces the amount of data that the user must prepare. The input required is a joint distribution of all the random variables in each period. Table I shows a typical independent scenario model specifying probabilities that sum to one down the first column and joint outcomes for each random variable across each row. Figure 1 shows the tree structure of 256 scenarios in the 4 model periods plus the end-effects period.

The scenario generator creates the scenario outcomes from the input data using several adjustments. The adjustments provide flexibility in specifying the lengths of periods and numbers of outcomes independent of the specification of the base distribution. In each period, the

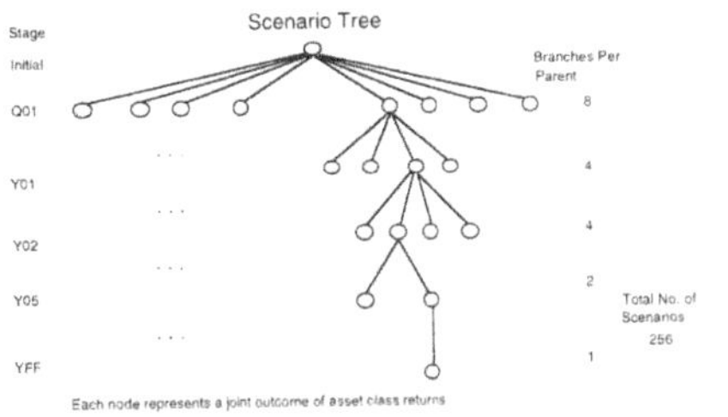

Figure 1. Structure of a tree of 256 scenarios.

scenario generator calculates the mean and standard deviation of each random return in the base distribution. A desired mean and standard deviation are calculated given the period of measurement of the base distribution and the length of the given period. For a base period of measurement of 4 quarters with the current period 1 quarter long, the desired mean equals the base mean divided by 4 and the desired standard deviation equals the base standard deviation divided by $\sqrt{4}$. It is assumed that the variance grows proportionally to time.

The base set of outcomes is aggregated to reduce the number of outcomes to the number desired for the given period. The conditional means of consecutive pairs of outcomes are computed, reducing the number of outcomes to half of the base set. Consecutive pairs of the resulting set are combined if further reduction is necessary. The base set of outcomes must be ordered (and contain a power-of-two multiple of the desired number of outcomes. The probabilities of the outcomes to be combined are summed, and the outcome value is the conditional mean of the two outcomes.

After reduction of the number of outcomes and adjustment for period length, the means of the random variables remain equal to the desired means. However, the resulting standard deviations might not equal the desired standard deviations. A variance adjustment is applied that simultaneously moves outcomes toward or away from the mean of the random variable until the desired variance is achieved. Outcomes are moved in proportion to their distances from the mean. By moving all outcomes, the overall general shape of the distribution is preserved; it is expanded from or contracted toward the mean by the desired amount.

The variance adjustment process is as follows:

$\bar{Z}$ = mean of random variable Z,

z_i(unadjusted) = outcome i before variance adjustment,

σ_Z^2(desired) = desired variance,

and

p_i = probability of outcome I.

Step 1. Calculate

$$\sigma_Z^2(\text{unadjusted}) = \sum_i p_i[z_i(\text{unadjusted}) - \bar{Z}]^2.$$

Step 2. Calculate the adjustment factor

$$\alpha = \sqrt{\frac{\sigma_Z^2(\text{desired})}{\sigma_Z^2(\text{unadjusted})}},$$

where $\alpha \geq 0$. If $\alpha = 1$ there is no adjustment.

Step 3. For all outcomes i, assign

$$z_i(\text{adjusted}) = \bar{Z} + \alpha(z_i(\text{unadjusted}) - \bar{Z}).$$

Step 4. Check that all adjusted outcomes z_i (adjusted) are greater than or equal to the lower bound z_{lb} for the random variable. If Step 3 results in the lowest outcome z_{lo} falling below the lower bound z_{lb} for the random variable, then set

$$\alpha = \frac{z_{lb} - \bar{Z}}{z_{lo}(\text{unadjusted}) - \bar{Z}},$$

and repeat Step 3.

This variance adjustment procedure is applied to each random variable individually. All outcomes are adjusted; the adjustment of any individual outcome tends to be small. Hence, the overall shape of the distribution tends to be preserved. When reducing the number of outcomes, some characteristics of the base distribution are lost. For example, in reducing the number of outcomes, correlations among the random variables will increase in magnitude. With only two outcomes, the correlations are $+1$ or -1. This procedure preserves the sign of the correlations of the base distribution. This methodology can be used to create scenarios from empirical data. Given the historical returns, equal probabilities for all outcomes could be assigned. This procedure preserves the historical means and variances of the returns.

The second scenario generation method implemented in the software constructs return outcomes using a factor model of asset returns. This captures the dependence among asset returns through elementary factors. Interest rate levels in adjacent periods are correlated across periods, which leads to dependence in interest rate-sensitive returns across periods. Three factors—interest rates, equity returns, and currency exchange rates—adequately capture the dependence among asset returns. The long-term government bond yield represents the interest factor, the return to the TOPIX index (the capitalization-weighted average of all stocks on the first section of the Tokyo Stock Exchange) represents the equity factor, and the yen versus U.S. dollar currency return represents the currency factor. Domestic bond, loan, and cash returns depend on the interest factor; domestic equity price returns depend on the equity factor; foreign equity return depends on the currency factor. Foreign bond return depends on both the interest and currency factors. The movements of the factors over time were modeled by a time-series model that captures intertemporal dependence.

The third method provided by the model's software allows the user complete flexibility in describing the structure and outcomes in the scenario tree. The tree may have arbitrary structure with differing numbers of branches per parent within a given period. The model takes the specified scenario tree as given and makes no adjustments to outcomes.

Chopra and Ziemba (1993) show that the use of past data, in particular, often yields poor mean estimates that can cause large errors in the objective value. Hence, the factor model and third method, econometric models, are preferred. For methods to massage data inputs to improve model performance see Hensel and Turner (1998). These studies are in a mean variance context. However, similar results obtain in stochastic programming although this model is less sensitive to such errors than mean-variance analysis.

2. END EFFECTS

The stochastic linear programming model (the base problem) has uncertainty in many coefficients, which are modeled through scenarios. Since each scenario has a discrete probability of occurrence for any finite horizon, the stochastic linear program is equivalent to a large deterministic linear program in extensive form (the grand linear program). The institution has an ongoing business, so their situation is well modeled as an infinite horizon problem. For a given fixed scenario that has no uncertainty, the problem is

$$
\begin{aligned}
&\min \sum_{t=1}^{\infty} \alpha_t c_t x_t,\\
&A_0 x_0 = b_0\\
&K_1 x_0 + A_1 x_1 = b_1\\
&\qquad K_2 x_1 + A_2 x_2 = b_2\\
&\qquad\qquad \ddots \qquad \vdots\\
&u_t \geqslant x_t \geqslant l_t, \quad t = 0, 1, 2, \ldots
\end{aligned}
$$

The matrices $A_0, A_1, \ldots$ *and the vector* b_0 are deterministic. The matrices $K_1, K_2, \ldots$ and the vectors $b_1, b_2, \ldots$ generally depend upon the random scenario that actually occurs. Fixing on a specific scenario gives a deterministic linear programming base problem. Its solution, for all scenarios properly averaged, provides the current allocation decision x_0 and a sequence of vectors $(x_1, x_2, \ldots)$ that are contingent on the actual outcomes of the random variables period by period.

Given the size of the problem with many variables and scenarios, it is not practical to consider the infinite horizon problem. An approximation that truncates the problem in period T will not have much impact on the early period decisions only if T as well as the discount rate γ are sufficiently large. Calculations showing this error, which is considerable, for given T and γ appear in Grinold (1980). A preferred approach is to consider the base problem up to period T and then add a steady-state terminal value term $d_T x_T$ to the objective function. This term and the constraints associated with it yield one more period in the base problem. Hence, the problem has $T + 1$ periods and, for reasonably sized T, is manageable. Grinold (1977, 1980, 1983) has studied various approaches for adding the steady-state period. Calculations, as well as economic intuition, favor the dual equilibrium technique. The basic idea is to assume that the dual variables of the T stage problem increase period by period in proportion to the assumed discount factor. Such an idea has great appeal since prices rise directly over time with an assumed inflation rate. Except for uncertainties in time, this is precisely what happens for periods 1 to T for sufficiently long T. The infinite horizon problem can then be approximated with a $T + 1$ period problem using the constant (time independent) parameters α, c, A, K, b, and δ. For periods $s = 1, 2, \ldots$ after T, it is assumed that the various coefficients in the base problem are:

$$
\begin{aligned}
\alpha_{T+s} c_{T+s} &= \alpha^{T+s} c,\\
A_{T+s} &= A,\\
K_{T+s} &= K,
\end{aligned}
$$

and

$$b_{T+s} = \delta^{s-1} b$$

where

$$0 < \alpha < 1,\ 0 \leqslant \delta,\ \text{and}\ \alpha\delta < 1.$$

The discount factor $\alpha_t = 1/(1 + \gamma_t)$ varies with period t only because the periods may be of varying lengths (quarterly vs. annually). Hence, it is assumed that the periods are at constant length, namely annual after period T. Then the coefficients in the objective and right-hand side grow as shown above. The matrices A_{T+s} are constants A and the K_{T+s} are constants K, assuming that there is only one scenario (the mean) past the horizon T.

The dual equilibrium approximate problem is

$$\min \sum_{t=1}^{T} \alpha_t c x_t + \frac{\alpha^{T+1}}{1-\alpha} c\bar{x},$$

subject to

$$
\begin{aligned}
&A_0 x_0 = b_0\\
&K_1 x_0 + A_1 x_1 = b_1\\
&\qquad K_2 x_1 + A_2 x_2 = b_2\\
&\qquad\qquad \ddots \qquad \vdots\\
&\qquad\qquad\qquad K_T x_{T-1} + A_T x_T = b_T\\
&\qquad\qquad\qquad\qquad K x_T + \frac{A + \alpha K}{1-\alpha}\bar{x} = \frac{1}{1-\alpha\delta} b,\\
&u \geqslant x_t \geqslant l, \quad t = 0, \ldots T, \quad u \geqslant \bar{x} \geqslant l.
\end{aligned}
$$

Table II

Dimensions of Implemented Problem with Loan Constraints

Per	BrPar	Scen	Assets	Alloc Var	Rows	Cols	Coeff	GLP:Rows	Cols	Coeff
INI	1	1	7	59	22	60	257	22	60	257
Q01	8	8	7	59	48	85	573	384	680	4,584
Y01	4	32	7	59	54	96	706	1,728	3,072	22,592
Y02	4	128	7	29	52	66	557	6,656	8,448	71,296
Y05	2	256	7	29	52	66	407	13,312	16,896	104,192
YFF	1	256	5	21	35	58	450	8,960	14,848	115,200
TOTAL					263	431	2,950	31,062	44,004	318,121

The variables $\bar{x}$ of the end-effects period are

$$\bar{x} = \sum_{s=1}^{\infty} (1 - \alpha)\alpha^{s-1} x_{T+s}.$$

Since $\Sigma_{s=1}^{\infty} (1 - \alpha)\alpha^{s-1} = 1$, the variables $\bar{x}$ are a convex combination of the post-horizon variables x_{T+s} for $s = 1, 2, \ldots$.

The model implemented for Yasuda Kasai has five periods, and the horizon period is at T = 5 years. The end-effect period YFF is designed to reduce the effects of ending the model at a finite horizon, while in reality the firm expects to operate indefinitely beyond the horizon. The methodology assumes that the data inputs of the model are in a steady state beyond the horizon. This assumption has implications primarily for the liability input data and places restrictions on this input.

Unfortunately, the data from the liability model described above do not satisfy the steady-state assumption. The maturity payments (the *P*s) do not reach steady-state by Year 5 but are still accelerating, reflecting the growth of the account during the earlier years of the data. Steady-state is reached when the growth in *P* equals the growth in flows *F*. One plus the common growth rate is the parameter δ. An unduly severe requirement on cash flow generation would be imposed if these data were used without adjustment.

Two adjustments must be made on the input data. First, the value for δ should be set equal to the one plus the growth in *F* from Year 5 to Year 6. Second, data should be adjusted so that the growth in *P* from Year 5 to Year 6 also equals this rate. (Because the inflow/payment data for the General Account grows at a constant rate, no modifications for that account are necessary.) The adjustment to the *F* data matrices amounts to a smoothing of the cash flows in later periods of the model. The procedure simply involves shifting the maturities of liabilities in later periods while keeping the total inflows as given.

3. COMPUTATIONS

Several versions of the RY model were formulated and analyzed. The largest model had 10 decision periods plus the end-effects period with 2,048 scenarios. This model was solved using a mainframe vector processor at the IBM T. J. Watson Research Center at Yorktown Heights, New York. The solution time was 26 hours. (Later experimentation cut this time considerably with several parallel processors.) Yasuda Kasai wished a model that they could solve on a single IBM RS/6000 Model 530 workstation in three hours or less, so they could do additional sensitivity and other calculations. The final model implemented had 4 decision periods plus the end-effects period with 256 scenarios.

Various stochastic programming and linear programming algorithms were tested. The model was implemented for Yasuda Kasai using the IBM Optimization Subroutine Library (OSL) interior point linear programming code with a simplex method finish-up provision.

The testing of various algorithms continued after implementation of the RY model in 1991. The comparison used IBM OSL functions and coding of the algorithms at Russell. Details of an experiment to compare the various approaches on an RS/6000 Model 550 follow. The following solution approaches were compared:

1. Progressive hedging: one scenario and multiple (grouped) scenarios at a time
2. Direct solve with OSL interior point code (using an interior point primal barrier method)
3. Direct solve with OSL's implementation of the simplex method
4. Benders decomposition (parallel code but running on a single processor)

The idea of the Rockafellar and Wets (1991) progressive hedging algorithm to use dual prices to solve for optimal first-period decision vectors based on single or multiple scenarios and combine the various decisions to obtain an optimal first period decision. The intuition of the method for this process is easy for decision makers to grasp and interpret.

The direct solve interior point method is based on a barrier method. Details of this algorithm and its solution steps appear in the IBM OSL documentation primal-dual with predictor-corrector. The simplex method can be used by itself or as a finishing phase to another algorithm. The OSL code has an automatic feature to switch to the simplex method after using the interior point method. The code developed at Russell for the single and grouped scenarios also has this feature. The Benders (1962) decomposition approach as applied to stochastic programming was developed by Van Slyke and Wets (1969) and is described in Wets (1988). Infanger (1994) has also tested the possibility of using the Benders decomposition on large scale

Table III
CPU Times for Various Algorithms Applied to the Solution of a Small, Medium, and Large Scale Five-Period Stochastic Program

Approaches		32 Scenarios	128 Scenarios	1,024 Scenarios
PH (6 iterations)	Single & simplex	6 min 27 sec		
PH (6 iterations)	Group & simplex	13 min 28 sec	41 min 46 sec	
Direct solve	Interior & simplex	5 min 29 sec	28 min 27 sec	35 hr 42 min 51 sec
Direct solve	Simplex only	9 min 4 sec	1 hr 5 min 28 sec	95 hr 30 min 36 sec
Benders	On one machine	22 min 56 sec	55 min 57 sec	11 hr 0 min 56 sec
Rows		6,593	16,609	123,425
Columns		9,896	23,912	174,480
Coefficients		6,871	162,207	1,198,263

stochastic programming problems for two and three stage problems.

Experiments were made with 32, 128, and 1024 scenario problems using a base LP with 275 rows, 435 columns, and 2945 coefficients. These "small, medium, and large" problems were all five-period problems with period by period scenario patterns of 1-8-4-1-1-1, 1-8-4-2-2-1, and 1-16-4-2-2-1, respectively.

The results provided the following conclusions.

1. For the small problem, progressive hedging with single scenarios is comparable to direct solve using the interior point method plus the simplex method to finish the optimization. Progressive hedging provides a better basis. However, the interior point method takes less time to produce the basis that is solved by the simplex method. The Benders decomposition was slow, and a parallel implementation did not improve it.

2. For the medium problem, the direct solve interior plus simplex was the fastest algorithm. Progressive hedging with grouped scenarios gives a better basis than the direct solve approach, but the interior point method is much faster. The Benders decomposition is more competitive.

3. For the large problem, the Benders decomposition was much faster than the other methods. The larger the problem, the greater is the advantage of the Benders decomposition approach over the other methods.

Although other researchers (see, e.g., Infanger 1994) performed different tests and did not compare as many different methods on problems with as many periods, the conclusion that the simplex method and progressive hedging are adequate for small to medium problems, and then for large problems the advantage shifts dramatically to the Benders decomposition, and is quite general and robust.

4. COMPARISON TO MEAN VARIANCE

Yasuda Kasai's previous methodology was to calculate portfolio weights period by period using a mean-variance model. We now compare the multistage stochastic programming model with a static mean-variance model that recomputes in each period. Table IV illustrates the main differences between the two models.

Six test cases were used to compare the models, as detailed in Table V. Two of the test cases were static, with only 1 period uncertainty with 8 and 16 scenarios, respectively. The other four test cases had different numbers of scenarios over the four periods plus the end-effects period.

The mean-variance calculations used the Russell Asset Allocation Model (RAAM), which is a quadratic programming optimizer developed at Russell based on the Markowitz formulation using Perold's (1984) algorithm. To make the two models comparable in terms of structure, certain assumptions were made for RAAM.

First, to made the risk and return assumptions comparable, the forecasted (f) scenarios from RY were used to generate the means, standard deviations, and correlations for RAAM. Two sets of scenarios were tested—16 and 8 scenarios. In the RY model, the loan model recalculates the price returns for fixed rate loans (RPLF). These adjusted returns were input to correct the means, standard deviations, and correlations for fixed rate loans used as inputs to the mean-variance model. No adjustments were made for the income gap in the mean-variance model. See Table VI.

The scenario methodology in the RY model preserves the mean and standard deviations when creating fewer scenarios. Changes occur in the correlation tables between

Table IV
Comparison of RY Stochastic Programming Model with a Mean-Variance Model

	RY	Mean-Variance
Objective	Piecewise Linear	Quadratic
Stages	Multiple with end-effects period	Single
Allocations	Dynamic	Static
Accounts	Multiple	Single
Risk Measures	Multiple Shortfalls	Variance

Table V
Test Cases

Case No.	INI	Q01	Y01	Y02	Y05	YFF
1	1	16	4	2	2	1
2	1	16	2	2	2	2
3	1		16			
4	1	8	4	4	2	1
5	1	8	4	2	2	2
6	1		8			
Scenario		f	f	s	s	s

16 and 8 scenarios. For example, the foreign equity correlations changed from 0.4 and −0.4 with cash and bonds to 0.8 and −0.8 for 16 versus 8 scenarios. The correlations are the same, except for REF because of the way the scenarios were created. The correlations are a product of the scenarios. The difference between the 16 and 8 scenario cases is only evident in the REF because the pairs do not change. In moving to four or two scenarios from eight, we can expect the correlation table to change for the other asset classes.

The next step in creating comparable structures between the RY model and RAAM was to add constraints to RAAM. Since RAAM could not handle multiple accounts in which asset classes are duplicated, the mean-variance runs were made for each account separately—General, Savings, First and Second Special Savings. For each account's problem, five Ministry of Finance constraints—total equity, total foreign investment, loans, tokkin, and foreign subsidiaries—were added.

Liabilities and cashflows were handled in RAAM using a minimum yield constraint set to the average level of interest growth g times the total liability balance L plus required profit Γ divided by the initial value of all the accounts. That is, $(gL_0 + \Gamma)/V_0$ was the minimum expected yield constraint for each account.

For each account, direct and indirect allocation classes were used in RAAM. The indirect allocation classes correspond to tokkin and foreign subsidiaries. Risk and return assumptions for a given asset class were the same for direct and indirect investment in the asset class. The expected yield on direct allocation classes was set equal to expected income return, while expected yield on indirect classes was set equal to expected total return. Loan constraints equivalent to 90 and 120 percent of the starting loan values were set.

Optimal solutions from RY employed Yasuda Kasai's standard set of costs and a set of zero costs. The standard set of costs defines Yasuda Kasai's sensitivity to certain goals or business risk. In the mean-variance framework, this is analogous to risk tolerance. By employing zero costs, RY maximizes wealth. The zero costs solutions are comparable to RAAM's highest risk solution given similar constraints.

There are various ways to compare models. One may build a larger meta model and then determine which of the simple models most accurately approximates the model. This is used with econometric models. Another approach is to formulate models based on a given situation and then compare the actual or simulated performance of them

Table VI
Correlation Matrix, Means, and Standard Deviations

	16 Scenarios (forecasted)							
	RCJ	RBJ	REJ	RLL	RLF	RBF	REF	g
RCJ	1.00							
RBJ	−1.00	1.00						
REJ	−0.23	0.23	1.00					
RLL	1.00	−1.00	−0.23	1.00				
RLF	−1.00	1.00	0.23	−1.00	1.00			
RBF	0.21	−0.21	−0.13	0.21	−0.21	1.00		
REF	0.40	−0.40	−0.20	0.40	−0.40	0.23	1.00	
g	1.00	−1.00	−0.23	1.00	−1.00	0.21	0.40	1.00
Mean	7.00	8.59	6.96	7.55	6.90	9.08	14.20	6.20
SD	0.43	4.35	11.66	0.30	0.38	16.97	22.50	0.30

	8 Scenarios (forecasted)							
	RCJ	RBJ	REJ	RLL	RLF	RBF	REF	g
RCJ	1.00							
RBJ	−1.00	1.00						
REJ	−0.23	0.23	1.00					
RLL	1.00	−1.00	−0.23	1.00				
RLF	−1.00	1.00	0.23	−1.00	1.00			
RBF	0.21	−0.21	−0.13	0.21	−0.21	1.00		
REF	0.80	−0.80	−0.41	0.80	−0.80	0.47	1.00	
g	1.00	−1.00	−0.23	1.00	−1.00	0.21	0.80	1.00
Mean	7.00	8.59	6.96	7.55	6.90	9.08	14.20	6.20
SD	0.43	4.35	11.66	0.30	0.38	16.97	22.50	0.30

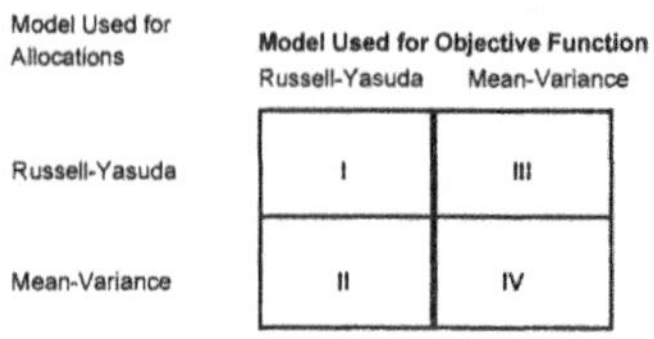

Figure 2. Models used to compare the stochastic and mean-variance models.

using standard statistical tests; see e.g., Kusy and Ziemba (1986). The approach used here was to compare the results of a four-way cross comparison using current data, where each of the two models was used for the allocations and these in turn were evaluated using the two different objective functions. These solutions are shown in Figure 2.

When comparing the RY Model runs I and II, the shortfalls and expected terminal wealth are important. When comparing the mean-variance runs III and IV, the portfolio means and variances are the relevant measures.

In choosing MV portfolios for comparison with RY, portfolios on the efficient frontier with similar risk and similar expected return as RY portfolios were selected. RAAM calculates the similar risk and return portfolios. Yasuda Kasai's risk tolerance was used. The consequence in MV was to examine two portfolios on the efficient frontier that were close to RY allocations—the similar risk and similar return portfolios shown in Figure 3.

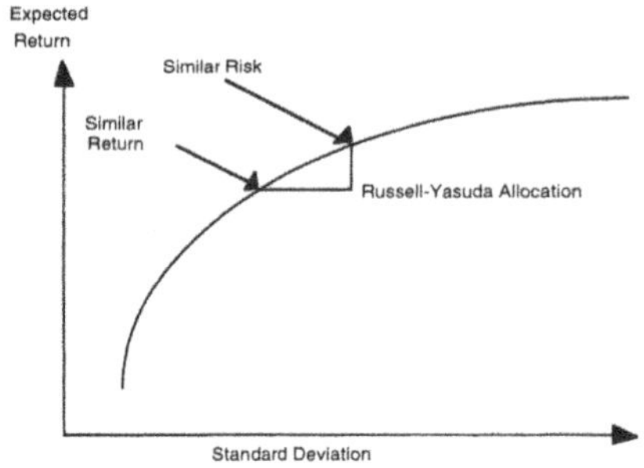

Figure 3. Comparisons of the RY Model to a mean-variance model.

There are six test cases and four model comparisons, for a total of 24 separate sets of calculations. The results from the six RY test cases (I of Figure 2) are summarized in Table VII. A typical allocation for case 2 with the 256 scenarios appears in Table VIII. The allocations are shown in percent by account so the columns add to 100 percent. For the multiperiod cases (1, 2, 4 and 5), the objective values ranged from −82,798 oku en (the objective functions unit values) for case 4 to −83,856.73 oku en for case 2. In comparing the 16 scenario cases, case 2 had the highest objective value, but a lower market value than case 1. Its advantage was in lower costs than case 1. In the 8 scenario cases, case 5 had both a higher expected market

Table VII
RY Test Cases (¥100 million)

	1	2	3	4	5	6
Market Value (−)	86102.02	86062.84	46459.87	85964.21	86135.05	46583.17
Shortfalls Q01–Y05						
Income (+)	2414.3	2206.07	153.02	2699.78	2305.37	137.84
Cash (+)	0.45	0.00	0.00	352.75	15.52	0.00
Reserve (+)	15.25	0.03	29.82	105.13	23.11	18.42
Shortfalls YFF						
Income (+)	0.00	0.00	0.00	2.61	0.23	0.00
Cash (+)	0.00	0.00	0.00	0.00	0.00	0.00
Reserve (+)	0.00	0.00	0.00	5.28	0.00	0.00
Total Shortfalls (+)	2430.00	2206.11	182.85	3165.56	2344.24	156.26
Objective Value (−)	83672.02	83856.73	46277.13	82798.65	83790.81	46426.91

Table VIII
Case 2,16f-2f-2s-2s-2s, RY Allocations in Percent by Account

	GD	GT	GC	SD	ST	SC	1D	1T	1L	2D	2T	2L	Total
CJ	0			28			41			0			31
LL	8			8			28			83			20
LF	21			25			31			0			27
BJ	41	0	0	39	0	0	0	0	0	0	0	0	17
EJ	3	0	0	0	0	0			0	17	0	0	1
BF	0	0	0	0	0	0	0	0	0	0	0	0	0
EF	27	0	0	1	0	0	0	0	0	0	0	0	4

Table IX
Risk and Return of Portfolios in RAAM (in percent)

Case Number	Portfolio	Total Rtn	Risk	Gen Rtn	Risk	Sav Rtn	Risk	SS1 Rtn	Risk	SS2 Rtn	Risk
1	R/Y	7.5	0.7	8.8	2.9	7.5	0.7	7.1	0.1	7.8	2.0
	Similar Run	7.5	0.5	8.8	2.8	7.5	0.7	7.2	0.0	7.8	0.3
	Similar Risk	7.6	0.7	8.8	2.9	7.6	0.7	7.3	0.1	8.3	2.0
2	R/Y	7.7	0.9	9.6	5.6	7.6	1.7	7.1	0.1	7.5	1.9
	Similar Rtn	7.6	0.9	9.6	5.4	7.6	0.9	7.2	0.0	7.6	0.0
	Similar Risk	7.7	0.9	9.7	5.6	8.1	1.7	7.3	0.1	8.3	2.0
3	R/Y	8.1	1.7	9.1	3.6	8.6	2.5	7.6	1.4	7.6	0.3
	Similar Rtn	8.1	1.5	9.1	3.5	8.6	2.4	7.6	0.7	7.6	0.0
	Similar Risk	8.2	1.7	9.1	3.6	8.6	2.5	8.1	1.4	7.8	0.3
4	R/Y	8.0	0.8	9.3	3.2	8.7	1.5	7.2	0.0	7.5	1.9
	Similar Rtn	8.0	0.7	9.3	3.2	8.7	1.5	7.2	0.0	7.6	0.0
	Similar Risk	8.0	0.8	9.3	3.2	8.7	1.5	7.2	0.0	8.3	1.9
5	R/Y	8.0	0.9	9.5	4.0	8.7	1.5	7.2	0.1	7.5	1.9
	Similar Rtn	8.0	0.7	9.5	3.6	8.7	1.5	7.2	0.0	7.6	0.0
	Similar Risk	8.2	0.9	9.5	4.1	8.7	1.5	7.2	0.0	8.3	1.9
6	R/Y	8.7	2.1	9.8	5.1	8.9	1.9	8.3	1.8	7.6	0.3
	Similar Rtn	8.7	1.8	9.8	5.1	8.9	1.9	8.3	1.2	7.6	0.0
	Similar Risk	8.7	2.1	9.8	5.1	8.9	1.9	8.5	1.8	7.9	0.3

value and lower costs than case 4. In the static cases, 6 had a higher market value and lower costs than did 3.

A comparison of allocations indicates that the cases with 16 initial branches in the tree (1–3) had more cash and less foreign equity than their counterparts with 8 initial branches. Correlations explain some of the differences between the 8 and 16 scenario cases. For example, foreign equity is a much better diversifier with −0.8 correlation to bonds and fixed-rate loans in the 8 scenario case (−0.4 in 16 scenario cases). In the 8 scenario cases, there are more bonds and fixed-rate loans and less cash.

The results from the six MV test cases (IV of Figure 2) are summarized in Table IX. RAAM's objective is based on the tradeoff between standard deviation risk and mean return. Different levels of risk and return on the efficient frontier correspond to different risk tolerances. The allocations from the RY model for the various accounts have differing risk tolerances in the mean-variance framework. These are a consequence of the constraints and objectives in the RY solution allocations. The General account return and risk are the most aggressive of the accounts. The First and Second Special Savings accounts have the more conservative risk/return profiles. For the Savings Account, test cases 4 through 6 representing the 8 scenarios have closer risk and return profiles for the similar risk and return portfolios than cases 1 through 3. This is reflected in the similarity of the allocations of those cases as well for the two portfolios. For case 2 for Category IV, similar return and similar risk allocations are similar.

When the RY allocations are input to RAAM as current allocations (Category III) the current allocation portfolio in the majority of cases lies close to the efficient frontier. Risk and expected return of the various portfolios is shown in Table IX. The total firm, General and Savings account allocations are often on the efficient frontier (cases 4 and 6). This is evident when the similar risk and return portfolios have the same risk and return as the RY portfolio. The Second Special Savings account's RY allocations are the least efficient portfolios; they have the greatest distance from the two efficient frontier portfolios.

The loan bounds were restrictive enough in the mean-variance model to constrain the problem so that the yield constraint was not binding. The constrained efficient frontier with loan bounds lay below the efficient frontier without loan bounds, but with the yield constraint. With the loan bounds there was enough expected income in each account (in the mean-variance model expected income is known with certainty and loan income ignored the income gap) that the universe of efficient and possible portfolios exceeded the yield hurdle. The 90/120-percent bounds on loan allocations combined with the high level of income make the yield constraint in RAAM irrelevant in the majority of cases.

The inefficiency of the solution of the Second Special Savings account may be the result of several factors. The level of loans provides enough income and total return to cover all types of shortfalls, especially given that the vast majority of liability payouts are beyond the end-effects period. The RY model may choose a less efficient portfolio in the Second Special Savings account so that it can use its flexibility to assist the other accounts. This is evident in case 2, where the model allocates foreign equity to the General account and the Second Special Savings account is only invested in loans and domestic equity.

RAAM is unable to distinguish among the investment types—direct, tokkin, and foreign Subsidiaries. This is shown in foreign equity and domestic bond allocations where there are equal divisions in the allocations or maximum allocations for each allocation type. In the similar return allocations for the General account, domestic bonds is split 22 percent in each direct and tokkin and foreign

Table X
Zero Cost Portfolios in RAAM

Case Number	Model	Total Rtn	Risk	Gen Rtn	Risk	Sav Rtn	Risk	SS1 Rtn	Risk	SS2 Rtn	Risk
4	R/Y	10.4	9.5	12.1	15.9	11.8	15.0	9.2	5.1	8.7	5.0
	MV Rtn	10.4	9.5	12.1	15.9	11.8	15.0	9.2	5.0	8.7	4.0
	MV Risk	10.4	9.5	12.1	15.9	11.8	15.0	9.2	5.1	8.7	4.0

equity is divided among direct, tokkin, and foreign subsidiaries, namely 16, 7, and 3 percent.

Additional testing of RY allocations in RAAM used zero costs. The risk profiles in RY with zero cost should be similar to the highest risk tolerance on the efficient frontier in MV; see Table X. As expected, the RY portfolios generated with zero costs did produce efficient and high risk/high return portfolios. Again, the Second Special Savings account portfolio was the least efficient of the RY portfolios in the mean-variance framework; see Table IX. These cases illustrate that the RY model with the same risk profile (zero cost or highest return objective) yields similar results to mean-variance in most accounts.

When mean-variance allocations (with similar return or similar risk) were input to RY model, the mean-variance fixed allocation had dramatically worse objective values in all cases; see Table XI. The difference in objective values in the static model comparisons is not as dramatic as the five-year model's objective values, but is still less than the optimal RY value.

While the MV allocations of similar risk and similar return portfolios are anchored by the current portfolio choice from RY solutions, there are substantial differences. RY optimizes across all accounts, while RAAM was restricted to each account. The flexibility in RY is evident in the cases where certain assets are found mostly in one account; see Table VIII for case 2. In case 2, the majority of foreign equity (EF) is found in the General account and Japanese equity is found in the Second Special Savings account and the General account. Japanese bonds are found in the General and Savings accounts.

The bulk of the difference in objective values comes from General account income shortfalls in year 5. For case 1 similar return portfolios the Y05 General Income shortfall is 87.4 percent of all shortfalls, and for the similar risk portfolio objective it is 87.9 percent. These General account income shortfalls were not part of a simultaneous overflow and shortfall.

Figure 4 shows the impact of the number of periods on the accuracy of the MV model in the RY objective when there are no loan bounds. The optimal objective value improves slightly for Case 1 from −83,672 to −85,850. The various period's values show the objective value from using the MV solution for that many periods and then the RY solution in the remaining periods. The longer the horizon the more inaccurate is the MV approximation. Even after one year, the mean-variance model gives extremely poor solutions.

The results show the impact of the multiperiod nature of the RY Model. The model reflects the decision-makers ability to change portfolios through time to react to changing circumstances. For example, different allocation decisions would be made two years hence, depending on whether the firm was in a strong or weak position. By fixing allocations, this flexibility is lost and its severity increases as more periods are fixed.

In the period sensitivity tests, two types of tests were made. The first was without loan bounds in all periods and the second was with loan bounds. The second set of tests were limited to no fixed allocations and fixed allocations in only the initial and quarter periods. The year 1 and subsequent models exceeded the maximum number of rows for the RY Model allowed when they included loan bounds. The initial and quarter one fixed models, loan bounds in the initial period were relaxed to 80 to 130 percent to be feasible with the previous period's loan values.

The more periods that are fixed with mean-variance allocations that change with new information only one period at a time, the less flexibility RY has and costs (increase leading to poorer objective values). In examining the small differences between no fixed allocations and fixed allocations only in the initial period that the model has nearly full recourse at quarter 1 to correct any errors in the initial allocation. With the first period being one quarter long followed by three quarters to year end, the

Table XI
Objective Value in RY (Yen 100 million)

Case Number	Scenarios -f-f-s-s-s	RY	RAAM Similar Return	RAAM Similar Risk
1	1-16-4-2-2-1	−83,672	51,765	45,326
2	1-16-2-2-2-2	−83,856	45,326	31,959
3	1--16	−46,277	−46,107	−46,115
4	1-8-4-4-2-1	−82,798	29,106	29,908
5	1-8-4-2-2-2	−83,790	28,699	29,624
6	1--8	−46,426	−46,107	−46,115

Note: No loan bounds were in place for RAAM allocation problems in RY.

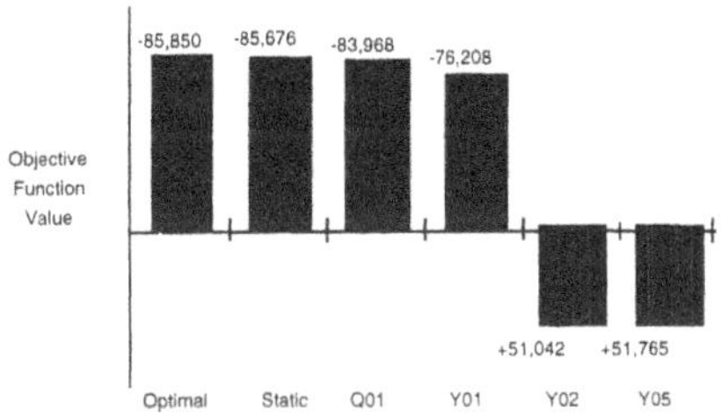

Figure 4. Effect of number of periods fixed with mean-variance allocations.

model has the flexibility (recourse) to reallocate the assets at quarter 1.

Loans are a major component of the model. The stickiness of the allocation to loans and the high expected income impact of the overall conservatism and efficiency of one account portfolios. Therefore, it was important to model the loan returns specially as was done in the RY Model.

To conclude, the RY solutions, which optimize across all accounts, always lie near the mean-variance efficient frontier. Sometimes they are on the frontier. The RAAM solutions have lower expected market value and high penalty costs in all cases. Even in the static case the MV solution is suboptimal.

5. EXPERIENCE AND BENEFITS OF THE MODEL

The model's software system has a modular structure with a matrix generator that creates a base linear program plus a set of random coefficient specifications for each period, a scenario generator that builds the decision tree structure and generates the random returns for each asset class, a liability generator that projects the random liabilities for each decision mode, a coefficient generator that combines the random coefficient specifications with the random variables to generate random coefficients, and a solver that generates the optimal solution using the optimization codes. The model's output consists of the optimal asset allocation (available by node and expected allocation per period), the expected balance and income statements, the objective function values including shortfall costs versus wealth accumulation, the probability of shortfall by type and period, and information concerning the regulatory constraints.

The model was used on a trial basis for the 1991 fiscal year (April 1, 1991 to March 31, 1992) and then in an integral way in Yasuda Kasai's business during the fiscal year 1992 and in subsequent years. The model has been operated by the financial planning department, which runs the asset-liability process for Yasuda Kasai. This process is outlined in Figure 5.

Yasuda Kasai have experienced both quantitative and qualitative benefits; see the summary below. A description of how the model fits into Yasuda Kasai's quarterly asset allocation process is useful to help explain the qualitative benefits.

The decision-making procedure of their asset allocation involves several meetings to develop the input data for the model. These include the market forecast meeting to determine the scenarios for the asset returns, the cash flow projection meeting to determine the scenarios for business sales and redemptions, the policy investment meeting, the income gain target meeting to set the goals (breakpoints and costs in the objective function) for income for their

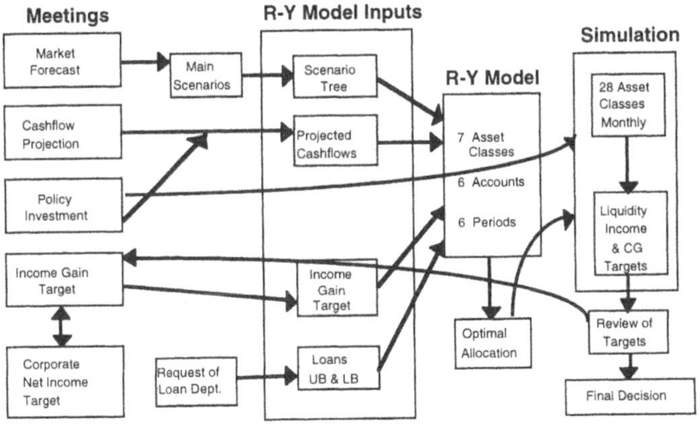

Figure 5. Yasuda Kasai's asset liability decision process.

policyholders, and the loan meeting to determine how much they will need to loan for business purposes and to set the minimums and maximums for investment purposes.

The financial planning department runs the RY Model using these inputs. The problem solved is large and difficult. The typical problem size is about 20,000 rows by about 30,000 columns. Using an IBM workstation, the problem takes about two hours to solve. The optimal asset allocation of seven assets is calculated for six accounts in each period. After the problem is solved, the optimal asset allocation of the RY Model is checked and justified using the simulation system ALM. If the risk and liquidity are acceptable to the company, the output of the RY Model is approved. Yasuda Kasai can rerun the model with different assumptions in only a few minutes given the hot start capability using the previous solution's basis. The model is at the very core of their asset allocation process; see Figure 5. The structuring of the RY Model was the beginning of Yasuda Kasai's investment process systemization. The RY Model has improved their decision-making process because decisions that are judgmental and decisions that are computational became synonymous.

Yasuda Kasai can estimate the risk they are facing by calculation of the probability and the actual size of losses occurring with various scenario possibilities. This is a great improvement for them because the previous mean-variance technology could not indicate how much business risk was implied in their portfolio. The model led to a much more organized and disciplined process that considered various possible future scenario paths. One can then diversify properly to avoid disastrous economic outcomes from extreme events. For example, the model suggested higher investments in bonds and other fixed income assets and less in stocks during the 1990 to 1992 severe decline of about 63 percent from top to bottom in the Japanese stock market, which led to much lower interest rates and gains in bonds; see Stone and Ziemba (1993).

6. SUMMARY OF BENEFITS OF THE RY MODEL

More realistic modeling capability. According to Mr. Kunihiko Sasamoto, Director and Deputy President of Yasuda Kasai, "the Russell-Yasuda Kasai model is at the core of all asset-liability work for the firm" because "traditional models such as Markowitz mean-variance cannot cope with the complexities of the business . . ."

Ease of Use. "The model provides a means for Yasuda Kasai to well define their risks in business terms. Risk is no longer restricted to an abstract, measure like standard deviation."

Improved financial performance. Compared to a performance benchmark established by Yasuda Kasai at the beginning of the fiscal year to measure the value added by the use of the model, the RY model increased their income by ¥9.5 billion (US$79 million) "securing enough income without sacrificing total return."

Improved other systems. Mr. Sasamoto adds that: "The model has provided an important side benefit by pushing the technology and efficiency of other asset management models in Yasuda Kasai forward to complement it."

Improved human judgment. "The Russell-Yasuda Kasai model has assisted Yasuda Kasai in determining when and how human judgment is best used in the asset-liability process."

Improved Competitive Position. "[T]he model will lead them to a more competitive position both retaining and gaining more new customers than their competitors."

Yasuda Kasai's main quantitative comparison is to compare their actual return both in terms of income received and total returns generated against a constant mix using the previous mean-variance strategy. It is assumed that they started using the model from the beginning of fiscal 1992.

In Yasuda Kasai's words, "As expected, the results are splendid. Our actual return, using the RY Model, outperformed the constant mix strategy by 42 basis points in income return and 5 basis points in total return over the last 2 years. This means 8.7 billion yen in income difference and 1.0 billion yen in total gain difference (US$79 million and US$9 million, respectively). The total return target in the model is at the 5-year horizon and the main intermediate goal is income return. So we expect even greater returns in the future. By using the model, we have succeeded in obtaining high income return without sacrificing total return. This was our main objective in implementing the RY Model."

The RY model is one of the largest applications of stochastic programming in financial services. The basic model structure is portable to other applications because of the generality of the technique and the flexibility in model generation. Discussion of other models made by Russell and others appears in Ziemba and Mulvey (1998).

Multistage stochastic programming models offer great potential for the analysis of the operations of various types of insurance and other financial institutions including governments. With modern workstations, large scale models are implementable in a variety of contexts.

ACKNOWLEDGMENT

Research on the Russell Yasuda-Kasai model was supported by The Yasuda Fire and Marine Insurance Company and by the Frank Russell Company. Some basic research related to this work by William Ziemba was partially supported by the Natural Sciences and Engineering Research Council of Canada and the U.S. National Science Foundation. This paper was presented at the Sixth International Conference on Stochastic Programming in Udine, Italy, and at the Universities of Abo Academy (Finland), Bergama, British Columbia, Cyprus, Erasmus, Hong Kong University of Science and Technology, National University of Singapore, Pennsylvania, Princeton and Stanford. Without implicating them, we would like to thank the project team members T. Eguchi, T. Kent, D. Myers, C. Stacy, M. Sylvanus, and A. Turner of Russell, T. Amaki, I. Harada, M. Harima, T. Morozumi, Y. Ohtani, K. Sasamoto, Y. Tayama, N. Ueda, K. Watanabe, and Y. Yazawa of Yasuda Kasai, and consultants C. Edirisinghe, A. King, K. Sawaki, and R. Wets for technical assistance. The results of this research were awarded second prize in the 1993 Franz Edelman Award for Management Science Achievement competition. Cariño et al. (1994), which focuses on the implementation and impact aspects of this research, was written for that competition. This paper and Cariño and Ziemba (1998), which discusses the technical aspects of the model and its use, are intended to be a full treatment of the model's construction and implementation.

REFERENCES

BENDERS, J. F. 1962. Partitioning Procedures for Solving Mixed-Variable Programming Problems. *Numerische Mathematic* **4**, 238–252.

CARIÑO, D. R., T. KENT, D. H. MEYERS, C. STACY, M. SYLVANUS, A. L. TURNER, K. WATANABE, AND W. T. ZIEMBA. 1994. The Russell-Yasuda Kasai Model: An Asset Liability Model for a Japanese Insurance Company Using Multi-stage Stochastic Programming. *Interfaces* **24**(1), 29–49.

CARIÑO, D. R. AND W. T. ZIEMBA. 1998. Formulation of the Russell-Yasuda Kasai Financial Planning Model. *Opns. Res.* **46**, 433–449.

CHOPRA, V. K. AND W. T. ZIEMBA. 1993. The Effect of Errors in Means, Variances and Covariances on Optimal Portfolio Choice. *J. Portfolio Mgmt.* Winter, 6–11.

GRINOLD, R. C. 1977. Finite Horizon Approximations of Infinite Horizon Linear Programs. *Math. Prog.* **12**, 1–17.

GRINOLD, R. C. 1980. Time Horizons in Energy Planning Models. In *Energy Policy Modeling: United States and Canadian Experiences*, Vol. II, 216–237. W. T. Ziemba and S. L. Schwartz (eds.), Martinus Nijhoff, Boston.

GRINOLD, R. C. 1983. Model Building Techniques for the Correction of End Effects in Multistage Convex Programs. *Opns. Res.* **31**, 407–431.

HENRIQUES, D. B. 1991. A Better Way to Track Your Assets. *The New York Times MONEY*, March 31, 11.

HENSEL, C. R. AND A. L. TURNER. 1998. Making Superior Asset Allocation Decisions: A Practicioner's Guide. In *Worldwide Asset and Liability Modeling.* W. T. Ziemba and J. M. Mulvey (eds.), Cambridge University Press, 62–83.

INFANGER, G. 1994. *Planning Under Uncertainty: Solving Large-Scale Stochastic Linear Programs.* The Scientific Press, Danvers, MA.

KUSY, M. I. AND W. T. ZIEMBA. 1986. A Bank Asset and Liability Management Model. *Opns. Res.* **34**(3), 356–376.

PEROLD A. F. 1984. Large Scale Portfolio Optimization. *Mgmt. Sci.* **30**, 1143–1160.

ROCKAFELLAR, R. T. AND R. J.-B. WETS. 1991. Scenarios and Policy Aggregation in Optimization under Uncertainty. *Math. O.R.* **16**, 119–147.

STONE, D. AND W. T. ZIEMBA. 1993. Land and Stock Prices in Japan. *J. Econ. Perspectives* **13**(3), 149–165.

VAN SLYKE, R. AND R. J.-B. WETS. 1969. L-shaped Linear Programs with Applications to Optimal Control and Stochastic Programming. *SIAM J. Appl. Math.* **17**, 638–663.

WETS, R. J.-B. 1988. Large Scale Linear Programming Techniques in Stochastic Programming. In *Numerical Techniques for Stochastic Optimization.* Y. Ermoliev and R. J.-B. Wets (eds.), Springer-Verlag, 65–93.

ZIEMBA, W. T. AND J. M. MULVEY. 1998. *Worldwide Asset and Liability Modeling.* Cambridge University Press.

Chapter 12

OR PRACTICE

The Innovest Austrian Pension Fund Financial Planning Model InnoALM*

Alois Geyer

University of Economics and Vienna Graduate School of Finance, Vienna, Austria, alois.geyer@wu-wien.ac.at

William T. Ziemba

Sauder School of Business, University of British Columbia, Vancouver, British Columbia, Canada V6T 1Z2, and Visiting Professor, Mathematical Institute, Oxford University, Oxford, United Kingdom 0X1 3LB, and ICMA Centre, University of Reading, Reading, United Kingdom RG6 6BA, wtzimi@mac.com

This paper describes the financial planning model InnoALM we developed at Innovest for the Austrian pension fund of the electronics firm Siemens. The model uses a multiperiod stochastic linear programming framework with a flexible number of time periods of varying length. Uncertainty is modeled using multiperiod discrete probability scenarios for random return and other model parameters. The correlations across asset classes, of bonds, stocks, cash, and other financial instruments, are state dependent using multiple correlation matrices that correspond to differing market conditions. This feature allows InnoALM to anticipate and react to severe as well as normal market conditions. Austrian pension law and policy considerations can be modeled as constraints in the optimization. The concave risk-averse preference function is to maximize the expected present value of terminal wealth at the specified horizon net of expected discounted convex (piecewise-linear) penalty costs for wealth and benchmark targets in each decision period. InnoALM has a user interface that provides visualization of key model outputs, the effect of input changes, growing pension benefits from increased deterministic wealth target violations, stochastic benchmark targets, security reserves, policy changes, etc. The solution process using the IBM OSL stochastic programming code is fast enough to generate virtually online decisions and results and allows for easy interaction of the user with the model to improve pension fund performance. The model has been used since 2000 for Siemens Austria, Siemens worldwide, and to evaluate possible pension fund regulation changes in Austria.

Subject classifications: scenarios; correlation matrices; pension fund planning; stochastic linear programming.
Area of review: OR Practice.
History: Received July 2003; revisions received January 2006, August 2006, January 2007, March 2007; accepted March 2007.

Introduction

The Siemens pension fund, established in 1998, is the largest corporate pension plan in Austria. More than 15,000 employees and 5,000 pensioners are members of the pension plan, with 510 million euro in assets under management as of December 1999. Innovest Finanzdienstleistungs AG, founded in 1998, is the investment manager of the Siemens pension plan and other institutional investors, with more than 7 billion euro in assets under management. The pension fund asset-liability management model InnoALM has been in use at Innovest since 2000. Meanwhile, it has become the only consistently implemented and fully integrated proprietary tool for assessing pension allocation issues within Siemens AG worldwide.

Several factors led Innovest to develop InnoALM, primarily the realization that changing demographics are creating a much higher ratio of retirees to workforce. Furthermore, the asset allocation constraints imposed by Austrian pension law are relaxed if a pension fund is using advanced modeling tools and proves adequate risk management capability. This makes it paramount that the pension plan be managed using systematic asset-liability management models as a tool in the decision-making process. A promising way to approach this was a multiperiod stochastic linear programming model.

InnoALM is one of the first implemented models to fully exploit the power of the multiperiod stochastic programming optimization approach in a European pension fund. The mathematical aspects of such models applied to asset-liability management are documented in Ziemba and Mulvey (1998), Gondzio and Kouwenberg (2001), and Wallace and Ziemba (2005). While following to some extent the work on the Russell-Yasuda insurance company planning models (Cariño et al. 1994, 1998; Cariño and Ziemba 1998), the application to European pension funds is new, and this model has new features such as state-dependent correlation matrices, fat-tailed asset return distributions, and output not in previous models. Zenios

*This chapter was originally published in: Geyer, A. & Ziemba, W. T. (2008). The Innovest Austrian Pension Fund Financial Planning Model InnoALM. *Operations Research*, 56(4), 797–810.

(1999) surveys large-scale asset-liability applications to bond and fixed-income portfolio management. Gondzio and Kouwenberg (2001) solved Dutch pension fund asset-liability management problems with millions of scenarios, constraints, and variables. Publicly available codes to solve large stochastic programming problems are detailed in Wallace and Ziemba (2005).

What is crucial are models that represent well the situation at hand, are user friendly, and provide the essential information quickly to those who need to make sound pension fund asset-liability decisions. The multiperiod stochastic programming approach includes more of the essential elements of the real problem faced by the pension plan than alternative approaches such as static mean-variance analysis (see, e.g., Sharpe and Tint 1990), continuous-time modeling (see, e.g., Campbell and Viceira 2002 and Rudolf and Ziemba 2004), shortfall risk minimization (see, e.g., Leibowitz and Henriksson 1988), and other approaches (see, e.g., Ziemba and Mulvey 1998). Key elements that make InnoALM superior to other models are the flexibility to formulate constraints and targets in combination with a broad and deep array of scenario-specific results. This allows Innovest to investigate path-dependent behavior of assets and liabilities as well as scenario-based risk assessment. Some of these aspects are illustrated in the application presented in §4.

InnoALM implements state-dependent correlation across asset classes, as asked for in discussions by Lo (1999) and Merton (2000). This feature allows the model to react to extreme events and to plan in advance to do so. Models that assume constant correlation matrices make a conceptual error that is one of the major factors appearing in most of the financial trading disasters of the 1990s and beyond, such as Orange County in 1994, Barrings in 1995, Niederhoffer in 1997 and 2006, Long Term Capital Management in 1998, the Tiger and Soros Hedge Funds in 2000, and Amarath in 2006. When funds are nondiversified and overleveraged, a plausible but low-probability extreme scenario can lead to a financial disaster. Consideration of the state-dependent correlations in advance should lead to portfolios that can react better to an extreme scenario and still produce good results when other, more probable scenarios occur. This feature is documented in the application presented in §4.

The paper briefly discusses the pension fund situation in Austria and Europe in §1. Section 2 develops the stochastic programming model formulation. Section 3 discusses the scenario generation and statistical inputs available for use in the model. Section 4 presents an illustrative application, using an example of a model formulation with five decision periods and four asset classes in various circumstances, including the difficult market conditions faced in 2000–2003. Section 5 provides conclusions and final remarks.

1. The Pension Fund Situation in Austria and Europe

The world's populations are aging rapidly. By 2030 there will be roughly a doubling from about 20% to about 40% of those 65 and older, the *retiree group*, compared to those 15–64, the *worker group*, in most countries of the world (see Bos 1994 or Roseveare et al. 1996). This demographic effect will have a major impact on public and private pension plans in Europe and across the world. European Union state pensions (usually labeled as Pillar 1) account for about 88% of total pension costs. While pay-as-you-go plans, where the contributions of current workers support current pensioners similar to U.S. social security, are the most threatened by aging populations, defined contribution plans are also at risk. Without changes, the pension payouts will grow from 10% of GDP in 1997 to over 15% of GDP in 2030 for many EU countries. Contribution rates must be raised significantly to enable the public social security system to cope. Reforms of the public pension systems will be necessary, together with an effective environment for Pillar 2 (company pensions) and Pillar 3 (private pension systems).

This paper describes a model for the effective operation Pillar 2 private pension funds in Austria. These funds usually work on a funded basis, where the pension benefits depend on an employment contract or the pursuit of a particular profession. Schemes are administered by private institutions, and benefits are not guaranteed by the state. Normally, contributions to such systems are made by the employer and, on an optional basis for additional benefits, by employees. Defined contribution plans (DCP), such as the Siemens pension plan for Austria, have fixed contributions, but the pensions are not fixed and the payout depends on the capital accumulation of the plan. Defined benefit plans (DBP) have payouts guaranteed by the company, and the contribution is variable, depending on the capital accumulation over time. For DCPs, which have become more popular, the employees and pensioners bear the risk of low asset returns. There is no direct financial risk for the employer, although with poor returns the employer would suffer negative image effects. For example, if there would be a headline "pensions for the Siemens' pensioners must be reduced by 3% in the next year," there would be reputation risk for Siemens.

The liability side of the Siemens pension plan consists of employees, for whom Siemens is contributing payments based on the DCP outline, and retired employees who receive pension payments. Contributions are computed on an individual level as a fixed fraction of salaries, which varies across employees. The set of retired employees is treated according to Austrian mortality and marital tables. Widows and widowers (a much smaller group) are entitled to 60% of the pension payments. Retired employees receive pension payments after reaching age 65 for men and 60 for women in accordance with the legal pension plan. Payments to retired employees are based on the individually

Geyer and Ziemba: *The Innovest Austrian Pension Fund Financial Planning Model InnoALM*
Operations Research 56(4), pp. 797–810, © 2008 INFORMS 799

accumulated contribution and the fund performance during active employment.

The actuarial computation of liabilities is based on the assumption that active employees are in steady state; that is, staff is replaced by a new employee with the same qualification and sex, which gives rise to the constant number of employees. Newly employed staff starts with less salary than retired staff, which implies that total contributions grow less rapidly than individual salaries. There exist agreements with employees such that the annual pension payments are based on a discount rate of 6% and the remaining life expectancy at the time of retirement. It is also agreed that these annuities grow by 1.5% annually to compensate for inflation. Hence, the wealth of the pension fund must grow by 7.5% per year to match liability commitments; see the InnoALM wealth target described in §2.

Some EU member states rely on quantitative restrictions on asset allocations to ensure proper pension fund investments. Such rules are usually established to protect the pensioners but also lead to weakly diversified asset holdings. For example, in 2002 Austria's pension funds had a relatively low share of only 13.4% in equities and almost 75% in fixed income (OECD 2004). However, the European Commission (1997) stressed the importance of a relaxation of restrictive quantitative rules on pension fund investing. The diversification of investments is more important than rules on different investments. Recent changes in Austrian pension regulation respond to this point and have made the InnoALM approach even more relevant. The rigid asset-based limits (e.g., not more than 40% in equities; at least 40% in Eurobonds) are relaxed for institutions that prove sufficient risk management expertise for both assets and liabilities of the plan. Thus, the implementation of a scenario-based asset allocation model at Innovest leads to more flexibility that allows for more risk tolerance, and should ultimately result in better long-term investment performance. In fact, some results of InnoALM have been used by the Austrian regulatory authorities to assess the potential risk stemming from less-constrained pension plans. The European Commission recommends the use of such modern asset and liability management techniques for pension planning, although the problem of high costs of such models is of concern. InnoALM is a model that responds to that recommendation and demonstrates that a small team of researchers with a limited budget can quickly produce a valuable modeling system that can be operated by nonstochastic programming specialists on a single PC.

2. Formulating the InnoALM as a Multistage Stochastic Linear Programming Model

The model determines the optimal purchases and sales for each of N assets in each of T planning periods. Typical asset classes used at Innovest are U.S., Pacific, European, and emerging market equities and U.S., U.K., Japanese, and European bonds. A concave risk-averse utility function is to maximize expected terminal wealth less convex penalty costs subject to linear constraints. The convex risk measure is approximated by a piecewise-linear function, so the model is a multiperiod stochastic linear program.

The nonnegative decision variables are wealth (after transactions) W_{it}, purchases P_{it}, and sales S_{it} for each asset ($i = 1, \ldots, N$). Purchases and sales are in periods $t = 0, \ldots, T-1$. Except for $t = 0$, purchases and sales are scenario dependent.

Wealth accumulates over time for a T period model according to

$$W_{i0} = W_i^{init} + P_{i0} - S_{i0}, \quad t = 0,$$

$$\widetilde{W}_{i1} = \tilde{R}_{i1} W_{i0} + \tilde{P}_{i1} - \tilde{S}_{i1}, \quad t = 1,$$

$$\widetilde{W}_{it} = \tilde{R}_{it} \widetilde{W}_{i,t-1} + \tilde{P}_{it} - \tilde{S}_{it}, \quad t = 2, \ldots, T-1, \quad \text{and}$$

$$\widetilde{W}_{iT} = \tilde{R}_{it} \widetilde{W}_{i,T-1}, \quad t = T.$$

W_i^{init} is the prespecified initial value of asset i. There is no uncertainty in the initialization period $t = 0$. Tildes denote scenario-dependent random parameters or decision variables. Returns are associated with time intervals. $\tilde{R}_{it}$ ($t = 1, \ldots, T$) are the (random) gross returns for asset i between $t-1$ and t. The scenario generation and statistical properties of returns are discussed in §3.

The budget constraints are

$$\sum_{i=1}^{N} P_{i0}(1+tcp_i) = \sum_{i=1}^{N} S_{i0}(1-tcs_i) + C_0, \quad t=0 \quad \text{and}$$

$$\sum_{i=1}^{N} \tilde{P}_{it}(1+tcp_i) = \sum_{i=1}^{N} \tilde{S}_{it}(1-tcs_i) + C_t, \quad t=1,\ldots,T-1,$$

where tcp_i and tcs_i denote asset-specific linear transaction costs for purchases and sales, and C_t is the fixed (nonrandom) net cashflow (inflow if positive).

Portfolio weights can be constrained over linear combinations (subsets) of assets or individual assets via

$$\sum_{i \in U} \widetilde{W}_{it} - \theta_U \sum_{i=1}^{N} \widetilde{W}_{it} \leqslant 0 \quad \text{and}$$

$$-\sum_{i \in L} \widetilde{W}_{it} + \theta_L \sum_{i=1}^{N} \widetilde{W}_{it} \leqslant 0, \quad t = 1, \ldots, T-1,$$

where θ_U is the maximum percentage and θ_L is the minimum percentage of the subsets U and L of assets $i = 1, \ldots, N$ included in the restrictions. The θ_Us, θ_Ls, Us, and Ls might be time dependent.

Risk is measured as a weighted discounted convex function of target violation shortfalls of various types in various periods. In a typical application, the deterministic wealth target $\overline{W}_t$ is assumed to grow by 7.5% in each year. The wealth targets are modeled via

$$\sum_{i=1}^{N} (\widetilde{W}_{it} - \tilde{P}_{it} + \tilde{S}_{it}) + \tilde{M}_t^W \geqslant \overline{W}_t, \quad t = 1, \ldots, T,$$

where $\widetilde{M}_t^W$ are nonnegative wealth target shortfall variables. The shortfall is penalized using a piecewise-linear convex risk measure using the variables and constraints

$$\widetilde{M}_t^W = \sum_{j=1}^{m} \widetilde{M}_{jt}^W, \quad t = 1, \ldots, T,$$

$$\widetilde{M}_{jt}^W \leqslant b_j - b_{j-1}, \quad t = 1, \ldots, T;\ j = 1, \ldots, m-1,$$

where $\widetilde{M}_{jt}^W$ is the wealth-target shortfall associated with segment j of the cost function, b_j is the jth breakpoint of the risk-measure function ($b_0 = 0$), and m is the number of segments of the function. A piecewise-linear approximation to the convex quadratic risk measure is used so the model remains linear. The appropriateness of the quadratic function is discussed below. Convexity guarantees that if $\widetilde{M}_{jt}^W > 0$, then $\widetilde{M}_{j-1,t}^W$ is at its maximum; and if $\widetilde{M}_{jt}^W$ is not at its maximum, then $\widetilde{M}_{j+1,t}^W = 0$.

Stochastic benchmark goals can also be set by the user and are similarly penalized for underachievement. The benchmark target $\widetilde{B}_t$ is scenario dependent. It is based on stochastic asset returns and fixed asset weights α_i defining the benchmark portfolio

$$\widetilde{B}_t = W_0 \sum_{j=1}^{t} \sum_{i=1}^{N} \alpha_i \widetilde{R}_{ij}.$$

The corresponding shortfall constraints are

$$\sum_{i=1}^{N} (\widetilde{W}_{it} - \widetilde{P}_{it} + \widetilde{S}_{it}) + \widetilde{M}_t^B \geqslant \widetilde{B}_t, \quad t = 1, \ldots, T,$$

where $\widetilde{M}_t^B$ is the benchmark target shortfall. These shortfalls are also penalized with a piecewise-linear convex risk measure.

If total wealth exceeds the target, a fraction $\gamma = 10\%$ of the exceeding amount is allocated to a reserve account and invested in the same way as other available funds. However, the wealth targets at future stages are adjusted. Additional nonnegative decision variables $\widetilde{D}_t$ are introduced and the wealth target constraints become

$$\sum_{i=1}^{N} (\widetilde{W}_{it} - \widetilde{P}_{it} + \widetilde{S}_{it}) - \widetilde{D}_t + \widetilde{M}_t^W$$

$$= \overline{W}_t + \sum_{j=1}^{t-1} \gamma \widetilde{D}_{t-j}, \quad t = 1, \ldots, T-1, \text{ where } \widetilde{D}_1 = 0.$$

Because pension payments are based on wealth levels, increasing these levels increases pension payments. The reserves provide security for the pension plan's increase of pension payments at each future stage.

The pension plan's objective function is to maximize the expected discounted value of terminal wealth in period T net of the expected discounted penalty costs over the horizon from the convex risk measures $c_k(\cdot)$ for the wealth and benchmark targets, respectively:

$$\text{Max } E\left[d_T \sum_{i=1}^{N} \widetilde{W}_{iT} - \lambda \sum_{t=1}^{T} d_t w_t \left(\sum_{k \in \{W, B\}} v_k c_k(\widetilde{M}_t^k) \right) \right].$$

Expectation is over T period scenarios S_T. The discount factors d_t are related to the interest rate r by $d_t = (1+r)^{-t}$. Usually, r is taken to be the three- or six-month treasury bill rate. The v_k are weights for the wealth and benchmark shortfalls, and the w_t are weights for the weighted sum of shortfalls at each stage normalized via

$$\sum_{k \in \{W, B\}} v_k = 1 \quad \text{and} \quad \sum_{t=1}^{T} w_t = T.$$

Such concave objective functions with convex risk measures date to Kusy and Ziemba (1986), were used in the Russell-Yasuda model (Cariño and Ziemba 1998), and are justified in an axiomatic sense in Rockafellar and Ziemba (2000). Nontechnical decision makers find the increasing penalty for target violations a good approach and easy to understand.

In the implementation of the model presented in §4, the penalty function $c_k(M^k)$ corresponds to a quadratic utility function. Kallberg and Ziemba (1983) show, for normally distributed asset returns, that varying the average Arrow-Pratt absolute risk-aversion index R_A traces out the whole spectrum of risk attitudes of all concave utility functions. The most aggressive behavior is log utility, which has $R_A = 1/\text{wealth}$, which is essentially zero. Typical 60–40 stock-bond pension funds have $R_A = 4$. The Kallberg-Ziemba (1983) results indicate that for computational purposes, the quadratic utility function $u(w) = w - R_A/2w^2$ will suffice and is easier to use in the optimization. The error in this approximation is close to zero and well below the accuracy of the data.

The parameter λ in the objective corresponds to $R_A/2$, which in the quadratic utility function is the weight assigned to risk measured in terms of variance. The objective function of the InnoALM model penalizes only wealth and benchmark target shortfalls. If the target growth is roughly equal to the average return of the portfolio, shortfalls measure only negative deviations from the mean, whereas variance is based on positive and negative deviations. This implies that shortfalls account for only about half of the variance. Therefore, to obtain results in agreement with a quadratic utility function, we use $\lambda = R_A$, rather than $R_A/2$, in the objective function. To obtain a solution to the allocation problem for general levels of total initial wealth w_0, we use the rescaled parameter $\lambda = R_A/w_0$ in the objective function.

Using a quadratic function, the penalty function $c_k(M^k)$ is

$$c_k(M^k) = \sum_{j=1}^{m} \widetilde{M}_{jt}^k (b_{j-1} + b_j), \quad \widetilde{M}_{jt}^k \leqslant b_j - b_{j-1}, \text{ with } b_0 = 0.$$

Geyer and Ziemba: *The Innovest Austrian Pension Fund Financial Planning Model InnoALM*
Operations Research 56(4), pp. 797–810, © 2008 INFORMS 801

Figure 1. Scenario tree with a 2-2-3 node structure (12 scenarios).

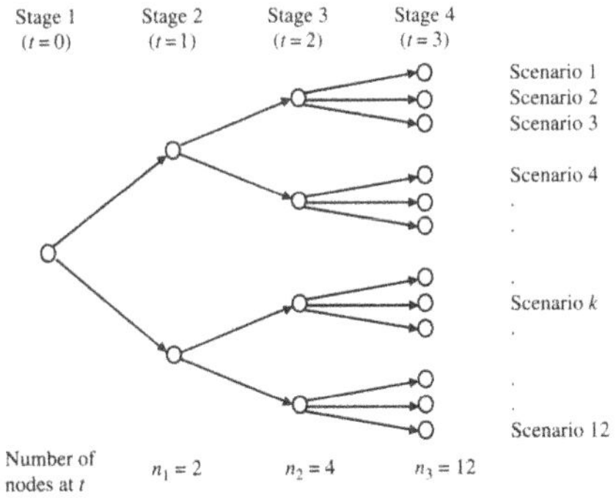

Uncertainty is modelled using multiperiod discrete probability scenarios using statistical properties of the assets' returns. A scenario tree is defined by the number of stages and the number of arcs leaving a particular node. Figure 1 shows a tree with a 2-2-3 node structure for a three-period problem with four stages and introduces some definitions and terminology. The tree always starts with a single node that corresponds to the present state ($t = 0$). Decisions are made at each node of the tree and depend on the current state, which reflects previous decisions and uncertain future paths. A single scenario s_t is a trajectory that corresponds to a unique path leading from the single node at stage 1 ($t = 0$) to a single node at t. Two scenarios s'_t and s''_t are identical until $t-1$ (i.e., $s'_{t-1} = s''_{t-1}$) and differ in subsequent periods $t, \ldots, T$. The scenario assigns specific values to all uncertain parameters along the trajectory, i.e., asset returns and benchmark targets for all periods. Given all T period scenarios S_T and their respective probabilities, one has a complete description of the uncertainty of the model.

Allocations are based on optimizing the stochastic linear program with IBM's optimization solutions library using the stochastic extension library (OSLE version 3). IBM has ceased all sales of this product in 2004. While existing installations of OSLE can still be used, new implementions require alternative software such as the open source project COIN-OR (see http://www.coin-or.org). The library uses the Stochastic Mathematical Programming System (SMPS) input format for multistage stochastic programs (see King et al. 2005). The *core-file* contains information about the decisions variables, constraints, right-hand sides, and bounds. It contains all fixed coefficients and dummy entries for random elements. The *stoch-file* reflects the node structure of the scenario tree and contains all random elements—i.e., asset and benchmark returns—and probabilities. Nonanticipatory constraints are imposed to guarantee that a decision made at a specific node is identical for all scenarios leaving that node, so the future cannot be anticipated. This is implemented by specifying an appropriate scenario structure in the stoch input file. The *time-file* assigns decision variables and constraints to stages. The required statements in the input files are automatically generated by the InnoALM system (see §4).

3. Scenario Generation and Statistical Inputs

The uncertainty of the random return and other parameters in InnoALM is modeled using discrete probability scenarios. These scenarios are approximations of the true underlying probability distributions. The accuracy of the set of scenarios chosen and the probabilities of these scenarios in relation to reality contribute greatly to model success. However, the scenario approach generally leads to superior investment performance even if there are errors in the estimations of both the actual scenario values and their probabilities. What the modeling effort attempts to do is to cover well the range of possible future evolution of the economic environment. Decisions take into account all these possible outcomes, weighted by their likelihood. This generally leads to superior performance of multiperiod stochastic programming models compared with other approaches, such as mean-variance analysis, fixed mix, stochastic control, stochastic programming with decision rules, etc. Studies showing this superiority, both in and out of sample, include Kusy and Ziemba (1986), Cariño and Turner (1998), Cariño et al. (1994, 1998), Cariño and Ziemba (1998), and Fleten et al. (2002).

Procedures for estimating the joint distribution of future bond and stock returns have been discussed by Chen et al. (1986), Keim and Stambaugh (1986), Ferson and Harvey (1993), Karolyi and Stultz (1996), and Bossaerts and Hillion (1999). Procedures for estimating discrete scenarios from joint multivariate bond and stock forecasting models have been discussed by Mulvey (1996), Jamshidian and Zhu (1997), Cariño et al. (1994, 1998), Cariño and Ziemba (1998), Zenios (1999), Høyland and Wallace (2001), Pflug (2001), and Roemisch and Heitsch (2003).

The scenarios in InnoALM are defined in terms of the distribution of asset returns and their first- and second-order moments. The latter can be prespecified by the user or estimated from the built-in database of historical returns. James-Stein estimates, which have frequently been suggested as the preferred approach, can be used to estimate mean returns; see, e.g., Jorion (1985), Hensel and Turner (1998), and Grauer and Hakansson (1998). See also MacLean et al. (2007) for an alternative approach using truncated estimators. For each asset the user can choose from the normal, the t-, or the historical (empirical) distribution.

Empirical asset returns over short horizons (up to one month) typically are not normally distributed but have fat tails and are skewed. Jackwerth and Rubinstein (1997) show how much fatter the implied probability left tails of

Table 1. Statistical properties of asset returns.

	Stocks Eur 1/70-9/00	Stocks Eur 1/86-9/00	Stocks US 1/70-9/00	Stocks US 1/86-9/00	Bonds Eur 1/86-9/00	Bonds US 1/86-9/00
Monthly returns						
Mean (% p.a.)	10.6	13.3	10.7	14.8	6.5	7.2
Std. dev. (% p.a.)	16.1	17.4	19.0	20.2	3.7	11.3
Skewness	−0.90	−1.43	−0.72	−1.04	−0.50	0.52
Kurtosis	7.05	8.43	5.79	7.09	3.25	3.30
Jarque-Bera test	302.6	277.3	151.9	155.6	7.7	8.5
Annual returns						
Mean (%)	11.1	13.3	11.0	15.2	6.5	6.9
Std. dev. (%)	17.2	16.2	20.1	18.4	4.8	12.1
Skewness	−0.53	−0.10	−0.23	−0.28	−0.20	−0.42
Kurtosis	3.23	2.28	2.56	2.45	2.25	2.26
Jarque-Bera test	17.4	3.9	6.2	4.2	5.0	8.7

the S&P500 have become since the 1987 worldwide stock market crash because of investor fear of large declines. t-distributions model fat tails well (see Glasserman et al. 2000). The degrees-of-freedom parameter has to be set to a small value (e.g., five). However, both the normal and the t-distribution are symmetric distributions and might therefore underestimate the downside risk of an asset or portfolio. Skewed t-distributions are an alternative to account for skewness and fat tails but were not considered in this model.

Pension fund planning models typically use rebalancing intervals that are much longer than one month. InnoALM can accommodate, e.g., weekly, monthly, annual, or longer rebalancing intervals. In the example in §4, annual and biannual periods are considered. Annual returns have distinctly different distributional properties than monthly returns (see Table 1). Given the difficulty associated with choosing an appropriate parametric distribution, we also use a nonparametric approach to generate random samples reflecting the shape of the historical return distribution.

To simulate the historical distribution for a single asset, we compute standardized annual returns y_t. We use (overlapping) annual returns from monthly data rather than monthly returns because the planning intervals in the example presented in §4 are in years, and thus the distribution of annual returns is more appropriate than the distribution of monthly returns. A single element of the simulated historical return distribution is computed as follows. First, a random number u is drawn from a uniform distribution. This random number is treated as a probability and the corresponding percentile z is computed from the standardized returns. The percentile is a random draw from the historical, standardized distribution with the property $P[y_t < z] = u$. Multiplying z by a prespecified standard deviation and adding a prespecified mean yields the random return used at a particular node in the scenario tree (see below). Sampling from standardized rather than observed returns allows us to simulate historical distributions with means and standard deviations that might differ from the historically observed sample statistics.

This approach yields a random sample that matches the shape of the historical (fat tailed and/or skewed) distribution. The size of the random sample that can be generated by this approach is not limited by the number of available historical observations because any desired number of percentiles could be computed from historical returns. The approach cannot produce values that are more extreme than historically observed returns, however.

State-dependent correlation matrices of InnoALM are a new feature and have not yet been used in pension planning or asset allocation models. InnoALM uses three different correlation matrices and corresponding sets of standard deviations. The choice of a specific correlation matrix depends on the level of stock return volatility. We distinguish "extreme" (or "crash") periods, "highly volatile" periods, and "normal" periods. Each of the three periods or regimes is assigned a probability of occurrence p^j ($j = 1, 2, 3$). Harvey (1991), Karolyi and Stulz (1996), Solnik et al. (1996), and Das and Uppal (2004) study changing correlation structures over time. To estimate correlations and standard deviations for the three regimes, we use the regression approach suggested by Solnik et al. (1996). Using monthly time series, we compute moving average (window length 36 months) estimates of correlations among all assets and standard deviations of U.S. equity returns. Correlations are regressed on U.S. stock return volatilities. The estimated regression equations are used to predict correlations for the three regimes (more details on this are presented in §4.1).

Correlated random returns are simulated using the following procedure. For each asset i, we generate n_t standardized random numbers z_{ti}, where n_t is the number of nodes in period t (see Figure 1). z_{ti} could have a normal, t-, or historical distribution, depending on the asset and the choice of the user. The n_t-dimensional vectors z_{ti} are used to compile the $n_t \times N$ matrix $\tilde{Z}$. The correlation among assets is modeled by multiplying the matrix $\tilde{Z}$ with the Cholesky decomposition of the correlation matrix C: $\tilde{Y} = \tilde{Z} \cdot chol(C)$. Thus, this procedure essentially uses a normal multivariate copula with normal or nonnormal marginals.

Geyer and Ziemba: *The Innovest Austrian Pension Fund Financial Planning Model InnoALM*
Operations Research 56(4), pp. 797–810, © 2008 INFORMS

Simulated gross returns for each asset are obtained by multiplying each column of $\tilde{Y}$ with the standard deviation σ_i of asset i and adding the asset's mean μ_i, where both are adjusted for the length τ_t of planning period t via

$$\tilde{R}_{ti} = (1+\mu_i)^{\tau_t} + \tilde{Y}_{ti}\sigma_i\sqrt{\tau_t}.$$

Mixing of correlations is obtained by generating three subsets of simulated returns as described, but using a different correlation matrix C^j in each subset yielding three sets of returns $\tilde{R}^j_{ti}$ $(j = 1, 2, 3)$. At any particular period, the set of all nodes n_t is randomly partitioned into three subsets corresponding to the three volatility regimes. We use all available nodes of a period to define the subsets (i.e., $n_t = k_1 \cdot k_2 \cdots k_t$, where k_i is the number of paths leaving from node $i-1$). The number of elements n^j_t in each set is determined by the prespecified probability p^j of the three regimes via $n^j_t = n_t p^j$, where n^j_t is rounded up to the nearest integer. All nodes n^j_t of a subset are used for moment-matching (e.g., if the node structure is 100-5-2 and $p^j = 0.1$, we have 10, 50, and 100 nodes available for regime j). The simulated returns $\tilde{R}^j_{ti}$ are randomly distributed within each of the three subsets, and the subsets are randomly distributed across all nodes in that period. A tag is assigned to each return to identify the associated regime for later use as described in §4.3. A pseudocode is included in the appendix to describe the procedure. It is well established empirically that short-term (daily or weekly) volatility is highly persistent. After extreme events, high levels of volatility are more likely than normal levels. However, estimating regime transition probabilities for annual or even longer intervals is not a trivial issue. Therefore, we assume that the probability for ending up in a particular regime is independent of the previous regime. If reliable regime transition probabilities were available, these could be included in applications of the model.

4. Implementation and Sample Results

Out of a large number of calculations and tests, we present examples that show interesting features of InnoALM but do not disclose any important proprietary aspects of InnoALM. The purpose of the sample application is to highlight the importance of considering mixing correlations, the impact of various assumptions about return distributions, and the effects of rebalancing as implied by the optimal solution. We also show the impact of constraints on the asset allocation as prescribed by Austria's pension law. Compared to the actual applications at Innovest the example is simplified, but the results highlight key lessons to be learned from inspecting the model's wealth and risk implications across time and across scenarios.

InnoALM has a user interface to select assets, and define the number of stages and the scenario node structure. The user can specify the wealth targets, cash inflows and outflows, and other parameters (e.g., risk aversion, constraints on asset weights, weights that define the benchmark target). Historical data on the asset classes considered are embedded into the model. This includes a monthly data set ranging from 1970 to January 2002 for equities (MSCI index) and from 1986 to January 2002 for bonds (JP Morgan index). The period October 2000 to January 2002 was reserved for out-of-sample tests (see §4.3). Statistical properties of returns can be computed from the historical database or specified by the user. Calculations are easy to make using various assumptions, such as those from the past 101 years in Dimson et al. (2002, 2006). Different parameters can be specified for each stage of the planning period.

Statistical analysis and simulation uses the GAUSS programming language (Aptech Systems, Inc., www.aptech.com). This language is also used to automatically generate the SMPS input files. This greatly facilitates experimenting with the model because there is no need to do any recoding or manipulating SMPS files if different assets are considered, a different node structure is assumed, or other modifications are made. The problem is solved with IBM's optimization solutions library using the stochastic extension library (OSLE version 3). The solution is written to an output file that is used to generate summary tables and graphs.

A typical application as described below, with 10,000 scenarios, takes about 7–8 minutes for simulation, generating SMPS files, solving and producing output on a 1.2 GHz Pentium III notebook with 376 MB RAM, although for some problems execution times can be 15–20 minutes.

4.1. Sample Application—Assumptions

To illustrate some of the model's features, we present results for an application with four asset classes (Stocks Europe, Stocks US, Bonds Europe, and Bonds US), and five periods (six stages). Periods 1 and 2 are one year in length, Periods 3 and 4 are two years in length, and Period 5 is four years long (10 years in total), which reflects Innovest's rebalancing policy. We assume discrete compounding, which implies that the mean return for asset i (μ_i) used in simulations is $\mu_i = \exp(\bar{y}+0.5\sigma^2)-1$, where $\bar{y}$ and σ^2 are mean and variance of log-returns. We generate 10,000 scenarios using a 100-5-5-2-2 node structure, which should provide sufficient detail about the distribution of assets and still allow for reasonable solution times. Using only a few branches and fitting distributions across all nodes may induce (unintended) serial correlation between stages. This might bias the results because of the implied return predictability. This shortcoming can be avoided with very large sample sizes (i.e., many branches), which was not feasible in this application. Initial wealth is 100 units, and the wealth target grows at an annual rate of 7.5%. No benchmark target and no cash inflows and outflows are considered in this sample application, and the interest rate is fixed at 5%. We use $R_A = 4$, which corresponds roughly with a simple static mean-variance model to a standard 60–40 stock-bond pension fund mix; see Kallberg and Ziemba (1983). Hence, it is appropriate for this application.

Assumptions about the statistical properties of log-returns (including dividends) are based on a sample of monthly data from January 1970 for stocks and from 1986 for bonds to September 2000. All asset returns are measured in nominal Euros. Summary statistics for monthly and annual log-returns are in Table 1. The U.S. and European equity means for the longer period 1970–2000 are much lower than for 1986–2000 and slightly less volatile. Table 1 shows that monthly stock returns are non-normal and negatively skewed. Monthly stock returns are fat-tailed, whereas monthly bond returns are close to normal (the critical value of the Jarque-Bera test for $\alpha = 0.01$ is 9.2).

However, for long-term planning models such as InnoALM with its one-year review period, properties of monthly returns are less relevant. The second panel of Table 1 contains statistics for annual returns. While average returns and volatilities remain about the same (we lose one year of data when we compute annual returns), the distributional properties change dramatically. While we still find negative skewness, there is no evidence for fat tails in annual returns except for European stocks (1970–2000).

The mean returns from this sample are comparable to the 1900–2000 mean returns estimated by Dimson et al. (2002, 2006). Their estimate of the nominal mean equity return for the United States is 12.0%, and that for Germany and the United Kingdom is 13.6% (the simple average of the two countries' means). The mean of bond returns is 5.1% for the United States and 5.4% for Germany and the United Kingdom.

Assumptions about means, standard deviations, and correlations for the applications of InnoALM appear in Table 2 and are based on the sample statistics presented in Table 1. Projecting future rates of returns from past data is difficult. We use the equity means from the period 1970–2000 because the period 1986–2000 had high stock returns that are not assumed to prevail in the long run. Thus, the results might be considered to be based on conservative assumptions. The asset classes Innovest uses are well diversified and therefore do not have an excessive amount of own-company (Siemens) stock. See Douglass et al. (2004) for an analysis of the problems that can arise in U.S. pension plans with high allocations to own-company stock that can be justified only by very low risk aversion or high expected own-company stock returns.

The correlation matrices in Table 2 for the three different regimes are based on the regression approach described above. Results for the estimated regression equations appear in Table 3. We consider three different regimes and assume that 10% of the time equity markets are extremely volatile, 20% of the time markets are characterized by high volatility, and 70% of the time markets are normal. The 35th percentile of U.S. equity return volatility located at the

Table 2. Means, standard deviations, and correlations assumptions.

		Stocks Europe	Stocks US	Bonds Europe	Bonds US
Normal periods (70% of the time)	Stocks US	0.755			
	Bonds Europe	0.334	0.286		
	Bonds US	0.514	0.780	0.333	
	Standard deviation	14.6	17.3	3.3	10.9
High volatility (20% of the time)	Stocks US	0.786			
	Bonds Europe	0.171	0.100		
	Bonds US	0.435	0.715	0.159	
	Standard deviation	19.2	21.1	4.1	12.4
Extreme periods (10% of the time)	Stocks US	0.832			
	Bonds Europe	−0.075	−0.182		
	Bonds US	0.315	0.618	−0.104	
	Standard deviation	21.7	27.1	4.4	12.9
Average period	Stocks US	0.769			
	Bonds Europe	0.261	0.202		
	Bonds US	0.478	0.751	0.255	
	Standard deviation	16.4	19.3	3.6	11.4
All periods	Mean	10.6	10.7	6.5	7.2

center of the 70% "normal" range defines "normal" periods. "Highly volatile" periods are based on the 80th volatility percentile and "extreme" periods on the 95th percentile. The associated correlations are computed using the results from Table 3 and reflect the return relationships that typically prevailed during those market conditions. For example, if the 35th percentile of volatility is 0.173 (p.a.) the expected correlation between U.S. and European stocks is $0.62 + 2.7 \cdot 0.173/\sqrt{12} = 0.755$. The correlations in Table 2 show a distinct pattern across the three regimes. Correlations among stocks tend to increase as stock return volatility rises, whereas the correlations between stocks and bonds tend to decrease. European bonds may serve as a hedge for equities during extremely volatile periods because bond and stock returns, which are usually positively correlated, are then negatively correlated.

A crucial aspect for Innovest is to choose appropriate return distributions. To facilitate this choice, we calculate and compare optimal portfolios for seven cases. We distinguish cases with and without mixing of correlations and consider normal, t-, and historical distributions. Cases NM, HM, and TM use mixing correlations. Case NM assumes normal distributions for all assets. Case HM uses the historical distributions of each asset, whereby we capture the skewness found for all annual asset returns (see Table 1). Case TM assumes t-distributions with five degrees of freedom for stock returns to account for their fat tails, whereas bond returns are assumed to have normal distributions. While t-distributions are not empirically justified for annual returns (see Table 1), we have made this assumption to investigate how the model can deal with severe (worse than

Geyer and Ziemba: The Innovest Austrian Pension Fund Financial Planning Model InnoALM
Operations Research 56(4), pp. 797–810, © 2008 INFORMS

Table 3. Regression equations relating asset correlations and U.S. stock return volatility (monthly returns; Jan. 1989–Sept. 2000; 141 observations).

Correlation between	Constant	Slope w.r.t. U.S. stock volatility	t-statistic of slope	R^2
Stocks Europe–Stocks US	0.62	2.7	6.5	0.23
Stocks Europe–Bonds Europe	1.05	−14.4	−16.9	0.67
Stocks Europe–Bonds US	0.86	−7.0	−9.7	0.40
Stocks US–Bonds Europe	1.11	−16.5	−25.2	0.82
Stocks US–Bonds US	1.07	−5.7	−11.2	0.48
Bonds Europe–Bonds US	1.10	−15.4	−12.8	0.54

"normal") market conditions, an aspect of key concern to Innovest and regulatory authorities. The cases NA, HA, and TA are based on the same distribution assumptions with no mixing of correlations matrices. Instead, the correlations and standard deviations used in these cases correspond to an "average" period where 10%, 20%, and 70% weights are used to compute averages of correlations and standard deviations used in the three different regimes. Comparisons of the average (A) cases and mixing (M) cases are mainly intended to investigate the effect of mixing correlations. Finally, in the case TMC, we maintain all assumptions of case TM but constrain asset weights according to Austria's pension law. Eurobonds must be at least 40% and equity at most 40%, and these constraints are binding. As mentioned above, those constraints can be relaxed if a pension fund is managed according to the standards of the regulating authority (mainly if certain risk measures are in an acceptable range). Comparisons of constrained and unconstrained results, as presented below, have been used by Austrian regulatory authorities to assess the potential effects of such constraints. We consider the unconstrained cases also because the associated effects of mixing correlations and varying distributions are more pronounced if constraints are omitted.

4.2. Sample Application—Results

Table 4 shows the optimal initial asset weights at stage 1 for the various cases. Table 5 shows results for the final stage. These tables show a distinct pattern: the mixing correlation cases initially assign a much lower weight to European bonds than the "average" period cases. Single-period, mean-variance optimization and the "average" period cases (NA, HA, and TA) suggest an approximate 45–55 mix between equities and bonds. The mixing correlation cases (NM, HM, and TM) imply a 65–35 mix. Investing in U.S. bonds is not optimal at stage 1, mainly due to the relatively high volatility of U.S. bonds. Chopra and Ziemba (1993) point out that the asset allocation is very sensitive to the accuracy of the estimated mean return. For example, assuming a mean return for U.S. stocks equal to the long-run mean of 12% as estimated by Dimson et al. (2002, 2006), the model invests 100% into U.S. and European equities. Conversely, a mean return for U.S. stocks of 9% implies a 30%–70% mix of equities and bonds.

Table 4. Optimal initial asset weights at stage 1 by case (percentage).

	Stocks Europe	Stocks US	Bonds Europe	Bonds US
Single-period, mean-variance optimal weights (average periods)	34.8	9.6	55.6	0.0
Case NA: no mixing (average periods) normal distributions	27.2	10.5	62.3	0.0
Case HA: no mixing (average periods) historical distributions	40.0	4.1	55.9	0.0
Case TA: no mixing (average periods) t-distributions for stocks	44.2	1.1	54.7	0.0
Case NM: mixing correlations normal distributions	47.0	27.6	25.4	0.0
Case HM: mixing correlations historical distributions	37.9	25.2	36.8	0.0
Case TM: mixing correlations t-distributions for stocks	53.4	11.1	35.5	0.0
Case TMC: mixing correlations historical distributions; constraints on asset weights	35.1	4.9	60.0	0.0

Table 5 shows that the distinction between "A" and "M" cases becomes less pronounced over time. However, European equities still have a consistently higher weight in the mixing cases than in no-mixing cases. This higher weight is mainly at the expense of Eurobonds. In general, the proportion of equities at the final stage is much higher than in the first stage because the expected portfolio wealth at later stages is far above the target wealth level (206.1 at stage 6), and the higher risk associated with stocks is less important (see §4.3). This can also be derived from Figure 2, which shows the wealth distribution across all stages for case TM. Extreme poorly performing scenarios (i.e., large shortfalls) do not seem to be a problem for the mixing correlation cases, as also indicated by the final column in Table 5. The constraints in case TMC lead to lower expected portfolio wealth throughout the horizon and to a higher shortfall probability than any other case. Calculations show that initial wealth would have to be 35% higher to compensate for the loss in terminal expected wealth due to those constraints. In all cases, the optimal weight of equities is much higher than the 13.4% in 2002 in Austria (OECD 2004).

The expected terminal wealth levels and the shortfall probabilities at the final stage make the difference between mixing and no-mixing cases even clearer (see Table 5).

Table 5. Expected portfolio weights at the final stage by case (percentage), expected terminal wealth, expected reserves, and the probability for wealth-target shortfalls (percentage) at the final stage.

	Stocks Europe	Stocks US	Bonds Europe	Bonds US	Expected terminal wealth	Expected reserves at stage 6	Probability of target shortfall	Probability shortfall >10%
NA	34.3	49.6	11.7	4.4	328.9	202.8	11.2	2.7
HA	33.5	48.1	13.6	4.8	328.9	205.2	13.7	3.7
TA	35.5	50.2	11.4	2.9	327.9	202.2	10.9	2.8
NM	38.0	49.7	8.3	4.0	349.8	240.1	9.3	2.2
HM	39.3	46.9	10.1	3.7	349.1	235.2	10.0	2.0
TM	38.1	51.5	7.4	2.9	342.8	226.6	8.3	1.9
TMC	20.4	20.8	46.3	12.4	253.1	86.9	16.1	2.9

Mixing correlations implies higher levels of terminal wealth and lower shortfall probabilities.

If the level of portfolio wealth exceeds the target, the surplus $\tilde{D}_j$ is allocated to a reserve account; see §2. The reserves in t are computed from $\sum_{j=1}^{t} \tilde{D}_j$ and are shown in Table 5 for the final stage. These values are in monetary units given an initial wealth level of 100. They can be put into context by comparing them to the wealth target (206.1 at stage 6). Expected reserves exceed the target level at the final stage by up to 16%. Depending on the scenario, the reserves can be as high as 1,800. Their standard deviation (across scenarios) ranges from five at the first stage to 200 at the final stage. The constraints in case TMC lead to a much lower level of reserves compared to the other cases, which implies, in fact, less security against future increases of pension payments.

Summarizing, the main lesson to be learned from this application is that scenario-dependent correlations imply higher levels of wealth, less risk, and more reserves than constant alternatives. We also find that optimal allocations, expected wealth, and shortfall probabilities are more affected by considering mixing correlations while the type of distribution (i.e., accounting for skewness or fat tails) has a smaller impact. The results illustrate the insights pension fund planners and regulating authorities can obtain from inspecting the model's wealth and risk implications across time and across scenarios.

Figure 2. Total wealth distribution over time for case TM.

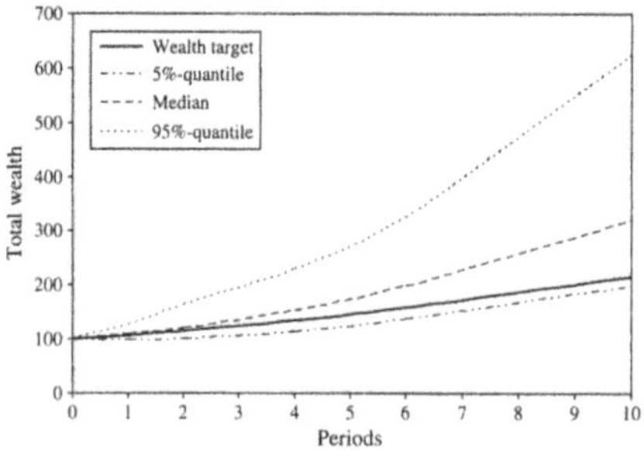

4.3. Model Tests

Because state-dependent correlations have a significant impact on allocation decisions, we further investigate their nature and their implications to test the model. While the focus of the previous section was to compare various stochastic assumptions and to highlight the model's benefits to Innovest, the purpose of the present section is to test the advantages of using mixing correlations in an out-of-sample context and a controlled experiment.

Positive effects on the pension fund performance and its risk profile induced by the stochastic, multiperiod planning approach will be realized only if the portfolio is dynamically rebalanced, as implied by the optimal scenario tree. We first illustrate the decision rule implied by the model. We form quintiles of wealth and compute the average optimal weights assigned to each quintile.

Figure 3 shows the distribution of weights for each of the five average levels of wealth for case TM at stage 2, which

Figure 3. Optimal TM weights conditional on quintiles of portfolio wealth at stage 2.

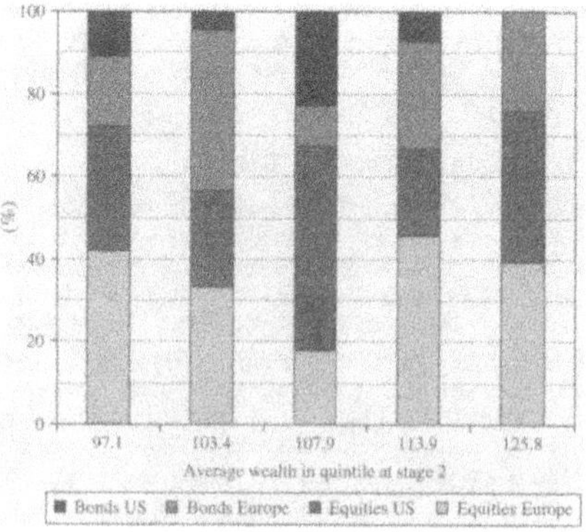

Geyer and Ziemba: The Innovest Austrian Pension Fund Financial Planning Model InnoALM
Operations Research 56(4), pp. 797–810, © 2008 INFORMS

depends on the wealth level in a specific way. For example, if average attained wealth is 103.4, which is slightly below the target, a very cautious strategy is chosen. Bonds have the highest weight in this case (almost 50%). In this situation, the model implies that the risk of even stronger underachievement of the target is to be minimized. If attained wealth is far below the target (97.1), the model implies more than 70% equities and a high share (10.9%) of relatively risky U.S. bonds. With such strong underachievement, there is no room for a cautious strategy to attain the target level again. If average attained wealth is close to the target 107.5 putting more money into U.S. assets (72.4%), which are more risky than the corresponding European assets, is acceptable because risk does not play a big role in that situation. For wealth levels above the target, most of the portfolio is switched to European assets, which are safer than U.S. assets, thereby preserving the high levels of attained wealth. These results follow the objective of the fund, although individual pension beneficiaries might have different preferences.

The decision rules implied by the optimal solution can be used to perform a test of the model using the following rebalancing strategy. Consider the 10-year period from January 1992 to January 2002. In the first month of this period, we assume that wealth is allocated according to the optimal solution for stage 1 (see Table 4). In each of the subsequent months, the portfolio is rebalanced as follows: we identify the current volatility regime (normal, highly volatile, or extreme) by comparing the U.S. stock return volatility estimated from the past 36 months of U.S. equity returns (see §3, p. 13) to the 35th, 80th, and 95th percentiles of volatility as defined in §4.1. The regime might have been identified incorrectly. Then, we search the scenario tree across all stages to find a node that corresponds to the current volatility regime (using the tags assigned to simulated return) and has the same or a similar level of wealth. Given the high short-run persistence of return covariance, it is plausible to assume that the current volatility and correlation regime prevails in the subsequent month and we use the optimal weights from that node to determine the rebalancing decision. For the no-mixing cases NA, TA, and HA, the information about the current volatility regime cannot be used to identify optimal weights. In those cases, we use the weights from a node with a level of wealth as close as possible to the current level of wealth.

Table 6 presents summary statistics for the complete sample time period and the out-of-sample time period October 2000 to January 2002. The mixing correlation solutions assuming normal and t-distributions (cases NM and TM) provide a higher average return with lower standard deviation than the corresponding nonmixing cases (NA and TA). The advantage might be substantial, as indicated by the 14.9% average return of TM compared to 10.0% for TA. The t-statistic for this difference is 1.7 and is significant at the 5% level (one-sided test). Using the historical distribution and mixing correlations (HM) yields a lower average return than no-mixing (HA). This result can be explained by a strong asymmetry in the pattern of conditional weights of HA (as shown in Figure 3 for TM) in favor of stocks, which contributes to the superior performance of HA compared to HM. In the constrained case TMC, the average return for the complete sample is in the same range as for the unconstrained cases. This is mainly due to relatively high weights assigned to U.S. bonds, which had high returns during the test period. The standard deviation of returns is much lower because the constraints imply a lower degree of rebalancing.

To emphasize the difference between the cases TM and TA, Figure 4 compares the cumulated monthly returns obtained from the rebalancing strategy for the two cases as well as the results of two buy-and-hold strategies. One of the buy-and-hold strategies assumes that the portfolio weights on January 1992 are fixed at the optimal TM weights throughout the test period, and the other uses the weights from single-period mean-variance analysis (see Table 4). Rebalancing on the basis of the optimal TM scenario tree provides a substantial gain when compared to the buy-and-hold strategies or the performance using TA results, where rebalancing does not account for different correlation and volatility regimes.

The results in Table 6 suggest that the TMC is the most attractive strategy after adjusting for risk (e.g., using a Sharpe ratio). However, such in- and out-of-sample comparisons depend on the observed asset returns and the test period. To isolate the potential benefits from considering state-dependent correlations, we performed the following controlled simulation experiment. Consider 10,000 10-year periods where simulated annual returns of the four assets are assumed to have the statistical properties summarized in Table 2. The means and standard deviations of simulated returns across all 100,000 years are equal to those given in the last two rows of Table 2. One of the 10 years is assumed to be an "extreme" year, two years correspond to "highly volatile" markets, and seven years are "normal" years using the corresponding correlation matrix and standard deviations from Table 2. Returns have normal, historical, or

Table 6. Results of asset allocation strategies using the decision rule implied by the optimal scenario tree.

	Complete sample 01/92–01/02		Out-of-sample 10/00–01/02	
	Mean	Std. dev.	Mean	Std. dev.
NA	11.6	16.1	−17.1	18.6
NM	13.1	15.5	−9.6	16.9
HA	12.6	16.5	−15.7	21.1
HM	11.8	16.5	−15.8	19.3
TA	10.0	16.0	−14.6	18.9
TM	14.9	15.9	−10.8	17.6
TMC	12.4	8.5	0.6	9.9

Figure 4. Cumulative monthly returns for different strategies.

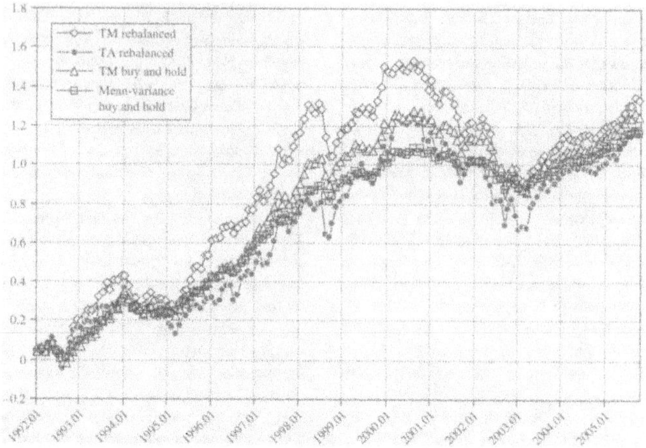

t-distributions. We compare rebalancing strategies that use the implied decision rules of the optimal scenario tree, as explained in the in- and out-of-sample tests above. Only the rebalancing strategies of the cases NM, HM, and TM are appropriate in this simulated environment because the strategies are based on the optimal solution derived from a stochastic tree with mixing correlations. The strategies for cases NA, HA, and TA are based on the optimal solution assuming an average correlation matrix. For simplicity, we assume that the current volatility regime is known in the mixing strategies.

Using this experiment, we assess the value of scenario-dependent correlation matrices by comparing NM to NA, HM to HA, and TM to TA (see Table 7). Case TMC is included to test the impact of constraints on asset weights. The average annual return over 10,000 repetitions using TM weights is 10.0%, compared with 9.51% using the TA weights. The mean difference has a t-statistic of 11.2, which indicates a highly significant advantage of using state-dependent correlations. The rebalancing strategy in case TM applies appropriate decision rules, while the strategy in case TA cannot respond adequately to different regimes. The expected wealth at the end of year 10 is 314.5 for TM, compared to only 292.7 for TA. The shortfall probability in case TM is also smaller. Similar differences can be observed by comparing the pairs NA-NM and HA-HM, although the advantage of the mixing cases is not uniform across distributions. For the constrained case TMC, we obtain an average return of only 8.06%, which indicates that the constraints imply insufficient rebalancing capacity. Thus, the relatively good performance of the TMC rebalancing strategy in the sample period 1992–2002 might have been positively biased by the favorable conditions during that time. Rebalancing strategies always outperform buy-and-hold strategies (e.g., 10% compared to 9.2% in case TM).

Table 7. Average annual returns, expected terminal wealth, and the probability for wealth-target shortfalls (percentage) for different rebalancing strategies.

	Average annual return (%)	Expected terminal wealth	Probability of target shortfall
NA	9.87	307.1	31.0
NM	9.98	313.3	30.7
HA	9.28	283.2	33.7
HM	9.53	294.3	32.8
TA	9.51	292.7	32.1
TM	10.0	314.5	30.1
TMC	8.06	231.9	38.0

Summarizing, the main implications derived from the model tests for practical applications are significant benefits of using scenario-dependent correlation matrices. The controlled experiments indicate that the advantages measured in terms of wealth and shortfall probabilities are not sample dependent.

5. Conclusions and Final Remarks

The model InnoALM provides an easy-to-use tool to help Austrian pension funds' investment allocation committees evaluate the effect of various policy choices in light of changing economic conditions and various goals, constraints, and liability commitments. The model includes

Geyer and Ziemba: The Innovest Austrian Pension Fund Financial Planning Model InnoALM
Operations Research 56(4), pp. 797–810, © 2008 INFORMS 809

features that reflect real investment practices. These include multiple scenarios, nonnormal distributions, and different volatility and correlation regimes. The model provides a systematic way to estimate in advance the likely results of particular policy changes and asset return realizations. This provides more confidence and justification to policy changes that might be controversial, such as a higher weight in equity and less in bonds than has traditionally been the case in Austria.

The model is an advance on previous models and includes new features such as state-dependent correlation matrices. Crucial to the success of the results are the scenario inputs and especially the mean return assumptions. The model has a number of ways to estimate such scenarios. Given good inputs, the policy recommendations can improve current investment practice and provide greater confidence to the asset allocation process. The following quote by Konrad Kontriner (member of the board) and Wolfgang Herold (senior risk strategist) of Innovest emphasizes the practical importance of InnoALM:

> "The InnoALM model has been in use by Innovest, an Austrian Siemens subsidiary, since its first draft versions in 2000. Meanwhile it has become the only consistently implemented and fully integrated proprietary tool for assessing pension allocation issues within Siemens AG worldwide. Apart from this, consulting projects for various European corporations and pensions funds outside of Siemens have been performed on the basis of the concepts of InnoALM.
>
> The key elements that make InnoALM superior to other consulting models are the flexibility to adopt individual constraints and target functions in combination with the broad and deep array of results, which allows to investigate individual, path-dependent behavior of assets and liabilities as well as scenario based and Monte-Carlo like risk assessment of both sides.
>
> In light of recent changes in Austrian pension regulation the latter even gained additional importance, as the rather rigid asset-based limits were relaxed for institutions that could prove sufficient risk management expertise for both assets and liabilities of the plan. Thus, the implementation of a scenario-based asset allocation model will lead to more flexible allocation restraints that will allow for more risk tolerance and will ultimately result in better long-term investment performance.
>
> Furthermore, some results of the model have been used by the Austrian regulatory authorities to assess the potential risk stemming from less-constraint pension plans."

Appendix. Pseudo-Code for Scenario Generation

```
SET N % number of assets
SET T % number of periods
SET cp, hp, np % probabilities for crash, high and normal regimes
SET m % T × N matrix of mean gross returns adjusted for period length
SET cs, hs, ns % T × N matrices of volatilities adjusted for period length
SET cc, hc, nc % N × N correlations for crash, high and normal regimes

FOR period = 1 to T
nz = n_nodes[period] % total number of nodes in the current period

COMPUTE nz × N matrix Z % antithetic random numbers with mean 0 and std.dev 1; Z can have normal, t- or historical distribution

DEFINE ic, ih, in % arrays with random pointers to rows of Z; ic, ih, and in have dimension CEIL(cp*nz), CEIL(hp*nz), and nz-CEIL(cp*nz)-CEIL(hp*nz); the joint index set is nonoverlapping; in each period a different set of random pointers is used

COMPUTE mean 0 returns with required correlation and volatility in each regime:
Y[ic,.] = (Z[ic,.]*CHOL(cc)).*cs[period,.]
Y[ih,.] = (Z[ih,.]*CHOL(hc)).*hs[period,.]
Y[in,.] = (Z[in,.]*CHOL(nc)).*ns[period,.]

COMPUTE R_period = m[period,.] + Y % gross returns for current period
ENDFOR
```

Acknowledgments

This research was supported by Innovest and the Natural Sciences and Engineering Research Council of Canada. Thanks to Melania Paunescu for computer help; Wolfgang Herold, Konrad Kontriner, and Johann Maurer for encouragement and support; Alan King and Alex Weissensteiner; the former area editor, Rick Rosenthal; the current area editor, Steve Graves; an anonymous associate editor, and the referees for helpful comments on earlier versions of this paper.

This paper was presented at the Hermes Centre of Excellence in Computational Finance and Economics, the Conference on Asset and Liability Management: From Institutions to Households, Nicosia, Cyprus, May 2001; the International Conference on Financial Engineering, E-Commerce and Supply Chain, Athens, Greece, May 2001; the Chicago Fed/DePaul University Finance Seminar, June 2001; the 9th International Conference on Stochastic Programming, Berlin, August 2001; the IFIP/IIASA/GAMM Workshop on Dynamic Stochastic Optimization, IIASA, Laxenburg, Austria, March 2002; Southampton University and Imperial College, September 2002; the Euro Working Group on Financial Modeling, Cyprus and University of Bergamo, November 2002; the SAID Business School, Oxford University, March 2003; the University of Zurich and the Mathematical Institute, Humboldt University, June 2003; the Operations Research Department of the ETH Zurich, July 2003; the Workshop on Asset Liability Management in Insurance in Vienna, September 2004; the University of Washington Statistics and Industrial Engineering Departments, June and November 2005; the Control Engineering Department, ETH, Zurich, October 2005; the 19th International Conference on Mathematical Programming, Rio de Janeiro, August 2006; the International Workshop on Forecasting and Risk Control, Chinese Academy of Sciences, Beijing, December 2006; the Mathematical Institute, Oxford University and the Department of Mathematics, University of Edinburgh, March 2007; Universities of Bergamo and Venice, May 2008; and Universities of Florence, Zurich, and Reading, June 2008.

References

Bos, E. 1994. World population projections 1994–95. The World Bank, Washington, D.C.

Bossaerts, P., P. Hillion. 1999. Implementing statistical criteria to select return forecasting models: What do we learn? *Rev. Financial Stud.* **12** 405–428.

Campbell, J. Y., L. M. Viceira. 2002. *Strategic Asset Allocation*. Oxford University Press, Oxford, UK.

Cariño, D. R., A. L. Turner. 1998. Multiperiod asset allocation with derivative assets. J. M. Mulvey, W. T. Ziemba, eds. *Worldwide Asset and Liability Modeling*. Cambridge University Press, Cambridge, UK, 182–204.

Cariño, D. R., W. T. Ziemba. 1998. Formulation of the Russell-Yasuda Kasai financial planning model. *Oper. Res.* **46** 433–449.

Cariño, D. R., D. H. Myers, W. T. Ziemba. 1998. Concepts, technical issues, and uses of the Russell-Yasuda Kasai financial planning model. *Oper. Res.* **46** 450–462.

Cariño, D. R., T. Kent, D. H. Myers, C. Stacey, M. Sylvanus, A. L. Turner, K. Watanabe, W. T. Ziemba. 1994. The Russell-Yasuda Kasai model: An asset/liability model for a Japanese insurance company using multistage stochastic programming. *Interfaces* **24**(1) 29–49.

Chen, N., R. Roll, S. A. Ross. 1986. Economic forces and the stock market. *J. Bus.* **59** 383–403.

Chopra, V., W. T. Ziemba. 1993. The effect of errors in mean and covariance estimates on optimal portfolio choice. *J. Portfolio Management* **19** 6–11.

Das, S. R., R. Uppal. 2004. Systemic risk and international portfolio choice. *J. Finance* **59** 2809–2834.

Dimson, E., P. Marsh, M. Staunton. 2002. *Triumph of the Optimists: 101 Years of Global Investment Returns*. Princeton University Press, Princeton, NJ.

Dimson, E., P. Marsh, M. Staunton. 2006. *Global Investment Returns Yearbook*. ABN-Ambro, London.

Douglass, J., O. Wu, W. T. Ziemba. 2004. Stock ownership decisions in DC pension plans. *J. Portfolio Management* (Summer) 92–100.

European Commission. 1997. Supplementary pensions in the single market. A Green Paper, COM 283, Brussels, Belgium.

Ferson, W. E., C. R. Harvey. 1993. The risk and predictability of international equity returns. *Rev. Financial Stud.* **6** 527–566.

Fleten, S.-S., K. Hoyland, S. W. Wallace. 2002. The performance of stochastic dynamic and fixed mix portfolio models. *Eur. J. Oper. Res.* **140** 37–49.

Glasserman, P., P. Heidelberg, P. Shahabuddin. 2000. Variance reduction techniques for value-at-risk with heavy-tailed risk factors. J. A. Joines, R. R. Barton, K. Kang, P. A. Fishwick, eds. *Proc. 2000 Winter Simulation Conf.*, Orlando, FL, 604–609.

Gondzio, J., R. Kouwenberg. 2001. High performance computing for asset-liability management. *Oper. Res.* **49** 879–891.

Grauer, R. R., N. H. Hakansson. 1998. Stein and CAPM estimators of the means in asset allocation. *Internat. Rev. Financial Anal.* **4** 35–66.

Harvey, C. R. 1991. The world price of covariance risk. *J. Finance* **46** 111–157.

Hensel, C. R., A. L. Turner. 1998. Making superior asset allocation decisions: A practitioner's guide. J. M. Mulvey, W. T. Ziemba, eds. *Worldwide Asset and Liability Modeling*. Cambridge University Press, Cambridge, UK, 62–83.

Høyland, K., S. W. Wallace. 2001. Generating scenario trees for multistage decision problems. *Management Sci.* **47** 295–307.

Jackwerth, J. C., M. Rubinstein. 1997. Recovering probability distributions from option prices. *J. Finance* **51** 1611–1631.

Jamshidian, F., Y. Zhu. 1997. Scenario simulation: Theory and methodology. *Finance and Stochastics* **1** 43–67.

Jorion, P. 1985. International portfolio diversification with estimation risk. *J. Bus.* **58** 259–278.

Kallberg, J. G., W. T. Ziemba. 1983. Comparison of alternative utility functions in portfolio selection problems. *Management Sci.* **29** 1257–1276.

Karolyi, A., R. Stultz. 1996. Why do markets move together? An investigation of US-Japan stock return comovements. *J. Finance* **51** 951–986.

Keim, D. B., R. F. Stambaugh. 1986. Predicting returns in the stock and bond markets. *J. Financial Econom.* **17** 357–390.

King, A. J., S. E. Wright, G. R. Parija, R. Entriken. 2005. The IBM stochastic programming system. S. W. Wallace, W. T. Ziemba, eds. *Applications of Stochastic Programming*. Series in Optimization, MPS SIAM, Philadelphia, 27–44.

Kusy, M. I., W. T. Ziemba. 1986. A bank asset and liability management model. *Oper. Res.* **34** 356–376.

Leibowitz, M. L., R. D. Henriksson. 1988. Portfolio optimization within a surplus framework. *Financial Analysts J.* **21** 43–51.

Lo, A. W. 1999. The three P's of total risk management. *Financial Analysts J.* **55** 13–26.

MacLean, L. C., W. T. Ziemba, M. Foster. 2007. Empirical Bayes estimation with dynamic portfolio models. *J. Banking Finance* **31** 3503–3523.

Merton, R. C. 2000. Finance and the role of financial engineering in the 21st century. Speech to the Research Centre of Financial Engineering. Institute of Economic Research, University of Kyoto, Kyoto, Japan, December 12.

Mulvey, J. M. 1996. Generating scenarios for the Towers Perrin investment system. *Interfaces* **26** 1–15.

OECD. 2004. Global pension statistics project: Measuring the size of private pensions with an international perspective. *Financial Market Trends* (8), Paris.

Pflug, G. C. 2001. Scenario tree generation for multiperiod financial optimization by optimal discretization. *Math. Programming Series B* **89** 251–257.

Rockafellar, R. T., W. T. Ziemba. 2000. Modified risk measures and acceptance sets. Working paper, Sauder School of Business, University of British Columbia, Vancouver, British Columbia, Canada.

Roemisch, W., H. Heitsch. 2003. Scenario reduction algorithms in stochastic programming. *Comput. Optim. Appl.* **24** 187–206.

Roseveare, D., W. Leibfritz, D. Fore, E. Wurzel. 1996. Aging populations, pension systems and government budgets: Simulation for 20 OECD countries. Economics Department Working Paper 168, OECD, Paris.

Rudolf, M., W. T. Ziemba. 2004. Intertemporal surplus management. *J. Econom. Dynamics Control* **28** 975–990.

Sharpe, W. F., L. G. Tint. 1990. Liabilities—A new approach. *J. Portfolio Management* **17** 5–10.

Solnik, B., C. Boucrelle, Y. Le Fur. 1996. International market correlation and volatility. *Financial Analysts J.* **52** 17–34.

Wallace, S. W., W. T. Ziemba, eds. 2005. Applications of stochastic programming. SIAM—Mathematical Programming Society Series on Optimization, SIAM, Philadelphia.

Zenios, S. A. 1999. High-performance computing for financial planning: The last ten years and the next. *Parallel Comput.* **25** 2149–2175.

Ziemba, W. T., J. M. Mulvey, eds. 1998. *Worldwide Asset and Liability Modeling*. Cambridge University Press, Cambridge, UK.

Section IV

Kelly Optimal Growth

Chapter 13

GROWTH VERSUS SECURITY IN DYNAMIC INVESTMENT ANALYSIS*,#

L. C. MacLEAN, W. T. ZIEMBA and G. BLAZENKO
School of Business Administration, Dalhousie University, Halifax, Nova Scotia, Canada B3H 1Z5
Faculty of Commerce, University of British Columbia, Vancouver, British Columbia, Canada V6T 1Z2
School of Business Administration, Simon Fraser University, Burnaby, British Columbia, Canada V5A 1S6

This paper concerns the problem of optimal dynamic choice in discrete time for an investor. In each period the investor is faced with one or more risky investments. The maximization of the expected logarithm of the period by period wealth, referred to as the Kelly criterion, is a very desirable investment procedure. It has many attractive properties, such as maximizing the asymptotic rate of growth of the investor's fortune. On the other hand, instead of focusing on maximal growth, one can develop strategies based on maximum security. For example, one can minimize the ruin probability subject to making a positive return or compute a confidence level of increasing the investor's initial fortune to a given final wealth goal. This paper is concerned with methods to combine these two approaches. We derive computational formulas for a variety of growth and security measures. Utilizing fractional Kelly strategies, we can develop a complete tradeoff of growth versus security. The theory is applicable to favorable investment situations such as blackjack, horseracing, lotto games, index and commodity futures and options trading. The results provide insight into how one should properly invest in these situations.
(CAPITAL ACCUMULATION; FRACTIONAL KELLY STRATEGIES; EFFECTIVE GROWTH-SECURITY TRADEOFF; BLACKJACK; HORSERACING; LOTTO GAMES; TURN OF THE YEAR EFFECT)

This paper develops an approach to the analysis of risky investment problems for practical use by individuals. The idea is to provide simple-to-understand two-dimensional graphs that provide essential information for intelligent investment choice. Although the situation studied is multiperiod, the approach is couched in a growth versus security fashion akin to the static Markowitz mean-variance portfolio selection tradeoff. The approach is a marriage of the capital growth literature of Kelly (1956), Breiman (1961), Thorp (1966, 1975), Hakansson (1971, 1979), Algoet and Cover (1988) and others, which emphasizes maximal growth, with the maximal security literature of Ferguson (1965), Epstein (1977), and Feller (1962). In §1, we formulate a general investment model and describe three growth measures and three security measures. The measures all relate to single-valued aggregates of the investment results over multiple periods such as the mean first passage time to a particular wealth level and the probability of doubling one's wealth before halving it. In §2, we model the investment process as a random walk. Then, using familiar procedures from probability theory, we can easily generate computable quantities which are usually close approximations to the measures of interest. To generate tradeoffs of growth versus security one can utilize fractional Kelly strategies as discussed in §3. A simple but powerful result is that a complete trade-off of growth versus security for the most interesting growth and security measures is implementable simply by choosing various fractional Kelly strategies. Theoretical justification for the fractional Kelly strategies in a multiperiod context can be made using a continuous time approach and log normality assumptions (see Li et al. 1990 and Wu and Ziemba 1990).

* Accepted by Stavros A. Zenios; received March 1991. This paper has been with the authors 4 months for 2 revisions.

#This chapter was originally published in: MacLean, L. C., Ziemba, W. T. & Blazenko, G. (1992). Growth versus Security in Dynamic Investment Analysis. *Management Science*, 38(11), 1562–1585.

Application of the theory to four favorable investment situations is made in §4. In each case the basic game or investment situation is unfavorable to the typical or average player. However, systems have been developed that beat the game in the sense that they have positive expected value. The question then remains how large should the wagers be and how confident is one that particular goals will be achieved. The various games, blackjack, horseracing, lotto games and the turn of the year effect differ markedly in their character. The size of the wagers vary from over half of one's fortune to less than one millionth of the fortune. The graphs that are outputted for each of these applications show how to trade off risk and return and provide crucial insight into how one should invest intelligently in these situations.

1. The Basic Investment Problem

An investor has initial wealth $y_0 \in \mathbb{R}$ and is facing n risky investments in periods 1, 2, $\ldots, t, \ldots$. The return on investments follows a stochastic process defined on the probability space (Ω, B, P) with corresponding product spaces (Ω^t, B^t, P^t). Given the realization history $\omega^{t-1} \in \Omega^{t-1}$, the investor's capital at the *beginning* of period t is $Y_{t-1}(\omega^{t-1})$. The investment in period t in each opportunity i, $i = 1, \ldots, n$, is $X_{it}(\omega^{t-1})$, $X_{it}(\omega^{t-1}) \leq Y_{t-1}(\omega^{t-1})$. The investment decisions in terms of proportions are $X_{it}(\omega^{t-1}) = p_{it}(\omega^{t-1})Y_{t-1}(\omega^{t-1})$ for $i = 1, \ldots, n$, and $p_t(\omega^{t-1}) = (p_{0t}(\omega^{t-1}), \ldots, p_{nt}(\omega^{t-1}))$, where $\sum_{i=0}^{n} p_{it}(\omega^t) = 1$ and $p_{0t}(\omega^{t-1})Y_{t-1}(\omega^{t-1})$ is the investment at time t in riskless cash-like instruments. In this general form the investment strategy $p_t(\omega^{t-1})$ depends on time and the history Ω^{t-1} of the investment process. The net return per unit of capital invested in i, $i = 1, \ldots, n$, given the outcome $\omega_t \in \Omega$, in period t is given by $K_{it}(\omega_t)$, $i = 1, \ldots, n$, $t = 1, \ldots$. The return on the risk-free asset is given by $K_{0t} = 0$. It is assumed that $K_{it}(\omega_t)$ is defined by the multiplicative model

$$K_{it}(\omega_t) = \alpha_i(t)E_i(\omega_t),$$

where $\alpha_i(t) > 0$ is the average time path and $E_i(\omega_i)$ is an independent error term. Special cases result when $\alpha_i(t) = \alpha_i$ or $\alpha_i(t) = \alpha_i^t$ for $t = 1, \ldots$. The error terms in this model are not autocorrelated. A more general approach would be to consider the conditional return at time t given the history ω^{t-1}, denoted by $K_{it}(\omega_t | \omega^{t-1})$. A Bayesian analysis with such a model is theoretically tractable, but it is not as suited to computations as the multiplicative model.

An investment environment is said to be favorable if $EK_i(\omega) > 0$ for some i. We are only concerned with favorable environments. The total return on investment is $R_{it}(\omega_i) = 1 + K_{it}(\omega_t)$, and the investment decisions are $p = (p_1, p_2(\omega^1), \ldots, p_t(\omega^{t-1}), \cdots)$. Then the accumulated wealth at the end of period t is

$$Y_t(p, \omega^t) = y_0 \prod_{s=1}^{t} \left(\sum_{i=0}^{n} R_{is}(\omega_s)p_{is}(\omega^{s-1}) \right), \qquad \omega^t \in \Omega^t, \qquad t = 1, \ldots. \tag{1}$$

For the stochastic capital accumulation process $\{Y_t(p)\}_{t=1}^{\infty}$ we are interested in characterizing the accumulation paths as the investment decisions vary. Consider the following measures of growth and security.

1.1. *Measures of Growth*

G1. $\mu_t(y_0, p) = EY_t(p)$. This is the mean accumulation of wealth at the end of time t. That is, how much do we expect to have, on average, after t periods.

G2. $\phi_t(y_0, p) = E \ln (Y_t(p)^{1/t})$. This is the mean exponential growth rate over t periods. It is a measure of how fast the investor is accumulating wealth. We also consider the long-run growth rate $\phi(p) = \lim_{t\to\infty} \phi_t(y_0, p)$.

G3. $\eta(y_0, p) = E\tau_{\{Y(p)\geq U\}}$. This is the mean first passage time τ to reach the set $[U, \infty)$. That is, how long on average does it take the investor to reach a specific level of wealth. For example, how long must the investor wait before he is a millionaire.

1.2. *Measures of Security*

S1. $\gamma_t(y_0, p) = \Pr[Y_t(p) \geq b_t]$. This is the probability that the investor will have a specific accumulated wealth $b_t \in \mathbb{R}$ at time t. That is, what are his chances of reaching a given target in a fixed amount of time. For example, what chance does the investor have of accumulating $200,000 one hundred days from now?

S2. $\alpha(y_0, p) = \Pr[Y_t(p) \geq b_t, t = 1, \cdots]$. This is the probability that the investor's wealth is above a specified path. Our concern for an investor is that his wealth will *fall back* too much in any period. He may want protection against losing more than, say, 10% of current wealth at any point in time.

S3. $\beta(y_0, p) = \Pr[\tau_{\{Y(p)\geq U\}} < \tau_{\{Y(p)\geq L\}}]$. This is the probability of reaching a goal U which is higher than his initial wealth y_0, before falling to a wealth level L which is less than y_0. For example, if $U = 2y_0$ and $L = y_0/2$, this is the probability of doubling before halving.

The rationale for the measures selected is to *profile* the growth and security dimensions of the accumulation process. In each case there is a natural pairing of the measures: (μ_t, γ_t) for accumulated wealth at a point in time; (ϕ, α) for the behavior of growth paths; and (η, β) for first passage to terminal or stopping states. The choice of profile (pair of measures) is largely a function of personal preference and problem context. It is expected that the information contained in each of the profiles would be useful in selecting an investment strategy.

The usual criterion for evaluating a decision rule is $t\phi_t(y_0, p)$, the expected log of accumulated wealth. When $K_{it}(\omega_t) = \alpha_i(t)E_i(\omega_t)$, $i = 1, \ldots, n$, $t = 1, \ldots$, then the log optimal strategy is *proportional*, $\bar{p}_{it}(\omega^{t-1}) = \bar{p}_{it}$. Furthermore, if $\bar{p}_i$, $i = 1, \ldots, n$, solves the one-period problem

$$\max\left\{E\ln\left(1+\sum_{i=1}^{n}E_i(\omega)p_i\right)\middle|\sum_{i=1}^{n}p_i\leq 1,\qquad p_i\geq 0,\qquad i=1\cdots,n\right\},$$

then $\bar{p}_{it} = \inf\{\alpha_i^{-1}(t)\bar{p}_i, 1\}$ for $i = 1, \ldots, n$, $t = 1, \ldots$. In the case where $\alpha_i(t) = \alpha_i$, $i = 1, \ldots, n$, the log optimal strategy is a fixed fraction (independent of time), and is referred to as the Kelly (1956) strategy.

Considering the other growth measures we find that the Kelly strategy (i) maximizes the long run exponential growth rate $\phi(y_0, p)$, and (ii) minimizes the expected time to reach large goals $\eta(y_0, p)$ (Breiman 1961, Algoet and Cover 1988). The main properties of the Kelly strategy are summarized in Table 1. The performance of the Kelly strategy on the security measures is not so favorable. As with any fixed fraction rule, the Kelly strategy never risks ruin, but in general it entails a considerable risk of losing a substantial portion of wealth.

In terms of security an optimal policy is often to keep virtually all wealth in the riskless asset (Eithier 1987). We will let $p_0 = (1, 0, \ldots, 0)$ be the extreme security strategy, where all assets are held in *cash*.

Our purpose is to monitor the growth and security measures as the investment decisions vary with the goal of balancing the measures to obtain a strategy which performs well on both the growth and security dimensions. For a particular (growth, security) combination, the complete set of values is given by the *graph* (see Figure 1)

$$U_i = \{(G_i(p), S_i(p)) \mid p \text{ is a feasible investment strategy}\}.$$

TABLE 1—PART 1

Main Properties for the Kelly Criterion

Good/Bad	Property	Reference
G	Maximizing $E \log X$ asymptotically maximizes the rate of asset growth.	Breiman (1961), Algoet and Cover (1988)
G	The expected time to reach a preassigned goal is asymptotically as X increases least with a strategy maximizing $E \log X_N$.	Breiman (1961), Algoet and Cover (1988)
G	Maximizing median $\log X$.	Ethier (1987)
B	False Property: If maximizing $E \log X_N$ almost certainly leads to a better outcome then the expected utility of its outcome exceeds that of any other rule provided n is sufficiently large. Counterexample: $u(x) = X$, $\frac{1}{2} < p < 1$, Bernoulli trials, $f = 1$ maximizes $EU(x)$ but $f^* = 2p - 1 < 1$ maximizes $E \log X_N$.	Thorp (1975)
G	The $E \log X$ bettor never risks ruin.	Hakansson and Miller (1975)
B	If the $E \log X$ bettor wins then loses or loses then wins he is behind. The order of win and loss is immaterial for one, two, . . . sets of trials.	$(1 + \gamma)(1 - \gamma)X_0 = (1 - \gamma^2)X_0 < 0$
G	The absolute amount bet is monotone in wealth.	$(\partial E \log X)/\partial W_0 > 0$
B	The bets are extremely large when the wager is favorable and the risk is very low.	Roughly the optimal wager is proportional to the edge divided by the odds. Hence for low risk situations and corresponding low odds the wager can be extremely large. For one such example, see Ziemba and Hausch (1985, pp. 159–160). There in a \$3 million race the optimal fractional wager on a 3–5 shot was 64%.

The most obvious points in U_i to identify are *efficient* points given by $(G_i(p_\alpha), S_i(p_\alpha)) \in U_i$ with

$$G_i(p_\alpha) = \max \{ G_i(p) \mid S_i(p) \geq \alpha, p \text{ feasible} \}.$$

Alternatively the efficient points are $(G_i(p_\beta), S_i(p_\beta))$ with

$$S_i(p_\beta) = \max \{ S_i(p) \mid G_i(p) \geq \beta, p \text{ feasible} \}.$$

Given the required level of security (or growth) the efficient points are undominated. The set of efficient points constitutes the *efficient frontier*.

Two key efficient points are the unconstrained optimal growth and optimal security points, respectively $(G_i(\bar{p}), S_i(\bar{p}))$ with $G_i(\bar{p}) = \max \{ G_i(p) \mid p \text{ feasible} \}$ and $(G_i(p_0), S_i(p_0))$ with $S_i(p_0) = \max \{ S_i(p) \mid p \text{ feasible} \}$. The optimal growth strategy is the Kelly strategy $\bar{p}$ and the optimal security strategy is the cash strategy p_0. These are both fixed fraction strategies. Other strategies yielding points on the efficient frontier would not typically be fixed fraction, but rather would be dynamic strategies, depending on current wealth and/or time. Gottlieb (1985) has derived such a strategy for the criteria of maximizing mean first passage time to a goal (G_3), subject to a high probability of reaching the goal (S_3).

TABLE 1—PART 2
Main Properties for the Kelly Criterion

Good/Bad	Property	Reference
B	One overbets when the problem data is uncertain.	Betting more than the optimal Kelly wager is dominated in a growth-security sense. Hence if the problem data provides probabilities, edges and odds that may be in error, then the suggested wager will be too large. This property is discussed in and largely motivates this paper.
B	The total amount wagered swamps the winnings—that is, there is much "churning."	Ethier and Tavaré (1983) and Griffin (1985) show that the Expected Gain/E Bet is arbitrarily small and converges to zero in a Bernoulli game where one wins the expected fraction p of games.
B	The unweighted average rate of return converges to half the arithmetic rate of return.	Related to property 5 this indicates that you do not seem to win as much as you expect; see Ethier and Tavare (1983) and Griffin (1985).
G	The $E\log X$ bettor is never behind any other bettor on average in 1, 2, . . . trials.	Finkelstein and Whitley (1981)
G	The $E\log X$ bettor has an optimal myopic policy. He does not have to consider prior to subsequent investment opportunities.	This is a crucially important result for practical use. Hakansson (1971b) proved that the myopic policy obtains for dependent investments with the log utility function. For independent investments and power utility a myopic policy is optimal.
G	The chance that an $E\log X$ wagerer will be ahead of any other wagerer after the first play is at least 50%.	Bell and Cover (1980)
G	Simulation studies show that the $E\log X$ bettor's fortune pulls way ahead of other strategies' wealth for reasonably-sized sequences of investments.	Ziemba and Hausch (1985)

Rather than trying to move from optimal growth to optimal security along the efficient frontier, we will consider the path generated by convex combinations of the optimal growth and optimal security strategies, namely

$$p(\lambda) = \lambda\bar{p} + (1-\lambda)p_0, \qquad 0 \leq \lambda \leq 1.$$

Clearly $p(\lambda)$ is a fixed fraction strategy and we will call it *fractional Kelly* since it blends part of the Kelly with the cash strategy. The fractional Kelly strategy is n-dimensional, specifying investments in all opportunities, and the key parameter is λ, which we can consider as a *tradeoff* index.

The path traced by the fractional Kelly strategies is

$$U_i^0 = \{(G_i(p(\lambda)), S_i(p(\lambda)))\,|\,0 \leq \lambda \leq 1\}.$$

The fractional Kelly path is illustrated in Figure 1. This path has attractive properties. First, it is easily *computable*, as shown in the next section. When λ varies from 0 to 1 we continuously trade growth for security. Although this tradeoff is not always efficient, it is *effective* in that we see a *monotone increase in security as we decrease growth*. However, the rate of change in growth or security with respect to λ is not constant and thus the Kelly path is curvilinear. In fact, MacLean and Ziemba (1990) established that the Kelly path is above the straight line (secant) joining the optimal growth and optimal security points. These properties are discussed in §3.

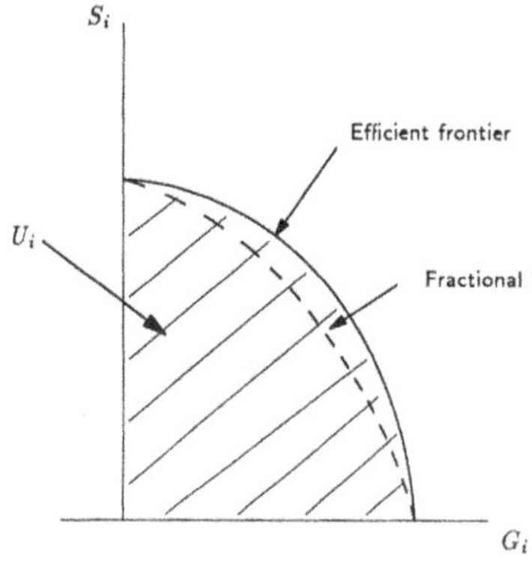

FIGURE 1. Graph of (Growth, Security) Profile Showing Efficient Frontier and Effective Path.

2. Computation of Measures

If we select a strategy which specifies our investment in the various opportunities and we stick with that strategy, then each of the measures described in §2 is easily computable. We will now develop the computational formulae. Since most of our discussion focuses on fractional Kelly strategies, we work with them. However, more general fixed strategies could be used.

Consider the fractional Kelly strategy $p(\lambda)$ and use the transformation

$$Z_t(p(\lambda), \omega^t) = \ln Y_t(p(\lambda), \omega^t).$$

From (1),

$$Z_t(p(\lambda), \omega^t) = z_0 + \sum_{s=1}^{t} \ln \left(\sum_{i=0}^{n} R_i(\omega_s) p_i(\lambda) \right) = Z_{t-1}(p(\lambda), \omega^{t-1}) + J(p(\lambda), \omega_t),$$

where $J(p(\lambda), \omega) = \ln (\sum_{i=0}^{n} R_i(\omega) p_i(\lambda))$ is a stationary jump process and $z_0 = \ln y_0$. Hence, Z_t, $t = 1, \ldots,$ is a random walk and we can evaluate the various measures of interest using this process. An alternative approach to evaluating these measures is presented in Ethier (1987) where the discrete time (and maybe discrete state) process $Y_t(p(\lambda))$ is approximated by geometric Brownian motion.

The mean wealth accumulation measure G1 is

$$\mu_t(y_0, p(\lambda)) = EY_t(p(\lambda)) = y_0 E \prod_{s=1}^{t} \left(\sum_{i=0}^{n} R_i(\omega_s) p_i(\lambda) \right) = y_0 \left(\sum_{i=0}^{n} \bar{R}_i p_i(\lambda) \right)^t, \quad (2)$$

where $\bar{R}_i = ER_i(w)$, $i = 0, \ldots, n$.

For the mean growth rate measure G2

$$\phi_t(y_0, p(\lambda)) = E \ln (Y_t(p(\lambda))^{1/t}) = 1/tEZ_t(p(\lambda))$$

$$= E \ln \left(\sum_{i=0}^{n} R_i(\omega) p_i(\lambda) \right) + \frac{1}{t} z_0 = EJ(p(\lambda), \omega) + \frac{1}{t} z_0, \quad (3)$$

which is an easy calculation to make.

For measure S1 assume the process

$$Z_t(p(\lambda), \omega^t) = z_0 + \sum_{s=1}^{t} J(p(\lambda), \omega_s)$$

has an approximate normal distribution. Using this approximation yields

$$\gamma_t(y_0, p(\lambda)) = 1 - F\left(\frac{b_t^* - E(Z_t(p(\lambda)))}{\sigma(Z_t(p(\lambda)))}\right), \tag{4}$$

where F is the cumulative for the standard normal, $b_t^* = \ln b_t$, and $E(Z_t(p(\lambda)))$, $\sigma(Z_t(p(\lambda)))$ are the mean and standard deviation respectively.

Measure S2 is given by

$$\alpha(y_0, p(\lambda)) = \Pr[Z_t(p(\lambda)) \geq b_t^*, t = 1, \cdots] \tag{5}$$

$$= \prod_{t=1}^{\infty} \Pr[Z_t(p(\lambda)) \geq b_t^* | Z_s(p(\lambda)) \geq b_s^*, s = 1, \ldots, t-1]$$

$$= \prod_{t=1}^{\infty} \alpha_t(z_0, p(\lambda)). \tag{6}$$

Then with $h_t(z_t | Z_s \geq b_s^*, s = 1, \ldots, t-1)$ the conditional density

$$\alpha_t = \int_{z_t \geq b_t^*} h_t(z_t | Z_s \geq b_s^*, s = 1, \ldots, t-1) dz_t$$

$$= \int_{z_t \geq b_t^*} \left\{ \int_{z_t - x \geq b_{t-1}^*} h_{t-1}(z_t - x | Z_s \geq b_s^*, s = 1, \ldots, t-1) \pi(x) dx \right\} dz_t,$$

where $\pi(x)$ is the density for $J(p(\lambda))$,

$$= \int_{z_t \geq b_t^*} \left\{ \int_{x \leq z_t - b_{t-1}^*} \frac{h_{t-1}(z_t - x | Z_s \geq b_s^*, s = 1, \ldots, t-2)}{\alpha_{t-2}} \pi(x) dx \right\} dz_t. \tag{7}$$

Equation (7) provides a sequential procedure to compute measure S2, requiring only the distribution from the previous stage and the jump probabilities.

For the other measures assume that the random variable $J(p(\lambda))$ has finite support given by the interval $[J_m(p(\lambda)), J_M(p(\lambda))]$. Consider measure S3

$$\beta(y_0, p(\lambda)) = \Pr[\tau_{\{Y(p(\lambda)) \geq U\}} < \tau_{\{Y(p(\lambda)) \leq L\}} | y_0].$$

Transforming to an additive process with $z = \ln y$ and letting

$$\beta(z, p(\lambda)) = \Pr[\tau_{\{Z(p(\lambda)) \geq \ln U\}} < \tau_{\{Z(p(\lambda)) \leq \ln L\}} | z]$$

yields

$$\beta(z_0, p(\lambda)) = E\{\beta(z_0 + J(p(\lambda)), p(\lambda))\}. \tag{8}$$

The expectation in (8) is over the random variable $J(p(\lambda))$. We must solve (8) for β subject to the boundary conditions

$$\beta(z, p(\lambda)) = 0 \quad \text{if} \quad z \leq \ln L \tag{8a}$$

$$\beta(z, p(\lambda)) = 1 \quad \text{if} \quad z \geq \ln U. \tag{8b}$$

A solution to (8) is of the form $\beta(z, p(\lambda)) = \sum_{k=1}^{s} A_k \theta_k^z$, where A_k are chosen to satisfy (8a, 8b) and the roots $\theta_1, \ldots, \theta_s$ satisfy the equation $E\theta^{J(p(\lambda))} = 1$. It is easy to show that there are two positive roots $\theta_1 = 1$ and $\theta_2 = \theta$, where $\theta_2 < 1$ or $\theta_2 > 1$ depending on whether $EJ(p(\lambda)) > 0$ or $EJ(p(\lambda)) < 0$ respectively. Similar to the methods discussed in Feller (1962, pp. 330–334), we take the minimum $J_m(p(\lambda)) < 0$ and maximum

TABLE 2
Computational Formulas for Growth Measures G1–G3 *and Security Measures* S1–S3

G1	$\mu_t(Y_0, p) = Y_0\left(\sum_{i=0}^{n} \bar{R}_i p_i\right)^t$
G2	$\phi(p) = E \ln\left(\sum_{i=0}^{n} R_i(\omega) p_i\right)$
G3	$\bar{\eta}(Z_0, p) = \frac{\theta^{Z_0}}{2EJ(p)}\left(\frac{U_*(p)}{\theta^{U_*(p)}} + \frac{U^*(p)}{\theta^{U^*(p)}}\right) - \frac{Z_0}{EJ(p)}$
S1	$\bar{\gamma}(Z_0, p) = 1 - F\left(\frac{b_t^* - Z_0 - tEJ(p)}{\sqrt{t}\sigma(J(p))}\right)$
S2	$\alpha(Z_0, p) = \prod_{t=1}^{\infty} \alpha_t(Z_0, p),$
	$\alpha_t(Z_0, p) = \sum_{Z_t \geq b_t^*}\left[\sum_{J_t \geq Z_t - b_{t-1}^*} \frac{G_{t-1}(Z_t - J_t(p))}{\alpha_{t-1}(Z_0, p)} \cdot \pi_i\right]$
S3	$\bar{\beta}(Z_0, p) = \frac{(\theta^{Z_0} - \theta^{U^*})(\theta^{U^*} - \theta^{L^*(p)}) + (\theta^{Z_0} - \theta^{L^*(p)})(\theta^{U^*(p)} - \theta^{L^*})}{2(\theta^{U^*(p)} - \theta^{L^*})(\theta^{U^*} - \theta^{L^*(p)})}$

$J_M(p(\lambda)) > 0$ jumps and find bounds on the solution by solving a simple system with the extreme boundary conditions satisfied as equalities. For the upper bound,

$$\beta(\ln L + J_m(p(\lambda)), p(\lambda)) = 0 \quad \text{and} \quad \beta(\ln U, p(\lambda)) = 1.$$

For the lower bound,

$$\beta(\ln L, p(\lambda)) = 0 \quad \text{and} \quad \beta(\ln U + J_M(p(\lambda)), p(\lambda)) = 1.$$

Let $L^* = \ln L$, $L^*(p(\lambda)) = \ln L + J_m(p(\lambda))$, $U^* = \ln U$, and $U^*(p(\lambda)) = \ln U + J_M(p(\lambda))$.

The bounds for measure S3 are then

$$\frac{\theta^{z_0} - \theta^{L^*}}{\theta^{U^*(p(\lambda))} - \theta^{L^*}} \leq \beta(y_0, p(\lambda)) \leq \frac{\theta^{z_0} - \theta^{L^*(p(\lambda))}}{\theta^{U^*} - \theta^{L^*(p(\lambda))}}. \tag{9}$$

For measure G3,

$$\eta(y_0, p(\lambda)) = E\tau_{\{Y(p(\lambda)) \geq U | y_0\}} = E\tau_{\{Z(p(\lambda)) \geq \ln U | z_0\}},$$

we use the recursive equation

$$\eta(z_0, p(\lambda)) = E\{\eta(z_0 + J(p(\lambda)), p(\lambda))\} + 1 \tag{10}$$

subject to the boundary condition

$$\eta(z, p(\lambda)) = 0 \quad \text{if} \quad z \geq \ln U. \tag{10a}$$

One solution to (10) is $\eta^*(z, p(\lambda)) = -z/(EJ(p(\lambda)))$. Any other solution can be written as $\eta(z, p(\lambda)) = \eta^*(z, p(\lambda)) + \Delta(z, p(\lambda))$ where $\Delta(z, p(\lambda))$ satisfies the system

$$\Delta(z, p(\lambda)) = E\{\Delta(z + J(p(\lambda)), p(\lambda))\}. \tag{10b}$$

Solutions of (10b) have the form $\Delta(z, p(\lambda)) = \sum A_k \theta_k^z$. Solutions of (10) are then

$$\eta(z, p) = \sum A_k \theta_k^z - z/(EJ(p(\lambda)))$$

where the A_k are chosen to satisfy the boundary conditions (10a). With $U_*(p(\lambda))$

$= \ln U - J_m(p(\lambda))$ we can solve the extreme boundary conditions as equalities, namely $\eta(U^*(p(\lambda)), p(\lambda)) = 0$ and $\eta(U_*(p(\lambda)), p(\lambda)) = 0$ yields the following bounds on G3:

$$\left[\frac{U_*(p(\lambda))}{EJ(p(\lambda))}\right]\left(\frac{\theta^{z_0}}{\theta^{U_*(p(\lambda))}}\right) - \frac{z_0}{EJ(p(\lambda))} \leq \eta(y_0, p(\lambda))$$

$$\leq \left[\frac{U^*(p(\lambda))}{EJ(p(\lambda))}\right]\left(\frac{\theta^{z_0}}{\theta^{U^*(p(\lambda))}}\right) - \frac{z_0}{EJ(p(\lambda))}. \quad (11)$$

The bounds in (9) and (11) are quite tight when the jumps are small relative to the initial wealth z_0.

Table 2 summarizes the formulas we can use to compute the six growth and security measures. For G3 and S3 we have bounds and the formulas given provide midpoint estimates of these bounds. A similar table appears in Ethier (1987) for the geometric Brownian motion model.

3. Effective Growth-security Tradeoff

The fact that the various growth and security measures can be easily evaluated for fractional Kelly strategies provides an opportunity to interactively investigate the performance of strategies for various measures and scenarios. The ability to evaluate various performance measures and determine a preferred strategy will depend on an *effective tradeoff* between complementary measures of growth and security. A tradeoff is effective if the loss of performance in one dimension (say growth) is compensated by a gain in the other dimension (security). In this section we establish that the tradeoff using fractional Kelly strategies is effective for each of the profile combinations. In calculating the rates of change for the various measures we will see that the tradeoff between growth and security is not constant for all λ, $0 \leq \lambda \leq 1$.

(i) *Rate Profile*: (ϕ, α).

LEMMA 3.1. *Suppose $p(\lambda)$ is a fractional Kelly strategy and $\bar{p}$ is the Kelly strategy. Then*

$$\frac{\partial\phi(y_0, p(\lambda))}{\partial\lambda} > 0, \qquad 0 \leq \lambda \leq 1.$$

PROOF. Consider the optimal growth strategy given by $\bar{p} = (\bar{p}_0, \ldots, \bar{p}_n)$, and the optimal security strategy $p_0 = (1, 0, \ldots, 0)$.

Then

$$p(\lambda) = (\lambda\bar{p}_0 + (1-\lambda), \ldots, \lambda\bar{p}_n) = (p_0(\lambda), \ldots, p_n(\lambda)) \qquad \text{and}$$

$$\frac{d}{d\lambda}p_0(\lambda) < 0, \qquad \frac{d}{d\lambda}p_i(\lambda) > 0, \qquad i = 1, \ldots, n.$$

We have the optimal growth problem

$$\max \phi(p(\lambda)) = \max E \ln\left(\sum_{i=0}^{n} R_{it}(\omega)p_i(\lambda)\right).$$

Then

$$\frac{\partial}{\partial p_0}\phi(p(\lambda)) = E\left(\frac{1 - \sum_{i=1}^{n} R_{it}(\omega)}{\sum_{i=0}^{n} R_{it}(\omega)p_i(\lambda)}\right) \qquad \text{and}$$

$$\frac{\partial^2}{\partial p_0^2}\phi(p(\lambda)) = -E\left[\frac{1 - \sum_{i=1}^{n} R_{it}(\omega)}{\sum_{i=0}^{n} R_{it}(\omega)p_i(\lambda)}\right]^2 < 0.$$

So $\phi(p(\lambda))$ is concave in p_0 and with $\bar{p}_0$ such that $\partial\phi(p(\lambda))/\partial p_0 = 0$, we have

$$\frac{\partial}{\partial p_0}\phi(p(\lambda)) < 0, \qquad p_0 < \bar{p}_0.$$

Therefore

$$\frac{d}{d\lambda}\phi(p(\lambda)) = \frac{dp_0}{d\lambda}\left(\frac{\partial}{\partial p_0}\phi(p(\lambda))\right) > 0 \qquad \text{and } \phi(p(\lambda)) \text{ is increasing in } \lambda. \qquad \square$$

LEMMA 3.2. *Let $p(\lambda)$ be a fractional Kelly strategy and* $\ln a < 0$ *be a given fallback rate. Then*

$$\frac{\partial}{\partial\lambda}\alpha(a, p(\lambda)) \le 0.$$

PROOF. We have for the security measure

$$\begin{aligned}\alpha(a, p(\lambda)) &= \text{Prob}\,[Y_t(p(\lambda)) \ge y_0 a^t,\ t = 1, \cdots]\\ &= \prod_{t\ge 1} \text{Prob}\,[Y_t(p(\lambda)) \ge a^t \mid Y_s(p(\lambda)) \ge a^s,\ s = 1, \ldots, t-1]\\ &= \prod_{t\ge 1} \alpha_t(a, p(\lambda)).\end{aligned}$$

Along any path $1, y_1, \ldots, y_{t-1}$ with $y_s \ge a^s$, $s = 1, \ldots, t-1$.

$$\alpha_t(a, p(\lambda)) = \text{Prob}\left[\ln\left(\sum R_{jt}(\omega)p_j(\lambda)\right) > \ln a - \frac{1}{t-1}\sum_{s=1}^{t-1} z_s\right],$$

where $z_s = \ln y_s$ and $\ln a - (t-1)^{-1}\sum_{s=1}^{t-1} z_s < 0$. With $b = \ln a - (t-1)^{-1}\sum z_s$ and $R_t p(\lambda) = \sum R_{jt}(\omega)p_j(\lambda)$ we have $\alpha_t(\lambda) \equiv$

$$\begin{aligned}\alpha_t(a, p(\lambda)) &= \text{Prob}\,[\ln(R_t p(\lambda)) \ge b]\\ &= \text{Prob}\,[\ln(\lambda R_t\bar{p} + (1-\lambda)R_t p_0) \ge b]\\ &= \text{Prob}\,[\lambda\ln(R_t\bar{p}) + (1-\lambda)\ln(R_t p_0) + \Delta \ge b]\\ &= \text{Prob}\left[\ln(R_t\bar{p}) \ge \frac{b-\Delta}{\lambda}\right] = 1 - F_t(x(\lambda)),\end{aligned}$$

where $x(\lambda) = (b - \Delta)/\lambda$ and F_t is the distribution function for the optimal growth process $\ln(R_t p_0)$.

Then $dx(\lambda)/d\lambda > 0$ and F nondecreasing imply $d\alpha_t(\lambda)/d\lambda \le 0$. Hence $d\alpha(a, p(\lambda))/d\lambda \le 0$. $\square$

Thus along the fractional Kelly path growth is increasing and security is decreasing and an *effective* tradeoff is possible.

(ii) *Wealth Profile*: (μ_t, γ_t).

LEMMA 3.3. *If $p(\lambda)$ is a fractional Kelly strategy then*

$$\frac{d}{d\lambda}\mu_t(p(\lambda)) > 0, \qquad 0 \le \lambda \le 1.$$

PROOF. We have

$$\frac{\partial}{\partial p_0}\mu_t(p(\lambda)) = E\frac{\partial}{\partial p_0}Y_t(p(\lambda)) = E\frac{\partial}{\partial p_0}\left[y_0\prod_{s=1}^{t}\left(\sum_{j=1}^{n}R_j(\omega_s)p_j(\lambda)\right)\right]$$

$$= E\left[y_0\sum_{r=1}^{t}\frac{\partial}{\partial p_0}\left(\sum_{j=0}^{n}R_j(\omega_r)p_j(\lambda)\right)\prod_{s\neq r}\left(\sum_{j=0}^{n}R_j(\omega_s)p_j(\lambda)\right)\right]$$

$$= -ty_0E[K(\omega_t)Y_{t-1}(\omega^{t-1})] = -ty_0(EK)(EY_{t-1}) < 0.$$

Then

$$\frac{d}{d\lambda}\mu_t(p(\lambda)) = \frac{dp_0(\lambda)}{d\lambda}\frac{\partial}{\partial p_0}\mu_t(p(\lambda)) > 0. \qquad \square$$

LEMMA 3.4. *Suppose $p(\lambda)$ is a fractional Kelly strategy and consider the growth rate $\alpha = 1$. Then*

$$\frac{d}{d\lambda}\gamma_t(y_0, p(\lambda)) < 0 \qquad \text{for} \qquad 0 \le \lambda < 1.$$

PROOF. We have

$$\gamma_t(y_0, p(\lambda)) = \text{Prob}\,[Y_t(p(\lambda)) \ge y_0a^t] = \text{Prob}\left[\sum_{s=1}^{t}\ln R_sp(\lambda) \ge t\ln a\right]$$

$$= \text{Prob}\left[\sum \ln(\lambda R_s\bar{p} + (1-\lambda)R_sp_0) \ge 0\right]$$

$$= \text{Prob}\left[\lambda\sum\ln(R_s\bar{p}) + \sum\Delta_s \ge 0\right] \qquad \text{where} \qquad \Delta_s > 0$$

$$= \text{Prob}\left[\sum\ln(R_s\bar{p}) \ge \frac{-\sum\Delta_s}{\lambda}\right]$$

$$= 1 - F^t(x_t(\lambda)),$$

where $x_t(\lambda) = (-\sum\Delta_s)/\lambda$ and F^t is the distribution function for $\sum_{s=1}^{t}\ln(R_s\bar{p})$. Then $(d/d\lambda)x(\lambda) > 0$ and F^t nondecreasing gives the desired result. $\square$

Hence for the wealth profile an *effective* tradeoff is possible along the fractional Kelly path.

(iii) *Stopping Rule Profile*: (η^{-1}, β). Our analysis of the stopping rule profile focuses on the computational formulas $\bar{\eta}(p(\lambda))$ and $\bar{\beta}(p(\lambda))$. Since we have upper and lower bounds for the true values, the accuracy of the approximation is easy to determine in a particular application. Our choice of strategy is based on the profile graph and that requires $\bar{\eta}$ and $\bar{\beta}$.

The formulas for $\bar{\eta}$ and $\bar{\beta}$ are based on the random walk $Z_t(p(\lambda))$ with jump process $J(p(\lambda))$. The process $J(p(\lambda))$ is *flexible* at the fractional Kelly strategy $p(\lambda)$ if the condition

$$\frac{L'^*(p(\lambda))\theta^{L^*(p(\lambda))}}{L^*(p(\lambda))\theta^{L^*(p(\lambda))}} < \frac{EJ'(p(\lambda))\theta^{J(p(\lambda))}}{EJ(p(\lambda))\theta^{J(p(\lambda))}} < \frac{U'^*(p(\lambda))\theta^{U^*(p(\lambda))}}{U^*(p(\lambda))\theta^{U^*(p(\lambda))}}$$

holds, where $\theta < 1$ is a positive root of the equation $E\theta(p(\lambda))^{J(p(\lambda))} = 1$, and prime denotes the derivative w.r.t. λ.

LEMMA 3.5. *Suppose $p(\lambda)$ is a fractional Kelly strategy and consider the wealth process $Y_t(p(\lambda))$, $t = 1, \cdots$ and the absorbing states $U = ky_0$, $L = k^{-1}y_0$, $k > 1$. If $J(p(\lambda))$ is flexible at $p(\lambda)$ then for $0 \le \lambda \le 1$*

$$\text{(i)} \qquad \frac{\partial}{\partial\lambda}\bar{\eta}(y_0, p(\lambda)) < 0,$$

$$\text{(ii)} \qquad \frac{\partial}{\partial\lambda}\bar{\beta}(y_0, p(\lambda)) < 0.$$

PROOF. (i) For the mean first passage time consider the lower bound

$$\eta^2(p(\lambda)) = \frac{U_*(p(\lambda))}{EJ(p(\lambda))\theta^{U_*(p(\lambda))}},$$

where without loss of generality assume $y_0 = 1$ ($z_0 = 0$). Then

$$\frac{\partial}{\partial p_0}\eta^2(p(\lambda)) = \frac{N^2(p(\lambda))}{D^2(p(\lambda))},$$

where $\quad D^2(p(\lambda)) = [EJ(p(\lambda))\theta^{U_*(p(\lambda))}]^2 \quad$ and

$$\begin{aligned} N^2(p(\lambda)) = {} & [EJ(p(\lambda))\theta^{U_*(p(\lambda))}J'_m(p(\lambda)) - U_*(p(\lambda))EJ'(p(\lambda))\theta^{U_*(p(\lambda))} \\ & - U_*(p(\lambda))EJ(p(\lambda))\theta^{U_*(p(\lambda))}J'_m(p(\lambda))\ln\theta \\ & - U_*(p(\lambda))EJ(p(\lambda))\theta^{U_*(p(\lambda))}U_*(p(\lambda))\theta'/\theta], \end{aligned}$$

where the prime denotes the first derivative w.r.t. p_0. Since $EJ'(p(\lambda)) < 0$ and $EJ(p(\lambda)) > 0$, $J'_m(p(\lambda)) > 0$, $\theta' < 0$, we get all terms in $N^2(p(\lambda))$ positive and $(\partial/\partial p_0)\eta^2(p(\lambda)) > 0$. In the same way for the upper bound $\eta^1(p(\lambda))$ we get $(\partial/\partial p_0)\eta^1(p(\lambda)) > 0$. With $(d/d\lambda)p_0(\lambda) < 0$ the average of the bounds yields (1).

(ii) For the first passage probability we utilize the upper bound

$$\beta^1(p(\lambda)) = \frac{1 - \theta^{L^*(p(\lambda))}}{\theta^{U^*} - \theta^{L^*(p(\lambda))}}.$$

Then the numerator of $(\partial/\partial p_0)\beta^1(p(\lambda))$ is

$$N(p(\lambda)) = (\theta^{U^*} - 1)\frac{\partial}{\partial p_0}\theta^{L^*(p(\lambda))} - (1 - \theta^{L^*(p(\lambda))})\frac{\partial}{\partial p_0}\theta^{U^*}.$$

We have $E\theta(p(\lambda))^{J(p(\lambda))} = 1$ and $(\partial/\partial p_0)E\theta(p(\lambda))^{J(p(\lambda))} = 0$ from which

$$\begin{aligned} \frac{\partial}{\partial p_0}\theta(p(\lambda)) &= -\theta(p(\lambda))\ln\theta(p(\lambda))[EJ'(p(\lambda))\theta^{J(p(\lambda))}/EJ(p(\lambda))\theta^{J(p(\lambda))}] \\ &= (-\theta(p(\lambda))\ln\theta(p(\lambda)))\psi(p(\lambda)). \end{aligned}$$

Then

$$\begin{aligned} \frac{\partial}{\partial p_0}\theta^{L^*(p(\lambda))} &= \theta^{L^*(p(\lambda))}\left(\frac{L^*(p(\lambda))}{\theta(p(\lambda))}\frac{\partial}{\partial p_0}\theta + \ln\theta\frac{\partial}{\partial p_0}L^*(p(\lambda))\right) \\ &= -L^*(p(\lambda))\theta^{L^*(p(\lambda))}\psi(p(\lambda))\ln\theta + L'^*(p(\lambda))\theta^{L^*(p(\lambda))}\ln\theta, \end{aligned}$$

and

$$\frac{\partial}{\partial p_0}\theta^{U^*} = U^*\theta^{U^*-1}\frac{\partial}{\partial p_0}\theta = -U^*\theta^{U^*}\psi(p(\lambda))\ln\theta.$$

Substituting into $N(p(\lambda))$ with a little algebra yields

$$N(p(\lambda)) = -(\theta^{U^*} - 1)L^*(p(\lambda))\theta^{L^*(p(\lambda))}\psi(p(\lambda)) \ln \theta$$
$$+ (1 - \theta^{L^*(p(\lambda))})U^*\theta^{U^*}\psi(p(\lambda)) \ln \theta$$
$$- (\theta^{U^*} - 1)L'^*(p(\lambda))\theta^{L^*(p(\lambda))} \ln \theta.$$

With $U = ky_0$ and $L = k^{-1}y_0$ it is easy to show that

$$\frac{U^*\theta^{U^*}}{1-\theta^{U^*}} < \frac{L(p(\lambda))\theta^{L^*(p(\lambda))}}{1-\theta^{L^*(p(\lambda))}}$$

and therefore

$$A = (1 - \theta^{L^*(p(\lambda))})U^*\theta^{u^*} > -(\theta^{U^*} - 1)L^*(p(\lambda))\theta^{L^*(p(\lambda))} = B.$$

We have, then, substituting B for A

$$N(p(\lambda)) > 2(1 - \theta^{U^*}) \ln \theta(L^*(p(\lambda))\theta^{L^*(p(\lambda))}\psi(p(\lambda)) + L'^*(p(\lambda))\theta^{L^*(p(\lambda))}) > 0$$

since J flexible at $p(\lambda)$ implies

$$L^*(p(\lambda))\theta^{L^*(p(\lambda))}\psi(p(\lambda)) + L'^*(p(\lambda))\theta^{L^*(p(\lambda))} < 0.$$

So

$$\frac{\partial}{\partial p_0}\beta^1 > 0.$$

With the same result for the lower bound and with $(d/d\lambda)p(\lambda) < 0$ we get (ii). □

The proof of the above lemma depends on the flexibility condition but not the requirement that the strategy be fractional Kelly. The significance of the fractional Kelly strategies is that the flexibility condition is always satisfied if it is satisfied for the Kelly strategy.

For the stopping rule profile $(\bar{\eta}^{-1}, \bar{\beta})$ we have along the fractional Kelly path growth increasing and security decreasing. The inverse of expected stopping time is a measure of growth since faster growth would imply getting to the target U sooner.

In summary, for each of the profile types we have the same type of behavior. The complementary measures, growth and security, move in opposite directions as we change the blend between the Kelly and cash strategies. This enables a continuous tradeoff between growth and security.

TRADEOFF THEOREM. *Suppose $p(\lambda)$ is a fractional Kelly strategy. Then for each profile there is an effective tradeoff between growth and security by varying λ, the tradeoff index.*

Additional theoretical results concerning these tradeoffs are presented in MacLean and Ziemba (1990).

Friedman (1982) seems to have first considered fractional Kelly strategies in the context of blackjack. His results are along the lines discussed in §4.1 below. Other references on fractional Kelly strategies are Gottlieb (1984); Ethier (1987); Li, MacLean and Ziemba (1990); and Wu and Ziemba (1990).

The tradeoff theorem in this section establishes the use of growth and security measures in determining an investment strategy. There are many possible tradeoffs depending upon the choice of measures and the parameters specified in these measures. Rather than further considering the preferred measures and tradeoff in theory, we will apply the concepts to some real world examples and explore the choice of investment decisions in practice.

4. Applications

The methods described in previous sections are now applied to a variety of well-known problems in gambling and investment. Rather than concentrating on the results in the tradeoff theorem, we will explore a variety of growth and security measures to see how interactively a satisfactory decision is achieved from both perspectives. In each case we emphasize a pair of measures (growth, security). There are a few points we should make about our approach to these applications. Satisfaction with a particular investment strategy will depend on many factors. The measures of performance we have described are helpful, but they are functions of *inputs* such as initial wealth, return distribution, and performance standards. We must vary those inputs in appropriate ways to see a decision rule under different scenarios. In cases where inputs are soft we may need many diverse scenarios.

Throughout the theory and examples we use fixed strategies. This is not to imply that the particular fixed strategy is used forever, but rather a statement that if all inputs remain constant we can predict the results from the fixed strategy. Of course, the inputs are dynamic and we would regularly (continuously) update the strategy and measures of performance based on new input data. This process is facilitated by easily computable measures.

4.1. *Blackjack*: (ϕ, β)

The game of blackjack seems to have evolved from several related card games in the 19th century. It became popular in World War I and has since reached enormous popularity. It is played by millions of people in casinos around the world. Billions of dollars are lost each year by people playing the game. A relatively small number of professionals and advanced amateurs, using various methods such as card counting, are able to beat the game. The object is to reach, or be close to, twenty-one with two or more cards. Scores above twenty-one are said to bust or lose. Cards two to ten are worth their face value, Jacks, Queens, and Kings are worth ten points and Aces are worth one or eleven at the player's choice. The game is called blackjack because an Ace and a ten-valued card was paid three for two and an additional bonus accrued if the two cards were the Ace of Spades and the Jack of Spades or Clubs. While this extra bonus has been dropped by current casinos, the name has stuck. Dealers normally play a fixed strategy of hit until

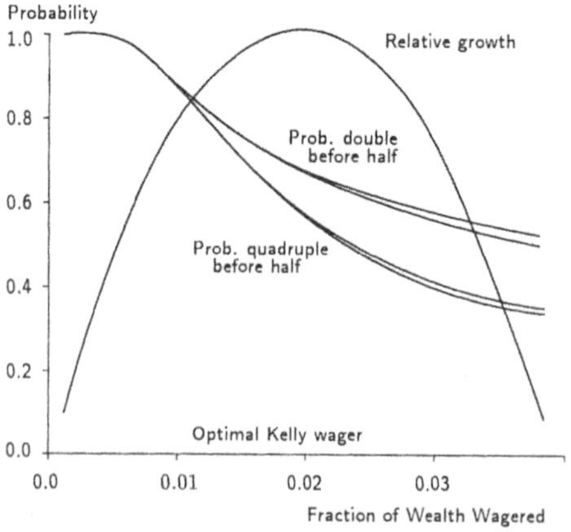

FIGURE 2. Probability of Doubling and Quadrupling before Halving and Relative Growth Rates Versus Fraction of Wealth Wagered for Blackjack (2% Advantage, $p = 0.51$ and $q = 0.49$).

TABLE 3

Growth Rates Versus Probability of Doubling before Halving for Blackjack

	λ		$\bar{\beta}(0, p)$ = P[Doubling before Halving]		$\phi(p)$ = Relative Growth Rate
Range for Blackjack Teams	0.1		0.999		0.19
	0.2		0.998		0.36
	0.3	↑	0.98	↑	0.51
	0.4	SAFER	0.94	LESS GROWTH	0.64
	0.5		0.89		0.75
	0.6	RISKIER	0.83	MORE GROWTH	0.84
	0.7	↓	0.78	↓	0.91
	0.8		0.74		0.96
	0.9		0.70		0.99
	1.0	KELLY	0.67		1.00
	1.5		0.56		0.75
Overkill → Too Risky	2.0		0.50		0.00

a seventeen is reached and then stay. A variation is whether or not a soft seventeen (an ace with cards totalling six) is hit. It is slightly better for the player if the dealer stands on soft seventeen. The house has an edge of 2–10% against typical players. For example, the strategy mimicking the dealer loses about 8% because the player must hit first and busts about 28% of the time ($0.28^2 \cong 0.08$).

In general, the edge for a successful card counter varies from about −10% to +10% depending upon the favorability of the deck. By wagering more in favorable situations and less or nothing when the deck is unfavorable, an average edge weighted by the size of the bet of about 2% is reasonable. Hence, an approximation that will provide us insight into the long-run behavior of a player's fortune is to simply assume that the game is a Bernoulli trial with a probability of success $\pi = 0.51$ and probability of loss $1 - \pi = 0.49$.

We then have $\Omega = \{0, 1\}$, $K(0, p) = p$ with probability π, and $K(1, p) = -p$ with probability $1 - \pi$. The mean growth rate is

$$E \ln(1 + K(\omega, p)) = \pi \ln(1 + p) + (1 - \pi) \ln(1 - p).$$

Simple calculus gives the optimal fixed fraction strategy: $p^* = 2\pi - 1$ if $EK > 0$; $p^* = 0$ if $EK \leq 0$. (This optimal strategy may be interpreted as the edge divided by the odds (1–1 in this case).) In general, for win or lose for two outcome situations where the size of the wager does not influence the odds, the same intuitive formula holds. Hence with a 2% edge betting on a 10–1 shot, the optimal wager is 0.2% of one's fortune.) The growth rate of the investor's fortune is

$$\phi(p) = \pi \ln(1 + p) + (1 - \pi) \ln(1 - p)$$

and this is shown in Figure 2. It is nearly symmetrical around $p^* = 0.02$. Security measure S3 is also displayed in Figure 2, in terms of the probability of doubling or quadrupling before halving. The bounds, from (5), are fairly sharp. Since the growth rate and the security are both decreasing for $p > p^*$, it follows that it is never advisable to wager more than p^*. However, one may wish to trade off lower growth for more security using a fractional Kelly strategy. Table 3 illustrates the relationship between the fraction λ and growth and security. For example, a drop from $p = 0.02$ to 0.01 for a 0.5 fractional Kelly strategy, drops the growth rate by 25%, but increases the chance of doubling before halving from 67% to 89%.

In the blackjack example we see how the additional information provided by the security measure $\beta(y_0, p)$ was valuable in reaching a final investment decision. In a flexible or adaptive decision environment, competing criteria would be balanced to achieve a satisfactory path of accumulated wealth. With this approach professional blackjack teams typically use a fractional Kelly wagering strategy with the fraction $\lambda = 0.2$ to 0.8. See Gottlieb (1985) for discussion including the use of adaptive strategies.

4.2. *Horseracing*: (μ_t, γ_t)

Suppose we have n horses entered in a race. Only the first three finishers have positive return to the bettor. For the remaining positions, you lose your bet. Then

$$\Omega = \{(1, 2, 3), \ldots, (i, j, k), \ldots, (n-2, n-1, n)\}$$

is the set of all outcomes with probability π_{ijk}. We wager the fractions p_{i1}, p_{i2}, p_{i3} of our fortune Y_0 on horse i to win, place, or show, respectively. One collects on a win bet only when the horse is first, on a place bet when the horse is first or second, and on a show bet when the horse is first, second, or third. The order of finish does not matter for place and show bets. The bettors, wagering on a particular horse, share the net pool in proportion to the amount wagered, once the original amount of the bets are refunded and the winning horses share the resulting profits. Let p be the $n \times 3$ matrix of wager fractions, where $\sum_{i=1}^{n} \sum_{j=1}^{3} p_{ij} \leq 1$. The return function for a particular (i, j, k) outcome is

$$K((i, j, k), p) = (QW - w_i)\frac{p_{i1}}{w_i} + \frac{(QP - P_i - P_j)}{2}\left(\frac{p_{i2}}{P_i} + \frac{p_{j2}}{P_j}\right)$$
$$+ \left(\frac{QS - S_i - S_j - S_k}{3}\right)\left(\frac{p_{i3}}{S_i} + \frac{p_{j3}}{S_j} + \frac{p_{k3}}{S_k}\right)$$
$$- \left(\sum_{l \neq i} p_{l1} + \sum_{l \neq i,j} p_{l2} + \sum_{l \neq i,j,k} p_{l3}\right),$$

where $Q = 1 -$ the track take, W_i, P_j and S_k are the total amounts bet to win, place, and show on the various horses, respectively, and $W = \sum W_i$, $P = \sum P_j$, $S = \sum S_k$.

As an example we will consider a simplified scheme where a wager is made on a single horse per race and there are five races occurring simultaneously across tracks (Hausch and Ziemba 1990). The required information on the races is given below. Each of the horses has an expected return on a \$1 bet of \$1.14, so this is a very favorable situation.

Race	Horse	Probability of Collecting on Wager	Odds
1	A	0.570	1–1
2	B	0.380	2–1
3	C	0.285	3–1
4	D	0.228	4–1
5	E	0.190	5–1

The Kelly strategy is

$$p^* = (p_0^*, p_1^*, p_2^*, p_3^*, p_4^*, p_5^*) = (0.8529, 0.0140, 0.0210, 0.0141, 0.0700, 0.0280).$$

So 1.4% of your fortune is bet on horse A in race 1. Using the growth measure $\mu_t(p)$ = mean accumulation of wealth, and the security measure $\gamma_t(p)$ = probability that accumulated wealth will exceed b_t, the Kelly strategy was compared to half Kelly and the fixed fraction strategies which bet 0.01, 0.05 and 0.10 respectively, distributed across

TABLE 4

$\gamma_t(Y_0, p)$ = Prob $Y_t(p)$ *Will Exceed* b_t (t = 700, Y_0 = 1000)

	Strategy − p				
				Proportional	
b_t	Kelly	0.5 Kelly	1%	5%	10%
500	0.940	0.992	1.000	0.915	0.518
1,000	0.892	0.961	0.980	0.856	0.517
5,000	0.713	0.691	0.061	0.631	0.358
10,000	0.603	0.445	0.003	0.512	0.304
100,000	0.231	0.028	0.000	0.148	0.141
$\mu_t(p)$*	$17,497	$8,670	$2,394	$10,464	$1,176

* The median is used here since $Y_t(p)$ is approximately log normal (skewed) (Ethier 1987).

horses in the proportions (0.1, 0.3, 0.3, 0.2, 0.1). These fixed fraction strategies are not fractional Kelly.

The results for $\mu_t(p)$ and $\gamma_t(p)$ are given in Table 4. The Kelly strategy with a 6% betting fraction and the 5% fixed fraction are similar, both having favorable growth and security. The smaller betting fractions provide slightly more security but have much less growth. Since the 10% strategy is beyond the Kelly fraction it has less growth and less security. An interesting point is that the total fraction bet is more significant than the distribution of the bets across the horses.

Implicit in the above example is the ability to identify races where there is a substantial edge in the bettor's favor. There has been considerable research into that question. Hausch et al. (1981) demonstrated the existence of anomalies in the place and show market. At thoroughbred racetracks about 2–4 profitable wagers with an edge of 10% or more exist on an average day. The profitable wagers occur mainly because: (1) the public has a distaste for the high probability-low payoff wagers that occur on short priced horses to place and show, and (2) the public's inability to properly evaluate the worth of place and show wagers because of their complexity—for example, in a ten-horse race there are 72 possible show finishes, each with a different payoff and chance of occurrence. In Hausch et al. (1981) and more fully in Hausch and Ziemba (1985) equations are developed that approximate the expected return and optimal Kelly wagers based on minimal amounts of data to make the edge operational in the limited time available at the track.

Ziemba and Hausch (1987) implement and discuss these ideas and explore various applications, extensions, simulations and results. A laymen's article discussing this appears in the May 1989 issue of *OMNI*. A survey of the academic literature on racetrack and other forms of sports betting is in Hausch and Ziemba (1992).

4.3. *Lotto Games*: (η, β)

Lotteries have been played since before the birth of Christ. Organizations and governments have long realized the enormous profits that can be made, based on the greed and hopes of the players. Lotteries tend to go through various periods of government control and when excessive abuses occur, they have often been shut down or outlawed, only to resurface later. Since 1964, there has been an unprecedented growth in lottery games in the United States and Canada. Current yearly sales are over thirty billion dollars, while net profits to various governmental bodies are well over ten billion dollars. Since the prizes are very large, the public cares little that the expected return per dollar wagered is only 40–50 cents. Typically, half the money goes to prizes, a sixth to expenses, and a third to profits. With such a low payback, it is exceedingly difficult to win at these games

TABLE 5
Lotto Games

		Case A		Case B	
Prizes	Probability of Winning	Prize	Contribution to Expected Value	Prize	Contribution to Expected Value
Jackpot	1/13,983,816	$6 M	42.9	$10 M	71.5
Bonus, 5/6⁺	1/2,330,636	$0.8	34.3	$1.2 M	51.5
5/6	1/55,492	M	9.0	$10,000	18.0
4/6	1/1,032	$5,000	14.5	$250	24.2
3/6	1/57	$150	17.6	$10	17.5
		$10			
			118.1		182.7
Edge			18.1%		82.7%
Optimal Kelly Bet			0.000,000,11		0.000,000,65
Optimal Number of Tickets Purchased per Draw with $10 M Bankroll			11		65

and the chances of winning any prize at all, let alone one of the big prizes, is very small. Is it possible to beat such a game with a scientific system? The only hope of winning is to wager on unpopular numbers in pari-mutuel lotto games. A lotto game is based on a small selection of numbers chosen by the players. Typically, games have forty to forty-nine numbers and you must choose five or six numbers. Management then draws the winning numbers and prizes typically accrue to those with three, four or more correctly matching numbers. By pari-mutuel, it is meant that the net pools for the various prizes are shared by those with winning tickets. Hence, if a small number of people, with so-called unpopular numbers, win a prize, it will be larger than if more people with popular numbers are sharing. Ziemba et al. (1986) investigated the Canadian 6/49, which played across the country, and other regional games. They found that numbers ending in nines and zeros and high numbers tended to be unpopular. Collections of unpopular numbers have a slight edge, a dollar wagered was worth more than a dollar on average, and this edge became fairly substantial when there was a large carryover. With a large carryover, that is, a jackpot pool that is steadily growing because the jackpot has not been won lately, the edge can be as high as 100% or more. Despite this promise, investors may still lose because of the very reasons that Chernoff found, essentially reverberation to the mean and gamblers ruin. Still, with such substantial edges, it is interesting to see how an investor might do playing such numbers over a long period of time.

Two realistic cases are developed in Table 5. Case A corresponds to the situation when the investor wagers only when there is a medium-sized carryover and the numbers that are drawn are quite unpopular. Case B corresponds to the situation where there is a huge carryover and the numbers drawn are the most unpopular. About one draw in every five to ten is similar to Case A and one draw in every twenty or more corresponds to Case B. Also, we have been generous in the suggested prizes. In short, we are giving the unpopular number system an at least fair chance to see if it has any hope of being a winning system in the long run. These cases correspond to the Canadian situation of paying the lotto winnings in cash up front tax free. The US situation of paying the lotto winnings over twenty years and taxing these winnings yields prizes with expected returns about one-third of those in Canada.

First we observe that the optimal Kelly wagers are miniscule. This is not surprising since for Case A, 77.2 cents of the $1.18 expected value and for Case B, $1.23 of the

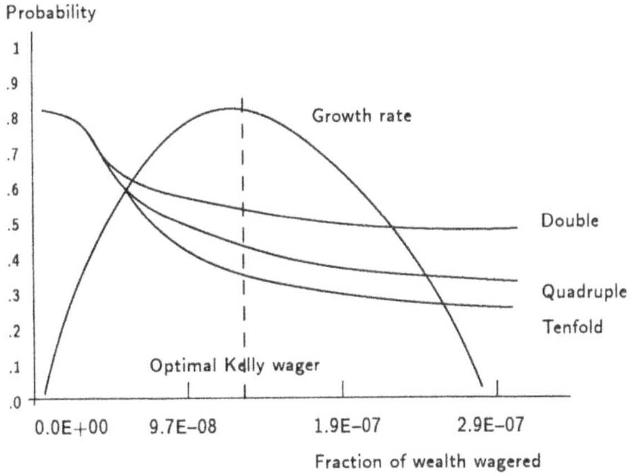

FIGURE 3. Probability of Doubling, Quadrupling and Tenfolding before Halving for Lotto 6/49, Case A.

$1.83 expected value, respectively, is composed of less than a one in a million chance of winning the jackpot or the bonus prize. One needs a bankroll of $1 million to justify even one $1 ticket for Case A and over $150,000 for Case B. If one had a bankroll of $10 million, the optimal Kelly wagers are just 11 and 65 $1 tickets respectively. Figures 3 and 4 show the chance that the investor will double, quadruple, or tenfold his fortune before it is halved, using Kelly and fractional Kelly strategies for Cases A and B respectively. For the Kelly strategies, these chances are 0.4 to 0.6 for Case A and 0.55 to 0.80 for Case B. With fractional Kelly strategies in the range of 0.00000004 and 0.00000025 or less, the chance of tenfolding one's initial fortune before halving it is 95% or more with Cases A and B respectively. This is encouraging, but it takes an average 294 and 55 billion

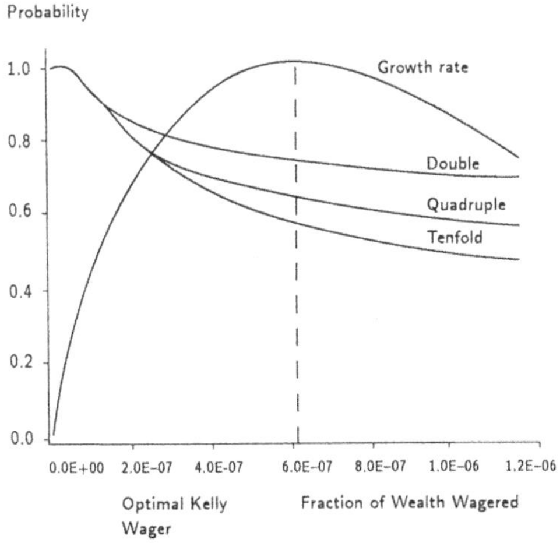

FIGURE 4. Probability of Doubling, Quadrupling and Tenfolding before Halving for Lotto 6/49, Case B.

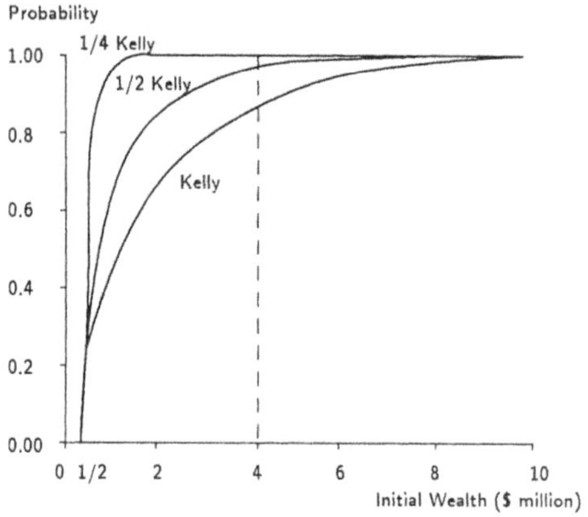

FIGURE 5. Probability of Reaching the Goal of \$10 Million before Falling to \$$\frac{1}{2}$ Million with Various Initial Wealth Levels for Kelly, $\frac{1}{2}$ Kelly and $\frac{1}{4}$ Kelly Wagering Strategies for Case A.

years, respectively, to achieve this goal. These calculations assume that there are 100 draws per year.

Figure 5 shows the probability of reaching \$10 million before falling to \$$\frac{1}{2}$ million for various initial wealth levels in the range \$$\frac{1}{2}$–\$10 million for Cases A and B with full Kelly, half Kelly and quarter Kelly wagering strategies. The results are encouraging to the millionaire lotto player especially with the smaller wagers. For example, starting with \$1 million there is over a 95% chance of achieving this goal with the quarter Kelly strategy for Cases A and B. Again, however, the time needed to do this is very long being 914 million years for Case A and 482 million years for Case B. More generally we have that Case A with full Kelly will take 22 million years, half Kelly 384 million years and quarter Kelly 915 million years. Case B with full Kelly will take 2.5 million years, half Kelly

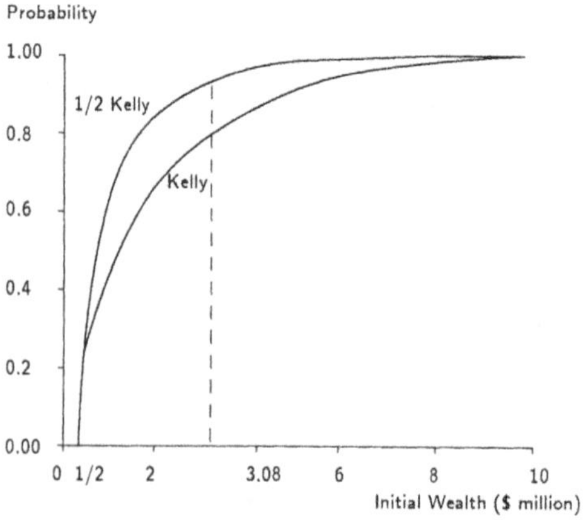

FIGURE 6. Probability of Reaching \$10 million before Falling to \$25,000 with Various Initial Wealth Levels for Kelly and $\frac{1}{2}$ Kelly Wagering Strategies for Case B.

19.3 million years and quarter Kelly 482 million years. It will take a lot less time to merely double one's fortune rather than tenfolding it, but it is still millions of years. For Case A it will take 4.6, 2.6 and 82.3 million years for full, half, and quarter Kelly, respectively. For Case B it will take 0.792, 2.6 and 12.7 million years for full, half and quarter Kelly.

Finally, we investigate the situation for the nonmillionaire wishing to become one. First, our aspiring gambler must pool his funds with some colleagues to get enough bankroll to proceed since at least $150,000 is needed for Case B and $1 million for Case A. Such a tactic is legal in Canada and in fact highly encouraged by the lottery corporations who supply legal forms for such an arrangement. For Case A, our player needs a pool of $1 million even if the group wagers only $1 per draw. Hence the situation is well modeled by Figure 5. Our aspiring millionaire "puts up" $100,000 along with nine other friends for the $1 million bankroll and when they reach $10 million each share is worth $1 million. The pool must play full Kelly and has a chance of success of nearly 50% before disbanding if they lose half their stake. Each participant does not need to put up the whole $100,000 at the start. Indeed, the cash outflow is easy to bankroll, namely 10 cents per week per participant. However, to have a 50% chance of reaching the $1 million goal each participant (and his heirs) must have $50,000 at risk. On average it will take 22 million years to achieve the goal.

The situation is improved for Case B players. First, the bankroll needed is about $154,000 since 65 tickets are purchased per draw for a $10 million wealth level. Suppose our aspiring nouveau riche is satisfied with $500,000 and is willing to put all but $25,000/2 or $12,500 of the $154,000 at risk. With one partner he can play half Kelly strategy and buy one ticket per Case B type draw. Figure 6 indicates that the probability of success is about 0.95. On average with initial wealth of $308,000 and full Kelly it will take $\frac{3}{4}$ million years to achieve this goal. With half Kelly it will take 2.7 million years and with quarter Kelly it will take 300 million years.

The conclusion then seems to be: millionaires who play lotto games can enhance their dynasties' long-run wealth provided their wagers are sufficiently small and made only when carryovers are reasonably large; and it is not possible for non-already-rich people, except in pooled syndicates, to use the unpopular numbers in a scientific way to beat the lotto and have confidence of becoming rich; moreover these aspiring millionaires are most likely going to be residing in a cemetery when their distant heir finally reaches the goal.

4.4. *Playing the Turn of the Year Effect with Index Futures:* (ϕ, β)

Ibbotson Associates (1986) have considered the actual returns received from investments in US assets with different levels of risk during the period 1926–1985. While small stocks outperformed common stocks by more than 4 to 1, in terms of the cumulative wealth levels, their advantage is totally in the last two decades and most of the gains are in the 1974+ bull market. These returns are before taxes so that the net return after taxes adjusted for inflation for the "riskless" investments and bonds may well be negative for many investors.

One way to invest in this anomaly in light of the Roll (1983) and Ritter (1988) results is to hold long positions in a small stock index and short positions in large stock indices, because the transaction costs are less than a tenth of that of trading the corresponding basket of securities. During the time of this study the March Value Line index was a geometric average of the prices of about 1,700 securities and emphasizes the small stocks while the S&P 500 is a value weighted index of 500 large stocks. Hence the VL/S&P special makes are long in small stocks and short in big stocks at the end of the year. Each point change in the index spread is worth $500. By January 15, the biggest gains are over and the risks increase. On average, the spread drops 0.92 points in this period with a

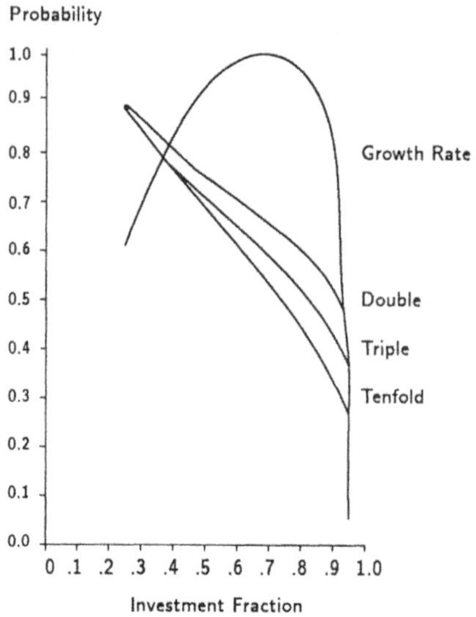

FIGURE 7. Turn of Year Effect: Relative Growth Rate and the Probability of Doubling, Tripling and Tenfolding before Halving for Various Fractional Kelly Strategies.

high variance. The projected gain from a successful trade is 0–5 points and averages 2.85 points or $1,342.50 per spread, assuming a commission of 1.5 × $55. On average, the December 15 to (−1) day gain on the spread, is 0.57 points. However, it was 1.05 in 1985 and 3.15 in 1986 which may reflect the fact that with the thin trading in the VL index, the market can be moved with a reasonably small number of players, who are learning about the success of this trade, i.e. the basis was bid up anticipating the January move. The average standard deviation of the VL/S&P spread was about 3.0. With a mean of 2.85 the following is an approximate return distribution for the trade:

Gain	7	6	5	4	3	2	1	0	−1
Probability	0.007	0.024	0.070	0.146	0.217	0.229	0.171	0.091	0.045

The optimal Kelly investment based on the return distribution is a shocking 74% of one's fortune! Such high wagers are typical for profitable situations with a small probability of loss. Given the uncertainty of the estimates involved and the volatility and margin requirements of the exchanges a much smaller wager is suggested.

Figure 7 displays the probability of doubling, tripling and tenfolding one's fortune before losing half of it, as well as the growth rates, for various fractional Kelly strategies. At fractional strategies of 25% or less the probability of tenfolding one's fortune before halving it exceeds 90% with a growth rate in excess of 50% of the maximal growth rate. Figure 8 gives the probability of reaching the distant goal of $10 million before ruining for Kelly, half Kelly and quarter Kelly strategies with wealth levels in the range of $0–$10 million. The results indicate that the quarter Kelly strategy seems very safe with a 99+% chance of achieving this goal.

These concepts were used in a $100,000 speculative account for a client of CARI Ltd., a Canadian investment management company. Five VL/S&P spreads were purchased to approximate a slightly less than 25% fractional Kelly strategy. Watching the market carefully, these were bought on December 17, 1986 at a spread of −22.18 which was

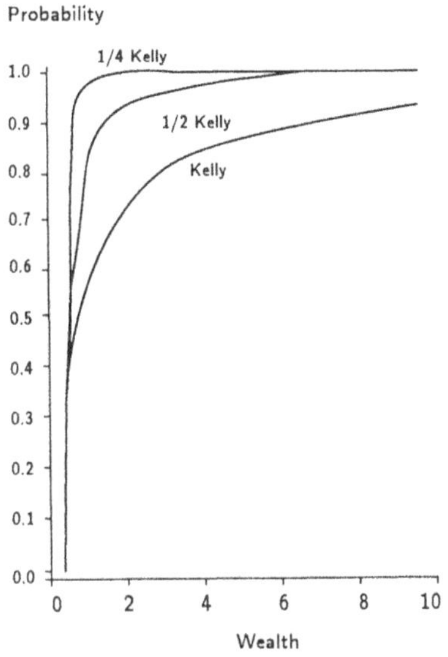

FIGURE 8. Turn of Year Effect: Probability of Reaching \$10 Million before Ruin for Kelly, $\frac{1}{2}$ Kelly and $\frac{1}{4}$ Kelly Strategies.

very close to the minimum that the spread traded at around December 15. The spread continued to gain and we cashed out at −16.47 on the 14th for a gain of 5.55 points per contract or \$14,278.50 after transactions costs.

A more detailed discussion of many of the issues in this section appears in Clark and Ziemba (1987), which was updated by Van der Cruyssen and Ziemba (1992a, b).[1]

[1] This research was partially supported by Natural Sciences and Engineering Research Council of Canada grants 5-87147 and A-3152 and by the U.S. National Science Foundation. Without implicating them we would like to thank T. Cover, S. Zenios, and the referees for helpful comments on earlier drafts of this paper.

References

ALGOET, P. H. AND T. M. COVER, "Asymptotic Optimality and Asymptotic Equipartition Properties at Log-optimum Investment," *Ann. Prob.*, 16 (1988), 876–898.

BELL, R. M., AND T. M. COVER, "Competitive Optimality of Logarithmic Investment," *Math. Oper. Res.*, 5, 2 (1980), 161-166.

BREIMAN, L., "Optimal Gambling System for Favorable Games," *Proc. 4th Berkeley Symposium on Math. Statistics and Prob.*, 1 (1961), 63–68.

CHERNOFF, H., "An Analysis of the Massachusetts Numbers Game," Technical Report No. 23, Department of Math., Massachusetts Institute of Technology, Cambridge, MA, 1980 shortened version published in *Math. Intelligence*, 3 (1981), 166–172.

CLARK, R. AND W. T. ZIEMBA, "Playing the Turn of the Year with Index Futures," *Oper. Res.*, 35 (1987), 799–813.

EPSTEIN, R. A., *The Theory of Gambling and Statistical Logic*, 2nd ed., Academic Press, New York, 1977.

ETHIER, S. N., "The Proportional Bettor's Fortune," *Proc. Seventh International Conf. on Gambling and Risk Taking*, Department of Economics, University of Nevada, Reno, NV, 1987.

———, AND S. TAVARÉ, "The Proportional Bettor's Return on Investment," *J. Appl. Prob.*, 20, 563–573.

FELLER, W., *An Introduction to Probability Theory and its Applications*, Vol. 1, 2d ed., John Wiley & Sons, New York, 1962.

FERGUSON, T. S., "Betting Systems which Minimize the Probability of Ruin," *J. Soc. Appl. Math.*, 13 (1965), 795–818.

FINKELSTEIN, M. AND R. WHITLEY, "Optimal Strategies for Repeated Games," *Adv. Appl. Prob.*, 13 (1981), 415–428.

FRIEDMAN, J., "Using the Kelly Criterion to Select Optimal Blackjack Bets," Mimeo, Stanford University, 1982.

GOTTLIEB, G., "An Optimal Betting Strategy for Repeated Games," Mimeo, New York University, 1984.

———, "An Analystic Derivation of Blackjack Win Rates," *Oper. Res.*, 33 (1985), 971–988.

GRIFFIN, P., "Different Measures of Win Rate for Optimal Proportional Betting," *Management Sci.*, 30, 12 (1985), 1540–1547.

HAKANSSON, N. H. "Capital Growth and the Mean-Variance Approach to Portfolio Selection," *J. Fin. Quant. Anal.*, 6 (1971a), 517–557.

———, "On Optimal Myopic Portfolio Policies With and Without Serial Correlation," *J. Business*, 44 (1971b), 324–334.

———, "Capital Growth and the Mean-Variance Approach to Portfolio Selection," *J. Fin. Quant. Anal.*, 6 (1971c), 517–557.

———, "Optimal Multi-Period Portfolio Policies," *Portfolio Theory, TIMS Studies in the Management Sciences*, Vol. 11, E. Elton and M. J. Gruber, Eds., North-Holland, Amsterdam, 1979.

——— AND B. L. MILLER, "Compound-Return Mean-Variance Efficient Portfolios Never Risk Ruin," *Management Sci.*, 22, 4 (1975), 391–400.

HAUSCH, D. AND W. T. ZIEMBA, "Transactions Costs, Extent of Inefficiencies, Entries and Multiple Wagers in a Racetrack Betting Model," *Management Sci.*, 31, 4 (1985), 381–392.

——— AND ———, "Arbitrage Strategies for Cross-Track Betting on Major Horse Races," *J. Business*, 63, 1 (1990), 61–78.

——— AND ———, "Efficiency of Sports and Lottery Betting Markets," In *New Palgrave Dictionary on Money and Finance*, J. Eatwell, P. Newman and M. Milgatel, Eds., Macmillan, London, 1992.

———, ——— AND M. RUBINSTEIN, "Efficiency of the Market for Racetrack Betting," *Management Sci.*, 27 (1981), 1435–1452.

IBBOTSON ASSOCIATES, *Stocks, Bonds, Bills and Inflation: Market Results for* 1926–1985, Ibbotson Associates, Chicago, IL, 1986.

KELLY, J., "A New Interpretation of Information Rate," *Bell System Technology J.*, 35 (1956), 917–926.

LI, Y., L. MACLEAN AND W. T. ZIEMBA, "Security Aspects of Optimal Growth Models with Minimum Expected Time Criteria," Mimeo, University of British Columbia, British Columbia, Canada, 1990.

MACLEAN, L. AND W. T. ZIEMBA, "Growth-Security Profiles in Capital Accumulation Under Risk," *Ann. Oper. Res.*, 31 (1990), 501–509.

RITTER, J. R., "The Buying and Selling Behavior of Individual Investors at the Turn of the Year: Evidence of Price Pressure Effects," *J. Finance*, 43 (1988), 701–719.

ROLL, R., "Was ist das? The Turn of the Year Effect and the Return Premia of Small Firms," *J. Portfolio Management*, 10 (1983), 18–28.

THORP, E. O., *Beat the Dealer*, 2d ed., Random House, New York, 1966.

———, "Portfolio Choice and the Kelly Criterion," In *Stochastic Optimization Models in Finance*, W. T. Ziemba and R. G. Vickson, Eds., Academic Press, New York, 1975.

VAN DER CRUYSSEN, B. AND W. T. ZIEMBA, "The Turn of the Year Effect," *Interfaces*, forthcoming (1992a).

——— AND ———, "Investing in the Turn of the Year Effect in the Futures Markets," *Interfaces*, forthcoming, (1992b).

WU, M. G. H. AND W. T. ZIEMBA, "Growth Versus Security Tradeoffs in Dynamic Investment Analysis," Mimeo, University of British Columbia, British Columbia, Canada, 1990.

ZIEMBA, W. T., "Security Market Inefficiencies: Strategies for Making Excess Profits in the Stock Market," TIMS Workshop on Investing in the Stock Market, 1986.

———, S. L. BRUMELLE, A. GAUTIER AND S. L. SCHWARTZ, *Dr. Z's 6/49 Lotto Guidebook*, Dr. Z Investments Inc., Vancouver, 1986.

——— AND D. B. HAUSCH, *Dr. Z's Beat the Racetrack*, William Morrow, New York (revised and expanded second edition of Ziemba-Hausch 1984), 1987.

——— AND ———, *Betting at the Racetrack*, Dr. Z Investments, Los Angeles, 1985.

Chapter 14

Time to wealth goals in capital accumulation[#]

LEONARD C. MacLEAN*†, WILLIAM T. ZIEMBA‡§ and YUMING LI¶

†School of Business Administration, Dalhousie University, Halifax, NS, Canada B3H 1Z5
‡Sauder School of Business, University of British Columbia, Vancouver, BC, Canada V6T 1Z2
§Department of Finance, Sloan School of Management, 50 Memorial Drive E52-410, Massachusetts Institute of Technology, Cambridge, MA 02142-1347, USA
¶School of Business, California State University, Fullerton, CA 92834, USA

(*Received 26 January 2004; in final form 15 April 2005*)

This paper considers the problem of investment of capital in risky assets in a dynamic capital market in continuous time. The model controls risk, and in particular the risk associated with errors in the estimation of asset returns. The framework for investment risk is a geometric Brownian motion model for asset prices, with random rates of return. The information filtration process and the capital allocation decisions are considered separately. The filtration is based on a Bayesian model for asset prices, and an (empirical) Bayes estimator for current price dynamics is developed from the price history. Given the conditional price dynamics, investors allocate wealth to achieve their financial goals efficiently over time. The price updating and wealth reallocations occur when control limits on the wealth process are attained. A Bayesian fractional Kelly strategy is optimal at each rebalancing, assuming that the risky assets are jointly lognormal distributed. The strategy minimizes the expected time to the upper wealth limit while maintaining a high probability of reaching that goal before falling to a lower wealth limit. The fractional Kelly strategy is a blend of the log-optimal portfolio and cash and is equivalently represented by a negative power utility function, under the multivariate lognormal distribution assumption. By rebalancing when control limits are reached, the wealth goals approach provides greater control over downside risk and upside growth. The wealth goals approach with random rebalancing times is compared to the expected utility approach with fixed rebalancing times in an asset allocation problem involving stocks, bonds, and cash.

Keywords: Capital accumulation; Wealth goals; Investment of capital

1. Introduction

In capital accumulation under uncertainty, a decision-maker must determine how much capital to invest in riskless and risky investment opportunities at each point in time. The investment strategy yields a stream of capital over time, with investment decisions made so that the distribution of wealth has desirable properties. An investment strategy which has generated considerable interest is the growth optimal or Kelly strategy, where the expected logarithm of wealth is maximized (Kelly 1956). The wealth distribution of this strategy has many attractive characteristics (see e.g. Hakansson 1970, 1971, Markowitz 1976, Hakansson and Ziemba 1995). As Breiman (1960, 1961), and Algoet and Cover (1988) have shown, the Kelly strategy maximizes the long run expected rate of growth of capital and minimizes the expected time to reach a fixed level of wealth for sufficiently large goals under mild conditions. Researchers such as Thorp (1975), Hausch *et al.* (1981), Grauer and Hakansson (1986, 1987), and Mulvey and Vladimirow (1992) have used the optimal growth strategy to compute optimal portfolio weights in multi-asset and worldwide asset allocation problems.

The literature considers the stream of capital following from an investment policy from either a wealth or a time perspective. In most situations the expected utility of accumulated capital at a fixed point in time is analysed. There is particular interest in the logarithm of accumulated capital, and the corresponding rate of capital growth. Alternatively, the growth rate can be viewed as the time it takes for accumulated capital to reach wealth milestones.

The distribution of accumulated capital to a fixed point in time and the distribution of the first passage

*Corresponding author. Email: lmaclean@mgmt.dal.ca

[#]This chapter was originally published in: MacLean, L. C., Ziemba, W. T. & Li, Y. (2005). Time to Wealth Goals in Capital Accumulation. *Quantitative Finance*, 5(4), 343–355.

time to a fixed level of accumulated capital are variables controlled by the investment decisions. The Kelly strategy maximizes the expected logarithm of accumulated capital or the expected growth rate. However, the strategy is very aggressive. As Hausch and Ziemba (1985) and Clark and Ziemba (1987) have demonstrated, the optimal portfolio weights in the risky assets given by this strategy tend to be so large for favourable investments that the chances of losing a substantial portion of wealth are very high, particularly if the probability estimates are in error. In the time domain, the chances are high that the first passage to subsistence wealth occurs before achieving the established wealth goals.

When the investor is more risk averse, then this can be reflected in the utility function choice. If the utility function has an Arrow–Pratt risk aversion parameter, e.g. the constant relative risk aversion (CRRA) utility, then the value of this parameter captures risk tolerance; see Kallberg and Ziemba (1983).

Another approach is to define a measure of risk which depends on the investment decision. A standard measure of risk is volatility as defined by the variance of wealth at a point in time or the variance of the passage time to a wealth target. Mean-variance analysis of wealth has been widely used to determine investment strategies; see Markowitz (1952, 1987). In the time domain the mean-variance approach yields different strategies. However, the logarithm of wealth and the first passage time have consistent mean-variance properties; see Burkhardt (1998).

An alternative to variance is to use a *downside risk measure* (Breitmeyer *et al.* 1999). MacLean *et al.* (1992) considered, as risk measures, quantiles for wealth, log-wealth and first passage time in identifying investment strategies which achieve capital growth with a required level of security. Security is defined as controlling downside risk. Growth is traded for security with fractional Kelly strategies. In discrete time models with general return distributions this strategy is generally suboptimal, but it has attractive wealth/time distribution properties. See MacLean and Ziemba (1999) for extensions of this research. The emphasis in that trade-off work is the properties of the wealth process for a given fraction. For example, the probability of reaching upper wealth U before lower wealth L is calculated for various strategies. In this paper, the reverse problem of finding a strategy which achieves a specified probability (risk) is studied.

The most common downside risk measure is Value at Risk (VaR) (Jorion 1997). VaR has been studied extensively (Artzner *et al.* 1999, Gaivoronski and Pflug 2005). Basak and Shapiro (2001) consider VaR in a model with CRRA utility. Although VaR is an industry standard it has weaknesses in controlling risk. The most serious shortcoming is the insensitivity to very large losses which have small probability—the essence of risk. Measures based on lower partial moments (incomplete means) such as CvaR (Rockafeller and Uryasev 2000) and convex risk measures based on target violations (Carino and Ziemba 1998, Rockafeller and Ziemba 2000) attempt to deal with this problem.

Similar to mean-variance, a variety of mean-risk problems have been studied. Bi-criteria problems such as maximizing expected logarithm of wealth subject to a VaR constraint are consistent with stochastic dominance, the traditional concept for ordering wealth distributions. (Ogryczak and Ruszczynski 2002).

There is, however, another issue complicating the measurement of risk and return, which is the estimation of parameters defining the returns distribution. The value of the risk/return measures in practice are estimates of the true values, and the error of the estimates of measures is very sensitive to errors in the estimation of the returns distribution. Furthermore, the sensitivity to estimation errors of expected value measures (mean, CVaR) is much greater than quantile measures (median, VaR).

In this paper parameter estimation and risk control are considered in a model where the filtration and control processes are separate. A dynamic stochastic model for asset prices is presented in section 2. The model is a generalization to the multi-asset case of the random coefficients model of Browne and Whitt (1996). The inclusion of many assets facilitates the estimation of model coefficients since the correlation between assets is related to the intrinsic model structure. The existence of latent factors generating price movements is implied by the equations for price dynamics. Alternatively, price parameters could be related to observable state variables, as is the case in the model of Xia (2001). (See also Brennan 1998)

Given the estimated price dynamics, an investment decision is made to control the path of future wealth. In section 3, an approach to control is developed based upon wealth levels as stopping rules. In practice, an investment portfolio cannot be continuously rebalanced and a realistic approach is to reconsider the investment decision at regular discrete time intervals (Rogers 2000). At each rebalance time, with additional data and a change in wealth, price parameters are re-estimated and a new investment strategy is developed. The process is illustrated in figure 1. The most significant aspect of the rebalancing is the accuracy of the estimated returns distribution. If forecasts are accurate, then wealth will accumulate as expected. If prices are not as forecast over the next hold interval then unacceptable wealth levels may result. To protect against that outcome *wealth limits* can be placed on the wealth process. If the wealth trajectory is within the limits, the wealth process is under control. However, the asset pricing model and the investment decisions are reconsidered when a control limit is reached. So rebalancing occurs at a random time rather than at a given point in time. Intervention occurs when the wealth trajectory is not proceeding as expected and it can be concluded that the investment decision does not fit the true securities price process.

Whether rebalancing occurs at fixed or random times, at the rebalancing the investor:

1. generates *new estimates* for returns distributions;
2. establishes *next wealth limits* for random time rebalancing, or the next *hold time* for the fixed rebalance interval;

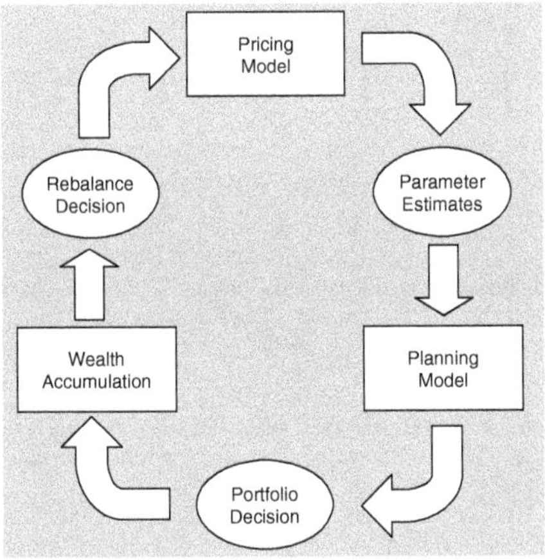

Figure 1. Dynamic investment process.

3. determines a *new investment strategy* based on the updated returns estimates, and control limits or hold time.

At a rebalance point, the decision on investment is based on accumulated wealth at a planning horizon. A number of bi-criteria decision models have been mentioned, but the model considered is maximization of expected utility at the horizon, with a negative power utility. It is significant that there exist wealth goals and an associated bi-criteria decision model which yields an identical investment strategy. Although demonstrated for the special case of negative power utility, this result is general, so that wealth goals reflect a wide range of preferences.

The wealth goals decision is put in the context of capital growth with security. So a strategy is determined which minimizes the expected time to the upper limit (*growth*) while maintaining a high probability of achieving the upper limit before falling to the lower limit (*security*). The optimal strategy for the power utility and growth–security models is shown to be *fractional Kelly*—a blend of the risk free (cash) strategy and the optimal growth strategy.

Although the negative power utility and wealth goals models are linked by the strategy, the approaches to risk are different. The expected utility model considers risk at the horizon, whereas the wealth goals model considers risk along the trajectory. In section 4, the wealth goals and power utility approaches are compared for the fundamental problem of investing in stocks, bonds, and cash over time. It is shown that there is an advantage from wealth goals, since rebalancing occurs at times indicated by the wealth trajectory, i.e. the wealth condition. This result is comparable to the superiority of condition based intervention in repairable systems (Aven and Jensen 1999). Appendix A contains proofs for propositions in the text.

2. Dynamic estimation of asset price distributions

In the dynamic investment process shown in figure 1, the returns on risky assets are re-estimated at the time of rebalancing a portfolio. The updated returns distributions are inputs to the investment decision models. In this section a linear pricing model is proposed where the estimation problem is separated from the control problem. The model is Bayesian, so that the updating of parameter estimates follows from Bayes theorem, and fits naturally into the dynamic investment process.

2.1. *Price model*

Suppose there are m risky assets, with $P_i(t)$ equal to the trading price of asset i at time t, $i=1,\dots,m$, and a riskless asset with rate of return r at time t. The risky asset prices are assumed to have a joint log-normal distribution. Letting $Y_i(t)=\ell n P_i(t)$, $i=0,\dots,m$, the price dynamics are defined by the stochastic differential equations

$$\begin{aligned} \mathrm{d}Y_0(t) &= r\,\mathrm{d}t, \\ \mathrm{d}Y_i(t) &= \alpha_i(t)\mathrm{d}t+\delta_i\,\mathrm{d}U_i, \quad i=1,\dots,m, \end{aligned} \tag{1}$$

where $\mathrm{d}U_i$, $i=1,\dots,m$, are independent standard Brownian motions. They represent the variation in price *specific* to each security. The other component of price variation is generated by the instantaneous mean rate of return $\alpha_i(t)$, $i=1,\dots,m$. Assume that $\alpha_i(t)$ is a random variable with distribution defined by

$$\alpha_i(t)=\mu_i+\gamma_i Z_i(t), \quad i=1,\dots,m. \tag{2}$$

The Z_i, $i=1,\dots,m$, are correlated Gaussian variables, with ρ_{ij} being the correlation between Z_i and Z_j. So the rates of return are correlated, with the covariance between $\alpha_i(t)$ and $\alpha_j(t)$ given by $\gamma_i\gamma_j\rho_{ij}$.

The price process defined by (1) and (2) is a variation on the Merton model (1992) with the condition that the rates α_i, $i=1,\dots,m$, are stochastic and the volatilities δ_i, $i=1,\dots,m$, are not stochastic. The intention is to emphasize uncertainty in the mean since errors in estimating the mean have by far the greatest impact on portfolio decisions (Chopra and Ziemba 1993). The asset prices in the model are correlated, with the correlation generated by the relationship between the random rates of return on assets. Presumably those rates of return are related through some *common factors*. The factors may be *latent*, as is assumed in this paper, or they may be observable state variables as presented by Xia (2001), who considers the single risky asset case.

If the model for prices is correct then the error in forecasting prices arises from errors in parameter estimates. Error from incorrect modeling may be confounded with estimation error, so attention to the correct model in an application may be significant. There are generalizations of (1) and (2) which can be incorporated into the approach developed in this section. For example, the rates of return could be defined by stochastic differential equations: $d\alpha_i(t) = \mu_i\,dt + \gamma_i\,dq_i$, where dq_i are correlated Brownian motions, $i = 1, \ldots, m$. Then $\alpha_i(t) = \alpha_i(0) + \mu_i t + \gamma_i\sqrt{t}Z_i(t)$, and the rates are dynamic. The assumption in (2) simplifies the presentation, so that formulation is followed, but reference to the dynamic linear model will be made where appropriate. With regard to the stationary process (2), *the model assumption applies until the next rebalance point*. That is, the distribution for the random rates is the same between rebalance points, but the distribution at the next point may change. The model in (2) can be considered as an approximation between rebalance points. When used with control limits, where rebalancing occurs when the actual prices depart from model forecasts, this is a useful approach.

From (1) and (2) the relevant distributions for asset prices follow. Let $Y(t) = (Y_1(t), \ldots, Y_m(t))'$, $\mu = (\mu_1, \ldots, \mu_m)'$, $\alpha = (\alpha_1, \ldots, \alpha_m)'$, $\Delta = \mathrm{diag}(\delta_1^2, \ldots, \delta_m^2)$, and $\Gamma = (\gamma_{ij})$, where $\gamma_{ij} = \gamma_i\gamma_j\rho_{ij}$

$$\text{(Prior)} \quad \alpha \sim N(\mu, \Gamma), \tag{3}$$

$$\text{(Conditional)} \quad (Y(t)|\alpha, \Delta) \sim N(\alpha t, t\Delta), \tag{4}$$

$$\text{(Marginal)} \quad Y(t) \sim N(\mu(t), \Sigma(t)), \tag{5}$$

where $\mu(t) = t\mu$ and $\Sigma(t) = t^2\Gamma + t\Delta = \Gamma(t) + \Delta(t)$.

The Bayesian pricing model defined by (3)–(5) has an alternative structural model representation. The prior covariance has a decomposition $\Gamma = \Lambda\Lambda'$, where Λ is an $m \times l$ matrix with $l \le m$. Consider the independent *latent factors* $F' = (F_1, \ldots, F_l)$, $F' \sim N(0, I)$, and the errors $\varepsilon'(t) = (\varepsilon_1(t), \ldots, \varepsilon_m(t))$, $\varepsilon'(t) \sim N(0, \Delta(t))$. Let $\Lambda(t) = t\Lambda$. Then the log prices at time t are

$$Y(t) = \mu(t) + \Lambda(t)F + \varepsilon(t). \tag{6}$$

From (6), $Y(t) \sim N(\mu(t), \Sigma(t))$, where $\Sigma(t) = \Lambda(t)\Lambda'(t) + \Delta(t)$. The relationship between prices is driven by underlying common factors which are unobserved. This manifests itself in rates of return, $\alpha = \mu + \Lambda F$, which are random.

The factor model in (6) has been the subject of numerous asset pricing studies, with the factors representing traded portfolio's in some cases (Campbell *et al.* 1997). Here, the factor model is used to define estimates for parameters in the inter-temporal pricing model of (1) and (2).

2.2. Bayes estimation

At the time an investor is rebalancing a portfolio, information is available on past realized securities prices. Consider the data available at time t, $\{Y(t), 0 \le s \le t\}$, and the corresponding filtration $F_t^Y = \sigma(Y(t), 0 \le s \le t)$, the σ-algebra generated by the process Y up to time t. Conditioned on the data, the distribution for the rate of return can be determined from Bayes theorem. That is,

$$\tilde{\alpha}(t) = \left(\alpha(t)|F_t^Y\right) \propto N(\hat{\alpha}(t), \hat{\Gamma}(t)), \tag{7}$$

where $\hat{\alpha}(t) = \mu(t) + (I - \Delta(t)\Sigma^{-1}(t))(\overline{Y}(t) - \mu(t))$, with

$$\overline{Y}(t) = \frac{1}{t}Y(t),$$

and

$$\hat{\Gamma}(t) = \frac{1}{t^2}\left(I - \Delta(t)\Sigma^{-1}(t)\right)\Delta(t).$$

The *Bayes estimate* for the rate of return $\alpha(t)$ is the conditional expectation $\hat{\alpha}(t) = E\tilde{\alpha}(t)$. This estimate is the minimum mean squared error forecast for the rate given the data. In the context of rebalancing, this is the planning value for α until the next decision time $t + \tau$ (when the stopping boundaries are reached or the fixed rebalance time occurs). Then, since no information is added in the hold interval, $E(\alpha(t)|F_t^Y) = E(E(\alpha(t)|F_{t+\tau}^Y)|F_t^Y)$, and the best estimate is $\hat{\alpha}(t)$ throughout the interval.

The Bayes estimate $\hat{\alpha}(t)$ has an appealing form. It is inherently dynamic, so that estimates can be updated as more information on prices is obtained. In particular, at the next rebalance time $t + \tau$, the posterior $\hat{\alpha}(t)$ becomes the next prior and Bayes theorem is used to update with the new information—$\overline{Y}(t + \tau)$. This approach is described in MacLean *et al.* (2004). There is another approach which emphasizes the current dynamics. The pricing model parameters (μ, Γ, Δ) are interpreted as values for the most recent rebalance cycle, and only data from that time interval is used in estimating the parameters. With control limits, the recent data contains information on a change in dynamics, and a change in prior parameters. The technique for implying the values for the prior parameters from data is empirical Bayes estimation.

To develop the estimation consider a rebalance interval $(0, t)$ and prices at the *discrete* times kt/n, $k = 0, \ldots, n$, with corresponding log prices $Y(k) := Y[(k/n)t]$. The change in log prices between times kt/n and $[(k+1)/n]t$ is $e(k) = Y(k) - Y(k-1)$, $k = 1, \ldots, n$. From the model equations

$$e(k) = \frac{t}{n}\alpha + \sqrt{\frac{t}{n}}\Delta^{1/2}Z, \quad k = 1, \ldots, n, \tag{8}$$

where $Z \sim N(0, I)$.

The increment vectors defined by (8) are independent and Gaussian for each k. The covariance matrix for each vector is

$$\Sigma_n(t) = \frac{t^2}{n^2}\Gamma + \frac{t}{n}\Delta = \Gamma_n(t) + \Delta_n(t),$$

and

$$\overline{Y}(t) = \frac{1}{n}\sum_{k=1}^{n} e(k)$$

Consider observed log prices on risky securities at the discrete time points: $\{Y_{ik}, i = 1, \ldots, m, k = 0, \ldots, n\}$. With $e_{ik} = Y_{ik} - Y_{i,k-1}$, the data on increments (first-order differences in log prices) are $\{e_{ik}, i = 1, \ldots, m, k = 1, \ldots, n\}$. Let the covariance matrix for the observed increments be S_m, the estimate of $\Sigma_n(t)$.

From the random effects model (8) the theoretical covariance is factored as $\Sigma_n(t) = \Gamma_n(t) + \Delta_n(t)$. If the rank $(\Gamma_n(t)) = l < m$, then the sample covariance matrix can be factored to produce estimates of $\Gamma_n(t)$ and $\Delta_n(t)$. In terms of the structural model for prices in (6), the assumption rank $(\Gamma_n(t)) = l < m$ is equivalent to the assumption *the number of latent factors l is strictly less than the number of risky assets m.*

Assuming $l < m$, a maximum likelihood factor analysis of S_{tn} with l factors will yield a *loading* matrix L_{tn} and a *specific error* matrix D_{tn}, where D_{tn} is diagonal. Since the number of factors is known, (L_{tn}, D_{tn}) is an efficient estimator of $(\Lambda_n(t), \Delta_n(t))$, with $\Lambda_n(t) = (t/n)\Lambda$ (Lawley and Maxwell 1971). Then $G_{tn} = L_{tn}L'_{tn}$ is an efficient estimator of $\Gamma_n(t)$.

The prior mean μ for the rates of return on securities in a rebalance interval needs to be estimated. If it is assumed that the rates have a *common prior mean*, i.e. $\mu_i = \mu, i = 1, \ldots, m$, then the overall mean $\bar{\bar{Y}}(t) = (1/I)\sum_{i=1}^{I} \bar{Y}_i(t)$ is an estimate of μ, where $\bar{Y}_i(t) = (1/t)Y_i(t)$. The assumption of a common value is consistent with a long run rate of return on securities. (Alternatively, securities in the same class could have a common mean, with differences between classes of securities.)

The discussion has identified estimates for all model parameters within a rebalance interval. The conditional distribution for securities prices can be estimated, and in particular the conditional mean rate of return for the next time interval can be forecast. Since the forecast is the Bayes formula with the prior parameters estimated from data it is an empirical Bayes estimate.

Proposition 1: *Let $Y_k, k = 0, \ldots, n$, be observations on the vector of log prices of risky assets at regular intervals of width t/n, with the statistics computed from first-order increments: S_{tn}, L_{tn}, D_{tn} and $\bar{\bar{Y}}_t$. Then $\hat{\Delta} = (n/t)D_{tn}$, $\hat{\Lambda} = (n/t)L_{tn}$ are estimates of the model parameters Δ and Λ, respectively. With $\hat{\Delta}(t) = t\hat{\Delta}, \hat{\Lambda}(t) = t\hat{\Lambda}$ and $S_t^* = \hat{\Lambda}(t)\hat{\Lambda}'(t) + \hat{\Delta}(t)$, an estimate for the conditional mean rate of return at time t is*

$$\hat{\alpha}_n(t) = \bar{\bar{Y}}(t) + (I - \hat{\Delta}(t)S_t^*)(\bar{Y}(t) - \bar{\bar{Y}}(t)) \tag{9}$$

Furthermore, the limit as $n \to \infty$ of $\hat{\alpha}_n(t)$ is $\hat{\alpha}(t)$.

The empirical Bayes estimate in (9) is a natural formulation given the proposed pricing model. If the model is correct then $\hat{\alpha}_n(t)$ has smaller mean squared error than well known estimates for the rate of return, such as the maximum likelihood estimate and the James–Stein estimate. If the model is correct but the number of latent factors is unknown, then there is additional estimation error from estimating that number. However, results from similar models indicate such error is small; see MacLean and Weldon (1996). If a dynamic model for rates, $\alpha_i(t) = \alpha_i(0) + \mu_i t + \gamma_i\sqrt{t}Z_i(t), i = 1, \ldots, I$, is the correct formulation then the approach described above can be modified to obtain empirical Bayes estimates for parameters. The modification involves calculating *second-order differences* to obtain a random effects model with iid second-order increments.

With this estimation procedure, an essential component of the dynamic investment process is in place. The next component, the planning model, will have the forecasts from the estimated model as inputs.

3. Portfolio planning models

Assuming that at a rebalance point the data has been filtered to obtain estimates for the parameters, the decision on how much capital to allocate to the various assets is now considered. The objective is to control the path of accumulated capital generated by the decision and the unfolding asset prices. The decision will be developed from the estimated price parameters whereas capital will accumulate from the true process. Of course, if the estimates used in computing a strategy are substantially in error, then the trajectory of wealth will not proceed as anticipated, but the trajectory may still be under control. At the rebalancing time t, there are estimates for the conditional rate of return $\hat{\alpha}(t)$, and the volatility $\hat{\Delta}(t)$, based on the methods of section 2. The forecast dynamics for the price process, conditional on the estimates for parameters, are

$$\mathrm{d}Y(t) = \hat{\alpha}(t)\mathrm{d}t + \hat{\Delta}^{1/2}(t)\mathrm{d}\hat{Z}, \tag{10}$$

where the innovations process $\mathrm{d}\hat{Z}$ is standard Brownian motion.

An investment strategy is a vector process

$$\{(x_0(t), X(t)), t \geq 0\} = \{x_0(t), (x_1(t), \ldots, x_m(t)), t \geq 0\}, \tag{11}$$

where $\sum_{i=0}^{m} x_i(t) = 1$ for any t, with $x_0(t)$ the investment in the risk-free asset. The proportions of wealth invested in the m risky assets are unconstrained since $x_0(t)$ can always be chosen, with borrowing or lending, to satisfy the budget constraint.

The forecast change in wealth from an investment decision $X(t)$ is determined by the conditional price process (10). Suppose the investor at time t has wealth $W(t)$ and let $\hat{\phi}_i(t) = \hat{\alpha}_i(t) + (1/2)\hat{\delta}_i^2(t)$, $i = 1, \ldots, m$. Then the forecast for the instantaneous change in wealth is

$$\mathrm{d}W(t) = \left[\sum_{i=1}^{m} x_i(t)(\hat{\phi}_i(t) - r) + r\right] W(t)\mathrm{d}t + W(t)\sum_{i=1}^{m} x_i(t)\hat{\delta}_i(t)\mathrm{d}Z_i, \tag{12}$$

where $\mathrm{d}Z_i$ is standard Brownian motion.

There is a *growth condition* which will be required of any *feasible* investment strategy:

$$X_t = \left\{X(t)\left|\left[\sum_{i=1}^{m} x_i(t)(\hat{\phi}_i(t) - r) + r - \frac{1}{2}\sum_{i=1}^{m} x_i^2(t)\hat{\delta}_i^2(t)\right] \geq 0\right.\right\}.$$

With a fixed mix strategy over the hold interval satisfying the growth condition, the forecast wealth process $W(\tau)$, $\tau \geq t$, defined by (12) follows geometric Brownian motion such that $W(\tau) \geq 0$.

To determine an investment decision which controls wealth, two approaches are considered. First, a model which considers preferences for wealth at the planning horizon is defined. The standard approach is to maximize expected utility at a planning horizon. Because of uncertainty in the parameters for the asset pricing model, parameters are re-estimated and decisions revised at regular intervals in time up to the horizon. In the second approach, the preferences at the horizon are used to develop wealth goals (limits). Then a wealth goals model is defined, which has an equivalent investment strategy. The contrast from the approaches comes from rebalancing times. The wealth goals approach involves a random hold interval, with stopping/rebalancing occurring when specified upper or lower wealth goals are reached.

The matching of preferences in the two approaches does not mean that the same fixed mix strategy is used for both models. The rebalance times are different, and therefore there are different parameter estimates used in the strategy calculation.

The link between the planning models is stochastic dominance. Wealth W_1 dominates wealth W_2 iff $Eu(W_1)$ is greater than or equal to $Eu(W_2)$, with strict inequality for at least one utility function $u \in U$. Orders of stochastic dominance are determined by classes of utilities. If $U_k = \{u|(-1)^{j-1}u^{(j)} \geq 0, j = 1, \ldots, k\}$, so that $U_1 \supset U_2 \supset \ldots$, then U_1 is the class of monotone utilities, U_2 the class of concave monotone utilities, …, and U_∞contains the CRRA utilities. Since the CRRA utilities are a limiting subset, they are a reasonable reference class.

There are alternative formulations of the various orders of stochastic dominance. In particular, first order is equivalent to dominance in the cumulative distribution of wealth. The wealth goals model will be defined on the distribution of wealth, and therefore is based on first-order dominance principles. However, it is a relaxation of first-order dominance in that it focuses on parts of the distribution in a bi-criteria problem.

3.1. Expected utility strategy with fixed rebalance times

Consider an investor whose objective is to maximize the expected utility of wealth at the end of a finite planning horizon T. To obtain an explicit solution we assume a constant relative risk aversion (CRRA) utility. The utility of wealth w is

$$U(w) = \frac{w^\beta}{\beta}, \quad \text{with } \beta < 1, \ \beta \neq 0.$$

At the current decision time, the parameters in the pricing model are estimated and an investment strategy is determined, conditional on those estimates. Consider the conditional CRRA wealth problem.

Definition 1: The conditional CRRA wealth problem at rebalance time t, with current wealth w_t, horizon T and estimated parameters $\hat{\alpha}(t), \hat{\Delta}(t)$, is to find the strategy $X(t) \in X_t$ which maximizes

$$E\left[\frac{W(T)^\beta}{\beta}\right],$$

where the forecast dynamics of wealth $W(t)$ are given by (12).

Proposition 2: *The optimal strategy for the conditional CRRA wealth problem is*

$$X^*(t) = \frac{1}{1-\beta}\hat{\Delta}^{-1}(t)(\hat{\phi}(t) - re). \tag{13}$$

As $\beta \to 0$ in definition 1 the utility is log and the efficient strategy is the benchmark optimal growth solution: $\tilde{X}(t) = \Delta^{-1}(\hat{\phi}(t) - re)$. The fraction $f = 1/(1-\beta)$ captures the aversion to risk (Pratt 1964). When $0 < \beta < 1$, the positive power utility case, the optimal portfolio invests more than the benchmark, with the over-investment financed through borrowing (levered strategies). Although the strategy $X^\beta(t), 0 < \beta < 1$, is optimal, it is problematic from the perspective of the distribution of terminal wealth $W(T)$. Let F_β be the distribution function for terminal wealth following strategy $X^\beta(t)$, with F_0 the terminal wealth distribution following the benchmark strategy. Distributions can be compared with the first-order stochastic dominance relation: F_{β_1}dominates F_{β_2} iff $F_{\beta_1}(w) \leq F_{\beta_2}(w)$ for $w \in R$ with strict inequality for some w.

Proposition 3: *The terminal wealth distribution F_0 for the benchmark portfolio first-order stochastically dominates the distribution F_β for $0 < \beta < 1$.*

This result provides a rationale for a restriction $\beta \leq 0$ to the negative power and log utility functions, and the resulting class of fractional Kelly strategies $p\tilde{X}(t)$, where $p \leq 1$. First-order stochastic dominance is defined on the class of all monotone utilities, of which the CRRA utility is a small subset. Imposing the first-order dominance condition on the fraction from a CRRA utility model is a restriction, but other work, where a risk constraint such as VaR is included in the expected CRRA utility model, has shown that levered strategies are excluded (Basak and Shapiro 2001).

The solution in (13) is independent of current wealth w_t and the planning horizon T.

The decision is sensitive to estimation and modeling error, and at regular intervals of width s model parameters are re-estimated using the empirical Bayes methodology.

The actual investment decision at times $t, t+s, \ldots,$ would change with the new estimates.

3.2. Wealth goals strategy and random rebalance times

The uncertainty in returns on investment, whether from natural variability, variability in underlying factors, or errors in estimation, is the motivation for strategies that control risk. In the conditional CRRA utility problem the risk associated with the forecast wealth at the horizon is controlled with the risk aversion parameter β, with the estimation risk controlled by regularly updating estimates for parameters. Updates are appropriate when there is evidence that current estimates are substantially in error. This concept of updating based on the gap between expected and actual processes suggests another way to control the wealth process. That is, to set control limits (or wealth goals), as is the practice in process control. The wealth goals are action levels so that the investment portfolio is rebalanced if either of the goals is reached. With wealth w_t at time t, the lower and upper wealth goals $\underline{w}_t$ and $\overline{w}_t$ are set, where $\underline{w}_t < w_t < \overline{w}_t$. If the investment strategy $X(t)$ is chosen, then the strategy is followed until either $\underline{w}_t$ or $\overline{w}_t$ is reached. At that point the portfolio is rebalanced. So new estimates are generated, new goals are set and a new strategy is chosen. Between rebalancing points a fixed mix strategy is followed. Information on prices is obtained between rebalance points, but it is only used when the accumulated information on actual prices signals that the forecasts for price movements are substantially in error, that is, when a control limit is reached.

The choice of wealth goals is an important component of the control process. Wealth goals can be an expression of preferences as naturally as a utility function. Our approach is to first consider the form of an investment strategy for *given wealth goals*, assuming the wealth goals are feasible, i.e. admit an investment strategy. Then a methodology for specifying goals based on expected utility is developed.

The risk and return characteristics of the wealth process have traditionally guided the choice of strategy $X(t)$. Within the wealth goals context, therefore:

(i) the chance of hitting the lower wealth goal should be small. That is, the *downside risk* should be controlled;
(ii) the upper wealth goal, the preferred target, should be reached as quickly as possible. That is, the *growth rate* of capital should be maximized.

To formalize downside risk in the wealth goals approach, consider

$T_w(X(t), w_t|\hat{\alpha}(t), \hat{\Delta}(t))$ = *first passage time to wealth w starting with wealth w_t at time t and following investment strategy $X(t)$, conditioned on the estimates for parameters at time t.*

Let the set of wealth goals be denoted by

$$B_t = \{b_t | b_t = (\underline{w}_t, \overline{w}_t), 0 < \underline{w}_t < w_t < \overline{w}_t\}.$$

For $b_t \in B_t$, downside risk for a strategy $X(t) \in X_t$ is measured by

$$\Re_{b_t}(X(t)) = \Pr\left[T_{\underline{w}}t\left(X(t), w_t|\alpha(t), \hat{\Delta}(t)\right) \leq T_{\overline{w}_t}\left(X(t), w_t|\hat{\alpha}(t), \hat{\Delta}(t)\right)\right]. \quad (14)$$

The risk is the probability the first passage time to $\underline{w}_t$ is smaller than the first passage time to $\overline{w}_t$.

Risk measures are associated with acceptance sets of capital accumulation paths (Artzner *et al.* 1999). Let $\Omega(X(t))$ be the set of all paths of $W(\tau), \tau \geq t$, and let $A(X(t))$ be the set of acceptable paths. If $A^c(X(t))$ is the complement, then the downside risk for $X(t)$ is $\Re(X(t)) = \sigma(A^c(X(t)))$. That is, the risk for a strategy is the probability measure of the unacceptable set of paths.

Desirable properties of risk measures have been considered in the literature. The following basic axioms for a *downside risk measure* are proposed in Breitmeyer *et al.* (1999).

A: (non-negativity) $\Re(X(t)) \geq 0$.
B: (normalization) If $A^c(X(t)) = \phi$, then $\Re(X(t)) = 0$.
C: (downside focus) If $A^c(X_1(t)) = A^c(X_2(t))$, then $\Re(X_1(t)) = \Re(X_2(t))$.
D: (monotonicity) If $A^c(X_1(t)) \subseteq A^c(X_2(t))$, then $\Re(X_1(t)) \leq \Re(X_2(t))$

Consider the measure in (14). From the growth condition defining feasible strategies, $X(t) \in X_t$, any path eventually reaches $\overline{w}_t$, and the *acceptance set* for the measure is defined as

$$A_{b_t}(X(t)) = \textit{paths of } W(\tau), \tau \geq t, \textit{ which reach } \overline{w}_t \textit{ before ever dropping to } \underline{w}_t.$$

Using this definition of acceptance sets, the risk measure defined in (14) satisfies axioms A–D.

With an appropriate risk measure defined in terms of wealth goals, risk can be controlled with a constraint on the measure. For control limits $b_t \in B_t$ and risk level $1-\gamma$, $0 \leq \gamma \leq 1$, feasible strategies $X(t) \in X_t$ are required to satisfy $\Re_{b_t}(X(t)) \leq 1-\gamma$.

The other characteristic of the wealth goals approach is the anticipation that the upper limit is reached as quickly as possible. With the expected time defined as

$$G_{b_t}(X(t)) = E\left\{T_{\overline{w}_t}(X(t), w_t|\hat{\alpha}(t), \hat{\Delta}(t))\right\}, \quad (15)$$

the objective is to minimize $G_{b_t}(X(t))$. Speed in the time domain is a growth measure. Suppose the random time to a fixed wealth goal $T_{\overline{w}_t}$ is mapped onto random wealth at a fixed time T by $W_T = \overline{w}_t \exp(T - T_{\overline{w}_t})$. Then, $E\{\ln W_T\} = [\ln \overline{w}_t + T] - E\{T_{\overline{w}_t}\}$. Minimizing the expected time to the wealth goal $\overline{w}_t$ is analogous to maximizing the expected log of wealth to the appropriate horizon T. The log optimal strategy maximizes the rate of growth of capital, so (15) is a capital growth criterion. With reference to first-order stochastic dominance, the expected log of wealth is equivalent to the median wealth, since wealth is lognormal.

With the risk-return characteristics specified by (14) and (15), a *Growth–Security* decision model can be defined. Security is the complement of risk, that is, $S_{b_t}(X(t)) = 1 - \Re_{b_t}(X(t))$.

Definition 2: For given control limits $b_t \in B_t$ and risk level $1-\gamma, 0 \leq \gamma \leq 1$, and estimates $\hat{\alpha}(t), \hat{\Delta}(t)$, the conditional Growth–Security strategy $X(t)$ is determined from the problem

$$\text{Minimize } \left\{G_{b_t}(X(t)) | S_{b_t}(X(t)) \geq \gamma, X(t) \in X_t\right\}. \quad (16)$$

Explicit expressions for the optimal solution to (16) will be developed for the geometric Brownian motion model. Consider the wealth process $W(\tau), \tau \geq t$, with forecast dynamics given by (12). Let

$$\psi_t(X(t)) = \sum_{i=1}^{m} x_i(t)(\hat{\phi}_i(t) - r) + r,$$

$$\sigma_t^2(X(t)) = \sum_{i=1}^{m} x_i^2(t)\delta_i^2(t), \varphi_t(X(t)) = 2\psi_t(X(t)) - \sigma_t^2(X(t)),$$

and

$$\theta_t(X(t)) = \frac{\varphi_t(X(t))}{\sigma_t^2(X(t))}.$$

The measures $G_{b_t}(X(t))$ and $S_{b_t}(X(t)) = 1 - \Re_{b_t}(X(t))$ for geometric Brownian motion are given by Karlin and Taylor (1981):

$$G_{b_t}(X(t)) = \frac{2\ln(\overline{w}_t/w_t)}{\varphi_t(X(t))}, \tag{17}$$

$$S_{b_t}(X(t)) = \frac{\left[1 - (\underline{w}_t/w_t)^{\theta_t(X(t))}\right]}{\left[1 - (\underline{w}_t/\overline{w}_t)^{\theta_t(X(t))}\right]}. \tag{18}$$

These expressions define growth and security in terms of the estimated parameters of the returns distribution and the control limits. Therefore, the growth–security strategy from (16) can be related to those inputs.

Proposition 4: *Suppose at rebalance time t, the investor has wealth w_t, parameter estimates $\hat{\alpha}(t), \hat{\Delta}(t)$, and the return on the risk-free asset is r. If control limits (wealth goals) are $b_t \in B_t$ and the risk level is $1-\gamma$, then the conditional growth–security efficient strategy at time t is $X_{b_t}^*(t) = (x_{1b_t}^*(t), \ldots, x_{mb_t}^*(t))'$ with*

$$X_{b_t}^*(t) = p_t(w_t, b_t, \gamma)\hat{\Delta}^{-1}(t)(\hat{\phi}(t) - re), \tag{19}$$

where e is a vector of ones.

The expression in (19) reveals the approach to risk control with wealth goals. The component $\tilde{X}(t) = \hat{\Delta}^{-1}(t)(\hat{\phi}(t) - re)$ is the *optimal growth* portfolio (Merton 1992), or the *Kelly strategy* (Kelly 1956) or the benchmark portfolio (Basak and Shapiro 2001). The function $p_t(w_t, b_t, \gamma)$ defines a fraction invested in the risky assets that depends on current wealth, wealth goals, and risk level. Hence, the strategy which is growth–security efficient is *fractional Kelly*, as is the case for CRRA utility. An expression for the investment fraction follows from proposition 4.

Corollory 1: *For wealth goals $b_t \in B_t$, the fraction of wealth invested in risky assets at the rebalancing time t is* $\min\{1, p_t\}$ for

$$p_t(w_t, b_t, \gamma) = h_t \cdot H_t(\tilde{X}(t)) + \sqrt{[h_t \cdot H_t(\tilde{X}(t))]^2 + \frac{2rh_t}{\sigma_t^2(\tilde{X}(t))}}, \tag{20}$$

where

$$H_t(\tilde{X}(t)) = \frac{[\psi_t(\tilde{X}(t)) - r]}{\sigma_t^2(\tilde{X}(t))},$$

$$h_t = \frac{[\log w_t - \log \underline{w}_t]}{[\log w_t - \log \underline{w}_t - \log y^*]},$$

and y^* is the minimum positive root of $\gamma y^{c+1} - y + (1-\gamma) = 0$ for

$$c_t = \frac{[\log \overline{w}_t - \log w_t]}{[\log w_t - \log \underline{w}_t]}.$$

The solutions to the conditional CRRA problem and the conditional G–S problem apply to one stage in the multistage investment process. Although the form of the solutions is fractional Kelly for both problems, there are differences. The CRRA solution is independent of current wealth and the planning horizon. The G–S solution depends on the current wealth and the horizon through the wealth goals. Both solutions depend on the estimates for price parameters.

3.3. *Wealth goals*

The dynamic investment process of figure 1 is almost complete. However, the specification of wealth goals in the G–S approach has not been addressed. The purpose in rebalancing is to develop a new investment policy when the current policy is not working. The method for determining goals in this analysis is based on preferences for wealth at the planning horizon as defined by the CRRA utility. A technique of *matched* strategies, which replicates the wealth preferences at the horizon, provides a fair comparison of the accumulated wealth for the contrasting models. That is, if expected utility is the standard, then performance of the G–S problem relative to that standard is studied. It is important to realize that the matching technique can be implemented with other standard problems. The wealth goals can be important milestones without reference to other problems.

Consider choices for β and $b_t = (\underline{w}_t, \overline{w}_t)$ which produce the same strategy, that is $p_t(w_t, b_t, \gamma) = 1/(1-\beta)$. From the definition of $p_t(w_t, b_t, \gamma)$, there are potentially many combinations of goals which are linked to the same β. Since the expected utility fraction invested in the benchmark portfolio is independent of current wealth, whereas the process control fraction depends on the current wealth w_t and the probability γ, the values w_t and γ will be fixed, and the $\beta \rightarrow b_t$ link explored. Consider, then, the conditional β-class of goals, with $w_t = w_t^0, \gamma = \gamma^0$

$$B_t^0(\beta) = \left\{b_t \middle| p_t(w_t^0, b_t, \gamma^0) = \frac{1}{1-\beta}\right\}. \tag{21}$$

The set $B_t^0(\beta) \subseteq B_t$ defines wealth goals with the same Arrow–Pratt relative risk aversion given the current wealth w_t^0 and risk probability γ^0. Proposition 5 establishes that such goals actually exist.

Proposition 5: *At the rebalance time t consider current wealth w_t^0, risk probability γ^0 and risk aversion* *parameter β. Assume that the benchmark portfolio satisfies the growth condition, i.e.*

$$\frac{\psi_t(\tilde{X}(t))}{\sigma_t^2(\tilde{X}(t))} > \frac{1}{2}.$$

Then $B_\tau^0(\beta)$ is non-empty for $\beta < 0$.

Consider the following *matching heuristic* for setting wealth goals at any rebalancing time τ:

1. $\overline{w}_\tau^* = E(W^{EU}(\tau + s))$ is the expected wealth at time $\tau + s$ with the CRRA strategy

$$X^*(\tau) = \frac{1}{(1-\beta)}\tilde{X}(\tau).$$

2. $\underline{w}_\tau^* = \max\{\underline{w}_\tau | b_\tau \in B_\tau^0(\beta)\}$.

Setting goals at $b_\tau^* = (\underline{w}_\tau^*, \overline{w}_\tau^*)$ maintains the investment fraction at $p_\tau = 1/(1-\beta)$ for any rebalancing time τ, and links the goals to the holding time s.

4. Comparisons

The accumulated capital from the wealth goals with random rebalancing times, and expected utility with fixed rebalancing times is now analysed for the fundamental problem of allocating investment capital to stocks, bonds and cash over time. The matching heuristic approach is used to insure the problems are comparable, with the main difference being rebalancing time.

Daily prices for stocks and bonds are simulated using the dynamic pricing model, discretized to days. If $P_i(t)$ is the price for asset i on day t, where $i=0$ (cash), 1 (stock), and 2 (bonds), then consider the increments $e_i(t) = \ln P_i(t+1) - \ln P_i(t)$, $i = 0, 1, 2$. From the model, $e_i(t) = \alpha_i + \delta_i Z_i(t)$, where $Z_i(t)$ are independent Gaussian variables. For cash returns, $\alpha_0 = \ln(1+r)$. It is assumed that (α_1, α_2) are Gaussian variables dependent on a single latent state variable. So $\alpha_i = \mu + \lambda_i F, i = 1, 2$, with F standard Gaussian. There is a simple structure to model parameters in this single factor case. If the covariance for risky asset log prices is Σ, The model implies $\Sigma = \Lambda\Lambda' + \Delta$, where $\Lambda = (\lambda_1, \lambda_2)'$ and $\Delta = \mathrm{diag}(\delta_1^2, \delta_2^2)$. The factor solution is

$$\Lambda = (\sqrt{\rho}\sigma_{11}, \sqrt{\rho}\sigma_{22})',$$
$$\Delta = \mathrm{diag}((1-|\rho|)\sigma_{11}^2, (1-|\rho|)\sigma_{22}^2),$$
$$\rho = \frac{\sigma_{12}}{\sigma_{11}\sigma_{22}}.$$

If the true covariance is known, then model parameters are specified and daily prices can be simulated. Conversely, if a sample covariance matrix is determined from a sequence of prices then the parameter values can be estimated using these equations. The estimates are empirical Bayes, based on the methods in section 2.

For the simulation of asset prices, data on yearly asset returns corresponding to the S&P500, Solomon Brothers bond index, and U.S. T-bills for 1980–1990 were used to generate seed parameters. Statistics on the associated

Table 1. Daily rates of return.

	Stocks	Bonds	Cash
Mean	0.00050	0.00031	0.00019
Variance	0.00062	0.00035	0
Covariance	0.00014		

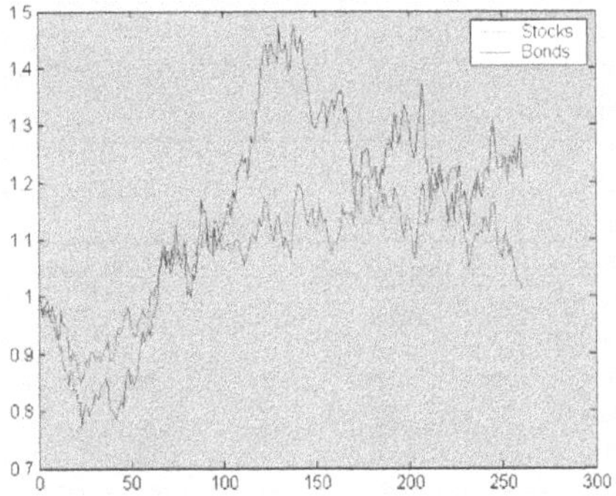

Figure 2. Daily prices for stocks and bonds.

daily returns are in table 1. The corresponding statistics for log-rates were used as seeds.

Daily prices were generated for one year (260 trading days) and this was repeated 200 times. The one year horizon is appropriate for the simulation since it provides sufficient time for differentiation of capital accumulation from the PC and EU strategies. The contrasting approaches to selecting an investment strategy were applied to each trajectory of prices. Initial parameter estimates were taken from average daily returns for the prior year, 1979. For expected utility, rebalancing (revising estimates of price model parameters; calculating new strategy) was done every 30 days. For process control, rebalancing occurs when control limits are reached. The estimation is based on the covariance matrix. To increase stability the covariance analysed at the jth rebalancing at time t is

$$\tilde{S}_j = \frac{t}{260}S_j + \frac{1-t}{260}\tilde{S}_{j-1}.$$

As time increases the updating is weighted to the observed covariance S. The procedure for setting limits (wealth goals) is described in section 4, where the process control fraction is maintained at $p_\tau = 1/(1-\beta)$.

The expected utility and wealth goals (process control) methods are shown for the trajectory of prices in figure 2. This trajectory has a volatile return on stock and is a useful example.

The expected utility strategies and portfolio values for the setting $1 - \beta = 1.1$ are given in table 2. The rebalancing occurred at 30 day intervals. The strategy emphasizes stocks and is quite stable. The return on the portfolio at the end of the year was 24%.

Table 2. Expected utility performance.

Time	Strategy		
	Stocks	Bonds	Port value
1	0.4670	0.1465	1
31	0.7439	−0.1319	0.8943
61	0.8688	−0.1770	0.9930
91	0.8963	−0.2292	1.1287
121	0.9701	−0.4437	1.4089
151	0.9432	−0.4726	1.3114
181	0.9864	−0.4900	1.2164
211	1.0125	−0.4181	1.1508
241	0.9820	−0.3989	1.2178

Table 3. Wealth goals performance.

Time	Strategy			Wealth limits	
	Stocks	Bonds	Port value	Upper	Lower
1	0.4670	0.1465	1	1.0112	0.5765
64	0.5805	0.1140	1.0148	1.0281	0.5309
65	0.6346	0.1010	1.0379	1.0526	0.5212
66	0.6656	0.0910	1.0562	1.0717	0.5196
67	0.6744	0.0864	1.0787	1.0946	0.5301
74	0.6804	0.0898	1.1065	1.1229	0.5427
88	0.7106	0.0671	1.1433	1.1615	0.5385
107	0.7566	−0.0011	1.1644	1.1844	0.5231
108	0.7889	−0.0509	1.1910	1.2127	0.5177
115	0.7995	−0.0936	1.2375	1.2603	0.5351
118	0.8060	−0.1302	1.2771	1.3006	0.5514
120	0.8089	−0.1571	1.3387	1.3634	0.5779
123	0.8242	−0.1957	1.3640	1.3898	0.5798
130	0.7864	−0.2152	1.4043	1.4290	0.6234

The process control methodology was run on the same trajectory, with settings $1-\beta = 1.1, 1-\gamma = 0.03$. Those results are presented in table 3. There is initially more frequent rebalancing with wealth goals, because of the volatility. When prices settle down, the fixed mix strategy does not change. The return at the end of the year was 42%. It is noteworthy that the return was monotone and the advantage of the PC strategy increases with time.

The comparison of the expected utility and process control approaches is the *expected wealth ratio* at the end of the year. The wealth ratio for each trajectory is the accumulated wealth with the process control strategy divided by the accumulated wealth with the expected utility strategy.

Table 4 presents mean wealth ratios for values for the CRRA utility parameter β, and the process control risk probability $1-\gamma$. The levered strategies $(0<\beta<1)$ are included, although those strategies are not growth–security efficient.

The wealth goals (process control) approach has a substantial advantage over expected utility, demonstrating the effect of accounting for current wealth (at the control limit) in determining a strategy. Since the PC strategy is determined (matched) from the EU strategy, the expected wealth advantage of being less risk averse (decreasing $1-\beta$) is embedded in the PC strategy, but the PC advantage over EU grows since the volatility is controlled by the upper and lower limits. As the security requirement is relaxed (γ decreasing) the expected wealth advantage for PC decreases. This results from the specific construction of the strategy, where the lower control limit drops with decreased γ and given upper control limit.

Table 4. Expected wealth ratios.

$1-\beta$	$1-\gamma$				
	0.01	0.02	0.03	0.04	0.05
1.15	1.291	1.290	1.289	1.265	1.264
1.10	1.322	1.321	1.320	1.298	1.293
1.05	1.365	1.364	1.359	1.340	1.337
1.00	1.410	1.408	1.403	1.384	1.381
0.95	1.460	1.459	1.457	1.443	1.433
0.90	1.523	1.522	1.520	1.507	1.491
0.85	1.608	1.608	1.607	1.602	1.584

The cases where $(1-\beta)<1$, the levered strategies, are high risk and are stochastically dominated as established in Proposition 4.

5. Conclusion

This paper considers the risk to accumulated capital in a multi-asset investment problem where the distribution of asset prices has random parameters. The basis for investment strategies is either process control, where wealth is controlled by upper and lower goals, or expected utility of terminal wealth at the horizon. In the process control approach, the portfolio is re-balanced when either wealth goal is reached.

At a re-balancing time the history of asset prices is used to update the conditional price distribution. An empirical Bayes estimator of distribution parameters is defined based on the observed correlation structure of asset prices. With the revised price distribution, new upper and lower wealth goals or the next re-balance time are selected and a new optimal strategy is derived. The process control strategy is growth–security efficient in the sense that it has maximum growth among strategies with a specified level of risk. Assuming a lognormal distribution for asset returns, the growth–security strategy is a blend of the risk-free portfolio and the optimal growth portfolio.

The wealth goals approach and the expected utility approach with constant relative risk aversion are compared. An equivalence between the wealth goals and the risk aversion parameter is developed. Although the alternative models have the same portfolio solution with the appropriate choices of parameter values, the wealth goals approach has the advantage of a direct control of downside risk and a re-balancing of the portfolio based on significant change in the price process and change in wealth. The benefit of intervening when the condition of wealth deviates from expectations rather than at regular intervals in time is clear. Re-balancing at specified points in time when wealth is proceeding as expected is analogous to *tampering* in process control, and typically introduces extra risk.

Acknowledgements

This work was presented at the Bachelier World Congress 2002, and seminars at The University of British Columbia and Dalhousie University. The authors wish to thank Yonggan Zhao for assistance with the computations. This research was supported by grants from the Natural Sciences and Engineering Research Council of Canada and the National Center of Competence in Research FINRISK, Swiss National Foundation.

Appendix A

This appendix contains proofs for the propositions in the paper.

Proposition 2: *The optimal strategy for the CRRA wealth problem is given by*

$$X^*(t) = \frac{1}{1-\beta}\hat{\Delta}^{-1}(t)(\hat{\phi}(t) - re). \tag{13}$$

Proof: The analysis is similar to theorem 6.2 in Janecek (1998). For investment strategy $X(t)$ the forecast dynamics of wealth are

$$dW(t) = \left[\sum_{i=1}^{m} x_i(t)(\hat{\phi}_i(t) - r) + r\right] W(t)\mathrm{d}t + W(t)\sum_{i=1}^{m} x_i(t)\hat{\delta}_i(t)\mathrm{d}Z_i.$$

With $X(\tau) = X(t)$ and $\hat{\phi}_i(\tau) = \hat{\phi}_i(t), \tau \geq t$, based on information to time t, integration from t to T gives the forecast wealth at the horizon

$$\hat{W}(T-t) = w_t \exp\left\{\left[\sum_{i=1}^{m} x_i(t)(\hat{\phi}_i(t) - r) + r - \frac{1}{2}\sum_{i=1}^{m} x_i^2(t)\hat{\delta}_i^2(t)\right] \times (T-t) + (T-t)^{1/2}\sum_{i=1}^{m} x_i(t)\hat{\delta}_i(t)Z_i\right\},$$

where $Z_i \sim N(0,1)$. The expected utility of wealth is

$$E\left[\frac{\hat{W}^\beta(T-t)}{\beta}\right] = \frac{1}{\beta}\left[w_t^\beta \exp\left\{\left[\sum_{i=1}^{m} x_i(t)(\hat{\phi}_i(t) - r) + r - \frac{1}{2}\sum_{i=1}^{m} x_i^2(t)\hat{\delta}_i^2(t)\right](T-t)\beta\right\}. E\exp\left\{\beta(T-t)^{1/2}\sum_{i=1}^{m} x_i(t)\hat{\delta}_i(t)Z_i\right\}\right].$$

Consider the expression

$$E\exp\left\{\beta(T-t)^{1/2}\sum_{i=1}^{m} x_i(t)\hat{\delta}_i(t)Z_i\right\} = \exp\left\{\frac{1}{2}\beta^2(T-t)\sum_{i=1}^{m} x_i^2(t)\hat{\delta}_i^2(t)\right\}.$$

Then

$$E\left[\frac{\hat{W}^\beta(T-t)}{\beta}\right] = \frac{1}{\beta}\left[w_t^\beta \exp\left\{(T-t)\beta\left[\sum_{i=1}^{m} x_i(t)(\hat{\phi}_i(t) - r) + r - \frac{1}{2}(1-\beta)\sum_{i=1}^{m} x_i^2(t)\hat{\delta}_i^2(t)\right]\right\}\right].$$

The first-order conditions

$$\frac{\partial}{\partial x_i(t)} E\left(\frac{\hat{W}^\beta(T-t)}{\beta}\right) = 0$$

reduce to

$$(\hat{\phi}_i(t) - r) - (1-\beta)x_i^*(t)\hat{\delta}_i(t) = 0, \quad i = 1, \ldots, I,$$

and $X^*(t)$ is as stated. □

Proposition 3: *The terminal wealth distribution F_0 for the benchmark portfolio first-order stochastically dominates the distribution F_β* for $0 < \beta < 1$.

Proof: Let $\psi(\tilde{X})$ and $\sigma(\tilde{X})$ be the instantaneous mean rate of return and standard deviation, respectively, of the optimal growth (benchmark) portfolio. Let $f = 1/(1-\beta)$ and define

$$\psi(X^\beta) = \psi(f) = f(\psi(\tilde{X}) - r) + r), \sigma^2(f) = f^2\sigma^2(\tilde{X})$$

and

$$\phi(f) = 2\psi(f) - \sigma^2(f).$$

Under the assumptions of the model, terminal wealth $W(t+T)$ from the strategy X^β is log-normally distributed with

$$F_\beta(w) = N\left[\frac{\ln\{(w/w_t) - [\phi(f)/2]\}T}{\sigma(f)\sqrt{T}}\right],$$

where N is the Gaussian cumulative distribution.

Since $\sigma^2(f)$ is increasing in f and $\phi(f)$ is decreasing in f for $f > 1$ (optimality of benchmark), the statement in the proposition follows. □

Proposition 4: *Suppose at rebalance time t, the investor has wealth w_t, forecast dynamics of asset prices given the history $\{Y_s, 0 \leq s \leq t\}$, and the return on the risk-free asset is r. If control limits (wealth goals) are $b_t \in B_t$ and the risk level is $1-\gamma$, then the growth–security efficient strategy at time t is $X_{b_t}^*(t) = (x_{1b_t}^*(t), \ldots, x_{mb_t}^*(t))'$ with*

$$X_{b_t}^*(t) = p_t(w_t, b_t, \gamma)\hat{\Delta}^{-1}(t)(\hat{\phi}(t) - re), \tag{19}$$

where e is a vector of ones.

Proof: Let $\underline{w}_t = w_t/k$ and $\overline{w}_t = k^c w_t$, where $k > 1$ and $c > 0$. For simplicity the time variable t is deleted. From (16) and (17) the growth–security efficiency problem is

$$\max_x\left\{\varphi(X)\left|\frac{1-k^{-\theta(X)}}{1-k^{(c+1)\theta(X)}} \geq \gamma,\ X \text{ feasible}\right.\right\}.$$

Letting $y = k^{-\theta(X)}$, the constraint requires $\gamma y^{c+1} - y + (1-\gamma) \geq 0$. Consider the minimum positive root y^* of the equation $\gamma y^{c+1} - y + (1-\gamma) = 0$, where $y^* \leq 1$ since $y^* = 1$ is a root. Then $\gamma y^{c+1} - y + (1-\gamma) \geq 0$ for $y \leq y^*$ and the constraint is satisfied if $k^{-\theta(X)} \leq y^*$ or

$$\theta(X) \geq -\left(\frac{\log y^*}{\log k}\right) = q^* \geq 0,$$

where q^* depends upon $\underline{w}_t, \overline{w}_t$, and γ. But $\theta(X) \geq q^*$ if $2\psi(X) - (1-q^*)\sigma^2(X) \geq 0$. Hence, the efficiency problem is

$$\max_x \{2\psi(X) - \sigma^2(X) | 2\psi(X) - (1+q^*)\sigma^2(X) \geq 0,\ X \text{ feasible}\}.$$

If X^* is a solution to this problem then it also solves, for optimal multiplier λ^*, the Lagrangian problem

$$\max_x L(X, \lambda^*),$$

where

$$L(X, \lambda^*) = 2\psi(X) - \sigma^2(X) + \lambda^*[2\psi(X) - (1+q^*)\sigma^2(X)].$$

The first-order conditions $\nabla_x L(X^*, \lambda^*) = 0$ imply that the optimal X^* satisfies the linear system

$$2(1+\lambda^*)(\hat{\phi}_i - r) - 2(1+\lambda^*(1+q^*))[x_i\delta_i^2] = 0, \quad i = 1, \ldots, I.$$

The solution to this system is $X^* = p_t(w_t, \underline{w}_t, \overline{w}_t, \gamma) \times \Delta^{-1}(\hat{\phi}(t) - re)$ where

$$p_t(w_t, \underline{w}_t, \overline{w}_t, \gamma) = \frac{1+\lambda^*}{1+\lambda^*(1+q^*)}.$$

□

Corollary 1: *For wealth goals $b_t \in B_t$, the fraction of wealth invested in risky assets at the rebalancing time t is* $\min\{1, p_t\}$ for

$$p_t(w_t, b_t, \gamma) = h_t \cdot H_t(\tilde{X}(t)) + \sqrt{[h_t \cdot H_t(\tilde{X}(t))]^2 + \frac{2rh_t}{\sigma_t^2(\tilde{X}(t))}}, \quad (20)$$

where

$$H_t(\tilde{X}(t)) = \frac{[\psi_t(\tilde{X}(t)) - r]}{\sigma_t^2(\tilde{X}(t))},$$

$$h_t = \frac{[\log w_t - \log \underline{w}_t]}{[\log w_t - \log \underline{w}_t - \log y^*]},$$

and y^* is the minimum positive root of $\gamma y^{c+1} - y + (1-\gamma) = 0$ for

$$c_t = \frac{[\log \overline{w}_t - \log w_t]}{[\log w_t - \log \underline{w}_t]}.$$

Proof: Clearly, $p_t \leq 1$, with

$$p_t = \frac{1+\lambda^*}{1+\lambda^*(1+q^*)} = 1$$

if $\lambda^* = 0$, i.e. when the constraint is not binding. If the security constraint is binding then X^* is a solution to $k^{-\theta(X)} = y^*$. Let $\tilde{X} = \Delta^{-1}(\hat{\phi} - re)$ and $X^* = p\tilde{X}$. Then the equation becomes

$$\left[\left(1 - \frac{\log y^*}{\log k}\right)\sigma^2(\tilde{X})\right]p^2 - 2[\mu(\tilde{X}) - r]p - 2r = 0.$$

The statement in the corollary follows. □

Proposition 5: *At the rebalance time t consider current wealth w_t^0, risk probability γ^0 and risk aversion parameter β. Assume that the benchmark portfolio satisfies the growth condition, i.e.*

$$\frac{\psi_t(\tilde{X}(t))}{\sigma_t^2(\tilde{X}(t))} > \frac{1}{2}.$$

It follows that $B_t^0(\beta)$ is non-empty for $\beta < 0$

Proof: From corollary 1, $p_t(w_t, b_t, \gamma) = 1/(1-\beta)$ implies

$$h_t = \frac{\sigma^2(\tilde{X})}{2r(1-\beta)^2 + 2H(\tilde{X})\sigma^2(\tilde{X})(1-\beta)} = K > 0.$$

Since

$$h_t(\underline{w}_t, \overline{w}_t) = \frac{\log w_t - \log \underline{w}_t}{\log w_t - \log \underline{w}_t - \log y^*},$$

any $(\underline{w}_t, \overline{w}_t) \in B_t^0(\beta)$ must satisfy the equation $h(\underline{w}_t, \overline{w}_t) = K$. From the assumption $\beta < 0$ and $\psi/\sigma^2 > 1/2$ it follows that $0 < K < 1$. The solution y^* of the equation $\gamma y^{C+1} - y + (1-\gamma) = 0$ has the property $y^* \uparrow 1$ as $\overline{w}_t \downarrow w_t$, for fixed $\underline{w}_t^0 < w_t$. So there exists $(\underline{w}_t^0, \overline{w}_t^*)$ such that $h(\underline{w}_t^0, \overline{w}_t^*) > K$. Also for fixed $\overline{w}_t^*, h(\underline{w}_t, \overline{w}_t^*) \downarrow 0$ as $\underline{w}_t \uparrow w_t$. That is, there is a $\underline{w}_t^*$ with $h(\underline{w}_t^*, \overline{w}_t^*) = K$. □

References

Algoet, P.H. and Cover, T.M., Asymptotic optimality and asymptotic equipartiation properties of log-optimum investment. *Annals of Probability*, 1988, **16**, 876–898.

Artzner, P., Delbaen, F., Eber, J. and Heath, D., Coherent measures of risk. *Mathematical Finance*, 1999, **9**, 203–228.

Aven, T. and Jensen, U., *Stochastic Models in Reliability*, 1999 (Springer: New York).

Basak, S. and Shapiro, A., Value at Risk based risk management: optimal policies and asset prices. *Review of Financial Studies*, 2001, **14**, 371–405.

Breiman, L., Investment policies for expanding business optimal in a long-run sense. *Naval Research Logistics Quarterly*, 1960, **7**, 647–651.

Breiman, L., Optimal gambling systems for favorable games, in *Proceedings of the 4th Berkeley Symposium on Mathematics, Statistics and Probability*, Vol. 1, 1961, pp. 63–68.

Breitmeyer, C., Hakenes, H., Pfingsten, A. and Rechtien, C., Learing from poverty measurement: an axiomatic approach to measure downside risk. Working Paper, University of Muenster, Germany, 1999.

Brennan, M.J., The role of learning in dynamic portfolio decisions. *European Finance Review*, 1998, **I**, 295–306.

Browne, S. and Whitt, W., Portfolio choice and the Bayesian Kelly criterion. *Advances in Applied Probability*, 1996, **28**, 1145–1176.

Burkhardt, T., A mean-variance of first passage time approach to portfolio selection in a lognormal world, in *the VIII International Conference on Stochastic Programming*, Vancouver, August, 1998.

Campbell, J., Lo, A. and MacKinlay, C., *The Econometrics of Financial Markets*, 1997 (Princeton University Press: Princeton, NJ).

Carino, D.R. and Ziemba, W.T., Formulation of the Russell Yasuda Kasai Financial Planning Model. *Operations Research*, 1998, **46**, 450–462.

Chopra, V.K. and Ziemba, W.T., The effect of errors in means, variances, and covariances on optimal portfolio choice. *Journal of Portfolio Management*, 1993, **19**, 6–11.

Clark, R. and Ziemba, W.T., Playing the turn-of-the-year effect with index futures. *Operations Research*, 1987, **35**, 799–813.

Gaivoronski, A. and Pflug, G., Value-at-risk in portfolio optimization: properties and computational approach. *Journal of Risk*, 2005, **7**(2), 1–31.

Grauer, R.R. and Hakansson, N.H., A half century of returns on levered and unlevered portfolios of stocks, bonds and bills, with and without small stocks. *Journal of Business*, 1986, **59**, 287–318.

Grauer, R.R. and Hakansson, N.H., Gains from international diversification: 1968–85 returns on portfolios of stocks and bonds. *Journal of Finance*, 1987, **42**, 721–739.

Hakansson, N.H., Optimal investment and consumption strategies under risk for a class of utility functions. *Econometrica*, 1970, **38**, 587–607.

Hakansson, N.H., Capital growth and the mean-variance approach to portfolio selection. *Journal of Financial and Quantitative Analysis*, 1971, **6**, 517–557.

Hakansson, N.H. and Ziemba, W.T., Capital growth theory. In *Finance*, edited by R.A. Jarrow, V. Maksimovic and W.T. Ziemba, pp. 65–86, 1995 (North-Holland: Amsterdam).

Hausch, D.B. and Ziemba, W.T., Transactions costs, extent of inefficiencies, entries and multiple wagers in a racetrack betting model. *Management Science*, 1985, **31**, 381–392.

Hausch, D.B. Ziemba, W.T. and Rubinstein, M., Efficiency of the market for racetrack betting. *Management Science*, 1981, **27**, 1435–1452.

Janecek, K., Maximum growth strategies in gambling and investment. Unpublished MSc thesis, Charles University, Prague, 1998.

Jorion, P., *Value-at-Risk: The Benchmark for Controlling Market Risk*, 1997 (Irwin: Chicago).

Kallberg, J.G. and Ziemba, W.T., Comparison of alternative utility functions in portfolio selection problems. *Management Science*, 1983, **29**, 1257–1276.

Karlin, S. and Taylor, H.M., *A Second Course in Stochastic Processes*, 1981 (New York: Academic Press).

Kelly, J., A new interpretation of information rate. *Bell System Technology Journal*, 1956, **35**, 917–926.

Lawley, D.N. and Maxwell, A.E., *Factor Analysis as a Statistical Method*, 1971 (Butterworths: London).

MacLean, L.C., Sanegre, R., Zhao, Y. and Ziemba, W.T., Capital growth with security. *Journal of Economic Dynamics and Control*, 2004, **28**, 937–954.

MacLean, L.C. and Weldon, K.L., Estimating multivariate random effects without replication. *Commun. Statist. Theory Meth.*, 1996, **24**, 1447–1469.

MacLean, L.C. and Ziemba, W.T., Growth versus security tradeoffs in dynamic investment analysis. *Annals of Operations Research*, 1999, **85**, 193–225.

MacLean, L.C., Ziemba, W.T. and Blazenko, G., Growth versus security in dynamic investment analysis. *Management Science*, 1992, **38**, 1562–1585.

Markowitz, H.M., Portfolio Selection. *Journal of Finance*, 1952, **7**, 77–91.

Markowitz, H.M., Investment for the long run: new evidence for an old rule. *Journal of Finance*, 1976, **31**, 1273–1286.

Markowitz, H.M., *Mean-variance Analysis in Portfolio Choice and Capital Markets*, 1987 (Basil Blackwell: New York).

Merton, R.C., *Continuous Time Finance*, 2nd ed., 1992 (Blackwell: Malden, MA).

Mulvey, J.M. and Vladimirou, H., Stochastic network programming for financial planning problems. *Management Science*, 1992, **38**, 1642–1664.

Ogryczak, W. and Ruszczynski, A., Dual stochastic dominance and related mean risk models. *SIAM Journal on Optimization*, 2002, **13**, 60–78.

Pratt, J.W., Risk aversion in the small and in the large. *Econometrica*, 1964, **32**, 122–136.

Rockafeller, R.T. and Uryasev, S., Optimization of conditional value-at-risk. *Journal of Risk*, 2000, **2**, 21–41.

Rockafeller, R.T. and Ziemba, W., Modified risk measures and acceptance sets. Mimeo. University of British Columbia, 2000.

Rogers, L.C.G., The relaxed investor and parameter uncertainty. *Finance and Stochastics*, 2000, **5**, 131–154.

Thorp, E.O., Portfolio choice and the Kelly criterion. In *Stochastic Optimization Models in Finance*, edited by W.T. Ziemba and R.G. Vickson, pp. 599–619, 1975 (Academic Press: New York).

Xia, Y., Learning about predictability: the effects of parameter uncertainty on dynamic asset allocation. *Journal of Finance*, 2001, **56**, 205–246.

Chapter 15

Long-term capital growth: the good and bad properties of the Kelly and fractional Kelly capital growth criteria[#]

LEONARD C. MACLEAN*†, EDWARD O. THORP‡§ and WILLIAM T. ZIEMBA¶⊥‖††

†School of Business, Dalhousie University, Halifax, NS, Canada
‡Edward O. Thorp and Associates, Newport Beach, CA, USA
§University of California, Irvine, CA, USA
¶University of British Columbia, Vancouver, BC, Canada
⊥Mathematical Institute, Oxford University, Oxford, UK
‖ICMA Centre, University of Reading, Reading, UK
††University of Bergamo, Bergamo, Italy

(*Received 17 June 2010; in final form 23 July 2010*)

The main advantage of the Kelly criterion, which maximizes the expected value of the logarithm of wealth period by period, is that it maximizes the limiting exponential growth rate of wealth. The main disadvantage of the Kelly criterion is that its suggested wagers may be very large because the Arrow–Pratt risk aversion, the reciprocal of current wealth, is small compared with other commonly chosen utility functions. Hence, the Kelly criterion is relatively risky in the short term. And although most of the time Kelly bettors will have a lot of final wealth after a long sequence of favorable bets, it is possible, through bad scenarios, to lose most of one's wealth. Hence, care in the use of Kelly and fractional Kelly strategies is crucial.

In the one asset two valued payoff case, the optimal Kelly wager is the edge (expected return) divided by the odds. If there are multiple assets in a continuous time model with a lognormal distribution for returns, the

*Corresponding author. Email: lmaclean@mgmt.dal.ca

[#]This chapter was originally published in: MacLean, L. C., Thorp, E. O. & Ziemba, W. T. (2010). Long-Term Capital Growth: The Good and Bad Properties of the Kelly and Fractional Kelly Capital Growth Criteria. *Quantitative Finance*, 10(7), 681–687.

Table 1. Average ratio of certainty equivalent loss for errors in means, variances and covariances. Source: Chopra and Ziemba (1993).

Risk tolerance*	Errors in means vs. covariances	Errors in means vs. variances	Errors in variances vs. covariances
25	5.38	3.22	1.67
50	22.50	10.98	2.05
75	56.84	21.42	2.68
	↓	↓	↓
	20	10	2
	Error mean	Error var	Error covar
	20	2	1

*Risk tolerance $= R_T(w) = 100/(1/2)R_A(w)$ where $R_A(w) = -u''(w)/u'(w)$.

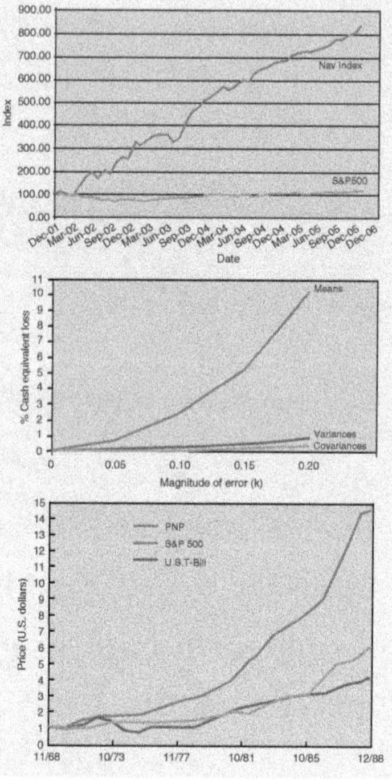

Figure 1. Mean percentage cash equivalent loss due to errors in inputs.

optimal *Kelly strategy* also has a return relative to risk structure. The investments in assets are given by the product of the inverse of the covariance matrix for the idiosyncratic component and the vector of excess returns. When the covariance matrix is diagonal, an assumption that MacKinley and Pastor (2000) support with evidence, the investment fractions in assets are proportional to the Sharpe ratios. The total fraction of wealth invested depends on the investor's aversion to risk.

In practice, estimates for the mean vector and covariance matrix are used in the calculation of the Kelly investments in assets. Chopra and Ziemba (1993), following earlier studies by Kallberg and Ziemba (1981, 1984), showed for mean–variance asset allocation problems that the mean is much more important than the variances and covariances. For allocations based on average risk aversion, errors in means versus errors in variances, covariances are about 20:2:1 in importance as measured by the cash equivalent value of final wealth. However, for low risk aversion such as log utility with risk aversion equal to $1/w$, the impact of estimation error was about 100:3:1. Also, the bets may be exceedingly large and risky for favorable Kelly bets. The covariance can be used to yield improved Stein-type estimates of the means (MacLean *et al.* 2007.)

So the Elog maximizing bettor must be very careful not to over bet because of inaccurate mean estimates. Table 1 and figure 1 show this and illustrate that the relative importance of mis-estimated parameters depends on the bettor's degree of risk aversion. The lower is the Arrow–Pratt risk aversion,

$$R_A = -\frac{u''(w)}{u'(w)},$$

the greater are the relative errors from incorrectly estimated means. Chopra (1993) further shows that portfolio turnover is larger for errors in the means than for errors in variances and covariances, but the effects are much less than for the cash equivalent performance as shown in figure 2. The impact of estimation errors can be moderated with a fractional Kelly strategy, where a fraction α, with $0 \leqslant \alpha \leqslant 1$, of the total Kelly proportion is allocated to risky assets and the rest to cash. In the lognormal case the fraction is directly linked to the Arrow–Pratt absolute and relative risk aversion parameter $R_R = wR_A(w) = 1 - \delta$ of the negative power utility function

$$u(w) = \delta w^{\delta}, \quad \text{for } \delta < 0, \text{ namely } \alpha = \frac{1}{1-\delta} = \frac{1}{R_R}.$$

A variation on this, which cuts back on investment capital, w, is the *discretionary wealth approach* (Wilcox 2003), where a fraction of wealth, c, is set aside at each investment decision for consumption or savings. This is a special type of fractional Kelly strategy, where

$$f = \frac{w-c}{w}.$$

Since log has $R_A(w) = 1/w$, which is close to zero, the Kelly bets may be exceedingly large and risky for favorable Kelly bets. MacLean *et al.* (2010a) present simulations of medium term Kelly, fractional Kelly and proportional betting strategies. The results show that with favorable investment opportunities, Kelly bettors attain

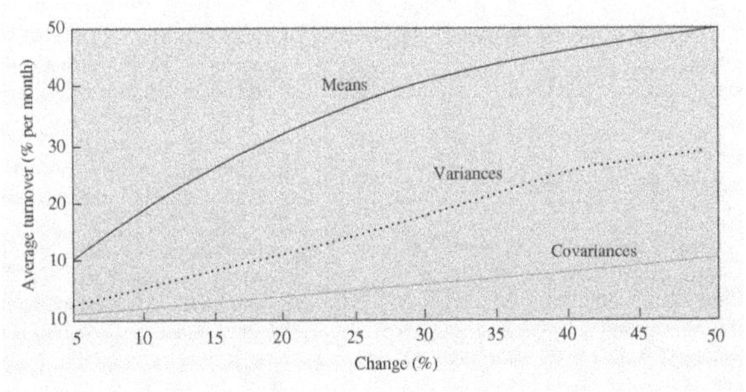

Figure 2. Average turnover for different percentage changes in means, variances and covariances. Source: Based on data from Chopra (1993).

large final wealth most of the time. But, because a long sequence of bad scenario outcomes is possible, any strategy can lose substantially, even if there are many independent investment opportunities and the chance of losing at each investment decision point is small. The Kelly and fractional Kelly rules, like all rules, are never a sure way of winning for every finite sequence.

Many great investors have used Kelly or fractional Kelly strategies. Three of them, Keynes, Buffett, and Soros, were long-term investors whose wealth paths were quite rocky but with good long-term outcomes. Our analyses suggest that Buffett and Soros seem to act similar to full Kelly bettors and Keynes like an 80% Kelly bettor with the negative power utility function $-w^{-0.25}$ (Ziemba 2003).

Graphs such as figure 3 show that growth is traded off for security with the use of fractional Kelly strategies and negative power utility functions. Log maximizes the long-run growth rate. Utility functions such as positive power that bet more than Kelly have more risk and lower growth, so they are growth-security dominated. Betting in this area invariably leads to disaster. One of the properties shown below that is illustrated in the graph is that for processes which are well approximated by continuous time, the growth rate becomes zero plus the risk free rate when one bets exactly twice the Kelly wager.

As you exceed the Kelly bets more and more, risk increases and long-term growth falls, eventually becoming more and more negative. Long Term Capital Management, Amarath and the Victor Niederhoffer funds are three of many real world instances in which overbetting led to disaster. See Ziemba and Ziemba (2007) for additional examples.

Thus long-term growth maximizing investors should bet Kelly (the expected log maximizing strategy period by period) or less. We call betting less than Kelly 'fractional Kelly', which is simply a blend of Kelly and cash. Consider the negative power utility function $\delta\omega^\delta$ for $\delta<0$. This utility function is concave and when $\delta\rightarrow 0$ it converges to log utility. As δ becomes more negative, the investor is less aggressive since his absolute

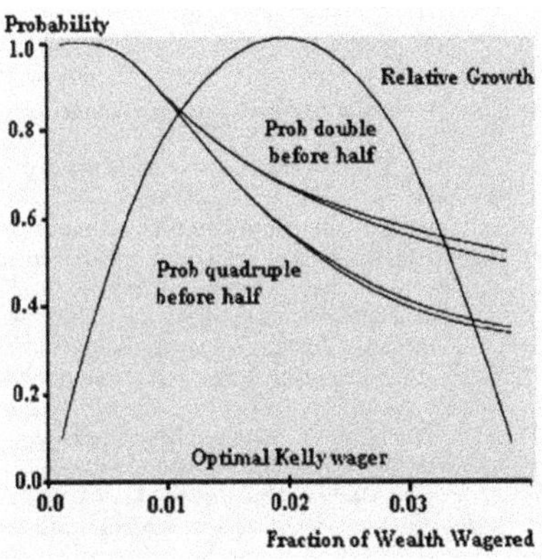

Figure 3. Continuous time approximation to the probability of doubling and quadrupling before halving and relative growth rates versus fraction of wealth wagered for Blackjack (2% advantage, $p=0.51$ and $q=0.49$). Source: MacLean and Ziemba (1999).

Arrow–Pratt risk aversion index is also higher. For the case of a stationary lognormal process and a given δ for utility function δw^δ with $\alpha=1/(1-\delta)$ between 0 and 1, the optimal portfolio has α invested in the Kelly portfolio and $1-\alpha$ invested in cash.

This handy formula relating the coefficient of the negative power utility function to the Kelly fraction is correct for lognormally distributed investment assets (MacLean *et al.* 2005). For example, half Kelly is $\delta=-1$ and quarter Kelly is $\delta=-3$. So if you want a less aggressive path than Kelly pick an appropriate δ. This formula does not apply more generally. For example, for coin tossing, where $Pr(X=1)=p$, $Pr(X-1)=q$, $p+q=1$,

$$f^*_\delta=\frac{p^{1/(1-\delta)}-q^{1/(1-\delta)}}{p^{1/(1-\delta)}+q^{1/(1-\delta)}}=\frac{p^\alpha-q^\alpha}{p^\alpha+q^\alpha},$$

which is not αf^*, where $f^* = p - q \geqslant 0$ is the Kelly bet. Thorp (2010) shows that, for non-lognormally distributed assets, this handy formula is not accurate.

We now list various important good and bad Kelly criterion properties.

The good properties

Good Maximizing expected utility, $E\log X$, asymptotically maximizes the rate of asset growth (Breiman 1961, Algoet and Cover 1988).

Good The expected time to reach a preassigned goal A is asymptotically least as A increases without limit with a strategy maximizing $E\log X_N$ (Breiman 1961, Algoet and Cover 1988, Browne 1997).

Good Under fairly general conditions, maximizing $E\log X$ also asymptotically maximizes median $\log X$ (Ethier 1987, 2004, 2010).

Good The $E\log X$ bettor never risks ruin (Hakansson and Miller 1975).

Good The absolute amount bet is monotone increasing in wealth.

Good The $E\log X$ bettor has an optimal myopic policy. He does not have to consider prior nor subsequent investment opportunities. This is a crucially important result for practical use. Hakansson (1971) proved that the myopic policy obtains for dependent investments with the log utility function. For independent investments and any power utility a myopic policy is optimal (Mossin 1968). In fact, past outcomes can be taken into account by maximizing the conditional expected logarithm given the past (Algoet and Cover 1988).

Good Simulation studies show that the $E\log X$ bettor's fortune pulls ahead of other 'essentially different' strategies' wealth for most reasonable-sized samples. Essentially different has a limited meaning. For example $g^* \geqslant g$ but $g^* - g = \epsilon$ will not lead to rapid separation if ϵ is small enough The key again is risk (Bicksler and Thorp 1973, Ziemba and Hausch 1986, MacLean *et al.* 2010a). General formulas are given by Aucamp (1993).

Good If you wish to have higher security by trading it off for lower growth, then use a negative power utility function, δw^δ, or fractional Kelly strategy. See MacLean *et al.* (2004), who show how to compute the coefficient to stay above a growth path at discrete points in time with given probability or to be above a given drawdown with a certain confidence limit. MacLean *et al.* (2009) add the feature that path violations are penalized with a convex cost function. See also Stutzer (2010) for a related but different model of such security.

Good Competitive optimality. Kelly gambling yields wealth X^* such that $E(X/X^*) \leqslant 1$, for all other strategies X. This follows from the Kuhn Tucker conditions. Thus by Markov's inequality, $Pr[X \geqslant tX^*] \leqslant 1/t$, for $t \geqslant 1$, and for all other induced wealth x. Thus an opponent cannot outperform X^* by a factor t with probability greater than $1/t$. This inequality can be improved when $t = 1$ by allowing fair randomization U. Let U be drawn according to a uniform distribution over the interval $[0, 2]$, and let U be independent of X^*. Then the result improves to $Pr[X \geqslant UX^*] \leqslant 1/2$ for all portfolios X. Thus fairly randomizing one's initial wealth and then investing it according to the Kelly criterion, one obtains a wealth UX^* that can only be beaten half the time. Since a competing investor can use the same strategy, probability 1/2 is the best competitive performance one can expect. Kelly gambling is the heart of the solution of this two-person zero sum game of who ends up with the most money. So X^* (actually UX^*) is competitively optimal in a single investment period (Bell and Cover 1980, 1988).

Good If X^* is the wealth induced by the log optimal (Kelly) portfolio, then the expected wealth ratio is no greater than one, i.e. $E(X/X^*) \leqslant 1$, for the wealth X induced by any other portfolio (Bell and Cover, 1980, 1988).

Good Super St Petersburg. Any cost c for the St Petersburg random variable X, $Pr[X = 2^k] = 2^{-k}$, is acceptable. But the larger the cost c, the less wealth one should invest. The growth rate G^* of wealth resulting from repeating such investments is

$$G^* = \max_{0 \leqslant f \leqslant 1} E\ln\left(1 - f + \frac{f}{c}X\right),$$

where f is the fraction of wealth invested. The maximizing f^* is the Kelly proportion (Bell and Cover 1980). The Kelly fraction f^* can be computed even for a super St Petersburg random variable $Pr[Y = 2^{2^k}] = 2^{-k}$, $k = 1, 2, \ldots,$ where $E\ln Y = \infty$, by maximizing the relative growth rate

$$\max_{0 \leqslant f \leqslant 1} E\ln\frac{1 - f + (f/c)Y}{(1/2) + (1/2c)Y}.$$

This is bounded for all f in [0, 1]. Now, although the exponential growth rate of wealth is infinite for all proportions f and it seems that all $f \in [0, 1]$ are equally good, the maximizing f^* in the previous equation guarantees that the f^* portfolio will asymptotically exponentially outperform any other portfolio $f \in [0, 1]$. Both investors' wealth have super exponential growth, but the f^* investor will exponentially outperform any other essentially different investor.

Some bad properties

Bad The bets may be a large fraction of current wealth when the wager is favorable and the risk of loss is very small. For one such example, see Ziemba and

Hausch (1986, pp. 159–160). There, in the inaugural 1984 Breeders' Cup Classic \$3 million race, the optimal fractional wager, using the Dr Z place and show system using the win odds as the probability of winning, on the 3–5 shot Slew of Gold was 64%. (See also the 74% futures bet on the January effect in MacLean *et al.* 1992.) Thorp and Ziemba actually made this place and show bet and won with a low fractional Kelly wager. Slew finished third but the second place horse Gate Dancer was disqualified and placed third. Wild Again won this race; the first great victory by the masterful jockey Pat Day.

Bad For coin tossing, any fixed fraction strategy has the property that if the number of wins equals the number of losses then the bettor is behind. For n wins and n losses and initial wealth W_0 we have $W_{2n} = W_0(1 - f^2)^n$.

Bad The unweighted average rate of return converges to half the arithmetic rate of return. Thus you may regularly win less than you expect. This is a consequence of weighting equally rather than by size of the wager (Ethier and Tavaré 1983, Griffin 1985).

Some observations

(1) For an i.i.d. process and a myopic policy, which results from maximizing expected utility in case the utility function is log or a negative power, the result is fixed fraction betting, hence fractional Kelly includes all these policies.

(2) A betting strategy is 'essentially different' from Kelly if $S_n \equiv \sum_{i=1}^{n} \mathrm{E}\log(1 + f_i^* X_i) - \sum_{i=1}^{n} \mathrm{E}\log(1 + f_i X_i)$ tends to infinity as n increases. The sequence $\{f_i^*\}$ denotes the Kelly betting fractions and the sequence $\{f_i\}$ denotes the corresponding betting fractions for the essentially different strategy.

(3) The Kelly portfolio does not necessarily lie on the efficient frontier in a mean–variance model (Thorp 1971). Markowitz (1976) argues that the Kelly Elog maximizing strategy is a limiting mean–variance portfolio. Roll (1973) tests the differences between Kelly and mean–variance portfolios and, for his assumptions and data, finds them closely related.

(4) Despite its superior long-run growth properties, Kelly, like any other strategy, can have a very poor return outcome. For example, making 700 wagers all of which have a 14% advantage, the least of which has a 19% chance of winning, can turn \$1000 into \$18. But with full Kelly 16.6% of the time \$1000 turns into at least \$100,000 (Ziemba and Hausch 1986). Half Kelly does not help much as \$1000 can become \$145 and the growth is much lower with only over \$100,000 final wealth 0.1% of the time. For more such calculations, see Bicksler and Thorp (1973) and MacLean *et al.* (2010a).

(5) Fallacy: If maximizing $\mathrm{E}\log X_N$ almost certainly leads to a better outcome, then the expected utility of its outcome exceeds that of any other rule provided N is sufficiently large. *Counterexample:* $u(x) = x$, $1/2 < p < 1$, Bernoulli trials $f = 1$ maximizes $Eu(x)$ but $f = 2p - 1 < 1$ maximizes $\mathrm{E}\log X_N$ (Samuelson 1971, Thorp 1971, 2006).

(6) It can take a long time for any strategy, including Kelly, to dominate an essentially different strategy. For instance, in continuous time with a geometric Wiener process, suppose $\mu_a = 20\%$, $\mu_b = 10\%$, $\sigma_a = \sigma_b = 10\%$. Then in five years, A is ahead of B with 95% confidence. But if $\sigma_a = 20\%$, $\sigma_b = 10\%$ with the same means, it takes 157 years for A to beat B with 95% confidence. As another example, in coin tossing suppose game A has an edge of 1.0% and game B 1.1%. It takes two million trials to have an 84% chance that game B dominates game A (Thorp 2006).

(7) Fractional Kelly, with fraction k, where $0 < k \leqslant 1$, applied to capital w_0, is equivalent to full Kelly applied to kw_0, with $(1 - k)w_0$ in cash. Question: For what other utility functions does such a decomposition hold? Lemma: It is true if the utility function $u(w)$ has the property $u(\lambda w) = f(\lambda)g(w)$. Proof: the solutions to $0 = u(\lambda x) = f(\lambda)g(w)$ are the solutions to $g(w) = 0$, which does not depend on λ. An example is $u(w) = -w^{-a}$. It is not known if the property in the lemma is also necessary.

The theory and practical application of the Kelly criterion is straightforward when the underlying probability distributions are fairly accurately known.† However, in investment applications this is usually not the case. Realized future equity returns may be very different from what one would expect using estimates based on historical returns. Consequently, practitioners who wish to protect capital above all, sharply reduce risk as their drawdown increases.

Prospective users of the Kelly criterion can check our list of good properties, bad properties and observations to test whether Kelly is well suited to their intended application. Given the extreme sensitivity of Elog calculations to errors in mean estimates, these estimates must be accurate and, to be on the safe side, the size of the wagers should be reduced.

For long-term compounders, the good properties dominate the bad properties of the Kelly criterion. But the bad properties may dampen the enthusiasm of naive prospective users of the Kelly criterion. The Kelly and fractional Kelly strategies are very useful if applied carefully with good data input and proper financial engineering risk control.

†With transactions and price pressures, one solves a simple stochastic program or, in the case of discrete probability distributions, a nonlinear program.

Acknowledgements

Special thanks go to Tom Cover, Michael Dempster and John Mulvey for helpful comments on an earlier draft of this paper. This is an expanded and updated discussion of a chapter in MacLean *et al.* (2010b).

References

Algoet, P.H. and Cover, T., Asymptotic optimality and asymptotic equipartition properties of log-optimum investment. *Ann. Probab.*, 1988, **16**(2), 876–898.

Aucamp, D., On the extensive number of plays to achieve superior performance with the geometric mean strategy. *Mgmt Sci.*, 1993, **39**, 1163–1172.

Bell, R.M. and Cover, T.M., Competitive optimality of logarithmic investment. *Math. Oper. Res.*, 1980, **5**, 161–166.

Bell, R.M. and Cover, T.M., Game-theoretic optimal portfolios. *Mgmt Sci.*, 1988, **34**(6), 724–733.

Bicksler, J.L. and Thorp, E.O., The capital growth model: an empirical investigation. *J. Financial Quant. Anal.*, 1973, **8**(2), 273–287.

Breiman, L., Optimal gambling system for favorable games, in *Proceedings of the 4th Berkeley Symposium on Mathematical Statistics and Probability*, 1961, pp. 63–68.

Browne, S., Survival and growth with a fixed liability: optimal portfolios in continuous time. *Math. Oper. Res.*, 1997, **22**, 468–493.

Chopra, V.K., Improving optimization. *J. Invest.*, 1993, **2**(3), 51–59.

Chopra, V.K. and Ziemba, W.T., The effect of errors in mean, variance and co-variance estimates on optimal portfolio choice. *J. Portfol. Mgmt*, 1993, **19**, 6–11.

Ethier, S., The proportional bettor's fortune, in *Proceedings of the 7th International Conference on Gambling and Risk Taking*, 1987.

Ethier, S., The Kelly system maximizes median fortune. *J. Appl. Probab.*, 2004, **41**, 1230–1236.

Ethier, S., *The Doctrine of Chances: Probabilistic Aspects of Gambling*, 2010 (Springer: Berlin).

Ethier, S. and Tavaré, S., The proportional bettor's return on investment. *J. Appl. Probab.*, 1983, **20**, 563–573.

Griffin, P., Different measures of win rates for optimal proportional betting. *Mgmt Sci.*, 1985, **30**, 1540–1547.

Hakansson, N.H., On optimal myopic portfolio policies with and without serial correlation. *J. Business*, 1971, **44**, 324–334.

Hakansson, N.H. and Miller, B., Compound-return mean–variance efficient portfolios never risk ruin. *Mgmt Sci.*, 1975, **22**, 391–400.

Janacek, K., Optimal growth in gambling and investing. MSc thesis, Charles University, Prague, 1998.

Kallberg, J.G. and Ziemba, W.T., Remarks on optimal portfolio selection. In *Methods of Operations Research, Oelgeschlager*, edited by G. Bamberg and O. Opitz, Vol. 44, pp. 507–520, 1981 (Gunn and Hain).

Kallberg, J.G. and Ziemba, W.T., Mis-specifications in portfolio selection problems. In *Risk and Capital*, edited by G. Bamberg and K. Spremann, pp. 74–87, 1984 (Springer: New York).

MacKinlay, A.C. and Pastor, L., Asset pricing models: implications for expected returns and portfolio selection. *Rev. Financial Stud.*, 2000, **13**(4), 883–916.

MacLean, L.C., Foster, M. and Ziemba, W.T., Covariance complexity and rates of return on assets. *J. Bank. Finance*, 2007, **31**(11), 3503–3523.

MacLean, L.C., Sanegre, R., Zhao, Y. and Ziemba, W.T., Capital growth with security. *J. Econ. Dynam. Control*, 2004, **28**(4), 937–954.

MacLean, L.C., Thorp, E.O., Zhao, Y. and Ziemba, W.T., Medium term simulations of the full Kelly and fractional Kelly investment strategies. In *The Kelly Capital Growth Investment Criterion: Theory and Practice*, edited by L.C. MacLean, E.O. Thorp, and W.T. Ziemba, 2010a (World Scientific: Singapore).

MacLean, L.C., Thorp, E.O. and Ziemba, W.T., editors, *The Kelly Capital Growth Investment Criterion: Theory and Practice*, 2010b (World Scientific: Singapore).

MacLean, L.C., Zhao, Y. and Ziemba, W.T., Optimal capital growth with convex loss penalties. Working Paper, Dalhousie University, 2009.

MacLean, L.C. and Ziemba, W.T., Growth versus security tradeoffs in dynamic investment analysis. *Ann. Oper. Res.*, 1999, **85**, 193–227.

MacLean, L.C., Ziemba, W.T. and Blazenko, G., Growth versus security in dynamic investment analysis. *Mgmt Sci.*, 1992, **38**, 1562–1585.

MacLean, L.C., Ziemba, W.T. and Li, Time to wealth goals in capital accumulation and the optimal trade-off of growth versus security. *Quant. Finance*, 2005, **5**(4), 343–357.

Markowitz, H.M., Investment for the long run: new evidence for an old rule. *J. Finance*, 1976, **31**(5), 1273–1286.

Mossin, J., Optimal multiperiod portfolio policies. *J. Business*, 1968, **41**, 215–229.

Roll, R., Evidence on the growth optimum model. *J. Finance*, 1973, **28**(3), 551–566.

Samuelson, P.A., The 'fallacy' of maximizing the geometric mean in long sequences of investing or gambling. *Proc. Natn. Acad. Sci.*, 1971, **68**, 2493–2496.

Stutzer, M., On growth optimality versus security against underperformance. In *The Kelly Capital Growth Investment Criterion: Theory and Practice*, edited by L.C. MacLean, E.O. Thorp, and W.T. Ziemba, 2010 (World Scentific: Singapore).

Thorp, E.O., Portfolio choice and the Kelly criterion, in *Proceedings of the Business and Economics Section of the American Statistical Association*, 1971, 215–224.

Thorp, E.O., The Kelly criterion in blackjack, sports betting and the stock market. In *Handbook of Asset and Liability Management*, edited by S.A. Zenios and W.T. Ziemba, pp. 385–428, 2006 (North-Holland: Amsterdam).

Thorp, E.O., Understanding the Kelly criterion. In *The Kelly Capital Growth Investment Criterion: Theory and Practice*, edited by L.C. MacLean, E.O. Thorp, and W.T. Ziemba, 2010 (World Scientific: Singapore).

Wilcox, J., Harry Markowitz and the discretionary wealth hypothesis. *J. Portfol. Mgmt*, 2003, **29**, 58–65.

Ziemba, R.E.S. and Ziemba, W.T., *Scenarios for Risk Management and Global Investment Strategies*, 2007 (Wiley: New York).

Ziemba, W.T., The stochastic programming approach to asset liability and wealth management. AIMR, Charlottesville, VA, 2003.

Ziemba, W.T., The symmetric downside risk Sharpe ratio and the evaluation of great investors and speculators. *J. Portfol. Mgmt*, 2005, **32**(1), 108–122.

Ziemba, W.T., Utility theory for growth versus security, Working Paper, 2009.

Ziemba, W.T. and Hausch, D.B., *Betting at the Racetrack*, 1986 (Dr. Z. Investments: San Luis Obispo, CA).

Appendix A:

In continuous time, with a geometric Wiener process, betting exactly double the Kelly criterion amount leads to a growth rate equal to the risk-free rate. This result is due to Stutzer (2010), Janacek (1998) and Thorp (2006), and possibly others. The following simple proof, under the further assumption of the Capital Asset Pricing Model, is due to Harry Markowitz.

In continuous time

$$g_p = E_p - \frac{1}{2} V_p,$$

where E_p, V_p and g_p are the portfolio expected return, variance and expected log, respectively. In the CAPM,

$$E_p = r_0 + (E_M - r_0)X,$$
$$V_p = \sigma_M^2 X^2,$$

where X is the portfolio weight, E_M is the expected market return, and r_0 is the risk-free rate. Collecting terms and setting the derivative of g_p with respect to X equal to zero yields

$$X = \frac{(E_M - r_0)}{\sigma_M^2},$$

which is the optimal Kelly bet with optimal growth rate

$$\begin{aligned} g^* &= r_0 + (E_M - r_0)^2 - \frac{1}{2}\left[\frac{(E_M - r_0)}{\sigma_M^2}\right]^2 \sigma_M^2 \\ &= r_0 + \frac{(E_M - r_0)^2}{\sigma_M^2} - \frac{1}{2}\left[\frac{(E_M - r_0)^2}{\sigma_M^2}\right] \\ &= r_0 + \frac{1}{2}\left[\frac{(E_M - r_0)}{\sigma_M}\right]^2. \end{aligned}$$

Substituting double Kelly, namely $Y = 2X$ for X above, into

$$g_p = r_0 + (E_M - r_0)Y - \frac{1}{2}\sigma_M^2 Y^2,$$

and simplifying yields

$$g_0 - r_0 = 2\left[\frac{(E_M - r_0)^2}{\sigma_M^2}\right] - \frac{4}{2}\left[\frac{(E_M - r_0)^2}{\sigma_M^2}\right] = 0.$$

Hence $g_0 = r_0$ when $Y = 2X$.

The CAPM assumption is not needed. For a more general proof and illustration, see Thorp (2006).

Section V

Sports Betting and Analytics

Chapter 16

EFFICIENCY OF THE MARKET FOR RACETRACK BETTING*,#

DONALD B. HAUSCH,† WILLIAM T. ZIEMBA‡ AND MARK RUBINSTEIN§

Many racetrack bettors have systems. Since the track is a market similar in many ways to the stock market one would expect that the basic strategies would be either fundamental or technical in nature. Fundamental strategies utilize past data available from racing forms, special sources, etc. to "handicap" races. The investor then wagers on one or more horses whose probability of winning exceeds that determined by the odds by an amount sufficient to overcome the track take. Technical systems require less information and only utilize current betting data. They attempt to find inefficiencies in the "market" and bet on such "overlays" when they have positive expected value. Previous studies and our data confirm that for win bets these inefficiencies, which exist for underbet favorites and overbet longshots, are not sufficiently great to result in positive profits. This paper describes a technical system for place and show betting for which it appears to be possible to make substantial positive profits and thus to demonstrate market inefficiency in a weak form sense. Estimated theoretical probabilities of all possible finishes are compared with the actual amounts bet to determine profitable betting situations. Since the amount bet influences the odds and theory suggests that to maximize long run growth a logarithmic utility function is appropriate the resulting model is a nonlinear program. Side calculations generally reduce the number of possible bets in any one race to three or less hence the actual optimization is quite simple. The system was tested on data from Santa Anita and Exhibition Park using exact and approximate solutions (that make the system operational at the track given the limited time available for placing bets) and found to produce substantial positive profits. A model is developed to demonstrate that the profits are not due to chance but rather to proper identification of market inefficiencies.
(FINANCE-PORTFOLIO; GAMES-GAMBLING)

1. The Racetrack Market

For the most part,[1] academic research on security markets has bypassed an interesting and accessible market—the racetrack for thoroughbred horses—with its highly standardized form of security—the tote ticket. The racetrack shares many of the characteristics of the archtypical securities market in listed common stocks. Moreover the racetrack gains further interest from its significant differences, and more importantly, because it is inherently a more elementary market context, lacking many of the dynamic features which complicate analysis of the stock market.

The "market" at the track in North America convenes for about 20 minutes, during which participants place bets on any number of the six to twelve horses in the following race. In a typical race, participants can bet on each horse, either to win, place or show.[2] The horses that finish the race first, second or third are said to finish

*Accepted by Vijay S. Bawa, former Departmental Editor; received April 3, 1980. This paper has been with the authors 2 months for 1 revision.

†Northwestern University.
‡University of British Columbia.
§University of California, Berkeley.

[1] For surveys, see Copeland and Weston [6], Fama [9], [10] and Rubinstein [22].

[2] Other bets such as the daily double (pick the winners in the first and second race), the quinella (pick the first two finishers regardless of order in a given race) and the exacta (pick the first two finishers in exact order in a given race) as well as various combinations are possible as well. Such bets are utilized by the public to construct low probability high payoff bets. For discussion of some of the implications of such bets see Rosett [21].

#This chapter was originally published in: Hausch, D. B., Ziemba, W. T. & Rubinstein, M. (1981). Efficiency of the Market for Racetrack Betting. *Management Science*, 27(12), 1435–1452.

"in-the-money." All participants who have bet a horse to win, realize a positive return on that bet only if the horse is first, while a place bet realizes a positive return if the horse is first or second, and a show bet realizes a positive return if the horse is first, second or third. Regardless of the outcome, all bets have limited liability. Unlike most casino games such as roulette, but like the stock market, security prices (i.e. the "odds") are jointly determined by all the participants and a rule governing transaction costs (i.e. the track "take"). To take the simplest case, for win, all bets across all horses to win are aggregated to form the win pool. If W_i represents the total amount bet by all participants on horse i to win, then $W = \sum_i W_i$ is the win pool and WQ/W_i is the payoff per dollar bet on horse l to win if and only if horse i wins, where $1 - Q$ is the percentage transaction costs.[3] If horse i does not win, the payoff per dollar bet is zero.

The track is "competitive" in the sense that every dollar bet on horse i to win, regardless of the identification of the bettor, has the same payoff. The "state contingent" price of a dollar received if and only if horse i wins is $\rho_i = (W_i/WQ)$ and the one plus riskless return is $1/\sum_i \rho_i = Q$, a number less than one. The interest rate at the track is thus negative and solely determined by the level of transactions costs. Thus, apart from an exogeneously set riskless rate, the participants at the track jointly determine the security prices. For example, by betting more on one horse than another, the state-contingent price of the first horse increases relative to the second, or alternatively the payoff per dollar bet decreases on the first relative to the second.

The rules for division of the place and show pools are slightly more complex than the win pool. Let P_j be the amount bet on horse j to place and $P \equiv \sum_j P_j$ be the place pool. Similarly S_k is the amount bet on horse k to show and the show pool is $S \equiv \sum_k S_k$. The payoff per dollar bet on horse j to place is

$$\begin{cases} 1 + [PQ - P_i - P_j]/(2P_j) & \text{if } \begin{cases} i \text{ is first and } j \text{ is second or} \\ j \text{ is first and } i \text{ is second} \end{cases} \\ 0 & \text{otherwise.} \end{cases}$$

Thus if horses i and j are first and second each bettor on j (and also i) to place first receives the amount of his bet back. The remaining amount in the place pool, after the track take, is then split evenly between the place bettors on i and j. The payoff to horse j to place is independent of whether j finishes first or second, but it is dependent on which horse finishes with it. A bettor on horse j to place hopes that a longshot, not a favorite, will finish with it.

The payoff per dollar bet on show is analogous

$$\begin{cases} 1 + [SQ - S_i - S_j - S_k]/(3S_k) & \text{if } \begin{cases} k \text{ is first, second or third} \\ \text{and finishes with } i \text{ and } j \end{cases} \\ 0 & \text{otherwise.} \end{cases}$$

In many ways the racetrack is like the stock market. A technical strategy based on discrepancies between the amounts bet on the same horses to win, place and show, is examined in this paper. Since a short position has a perfectly negative correlated outcome to the result of normal bet a given horse can be "shorted" by buying tickets on all the other horses in a race.

The racetrack also differs from the stock market in important ways. In the stock market, an investor's profit depends not only on the initial price he pays for a security,

[3]The actual transactions cost is more complicated and is described below.

but also on what some other investor is willing to pay him for it when he decides to sell. Thus his profit depends not only on how well the underlying firm does in terms of earnings over the time he holds its stock (i.e. supply uncertainty), but also on how other investors value that stock in the future (i.e. demand uncertainty). Given the initial price, both the nature and behavior of other market participants determine his profit. Thus current stock prices might depend not only on "fundamental" factors but also on market "psychology"—the tastes, beliefs, and endowments of other investors, etc. In contrast once all bets are placed at the track prior to a given race (i.e. initial security prices are given), the result of the race and the corresponding payoffs depend only on nature. There is no demand uncertainty at the track.

2. Previous Work on Racetrack Efficiency

A market is efficient if current security prices fully reflect all available relevant information. If this is the case, experts should not be able to achieve higher than average returns with regularity. A number of investigators have demonstrated that the New York Stock Exchange and other major security markets are efficient and so-called experts in fact achieve returns when adjusted for risk that are no higher than those that would be received from random investments (see Copeland and Weston [6], Fama [9], [10] and Rubinstein [22] for discussion, terminology, and relevant references). For an exception see Downes and Dyckman [7].

Snyder [24] provided an investigation of the efficiency of the market for racetrack bets to win. The question Snyder poses is whether or not bets at different odds levels yield the same average return. The rate of return for odds group i is

$$R_i = \frac{N_i^*(O_i + 1) - N_i}{N_i}$$

where N_i and N_i^* are the number of horses, and the number who won, respectively, at odds $O_i = (WQ/W_i - 1)$. A weakly-efficient market in Snyder's sense would set $R_i = Q$ for all i, where $1 - Q$ is the percentage track take. His results as well as those of Fabricant [8], Griffith [12], [13], McClothlin [18], Seligman [23] and Weitzman [27] suggest that there are "strong and stable biases but these are not large enough to make it possible to earn a positive profit" [24; 1110]. In particular, extreme favorites tend to be under bet and longshots overbet. The combined results of several studies comparing over 30,000 races are summarized in Table 1.

TABLE 1 (Snyder [24])

Rates of Return on Bets to Win by Grouped Odds, Take Added Back

	Midpoint of grouped odds							
Study	0.75	1.25	2.5	5.0	7.5	10.0	15.0	33.0
Fabricant	11.1[a]	9.0[a]	4.6[a]	− 1.4	− 3.3	− 3.7	− 8.1	− 39.5[a]
Griffith	8.0	4.9	3.1	− 3.1	− 34.6[a]	− 34.1[a]	− 10.5	− 65.5[a]
McGlothlin	8.0[b]	8.0[a]	8.0[a]	− 0.8	− 4.6	− 7.0[b]	− 9.7	− 11.0
Seligman	14.0	4.0	− 1.0	1.0	− 2.0	− 4.0	− 7.8	− 24.2
Snyder	5.5	5.5	4.0	− 1.2	3.4	2.9	2.4	− 15.8
Weitzman	9.0[a]	3.2	6.8[a]	− 1.3	− 4.2	− 5.1	− 8.2[b]	− 18.0[a]
Combined	9.1[a]	6.4[a]	6.1[a]	− 1.2	− 5.2[a]	− 5.2[a]	− 10.2[a]	− 23.7[a]

[a] Significantly different from zero at 1% level or better.
[b] Significantly different from zero at 5% level or better.

Since the track take averages about 18%, the net rate of return for any strategy which consistently bets within a single odds category is −9% or less. For horses with odds averaging 33 the net rate of return is about −42%.

Conventional financial theory does not explain these biases because it is usual to assume that as nondiversifiable risk (e.g. variance) rises expected return rises as well. In the win pool expected return declines as risk increases. An explanation consistent with the expected utility hypothesis is that investors (as a composite) are risk lovers and behave as if the betting opportunities are limited to a single race. Weitzman [27] and Ali [1] have estimated such utility functions. Ali's estimated utility function over wealth w is the convex function

$$u(x) = 1.91 w^{1.1784} \qquad (R^2 = .9981),$$

which has increasing absolute risk aversion. Thus by the Arrow-Pratt [3], [19] theory investors will take more risk as their wealth declines. This explains the common phenomenon that bettors, when losing, tend to bet more and more on longer odds horses in a desperate attempt to recoup earlier losses. Moreover, since u is nearly linear for large w investors are nearly risk neutral at such wealth levels.

A second explanation is that gamblers simply prefer low probability high prize combinations (i.e. longshots) to high probability low prize combinations. Besides the possible gains involved, gamblers have egos associated with analyzing racing forms and pitting one's predictions against others. Luck and entertainment as well are largely absent in betting favorites. The thrill is to successfully detect a moderate or long odds winner and thus confirm one's ability to outperform the other bettors. Such a scenario is consistent with the data and leads to the biases. Rosett [21] provides an analysis of ways to construct low probability high prize bets through parlays and other combinations that can be used to avoid the longshot tail bias problem and to take advantage of the favorite bias. In an effort to capitalize on this market many tracks feature such bets in the form of the daily double, the exacta and the quinella. However, none of these schemes appear to yield bets with positive net returns.[4]

Other studies of racetrack efficiency have been conducted by Ali [2], Figlewski [11] and Snyder [24]. Ali shows that the win market is efficient in the sense that independently derived bets with identical probabilities of winning do in fact have the same odds in a statistical sense. His analysis utilizes daily double bets and the corresponding parlays, i.e. bet the proceeds if the chosen horse wins the first race on the chosen horse in the second race, for 1089 races. Figlewski, using a multinomial logit probability model to measure the information content of the forecasts of professional handicappers and data from 189 races at Belmont in 1977, found that these forecasts do contain considerable information but the track odds generated by bettors discount almost all of it. Snyder provided strong form efficiency tests of the form: are there persons with special information that would allow them to outperform the general public? He found using data on 846 races at Arlington Park in Chicago that forecasts from three leading newspapers, the daily racing form and the official track handicapper did not lead to bets that outperformed the general public.

[4] For an entertaining account of an "expert" who was able to achieve positive net returns over a full racing season, see Beyer [5]. See also Vergin [26].

3. Proposed Test

The studies described in §2 examine racetrack efficiency with respect to the win pool only. In this paper our concern is with the efficiency of the place and show pools relative to the win pool and with the development of procedures to best capitalize on potential inefficiencies between these three "markets." We utilize the following definition of weak-form efficiency: the market is weakly-efficient if no individual can earn positive profits using trading rules based on historical price information. In Baumol's [4; 46] words ... "all opportunities for profit by systematic betting are eliminated". Our analysis utilizes the following two data sets: 1) Data Set 1: all dollar bets to win, place and show for the 627 races over 75 days involving 5895 horses running in the 1973/74 winter season at Santa Anita Racetrack in Arcadia, California, collected by Mark Rubinstein; and 2) Data Set 2: all dollar bets to win, place and show for the 1065 races over 110 days involving 9037 horses running in the 1978 summer season at Exhibition Park, Vancouver, British Columbia, collected by Donald B. Hausch and William T. Ziemba.

In the analysis of the efficiency of the win pool one may compare the actual frequency of winning with the theoretical probability of winning as reflected through the odds. Similar analyses are possible for the place and show pools once an estimate of the theoretical probabilities of placing and showing for all horses is available. There is no unique way to obtain these estimates. However, very reasonable estimates obtain from the natural generalization of the following simple procedure. Suppose three horses have probabilities to win of 0.5, 0.3, and 0.2, respectively. Now if horse 2 wins, a Bayesian would naturally expect that the probabilities that horses 1 and 3 place (i.e. win second place) are 0.5/0.7 and 0.2/0.7, respectively. In general if q_i $(i = 1, \ldots, n)$ is the probability horse i wins, then the probability that i is first and j is second is

$$(q_i q_j)/(1 - q_i) \tag{1}$$

and the probability that i is first, j is second and k is third is

$$q_i q_j q_k/(1 - q_i)(1 - q_i - q_j). \tag{2}$$

Harville [14] gives an analysis of these formulas. Despite their apparent reasonableness they suffer from at least two flaws:

1) no account is made of the possibility of the "Silky Sullivan" problem; that is, some horses generally either win or finish out-of-the-money—for example, see footnote 5 in [15]; for these horses the formulas greatly over-estimate the true probability of finishing second or third; and

2) the formulas are not derivable from first principles involving individual horses running times; even independence of these random variables $T_1, \ldots, T_n$ is neither necessary nor sufficient to imply the formulas.

In addition to assuming (1) and (2) we assume that

$$q_i = W_i \Big/ \sum_{i=1}^{n} W_i. \tag{3}$$

That is, the win pool is efficient. The discussion above, of course, indicates that this assumption is suspect in the tails and this is discussed below. Table 2a–c compares the actual versus theoretical probability of winning, placing and showing for data set 2.

Similar tables for data set 1 appear in King [17]; see also Harville [14]. The usual tail biases appear in Table 2a (although they are not significant at the 5% confidence level). One has reverse tail biases in the finishing second and third probabilities, see Tables 2b, c in [15]. This occurs because if the probability to win is overestimated (underestimated) and probabilities sum to one it is likely that the probabilities of finishing second and third would be underestimated (overestimated). Tables 2b, c, indicate how these biases tend to cancel when they are aggregated to form the theoretical probabilities and frequencies of placing and showing.[5]

TABLE 2

Actual vs. Theoretical Probability of Winning, Placing and Showing: Exhibition Park 1978

(a)

Theoretical Probability of Winning	Number of Horses	Average Theoretical Probability	Actual Frequency of Winning	Estimated Standard Error
0.000 –0.025	540	0.019	0.016	0.005
0.026 –0.050	1498	0.037	0.036	0.005
0.051 –0.100	2658	0.073	0.079	0.005
0.101 –0.150	1772	0.123	0.126	0.008
0.151 –0.200	1199	0.172	0.156	0.010
0.201 –0.250	646	0.223	0.227	0.016
0.251 –0.300	341	0.272	0.263	0.024
0.301 –0.350	199	0.323	0.306	0.033
0.351 –0.400	101	0.373	0.415	0.049
0.401 +	83	0.450	0.469	0.055
	9037			

(b)

Theoretical Probability of Placing	Number of Horses	Average Theoretical Probability	Actual Frequency of Placing	Estimated Standard Error
0.000 –0.025	21	0.022	0.000*	0.000
0.026 –0.050	391	0.040	0.030	0.009
0.051 –0.100	1394	0.075	0.080	0.007
0.101 –0.150	1335	0.124	0.152*	0.010
0.151 –0.200	1295	0.174	0.174	0.011
0.201 –0.250	1057	0.223	0.243	0.013
0.251 –0.300	871	0.274	0.304	0.016
0.301 –0.350	772	0.323	0.314	0.017
0.351 –0.400	580	0.373	0.313*	0.019
0.401 –0.450	420	0.424	0.395	0.024
0.451 –0.500	321	0.472	0.457	0.028
0.501 –0.550	202	0.523	0.415*	0.035
0.551 –0.600	149	0.573	0.483*	0.041
0.601 –0.650	114	0.623	0.570	0.046
0.651 –0.700	51	0.672	0.627	0.068
0.701 –0.750	41	0.721	0.731	0.069
0.751 +	23	0.792	0.782	0.086
	9037			

[5]Since it is the accuracy of these probabilities rather than the q_i's that is of crucial importance in the calculations and model below this canceling provides some justification for omitting the tail biases in (3). In practice, bets are only made on horses with expected returns considerably above 1, e.g., 1.16 at Santa Anita. Modification of the q_i to include these biases might change the 1.16 to 1.14, for example. See also the discussion below and in §§4 and 5.

TABLE 2 (continued)

Actual vs. Theoretical Probability of Winning, Placing and Showing: Exhibition Park 1978

(c) Theoretical Probability of Showing	Number of Horses	Average Theoretical Probability	Actual Frequency of Showing	Estimated Standard Error
0.000 -0.025	0	—	—	—
0.026 -0.050	55	0.043	0.036	0.025
0.051 -0.100	592	0.078	0.081	0.011
0.101 -0.150	895	0.125	0.165*	0.012
0.151 -0.200	909	0.175	0.195	0.013
0.201 -0.250	799	0.224	0.292*	0.016
0.251 -0.300	885	0.275	0.289	0.015
0.301 -0.350	794	0.324	0.346	0.017
0.351 -0.400	703	0.374	0.398	0.018
0.401 -0.450	655	0.425	0.433	0.019
0.451 -0.500	617	0.475	0.452	0.020
0.501 -0.550	542	0.524	0.477*	0.021
0.551 -0.600	396	0.573	0.477*	0.025
0.601 -0.650	375	0.624	0.599	0.025
0.651 -0.700	264	0.672	0.609*	0.030
0.701 -0.750	206	0.722	0.582*	0.034
0.751 -0.800	154	0.773	0.655*	0.038
0.801 -0.850	113	0.821	0.752	0.041
0.851 -0.900	53	0.873	0.830	0.052
0.901 +	30	0.925	0.833	0.068
	9037			

[a]Categories when the theoretical probability and the actual frequency are different at the 5% significance level are denoted by *'s. The estimated standard error is $(s^2/N)^{\frac{1}{2}}$ where the actual frequency sample variance $s^2 = N(E(X^2) - (EX)^2)/(N-1)$. Since the X_i are either 0 or 1, $E(X^2) = EX$ and $s^2 = N(EX - (EX)^2)/(N-1)$.

Formulas (1)–(3) can be used to develop procedures that yield net rates of return for place and show betting that are higher than expected (i.e.–18%) and indeed make positive profits. As a first step towards development of a "system" we present the results on the two data sets of \$1 bets when the theoretical expected return is α for varying α. The expected return from a \$1 bet to place on horse l is[6,7]

$$EX_l^p \equiv \sum_{\substack{j=1\\ j\neq l}}^{n}\left(\frac{q_l q_j}{1-q_l}\right)\left[1+\frac{1}{20}\mathrm{INT}\left\{\left(\frac{Q(P+1)-(1+P_l+P_j)}{2}\right)\left(\frac{1}{1+P_l}\right)\times 20\right\}\right]$$
$$+\sum_{\substack{i=1\\ i\neq l}}^{n}\left(\frac{q_i q_l}{1-q_i}\right)\left[1+\frac{1}{20}\mathrm{INT}\left\{\left(\frac{Q(P+1)-(1+P_i+P_l)}{2}\right)\left(\frac{1}{1+P_l}\right)\times 20\right\}\right], \tag{4}$$

[6]The expressions (4) and (5) give the marginal expected return for an additional \$1 bet to place or show on horse l. To obtain the average expected rates of return one simply replaces $(1+p_l)$ and $(1+s_l)$ in these expressions by p_l and s_l, respectively. From a practical point of view with usual track data these quantities are virtually identical.

[7]A further complication, not reflected in (4) and (5) below, is that a \$2 winning bet must return at least \$2.10. Hence in these "minus pools" involving an extreme favorite the track's take is less than $1 - Q$.

where Q is 1 minus the track take, $P \equiv \sum P_i$ is the place pool, P_i is bet on horse i to place and INT(Y) means the largest integer not exceeding Y. In (4) the quantities P and P_i are the amounts bet before an additional \$1 is bet; similarly with S and S_i in (5), below. The expressions involving INT take into account the fact that \$2 bets return payoffs rounded down to the nearest \$0.10. The two expressions represent the expected payoffs if l is first or second, respectively. Similarly the expected payoff from a \$1 bet to show on horse l is

$$
\begin{aligned}
EX_l^s \equiv & \sum_{\substack{j=1\\ j\neq l}}^{n} \sum_{\substack{k=1\\ k\neq l,j}}^{n} \frac{q_l q_j q_k}{(1-q_l)(1-q_l-q_j)} \\
& \times \left[1 + \frac{1}{20} \mathrm{INT} \left\{ \left(\frac{Q(S+1) - (1+S_l+S_j+S_k)}{3} \right) \left(\frac{1}{1+S_l} \right) \times 20 \right\} \right] \\
& + \sum_{\substack{i=1\\ i\neq l}}^{n} \sum_{\substack{k=1\\ k\neq i,l}}^{n} \frac{q_i q_l q_k}{(1-q_i)(1-q_i-q_l)} \\
& \times \left[1 + \frac{1}{20} \mathrm{INT} \left\{ \left(\frac{Q(S+1) - (1+S_i+S_l+S_k)}{3} \right) \left(\frac{1}{1+S_l} \right) \times 20 \right\} \right] \\
& + \sum_{\substack{i=1\\ i\neq l}}^{n} \sum_{\substack{j=1\\ j\neq l,i}}^{n} \frac{q_i q_j q_l}{(1-q_i)(1-q_i-q_j)} \\
& \times \left[1 + \frac{1}{20} \mathrm{INT} \left\{ \left(\frac{Q(S+1) - (1+S_i+S_j+S_l)}{3} \right) \left(\frac{1}{1+S_l} \right) \times 20 \right\} \right], \qquad (5)
\end{aligned}
$$

where $S \equiv \sum S_i$ is the show pool, S_i is bet on horse i to show and the three expressions represent the expected payoffs if l is first, second and third, respectively.

Naturally one would expect that positive profits would not be obtained, given the inherent inaccuracies in assumptions (1)–(3), unless the theoretical expected return α was significantly greater than 1. However we might hope that the actual rate of return would at least increase with α and be somewhat near α. Table 3 indicates this is true for both data sets. The perverse behavior for high α in the place pool is presumably a small sample phenomenon. Additional calculations along these lines appear in Harville [14].

4. A Betting Model

The results in Table 3 give a strong indication that there are significant inefficiencies in the place and show pools and that it is possible not only to achieve above average returns but to make substantial profits. In this section we develop a model indicating not only which horses should be bet but how much should be bet taking into account investor preferences and wealth levels and the effect of bet size on the odds.

We consider an investor having initial wealth w_0 contemplating a series of bets. It is

TABLE 3

Results of Betting \$1 to Place or Show on Horses with a Theoretical Expected Return of at Least α

Exhibition Park

	Place			Show		
α	Number of Bets	Total Net Profit (\$)	Net Rate of Return (%)	Number of Bets	Total Net Profit (\$)	Net Rate of Return (%)
1.04	225	5.10	2.3	612	33.20	5.4
1.08	126	− 10.10	−8.0	386	53.50	13.9
1.12	69	11.10	16.1	223	40.80	18.3
1.16	40	5.10	12.8	143	26.30	18.4
1.20	18	5.30	29.4	95	21.70	22.8
1.25	11	−2.70	−24.5	44	11.20	25.5
1.30	3	−3	− 100.0	27	10.80	40.0
1.50	0	0	—	3	6	200.0

Santa Anita

	Place			Show		
α	Number of Bets	Total Net Profit (\$)	Net Rate of Return (%)	Number of Bets	Total Net Profit (\$)	Net Rate of Return (%)
1.04	103	12.30	11.9	307	− 18.00	− 5.9
1.08	52	12.80	24.6	162	6.90	4.3
1.12	22	9.20	41.8	89	3.00	3.4
1.16	7	2.30	32.9	46	12.40	27.0
1.20	3	− 1.30	−43.3	27	6.20	23.0
1.25	0	0	—	9	6.00	66.7
1.30	0	0	—	5	5.10	102.0
1.50	0	0	—	0	0	—

natural to suppose that the investor would wish to maximize the long run rate of asset growth and thus employ the so-called Bernoulli capital growth model; see Ziemba and Vickson [28] for references and discussion of various assumptions and results. We use the following result: if in each time period $t = 1, 2, \ldots$ there are I investment opportunities with returns per unit invested denoted by the random variables $x_{t1}, \ldots, x_{tI}$, where the x_{ti} have finitely many distinct values and for distinct t the families are independent, then maximizing $E \log \sum \lambda_{ti} x_{ti}$, s.t. $\sum \lambda_{ti} \leqslant w_t$, $\lambda_{ti} \geqslant 0$ maximizes the asymptotic rate of asset growth. The assumptions are quite reasonable in a horseracing context because there are a finite number of return possibilities and the race by race returns are likely to be nearly independent since different horses will be running (although the jockeys and trainers may not be).

The second key feature of the model is that it considers an investor's ability to influence the odds by the size of his bets.[8] This yields the following model to calculate

[8]The first model to include this feature seems to be Isaacs [16]. Only win bets are considered with linear utility, and he is able to determine the exact solution in closed form. His model may be useful in situations where the perfect market assumption (3) is violated or where special expertise leads one to believe their estimates of the q_i are better than those of the other bettors.

the optimal amounts to bet for place and show.

$$\underset{\{p_l\}\{s_l\}}{\text{Maximize}} \sum_{i=1}^{n} \sum_{\substack{j=1\\ j\neq i}}^{n} \sum_{\substack{k=1\\ k\neq i,j}}^{n} \frac{q_i q_j q_k}{(1-q_i)(1-q_i-q_j)} \log \left[\begin{array}{l} \dfrac{Q(P+\sum_{l=1}^{n} p_l)-(p_i+p_j+P_i+P_j)}{2} \\ \quad \times \left(\dfrac{p_i}{p_i+P_i} + \dfrac{p_j}{p_j+P_j} \right) \\ + \dfrac{Q(S+\sum_{l=1}^{n} s_l)-(s_i+s_j+s_k+S_i+S_j+S_k)}{3} \\ \quad \times \left(\dfrac{s_i}{s_i+S_i} + \dfrac{s_j}{s_j+S_j} + \dfrac{s_k}{s_k+S_k} \right) \\ \quad + w_0 - \sum_{\substack{l=1\\ l\neq i,j,k}}^{n} s_l - \sum_{\substack{l=1\\ l\neq i,j}}^{n} p_l \end{array} \right] \tag{6}$$

$$\text{s.t.} \sum_{l=1}^{n} (p_l + s_l) \leqslant w_0, \qquad p_l \geqslant 0, s_l \geqslant 0, l = 1, \ldots, n,$$

where $Q = 1 -$ the track take, W_i, P_j and S_k are the total dollar amounts bet to win, place and show on the indicated horses by the crowd, respectively, $W \equiv \sum W_i$, $P \equiv \sum P_j$ and $S \equiv \sum S_k$ are the win, place and show pools, respectively, $q_i \equiv W_i / W$ is the theoretical probability that horse i wins, w_0 is initial wealth and p_l and s_l are the investor's bets to place and show on horse l, respectively.

The formulation (6) maximizes the expected logarithm of final wealth considering the probabilities and payoffs from all possible horserace finishes. It is exact except for the minor adjustment made that the rounding down to the nearest \$0.10 for a two dollar bet, see (4) and (5), is omitted.[9] For the values of $\alpha \geqslant 1.16$ it was observed that in a given race at most three p_l and three s_l were nonzero. When (6) is then simplified it can be solved in less than 1 second of CPU time.[10] A discussion of the generalized concavity properties of (6) will appear in a forthcoming paper by Kallberg and Ziemba.

The results are illustrated by function 1 in Figures 1 and 2 for the two data sets using an initial wealth of \$10,000. In both cases the bets produced from (6) lead to well above average returns and to positive profits.[11] These results may be contrasted with random betting; function 2 in Figures 1 and 2. Intuition suggests that Santa Anita with its larger betting pools would have more accurate estimates of the q_i than would be obtained at Exhibition Park. Hence positive profits would result from lower values of α. The results bear this out and only horses with $\alpha \geqslant 1.20$ for Exhibition Park were considered for possible bets. Generally speaking the bets are usually favorites and almost always on those horses with maximum $(W_i/W)/(P_i/P)$ and $(W_i/W)/(S_i/S)$

[9]It is possible to include this feature in (6) but it greatly complicates the solution procedure (e.g. differentiability is lost) with little added gain in accuracy.

[10]All calculations were made on UBC's AMDAHL 470V6 Model II computer using a code for the generalized reduced gradient algorithm.

[11]The procedure was to calculate the optimal bets to place and show in each race using (6) with the present wealth level. The results of the race and the actual payoffs that reflect the track's take and breakage are known. The payoff for our investor's bets were calculated using all the bets of the crowd plus the bets of our investor taking into account the track's take and breakage, i.e. the payoffs are thus those that would have occurred had our investor actually made his bets. The wealth level was then adjusted to reflect the race's gain or loss and the procedure continued for all races.

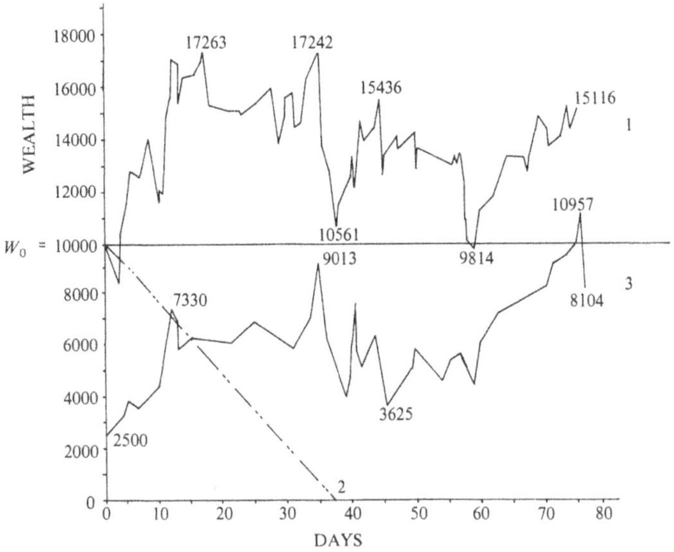

[1]Results from expected log betting to place and show when expected returns are 1.16 or better with initial wealth \$10,000.

[2]Approximate wealth level history for random horse betting. Total dollars bet is as in system 1 (\$116,074). Track payback is 82.5%, therefore final wealth level is \$10,000 − 0.175(\$116.074) = −\$10,313 (Note: breakage is not taken into consideration)

[3]Results from using the Exhibition Park approximate regression scheme (with initial wealth \$2,500) at Santa Anita.

FIGURE 1. Wealth Level Histories for Alternative Betting Schemes; Santa Anita: 1973/74 Season.

ratios. These ratios of the theoretical probability of winning to the track take unadjusted odds to place or show form a type of cost-benefit ratio that provides a first approximation to α. This is discussed further in §5, below. Most of the bets are to show and one tends to bet only about once per day. The numbers of bets and their size distribution are presented in Table 4. As expected, the influence on the odds made by our investor's bets is much greater at Exhibition Park hence the bets there tend to be much smaller than at Santa Anita. However, even there about 10% of the bets exceed \$1000.

The log formulation has absolute risk aversion $1/w$, which for wealth around \$10,000 is virtually zero. Zero absolute risk aversion is, of course, achieved by linear utility. One then will bet on the horse (or horses) with the highest α until the influence on the odds drops this horse (or horses) below another horse's α, etc., continuing until there are no favorable bets or the betting wealth has been fully utilized. The results of such linear utility betting with $w_0 = \$10,000$ are: at Exhibition Park with $\alpha \geqslant 1.20$ final wealth is \$14,818; at Santa Anita with $\alpha \geqslant 1.16$ final wealth is \$10,910. Such a strategy is a very risky one and leads to some very large bets. The log function has the distinct advantage that it implies negative infinite utility at zero wealth hence bets having any significant probability of yielding final wealth near zero are avoided.

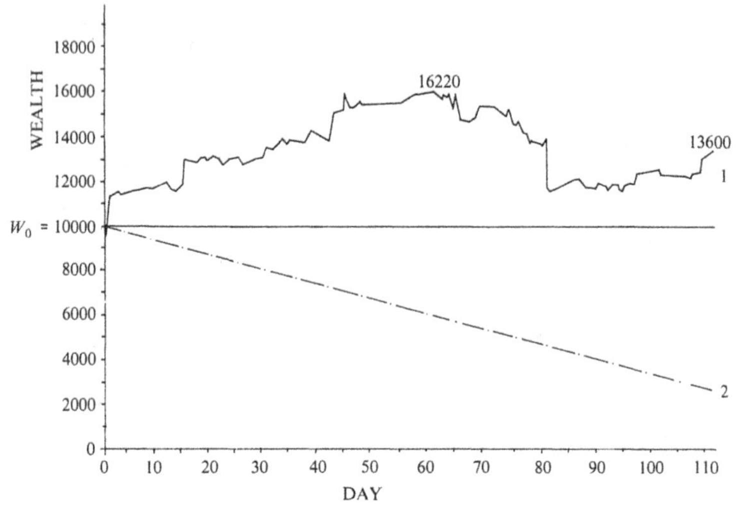

[1]Results from expected log betting to place and show when expected returns are 1.20 or better with initial wealth $10,000.

[2]Approximate wealth level history for random horse betting. Total dollars bet is as in system 2 ($8461). Track payback is 81.9% therefore final wealth level is $10,000 − 0.181($38461) = $3,035. (Note: Breakage is not taken into consideration.)

FIGURE 2. Wealth Level Histories for Alternative Betting Schemes; Exhibition Park: 1978 Season.

TABLE 4

Size Distribution of Bets, w_0 = $10,000, Log Utility

	Santa Anita				Exhibition Park			
	Place		Show		Place		Show	
Size	% of Bets	% of $Bet	% of Bets	% of $Bet	% of Bets	% of $Bet	% of Bets	% of $Bet
0–50	7.1	0.3	2.6	0.1	29.4	3.6	17.0	1.0
51–100	0	0	1.3	0.1	23.5	6.7	13.8	2.8
101–200	0	0	3.9	0.4	5.9	2.9	22.3	9.3
201–300	21.4	6.1	5.2	1.0	5.9	4.4	14.9	10.3
301–500	7.1	3.2	9.1	2.6	23.5	30.6	8.5	9.1
501–700	14.3	10.3	13.0	5.7	0	0	6.4	10.5
701–1000	14.3	14.4	7.8	4.8	0	0	7.4	17.5
> 1001	35.8	65.7	57.1	85.3	11.8	51.8	9.7	39.5
	n = 14	$11,932	n = 77	$104,142	n = 17	$4,954	n = 94[a]	$33,507

Total Place Bets; Total Show Bets; Total Santa Anita Bettings = $116,074

Total Place Bets; Total Show Bets; Total Exhibition Park Betting = $38,461

[a]Two of these bets had $EX_s^l \geqslant 1.20$ and $s_l^* = 0$.

5. Making the System Operational

The calculations reported in Figures 1 and 2 were made under the assumption that the investor is free to bet once all other bettors have placed their bets. In practice one can only attempt to be one of the last bettors.[12] There is a natural tradeoff between placing a bet too early and increasing the inaccuracies and running the possibility of arriving too late at the betting window to place a bet.[13] The time just prior to the beginning of a race is crucial since many bets are typically made then including the so called "smart money" bets made very close to the beginning of the race so their impact on other bettors is minimized. It is thus extremely important that the investor be able to perform all calculations necessary to place the bet(s) very quickly. Typically, since tracks have neither public phones nor electricity, calculations can at most utilize battery operated calculators or possibly a battery operated special purpose computer. Even if computing times were negligible the very act of punching in the data needed for an exact calculation is too time-consuming since it takes more than one minute. Therefore, in practice, approximations that utilize a limited number of input data elements are required. Several types of approximations are possible such as the tabular rules of thumb developed by King [17] or the regression procedures suggested here. Our procedure indicates whether or not a bet to place or show is warranted and at what level using the following eight data inputs: w_0, W_{i*}, P_{i*}, Q_{j*}, S_{j*}, W, P and S, where i^* is an i for which $(W_i/W)/(P_i/P)$ is maximized and j^* is a j for which $(W_j/W)/(S_j/S)$ is maximized. It is easy to determine i^* and j^*, particularly since i^* often equals j^*, by inspection of the tote board. The approximation supposes that the only possible bets are i^* to place and j^* to show. The regressions, as given below, must be calibrated to a given track and initial wealth level. As a prelude to actual betting the regressions were calibrated at Exhibition Park for $w_0 = \$2500$. For calculated i^* the expected return on a \$1 bet to place is approximated by

$$E\tilde{X}_{i*}^{P} = 0.39445 + 0.51338\,\frac{W_{i*}/W}{P_{i*}/P}, \qquad R^2 = 0.776. \tag{7}$$

If $E\tilde{X}_{i*}^{P} \geqslant 1.20$ then the optimal bet to place is approximated by

$$\begin{aligned} p_{i*} = {} & -459.32 + 1715.6q_{i*} - 0.042518q_{i*}P - 7440.1q_{i*}^2 \\ & + 13791q_{i*}^3 + 0.10247P_{i*} + 49.572\ln w_0, R^2 = 0.954. \end{aligned} \tag{8}$$

Similarly for j^* the expected return on a \$1 bet to show is approximated by

$$E\tilde{X}_{j*}^{S} = 0.64514 + 0.32806\,\frac{W_{j*}/W}{S_{j*}/S}, \qquad R^2 = 0.650. \tag{9}$$

[12] The model as developed in this paper utilizes an inefficiency in the place and show pools to yield positive profits. An investor's bets are determined by his wealth level as well as the profitability of one or more such bets. There may or may not exist "enough" inefficiency to provide positive profits for additional investors using a system of this nature. In the context of the Isaac's model, for win bets with linear utility, Thrall [25] showed that if there were positive profits to be made and each new investor was aware of all previous investor's bets then the profits for these various bettors are shared and in the limit become zero. It is likely that a similar result obtains for the model discussed here.

[13] At some tracks, such as Santa Anita, betting ends precisely at post time when the electric totalizator machines are shut off. At other tracks including Exhibition Park, betting ends when the horses enter the starting gate which may be 2 or even 3 minutes past the post time.

If $E\tilde{X}_j^s \geqslant 1.20$ then the optimal bet to show is approximated by

$$s_{j*} = -660.97 - 867.69q_{j*} + 0.25933q_{j*}S + 3715.2q_{j*}^2$$
$$-0.19572S_{j*} + 77.014 \ln w_0, \qquad R^2 = 0.970. \tag{10}$$

All the coefficients in (7)–(10) are highly significant at levels not exceeding 0.05. Utilizing the equations (7)–(10) results in a scheme in which the data input and execution time on a modern hand held programmable calculator is about 35 seconds.

The results of utilizing this method on the Exhibition Park data with initial wealth of \$2500 are shown in Figure 3, functions 1 and 2. Using the exact calculations yields a final wealth of \$5197 while the approximation scheme has an even higher final wealth of \$7698. The approximation scheme leads to 63 more bets (174 versus 111) than the exact calculation. Since these bets had a positive net return the total profit of the approximation scheme exceeds that of the exact calculation. Thus, it is clear that one would maximize profits with a cutoff rule below the conservative level of 1.20. The size distribution of bets from the exact and approximate solutions are remarkably similar; see Table 6 in [15].

For place there were 17 bets where EX^p exceeded or equalled 1.20 of which 7 (41%) were in the money. Only 2 of these 17 bets were not chosen by the regression. However 14 horses were chosen for betting by the regressions even though their "true" EX^p was less than 1.20. Most of these had "true" EX^p values close to 1.20 and were favorites. Four of these horses (29%) were in the money. For show there were 94 bets where EX^s exceeded or equalled 1.20 of which 52 (55%) were in the money. Only 8 of these were

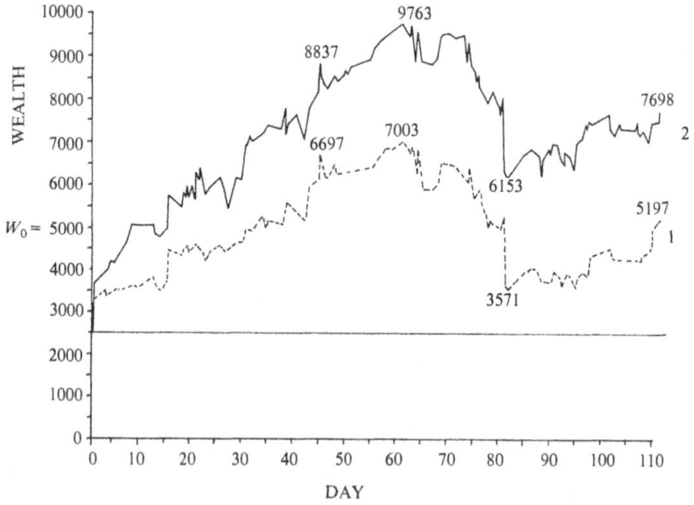

[1] Results from expected log betting to place and show when expected returns are 1.20 or better with initial wealth \$2,500.

[2] Results from using the approximate regression scheme with initial wealth \$2,500.

FIGURE 3. Wealth Level Histories for Exact and Approximate Regression Betting Schemes; Exhibition Park: 1978 Season.

overlooked by the regressions while 59 bets with "true" EX^s values less than 1.20 were chosen by the regressions. Of these 39 (66%) were in the money.

The regression method is a simple procedure that seems to work well. For example using it on the Santa Anita data (without reestimating the coefficients) indicates that initial wealth of \$2500 would yield a final wealth of \$8104; see function 3 in Figure 1. Conceivably, there are many possible refinements using fundamental information that could be added. Many of these refinements as well as discussion of the results of actual betting will appear in a forthcoming book by Ziemba and Hausch. One such refinement is the supposition that the win market is more efficient under normal fast track conditions and less efficient when the track is slow, muddy, heavy, wet, sloppy, etc. Bets were made on 87 of the 110 days at Exhibition Park; of these 57 days had a fast track. Using the regressions yields "fast track" bets of \$32,501 returning \$38,364 for a net profit of \$5863. On the nonfast days the regressions suggest bets of \$17,180 returning \$16,515 for a loss of \$665. Hence this refinement decreases the time spent at the track and increases the net profit from \$5198 to \$5863.

6. Implementation and Reliability of the System

The model presented in this paper assumed that one can utilize the betting data that prevails at the end of the betting period, say t, to calculate optimal bets. In practice, however, even with the approximations given by (7)–(10), one requires about 1–1.5 minutes to physically calculate the optimal bets and place them. Thus one can only utilize betting information from τ ($\approx t - 1.5$). Hence bets that were optimal at τ may not be as profitable at t. Some evidence by Ritter [20] seems to indicate that the odds on the expost favorite at t often decrease from τ to t. In which case an optimal bet at τ may be a poor bet at t. Ritter investigated the systems: bet on i^* if $(P_{i*}/P/(W_{i*}/W)$ $\leqslant 0.7$ and on j^* if $(S_{j*}/S)/(W_{j*}/W) \leqslant 0.7$. (For comparison equations (7) and (9) indicate the more restrictive constraints 0.6373 and 0.5912, respectively, instead of 0.7. The less restrictive Ritter constraints yield about three times as many bets as (7) and (9) indicate.) Using a sample of 229 harness races at Sportsman's Park and Hawthorne Park in Chicago he found that with \$2 bets these systems gained 24% and 16%, respectively. But a 15% advantage shrunk to -1% if one uses the τ bets with a random shock over the τ to t period (for the show bets for the 95 races at Hawthorne with a 0.65 cutoff). There are some difficulties with the design of Ritter's experiment, such as the small sample, the inclusion of only \$2 bets and the use of a random shock rather than an estimate of usual trends from τ to t, etc., however, his results point to the difficulty of actually making substantial profits in a racetrack setting.

An attempt was made during the summer 1980 racing season at Exhibition Park to implement the proposed system and observe the "end of betting problem." Nine racing days were attended during which 90 races were run. At $t-2$ minutes the win, place, and show data were recorded on any horse that, through equations (7) and (9), warranted a bet. Equations (8) and (10) were then used on this data to determine the regression estimates of the optimal bets. Updated toteboard data on these horses were recorded until the end of betting to determine if the horse remained a system bet. Results of this experiment are shown in Table 5 where: 1) an initial wealth of \$2500 is assumed; 2) size of bet calculations are done on data at $t-2$ minutes; and 3) returns are based on final data. Twenty-two bets were made that yielded final wealth of \$3716 for a profit of \$1216. Actual betting was not done but by making the calculations two minutes before the end of betting allows 1.5 minutes to place the bet, more than

TABLE 5

Results from Summer 1980 *Exhibition Park Betting*

Date	Race	Regression estimate of expected return per dollar, 2 minutes before end of betting	Regression estimate of expected return per dollar, at the end of betting	Regression estimate of optimal bet 2 minutes before end of betting	Finish	Net return based on final data with consideration of our bets affecting odds	Final wealth
							$2500
July 2	9	120	122	$19,SHOW ON 4	5-6-7	− $19	2481
"	10	120	123	72,SHOW ON 8	8-1-2	72	2553
July 9	7	121	110	292,SHOW ON 1	2-7-1	131	2684
"	10	135	122	248,PLACE ON 1	1-6-2	260	2944
July 16	6	131	122	487,PLACE ON 9 }	9-8-6	536 } 682	3626
		139	117	292,SHOW ON 9 }		146 }	
"	7	125	127	7,SHOW ON 1	5-2-8	− 7	3619
July 23	3	149	149	30,SHOW ON 2	2-10-7	92	3711
"	4	139	134	573,SHOW ON 10	6-10-4	201	3912
July 30	8	121	111	215,PLACE ON 4	4-1-5	129	4041
"	9	123	125	591,SHOW ON 6	8-1-5	− 591	3450
Aug 6	6	128	112	39,SHOW ON 4	4-3-1	59	3509
"	9	124	103	51,SHOW ON 2	4-1-3	− 51	3458
Aug 8	1	121	132	87,SHOW ON 1	1-10-4	139	3597
"	3	127	111	635,SHOW ON 3	3-4-7	127	3724
"	4	126	113	126,SHOW ON 2	2-7-1	82	3806
Aug 11	8	121	112	94,SHOW ON 8	8-6-2	113	3919
"	9	131	130	688,SHOW ON 5	5-3-4	138	4057
Aug 13	3	128	106	33,SHOW ON 2	1-6-7	− 33	4024
"	6	131	122	205,SHOW ON 5	5-8-4	144	4168
"	7	134	133	511,SHOW ON 6	8-5-9	− 511	3657
"	10	123	109	108,SHOW ON 5	3-5-1	59	3716

enough time. Note in Table 5 that many systems bets at $t-2$ were not system bets at t, however all had regression expected returns of more than one.

An important question concerns the reliability of the results: are the results true exploitations of market inefficiencies or could they be obtained simply by chance? This question is investigated utilizing a simple model which was suggested to us by an anonymous referee. The first application is concerned with an estimate of the probability that the system's theory is vacuous and indeed the observations conform to specific favorable samples from a random betting population. The second application estimates the probability of not making a positive profit. The calculations utilize the 1980 Exhibition Park data; see Table 5.

Let π be the probability of winning a bet in each trial and

$$X_i = \begin{cases} 1 + w & \text{if the bet is won,} \\ 0 & \text{otherwise,} \end{cases}$$

be the return from a $1 bet in trial i. In n trials, the probability of winning at least $100y\%$ of the total bet is

$$\Pr\left[\frac{1}{n}\left(\sum_{i=1}^{n} X_i\right) - 1 > y\right]. \tag{11}$$

Assume that the trials are independent. Since the X_i are binomially distributed (11) can be approximated by a normal probability distribution as

$$1 - \Phi\left[\frac{\sqrt{n}\,\{y - (1+w)\pi + 1\}}{(1+w)\pi\sqrt{(1-\pi)/\pi}}\right] \tag{12}$$

where Φ is the cumulative distribution function of a standard $N(0,1)$ variable. The observed probability of winning a bet, weighted by size of bet made, yields 0.771 as an estimate of π. If the systems theory was vacuous and random betting was actually being made then $(1+w)\pi = 0.83$ since the track's payback is approximately 83%. The 22 bets made totalled \$5304 and resulted in a profit of \$1216 for a rate of return of 22.9%. Using equation (12) with $n = 22$, gives 3×10^{-5} as the probability of making 22.9% through random betting.

Suppose that the 1980 Exhibition Park results represent typical system behavior so $\pi = 0.771$ and $(1+w)\pi = 1.229$. In n trials the probability of making a non-positive net return is

$$\Pr\left[\frac{1}{n}\left(\sum_{i=1}^{n} X_i\right) - 1 < 0\right] \tag{13}$$

which can be approximated as

$$\Phi\left[\frac{\sqrt{n}\,(1 - (1+w)\pi)}{(1-w)\pi\sqrt{(1-\pi)/\pi}}\right] = \Phi(-0.342\sqrt{n}). \tag{14}$$

For $n = 22$ this probability is only 0.054 and for $n = 50$ and 100 this probability is 0.008 and 0.0003, respectively. Thus it is reasonable to suppose that the results from the 1980 Exhibition Park data (as well as the 1978 Exhibition Park and 1973/1974 Santa Anita data with their larger samples) represent true exploitation of a market inefficiency.[14]

[14]Without implicating them we would like to thank Michael Alhadeff of Longacres Racetrack in Seattle, the American Totalizator Corporation and the staff of the Jockey Club at Exhibition Park in Vancouver for helping us obtain the data used in this study, and M. J. Brennan and E. U. Choo for helpful discussions. Thanks are also due to V. S. Bawa, J. R. Ritter, and two anonymous referees for helpful comments on an earlier draft of this paper. This paper is a condensation of [15].

References

1. Ali, M. M., "Probability and Utility Estimates for Racetrack Bettors," *J. Political Economy*, Vol. 85 (1977), pp. 803–815.
2. ———, "Some Evidence of the Efficiency of a Speculative Market," *Econometrica*, Vol. 47, No. 2 (1979), pp. 387–392.
3. Arrow, K. J., *Aspects of the Theory of Risk Bearing*, Yrjö Jahnsson Foundation, Helsinki, 1965.
4. Baumol, W. J., *The Stock Market and Economic Efficiency*, Fordham Univ. Press, New York, 1965.
5. Beyer, A., *My \$50, 000 Year at the Races*, Harcourt, Brace, Jovanovitch, New York, 1978.
6. Copeland, J. E. and Weston, J. F., *Financial Theory and Corporate Policy*, Addison-Wesley, Reading, Mass., 1979.
7. Downes, D. and Dyckman, T. R., "A Critical Look at the Efficient Market Empirical Research Literature as it Relates to Accounting Information," *Accounting Rev.* (April 1973), pp. 300–317.
8. Fabricant, B. F., *Horse Sense*, David McKay, New York, 1965.

9. FAMA, E. F., "Efficient Capital Markets: A Review of Theory and Empirical Work," *J. Finance*, Vol. 25 (1970), pp. 383–417.
10. ———, *Foundations of Finance*, Basic Books, New York, 1976.
11. FIGLEWSKI, S., "Subjective Information and Market Efficiency in a Betting Model," *J. Political Economy*, Vol. 87 (1979), pp. 75–88.
12. GRIFFITH, R. M., "Odds Adjustments by American Horse Race Bettors," *Amer. J. Psychology*, Vol. 62 (1949), pp. 290–294.
13. ———, "A Footnote on Horse Race Betting," *Trans. Kentucky Acad. Sci.*, Vol. 22 (1961), pp. 78–81.
14. HARVILLE, D. A., "Assigning Probabilities to the Outcomes of Multi-Entry Competitions," *J. Amer. Statist. Assoc.*, Vol. 68 (1973), pp. 312–316.
15. HAUSCH, D. B., ZIEMBA, W. T. AND RUBINSTEIN, M. E., "Efficiency of the Market for Racetrack Betting," U.B.C. Faculty of Commerce, W. P. No. 712, September 1980.
16. ISAACS, R., "Optimal Horse Race Bets," *Amer. Math. Monthly* (1953), pp. 310–315.
17. KING, A. P., "Market Efficiency of a Multi-Entry Competition," MBA essay, Graduate School of Business, University of California, Berkeley, June 1978.
18. MCGLOTHLIN, W. H., "Stability of Choices Among Uncertain Alternatives," *Amer. J. Psychology*, Vol. 63 (1956), pp. 604–615.
19. PRATT, J., "Risk Aversion in the Small and in the Large," *Econometrica*, Vol. 32 (1964), pp. 122–136.
20. RITTER, J. R., "Racetrack Betting: An Example of a Market with Efficient Arbitrage," mimeo, Department of Economics, University of Chicago, March 1978.
21. ROSETT, R. H., "Gambling and Rationality," *J. Political Economy*, Vol. 73 (1965), pp. 595–607.
22. RUBINSTEIN, M., "Securities Market Efficiency in an Arrow-Depreu Market," *Amer. Econom. Rev.*, Vol. 65, No. 5 (1975), pp. 812–824.
23. SELIGMAN, D., "A Thinking Man's Guide to Losing at the Track," *Fortune*, Vol. 92 (1975), pp. 81–87.
24. SNYDER, W. W., "Horse Racing: Testing the Efficient Markets Model," *J. Finance*, Vol. 33 (1978), pp. 1109–1118.
25. THRALL, R. M., "Some Results in Non-Linear Programming," *Proc. Second Sympos. in Linear Programming*, Vol. 2, National Bureau of Standards, Washington, D. C., January 27–29, 1955, pp. 471–493.
26. VERGIN, R. C., "An Investigation of Decision Rules for Thoroughbred Race Horse Wagering," *Interfaces*, Vol. 8, No. 1 (1977), pp. 34–45.
27. WEITZMAN, M., "Utility Analysis and Group Behaviour: An Empirical Study," *J. Political Economy*, Vol. 73 (1965), pp. 18–26.
28. ZIEMBA, W. T. AND VICKSON, R. G., eds., *Stochastic Optimization Models in Finance*, Academic Press, New York, 1975.

Chapter 17

Donald B. Hausch
University of Wisconsin—Madison

William T. Ziemba
University of British Columbia

Arbitrage Strategies for Cross-Track Betting on Major Horse Races*

Cross-track betting permits bettors to place wagers at their local tracks on a race being run at another track. Since each track operates a separate betting pool, the odds can vary across the tracks. The data suggest that the odds vary, and they often vary dramatically, allowing arbitrage opportunities. This article employs a risk-free arbitrage model to demonstrate the cross-track inefficiency and recommends an optimal capital growth model for exploiting it. A simpler method is proposed for a single bettor at a single cross track. The results indicate that these methods would have worked well in practice on a number of recent Triple Crown races.

I. Introduction

Racetracks and securities markets have many characteristics in common. A difference, though, is their complexity; the racetrack is really a sequence of markets that are relatively simple, short-lived, and, for the most part, independent. This "market-in-miniature" feature makes the racetrack attractive for tests of market efficiency, especially since, as Thaler and Ziemba (1988, p. 162) suggest, "one can argue that wagering markets have a better chance [than securities markets] of being efficient because the conditions (quick, repeated feedback) are those which usually facilitate learning." The many empirical racetrack studies support a weak form of efficiency for some of the available wagers, while other types of wagers seem not to be efficient. These studies are reviewed in Section II.

This article studies cross-track betting, a relatively new form of wagering. It allows bettors to wager at their track (a cross track) on a race

* Without implicating them, we would like to thank Bruce Fauman and Fraser Rawlinson. Also, we greatly appreciate the data supplied by a number of U.S. racetracks, and we wish to thank Victor Lespinasse for suggesting the one-track model.

*This chapter was originally published in: Hausch, D. B. & Ziemba, W. T. (1990). Arbitrage Strategies for Cross-Track Betting on Major Horse Races. *Journal of Business*, 63(1), 61–78.

TABLE 1 **Home-Track and Cross-Track Betting, Kentucky Derby**

Year	Home-Track Attendance	No. Cross Tracks	Home-Track Betting ($)	Cross-Track Betting ($)
1982	141,009	...	5,011,575	...
1983	134,444	...	5,546,977	...
1984	126,453	24	5,420,787	13,521,146
1985	108,573	32	5,770,074	14,474,555
1986	123,819	56	6,165,119	19,776,332
1987	130,532	73	6,362,673	20,829,236
1988	137,694	93	7,427,389	24,449,058

being run at another track (the home track). Since cross-track betting tends to be limited to major races, it gives the racing public an opportunity to bet on some of the world's finest racehorses. This makes it very popular with the public. Cross-track wagering can lead to increased attendance and revenues at the cross tracks and add to the revenues of the home track through a fee (usually 5% of the handle) paid by the cross tracks. Thus, all the tracks can increase profits.[1]

Separate pools for each track means the payoffs at the various tracks can differ.[2] Due to the costs of arbitrage in this setting, market efficiency across the tracks would, for practical purposes, allow some differences across the various sets of track odds. Considerable differences, however, would suggest the possibility of a market inefficiency. The data demonstrate that considerable differences do occur. For example, a $2.00 win ticket on Ferdinand, the winner of the 1986 Kentucky Derby, paid from $13.20 at Fairplex in Pomona, California, to $90.00 at Evangeline Downs in Lafayette, Louisiana.[3] Obviously, bettors would have preferred their win bets on Ferdinand to be made at

1. For an example of this effect, consider the home-track and cross-track betting on the Kentucky Derby (see table 1). The introduction in 1984 of cross-track betting on this race has greatly increased total Derby wagering. At the same time, cross-track betting seems to have had, at worst, only a minor effect on home-track wagering. The cross tracks' revenues can increase also. For instance, Illinois set a one-day pari-mutuel record on Kentucky Derby Day, 1987. Cross-track betting on the Derby accounted for $1,326,239 of the $4,534,879 wagered that day in the state. Another example is Calder Race Course in Florida. They set all-time revenue and attendance records on Kentucky Derby Day, 1985. Attendance was 23,105, and $2,775,645 was wagered, $562,453 of it on the Derby.

2. In some cases, all the wagers at the various tracks are summed. Then, on the basis of these summed values, identical payoffs are made at all the tracks. This is often called "intertrack" wagering and typically the tracks are within one state. Intertrack wagering will not be considered here.

3. These extreme payoffs are not just limited to the smaller tracks. Two large-track examples are Hollywood Park, where Ferdinand paid $16.80, and Woodbine Racetrack in Toronto where he paid $79.60. Alysheba, the 1987 Kentucky Derby winner, paid from $15.80 at Hollywood Park, California to $30.20 at Beulah Park, Ohio. Winning Colors, the 1988 derby winner, paid $7.40 at Pimlico Race Course, Maryland, and $10.40 at Beulah Park.

Evangeline Downs. The nature of the pari-mutuel betting system requires that if Ferdinand paid less at Fairplex than at Evangeline Downs, then another horse, were it to have won, would have paid more at Fairplex than at Evangeline Downs. Thus, if we are able both to learn the odds and place our bets at various tracks, it appears that significant arbitrage opportunities may exist.

Section III develops a risk-free arbitrage model to demonstrate this cross-track inefficiency. The optimal capital growth model is studied in Section IV on the general cross-track problem and, in Section V, on a simpler one-track problem. These models are tested on data from several recent Triple Crown races. A final discussion is in Section VI.

II. Efficiency of the Various Betting Markets

Among the possible wagers at the track are the so-called straight wagers to win, place, and show. They pay off when one's horse is at least first, second, or third, respectively. The "exotic" wagers include quinellas (requiring one to name the first two horses), exactors (requiring the first two horses in the correct order), trifectas (requiring the first three horses in the correct order), and daily doubles (requiring the winners of two consecutive races). Tracks have also extended the daily-double concept to picking the winners of three, four, six, and even nine consecutive races. These are very low-probability bets that can have tremendous payoffs, and they are very popular with the racing public. Before exotic wagering was offered by the tracks, bettors could use parlays and other combinations of wagers to construct low-probability/high-payoff situations. Rosett (1965) analyzed these possibilities and demonstrated that, except for extreme long shots, the bettors were rational in the sense that a simple bet would not be made if a parlay with the same probability of success had a greater return. Similarly, Ali (1973) showed that the return on a daily double is not significantly different from the return on what is an identical wager, the corresponding parlay of win bets.

Unlike typical casino games, where the odds are fixed, the odds at the track are determined by the relative amounts the bettors wager on the horses and by the track's transactions costs (the track's take and breakage). Thus, "prices" are determined at the track much like they are in securities markets. Let

n = the number of horses in a race;
T = the number of tracks accepting wagers on the race;
W_i^t = the total amount bet by the public at track t on horse i to win ($i = 1, \ldots, n$ and $t = 1, \ldots, T$);
$W^t = \Sigma_i W_i^t$ = the win pool at track t; and
Q^t = track t's payback proportion (typically from .80 to .86).

Then the payoff per dollar bet to win on horse i at track t is

$$\begin{cases} Q^tW^t/W_i^t & \text{if horse } i \text{ wins,} \\ 0 & \text{otherwise.} \end{cases} \tag{1}$$

To determine the place payoff let P_i^t be the amount bet to place on horse i at track t and let $P^t = \Sigma_i P_i^t$ be track t's place pool. The payoff per dollar bet to place on horse i at track t is

$$\begin{cases} 1 + (Q^tP^t - P_i^t - P_j^t)/(2P_i^t) & \text{if the first two horses are } i \text{ and } j, \\ 0 & \text{if horse } i \text{ is not first or second.} \end{cases} \tag{2}$$

Thus, the track keeps $(1 - Q^t)P^t$ and the place bets on i and j are repaid. The remainder, the losing bets minus the track take, is then split evenly between those who bet on i and those who bet on j. The share for i bettors is then divided on a per-dollar-bet basis. The place payoff on i does not depend on whether i was first or second but it does depend on which horse j was the other top finisher. In a similar fashion the payoff per dollar bet to show on horse i at track t is

$$\begin{cases} 1 + (Q^tS^t - S_i^t - S_j^t - S_k^t)/(3S_i^t) & \text{if the first three horses are } i, j, \text{ and } k, \\ 0 & \text{if horse } i \text{ is not at least third.} \end{cases} \tag{3}$$

Here S_i^t is the show bet on horse i by the public at track t, and $S^t = \Sigma_i S_i^t$ is track t's show pool. It is possible that $(Q^tS^t - S_i^t - S_j^t - S_k^t)/(3S_i^t)$ is less than 0.05, or even negative. In these cases, called minus pools, the track usually agrees to pay \$0.05 profit for each dollar wagered. Minus pools can also occur in the win and place markets, but are much less common. Equations (1)–(3) ignore breakage, the additional charge that results from the track rounding all payoffs down to the nearest 5 or 10 cents on the dollar.[4]

If prices reflect all available information then a market is said to be efficient (see Fama 1970). There are two conclusions that can be drawn from the many studies of win market efficiency (see, for instance, Ali [1977]; and Snyder [1978]). First, the North American public underbets favorites and overbets longshots, and this bias appears across the many years that data have been collected and across all sizes of racetrack betting pools.[5] Second, despite its strength and stability, this bias is almost always less than the track take and thus it cannot be exploited to achieve positive profits. Figure 1 illustrates the favorite/longshot

4. Breakage may seem like a relatively minor cost, but we (Ziemba and Hausch 1987) demonstrate that it can have a dramatic long-run effect on a bettor's fortune.

5. Busche and Hall (1988) demonstrate an opposite bias for Hong Kong bettors. Contrary to the North American bettors, Hong Kong bettors tend to overbet favorites and underbet long shots—a bias that is consistent with risk aversion.

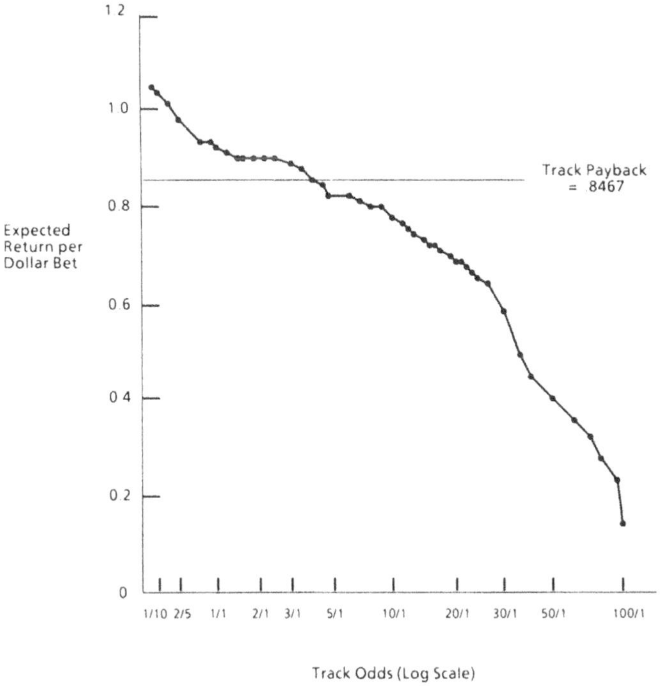

FIG. 1.—Expected return per dollar bet versus odds level: aggregation of studies involving more than 50,000 races. (Source.—Ziemba and Hausch 1986.)

bias and shows that the track take (assumed to be 15.33%, as it is in California) is sufficiently large to preclude profits. The one profitable exception is extreme favorites at odds of 3–10 or less. However, they are relatively rare. Thus, if we define a market to be weakly efficient (see Fama 1970), if no one can devise a profitable trading rule based on historical price information, the win market is, for practical purposes, weakly efficient.

Hausch, Ziemba, and Rubinstein (1981) tested the efficiency of the place-and-show markets. They assumed:

ASSUMPTION 1. If q_i is the probability that horse i wins, then the probability that i is first and j is second is $q_i q_j/(1 - q_i)$, and the probability that i is first, j is second, and k is third is

$$q_i q_j q_k/[(1 - q_i)][(1 - q_i - q_j)].$$

(These formulas were developed and tested by Harville [1973].)[6]

6. Henery (1981) and Stern (1987) show that these equations can be derived by associating with each horse an independent exponential random variable with a scale

Assumption 2. The win market is efficient, so the win odds can be used to estimate q_i.

Using these two assumptions and equations (2) and (3), Hausch, Ziemba, and Rubinstein (1981) were able to identify horses that were underbet to place or show. The optimal capital growth model then determined the place-and-show wagers that maximized the expected rate of growth of one's bankroll. Since the exact model is a complicated nonlinear optimization problem that is difficult to solve at the track, Hausch, Ziemba, and Rubinstein (1981) developed simple regression approximations with quite minimal data-entry requirements. Their empirical studies on two seasons of racing data indicated that significant returns on the order of 11% were possible in the place-and-show markets. We (Hausch and Ziemba 1985; Ziemba and Hausch 1987) extended Hausch, Ziemba, and Rubinstein's (1981) results to provide further evidence of the place-and-show inefficiency. We (Ziemba and Hausch 1986) and Asch and Quandt (1987) studied inefficiency of the exotic markets. Asch, Malkiel, and Quandt (1984, 1986) investigated whether a drop in the odds late in the betting period might reflect inside information and thereby point to wagers that may have positive expected returns. Their results suggest that this is not the case, however. A more thorough literature survey is in Thaler and Ziemba (1988) and Hausch and Ziemba (1990). The latter also studies racing outside of North America.

III. Inefficiency of the Win Market and the Risk-free Hedging Model

The literature has demonstrated weak efficiency of the win market at a single track, despite a favorite/longshot bias. To test whether this weak efficiency is maintained across the win markets with cross-track betting, data were collected on several recent Triple Crown races. Although cross-track betting is becoming more popular, it tends to be restricted to major races. The best known of these are the Triple Crown races: the Kentucky Derby at Churchill Downs on the first Saturday in May, the Preakness Stakes at Pimlico Race Course 2 weeks later, and the Belmont Stakes at Belmont Park 3 weeks after that.

A simple problem is considered first. Allowing only win betting, what is the minimum amount that our bettor must wager to ensure the return of $1.00 regardless of which horse wins the race? The solution to this problem is, for each horse, to identify the track that has it at the longest odds and bet just enough to receive $1.00 if it wins. The solution involves no estimation of the horses' win probabilities. If this

parameter equal to the inverse of its win probability. Then, any ordering of the random variables is just the Harville formulas. Stern also develops alternative ordering formulas using gamma distributions that are more accurate but more complicated.

TABLE 2 Projected Win Payoffs, 1983 Preakness

Horse No.	Highest Win Return (on a $1 Bet)	Track	$ Amount of Wager That Will Return $1
1	29.40	Louisiana Downs	.0340
2	12.70	Louisiana Downs	.0787
3	34.60	Los Alamitos	.0289
4	169.90	Hollywood	.0059
5	56.90	Louisiana Downs	.0176
6	5.70	Louisiana Downs	.1754
7	10.60	Pimlico	.0943
8	76.60	Louisiana Downs	.0131
9	116.10	Hollywood	.0086
10	2.20	Los Alamitos	.4545
11	40.60	Los Alamitos	.0246
Total			.9356

solution were employed at one track, then our bettor would have to pay $1/Q$ dollars (an amount greater than $1.00) to ensure a return of $1.00. With the opportunity of betting at several tracks, each with a different set of odds, we may be able to lower this minimum amount to below $1.00. To see how this system works, consider the 1983 Preakness. The final win odds were collected from 11 tracks that allowed wagering on this race.[7] The highest of the 11 win payoffs on horse number 1 was $29.40 per dollar wagered at Louisiana Downs. Thus, a win bet of $0.0340 there would have returned $1.00 when, in fact, horse number 1, Deputed Testamony, won the race. This wager and those on the other horses are presented in table 2.

Thus, by wagering $0.9356, our bettor is guaranteed $1.00 regardless of who wins the race. This is a certain profit of $0.0644 per $0.9356 wagered, or a guaranteed return of 6.9% rate of return in a 2-minute race.

Obviously, "risk-free" arbitrage is not possible. Implementing the system requires that the track odds be sent to a central decision maker several minutes before the end of betting, and during that time the odds can change. The system does, however, demonstrate the large discrepancies in betting across the tracks and shows how simple it can be to take advantage of them. Table 3 presents the results of applying the system to the data from other Triple Crown races.

Three of the races had insufficient variance in the win odds across

7. The number of outlets involved in cross-track betting has increased over the years. The 1985 Kentucky Derby had betting at 32 outlets, including New York City's off-track betting (OTB). The 1985 Preakness and Belmont had 28 and 41 outlets, respectively. For 1988, the number of outlets for these three races were, respectively, 93, 87, and 76. We requested the final win, place, and show data from the outlets that we knew had accepted wagers. Response rates tended to be low and, in some cases, the data were no longer available, having been stored for only a short period. All the data received were used in the analysis.

TABLE 3 **Risk-free Hedging Model Results**

Race	No. Horses in Race	No. Tracks	% Profit
Preakness:			
1982	7	5	.0
1983	11	11	6.9
1984	10	4	.0
1985	11	7	2.5
Belmont:			
1982	11	5	13.6
1983	12	9	8.5
1984	11	2	.0
1985	9	11	5.0
Kentucky Derby:			
1984*	12	7	.1
1985	12	6	10.1
Average			4.7

* Cross-track betting on the Kentucky Derby did not begin until 1984.

the tracks to allow a risk-free profit. This is not surprising for the 1984 Belmont because we had data from only two tracks. Also, the results for the 1982 and 1984 Preakness are based on only five and four tracks, respectively. In these three races our bettor would obviously make no wagers. These three races giving a 0% return together with the other seven races have an average risk-free profit of 4.7%. This rate of profit is for the certain return of \$1.00. As the required certain return increases, then the wagers begin to affect the odds and this rate of profit will decrease.[8]

8. This "certain return" scheme can be extended to include place-and-show betting. Let R_i^t be the return on a \$1.00 win bet on horse i at track t when i wins. Similarly, let R_{ij}^t be the return on a \$1.00 place bet on i at track t when i and j are the top two finishers, and let R_{ijk}^t be the return on a \$1.00 show bet on i at track t when i, j, and k are the top three finishers. Formulas (1)–(3), corrected for breakage, determine R_i^t, R_{ij}^t and R_{ijk}^t. The decision variables are amounts to wager to win, place, and show on horse i at track t and are represented, respectively, by w_i^t, p_i^t, and s_i^t. There is a constraint for each ijk finish that requires a return of \$1.00, should that finish occur. The following formulation ignores our effect on the odds and, while this effect is negligible for a return of \$1.00, it should be included for larger required returns. The formulation that determines the minimum expenditure for a certain return of at least \$1.00 is

$$\text{minimize} \sum_{t=1}^{T} \sum_{i=1}^{n} (w_i^t + p_i^t + s_i^t),$$

subject to

$$\sum_{t=1}^{T} (R_i^t w_i^t + R_{ij}^t p_i^t + R_{ji}^t p_j^t + R_{ijk}^t s_i^t + R_{jik}^t s_j^t + R_{kij}^t s_k^t) \geq 1 \quad \text{for each } i, j, k,$$

$$w_i^t, p_i^t, s_i^t \geq 0 \quad \text{for all } i = 1, \ldots, n \text{ and } t = 1, \ldots, T.$$

This linear program has a large number of constraints; with n horses there are $n(n-1)(n-2)$ possible ijk finishes and, consequently, $n(n-1)(n-2)$ constraints. (The dual program has $3Tn$ constraints, however.) Interestingly, even with the possibility of place-and-show betting, betting only to win, as in Sec. III, may be optimal. The 1982

IV. The Optimal Capital Growth Model

Section III demonstrated an inefficiency in cross-track betting. We now propose and test an "optimal" wagering strategy for this inefficiency. Bettors at the racetrack appear to have many different objectives and, therefore, employ many different wagering strategies. Two quite reasonable long-term objectives, however, are (1) to maximize the expected rate of growth of one's bankroll, and (2) to minimize the expected time to reach some specified large wealth level. Breiman (1961) proved that both of these objectives are asymptotically satisfied by maximizing, on a myopic period-by-period basis, the expected logarithm of one's final wealth. This approach is termed the optimal capital growth model, and its theoretical justification for the logarithmic utility function has been well studied (see Ziemba and Vickson [1975] for references and a discussion of its assumptions and results). A simulation by us (Ziemba and Hausch 1986) suggests that this strategy not only performs well asymptotically but over a year of wagering it can also be expected to outperform other commonly used betting strategies. Other attractive features of the capital growth model are that one's effect on the odds can be accounted for and bet size is monotone in wealth. On the negative side, though, the recommended bets can be very large. Indeed, the Arrow-Pratt absolute risk-aversion index is wealth^{-1}, which is close to zero for large wealth.

Let w_0 be our bettor's initial wealth and q_{ijk} the probability that i is first, j is second, and k is third. Also, let $P_{ij}^t = P_i^t + P_j^t$ and $S_{ijk}^t = S_i^t + S_j^t + S_k^t$. The optimal capital growth model is[9]

$$\max_{\{w_\ell^t, p_\ell^t, s_\ell^t\}} \sum_{i=1}^{n} \sum_{\substack{j=1\\ j\neq i}}^{n} \sum_{\substack{k=1\\ k\neq i,j}}^{n} q_{ijk} \log \Bigg[w_0 + \sum_{t=1}^{T} \Bigg\{ \Bigg[Q^t\Big(W^t + \sum_{\ell=1}^{n} w_\ell^t\Big) - (W_i^t + w_i^t) \Bigg] \Bigg(\frac{w_i^t}{W_i^t + w_i^t} \Bigg) + \frac{\Big[Q^t\Big(P^t + \sum_{\ell=1}^{n} p_\ell^t\Big) - (P_{ij}^t + p_i^t + p_j^t) \Big]}{2}$$

Preakness (with 7 × 6 × 5 = 210 constraints) is one example of this. The reason for no place-or-show betting at optimum seems to be a coordination problem. Win bets return one and only one positive amount and these payoffs are mutually exclusive. Thus, a return of $1.00 can be efficiently guaranteed with win bets. Place-and-show bets, however, tend to have many different possible payoffs, and collecting on them is not mutually exclusive. These differences make it difficult to efficiently choose place-and-show bets over the win bets.

9. It is very simple to include exotic wagering in this capital growth model. It was formulated to consider only win, place, and show betting, though, because that was the only available data for testing the model.

$$\times \left(\frac{p_i^t}{P_i^t + p_i^t} + \frac{p_j^t}{P_j^t + p_j^t}\right)$$

$$+ \frac{\left[Q^t\left(S^t + \sum_{\ell=1}^{n} s_\ell^t\right) - \left(S_{ijk}^t + s_i^t + s_j^t + s_k^t\right)\right]}{3}$$

$$\times \left(\frac{s_i^t}{S_i^t + s_i^t} + \frac{s_j^t}{S_j^t + s_j^t} + \frac{s_k^t}{S_k^t + s_k^t}\right)$$

$$- \left(\sum_{\substack{\ell=1 \\ \ell \neq i}}^{n} w_\ell^t + \sum_{\substack{\ell=1 \\ \ell \neq i,j}}^{n} p_\ell^t + \sum_{\substack{\ell=1 \\ \ell \neq i,j,k}}^{n} s_\ell^t\right)\Bigg\}\Bigg],$$

subject to

$$\sum_{t=1}^{T} \sum_{\ell=1}^{n} (w_\ell^t + p_\ell^t + s_\ell^t) \leq w_0,$$

$$w_\ell^t \geq 0,\ p_\ell^t \geq 0,\ s_\ell^t \geq 0, \quad t = 1, \ldots, T,\ \ell = 1, \ldots, n.$$

This model requires estimates of the win probabilities for each horse. The efficiency studies of the win market have indicated that the public's win odds, adjusted for the favorite/longshot bias, provide good estimates of these probabilities. However, with cross-track wagering we not only have a different set of win odds for each participating track but, as demonstrated by the Ferdinand example in Section I and the risk-free hedging model in Section III, these odds can vary considerably. Rather than take a weighted average of all the tracks' odds to arrive at a set of win probabilities, we decided to use only the home track's odds.[10] This decision was based on a perceived informational advantage that the home-track public has over the bettors at the cross tracks, an advantage that results from several factors: (1) since these races were run near the end of the day's racing, the home-track public had watched the jockeys perform in, perhaps, several races already, they had observed the condition of the track and possibly noted any track biases, and they saw the horses in the paddock and in the parade to post; (2) the home crowd knows better if their track tends to favor front-runners or late chargers; and (3) since the home track is usually a larger track that has many major races, its public is more likely to have seen some of these horses race earlier in the season. Further, the studies supporting win-market efficiency have all involved home-track odds. Thus, we assume win-market efficiency at the home track and,

10. This decision was not the result of any analysis of the data. There are only a few cross-track races each year and the required data for each race are the final tote-board figures from several of the racetracks permitting this betting. These difficulties led to data on only 10 races being collected, much less than would be required for any analysis.

TABLE 4 1982 Preakness

Horse	Finish	Pimlico's Win Odds	Win Probability
1. Reinvested	. . .	7.6–1	.090
2. Cut Away	3d	41.6–1	.011
3. Water Bank	. . .	12.0–1	.056
4. Bold Style	. . .	26.2–1	.023
5. Laser Light	. . .	5.3–1	.125
6. Linkage	2d	.5–1	.597
7. Aloma's Ruler	1st	6.9–1	.098

after adjusting for the favorite/longshot bias in figure 1, use the home-win odds to estimate win probabilities. Since this win-market efficiency is not necessarily maintained at the cross tracks, the model can then include possible win betting at the cross tracks. The 1982 Preakness Stakes will be used to illustrate this model. Table 4 lists the race's entrants and their odds.

Aloma's Ruler's 6.9–1 win odds meant that, when he won, each dollar wagered on him was returned with an additional $6.90 profit. Linkage was the crowd's favorite. His 0.5–1 win odds meant that, had he won, he would have returned $1.50 per dollar wagered on him. After adjusting the win probabilities for the favorite/longshot bias, the probabilities were then normalized to sum to one. These probabilities and equation (1) adjusted for breakage allow the calculation of the expected return on an additional dollar bet to win for each horse i at each track t. Similarly, the Harville formulas in assumption 1 and equations (2) and (3), also adjusted for breakage, allow the calculation of the expected returns on place-and-show bets (see Hausch, Ziemba, and Rubinstein 1981). We received final win, place, and show figures from four of the tracks that allowed betting on the 1982 Preakness: Golden Gate and Los Alamitos in California, Centennial in Colorado, and Penn National in Pennsylvania. The calculated expected returns on the various bets at the four tracks are presented in table 5.

If a track has a payback proportion of, say, 0.85 then the average return on $1.00 bets, ignoring breakage, will be $0.85. With breakage, it will be somewhat less than $0.85. For individual horses the expected returns from table 5 vary from 0.181 (show bet on horse 2 at Golden Gate) to 1.336 (place bet on horse 6 at Los Alamitos). Of particular interest are the expected returns exceeding 1.00 since those indicate the wagers that have a positive expected profit. We restricted our attention to wagers with expected returns of at least 1.10. They are the highlighted expected returns in table 5. If the probability estimates of this model were exact, then this 1.10 cutoff could result in suboptimal wagering, particularly since diversification can even lead to the inclusion of wagers with negative expected profits. Hausch, Ziemba, and

TABLE 5 **Expected Returns, Cross-Track Betting on 1982 Preakness**

	Horse						
	1	2	3	4	5	6	7
Finish	. . .	3	. . .	. . .	. . .	2	1
Win probability	.090	.011	.056	.023	.125	.597	.098
Expected return on a $1 bet to win:							
Golden Gate	.837	.246	.437	.708	.788	.955	1.000
Centennial	.900	.389	.370	.570	.825	.836	1.147*
Los Alamitos	.666	.391	.347	.777	.713	1.015	1.196*
Penn National	.954	.484	.588	1.109*	.650	.896	.755
Expected return on a $1 bet to place:							
Golden Gate	.749	.193	.349	.582	.669	1.149*	.880
Centennial	.769	.238	.260	.329	.719	1.084	1.120*
Los Alamitos	.794	.233	.277	.556	.778	1.336*	.888
Penn National	.673	.399	.391	.737	.586	1.101*	.731
Expected return on a $1 bet to show:							
Golden Gate	.837	.181	.405	.413	.817	1.153*	.996
Centennial	.747	.197	.340	.252	.803	1.008	1.138*
Los Alamitos	.890	.200	.392	.341	1.180*	1.293*	.873
Penn National	.710	.235	.451	.388	.769	1.099	.793

NOTE.—In this table, horses 2, 6, and 7 are Cut Away, Linkage, and Aloma's Ruler, respectively.
* Highlighted expected returns (returns of at least 1.10).

Rubinstein (1981) found, however, that due to the approximations in the model it was more profitable to wager only if the expected return was well in excess of 1.00. For large tracks and races of the quality of these Triple Crown races, a minimum expected return of 1.10 is reasonable.

The capital growth model was run on the data from these cross tracks. Table 6 presents the optimal portfolio of wagers assuming a 1.10 expected return cutoff and an initial wealth of $2,500. This portfolio has wagers totaling $2,437 at all four tracks and its certainty equivalent can be calculated as $432. Since the first three finishers of this race were horses 7, 6, and 2, our bettor would collect on the win, place, and show bets on horse 7 and the place and show bets on horse 6, for a return of $3,716.90 and a profit of $1,279.90. The payoffs in this table account for our bettor's effect on the odds. For example, the actual payoff per $1.00 bet to show on horse 7 at Centennial was $2.70. However, our bettor's $83 show bet at this track would have lowered this payoff to $2.50. The latter payoff was used to determine our bettor's return.

Table 5 supposes only $1.00 is wagered. Thus, even though one track may have a higher expected return to, say, show on some horse than another track has, it can be that our bettor will make show wagers at

TABLE 6 Optimal Capital Growth Wagers, Cross-Track Betting on 1982 Preakness

Horse	Bet	Track	Expected Return	$ Bet	$ Payoff per $1 Bet	$ Total Return	$ Profit
4	Win	P.N.	1.109	14	...	...	- 14.00
7	Win	L.A.	1.196	40	12.00	480.00	440.00
6	Place	L.A.	1.336	855	1.50	1282.50	427.50
7	Place	Cen.	1.120	46	3.30	151.80	105.80
5	Show	L.A.	1.180	172	...	...	- 172.00
6	Show	G.G.	1.153	571	1.30	742.30	171.30
6	Show	L.A.	1.293	656	1.30	852.80	196.80
7	Show	Cen.	1.138	83	2.50	207.50	124.50
Totals				2,437		3,716.90	1,279.90

NOTE.—P.N. = Penn National; L.A. = Los Alamitos; Cen. = Centennial; G.G. = Golden Gate.

both tracks because of the bettor's effect on the odds. This happened at Golden Gate and Los Alamitos. Horse 6 had expected returns of 1.153 and 1.293 at these tracks and the optimal show bets were $571 and $656 at them, respectively. With these wagers, it must be that the addition to expected utility from an additional dollar bet to show will be the same at the two tracks.[11]

The capital growth model was studied with cross-track data on the other Triple Crown races. In each case it was assumed that the initial wealth was $2,500. The results of these races and the 1982 Preakness are given in table 7.

Despite losses on two of the races, including a huge loss on the 1984 Preakness, there was a total profit of $2,647.80 for a 15% return on money wagered. Average profits were $264.78. The standard error of the mean is $342, so no statistically significant statements can be made about positive profits on the basis of these results. Studying the expected returns suggests that many of the profitable overlays occur because of regional biases. For instance, Conquistador Cielo, the winner of the 1982 Belmont Stakes, raced his entire career on the East Coast. The West Coast bettors were less familiar with him, while on the East Coast he was, for many, a sentimental favorite. In the Belmont Stakes he tended to be sent off at lower odds at the East Coast tracks. When he won he paid from $5.80 to win at Commodore Downs in Pennsylvania to $15.40 at Los Alamitos in California. Another example is Tolomeo, the English colt that won the 1983 Arlington Million. His odds were 4–1 in England and 38–1 at Arlington Park in

11. This marginal utility can be complicated because a component of the expected return on an additional dollar bet to show on horse 6 at Los Alamitos is the positive effect that it has on the return to the show bet on horse 5 at Los Alamitos if 6 finishes out of the money.

TABLE 7 Results of Optimal Capital Growth Model on Triple Crown Races

Race	No. Horses in Race	No. Tracks	No. Wagers	Total Wagers ($)	Certainty Equivalent ($)	No. Wagers Won	Return ($)	Profit ($)
Preakness:								
1982	7	4	8	2,437	432	6	3,716.90	1,279.90
1983	11	8	13	1,949	325	1	1,647.30	−301.70
1984	10	3	8	2,282	371	0	0.00	−2,282.00
1985	11	6	11	1,817	325	4	2,014.40	197.40
Belmont:								
1982	11	4	20	942	305	5	1,880.40	938.40
1983	12	7	20	2,452	469	6	2,578.80	126.80
1984	11	2	3	1,371	317	1	2,331.00	960.00
1985	9	9	15	471	73	1	78.30	−392.70
Kentucky Derby:								
1984	12	6	13	2,027	340	5	3,027.20	1,000.20
1985	12	6	7	1,973	350	3	3,094.50	1,121.50
Totals			118	17,721	3,307	32	20,368.80	2,647.80

Illinois. This observation and table 7 suggest that a high expected return is possible even with only a few carefully selected cross tracks.

The Triple Crown races are the most widely publicized of the North American horse races. Thus, one might expect that other less publicized cross-track races would have even more divergence in the odds across the tracks. If so, they should have an even greater potential for expected profits.

A major assumption of this model is that after all other bettors have made their wagers our bettor (1) learns the tote-board information at each track, (2) runs the capital growth model, and (3) communicates the optimal wagers to agents at each track, who then make the wagers. Obviously this is extremely difficult, if not impossible, in practice, never mind any legal concerns. Just learning the tote-board information at each track is difficult because there are no pay phones inside the racetrack grounds. A central decision maker and the agents communicating with cellular phones is feasible but still requires a significant amount of time. Unfortunately, though, odds may change in the last few minutes of betting, and profitable bets a few minutes before the end of betting may not be profitable based on the final odds. Hausch, Ziemba, and Rubinstein (1981) studied the odds changes in the last 2 minutes of betting and found that expected returns did change somewhat but profitable place-and-show bets 2 minutes from the end tended to remain profitable based on final odds. However, the agents in this model, because of its extra complications, would probably have to report odds more premature than those 2 minutes before the end of betting. The results given in this article, then, may overestimate the profits possible in practice. Additionally, our profit figures do not account for the costs of implementing this procedure—the agents and other costs at each cross track, the long-distance phone calls, and the computer time.

V. Testing the One-Track Capital Growth Model

Implementing the previous section's capital growth model is certainly difficult. However, when the race is televised from the home track there are simpler versions of this scheme possible for one bettor at one track. Our bettor, with a portable television at the cross track, can view the home odds when they are shown on TV. With these odds giving "true" win probabilities, our bettor can search for overlays at the cross track. A flat bet to win could be made on horses going off at longer odds than at the home track, or a sophisticated bettor could also bring a portable computer to the track and run the capital growth model described in Section IV for one track, that is, $T = 1$. This latter scheme is tested here with the Triple Crown race data.

As an example, consider the 1984 Kentucky Derby simulcast at

TABLE 8 **Optimal Wagers Based on One-Track Capital Growth Model, 1984 Kentucky Derby**

Wager Type	Horse	Expected Return	\$ Optimal Bet	\$ Payoff on a \$1 Bet	\$ Realized Return	\$ Profit
Win	2	1.236	15	...	...	−15.00
Win	10	1.159	...	5.60	...	...
Place	2	1.153	...	...	...	...
Place	10	1.410	249	3.70	921.30	672.30
Show	2	1.353	261	...	...	−261.00
Show	10	1.275	295	2.50	737.50	442.50
Totals			820		1,658.80	838.80

Golden Gate Fields in Albany, California. Using the win odds televised from Churchill Downs, Golden Gate had six wagers with expected returns exceeding 1.10. With a wealth of \$2,500, the capital growth model yields the optimal wagers shown in table 8.

This portfolio has four wagers totaling \$820. The win bet on horse number 10 and the place bet on horse number 2 are zero even though they have expected returns exceeding 1.10. This is because the possibility of number 2 doing well in the race is better accounted for with the higher returning win-and-show bets on him. Also, the possibility of number 10 doing well is better accounted for with the higher returning place-and-show bets on him. Swale, number 10, won the 1984 Derby, followed by Coax Me Chad and At The Threshold for a 10-12-9 finish. Therefore, only the place-and-show bets on Swale paid off for a return of \$1,658.80 and a profit of \$838.80.

Table 9 presents the results of this one-track model on the other races. The average wagers on a race varied from \$78.33 to \$1,173.25 and the average profits varied from −\$868.67 to \$824.10. The average of these 10 average profits was \$69.97 or 9.2% on the money wagered. Again, there is such variability in the profits that, without additional data, no statistically significant statements can be made about positive expected profits.

VI. Final Discussion

There is considerable evidence that the win market at the racetrack is weakly efficient. A risk-free arbitrage model is presented that demonstrates that this is not the case with cross-track wagering. The mispricing by the public at the cross tracks may be due partly to their more limited access to information relative to those attending the home track. Also, some of the variance in the odds across the tracks may be due to certain horses being more familiar to bettors in certain regions of North America. The optimal capital growth model suggests that the

TABLE 9 Results of One-Track Capital Growth Model on Triple Crown Races

Race	No. of Cross Tracks	Average Cross-Track Wager ($)	Average Cross-Track Realized Return ($)	Average Cross-Track Profit ($)
Preakness:				
1982	4	1,173.25	1,724.80	551.55
1983	8	909.25	353.79	−555.46
1984	3	868.67	.00	−868.67
1985	6	799.67	789.37	−10.30
Belmont:				
1982	4	407.25	639.02	231.78
1983	7	532.71	488.63	−44.08
1984	2	1,158.00	1,982.10	824.10
1985	9	78.33	7.80	−70.53
Kentucky Derby:				
1984	6	520.67	884.92	364.25
1985	6	1,161.33	1,438.42	277.08
Average	5.5	760.91	830.88	69.97

discrepancies across the tracks can allow profits, but further work is needed to demonstrate significant profits. A simpler version of the optimal capital growth model for one bettor at one cross track also demonstrates the possibility of profit.

References

Ali, M. M. 1977. Probability and utility estimates for racetrack bettors. *Journal of Political Economy* 85 (August): 803–15.

Ali, M. M. 1979. Some evidence of the efficiency of a speculative model. *Econometrica* 47 (March):387–92.

Asch, P.; Malkiel, B. G.; and Quandt, R. E. 1984. Market efficiency in racetrack betting. *Journal of Business* 57 (April): 165–75.

Asch, P.; Malkiel, B. G.; and Quandt, R. E. 1986. Market efficiency in racetrack betting: Further evidence and a correction. *Journal of Business* 59 (January): 157–60.

Asch, P., and Quandt, R. E. 1987. Efficiency and profitability in exotic bets. *Economica* 59 (August): 289–98.

Breiman, L. 1961. Optimal gambling systems for favorable games. In *Proceedings of the Fourth Berkeley Symposium*, pp. 65–68. Berkeley: University of California Press.

Busche, K., and Hall, C. D. 1988. An exception to the risk preference anomaly. *Journal of Business* 61 (July): 337–46.

Fama, E. F. 1970. Efficient capital markets: A review of theory and empirical work. *Journal of Finance* 25 (May): 383–417.

Harville, D. A. 1973. Assigning probabilities to the outcomes of multi-entry competitions. *Journal of the American Statistical Association* 68 (June): 312–16.

Hausch, D. B., and Ziemba, W. T. 1985. Transactions costs, extent of inefficiencies, entries, and multiple wagers in a racetrack betting model. *Management Science* 31 (April): 381–94.

Hausch, D. B., and Ziemba, W. T. (eds.). 1990, in press. *Efficiency of Racetrack Betting Markets*. New York: Academic Press.

Hausch, D. B.; Ziemba, W. T.; and Rubinstein, M. 1981. Efficiency of the market for racetrack betting. *Management Science* 27 (December): 1435–52.

Henery, R. J. 1981. Permutation probabilities as models for horse races. *Journal of the Royal Statistical Society*, ser. B, 43:86–91.

Rosett, R. H. 1965. Gambling and rationality. *Journal of Political Economy* 73 (December): 595–607.

Snyder, W. W. 1978. Horse racing: Testing the efficient markets model. *Journal of Finance* 33 (September): 1109–18.

Stern, H. S. 1987. Gamma processes, paired comparisons and ranking. Ph.D. dissertation. Stanford, Calif.: Stanford University, Department of Statistics.

Thaler, R., and Ziemba, W. T. 1988. Parimutuel betting markets: Racetracks and lotteries. *Journal of Economic Perspectives* 2 (Spring): 161–74.

Ziemba, W. T., and Hausch, D. B. 1986. *Betting at the Racetrack*. New York: Norris M. Strauss.

Ziemba, W. T., and Hausch, D. B. 1987. *Dr. Z's Beat the Racetrack*. New York: Morrow.

Ziemba, W. T., and Vickson, R. G. (eds.). 1975. *Stochastic Optimization Models in Finance*. New York: Academic Press.

Section VI

Market Crashes

Chapter 18

Stock market crashes in 2007–2009: were we able to predict them?[#]

SÉBASTIEN LLEO*† and WILLIAM T. ZIEMBA‡§¶

†Finance Department and Value and Persuasion Research Centre, Reims Management School, 59 rue Pierre Taittinger, 51100 Reims, France
‡University of British Columbia, Vancouver, BC, Canada
§Mathematical Institute, Oxford University, Oxford, UK
¶ICMA Centre, University of Reading, Reading, UK

(*Received 28 September 2011; in final form 3 July 2012*)

1. Background

The second author started using the bond stock earnings yield differential (BSEYD) model while in Tokyo consulting at the Yamaichi Research Institute in 1988. The model relates the yield on stocks (measured by the ratio of earnings to stock prices) to the yield on nominal Treasury bonds. The theory behind the model is that an optimal asset allocation between stocks and bonds is related to their relative yields and when the bond yield is too high, a market adjustment is needed and there is a shift out of stocks into bonds. If the adjustment is large, it causes an equity market correction (a decline of 10% within one year). Hence, there is a short-term negative equity risk premium (ERP). A study of the October 1987 stock market crash illustrated the model and it was from this episode that the model was discovered by Ziemba's crash study group. Table 1 and figure 1 show that the model went into the danger zone, i.e. the measure was above an upper confidence limit, in April 1987, with a spread of 3.39. The S&P500 was then at 289.32. By the end of September the S&P500 was at 318.66 with the measure higher at 4.14. After the crash at the end of October, the S&P500 had fallen to 245.01 with the spread falling out of the danger zone to 1.64. Table 1 shows beginning of month values. Continuous daily values are given in figure 1 and one sees a sharp move up in the measure to 4.42 in September 1987, way above the upper limit.

There are various ways that one can compute the upper and lower limits, but experience has shown that, with the

*Corresponding author. Email: sebastien.lleo@reims-ms.fr

[#]This chapter was originally published in: Lleo, S. & Ziemba, W. T. (2012). Stock Market Crashes in 2007–2009: Were We Able to Predict Them? *Quantitative Finance*, 12(8), 1161–1187.

various approaches, all of which use out-of-sample prior data, one usually comes to the same conclusion. In figure 1, the limits are simply the trailing mean plus or minus the standard deviation measure such that the one-sided limits hold 95% of the probability.†

2. Moving average and signal chart

In the following sections we use a moving average and a rolling horizon standard deviation to establish the confidence levels. The h-day moving average at time t, μ_t^h, and the corresponding rolling horizon standard deviation, σ_t^h, are given by

$$\mu_t^h = \frac{1}{h}\sum_{i=0}^{h-1} x_{t-i},$$

$$\sigma_t^h = \sqrt{\frac{1}{h-1}\sum_{i=0}^{h-1}(x_{t-i} - \mu_t^h)^2}.$$

Using rolling horizon means and standard deviations provides data consistency. This is used to compute confidence levels for the BSEYD measure. In particular, the rolling horizon mean and standard deviation are not overly sensitive to the starting date of the bond yield or stock market data, or to the overall number of data points. However, the choice of the horizon parameter h is subjective.

For our analysis of the US market, we use a five year horizon, therefore $h = 1260$, as longer time horizons tend to generate a robust signal and eliminate false positives. Of course, five years of historical bond and stock data may be a difficult requirement outside of major markets. For Iceland and China, we use a one year rolling horizon, but tighten the confidence level in order to eliminate false positives.

The idea behind the BSEYD model is that a crash signal should occur whenever

$$BSEYD(t) > CL(t),$$

where $CL(t)$ represents a one-tail confidence level. The level CL acts as a time-varying threshold for the crash signal. Therefore, a crash signal should occur whenever

$$SIGNAL(t) := BSEYD(t) - CL(t) > 0.$$

Graphically, the threshold for the crash signal is now a horizontal line with value 0, discussed in section 5 and shown below in figures 5, 6(b), 13 and 18. These graphs show a calculation of $SIGNAL(t)$ based respectively on a standard one-tail 95% confidence level and on an application of Cantelli's inequality.

An examination of the BSEYD spread distributions reveals their non-normal nature (see figures 3, 7, 11 and 19). As a result, standard confidence intervals which are based on a Gaussian assumption may prove inaccurate. In this case, we use Cantelli's inequality, a one-sided version of Chebyshev's inequality, to derive a 'worst case' confidence level (see, for example, problem 7.11.9 of Grimmett and Stirzaker (2001)).

Cantelli's inequality relates the probability that the distance between a random variable X and its mean μ exceeds a number $k > 0$ of standard deviations σ to this distance as

$$P[X - \mu \geq k\sigma] \leq \frac{1}{1+k^2},$$

or, alternatively,

$$P\left[X - \mu \geq \sigma\sqrt{\frac{1}{\alpha} - 1}\right] \leq \alpha,$$

where $\alpha = 1/(1+k^2)$. The parameter α provides an upper bound for a one-tailed confidence level on any

Table 1. S&P500 index, PE ratios, government bond yields and the yield premium over stocks, January 1984 to August 1988.

		S&P index	PER	(a) 30 yr G bd	(b) 1/pe (%)	(a)–(b)
1986	Jan	208.19	14.63	9.32	6.84	2.48
	Feb	219.37	15.67	8.28	6.38	1.90
	Mar	232.33	16.50	7.59	6.06	1.53
	Apr	237.98	16.27	7.58	6.15	1.43
	May	238.46	17.03	7.76	5.87	1.89
	Jun	245.30	17.32	7.27	5.77	1.50
	Jul	240.18	16.31	7.42	6.13	1.29
	Aug	245.00	17.47	7.26	5.72	1.54
	Sep	238.27	15.98	7.64	6.26	1.38
	Oct	237.36	16.85	7.61	5.93	1.68
	Nov	245.09	16.99	7.40	5.89	1.51
	Dec	248.60	16.72	7.33	5.98	1.35
1987	Jan	264.51	15.42	7.47	6.49	0.98
	Feb	280.93	15.98	7.46	6.26	1.20
	Mar	292.47	16.41	7.65	6.09	1.56
	Apr	289.32	16.22	9.56	6.17	3.39
	May	289.12	16.32	8.63	6.13	2.50
	Jun	301.38	17.10	8.40	5.85	2.55
	Jul	310.09	17.92	8.89	5.58	3.31
	Aug	329.36	18.55	9.17	5.39	3.78
	Sep	318.66	18.10	9.66	5.52	4.14
	Oct	280.16	14.16	9.03	7.06	1.97
	Nov	245.01	13.78	8.90	7.26	1.64
	Dec	240.96	13.55	9.10	7.38	1.72
1988	Jan	250.48	12.81	8.40	7.81	0.59
	Feb	258.10	13.02	8.33	7.68	0.65
	Mar	265.74	13.42	8.74	7.45	1.29
	Apr	262.61	13.24	9.10	7.55	1.55
	May	256.20	12.92	9.24	7.74	1.50
	Jun	270.68	13.65	8.85	7.33	1.52
	Jul	269.44	13.59	9.18	7.36	1.82
	Aug	263.73	13.30	9.30	7.52	1.78

Source: (Ziemba and Schwartz 1991).

†Using a different index rather than the S&P500 leads to the same conclusion, but slightly different results. Berge *et al.* (2008) used the MSCI index. The danger zone was entered in May 1987 and the correction occurred in October, four months later. During June, July and August, investors kept rebalancing their portfolios from the bond to the equity market (MSCI TRI + 13.87% over the quarter), then the equity market fell 31.80% in the following quarter (September to November 1987) with the major decline occurring in October.

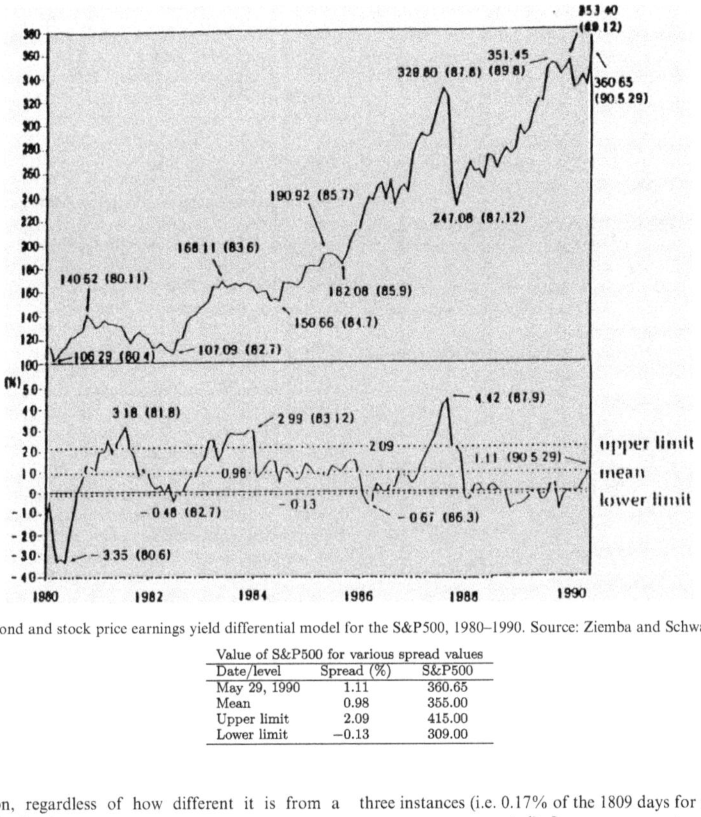

Figure 1. Bond and stock price earnings yield differential model for the S&P500, 1980–1990. Source: Ziemba and Schwartz (1991).

Value of S&P500 for various spread values

Date/level	Spread (%)	S&P500
May 29, 1990	1.11	360.65
Mean	0.98	355.00
Upper limit	2.09	415.00
Lower limit	−0.13	309.00

distribution, regardless of how different it is from a Normal distribution.

We use Cantelli's inequality with a one-tail confidence level to assess the relative strength of a signal. Using the one-tail confidence level, we obtain the crash signal. We then find the Cantelli probability α giving us a similar signal date to the Gaussian approach. To generate the same signal as a standard 95% confidence level, we need to select $\alpha = 27\%$ in Cantelli's inequality. Similarly, to generate the same signal as a standard 99% confidence level, we need to select $\alpha = 15.60\%$.

In the case of China, as discussed in section 3, we used a standard 99% confidence level to determine the signal. Based on Cantelli's inequality, we expect in the worst case to have a crash signal 15.60% of the time. Retrospectively, Cantelli's inequality is rather severe since it places the threshold for a signal at a BSEYD spread of 3% or above, on 372 consecutive trading days from June 9, 2005 to June 30, 2012 (i.e. 20.56% of the 1809 days for which this measure was computed). By contrast, if we consider the distribution over the entire period, we observe that the spread only exceeded 2.5% on three instances (i.e. 0.17% of the 1809 days for which this measure was computed). In summary, a standard 99% confidence level would have been sufficient to determine a clear crash signal.

In the case of Iceland, as discussed in section 4, we use a 95% confidence level to determine the signal; Cantelli's inequality suggests a worst case probability that 27% of observations could result in a signal. However, lowering the Cantelli probability α from 27% to 20% (corresponding roughly to a standard 97.7% confidence level) does not result in a significant loss of responsiveness of the signal, at least for Glitnir and Kaupthing (see figures 13(b) and (d)).

In the case of the United States, as discussed in section 5, our analysis covers a standard one-tail 95% normal distribution based confidence level and application of Cantelli's inequality. The conclusions are similar: over the period January 1, 1995 to October 19, 2011, two crash signals occurred: one in June 1999 and the other on June 14, 2007 (as discussed in section 5).

Lleo and Ziemba (2012) give an historical account of his use of this model from 1988 to 2011 in the US, Japan and other countries. The signal was in the danger zone 12 times from 1948 to 1988 and each of these times the Nikkei Stock Average index fell at least 10% from the level when the signal was reached. During this 40-year period, the index had 20 such falls, of which eight occurred for reasons other than high interest rates relative to earnings. The BSEYD model also predicted the −56% crash that started in January 1990 with a signal further in the danger zone than at any previous time since 1948.

The Fed model, which is the ratio not the difference like the original model, is mathematically equivalent to this model, as will now be shown.

The Fed model in its original 1996 form states the dependence of a fair stock price level $\tilde{p}(t)$ at time t to the expected earnings $E(t)$ and the most liquid (10- or 30-year) Treasury bond rate $r(t)$. Earnings expectations are incorporated in prices and discounted via

$$\tilde{p}(t) = \frac{E(t)}{r(t)}, \quad t = 1, 2, \ldots. \tag{1}$$

Equity earnings per share $\gamma(t)$ is the expected earnings for a unit investment in the stock market with equity shares $S(t)$, namely

$$\gamma(t) := \frac{E(t)}{S(t)}.$$

Then

$$S(t) = \frac{E(t)}{\gamma(t)}.$$

There is a direct relationship between the equity yield in (2) below and the long bond rate in (1). The ratio of the current market value to the theoretical value is the Fed model bond stock yield ratio

$$BSYR(t) := \frac{S(t)}{\tilde{p}(t)} = \frac{E(t)/\gamma(t)}{E(t)/r(t)} = \frac{r(t)}{\gamma(t)}. \tag{2}$$

The bond stock earnings yield differential that we focus on in this paper is related to the valuation measure and the equity yield via

$$\frac{S(t)}{\tilde{p}(t)} - 1 = \frac{BSEYD(t)}{\gamma(t)},$$

$$BSEYD(t) = \left[\frac{S(t)}{\tilde{p}(t)} - 1\right]\gamma(t) = [BSYR(t) - 1]\gamma(t).$$

This differential reflects the difference between the current market value and its theoretical value. A more theoretically sound motivation for the predictive ability of the BSEYD uses the basic Gordon growth Dividend Discount Model (see, for example, (Damodaran (2012)), where E/P is the forward earnings yield (which Schwartz and Ziemba (2000) show is the best predictor of at least individual Japanese stock prices), and

$$E/P - \text{nominal yield} = \text{equity risk premium} - \text{real growth} - \text{inflation}.$$

Therefore, the BSEYD can be used as a proxy for the unobservable right-hand-side economic variables.

For a given equity yield, the BSEYD and BSYR can be used to identify zones of under and over valuation and forecast possible forthcoming market adjustments.

Koivu *et al.* (2005) study the Fed model using a dynamic vector equilibrium correction model with data from 1980 to 2003 for the US, UK and Germany to show that the Fed model had predictive power in forecasting equity prices, earnings and bond yields. The model has been successful in predicting market turns, but in spite of its empirical success and simplicity, the model has been justifiably criticized. First, it does not consider the role played by time-varying risk premiums in the portfolio selection process, while it does consider a risk free government interest rate as the discount factor of future earnings. More seriously, the inflation illusion (the possible impact of inflation expectations on the stock market) as suggested by Modigliani and Cohn (1979) is not taken into consideration. Secondly, the model assumes the comparability of earning price ratios, a real quantity, with a nominal, bond-induced interest rate (Asness (2000, 2003), Ritter and Warr (2002) and Campbell and Vuolteenaho (2004) discuss these issues). Consigli *et al.* (2009) propose a stochastic model of equity returns based on an extension of the model that includes a risk premium in which market corrections are endogenously generated by the bond–stock yield difference. The model accommodates both cases of prolonged yield deviations leading to a long series of small declines in the equity market and the case, peculiar to recent speculative bubbles, of a series of corrections over limited time periods. The inclusion of the yield differential as a key driver of the market correction process is tested and the model is validated with market data.

Many of the critics focus on: (1) the short-term predicability that we know is weak (e.g., Giot and Petitjean (2008)), (2) simply do not focus on the long-run value of the measure, or (3) dismiss it outright because of the nominal versus real (minor) flaw (e.g., Montier (2011)). Consigli *et al.* (2009) use the model to estimate the current fair value of the S&P500. Of course, market and fair value can diverge for long periods. However, our concern here is whether or not the model actually predicts stock market crashes, stock market rallies and good times to be in and out of stock markets. Berge *et al.* (2008) discuss the latter issue and found for five countries (US, Germany, Canada, UK and Japan) that the strategy that says stay in the market when the indicator is not in the danger zone, and move to cash otherwise, provides about double the final wealth with less variance and a higher Sharpe ratio than a buy-and-hold strategy during 1975–2005 and 1980–2005. There is some limited predictability of stock market increases, but the evidence supports that the better use of the model is to predict crashes. In this paper we study the period 2007–2009 for the US, China and Iceland, all of which had large crashes. Shiller (2006) observes, as we have in the past, that low PE periods seem to lead to higher future stock prices and high PE periods to lower future prices. But the evidence is that PE levels by themselves are not enough to call the crashes. The argument here is that it is usually the interplay of interest rates (measured by the long bond) with PE ratios that gives the crash signal.

3. The Chinese Shanghai stock market crash

Figure 2 shows the rise of the Shanghai stock index from January 2000 to June 2012. The market bottomed at 1011.50 on July 11, 2005. It then rose six-fold to peak at 6092.06 on October 16, 2007. Then there was a crash of 11.98% from 5180.51 to 4559.75 over the two-day period January 21 and 22 followed by another 7.19% fall from 4761.69 to 4419.29 on January 28, 2008. Ultimately, the index fell to 1706.70 on November 4, 2008, a decline of over two-thirds from the peak and 23.09% and 29.93% from respectively the December 12, 2006 and December 25, 2006 BSEYD danger signals at 2218.95 and 2435.76. Table 2 discusses highlights for the Shanghai index from 2005–12.

Did the BSEYD model predict this crash? First, figure 3 shows that the BSEYD measure is not normally distributed with fat right, and even fatter left, tails. The biggest declines are much larger than the biggest increases.

Figure 4(a) and (b) show that the model did in fact predict the crash. See also the signals hitting the danger level in figures 5 and 6. This is a typical application of the model. The signal goes into the danger zone, then the market continues higher, but within 4 to 12 months there is a crash of 10% + from the value at the initial signal. In this case, the decline is much higher than 10%. Figure 4(a) uses a 95% confidence one-sided moving-average interval using prior data out of sample. The danger signal occurred on December 12, 2006, some 10 months before the stock market peak with the index at 6092.06 on October 16, 2007. Figure 4(b) uses a 95% one-sided confidence interval and gives the first danger signal on December 12, 2006 with the index at 2218.95. With a 99% one-sided confidence interval, the danger signal was reached on December 25, 2006 with the index at 2435.76. The ultimate fall was to 1706.70 on November 4, 2008, about 30% below the index value of 2218.95 or 2435.76 of the crash signals. These signals and the decline were a bit different from the usual case as it took almost two years to get the 10% plus crash and, in the meantime, the market almost tripled in value before the ultimate crash.

Figure 4 also illustrates the importance of the confidence level in relation to the rolling horizon of the moving average and the shape of the spread distribution. As pointed out in section 2, a short time horizon of one year, combined with a lower confidence level of 95% and the non-Gaussian nature of the spread distribution, may result in false positives. An *ex-post* analysis reveals that the Gaussian-based 95% confidence spread for the Shanghai Stock Exchange Composite index over the entire period equals 1.78% (figure 7). However, the actual 95% confidence level of the empirical distribution is 2.18%. In fact, a full 9.32% of all actual observations occur at or above 1.78%, a marked contrast from the 5% predicted by the Gaussian distribution. However, raising the confidence level to 99% or increasing the rolling horizon does help reduce the impact of the shape of the distribution on the signal.

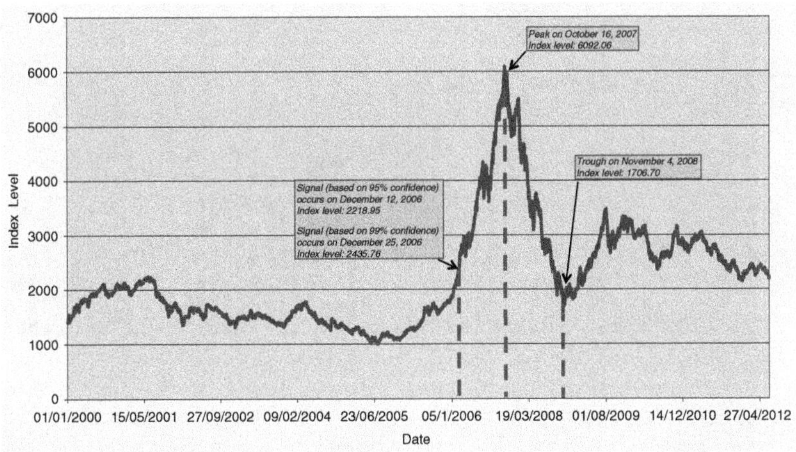

Figure 2. The Shanghai stock exchange composite index, January 2000 to June 30, 2012.

Table 2. Highlights on the Shanghai Stock Index, 2005–2012.

Date	Index value	Comment
Dec 31, 2004	1266.50	
May 23, 2005	1070.84	The index was down 15.4% year-to-date
Jul 11, 2005	1011.50	Market bottom
Dec 31, 2005	1161.06	The index was down 8.3% in 2005
Dec 12, 2006	2218.95	95% confidence BSEYD crash signal occurs
Dec 25, 2006	2435.76	99% confidence BSEYD crash signal occurs
Dec 31, 2006	2675.47	The index was up 130.4% in 2006
May 29, 2007	4334.92	Local high of the market. The market was up 62% year-to-date
Jul 5, 2007	3615.87	Local low of the market. The market was still up 35.1% year-to-date
Oct 16, 2007	6092.06	Highest historical market close. The market was up 127.7% year-to-date
Nov 28, 2007	4803.39	Local low of the market. The market was still up 79.5% year-to-date
Dec 31, 2007	5261.56	Index was up 96.7% in 2007, but down 13.6% from its peak in October
Jan 14, 2008	5497.90	Local high of the market
Jan 18, 2008	5180.51	The index closes the week at 5180.51, which is 5.8% lower than its local high on Jan 14
Jan 21, 2008	4914.43	The index experiences a one-day drop of 5.1% from 5180.51 to 4914.43
Jan 22, 2008	4559.75	The index experiences declines by 7.2% on this day, opening at 4914.43 to close at 4559.75
Jan 25, 2008	4761.69	The index recovers slightly to close the week at 4761.69
Jan 28, 2008	4419.29	The index drops by 7.2% from 4761.69 to 4419.29
Apr 18, 2008	3094.67	Local low of the market
May 5, 2008	3761.01	Local high of the market
Nov 4, 2008	1706.70	Global market minimum. The market was down by 72% peak to trough and 23.09% and 29.93% from the December 12 and 25 danger signal levels
Dec 31, 2008	1820.81	The market was down 65.4% in 2008
Aug 3, 2009	3471.44	Local high of the market. The market was up 103.4% from the trough
Aug 31, 2009	2667.75	Local low of the market
Nov 23, 2009	3338.66	Local high of the market
Dec 31, 2009	3277.14	The market was up 80% in 2009
Jul 5, 2010	2363.95	Local low of the market
Dec 31, 2010	2808.08	The market was down 14.3% in 2010
Jun 30, 2011	2762.08	The market was down about 1% year-to-date
Dec 31, 2011	2199.42	The market was down about 22% in 2011
Jun 30, 2012	2225.43	The market was up about 1% year-to-date

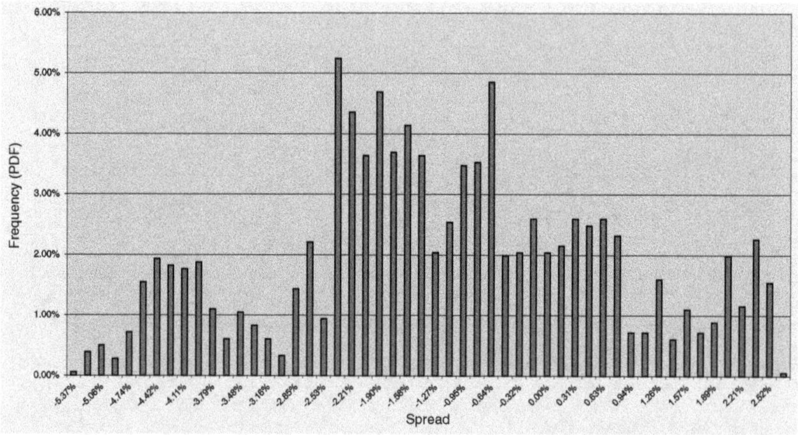

Figure 3. Spread distribution of the BSEYD measure on the Shanghai Stock Exchange Composite.

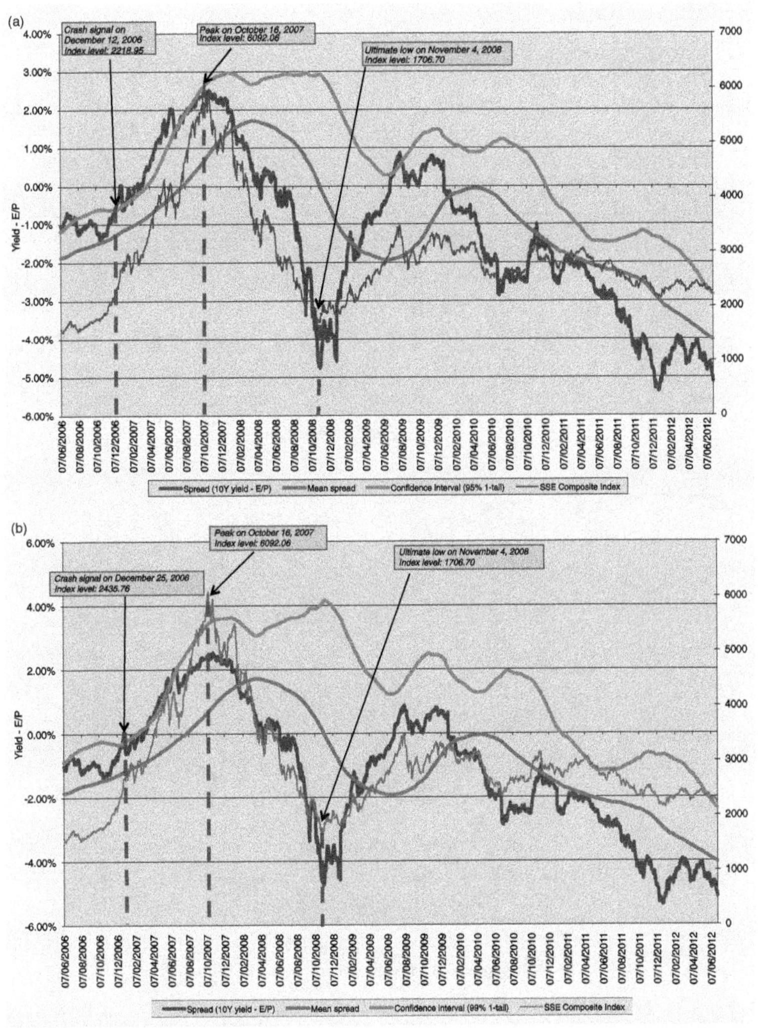

Figure 4. BSEYD danger signals for the Shanghai Stock Exchange Composite, 95% and 99% confidence: (a) First signal occurs on December 12, 2006. The market reaches its peak on October 16, 2007 and ultimate low on November 4, 2008 based on 95% confidence and (b) First signal occurs December 25, 2006. The market reaches its peak on October 16, 2007 and ultimate low on November 4, 2008 based on 99% confidence.

4. The Icelandic stock market crash

Iceland is a small country with only about 300 000 people. From 2002 to 2007, the economy and asset prices rose dramatically, with much leveraging of investments, especially by the banks. This led to high interest rates of about 10% long term and 16% short term. Eventually, it all collapsed in the wake of the 2007–2009 worldwide financial crisis. The decline was a massive crash of −95% in the equity index and a currency collapse.

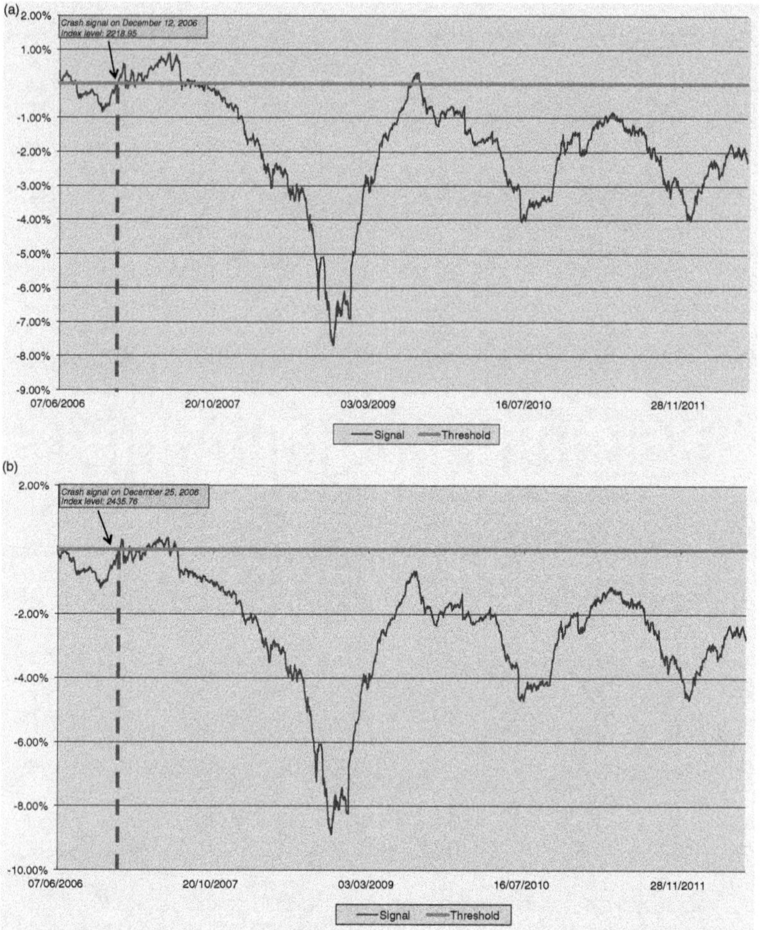

Figure 5. BSEYD danger signals for the Shanghai Stock Exchange Composite. Signals at 95% and 99% confidence: (a) Signal occurs on December 12, 2006 based on 95% confidence (b) Signal occurs on December 25, 2006 based on 99% confidence.

The equity index (see table 3) had 15 stocks in it with three of the banks having very high weighting: Kaupthing (26.5%), Lansbanki (13.0%) and Glitnir (12.3%) were more than half the market capitalization, and Actavis Banki had 9.9% and FL Banki another 6.7%. So the banks were close to two-thirds of the index value. In addition, index funds that tracked the market actually slightly over weighted these banks to yield higher returns.

Figure 8 shows the dramatic rise of the stock market, particularly since 2002. Similarly, figure 9 shows how quickly the crash occurred. However, the notable sharp sell-offs were, to a large extent, blips before the big crash and there was a question as to whether these investments could continue to produce similar returns and, if not, whether that would prompt investors to seek other markets.

Figure 10 shows that, in the autumn of 2007, the long bond interest rates rose above 10% and that, with an increase in the PE ratio respectively to 10.91 for Glitnir, as of October 10, 11.09 for Kaupthing, as of October 11, and 9.94 for Lansbanki as of October 17, the BSEYD

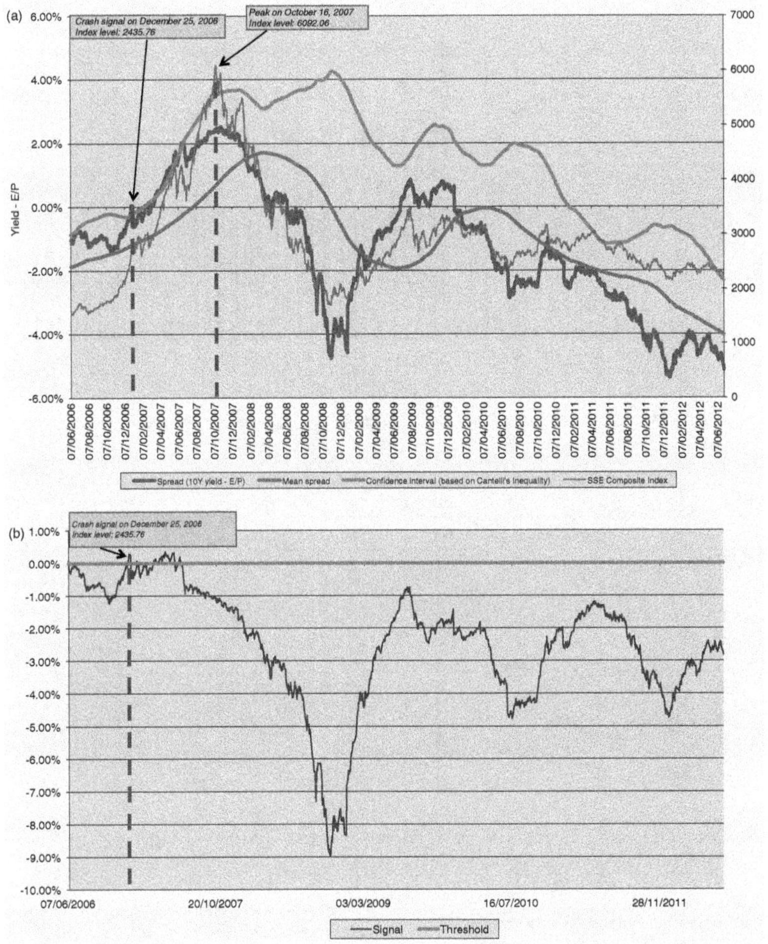

Figure 6. BSEYD Cantelli danger signals for the Shanghai Stock Exchange Composite: (a) First signal occurs on December 25, 2006. The market reaches its peak on October 16, 2007, (b) Signal occurs on December 25, 2006 (based on Cantelli's inequality, $\alpha = 15\%$).

spread signal did predict the massive crash. The market peaked at 8174.28 on July 18, 2007, starting in 2002 at 1180.75. Then it fell to 5803.55 by the end of December 2007. The complete collapse came in 2008, with the market falling by about 90% by the end of 2008 to 581.76 and by about – 95% to the ultimate bottom on February 2, 1010 at 491.58. As of June 30, 2012 the market had fallen to 677.75, 92% below its historical high. Table 4 summarizes the year-by-year story and figure 9 shows the index values from 1998 to June 30, 2012.

Figure 11 shows the BSEYD spreads for the three top banks and figures 12 and 13 show the bond–stock earnings yield crash measure from June 2004 to December 2008 for the three largest banks. Like China, the BSEYD distributions of these three largest banks are not normally distributed and have very fat left tails.

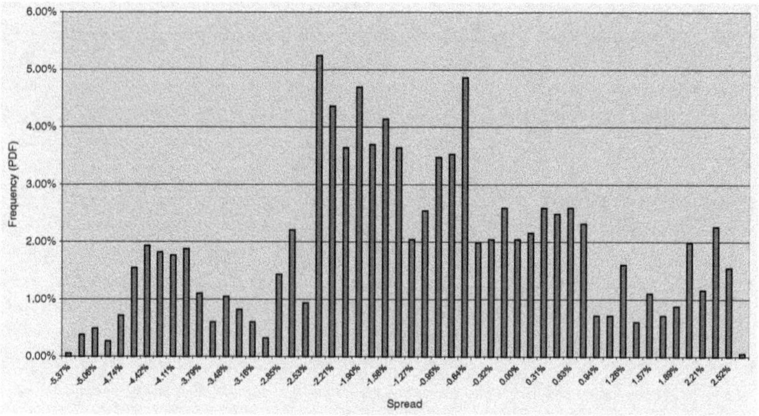

Figure 7. Spread distribution of the BSEYD measure on the Shanghai Stock Exchange Composite using the Cantelli inequality.

Table 3. Stock market index.

Weights				Real rates of return		
Company		Fund	Index		Fund	Index
1	Kaupthing Banki hf.	27.2%	26.5%	2005	56.5%	54.5%
2	Landsbanki Islands hf.	13.1%	13.0%	2004	49.1%	47.2%
3	Glitnir Banki hf.	12.5%	12.3%	2003	42.7%	40.7%
4	Straumur Burôarás Fjárfes	8.9%	8.9%	2002	20.7%	19.2%
5	Actavis Banki hf.	10.1%	9.9%	2001	−16.4%	−16.6%
6	FL Banki hf.	6.3%	6.2%	2000	−16.7%	−17.2%
7	Bakkavör Group hf.	4.0%	4.1%	1999	36.7%	36.4%
8	Avion Group hf.	3.7%	3.7%	1998	6.3%	3.4%
9	Mosaic Fashions hf.	2.7%	2.6%	1997	9.0%	10.2%
10	Ossurhf.	2.2%	2.2%	1996	44.1%	57.3%
11	Tryggingami9t69in hf.	2.1%	2.0%	1995	33.4%	31.1%
12	Dagsbrúnhf.	1.5%	1.5%			
13	Alfrescahf.	1.2%	1.2%			
14	FjarfestingafelagiBAtorka	1.0%	1.0%			
15	Grandi hf.	1.0%	1.0%			

Note: Over the period, inflation averaged 2–4%, implying that the nominal rates of return would have been slightly higher.
Source: Glitner (2006).

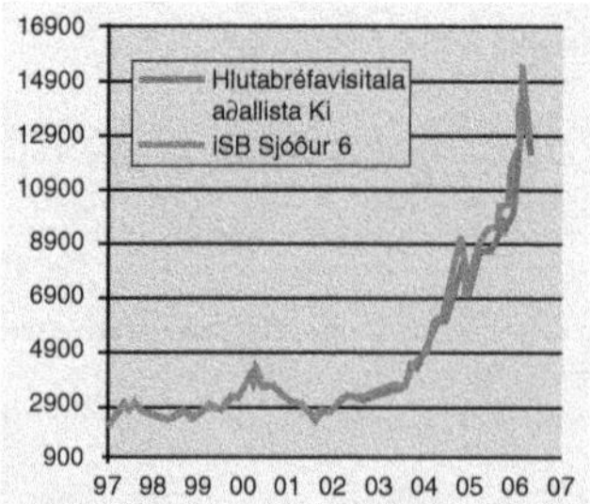

Figure 8. The 15 stocks in the Iceland equity index and their growth in real terms from 1997 to 2006. Source: Glitner (2006).

Finally, the question of whether or not the bond–stock earnings yield model predicted the crash is studied in figure 12(a), (c) and (e), which use 95% one-sided confidence intervals using moving averages. These graphs show that the crash was predicted. For Kaupthing, the danger zone was penetrated on September 28, 2007, two months after the July 18 peak and less than a month before the November 11 crash. For Glitnir, the signal was much earlier on October 17, 2006, some 13 months before the crash. Finally, for Lansbanki, the danger signal was on February 13, 2007. Figure 12(b), (d) and (f) show the BSEYM using Cantelli's inequality to account for the non-normality of the BSEYD measure. Figure 13 shows the signal dates. We focus on the largest banks because they led the market into the collapse and they are a majority of the index weighting. The smallest cap stocks in the index

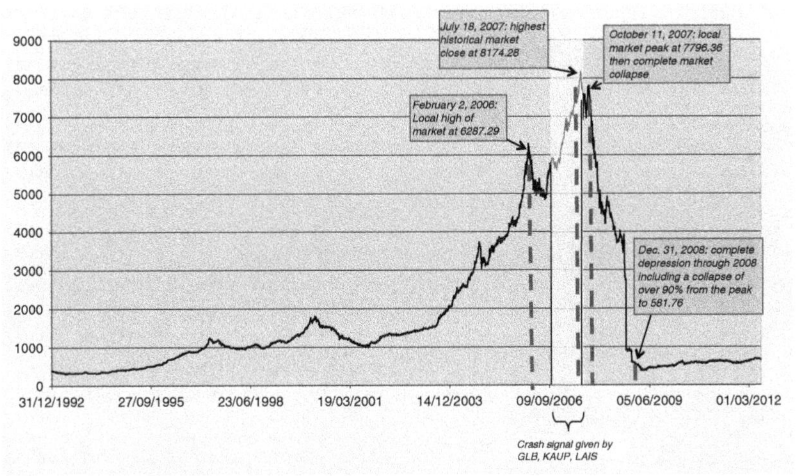

Figure 9. OMX Iceland all share price index, 1993 to June 30, 2012.

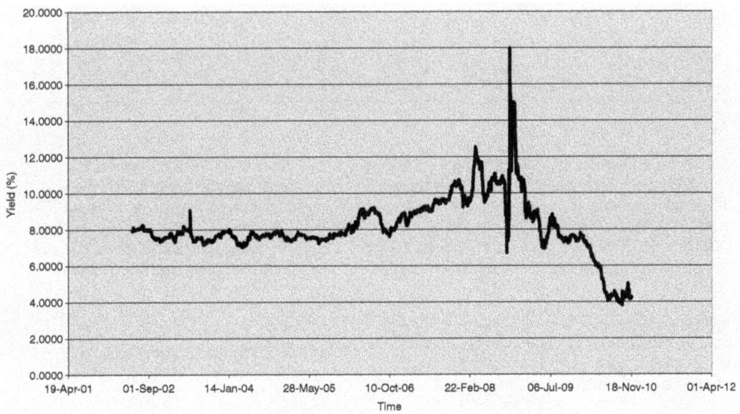

Figure 10. Iceland Treasury note (long bond) maturing May 17, 2013.

were in the danger zone in 2006, but not those of the large banks, and the overall index was not in the danger zone then, as is discussed by Ziemba and Ziemba (2007).

In summary, we make some comments on the crash signals for the three largest Icelandic banks.

Glitnir:

- Signal from September 15, 2003 until December 23, 2003: on October 12, 2004, the share price reached 11.90. By November 2, 2004, the share had gone down to 10, a 15.97% drop.
- Faint signal from November 17, 2004 until November 19, 2004 and December 6, 2004: on February 18, 2005, the share price fell to 11.60. By March 3, 2005, the share had gone down to 11.60, a 7.20% drop.
- Signal from November 22, 2005 until February 24, 2006 (with some interruptions): on October 12, 2004, the share price reached 22.60. By April 19, 2006, the share had gone down to 16.50, a 26.99% drop.

Table 4. Highlights for the Iceland stock index ICEXI-OMZ 1998–2011 with a start value of 1000 on December 31, 1997.

Date	Index value	Comment
Feb 11, 1998	977.58	
Dec 31, 1998	1046.58	
Dec 31, 1999	1511.86	Gain of 44.5% in 1999
Dec 31, 2000	1303.31	}
Dec 31, 2001	1180.75	} Weak market during US stock market weak period
Dec 31, 2002	1436.22	}
Dec 31, 2003	2064.05	Gain of 43.7% in 2003
Dec 31, 2004	3173.91	Gain of 53.8% in 2004
Dec 31, 2005	5107.49	Gain of 60.9% in 2005
Feb 2,2006	6287.29	Local high of market
Aug 2, 2006	4854.95	Local low of market
Dec 31, 2006	5857.50	Gain of 14.7% in 2006
Jul 18, 2007	8174.28	Global highest historical market close
Aug 16, 2007	6931.69	Market falls to local lows on day of US stock market turmoil when long–short funds had heavy losses
Oct 11, 2007	7796.36	Local market peak then complete market collapse
Dec 31, 2007	5803.35	Market down just slightly (−0.9%) in 2007 but 29% below the July 18, 2007 peak
Dec 31, 2008	581.76	Complete depression including a collapse of over 90% from the peak
Dec 31, 2009	496.48	Further fall in 2009
Feb 2, 2010	491.58	Global historical bottom of market
Nov 30, 2010	579.17	The market rallied back to make the yearly return nearly positive
Dec 31, 2010	569.19	Gain of 15.8% since global historical bottom but the index was still 93.0% below its historical high
Jan 31, 2011	624.97	Gain of 9.8% in January 2011
Jun 30, 2011	604.95	Gain of 23.0% since the global historical bottom but the index was still 92.5% below its historical high
Dec 31, 2011	567.77	Gain of 15% since the global historical bottom but the index was still 93% below its historical high
Jun 30, 2012	677.75	Gain of 38% since the global historical bottom but the index was still 92% below its historicalhigh

- Signal from October 17, 2006 (with a PE ratio of 22.30) until December 27, 2006: announces the market crash.
- Signal from December 28, 2007 until January 8, 2008.
- Signal from March 26, 2008 until April 10, 2008.

The crash signal analysis is basically according to the script except for the faint signal between November 17, 2004 until November 19, 2004 and December 6, 2004, for which we do not have a better explanation.

Kaupthing:

- Signal from February 7, 2006 until February 24, 2006: on October 26, 2006, the share price reached 868. By November 28, 2006, the share had fallen to 785, a 9.56% drop.
- The market reaches its peak on July 18, 2007 and a crash occurred on November 11, 2007.
- Signal from September 28, 2007 until November 5, 2007.
- Signal from March 26, 2008 until April 4, 2008.

Lansbanki:

- Signal from January 15, 2004 until March 4, 2004: on October 11, 2004, the share price reached 15.28. By November 2, 2004, the share had fallen to 10.85, a 28.98% drop.
- Signal from August 30, 2005 until December 29, 2005 (with minor interruptions): on February 16, 2006, the share price reached 30.56. By May 3, 2006, the share had fallen to 20.05, a 34.39% drop.
- Signal from February 13, 2007 until March 13, 2007 and from March 30, 2007 until June 28, 2007: market crash signal.
- The market reaches its peak on October 17, 2007.

The crash model works out well for Lansbanki: the signal identifies the market crashes and two large declines. Although the signal could be clearer for Glitnir and Kaupthing, we do not observe any false positives.

5. The US 2007–2009 crash

In this section we investigate whether or not the bond–stock measure predicted the US 2007–2009 crash, including the devastating September 2008 to March 2009 period. Table 6 shows the BSEYM at various periods from 2006 to 2011. In 2006, the weak economy led the Fed to dramatically reduce short-term interest rates,

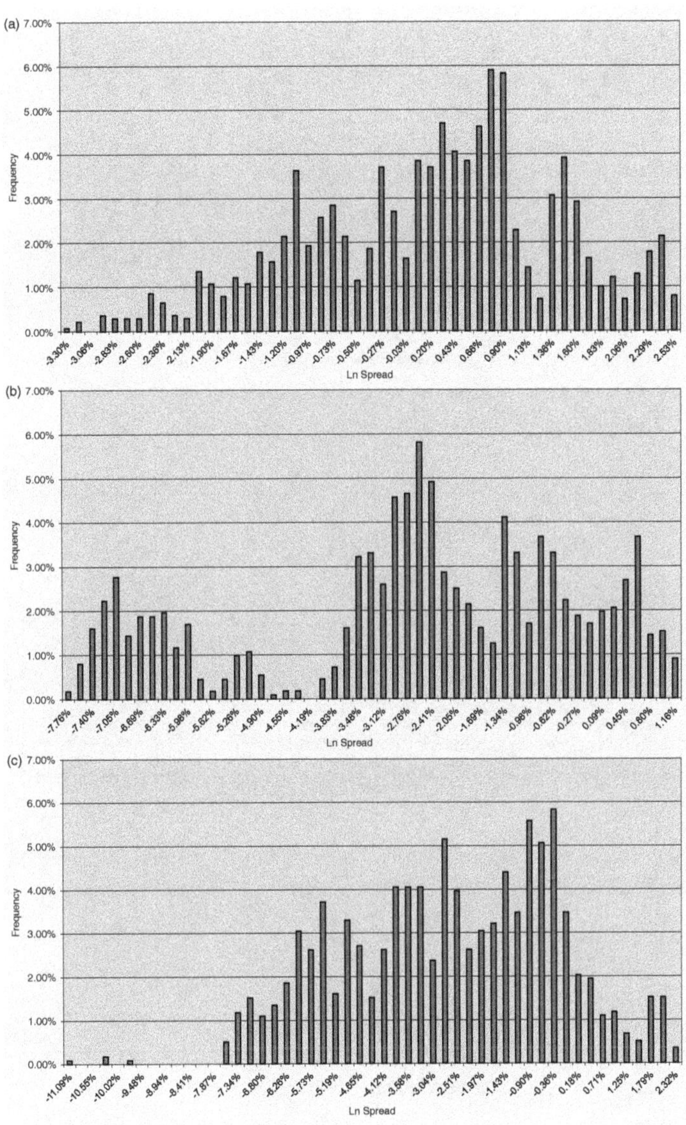

Figure 11. BSEYM spread distributions, Iceland: (a) Glitnir, (b) Kaupthing and (c) Lansbanki, MA.

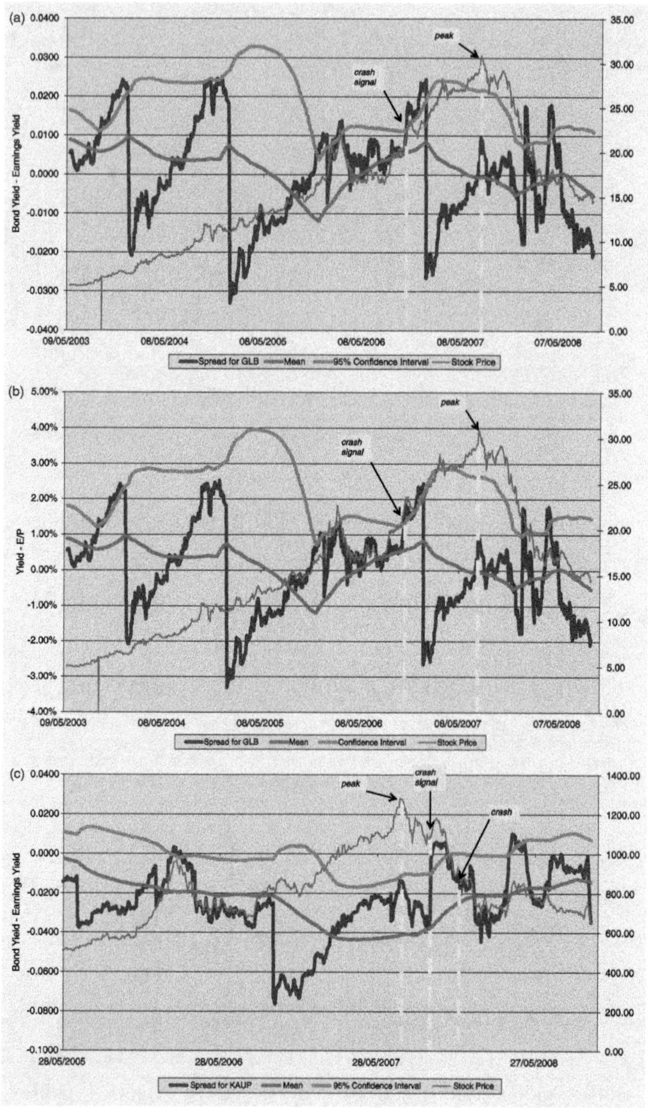

Figure 12. BSEYD crash indicators, Iceland: (a) BSEYD chart (indicator at 95% confidence): Glitnir. First crash signal occurs around October 17, 2006. The market reaches its peak on July, 20, 2007, (b) BSEYD chart (indicator using Cantelli's inequality, 20%): Glitnir. First crash signal occurs on October 17, 2006. The market reaches its peak on July, 20, 2007, (c) BSEYD chart (indicator at 95% confidence): Kaupthing. First signal occurs around October 2, 2007. The market reaches its peak on July 18, 2007 and a crash occurred on November 11, 2007, (d) BSEYD chart (indicator using Cantelli's inequality, 20%): Kaupthing. First crash signal occurs on October 2, 2007. The market reaches its peak on July 18, 2007 and a crash occurred on November 11, 2007, (e) BSEYD chart (indicator at 95% confidence): Lansbanki. First crash signal occurs around February 13, 2007. The market reaches its peak on October 17, 2007 and (f) BSEYD chart (indicator using Cantelli's inequality, 20%): Lansbanki. Faint crash signal throughout the first half of 2007. The market reaches its peak on October 17, 2007.

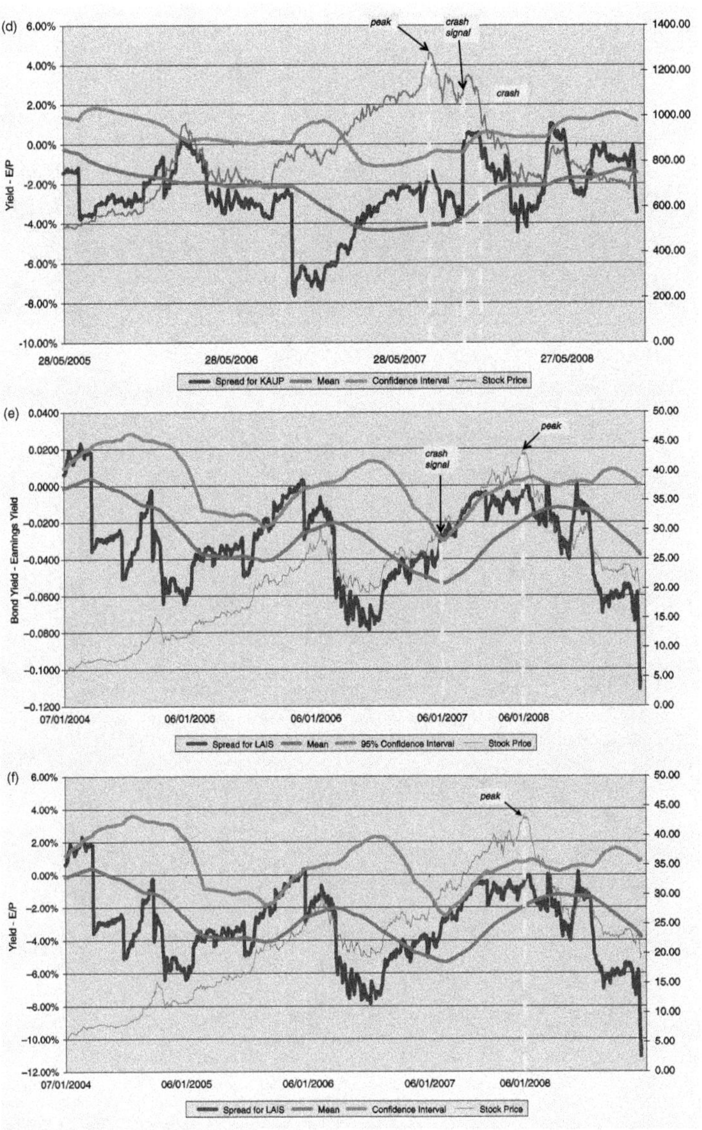

Figure 12. Continued.

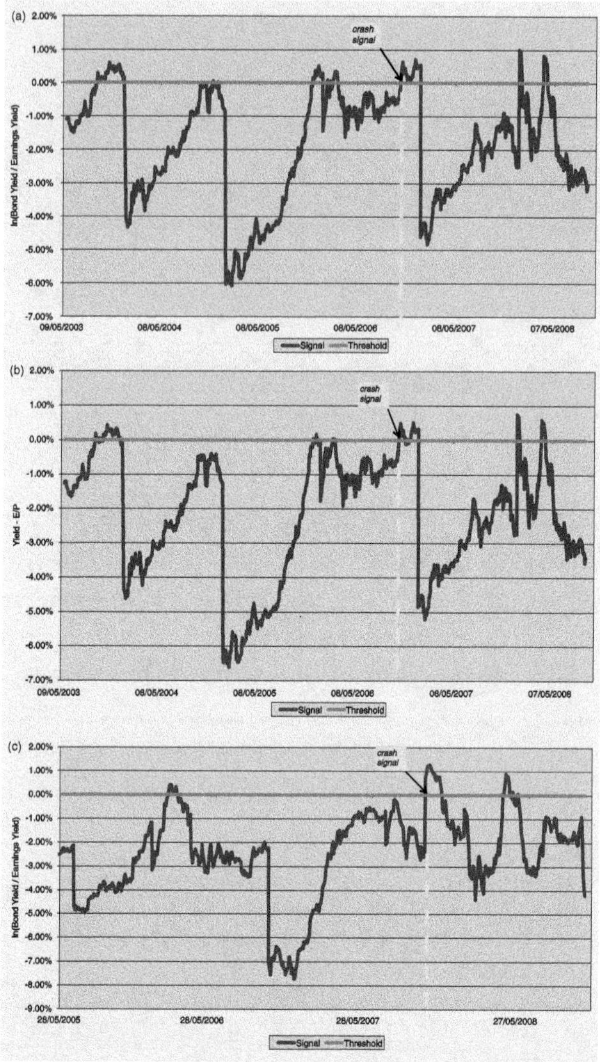

Figure 13. Crash indicators, Iceland: (a) Crash signal indicator (based on 95% confidence): Glitnir. First crash signal occurs around October 17, 2006. The market reaches its peak on July, 20 2007, (b) Signal chart (indicator using Cantelli's Inequality, 20%): Glitnir. First crash signal occurs on October 17, 2006. The market reaches its peak on July, 20 2007, (c) Signal chart (95% confidence): Kaupthing. First crash signal occurs around October 2, 2007. The market reaches its peak on July 18, 2007 and a crash occurred on November 11, 2007, (d) Signal chart (indicator using Cantelli's inequality, 20%): Kaupthing. First crash signal occurs on October 2, 2007. The market reaches its peak on July 18, 2007 and a crash occurred on November 11, 2007, (e) Signal chart (95% confidence): Lansbanki. First crash signal occurs around February 13, 2007. The market reaches its peak on October 17, 2007 and (f) Signal chart (indicator using Cantelli's inequality, 20%): Lansbanki. Faint crash signal throughout the first half of 2007. The market reaches its peak on October 17, 2007.

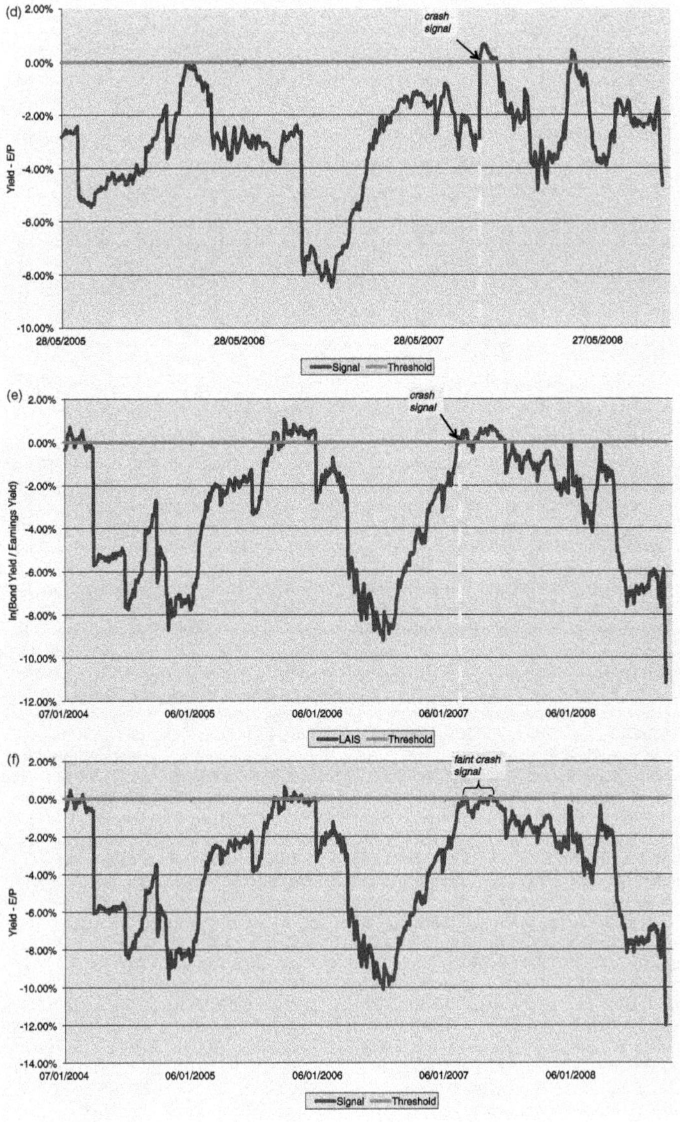

Figure 13. Continued.

Table 5. Long-bond (10 yr) versus earning yield differentials for major countries, July 12, 2006.

	S&P500	FTSE200	Nikkei225	CAC40	DAX30
Index	1259	5861	15,249	4942	5638
A) PE ratio	16.86	16.61	36.26	13.82	13.33
B) Stock return (1/A) (%)	5.93	6.02	2.76	7.24	7.50
C) Bond return (10 yr) (%)	5.10	4.67	1.94	4.10	4.09
D) Crash signal (C–B)	−0.83	−1.35	−0.82	−3.14	−3.41

Source: Ziemba and Ziemba (2007)

Table 6. Bond–stock yield model calculations leading up to the 2007–2009 crisis in the S&P500.

Date	Long bond (10 years)	Trailing PE	1/PE (%)	B–Y(pe)
Feb-06	4.49	20.00	5.00	(0.56)
Jun-07	5.15	17.00	5.98	(0.74)
Jun-08	4.14	18.00	5.55	(1.41)
May-09	3.70	33.30	3.00	0.70
May-10	3.41	20.47	4.89	(1.48)
Feb-11	3.59	23.83	4.20	(0.61)

which tended to drop the long-term rates that we use in the BSEYM calculations.

Table 5 considers the measure in five major countries on July 12, 2006. None of these major markets were in the danger zone then. Table 6 for the S&P500 has the calculations for the years from 2006 to 2011 on trailing price–earnings ratios that are usually used for these calculations and for 2011 which uses Shiller's average inflation-adjusted earnings from the previous 10 years. Figure 16(a) and (b) show the S&P500 PE ratios (Shiller's calculation method) and the 10-year Treasury bond yield.

Ex post it is clear that this stock market crash had a lot of components such as the first decline in aggregate US housing prices in more than 30 years, a subprime market collapsing because home buyers could not cover their mortgages, lots of suspect AAA-rated top tranches of securitization of these mortgages, and then a credit squeeze with much counterparty credit risk. As a result, firms were unwilling to lend money to others, including supposedly sound financial institutions, which led to the collapse of many large and previously sound financial institutions, such as Bear Stearns, Freddie Mac, Fannie May and, the killer for the market, Lehman Brothers.

Table 7 lists some of the main events regarding the S&P500 from 2006 to 2012. There are numerous books concerning this period plus many articles and columns (see, for example, Ziemba's several contributions in *Wilmott*). Starting in June 2007, Ziemba designed strategies and traded for an offshore BVI-based hedge fund group whose hedge funds had investments in Bear Stearns and in June 2007 asked for their money back. The process took three months and gave the fund manager a strong signal of danger. As an astute trader, he hedged and studied carefully the market situation through technical indicators that he has developed. Ziemba remembers his view formed in the summer of 2007 that "this is the big one" … "eventually the market will go to 660 on the S&P500". In the fall of 2007 the S&P500 was about 1500 (see figure 14). So this was a rather bold call, but a private one, and it turned out to be very accurate. Nouriel Roubini was boldly predicting a serious financial meltdown starting in 2006, when the housing market was beginning its decline (see figure 15(a), which gives the Case Shiller Home Price Index as of July 24, 2008). There was a sharp decline from 2005 to 2008. Roubini and other bears, such as Robert Shiller, are still (July 2012) pessimistic about the economy, real estate and financial markets. Figure 15(b) and (d) show the S&P Case Shiller index level and year-on-year change up until April 2012. Dropping real estate values have several depressive effects, such as homeowners can no longer use house price gains to fund consumption, foreclosures, etc. The March 2009 low closing was 676.53, with an intra-day low of 660 on March 6. The subsequent rally has doubled the S&P500 to 1320.64 as of the end of June 2011. There is considerable discussion regarding whether or not this rally is low-interest-rate-related to the Fed's quantitative easing, or is the only game in town since real estate, bonds and cash look unattractive. This is a case when the BSEYM signaled the rise in stock prices. A volatile period followed the rally, with a drop in the level of the S&P500 in August and September 2009 followed by a stabilization in October.

Did the BSEYD model predict the US crash? Figures 17 and 18 show that it did on June 14, 2007. As with China and Iceland, the BSEYD measure is not normally distributed, but rather its distribution has fat tails, especially on the downside, as shown in figure 19. The 95% confidence graph for the crash danger signal is shown in figure 17(a). The Cantelli inequality version of the model (figure 17(b)) gives the danger signal on the same day, namely June 14, 2007 (see also figures 18(a) and (b))).

Let us go back to the BSEYM and consider table 8, which was published in the Maudlin weekly newsletter,

Table 7. Highlights of the S&P500, January 1, 2006 to June 30, 2012.

Date	Index value	Comment
Dec 31, 2005	1248.29	
Aug 31, 2006	1303.82	Gain of 4.4% year-to-date
Dec 31, 2006	1418.30	Gain of 13.6% in 2006
Feb 26, 2007	1437.50	Local high of market
Mar 1, 2007	1374.12	Local low of market
Jun 7, 2007	1480.72	Bear Stearns suspends redemptions from one of its hedge funds
Jun 14, 2007	1522.97	BSEYD crash signal occurs
Jul 13, 2007	1552.50	Local high of market
Jul 31, 2007	1455.27	Bear Stearns liquidates two hedge funds
Aug 16, 2007	1411.27	Local low of market
Oct 9, 2007	1565.15	Market peak. Gain of 10.4% year-to-date
Dec 31, 2007	1468.35	Gain of 3.5% in 2007
Mar 17, 2008	1276.60	Local low of market
Sep 15, 2008	1192.70	Lehman Brothers files for bankruptcy protection
Sep 30, 2008	1166.36	Market down by 20.6% year-to-date
Oct 10, 2008	899.22	Local low of market
Oct 31, 2008	968.75	Market down by 16.9% in October
Dec 31, 2008	903.25	Market down by 38.5% in 2008
Mar 9, 2009	683.38	Lowest intra-day: 666.79
Mar 9, 2009	676.53	Market trough. The market was down by 56.8% peak to trough
Jul 28, 2009	979.62	Date Shepherd claimed that the S&P500 had a 723 PE ratio based on reported (real earnings) to the SEC on 10Q forms
Dec 31, 2009	1115.10	Market was down by 23.5% in 2009, but up by 64.8% since trough
Apr 23, 2010	1217.28	Local high
Jul 2, 2010	1022.58	Local low
Dec 31, 2010	1257.64	Gain of 12.8% in 2010, and of 23% since the local low of July 2, 2010
May 10, 2011	1357.16	Local high. Gain of 7.91% year-to-date and of 32.72% since the local low of July 2, 2010
Dec 31, 2011	1257.60	The index ends the year flat, but is still down 7.3% from the local high of May 10, 2010
Jun 30, 2012	1362.16	Gain of 8.3% year-to-date

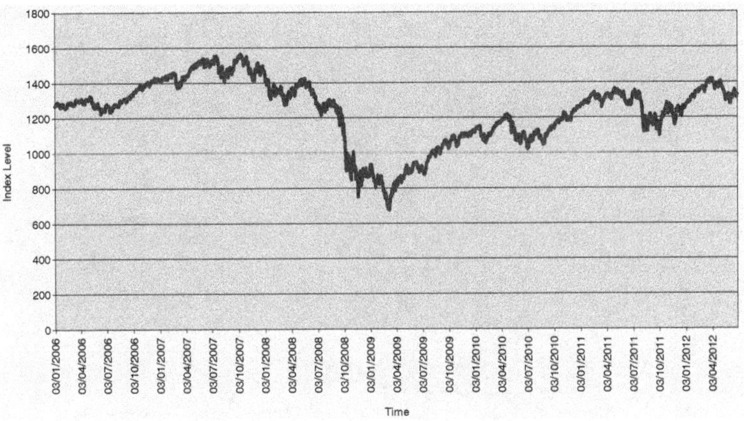

Figure 14. The S&P500, January 1, 2006 to June 30, 2012.

which had 1.5 million subscribers in May 2009, and discuss whether or not it called the September 2008 to March 2009 crash. Figure 20 shows the S&P500 during this 2007–2009 period. Table 8 has the S&P500 2008 estimated earnings and 2009 forecast earnings. On July 25, 2008, the S&P500 earnings for 2008 were estimated to be 72.00, with the S&P500 at 1257.76, which gives a PE ratio of 17.47—not high enough to signal the September 2008 to March 2009 crash. But by February 20, 2009, the 2008 earnings were estimated to be only 26.23. With the

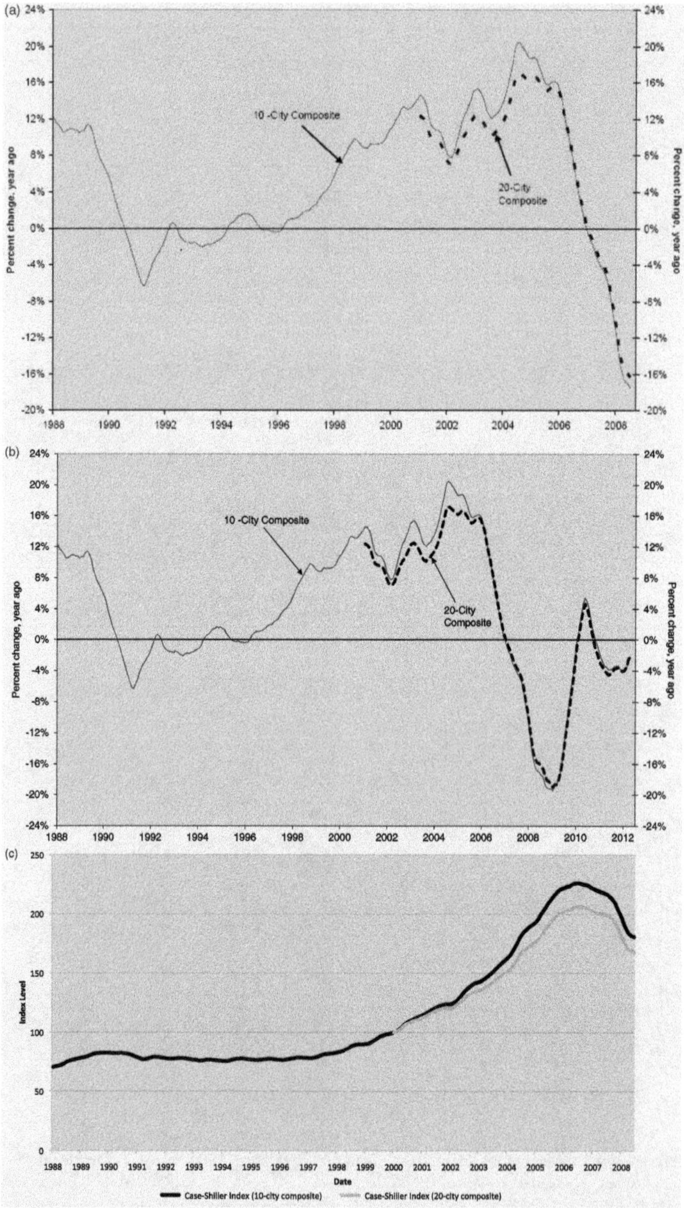

Figure 15. S&P/Case Shiller index: (a) Case Shiller Index: year-on-year percentage change (1988–2008), (b) S&P/Case Shiller Index: year-on-year percentage change(1988–2012), (c) S&P/Case Shiller Index level (1988–2008) and (d) S&P/Case Shiller Index level (1987–2012).

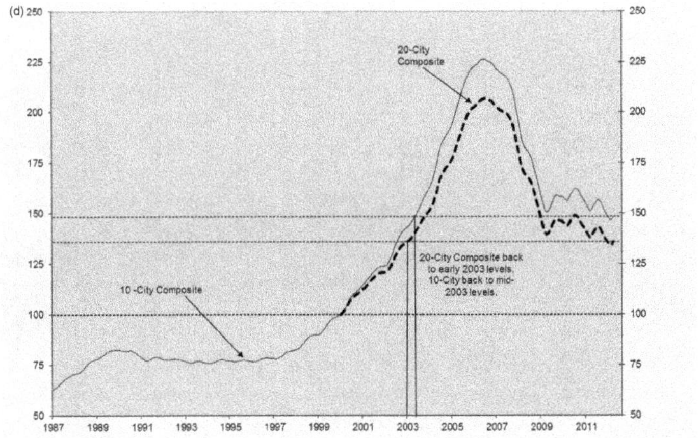

Figure 15. Continued.

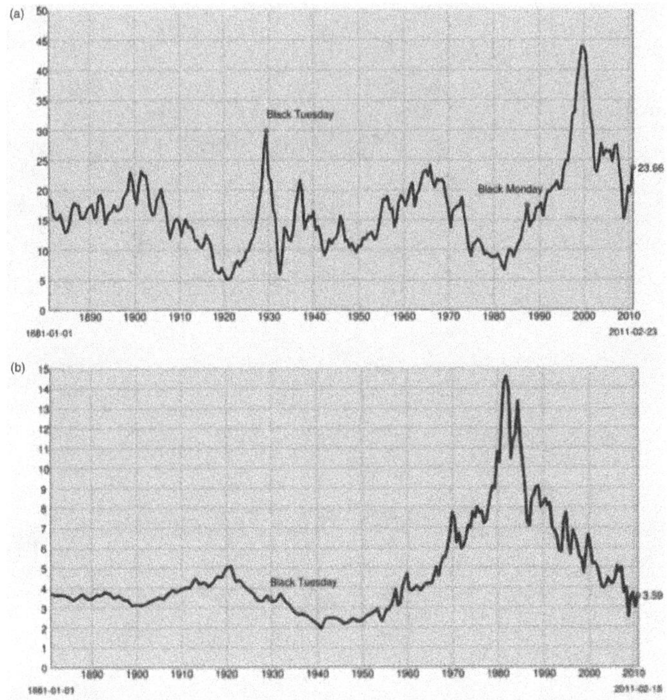

Figure 16. S&P500 and 10-year Treasury bond yields, January 1, 1881 to February 23, 2011: (a) S&P500 price earnings ratios and (b) Treasury bond yield. Source: Robert Shiller data.

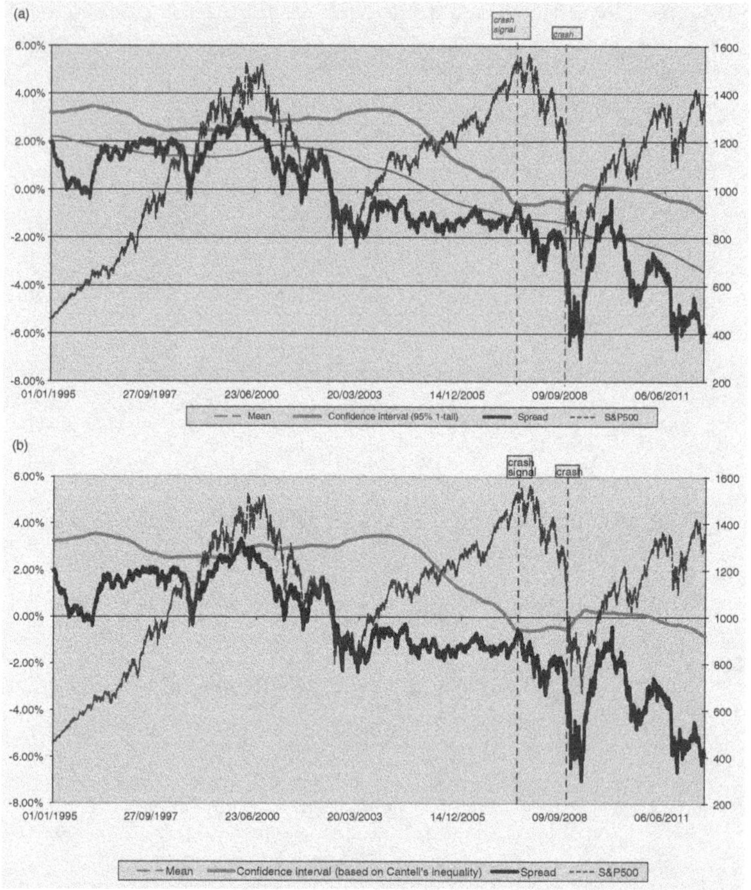

Figure 17. Crash indicators, US: (a) Crash indicator (95% confidence: s&p500 MA. Signal occurs on June 14, 2007. The market reaches its peak on October 9, 2007 and crashes in September 2008) and (b) Crash indicator (Cantelli's inequality): S&P500, MACI. Signal occurs on June 14, 2007. The market reaches its peak on October 9, 2007 and crashes in September 2008.

S&P500 at 770.05 on that day the trailing PE ratio was 29.36, which gives a BSEYD value of $2.78 - (100/29.36) = -0.626$.

Shepherd (2009) has the S&P500 PE ratio at 723 on July 28, 2009, four months into the rally that began in March 2009! The S&P500 was then 979.62, up nearly 50% from the March lows. This high PE ratio was based on reported real earnings from SEC 10Q filings. So what do we conclude here? Our conclusion is shown in figure 21. The BSEYD model did not give any additional sell signals during 2008. The signal was on June 14, 2007 with the index at 1522.97 and the crash occurred in various phases with closing peak of 1565.15 on October 9, 2007 and a closing low of 676.53 on March 9, 2009, down some 56.8% from the peak. The conclusions are similar: over the period January 1, 1995 to June 30, 2012, two BSYED crash signals occurred, one in June 1999 and the other in June 2007.

6. Logarithmic model

Koivu *et al.* 2005) use a logarithmic version of the BSEYD model. The question is does that model suggest

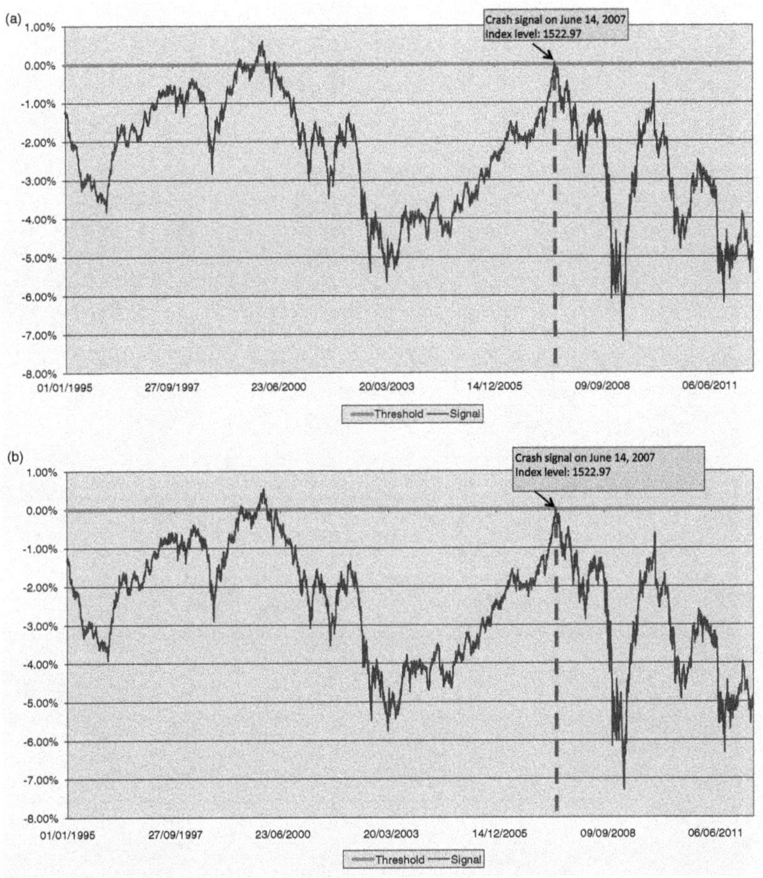

Figure 18. Signal occurs on June 14, 2007: (a) Based on a standard one-tail 95% confidence level, moving-average normal distribution assumption and (b) Based on a standard one-tail 95% confidence level, moving-average fat tail distribution, Cantelli's inequality assumption.

anything new for our analysis? The logarithmic model is based on the logarithm of the Fed model bond stock yield ratio, via

$$\ln BSEYR(t) = \ln\left(\frac{r(t)}{\gamma(t)}\right) = \ln r(t) - \ln \gamma(t).$$

For China and Iceland, both measures produce similar results which are available from the authors. The pattern and timing of the crash signals nearly coincide for all three Icelandic banks. In China, the lnBSEYR generates a slightly earlier signal than the BSEYD.

In the US, the result of the lnBSEYR and of the BSEYD measures are also broadly similar. A signal precedes both the internet-related crash of 2000 and the credit crunch crash of 2008 (see figures 22–24). In addition, the logarithmic lnBSEYR(t) measure generates a signal in April 1998, ahead of a 19% decline from July 17 to August 31. However, neither measure predicted the market decline of 2002. This is a combined result of the relatively low level reached by the two measures in 2001 compared with 1999, and of the increase in the confidence level starting in 2000.

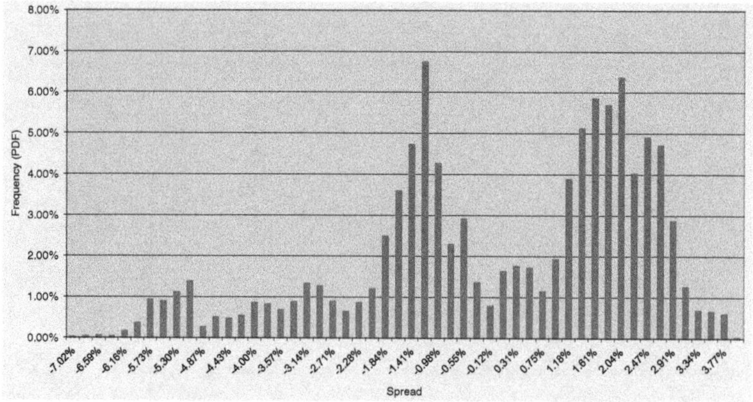

Figure 19. Spread distribution of the BSEYD measure on the S&P500.

Table 8. Earnings revisions for 2008 and 2009; analysts estimates of earnings in dollars.

		... and estimates for 2009	
Date	Earnings	Date	Earnings
Mar 2007	92.00	Mar 20, 2008	81.52
Dec 2007	84.00	Apr 9, 2008	72.60
Feb 2008	71.20	Jun 25, 2008	70.13
Jun 1, 2008	68.93	Sep 10, 2008	48.52
Jul 25, 2008	72.00	Aug 29, 2008	64.44
Sep 30, 2008	60.00	Feb 1, 2009	42.00
Oct 15, 2008	54.82	Feb 20, 2009	32.41
Feb 20, 2009	26.23	Apr 10, 2009	28.51
Apr 10, 2009	14.88		

Source: Mauldin (2009).

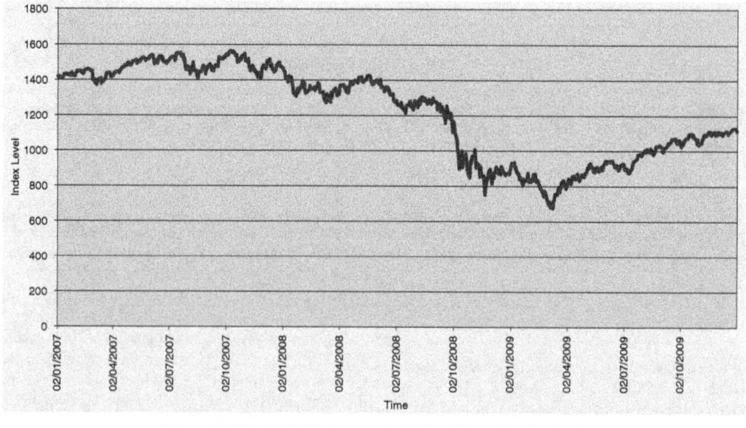

Figure 20. The S&P500, January 1, 2007 to December 31, 2009.

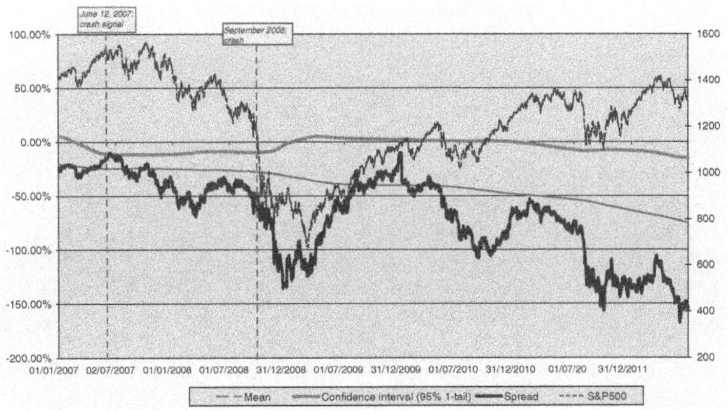

Figure 21. Crash indicator (95% confidence): S&P500, January 1, 2007 to June 30, 2012.

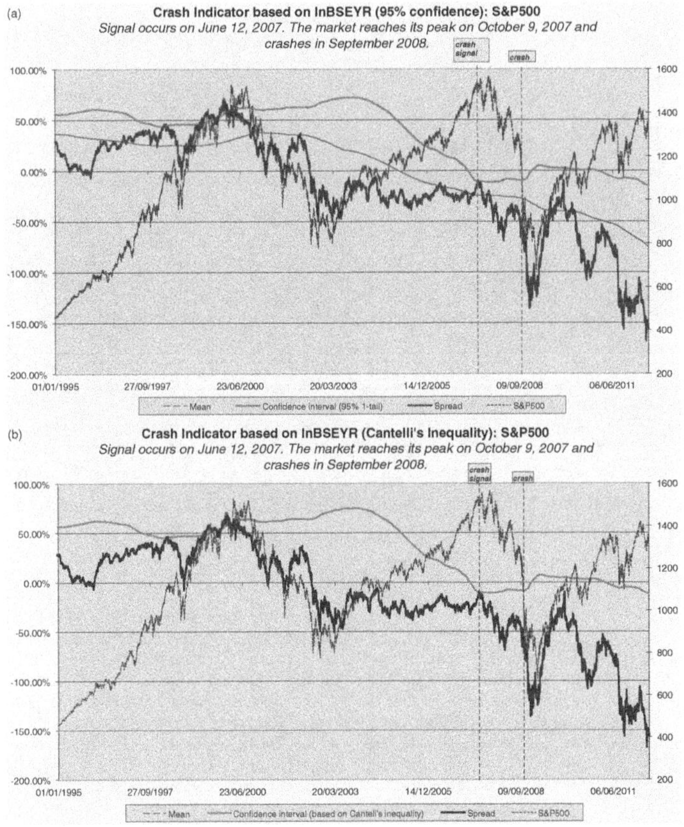

Figure 22. Crash indicators, US. (a) and (b).

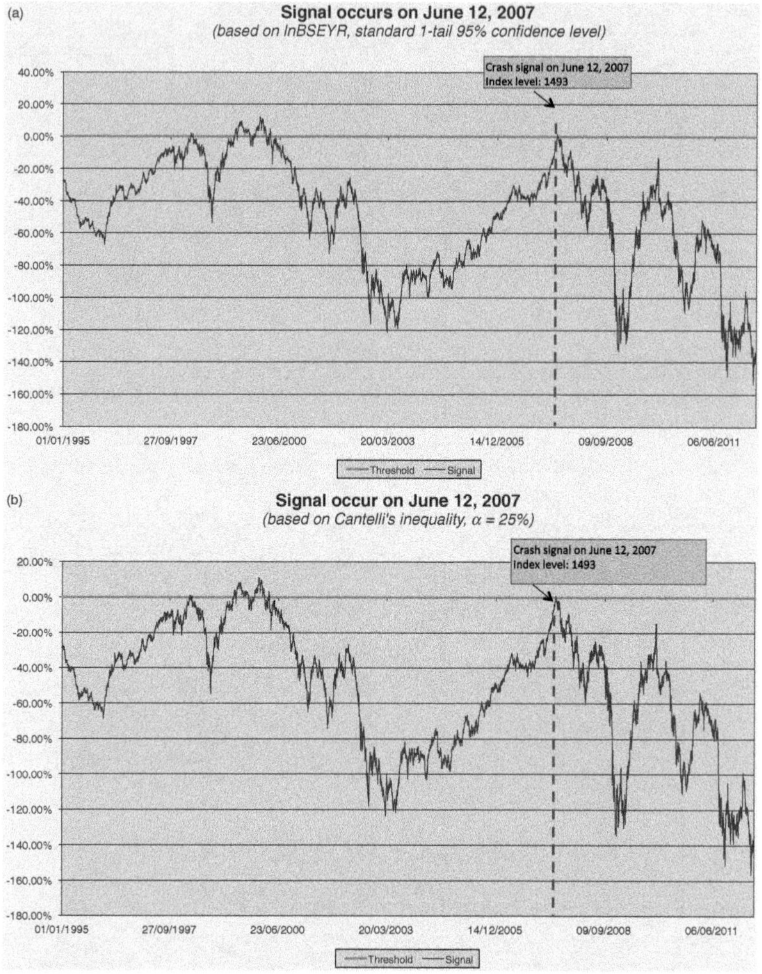

Figure 23. Signal occurs on June 14, 2007. (a) and (b).

7. Final remarks

The bond stock earnings yield model has been shown to be useful in a number of contexts. First, using it for being in or out of the market over long investment periods has been shown to produce about double the returns of buy and hold with lower risk in five major countries. Secondly, over the years, the model has predicted many significant stock market crashes such as those in China, Iceland and the US during 2007–2009. Finally, it has a possible, but less clear, use concerning when to re-enter markets after a crash. This is a topic the authors will consider in future research.

The measure does not call all crashes, just the ones with high interest rates relative to earnings. Other crashes such as the August–September 2011 turbulence can occur for other reasons, such as the European debt crisis and the political stalemate in Washington.

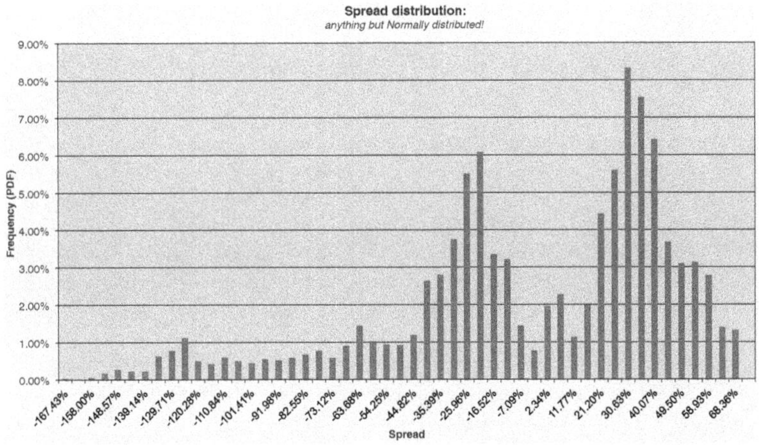

Figure 24. Spread distribution of the lnBSEYD measure on the S&P500.

Acknowledgements

This article was presented at the International Conference on Risk Management, Amsterdam, The Korea Advanced Institute for Science and Technology, the Izmir Options Exchange Turkey, Stanford University, Luiss Guido Carli University and Rensselaer Polytechnic Institute.

References

Asness, C., Stocks versus bonds: Explaining the equity risk premium. *Financ. Anal. J.*, 2000, March/April, 96–113.

Asness, C., Fight the Fed model: The relationship between future returns and stock and bond market yields. *J. Portfol. Mgmt*, 2003, Fall, 11–24.

Berge, K., Consigli, G. and Ziemba, W.T., The predictive ability of the bond stock earnings yield differential. *J. Portfol. Mgmt*, 2008, Spring, 63–80.

Campbell, J.Y. and Vuolteenaho, T., Inflation illusion and stock prices. *Am. Econ. Rev., Pap. Proc.*, 2004, **94**, 19–23.

Consigli, G., MacLean, L.C., Zhao, Y. and Ziemba, W.T., The bond–stock yield differential as risk indicator in financial markets. *J. Risk*, 2009, **11**(3), 1–22.

Damodaran, A., *Investment Valuation: Tools and Techniques for Determining the Value of Any Asset*, 3rd ed., 2012 (Wiley: New York).

Giot, P. and Petitjean, M., Short-term market timing using the bond–equity yield ratio. *Eur. J. Finance*, 2008, April–June, 365–384.

Glitner, List of available funds, 2006, May.

Grimmett, G. and Stirzaker, D., *Probability and Random Processes*, 2001 (Oxford University Press: Oxford).

Koivu, M., Pennanen, T. and Ziemba, W.T., Cointegration analysis of the FED model. *Finance Res. Lett.*, 2005, **2**, 248–256.

Lleo, S. and Ziemba, W.T., Some historical perspectives on the Bond–Stock Yield Model for crash prediction around the world. Technical Report, 2012.

Mauldin, J., May 'Outside the Box' newsletter, 2009.

Modigliani, F. and Cohn, R., Inflation, rational valuation and the market. *Financ. Anal. J.*, 1979, **35**, 24–44.

Montier, J., The seven immutable laws of investing. *John Mauldin's Outside the Box*, March 11, 2011.

Ritter, J.R. and Warr, R.S., The decline of inflation and the bull market of 1982–1999. *J. Financ. Quantit. Anal.*, 2002, **37**, 29–61.

Schwartz, S.L. and Ziemba, W.T., Predicting returns on the Tokyo stock exchange. In *Security Market Imperfections in World Wide Equity Markets*, pp. 492–511, 2000 (Cambridge University Press: Cambridge).

Shepherd, C., S&P500 ratio is now at 723, 2009. Available online at: www.trendinvestor.info

Shiller, R., Irrational exuberance revisited. *CFA Inst. Conf. Proc. Q.*, 2006, **23**(3), 16–25.

Ziemba, R.E.S. and Ziemba, W.T., *Scenarios for Risk Management and Global Investment Strategies*, 2007 (Wiley: New York).

Ziemba, W.T. and Schwartz, S.L., *Invest Japan*, 1991 (Probus: Chicago).

Chapter 19

Land and stock bubbles, crashes and exit strategies in Japan circa 1990 and in 2013[#]

A. N. SHIRYAEV†, M. V. ZHITLUKHIN†‡ and W. T. ZIEMBA*§¶||††

†Department of Probability and Statistics, Steklov Mathematical Institute, Moscow, Russia
‡Laboratory of Quantitative Finance, Higher School of Economics (HSE), Moscow, Russia
§Sauder School of Business, University of British Columbia, Vancouver, Canada
¶School of Social Sciences, University of Manchester, Manchester, UK
||Business School, Sabanci University, Istanbul, Turkey
††Systemic Risk Centre, London School of Economics, London, UK

(Received 13 January 2014; accepted 13 November 2014)

We study the land and stock markets in Japan circa 1990 and in 2013. While the Nikkei stock average in the late 1980s and its −48% crash in 1990 is generally recognized as a financial market bubble, a bigger bubble and crash was in the land market. The crash in the Nikkei which started on the first trading day of 1990 was predictable in April 1989 using the bond-stock earnings yield model which signalled a crash but not its exact moment. We show that it was possible to use the changepoint detection model based solely on price movements for profitable exits of long positions both circa 1990 and in 2013.

Keywords: Bubble; Change point detection; Bond-stock model; Nikkei stock average; Golf course membership index

JEL Classification: G01, C11

1. Introduction

The crash of the Japanese stock market in the 1990s and the land markets beginning in 1991 ushered in two decades of deflation, weak economic markets and a lost generation of young people. Various Japanese policies and regulatory constraints exacerbated the poor economic situation and never resolved the basic problem of overleveraging and excessive debt that was a major part of the 1980s' build-up.

Our purpose here is not to discuss these issues, including the policy not to let the bankrupt companies and individuals go into bankruptcy and start over, so that the successful ones would continue and the failures would exit the market or restructure. Rather, our concern is with two issues. First, was it possible to predict the crash and secondly, could investors have exited the market unscathed with most of their gains or actually shorted the market successfully using a model based solely on prices? We assume that there was a bubble in both the stock market measured by the Nikkei225, and the land market proxied by the golf course membership indices in various parts of Japan, but we do not need there to be an official bubble‡‡ for our results to hold.

Section 2 investigates the question whether or not the Japanese stock market crash was indeed predictable. French and Poterba (1991) and Ziemba and Schwartz (1991) use similar growth models to first justify the high prices of Japanese stocks at that time and the same models to indicate that with different weaker growth parameters a much lower equilibrium stock market price was predicted. Ziemba and Schwartz (1991) further showed that a long bond minus the reciprocal of past earnings to price ratio model did predict the 1990 crash with a danger signal in April 1989. That model derived from the 1987 US stock market crash predicted correctly 12/12 10%+ declines of the 20 such declines from 1948 to 1988 (i.e. the model was in the danger zone 12 times and each time the stock market fell at least 10% from the initial level when the danger signal occurred). The other eight declines were for other reasons than

*Corresponding author. Email: wtzimi@mac.com

This paper is dedicated to the memory of Professor Merton H. Miller who encouraged Ziemba to further study of the golf course membership index markets.

‡‡Tests of whether a market is a bubble or not have been studied by Stiglitz (1990) and the papers in that issue of the *Journal of Economic Perspectives* and by Camerer (1989), Scheinkman and Xing (2003), Jarrow *et al.* (2011), Evanoff *et al.* (2012), Anderson *et al.* (2013), Phillips *et al.* (2013) among others.

[#]This chapter was originally published in: Shiryaev, A. N., Zhitukhin, M. V. & Ziemba, W. T. (2015). Land and Stock Bubbles, Crashes and Exit Strategies in Japan Circa 1990 and in 2013. *Quantitative Finance*, 15(9), 1449–1469.

high price earnings ratios compared to high long bond interest rates.

This paper discusses the BSEYD (bond stock earnings yield differential) model applied to Japan. A survey of the application of the BSEYD model to US and other markets since it was discovered in 1988 is in Lleo and Ziemba (in press). The prediction of stock market crises and crashes has been studied by many authors. Major contributions using different models have been made by Buffett (2001), Corcos *et al.* (2002), Kindleberger and Aliber (2011), Reinhart and Rogoff (2009), Shiller (2009), Sornette (2003), Sornette (2004), Sornette and Zhou (2002), Weigand and Irons (2007), Yan *et al.* (2012b) and Yan *et al.* (2012a).

Section 3 describes the changepoint model that we use to determine exits and short entries in bubble-type markets. Section 4 applies the model to the Japanese stock market proxied by the Nikkei225 stock average which is price weighted similar to the 30 stock Dow Jones average. Section 5 applies the model to the golf course membership markets in various regions of Japan. Section 6 considers the overall land markets in Japan from 1955 to 1990 before the crash with some discussion regarding this market since 1990. Section 7 considers the 2013 Nikkei market. Section 8 discusses the use of the model for short selling. Section 9 concludes.

2. Was the 1990 Japanese stock market crash predictable?

Starting on the first trading day of 1990, the Nikkei stock average (Nikkei) declined. When it bottomed, the market had fallen 48% from 38 916 at the end of December 1989 to 20 222 on 1 October, 1990. This section presents the bond stock earnings yield model that suggested a danger signal in April 1987. This is based on too high interest rates relative to earnings yield, namely the trailing reciprocal of the price–earnings ratio.

In May 1988 I (Ziemba) was invited by Yamaichi Securities to interview to be the first Yamaichi visiting professor of finance at the University of Tsukuba, a Japanese national university. Yamaichi wished to try to establish the study of finance, especially investments, in Japanese universities, which was not generally taught. They established a five-year programme with five such visiting professors in succession. My teaching at the university (investments, security market anomalies, futures and options) was supplemented with a two-day a week consulting position in Tokyo some 60 kilometres southwest of Tsukuba at the Yamaichi Research Institute of Yamaichi Securities, then the fourth largest securities firm in Japan and the sixth largest in the world. In my interview I asked if I could study market imperfections (anomalies) and stock market crashes in two study groups with some of the young Yamaichi Research Institute employees who also came up to Tsukuba for my classes.

My proposal was accepted and each study group with about 10 eager young students in each group proceeded by me giving lectures on the US experience and they helping me investigate the Japanese situation. We focused on the postwar period 1948–1988 and much of what I learned appears in the book *Invest Japan*, Ziemba and Schwartz (1991) and the 1989–1993 research papers of Ziemba, including Schwartz and Ziemba (2000) and Stone and Ziemba (1993). My wife Sandra L. Schwartz and I also wrote the book *Power Japan* (1992) that discussed the Japanese economy. Sandra had a pretty good idea right away that the Japanese policies that led to astronomically high land and stock prices and massive trade surpluses would lead to disaster and they would eventually lose most of the money that they received from selling cars, stereos and the like. We made a list of prestige buildings that the Japanese overpaid for in the 1987–1989 era in *Power Japan*. Even at the height of their economic power in 1989 only 3% of Japanese assets were invested abroad.

My study groups started in August 1988 and ended a year later. I was asked to remain as a consultant for the fall of 1988 to complete a factor model discussed in Ziemba and Schwartz (1991) and Schwartz and Ziemba (2000) which was originally presented at a Berkeley Program in Finance meeting in Santa Barbara in September 1992. The factor model used anomaly ideas, such as mean reversion, momentum and value embedded in 30 variables to separate and rank stocks by their future mean performance from best to worst for all the 1000+ stocks on the Tokyo Stock Exchange first section which was about 86% of the total capitalization of the Japanese stock market. The model performed well out of sample so was useful for hedge fund long–short trading as well as long only investing. The hedge fund Buchanan Partners in London discovered the model which was discussed in *Invest Japan* when they bought a copy of the book and hired me to consult with them in their warrant trading which was largely long underpriced warrants and short overpriced stocks. Their trading was successful and the model, which was estimated using data during a stock market rise, still worked when the decline came, since variables such as earnings were the key drivers of the returns. An update of Japanese anomalies to 1994 appears in Comolli and Ziemba (2000). Ziemba's Japanese, US and other anomaly papers are reprinted in Ziemba (2012).

In the crash study group, I came up with a simple model in 1988 with only a single variable that being the difference between stock and bond rates of return. The idea was that stocks and bonds compete for investment dollars and, when interest rates are low, stocks are favoured and when interest rates are high, bonds are favoured. The main thing that I wished to focus on is that when the measure, the difference between these two rates, the long bond yield minus the earnings yield (the reciprocal of the price earnings ratio), was very large, then there was a high chance of a stock market crash, namely a 10%+ fall in the index within one year. The model explains the October 1987 crash. That application is how this idea came to me. Table 1 and figure 1 show this. The boxes indicate that there is extreme danger in the stock market because 30-year government bond yields are very much higher than usual stock market yields measured by the reciprocal of the last year's reported price–earnings ratio. These high interest rates invariably lead to a stock market crash. Here, the danger indicator moved across a statistical 95% confidence line in April 1987.† The market ignored this signal but did eventually crash in October 1987. While Table 1 uses S&P500 data and Berge *et al.* (2008) use

†For a study of this measure for staying in or exiting stock markets from 1975 and 1980 to 2005 in five major countries (US, Japan, UK, Germany and Canada), see Berge *et al.* (2008). In each country final wealth under the strategy in cash in the danger periods (about 20% of the time) is about double the buy and hold strategy with lower standard deviation risk.

Table 1. S&P500 index, PE ratios, government bond yields and the yield premium over stocks, January 1986 to August 1988.

		S&P Index	PER	(a) 30 Yr G bd	(b) 1/pe,%	(a)–(b)
1986	Jan	208.19	14.63	9.32	6.84	2.48
	Feb	219.37	15.67	8.28	6.38	1.90
	Mar	232.33	16.50	7.59	6.06	1.53
	Apr	237.98	16.27	7.58	6.15	1.43
	May	238.46	17.03	7.76	5.87	1.89
	Jun	245.30	17.32	7.27	5.77	1.50
	Jul	240.18	16.31	7.42	6.13	1.29
	Aug	245.00	17.47	7.26	5.72	1.54
	Sep	238.27	15.98	7.64	6.26	1.38
	Oct	237.36	16.85	7.61	5.93	1.68
	Nov	245.09	16.99	7.40	5.89	1.51
	Dec	248.60	16.72	7.33	5.98	1.35
1987	Jan	264.51	15.42	7.47	6.49	0.98
	Feb	280.93	15.98	7.46	6.26	1.20
	Mar	292.47	16.41	7.65	6.09	1.56
	Apr	289.32	16.22	9.56	6.17	3.39
	May	289.12	16.32	8.63	6.13	2.50
	Jun	301.38	17.10	8.40	5.85	2.55
	Jul	310.09	17.92	8.89	5.58	3.31
	Aug	329.36	18.55	9.17	5.39	3.78
	Sep	318.66	18.10	9.66	5.52	4.14
	Oct	280.16	14.16	9.03	7.06	1.97
	Nov	245.01	13.78	8.90	7.26	1.64
	Dec	240.96	13.55	9.10	7.38	1.72
1988	Jan	250.48	12.81	8.40	7.81	0.59
	Feb	258.10	13.02	8.33	7.68	0.65
	Mar	265.74	13.42	8.74	7.45	1.29
	Apr	262.61	13.24	9.10	7.55	1.55
	May	256.20	12.92	9.24	7.74	1.50
	Jun	270.68	13.65	8.85	7.33	1.52
	Jul	269.44	13.59	9.18	7.36	1.82
	Aug	263.73	13.30	9.30	7.52	1.78

Source: Ziemba and Schwartz (1991).

the US MSCI, both reach the same conclusion. There was a similar signal ignored by most investors in the US S&P500 in 1999 and then a crash that began in August 2000 and a weak stock market in 2001/02 which is discussed in Ziemba (2003).†

In 1988–1989, I asked one of my young colleagues in my crash study group, Sugheri Iishi, to check this for Japan. There were twenty 10% plus crashes during the 40 years, 1948–1988, see table 2. We found that whenever this measure was in the danger zone (that is outside a 95% confidence band), there was a crash of 10% or more from the current level within one year. Not all crashes had the measure in the danger zone, but whenever it was there, it was a crash with no misses. That model was 12/12.

So, the measure was successful at predicting future crashes—but when and how deep there was no precise way to know. However, long-run mean reversion (Poterba and Summers (1985)) suggests that the longer the bull run is and the more overpriced the measure is, the longer and deeper the decline will probably be. Then, one can use the measure as part of an econometric system to estimate future scenarios. The rest of this paper presents a model to exit or enter such markets.

Each time the spread exceeded the 4.23 cut-off (which was higher than 95% confidence), there was a crash. The measure was way in the danger zone in late 1989 and the decline (the 21st crash) began on the first trading day of 1990 with the Nikkei stock average peaking at 38 916. See figure 2. It is too bad Yamaichi's top management did not listen to Iishi when I sent him up to explain our results in Japanese; there was much greater danger in the market than they thought in 1989. By 1999, Yamaichi Securities was bankrupt and ceased to exist. Figure 3 shows why this happened because too high interest rates in 1990 that completely crushed the economy.

The model also indicated that the valuation was still high as of 29 May, 1990 at 4.88. Not much later, the 22nd crash began. Interestingly, at the bottom of the 22nd crash on 1 October, 1990, the Nikkei was at 20 222, which was almost exactly the mean. Meanwhile, the same calculation on 29 May, 1990, for the S&P500 is shown in figure 1. Indeed, it was cheap, that is below the mean, since the September 1987 peak of 4.42. The 29 May, 1990 value of 1.11 was, however, slightly above the mean level and the highest since the late fall of 1987.

Japan has had weak stock and land markets for 23 years, since the beginning of 1990. There are many factors for this that are political as well as economic. But the rising interest rates for eight full months until August 1990 shown in figure 3 is one of them. This extreme tightening of an overleveraged economy was too much. Cheap and easily available money, which caused the big run-up in asset prices in the 1980s turned into expensive and unavailable money in the 1990s.

3. The changepoint detection model for exit bubble-type markets

The finance and economics literature has research on identifying and timing bubbles. Trading bubble-type markets is difficult. It is known that famed bubble trader George Soros shorted the Japanese market too soon in 1988 and lost about \$1 billion. As shown in section 2, Ziemba's BSEYD model suggested an exit danger signal in April 1989 with the decline in 1990 of some −48% starting on the first trading day of 1990.

There are, however, some studies such as those referenced in section 1, which mostly focus on determining if a particular market is a bubble or not. What we mean by a bubble is a price that is going up just because it is going up! That is one where the price exceeds the fair value.

In this paper, we present a Bayesian changepoint detection model that seems to work well timing when to exit a long position. We apply the model to Japanese stock and land markets—the latter proxied by the golf course membership market, which has weekly transaction data. The Nikkei225 data is daily. We do not attempt to use the model for various types of land, since there is no frequent data available.

The basic idea is that there is a fast rate of growth in prices, then a peak and then a fast decline. The model tries to exit near the peak in prices. It is based on the mathematical theory of *changepoint detection* (or *disorder detection*) for stochastic

†Later Yardeni (1997) reported on a related Fed model which is a special case to the difference model used here. See Lleo and Ziemba (2013) where critiques of the difference model are also presented and discussed. Our aim here is the answer the question: does the model actually predict stock market crashes?

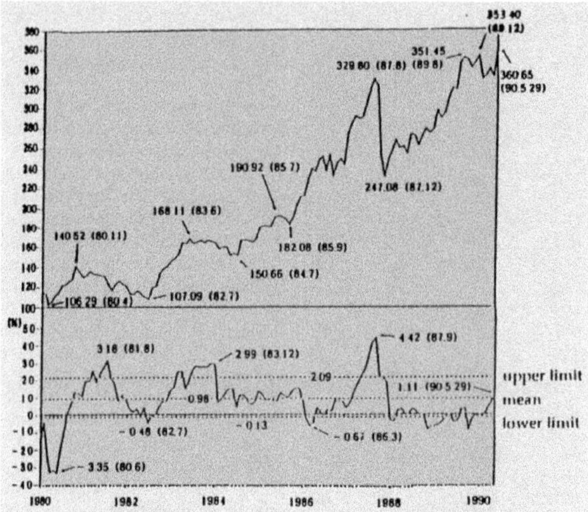

Value of S&P500 for various spread values		
Date/level	Spread, %	S&P500
May 29, 1990	1.11	360.65
Mean	0.98	355.00
Upper limit	2.09	415.00
Lower limit	-0.13	309.00

Figure 1. Bond and stock yield differential model for the S&P500, 1980–1990. Source: Ziemba and Schwartz (1991).

Table 2. The twenty corrections of 10% or more on the NSA from 1949 to 1988.

	Index Value			Date		
	Peak	Valley	% decrease	Peak	Valley	# Months
1	176.89	85.25	−51.8	01-Sep-49	06-Jul-50	11
2	474.43	295.18	−37.8	4-Feb-53	1-Apr-53	2
3	366.69	321.79	−12.2	6-May-53	3-Jun-53	1
4	595.46	471.53	−20.8	4-May-57	27-Dec-57	8
5	1,829.74	1,258.00	−31.2	18-Jul-61	19-Dec-61	5
6	1,589.76	1,216.04	−23.5	14-Feb-62	29-Oct-62	9
7	1,634.37	1201.26	−26.5	5-Apr-63	18-Dec-63	9
8	1,369.00	1,020.49	−25.5	3-Jul-64	12-Jul-65	13
9	1,588.73	1,364.34	−14.1	1-Apr-66	15-Dec-66	8
10	1,506.27	1,250.40	−17.0	1-Mar-67	11-Dec-67	9
11	2,534.45	1,929.64	−23.9	6-Apr-70	27-May-70	2
12	2,740.98	2,227.25	−18.7	13-Aug-71	20-Oct-71	3
13	5,359.74	3,355.13	−37.4	24-Jan-73	9-Oct-74	21
14	4,564.52	3,814.02	−16.4	12-May-75	29-Sep-75	5
15	5,287.65	4,597.26	−13.1	5-Sep-77	24-Nov-77	3
16	8,019.14	6,849.78	−14.6	17-Aug-81	1-Oct-82	14
17	11,190.17	9,703.35	−13.3	4-May-84	23-Jul-84	3
18	18,936.24	15,819.58	−16.5	20-Aug-86	22-Oct-86	2
19	25,929.42	22,702.74	−12.4	17-Jun-87	22-Jul-87	1
20	26,646.43	21,036.76	−21.1	14-Oct-87	11-Nov-87	1
Average			−0.224			6.5

Source: Yamaichi research institute.

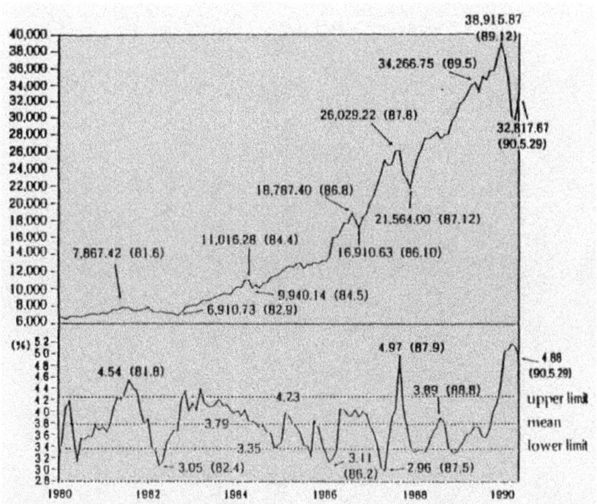

Value of Nikkei for various spread values

Date/level	Spread, %	Nikkei
May 29, 1990	4.88	32,818
Mean	3.79	20,022
Upper limit	4.23	23,754
Lower limit	3.35	17,303

Figure 2. Bond and stock yield differential model for Nikkei, 1980–1990. Source: Ziemba and Schwartz (1991).

processes. A changepoint of a stochastic process is an unknown moment of time when its probabilistic structure changes (e.g. the mean value changes from a positive number to a negative one). The theory studies statistics that allow to detect such changes after they happen.

Changepoint detection methods have been successfully applied in production quality control, radiolocation, information security, and have shown their usefulness. Their history goes back to the pioneering work of Shewhart (1925), and the first fundamental results by Page, Roberts, Shiryaev and others of 1950–1960s. Surveys of the history and the recent developments in this field can be found in e.g. the introduction to the book by Poor and Hadjiljadis (2009).

In the financial context, a changepoint may represent a moment when the market starts to decline. It can be identified with a moment of time when the trend of the sequence of the market's index value becomes negative. The objective of the model is to detect this change after it occurs and to close a long position maximizing the gain measured by a given utility function.

We emphasize that the changepoint model does not *predict* a decline of price, but considers the problem to detect it *after* it has started, taking into account that temporal declines may be caused by the volatility of the price rather than a real change of the trend. In particular, such a decline need not necessarily be caused by a crash of a bubble, but can be due to e.g. a structural change in an economy or bad news for a company. Thus, we do not need the price process to be a bubble in terms of one definition or another.

3.1. The description of the model

The model describes the evolution of the value S of an index at moments of time $t = 0, 1, \ldots, T$ driven by a geometric Gaussian random walk with logarithmic mean and variance (μ_1, σ_1^2) up to an unknown moment of time θ and (μ_2, σ_2^2) after θ. The moment θ will be interpreted as the point when the trend of the index changes from an increasing to a decreasing, and is called a *changepoint*. In this paper, we provide only a brief exposition, details can be found in Zhitlukhin (2013); a continuous-time analogue was considered by Shiryaev and Zhitlukhin (2012).

Let $\xi = (\xi_t)_{t=0}^T$ be a sequence of i.i.d.† standard normal random variables defined on a probability space $(\Omega, \mathcal{F}, \mathsf{P})$. The sequence $S = (S_t)_{t=0}^T$ is defined by its logarithmic increments via

$$S_0 = 1, \qquad \log \frac{S_t}{S_{t-1}} = \begin{cases} \mu_1 + \sigma_1 \xi_t, & t < \theta, \\ \mu_2 + \sigma_2 \xi_t, & t \geq \theta, \end{cases}$$

where $\mu_1, \mu_2 \in R$, $\sigma_1, \sigma_2 > 0$ are known parameters. The choice of $S_0 = 1$ means that all the prices are expressed

†Independent and identically distributed.

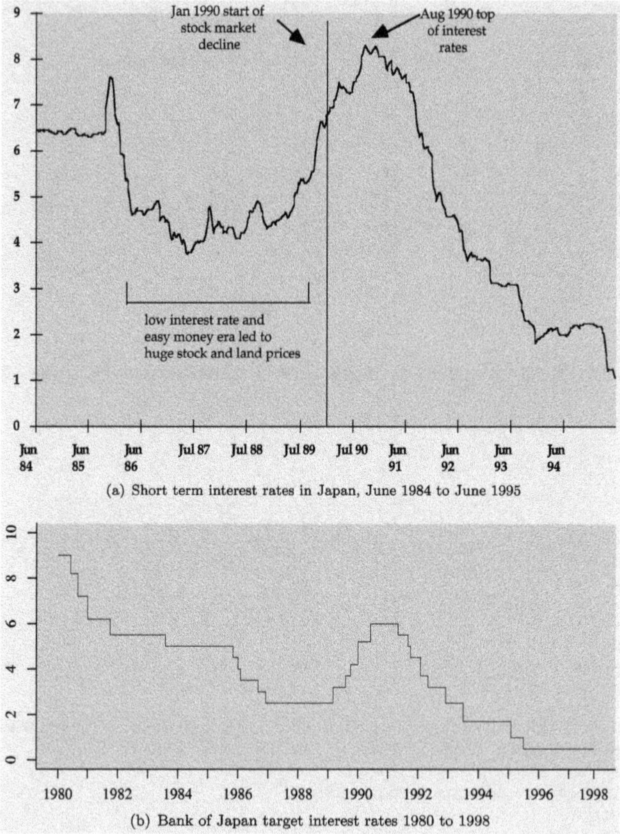

(a) Short term interest rates in Japan, June 1984 to June 1995

(b) Bank of Japan target interest rates 1980 to 1998

Figure 3. Interest rates in Japan.

relatively to the price at time $t = 0$, which does not reduce the generality of the model.

It is assumed that θ is a random variable defined on $(\Omega, \mathcal{F}, \mathsf{P})$, independent of the sequence ξ_t and taking values in the set $\{1, 2, \ldots, T+1\}$ with known prior probabilities $p_t = \mathsf{P}(\theta = t)$. The value p_1 is the probability that the changepoint appears from the beginning of the sequence S_t, and p_{T+1} is the probability that the changepoint does not appear within the time horizon $[0, T]$. The prior distribution function of θ is denoted by $G(t) = p_1 + p_2 + \ldots + p_t$.

Let $U_\alpha\colon R_+ \to R$, $\alpha \le 0$, be the family of negative power and logarithmic utility functions:†

$$U_\alpha(x) = -x^\alpha \text{ for } \alpha < 0, \qquad U_0(x) = \log x.$$

The problem consists in finding the moment of time τ which maximizes the utility from closing a long position provided one opens it at time $t = 0$ and needs to close before $t = T$.

Let $\mathbb{F} = (\mathcal{F}_t)_{t=0}^T$, $\mathcal{F}_t = \sigma(S_u;\ u \le t)$ be the filtration generated by the process S. By definition, a moment τ when one closes the position should be a *stopping time* of the filtration $\mathbb{F}$, i.e. τ should be a random variable taking values in the set $\{0, 1, \ldots, T\}$ such that $\{\omega : \tau(\omega) \le t\} \in \mathcal{F}_t$ for any $t = 0, \ldots, T$. The class of all stopping times $\tau \le T$ of $\mathbb{F}$ is denoted by $\mathfrak{M}$. The notion of a stopping time reflects the concept that a decision to close the position at time t should be based only on the information obtained from the observed values $S_0, S_1, \ldots, S_t$ and should not rely on the future values S_{t+1}, S_{t+2}, which are unknown at time t.

The problems of optimal closing of a long positions with respect to the utility function U_α is formulated as the *optimal stopping problem*

†These functions are from capital growth theory and are known to maximize long run asymptotic growth of wealth; see e.g. Kelly (1956), Breiman (1961), and MacLean *et al.* (2010). Log is full Kelly and negative power are fractional Kelly strategies blending cash with the max Elog portfolio to lower risk and the long-run growth rate.

$$V_\alpha = \sup_{\tau \in \mathfrak{M}} \mathsf{E} U_\alpha(S_\tau). \tag{1}$$

Its solution consists in finding the *optimal stopping time* τ_α, at which the supremum is attained (it is shown that such a stopping time exists).

Note that we focus on maximizing the expected utility $\mathsf{E}U_\alpha(S_\tau)$, but not on obtaining τ that will be close to θ in some sense, e.g. that minimizes $\mathsf{E}|\tau - \theta|$ or $\mathsf{E}(\tau - \theta)^2$. The latter approaches are more common in the literature on changepoint detection (which considers not only financial applications), but in our particular problem the setting of utility maximization seems more natural as it is directly interpreted as the profit obtained from trading.

It is assumed that $\mu_1 > -\alpha\sigma_1^2/2$ and $\mu_2 < -\alpha\sigma_2^2/2$. Under these assumptions the sequence $\{U_\alpha(S_t)\}_t$ increases on average if the logarithmic increments of S are i.i.d. $\mathcal{N}(\mu_1, \sigma_1^2)$ random variables, and decreases on average if they are i.i.d. $\mathcal{N}(\mu_2, \sigma_2^2)$ random variables. Consequently, the random variable θ represents the moment of time when the index value starts to decrease.

In order to formulate our main result, Theorem 1, we introduce auxiliary notation. Let $\psi = (\psi_t)_{t=0}^T$ denote the Shiryaev–Roberts statistic of the sequence of values S_t:

$$\psi_0 = 0, \quad \psi_t = \frac{\sigma^1}{\sigma^2}(p_t + \psi_{t-1})\, e^{\frac{(X_t-\mu_1)^2}{2\sigma_2^2} - \frac{(X_t-\mu_2)^2}{2\sigma_2^2}}, \quad t = 1, \ldots, T.$$

where $X = (X_t)_{t=1}^T$ denote the logarithmic increments of the index values, $X_t = \log(S_t/S_{t-1})$.

Define recurrently the family of functions $V_\alpha(t, x)$ for $\alpha \le 0$, $t = T, T-1, \ldots, 0$, $x \ge 0$ as follows:

$$\begin{aligned} V_\alpha(T, x) &\equiv 0, \quad V_\alpha(t, x) \\ &= \max\Big\{0,\ \beta^t\Big[\tfrac{(\gamma-1)}{\alpha}(x + p_{t+1}) \\ &\quad + \frac{(\beta-1)}{\alpha}(1 - G(t+1))\Big] + f_\alpha(t, x)\Big\}, \end{aligned} \tag{2}$$

with $\beta = e^{\alpha\mu_1 + \alpha^2\sigma_1^2/2}$, $\gamma = e^{\alpha\mu_2 + \alpha^2\sigma_2^2/2}$, where for $\alpha = 0$ we let $(\beta - 1)/\alpha = \mu_1$, $(\gamma - 1)/\alpha = \mu_2$, and the function

$$\begin{aligned} &f_\alpha(t, x) \\ &= \frac{1}{\sigma_1\sqrt{2\pi}} \int_{\mathbb{R}} V_\alpha\left(t+1,\ \frac{\sigma_1}{\sigma_2}(p_{t+1} + x)e^{\frac{(z-\mu_1)^2}{2\sigma_1^2} - \frac{(z-\mu_2)^2}{2\sigma_2^2}}\right) \\ &\quad \times e^{-\frac{(z-\mu_1-\alpha\sigma_1^2)^2}{2\sigma_1^2}}\, dz. \end{aligned}$$

THEOREM 3.1 (Zhitlukhin (2013), Chapter 3) *The following stopping time is optimal in problem* (1):

$$\tau_\alpha^* = \inf\{0 \le t \le T : \psi_t \ge b_\alpha^*(t)\}, \tag{3}$$

where the stopping boundary $b_\alpha^*(t)$, $t = 0, \ldots, T$, *is*

$$b_\alpha^*(t) = \inf\{x \ge 0 : V_\alpha(t, x) = 0\}.$$

Theorem 3.1 states that the optimal stopping time is the first moment of time when the Shiryaev-Roberts statistic exceeds the time-dependent threshold $b_\alpha^*(t)$. To find the function $b_\alpha^*(t)$ numerically, one first computes recurrently the functions $V_\alpha(t, x)$ for $t = T, T-1, \ldots, 0$ and then finds their minimal roots $x \ge 0$. The algorithm is described in Zhitlukhin (2013) along with the estimation of its computational error.

Remark 3.1 Let us clarify the intuition behind the changepoint detection scheme. Note that it is possible to express the optimal stopping time through the *posterior probability process* $\pi = (\pi_t)_{t=0}^T$ defined as the conditional probability $\pi_t = \mathsf{P}(\theta \le t \mid \mathcal{F}_t)$, the probability that the changepoint has happened given the information from the sequence of prices observed up to time t. From Bayes formula (see details in Zhitlukhin (2013)),

$$\psi_t = \frac{\pi_t}{1 - \pi_t}(1 - G(t)), \qquad \pi_t = \frac{\psi_t}{\psi_t + 1 - G(t)}.$$

Consequently, the optimal stopping time in problem (1) can be represented in the form

$$\begin{aligned} \tau_\alpha^* &= \inf\{0 \le t \le T : \pi_t \ge \tilde{b}_\alpha^*(t)\}, \text{ where } \tilde{b}_\alpha^*(t) \\ &= \frac{b_\alpha^*(t)}{b_\alpha^*(t) + 1 - G(t)}. \end{aligned}$$

In other words, one should close a long position as soon as he/she becomes sufficiently confident that the changepoint has already happened, which quantitatively means the posterior probability π_t exceeds the threshold $\tilde{b}_\alpha^*(t)$. The exact form of the threshold is such that the corresponding stopping rule maximizes $\mathsf{E}_\alpha(S_\tau)$ according to (1).

In the formulation of the Theorem, we prefer to use the statistic ψ_t as it results in a simpler expression, though, it can be equivalently formulated in terms of π_t.

The proof of the Theorem is based on a reduction of the problem V_α to a Markov optimal stopping problem for the process ψ_t. It turns out that

$$V_0 = \sup_{\tau \in \mathfrak{M}} \mathsf{E}^{Q^0}\left[\sum_{s=1}^{\tau} F_0(s, \psi_s)\right],$$

$$V_\alpha = \frac{|\alpha|}{\beta} \sup_{\tau \in \mathfrak{M}} \mathsf{E}^{Q^\alpha}\left[\sum_{s=1}^{\tau} F_\alpha(s, \psi_s)\right] - 1 \ \text{ for } \alpha < 0,$$

where Q^α is the probability measure such that the logarithmic returns X_t are i.i.d. $\mathcal{N}(\mu_1 + \alpha\sigma_1^2, \sigma_1^2)$ random variables (it is possible to write explicitly the Radon-Nikodym density of Q^α with respect to the original probability measure P), and the functions F_α are given by

$$F_0(t, x) = \mu_2 x + \mu_1(1 - G(t)),$$

$$F_\alpha(t, x) = \beta^t\Big[\tfrac{(\beta - \beta/\gamma)}{\alpha}x + \tfrac{(\beta-1)}{\alpha}(1 - G(t))\Big] \text{ for } \alpha \ne 0.$$

The optimal stopping problem V_α is solved by the standard technique (see Peskir and Shiryaev 2006 or Robbins *et al.* 1971). Introduce the value function $V_\alpha(t, x) = \sup_{\tau \le T-t} \mathsf{E}^{Q^\alpha}\Big[\sum_{s=1}^{\tau} F_\alpha(t + s, \psi_{t+s}) \mid \psi_t = x\Big]$, which is equal to the maximal expected utility that is possible to obtain if the observation of ψ_s is started at time t with the value $\psi_t = x$ (assuming the sum is equal to zero when $\tau = 0$). In particular, $V_0 = V_0(0, 0)$, $V_\alpha = \frac{|\alpha|}{\beta} V_\alpha(0, 0) - 1$. Due to the Markov structure of the sequence ψ_t, it is known that the optimal stopping time is the first moment of time when one is indifferent between continuing observing ψ_t and stopping immediately, i.e. when $V_\alpha(t, \psi_t) = 0$. We prove that $V_\alpha(t, x)$ is monotone in x, which results in the optimal stopping time of the form (3). The function $V_\alpha(t, x)$ is computed by backward induction, which results in the recurrent relation (2).

Remark 3.2 In this paper, we focused on the simplest model of prices, the geometric random walk. Its limitations and drawbacks are well known, and the use of more advanced models (e.g. with fat-tailed returns and non-constant volatility) could possibly improve the accuracy of changepoint detection. On the other hand, it will introduce additional parameters and the need to estimate or predict their values after the change of regime. These possible improvements are left for further research.

3.2. Application of the model to market data

We observe an index such that initially its value has a positive trend. The time interval between two consecutive index values can be arbitrary. It is assumed that a long position is opened at time $t = 0$ and should be closed by a fixed time $t = T$. The aim is to find the right moment when to close the position.

The observable values of the index are represented by the sequence $S_0, S_1, \ldots, S_T$, which is assumed to follow the above model of a geometric Gaussian random walk with a changepoint. In the applications below, we assume θ is uniformly distributed in the set $\{1, 2, \ldots, T\}$, which in some sense corresponds to the 'worst case' (since the uniform distribution has the maximum entropy among all distributions on a finite set).

The parameters μ_1, σ_1 of the model are estimated using from the past data $S_0, S_{-1}, S_{-2}, \ldots, S_{-t_0}$, where t_0 is some fixed constant, assuming that the logarithmic increments of the sequence $\{S_t\}_{t=-t_0}^{0}$ are i.i.d $\mathcal{N}(\mu_1, \sigma_1)$ random variables.

The choice of the values μ_2 and σ_2 is subjective, as we do not know the 'future' values of the drift and volatility after they change. In the applications below, we let $\sigma_2 = \sigma_1$ and consider several choices of the drift parameter†: $\mu_2 = -0.5\mu_1$, $\mu_2 = -\mu_1, \mu_2 = -2\mu_1, \mu_2 = -3\mu_1$ and $\mu_2 = -5\mu_1$, which, however, do not give any significantly different results.

We also vary the utility function U_α and the final moment of time T, and apply the model to $U_0(x) = \log x$, $U_{-1/2}(x) = -1/\sqrt{x}$ and $U_{-1}(x) = -1/x$ (i.e. the full Kelly rule, the 2/3 Kelly rule and the half Kelly rule assuming log normally distributed asset) and T corresponding to the end of 1992, 1990 and 1989 for the 1990 crash and T corresponding to the end of 2013 for the recent Nikkei225 data. When T corresponds to the end of 1989 no crash occurs on the observable time horizon, so the model should close the position close to the global maximum.

4. The Japanese stock market bubble

4.1. Background

The Japanese stock market was closed after World War II ended in 1945 until its reopening in 1948. From 1948 to 1988, there was a huge rise in the stock market measured by the Nikkei225 price weighted stock index as well as the Topix value weighted index of more than 1000 stocks. A steady increase in quality and quantity of equipment and automobiles of various kinds led to an enormous inflow of financial assets. These in turn were invested primarily in Japanese stocks and land. The land and stock markets were greatly intertwined as discussed by Ziemba (1991) and Stone and Ziemba (1993); see also section 6. To get an idea of the price pressure on Japanese land prices, consider that in the late 1980s:

- some 120 million people lived in Japan in an area the size of Montana,
- only 5% of the land was used to house the people, buildings and factories because most of the land is mountainous,
- most of the land was owned by large corporations but 60% of Japanese families and 55% of those in Tokyo owned their own home,
- there was massive savings by households,
- only some 3% of Japanese assets were invested abroad despite great fear in the west, and some very public purchases at inflated prices of expensive property such as the Pebble Beach golf course,
- low interest rates in the mid-to-late 1980s fuelled the stock and land booms,
- the Nikkei225 rose 220 times in yen and 550 times in US dollars from 1948 to 1988, yet there were twenty 10%+ declines in the Nikkei225, see table 2.

Figure 4 shows the Nikkei stock average from 1984 to 2014 and figure 3(b) shows the Bank of Japan target interest rate from 1980 to 1998.

The Nikkei peaked at the end of December 1989 at 39 816. In section 2, the bond stock earnings yield model was shown to go into the danger zone in April 1989. This model suggested that a large decline or crash was coming, but not when. To apply the changepoint detection model a maximum final time horizon needs to be specified. We apply it for three time horizons, namely to the ends of 1989, 1990 and 1992. In section 6, we apply the model to the Nikkei225 in 2013.

4.2. Nikkei stock average in the 1980–1990s

The model was applied to the Nikkei stock average with six different starting dates (January 1987, July 1987, July 1988, January 1989, July 1989, October 1989), four different values of the ratio μ_2/μ_1 ($-0.5, -1.0, -2.0, -5.0$), three different utility functions $U_0(x) = \log x, U_{-1/2}(x) = 1/\sqrt{x}, U_{-1}(x) = -1/x$ and three different time horizons (the ends of 1989, 1990, and 1992). In all the cases, $\sigma_2 = \sigma_1$.

The prices are daily closing prices; the parameters μ_1 and σ_1 are estimated using the 100 previous index values before the entering date. The data appears in tables 3–5 and figure 5. The tables show the exit dates obtained by applying the model for the corresponding values of the parameters, and the ratio of the price at these dates to the maximal closing price (on December 29, 1989). The figures present the four entry dates in 1988–1989 marked by blue circles and the corresponding exit dates marked by red squares for the value of the parameters $\alpha = 0$,

†It is well known that getting the means right is much more important than the variances, see Chopra and Ziemba (1993). Thus we focus on the analysis of the performance of the model for various drift values, but we assume that the variance stays constant.

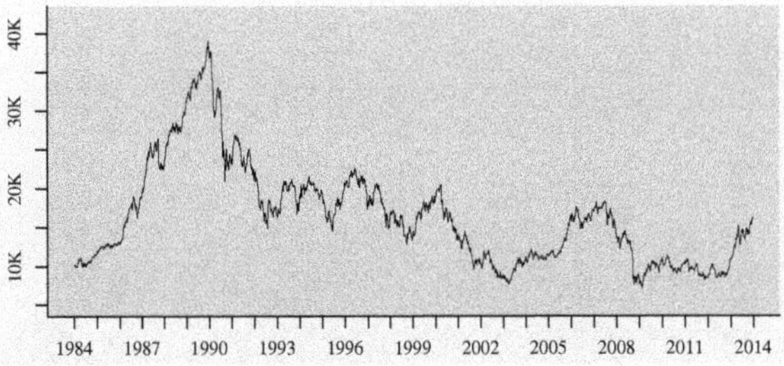

Figure 4. Nikkei-225 from 1984 to 2013.

Table 3. The exit dates for Nikkei stock average, T = end of 1990.

Enter	μ_1	σ	$\lvert\mu_2/\mu_1\rvert$			
			0.5	1.0	2.0	5.0
$\alpha = 0.0$						
26.12.86	0.00086	0.01300	26.02.90 (85.6%)	26.02.90 (85.6%)	23.02.90 (89.7%)	20.10.87 (56.3%)
30.06.87	0.00191	0.01114	23.02.90 (89.7%)	11.11.87 (54.1%)	20.10.87 (56.3%)	20.10.87 (56.3%)
30.06.88	0.00163	0.00585	16.01.90 (94.7%)	16.01.90 (94.7%)	16.01.90 (94.7%)	16.01.90 (94.7%)
28.12.88	0.00064	0.00634	26.02.90 (85.6%)	23.02.90 (89.7%)	21.02.90 (91.8%)	18.01.90 (94.4%)
30.06.89	0.00039	0.00602	26.02.90 (85.6%)	23.02.90 (89.7%)	21.02.90 (91.8%)	16.01.90 (94.7%)
29.09.89	0.00045	0.00497	26.02.90 (85.6%)	21.02.90 (91.8%)	21.02.90 (91.8%)	16.01.90 (94.7%)
$\alpha = -0.5$						
26.12.86	0.00086	0.01300	26.02.90 (85.6%)	23.02.90 (89.7%)	23.02.90 (89.7%)	20.10.87 (56.3%)
30.06.87	0.00191	0.01114	26.02.90 (85.6%)	10.11.87 (55.7%)	20.10.87 (56.3%)	20.10.87 (56.3%)
30.06.88	0.00163	0.00585	16.01.90 (94.7%)	16.01.90 (94.7%)	16.01.90 (94.7%)	16.01.90 (94.7%)
28.12.88	0.00064	0.00634	26.02.90 (85.6%)	23.02.90 (89.7%)	21.02.90 (91.8%)	16.01.90 (94.7%)
30.06.89	0.00039	0.00602	26.02.90 (85.6%)	23.02.90 (89.7%)	21.02.90 (91.8%)	16.01.90 (94.7%)
29.09.89	0.00045	0.00497	26.02.90 (85.6%)	21.02.90 (91.8%)	21.02.90 (91.8%)	16.01.90 (94.7%)
$\alpha = -1.0$						
26.12.86	0.00086	0.01300	23.02.90 (89.7%)	23.02.90 (89.7%)	11.11.87 (54.1%)	20.10.87 (56.3%)
30.06.87	0.00191	0.01114	04.01.88 (54.5%)	10.11.87 (55.7%)	20.10.87 (56.3%)	20.10.87 (56.3%)
30.06.88	0.00163	0.00585	18.01.90 (94.4%)	18.01.90 (94.4%)	16.01.90 (94.7%)	16.01.90 (94.7%)
28.12.88	0.00064	0.00634	26.02.90 (85.6%)	23.02.90 (89.7%)	21.02.90 (91.8%)	16.01.90 (94.7%)
30.06.89	0.00039	0.00602	26.02.90 (85.6%)	23.02.90 (89.7%)	21.02.90 (91.8%)	16.01.90 (94.7%)
29.09.89	0.00045	0.00497	26.02.90 (85.6%)	21.02.90 (91.8%)	21.02.90 (91.8%)	16.01.90 (94.7%)

$\mu_2 = -\mu_1$. The graphs are normalized in a such way that the price on the first trading day of 1984 is 100.

The results show for $\alpha = 0$ (log utility) exits from 54.5% of the maximum for entries in 1987 to 94.7% for entries in 1988 and 85.6% for entries in 1989 of the global maximum of the market. When $T = 1989$, the exit percent of peak value depends mostly on the entry time. Later entries exit closer to the peak. The $T = 1992$ results vary greatly depending on the entry date with the early entry dates exiting well below the peak and later entry dates exiting closer to the global maximum. The choice of α and the value of the ratio μ_1/μ_2 does not change the results as we are just searching for the exit point, not trading after that, see tables 3–5. In general the change point model yields a profit based on the entry and exit points; see figure 5(a) and (b). But it is possible that late entries close to the peak as in figure 5(b) with $T = 1992$ result in a trading loss because of the sharp decline after the peak.

5. The Japanese golf course membership market

5.1. *Background*

In 1989 there were more than 400 golf courses in Japan with a total value more than US$300 billion, a value larger than the Australian stock exchange capitalization of A$250 billion. Memberships, which cost as much as US$8 million, allowed play at a reduced cost plus the right to bring guests to play for a higher fee. However, their main value was not the ability to play golf, but their share of the land occupied by the course and as an instrument to play the land market for relatively low stake with liquidity. These memberships were actively traded as speculative investments whose market was maintained by six market makers in Tokyo and Osaka. Weekly data was available in various areas of Japan since the beginning of 1982. This data was the best widely available data series on land prices in Japan and forms an ideal source for many types of analyses.

Table 4. The exit dates for Nikkei stock average, T = end of 1989.

Enter	μ_1	σ	$\|\mu_2/\mu_1\|$ 0.5	1.0	2.0	5.0
$\alpha = 0.0$						
26.12.86	0.00086	0.01300	23.08.89 (89.7%)	17.07.89 (86.0%)	11.11.87 (54.1%)	20.10.87 (56.3%)
30.06.87	0.00191	0.01114	11.11.87 (54.1%)	20.10.87 (56.3%)	20.10.87 (56.3%)	20.10.87 (56.3%)
30.06.88	0.00163	0.00585	29.06.89 (84.7%)	16.10.89 (88.6%)	16.10.89 (88.6%)	16.10.89 (88.6%)
28.12.88	0.00064	0.00634	16.10.89 (88.6%)	07.09.89 (87.8%)	07.09.89 (87.8%)	12.10.89 (89.4%)
30.06.89	0.00039	0.00602	07.11.89 (90.6%)	12.10.89 (89.4%)	06.09.89 (88.1%)	30.08.89 (88.6%)
29.09.89	0.00045	0.00497	19.12.89 (98.8%)	11.12.89 (97.0%)	16.10.89 (88.6%)	12.10.89 (89.4%)
$\alpha = -0.5$						
26.12.86	0.00086	0.01300	17.07.89 (86.0%)	29.06.89 (84.7%)	10.11.87 (55.7%)	20.10.87 (56.3%)
30.06.87	0.00191	0.01114	11.11.87 (54.1%)	20.10.87 (56.3%)	20.10.87 (56.3%)	20.10.87 (56.3%)
30.06.88	0.00163	0.00585	06.09.89 (88.1%)	16.10.89 (88.6%)	16.10.89 (88.6%)	16.10.89 (88.6%)
28.12.88	0.00064	0.00634	12.10.89 (89.4%)	07.09.89 (87.8%)	06.09.89 (88.1%)	08.09.89 (87.7%)
30.06.89	0.00039	0.00602	07.11.89 (90.6%)	12.10.89 (89.4%)	06.09.89 (88.1%)	30.08.89 (88.6%)
29.09.89	0.00045	0.00497	19.12.89 (98.8%)	11.12.89 (97.0%)	16.10.89 (88.6%)	12.10.89 (89.4%)
$\alpha = -1.0$						
26.12.86	0.00086	0.01300	28.06.89 (85.4%)	15.06.89 (84.6%)	20.10.87 (56.3%)	20.10.87 (56.3%)
30.06.87	0.00191	0.01114	11.11.87 (54.1%)	20.10.87 (56.3%)	20.10.87 (56.3%)	20.10.87 (56.3%)
30.06.88	0.00163	0.00585	07.09.89 (87.8%)	16.10.89 (88.6%)	16.10.89 (88.6%)	16.10.89 (88.6%)
28.12.88	0.00064	0.00634	12.10.89 (89.4%)	07.09.89 (87.8%)	06.09.89 (88.1%)	07.09.89 (87.8%)
30.06.89	0.00039	0.00602	06.11.89 (91.1%)	12.10.89 (89.4%)	06.09.89 (88.1%)	30.08.89 (88.6%)
29.09.89	0.00045	0.00497	15.12.89 (98.3%)	11.12.89 (97.0%)	16.10.89 (88.6%)	12.10.89 (89.4%)

Table 5. The exit dates for Nikkei stock average, T = end of 1992.

Enter	μ_1	σ	$\|\mu_2/\mu_1\|$ 0.5	1.0	2.0	5.0
$\alpha = 0.0$						
26.12.86	0.00086	0.01300	06.08.90 (73.5%)	02.04.90 (72.0%)	22.03.90 (76.7%)	19.03.90 (80.3%)
30.06.87	0.00191	0.01114	26.02.90 (85.6%)	11.11.87 (54.1%)	20.10.87 (56.3%)	20.10.87 (56.3%)
30.06.88	0.00163	0.00585	21.02.90 (91.8%)	21.02.90 (91.8%)	18.01.90 (94.4%)	16.01.90 (94.7%)
28.12.88	0.00064	0.00634	19.03.90 (80.3%)	13.03.90 (83.8%)	26.02.90 (85.6%)	23.02.90 (89.7%)
30.06.89	0.00039	0.00602	22.03.90 (76.7%)	14.03.90 (83.1%)	26.02.90 (85.6%)	23.02.90 (89.7%)
29.09.89	0.00045	0.00497	14.03.90 (83.1%)	26.02.90 (85.6%)	23.02.90 (89.7%)	23.02.90 (89.7%)
$\alpha = -0.5$						
26.12.86	0.00086	0.01300	02.04.90 (72.0%)	02.04.90 (72.0%)	20.03.90 (79.2%)	11.11.87 (54.1%)
30.06.87	0.00191	0.01114	04.01.88 (54.5%)	10.11.87 (55.7%)	20.10.87 (56.3%)	20.10.87 (56.3%)
30.06.88	0.00163	0.00585	21.02.90 (91.8%)	21.02.90 (91.8%)	21.02.90 (91.8%)	16.01.90 (94.7%)
28.12.88	0.00064	0.00634	19.03.90 (80.3%)	26.02.90 (85.6%)	26.02.90 (85.6%)	23.02.90 (89.7%)
30.06.89	0.00039	0.00602	22.03.90 (76.7%)	14.03.90 (83.1%)	26.02.90 (85.6%)	23.02.90 (89.7%)
29.09.89	0.00045	0.00497	14.03.90 (83.1%)	26.02.90 (85.6%)	23.02.90 (89.7%)	21.02.90 (91.8%)
$\alpha = -1.0$						
26.12.86	0.00086	0.01300	02.04.90 (72.0%)	22.03.90 (76.7%)	19.03.90 (80.3%)	11.11.87 (54.1%)
30.06.87	0.00191	0.01114	04.01.88 (54.5%)	10.11.87 (55.7%)	20.10.87 (56.3%)	20.10.87 (56.3%)
30.06.88	0.00163	0.00585	21.02.90 (91.8%)	21.02.90 (91.8%)	21.02.90 (91.8%)	16.01.90 (94.7%)
28.12.88	0.00064	0.00634	19.03.90 (80.3%)	26.02.90 (85.6%)	26.02.90 (85.6%)	23.02.90 (89.7%)
30.06.89	0.00039	0.00602	20.03.90 (79.2%)	13.03.90 (83.8%)	26.02.90 (85.6%)	23.02.90 (89.7%)
29.09.89	0.00045	0.00497	13.03.90 (83.8%)	26.02.90 (85.6%)	23.02.90 (89.7%)	21.02.90 (91.8%)

Rachev and Ziemba (1992) modelled the price changes as stable variants. The tails had considerable mass and the distributions were considered to have fat tails with a characteristic exponent about 1.4. This is consistent with the hypothesis that there was a speculative bubble in the late 1980s and the subsequent crash in 1990–1992.

Figure 6 shows the golf course membership GCM prices in various regions of the country: the western and the eastern parts of Japan, the Tokyo area and the nationwide average. The golf course memberships market was a much bigger bubble than the stock market.

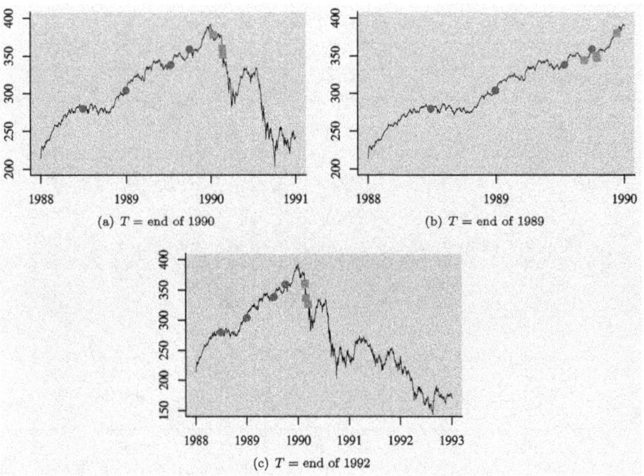

Figure 5. The results for the Nikkei index, base January 4, 1984: the enter (blue circles) and exit (red squares) dates for the values of the parameters $\alpha = 0.0$, $\mu_2 = -\mu_1$.

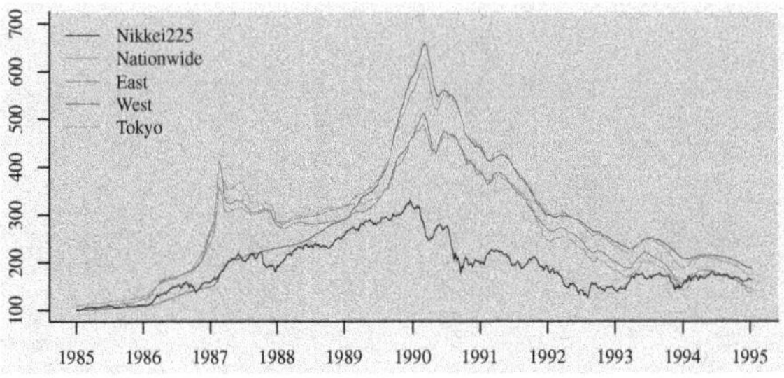

Figure 6. Graphs of the golf course membership prices in various areas of Japan and the Nikkei stock average, 1985–1995, with the 1985 values as 100%.

5.2. Application of the changepoint detection method

We applied the changepoint detection method to the golf prices for four different entering dates (July 1988, January 1989, July 1989, October 1989), four different values of the ratio μ_2/μ_1 $(-0.5, -1.0, -2.0, -5.0)$ and the three utility functions $U_0(x) = \log x$, $U_{-1/2}(x) = -x^{-1/2}$, $U_{-1}(x) = -1/x$. In all the cases, $\sigma_2 = \sigma_1$. We use weekly data, and the parameters μ_1 and σ_1 are estimated using the 20 previous index weekly values before the enter date. Same as in the previous section, we consider the time horizon T of the model corresponding to the end of 1989, 1990 and 1992.

The results are displayed in tables 6–17 with the same notation as the previous section.

In all cases with $T = 1990$, the model exits well above 90% of the global maximum price and all exits produced profits, see figure 7. When T=1989, before the global peak in prices, the exits are near the top but not as high, about 88% of the peak with all the exits producing trading profits; see figure 8. When $T = 1992$, the results are similar to $T = 1990$ as shown in figure 9. The exits are very close (96–98%) to the peak and all entries had trading gains. See the discussion in section 6 about lags in prices with stocks leading golf course membership prices, leading all land declines in 1990–1991.

Remark 5.1 Compared with the stock market bubble, the changepoint model applied to the golf course membership index exits almost immediately after the peak. One reason for that is the higher signal-to-noise ratio μ_1/σ (see tables 3–5 and 6–17): the statistic ψ_t increases 'faster' when the drift switches to the value μ_2 from μ_1, as observed from the formula for ψ_t. Also we use *weekly* data for the golf market, so one period in changepoint detection delay in t-time corresponds to a week in calendar time, while for the stock market *daily* data is used.

Table 6. Nationwide GCM prices, T = end of 1990.

Enter	μ_1	σ	$\lvert\mu_2/\mu_1\rvert$ 0.5	1.0	2.0	5.0
$\alpha = 0.0$						
26.06.88	0.00237	0.00280	25.03.90 (98.0%)	18.03.90 (98.9%)	18.03.90 (98.9%)	18.03.90 (98.9%)
25.12.88	0.00296	0.00228	18.03.90 (98.9%)	18.03.90 (98.9%)	18.03.90 (98.9%)	18.03.90 (98.9%)
25.06.89	0.00595	0.00347	18.03.90 (98.9%)	18.03.90 (98.9%)	18.03.90 (98.9%)	01.04.90 (95.0%)
24.09.89	0.01300	0.00689	25.03.90 (98.0%)	25.03.90 (98.0%)	25.03.90 (98.0%)	01.04.90 (95.0%)
$\alpha = -0.5$						
26.06.88	0.00237	0.00280	25.03.90 (98.0%)	18.03.90 (98.9%)	18.03.90 (98.9%)	18.03.90 (98.9%)
25.12.88	0.00296	0.00228	18.03.90 (98.9%)	18.03.90 (98.9%)	18.03.90 (98.9%)	18.03.90 (98.9%)
25.06.89	0.00595	0.00347	18.03.90 (98.9%)	18.03.90 (98.9%)	18.03.90 (98.9%)	01.04.90 (95.0%)
24.09.89	0.01300	0.00689	25.03.90 (98.0%)	25.03.90 (98.0%)	25.03.90 (98.0%)	01.04.90 (95.0%)
$\alpha = -1.0$						
26.06.88	0.00237	0.00280	25.03.90 (98.0%)	18.03.90 (98.9%)	18.03.90 (98.9%)	18.03.90 (98.9%)
25.12.88	0.00296	0.00228	18.03.90 (98.9%)	18.03.90 (98.9%)	18.03.90 (98.9%)	18.03.90 (98.9%)
25.06.89	0.00595	0.00347	18.03.90 (98.9%)	18.03.90 (98.9%)	18.03.90 (98.9%)	01.04.90 (95.0%)
24.09.89	0.01300	0.00689	18.03.90 (98.9%)	25.03.90 (98.0%)	25.03.90 (98.0%)	01.04.90 (95.0%)

Table 7. East Japan GCM prices, T = end of 1990.

Enter	μ_1	σ	$\lvert\mu_2/\mu_1\rvert$ 0.5	1.0	2.0	5.0
$\alpha = 0.0$						
26.06.88	0.00165	0.00361	25.03.90 (96.7%)	25.03.90 (96.7%)	18.03.90 (98.2%)	18.03.90 (98.2%)
25.12.88	0.00182	0.00311	25.03.90 (96.7%)	18.03.90 (98.2%)	18.03.90 (98.2%)	18.03.90 (98.2%)
25.06.89	0.00446	0.00455	18.03.90 (98.2%)	18.03.90 (98.2%)	18.03.90 (98.2%)	18.03.90 (98.2%)
24.09.89	0.01191	0.00639	18.03.90 (98.2%)	18.03.90 (98.2%)	18.03.90 (98.2%)	01.04.90 (93.7%)
$\alpha = -0.5$						
26.06.88	0.00165	0.00361	25.03.90 (96.7%)	25.03.90 (96.7%)	18.03.90 (98.2%)	18.03.90 (98.2%)
25.12.88	0.00182	0.00311	25.03.90 (96.7%)	18.03.90 (98.2%)	18.03.90 (98.2%)	18.03.90 (98.2%)
25.06.89	0.00446	0.00455	18.03.90 (98.2%)	18.03.90 (98.2%)	18.03.90 (98.2%)	18.03.90 (98.2%)
24.09.89	0.01191	0.00639	18.03.90 (98.2%)	18.03.90 (98.2%)	18.03.90 (98.2%)	01.04.90 (93.7%)
$\alpha = -1.0$						
26.06.88	0.00165	0.00361	25.03.90 (96.7%)	25.03.90 (96.7%)	18.03.90 (98.2%)	18.03.90 (98.2%)
25.12.88	0.00182	0.00311	25.03.90 (96.7%)	18.03.90 (98.2%)	18.03.90 (98.2%)	18.03.90 (98.2%)
25.06.89	0.00446	0.00455	18.03.90 (98.2%)	18.03.90 (98.2%)	18.03.90 (98.2%)	18.03.90 (98.2%)
24.09.89	0.01191	0.00639	18.03.90 (98.2%)	18.03.90 (98.2%)	18.03.90 (98.2%)	01.04.90 (93.7%)

6. The overall Japanese land market, 1955–2013

Figures 10 and 11 and table 18 give the Japan Real Estate Institute's land indices for the six largest cities, and for all of Japan for commercial, housing, industrial and total land for each six month period from 1955 to 2013. The figures also gives the yearly rate of changes. The six largest cities are Tokyo, Yokohama, Osaka, Nagoya, Kobe and Kyoto.

The country wide indices are based on 140 cities. The data are appraisal based which tends to smooth the price levels and lag the market. Simple averages of samples of 10 lots in each city form the indices which were normalized at 100 as of 1985. The sampling procedure separates land into high, medium and low grades reflecting location, social circumstances, yield, etc. The sampling procedure selects lots randomly and equally from each of these three classes.

Table 18 also indicates that the price increase has been largest in the six largest cities. Despite large rises in the 1980s, the relative gain in the period 1955–1970 was much larger than from 1970 to the circa 1990 peak. For land in the whole country, the 1955–1970 period produced gains of about 15 times the 1955 values. These prices then increased only about fourfold in the ensuing 20. In the six largest cities, the increase was also much larger in the 1955–1970 period versus the next two decades.

Land values in the six largest cities outpaced the Consumer Prices Index (CPI) by 20 from 1955 to 1990. In the Ginza district of Tokyo, each square metre of land was worth well over US$200 000 with some plots approaching $300 000. Choice downtown land in Tokyo sold for the equivalent of nearly a billion dollars an acre. At neighbouring land prices, the value of land under the Emperor's palace and garden in Tokyo equalled

Table 8. West Japan GCM prices, T = end of 1990.

Enter	μ_1	σ	$\lvert\mu_2/\mu_1\rvert$ 0.5	1.0	2.0	5.0
$\alpha = 0.0$						
26.06.88	0.00342	0.00235	25.03.90 (99.1%)	25.03.90 (99.1%)	25.03.90 (99.1%)	01.04.90 (96.4%)
25.12.88	0.00497	0.00349	25.03.90 (99.1%)	25.03.90 (99.1%)	01.04.90 (96.4%)	01.04.90 (96.4%)
25.06.89	0.00849	0.00715	01.04.90 (96.4%)	01.04.90 (96.4%)	01.04.90 (96.4%)	01.04.90 (96.4%)
24.09.89	0.01474	0.01141	01.04.90 (96.4%)	01.04.90 (96.4%)	01.04.90 (96.4%)	11.11.90 (69.6%)
$\alpha = -0.5$						
26.06.88	0.00342	0.00235	25.03.90 (99.1%)	25.03.90 (99.1%)	25.03.90 (99.1%)	01.04.90 (96.4%)
25.12.88	0.00497	0.00349	25.03.90 (99.1%)	25.03.90 (99.1%)	01.04.90 (96.4%)	01.04.90 (96.4%)
25.06.89	0.00849	0.00715	01.04.90 (96.4%)	01.04.90 (96.4%)	01.04.90 (96.4%)	01.04.90 (96.4%)
24.09.89	0.01474	0.01141	01.04.90 (96.4%)	01.04.90 (96.4%)	01.04.90 (96.4%)	11.11.90 (69.6%)
$\alpha = -1.0$						
26.06.88	0.00342	0.00235	25.03.90 (99.1%)	25.03.90 (99.1%)	25.03.90 (99.1%)	01.04.90 (96.4%)
25.12.88	0.00497	0.00349	25.03.90 (99.1%)	25.03.90 (99.1%)	01.04.90 (96.4%)	01.04.90 (96.4%)
25.06.89	0.00849	0.00715	01.04.90 (96.4%)	01.04.90 (96.4%)	01.04.90 (96.4%)	01.04.90 (96.4%)
24.09.89	0.01474	0.01141	01.04.90 (96.4%)	01.04.90 (96.4%)	01.04.90 (96.4%)	11.11.90 (69.6%)

Table 9. Tokyo GCM prices, T = end of 1990.

Enter	μ_1	σ	$\lvert\mu_2/\mu_1\rvert$ 0.5	1.0	2.0	5.0
$\alpha = 0.0$						
26.06.88	0.00173	0.00367	25.03.90 (96.5%)	18.03.90 (98.3%)	18.03.90 (98.3%)	09.04.89 (65.8%)
25.12.88	0.00278	0.00851	01.04.90 (94.1%)	01.04.90 (94.1%)	25.03.90 (96.5%)	25.03.90 (96.5%)
25.06.89	0.00189	0.00577	01.04.90 (94.1%)	25.03.90 (96.5%)	25.03.90 (96.5%)	18.03.90 (98.3%)
24.09.89	0.00759	0.00821	25.03.90 (96.5%)	25.03.90 (96.5%)	25.03.90 (96.5%)	01.04.90 (94.1%)
$\alpha = -0.5$						
26.06.88	0.00173	0.00367	25.03.90 (96.5%)	18.03.90 (98.3%)	18.03.90 (98.3%)	09.04.89 (65.8%)
25.12.88	0.00278	0.00851	01.04.90 (94.1%)	01.04.90 (94.1%)	25.03.90 (96.5%)	25.03.90 (96.5%)
25.06.89	0.00189	0.00577	01.04.90 (94.1%)	25.03.90 (96.5%)	25.03.90 (96.5%)	18.03.90 (98.3%)
24.09.89	0.00759	0.00821	25.03.90 (96.5%)	25.03.90 (96.5%)	25.03.90 (96.5%)	01.04.90 (94.1%)
$\alpha = -1.0$						
26.06.88	0.00173	0.00367	25.03.90 (96.5%)	18.03.90 (98.3%)	18.03.90 (98.3%)	09.04.89 (65.8%)
25.12.88	0.00278	0.00851	01.04.90 (94.1%)	01.04.90 (94.1%)	25.03.90 (96.5%)	25.03.90 (96.5%)
25.06.89	0.00189	0.00577	01.04.90 (94.1%)	25.03.90 (96.5%)	25.03.90 (96.5%)	18.03.90 (98.3%)
24.09.89	0.00759	0.00821	25.03.90 (96.5%)	25.03.90 (96.5%)	25.03.90 (96.5%)	01.04.90 (94.1%)

that of all California or of Canada. The total land value in Japan in 1990 was about 4.1 times that of the whole United States. Japanese land was worth some ¥2180 trillion as of the end of 1989. This compares with a value of ¥1050 trillion at the end of 1985. Using an exchange rate of ¥143.76 per dollar at the end of 1989, gave a land value of $15.16 trillion. As of September 1990, all land had an index of 203.1, up 16.2% from September 1989.

With an end of 1990 exchange rate of 135.40, total Japanese land values were in the $18.7 trillion range in late 1990. The average acre of land in Japan was worth fully 100 times the average acre in the US. So even though the US has about 25 times more land than Japan, its 1990 total value was less than a fourth as much. Essentially half the world's land value at 1987–1990 prices was accounted for by Japanese land! It also accounted for about 20% of the total non-human capital asset value in the world. Simple houses in Tokyo rented for more than $10 000 per month and cost in the millions. Office space for sale in Tokyo's financial district cost nearly $75 000 per square foot. Some luxury apartments in Tokyo rented for well over $20 000 per month.

In 1988 Tokyo's land value alone was about $7.7 trillion, or about half the land value of the whole country. To understand how much this is we can do a idealized experiment. Let's borrow on it up to 80% of its value. Banks in Tokyo commonly provided such loans based on land security until the high interest rates of late 1989 into 1990. From 1987 to 1989, the interest rates on loans secured by land were 5.7% and 6.6% for variable and fixed rate loans, respectively. We would then have almost enough money to purchase all the land in the US for

Table 10. Nationwide GCM prices, T = end of 1989.

Enter	μ_1	σ	$\lvert\mu_2/\mu_1\rvert$			
			0.5	1.0	2.0	5.0
$\alpha = 0.0$						
26.06.88	0.00237	0.00280	17.12.89 (87.8%)	17.12.89 (87.8%)	03.12.89 (85.5%)	19.11.89 (83.0%)
25.12.88	0.00296	0.00228	17.12.89 (87.8%)	10.12.89 (86.5%)	03.12.89 (85.5%)	12.11.89 (82.2%)
25.06.89	0.00595	0.00347	17.12.89 (87.8%)	17.12.89 (87.8%)	10.12.89 (86.5%)	19.11.89 (83.0%)
24.09.89	0.01300	0.00689	17.12.89 (87.8%)	17.12.89 (87.8%)	03.12.89 (85.5%)	12.11.89 (82.2%)
$\alpha = -0.5$						
26.06.88	0.00237	0.00280	17.12.89 (87.8%)	10.12.89 (86.5%)	03.12.89 (85.5%)	12.11.89 (82.2%)
25.12.88	0.00296	0.00228	17.12.89 (87.8%)	10.12.89 (86.5%)	03.12.89 (85.5%)	12.11.89 (82.2%)
25.06.89	0.00595	0.00347	17.12.89 (87.8%)	10.12.89 (86.5%)	03.12.89 (85.5%)	12.11.89 (82.2%)
24.09.89	0.01300	0.00689	17.12.89 (87.8%)	10.12.89 (86.5%)	03.12.89 (85.5%)	12.11.89 (82.2%)
$\alpha = -1.0$						
26.06.88	0.00237	0.00280	17.12.89 (87.8%)	10.12.89 (86.5%)	03.12.89 (85.5%)	12.11.89 (82.2%)
25.12.88	0.00296	0.00228	17.12.89 (87.8%)	10.12.89 (86.5%)	03.12.89 (85.5%)	12.11.89 (82.2%)
25.06.89	0.00595	0.00347	17.12.89 (87.8%)	10.12.89 (86.5%)	03.12.89 (85.5%)	12.11.89 (82.2%)
24.09.89	0.01300	0.00689	17.12.89 (87.8%)	10.12.89 (86.5%)	03.12.89 (85.5%)	12.11.89 (82.2%)

Table 11. East Japan GCM prices, T = end of 1989.

Enter	μ_1	σ	$\lvert\mu_2/\mu_1\rvert$			
			0.5	1.0	2.0	5.0
$\alpha = 0.0$						
26.06.88	0.00165	0.00361	17.12.89 (88.0%)	17.12.89 (88.0%)	10.12.89 (86.7%)	19.11.89 (84.3%)
25.12.88	0.00182	0.00311	17.12.89 (88.0%)	10.12.89 (86.7%)	03.12.89 (85.6%)	12.11.89 (83.7%)
25.06.89	0.00446	0.00455	17.12.89 (88.0%)	17.12.89 (88.0%)	10.12.89 (86.7%)	19.11.89 (84.3%)
24.09.89	0.01191	0.00639	17.12.89 (88.0%)	17.12.89 (88.0%)	10.12.89 (86.7%)	19.11.89 (84.3%)
$\alpha = -0.5$						
26.06.88	0.00165	0.00361	17.12.89 (88.0%)	10.12.89 (86.7%)	03.12.89 (85.6%)	12.11.89 (83.7%)
25.12.88	0.00182	0.00311	17.12.89 (88.0%)	10.12.89 (86.7%)	03.12.89 (85.6%)	12.11.89 (83.7%)
25.06.89	0.00446	0.00455	17.12.89 (88.0%)	10.12.89 (86.7%)	03.12.89 (85.6%)	12.11.89 (83.7%)
24.09.89	0.01191	0.00639	17.12.89 (88.0%)	10.12.89 (86.7%)	03.12.89 (85.6%)	12.11.89 (83.7%)
$\alpha = -1.0$						
26.06.88	0.00165	0.00361	17.12.89 (88.0%)	10.12.89 (86.7%)	03.12.89 (85.6%)	12.11.89 (83.7%)
25.12.88	0.00182	0.00311	17.12.89 (88.0%)	10.12.89 (86.7%)	03.12.89 (85.6%)	12.11.89 (83.7%)
25.06.89	0.00446	0.00455	17.12.89 (88.0%)	10.12.89 (86.7%)	03.12.89 (85.6%)	12.11.89 (83.7%)
24.09.89	0.01191	0.00639	17.12.89 (88.0%)	10.12.89 (86.7%)	03.12.89 (85.6%)	12.11.89 (83.7%)

$3.7 trillion and all the stock on the New York, American and NASDAQ over-the-counter stock exchanges for about $2.6 trillion in an all-cash transaction. Obviously, one could not sell all of Tokyo's land for $7.7 trillion quickly, nor would a group of banks undertake such a large loan, but this was the value of land prices in fiscal 1987. In Tokyo, about 2% of land changed hands each year. The price was kept up and bid higher because of the excess of demand over supply.

A staggering 56% of the national wealth of Japan was land. The 1990 percentage was even higher since there was a huge price increase in 1986 and steady rises since then. Land turnover was very small as the Japanese believe in holding land whenever possible. This was reinforced by the tax system which encourages the purchase of more land and discourages land sales. The population in per unit of habitable area was 30 times higher in Japan than the US. The GNP and energy consumption per habitable area were also much higher in Japan than in the US (though the energy per unit GNP was much lower in Japan), see table 19. This put upward pressure on land prices.

Boone (1989) developed several models in an attempt to rationalize the high land values in Japan from an economic point of view. He found that if Japan's GNP growth exceeded that in the US by about 2% per year forever, then land prices 100 times higher in Japan than in the US are consistent with the economic model.

High interest rates which led to a sharp fall in stock prices in 1990 did not lead to any decline in land prices until 1991 as shown in Figures 10 and 11. However, there was a sharp decline in speculative land such as golf course membership and condos, see Stone and Ziemba (1993). As interest rates rise, land demand fell but in Tokyo, with virtually no new

Table 12. West Japan GCM prices, T = end of 1989.

Enter	μ_1	σ	$\lvert\mu_2/\mu_1\rvert$			
			0.5	1.0	2.0	5.0
$\alpha = 0.0$						
26.06.88	0.00342	0.00235	24.12.89 (88.8%)	17.12.89 (87.0%)	10.12.89 (85.7%)	19.11.89 (81.0%)
25.12.88	0.00497	0.00349	17.12.89 (87.0%)	10.12.89 (85.7%)	03.12.89 (85.0%)	12.11.89 (79.9%)
25.06.89	0.00849	0.00715	17.12.89 (87.0%)	17.12.89 (87.0%)	03.12.89 (85.0%)	19.11.89 (81.0%)
24.09.89	0.01474	0.01141	17.12.89 (87.0%)	10.12.89 (85.7%)	03.12.89 (85.0%)	12.11.89 (79.9%)
$\alpha = -0.5$						
26.06.88	0.00342	0.00235	17.12.89 (87.0%)	10.12.89 (85.7%)	03.12.89 (85.0%)	12.11.89 (79.9%)
25.12.88	0.00497	0.00349	17.12.89 (87.0%)	10.12.89 (85.7%)	03.12.89 (85.0%)	12.11.89 (79.9%)
25.06.89	0.00849	0.00715	17.12.89 (87.0%)	10.12.89 (85.7%)	03.12.89 (85.0%)	12.11.89 (79.9%)
24.09.89	0.01474	0.01141	17.12.89 (87.0%)	10.12.89 (85.7%)	03.12.89 (85.0%)	12.11.89 (79.9%)
$\alpha = -1.0$						
26.06.88	0.00342	0.00235	17.12.89 (87.0%)	10.12.89 (85.7%)	03.12.89 (85.0%)	12.11.89 (79.9%)
25.12.88	0.00497	0.00349	17.12.89 (87.0%)	10.12.89 (85.7%)	03.12.89 (85.0%)	12.11.89 (79.9%)
25.06.89	0.00849	0.00715	17.12.89 (87.0%)	10.12.89 (85.7%)	03.12.89 (85.0%)	12.11.89 (79.9%)
24.09.89	0.01474	0.01141	17.12.89 (87.0%)	10.12.89 (85.7%)	03.12.89 (85.0%)	12.11.89 (79.9%)

Table 13. Tokyo GCM prices, T = end of 1989.

Enter	μ_1	σ	$\lvert\mu_2/\mu_1\rvert$			
			0.5	1.0	2.0	5.0
$\alpha = 0.0$						
26.06.88	0.00173	0.00367	17.12.89 (91.3%)	17.12.89 (91.3%)	09.04.89 (65.8%)	09.04.89 (65.8%)
25.12.88	0.00278	0.00851	10.12.89 (89.0%)	10.12.89 (89.0%)	03.12.89 (88.2%)	12.11.89 (83.9%)
25.06.89	0.00189	0.00577	17.12.89 (91.3%)	10.12.89 (89.0%)	03.12.89 (88.2%)	12.11.89 (83.9%)
24.09.89	0.00759	0.00821	17.12.89 (91.3%)	10.12.89 (89.0%)	10.12.89 (89.0%)	12.11.89 (83.9%)
$\alpha = -0.5$						
26.06.88	0.00173	0.00367	17.12.89 (91.3%)	10.12.89 (89.0%)	09.04.89 (65.8%)	09.04.89 (65.8%)
25.12.88	0.00278	0.00851	10.12.89 (89.0%)	10.12.89 (89.0%)	03.12.89 (88.2%)	12.11.89 (83.9%)
25.06.89	0.00189	0.00577	17.12.89 (91.3%)	10.12.89 (89.0%)	03.12.89 (88.2%)	12.11.89 (83.9%)
24.09.89	0.00759	0.00821	17.12.89 (91.3%)	10.12.89 (89.0%)	03.12.89 (88.2%)	12.11.89 (83.9%)
$\alpha = -1.0$						
26.06.88	0.00173	0.00367	17.12.89 (91.3%)	10.12.89 (89.0%)	09.04.89 (65.8%)	09.04.89 (65.8%)
25.12.88	0.00278	0.00851	10.12.89 (89.0%)	10.12.89 (89.0%)	03.12.89 (88.2%)	12.11.89 (83.9%)
25.06.89	0.00189	0.00577	17.12.89 (91.3%)	10.12.89 (89.0%)	03.12.89 (88.2%)	12.11.89 (83.9%)
24.09.89	0.00759	0.00821	17.12.89 (91.3%)	10.12.89 (89.0%)	03.12.89 (88.2%)	12.11.89 (83.9%)

supply, demand still greatly exceeded supply. At the same time supply declines with higher interest rates as development costs are curtailed. All the incentives favoured holding land and not even developing it. As Canaway (1990) pointed out, land held less than five years was taxed at fully 52% of its sale value. Meanwhile, yearly taxes paid to hold land were about 0.05–0.10% of its current value. Even upon death it paid to borrow money which was deductible at full value while land was valued at about half its market value. Hence, inheritance taxes are minimized. Canaway argued that in a major crash the stock market will go first, then the economy and finally the land markets. Our results confirm this.

7. Applying the model to the Nikkei in 2013

In 2013, a policy to devalue the usually strong yen led to a large increase in stock prices. Since the −48% crash in 1990, the Nikkei has had its ups and downs but, as shown in figure 4, it has never really recovered to the 1990 peak.

We apply the changepoint detection model to the Nikkei225 with T corresponding to the end of 2013. Table 20 shows the exits from the market past the 2013 local peak, and figure 12 illustrates the results for the parameters $\alpha = 0$, $\mu_2 = -\mu_1$, using data to October 2013. All the entries have exits with profits.

Table 14. Nationwide GCM prices, T = end of 1992.

Enter	μ_1	σ	$\lvert\mu_2/\mu_1\rvert$			
			0.5	1.0	2.0	5.0
$\alpha = 0.0$						
26.06.88	0.00237	0.00280	25.03.90 (98.0%)	25.03.90 (98.0%)	18.03.90 (98.9%)	18.03.90 (98.9%)
25.12.88	0.00296	0.00228	18.03.90 (98.9%)	18.03.90 (98.9%)	18.03.90 (98.9%)	18.03.90 (98.9%)
25.06.89	0.00595	0.00347	18.03.90 (98.9%)	18.03.90 (98.9%)	18.03.90 (98.9%)	01.04.90 (95.0%)
24.09.89	0.01300	0.00689	25.03.90 (98.0%)	25.03.90 (98.0%)	01.04.90 (95.0%)	01.04.90 (95.0%)
$\alpha = -0.5$						
26.06.88	0.00237	0.00280	25.03.90 (98.0%)	25.03.90 (98.0%)	18.03.90 (98.9%)	18.03.90 (98.9%)
25.12.88	0.00296	0.00228	18.03.90 (98.9%)	18.03.90 (98.9%)	18.03.90 (98.9%)	18.03.90 (98.9%)
25.06.89	0.00595	0.00347	18.03.90 (98.9%)	18.03.90 (98.9%)	18.03.90 (98.9%)	01.04.90 (95.0%)
24.09.89	0.01300	0.00689	25.03.90 (98.0%)	25.03.90 (98.0%)	01.04.90 (95.0%)	01.04.90 (95.0%)
$\alpha = -1.0$						
26.06.88	0.00237	0.00280	25.03.90 (98.0%)	25.03.90 (98.0%)	18.03.90 (98.9%)	18.03.90 (98.9%)
25.12.88	0.00296	0.00228	18.03.90 (98.9%)	18.03.90 (98.9%)	18.03.90 (98.9%)	18.03.90 (98.9%)
25.06.89	0.00595	0.00347	18.03.90 (98.9%)	18.03.90 (98.9%)	18.03.90 (98.9%)	01.04.90 (95.0%)
24.09.89	0.01300	0.00689	25.03.90 (98.0%)	25.03.90 (98.0%)	01.04.90 (95.0%)	01.04.90 (95.0%)

Table 15. East Japan GCM prices, T = end of 1992.

Enter	μ_1	σ	$\lvert\mu_2/\mu_1\rvert$			
			0.5	1.0	2.0	5.0
$\alpha = 0.0$						
26.06.88	0.00165	0.00361	01.04.90 (93.7%)	25.03.90 (96.7%)	25.03.90 (96.7%)	18.03.90 (98.2%)
25.12.88	0.00182	0.00311	25.03.90 (96.7%)	25.03.90 (96.7%)	18.03.90 (98.2%)	18.03.90 (98.2%)
25.06.89	0.00446	0.00455	25.03.90 (96.7%)	25.03.90 (96.7%)	18.03.90 (98.2%)	25.03.90 (96.7%)
24.09.89	0.01191	0.00639	18.03.90 (98.2%)	18.03.90 (98.2%)	25.03.90 (96.7%)	01.04.90 (93.7%)
$\alpha = -0.5$						
26.06.88	0.00165	0.00361	01.04.90 (93.7%)	25.03.90 (96.7%)	25.03.90 (96.7%)	18.03.90 (98.2%)
25.12.88	0.00182	0.00311	25.03.90 (96.7%)	25.03.90 (96.7%)	18.03.90 (98.2%)	18.03.90 (98.2%)
25.06.89	0.00446	0.00455	25.03.90 (96.7%)	25.03.90 (96.7%)	18.03.90 (98.2%)	25.03.90 (96.7%)
24.09.89	0.01191	0.00639	18.03.90 (98.2%)	18.03.90 (98.2%)	25.03.90 (96.7%)	01.04.90 (93.7%)
$\alpha = -1.0$						
26.06.88	0.00165	0.00361	01.04.90 (93.7%)	25.03.90 (96.7%)	25.03.90 (96.7%)	18.03.90 (98.2%)
25.12.88	0.00182	0.00311	25.03.90 (96.7%)	25.03.90 (96.7%)	18.03.90 (98.2%)	18.03.90 (98.2%)
25.06.89	0.00446	0.00455	25.03.90 (96.7%)	25.03.90 (96.7%)	18.03.90 (98.2%)	25.03.90 (96.7%)
24.09.89	0.01191	0.00639	18.03.90 (98.2%)	18.03.90 (98.2%)	25.03.90 (96.7%)	01.04.90 (93.7%)

8. Short selling the Nikkei portfolio

Would it be possible to apply the changepoint detection theory to profit from the price decline by short selling the index portfolio when the changepoint is detected?

Consider the method which consists in selling short the index portfolio when the crash of the bubble is detected, and finding the stopping time τ to buy the portfolio back which *minimizes* $\mathsf{E}\log(S_\tau)$†. The latter problem is equivalent to maximizing $\mathsf{E}\log(1/S_\tau)$ and reduces to Theorem 3.1 with $\tilde{S}_t = 1/S_t$. We applied this method to the Nikkei index portfolio in 1990 and 2013 with short selling on 16.01.90, 21.02.90, 23.02.90, and 30.05.13, 03.06.13, which are the dates when the crashes are detected by the changepoint model with parameters $\alpha = 0$ and $\mu_2 = -\mu_1$ (see tables 3 and 20). In the problem of minimizing $\mathsf{E}\log(S_\tau)$, we set $\mu_1 = -\hat{\mu}$, $\sigma = \hat{\sigma}$, where $\hat{\mu}$ and $\hat{\sigma}$ are the estimated parameters of the drift and volatility of the log prices during the 100 trading days before the market peaks on 29 December 1989 and 22 March 2013. The value of μ_2 varies through $\mu_2 = -0.5\mu_1, -\mu_1, -2\mu_1, -3\mu_1, -5\mu_1$, and T corresponds to the end of 1990 and 2013, respectively.

The exit dates obtained for both 1990 and 2013 do not depend on the entry dates. For 1990, we get 11.05.90 for $\mu_2 = -0.5\mu_1$, 07.05.90 for $\mu_2 = -\mu_1$, 09.04.90 for $\mu_2 = -2\mu_1$ and 26.03.90 for $\mu_2 = -3\mu_1$ and $\mu_2 = -5\mu_1$. The corresponding daily closing prices are 31512, 30956, 30398 and 31840, while the entry prices are 36 850 (on 16.01.90), 35 734 (21.02.90) and 34891 (23.02.90); the local trough was on 2 April, 1990 at 28002. Thus, the strategy was profitable in this case.

†Other utility functions can be considered in a similar way.

Table 16. West Japan GCM prices, T = end of 1992.

Enter	μ_1	σ	$\|\mu_2/\mu_1\|$ 0.5	1.0	2.0	5.0
$\alpha = 0.0$						
26.06.88	0.00342	0.00235	25.03.90 (99.1%)	25.03.90 (99.1%)	25.03.90 (99.1%)	01.04.90 (96.4%)
25.12.88	0.00497	0.00349	01.04.90 (96.4%)	01.04.90 (96.4%)	01.04.90 (96.4%)	01.04.90 (96.4%)
25.06.89	0.00849	0.00715	01.04.90 (96.4%)	01.04.90 (96.4%)	01.04.90 (96.4%)	01.04.90 (96.4%)
24.09.89	0.01474	0.01141	08.04.90 (94.5%)	08.04.90 (94.5%)	08.04.90 (94.5%)	08.11.92 (38.9%)
$\alpha = -0.5$						
26.06.88	0.00342	0.00235	25.03.90 (99.1%)	25.03.90 (99.1%)	25.03.90 (99.1%)	01.04.90 (96.4%)
25.12.88	0.00497	0.00349	01.04.90 (96.4%)	01.04.90 (96.4%)	01.04.90 (96.4%)	01.04.90 (96.4%)
25.06.89	0.00849	0.00715	01.04.90 (96.4%)	01.04.90 (96.4%)	01.04.90 (96.4%)	01.04.90 (96.4%)
24.09.89	0.01474	0.01141	08.04.90 (94.5%)	01.04.90 (96.4%)	08.04.90 (94.5%)	08.11.92 (38.9%)
$\alpha = -1.0$						
26.06.88	0.00342	0.00235	25.03.90 (99.1%)	25.03.90 (99.1%)	25.03.90 (99.1%)	01.04.90 (96.4%)
25.12.88	0.00497	0.00349	01.04.90 (96.4%)	01.04.90 (96.4%)	01.04.90 (96.4%)	01.04.90 (96.4%)
25.06.89	0.00849	0.00715	01.04.90 (96.4%)	01.04.90 (96.4%)	01.04.90 (96.4%)	01.04.90 (96.4%)
24.09.89	0.01474	0.01141	01.04.90 (96.4%)	01.04.90 (96.4%)	08.04.90 (94.5%)	08.11.92 (38.9%)

Table 17. Tokyo GCM prices, T = end of 1992.

Enter	μ_1	σ	$\|\mu_2/\mu_1\|$ 0.5	1.0	2.0	5.0
$\alpha = 0.0$						
26.06.88	0.00173	0.00367	01.04.90 (94.1%)	25.03.90 (96.5%)	25.03.90 (96.5%)	09.04.89 (65.8%)
25.12.88	0.00278	0.00851	15.04.90 (89.7%)	08.04.90 (92.2%)	01.04.90 (94.1%)	01.04.90 (94.1%)
25.06.89	0.00189	0.00577	08.04.90 (92.2%)	01.04.90 (94.1%)	01.04.90 (94.1%)	25.03.90 (96.5%)
24.09.89	0.00759	0.00821	01.04.90 (94.1%)	25.03.90 (96.5%)	25.03.90 (96.5%)	01.04.90 (94.1%)
$\alpha = -0.5$						
26.06.88	0.00173	0.00367	01.04.90 (94.1%)	25.03.90 (96.5%)	25.03.90 (96.5%)	09.04.89 (65.8%)
25.12.88	0.00278	0.00851	15.04.90 (89.7%)	08.04.90 (92.2%)	01.04.90 (94.1%)	01.04.90 (94.1%)
25.06.89	0.00189	0.00577	08.04.90 (92.2%)	01.04.90 (94.1%)	01.04.90 (94.1%)	25.03.90 (96.5%)
24.09.89	0.00759	0.00821	01.04.90 (94.1%)	25.03.90 (96.5%)	25.03.90 (96.5%)	01.04.90 (94.1%)
$\alpha = -1.0$						
26.06.88	0.00173	0.00367	01.04.90 (94.1%)	25.03.90 (96.5%)	25.03.90 (96.5%)	09.04.89 (65.8%)
25.12.88	0.00278	0.00851	15.04.90 (89.7%)	08.04.90 (92.2%)	01.04.90 (94.1%)	01.04.90 (94.1%)
25.06.89	0.00189	0.00577	08.04.90 (92.2%)	01.04.90 (94.1%)	01.04.90 (94.1%)	25.03.90 (96.5%)
24.09.89	0.00759	0.00821	01.04.90 (94.1%)	25.03.90 (96.5%)	25.03.90 (96.5%)	01.04.90 (94.1%)

Table 18. Increase of land prices, 1955–1990, %.

	Nationwide				6 largest cities			
	Total	Commercial	Residential	Industrial	Total	Commercial	Residential	Industrial
1955–1990	65.5	59.6	81.2	56.7	178.8	127.7	219.1	150.8
1955–1970	15.1	14.5	15.5	15.8	18.7	11.0	20.2	23.6
1970–1990	4.3	4.1	5.2	3.6	9.6	11.6	10.8	6.4

Source: Japan real estate institute.

In 2013, for the both entry dates the exits are 05.07.13 for $\mu_2 = -0.5\mu_1$, 02.07.90 for $\mu_2 = -\mu_1$, $\mu_2 = -\mu_1, -2\mu_1, -3\mu_1$ and 01.07.13 for $\mu_2 = -5\mu_1$. The corresponding daily closing prices, 14309.97, 14098.74 and 13852.50 are close to the local minimum at 12445.38 (13 June 2013), however, the strategy was unprofitable.

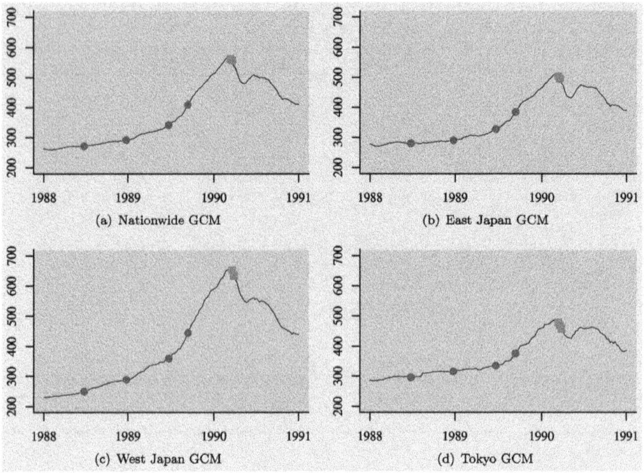

Figure 7. The results for the GCM prices when T = end of 1990: the enter (blue circles) and exit (red squares) dates for the values of the parameters $\alpha = 0.0$, $\mu_2 = -\mu_1$.

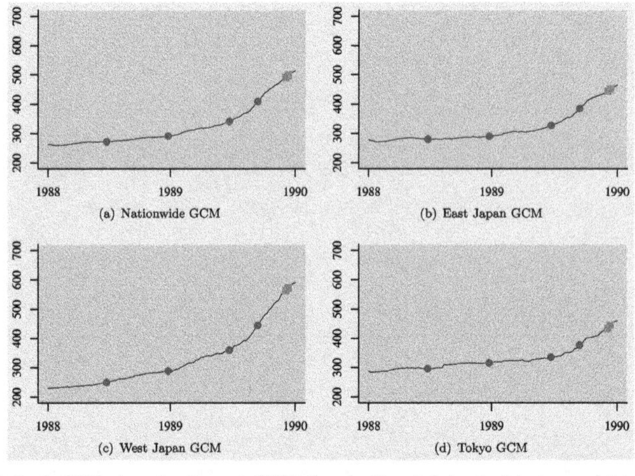

Figure 8. The results for the GCM prices when T = end of 1989: the enter (blue circles) and exit (red squares) dates for the values of the parameters $\alpha = 0.0$, $\mu_2 = -\mu_1$.

One can use these results to develop a multi-changepoint detection model, which buys (sells short) assets when the signal-to-noise ratio is high and positive (respectively, negative with large absolute value) and sells (buys) after it detects a changepoint, repeating this procedure continuously in time. We leave the analysis of this strategy for future research. The substantial difficulty here consists in the estimation of the risk of such a strategy, since our assumptions (mainly, log-normal returns with constant parameters, and the loose method of choosing T) do not allow an accurate quantitative prediction of the strategy performance. A theoretical result for a multiple changepoint model for a Brownian motion, which is a continuous-time analogue of our model, was obtained by Gapeev (2010).

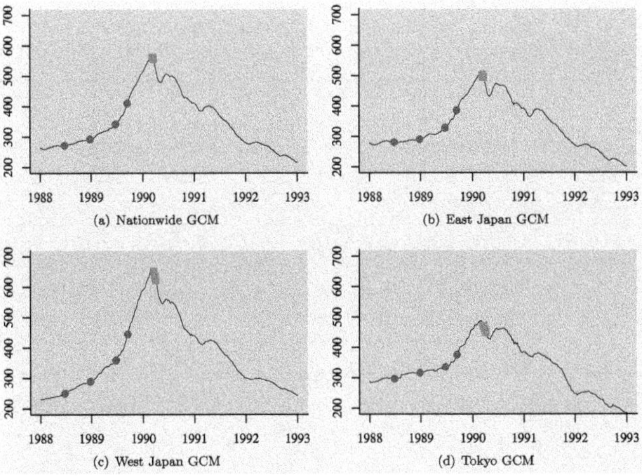

Figure 9. The results for the GCM prices when T = end of 1992: the enter (blue circles) and exit (red squares) dates for the values of the parameters $\alpha = 0.0$, $\mu_2 = -\mu_1$.

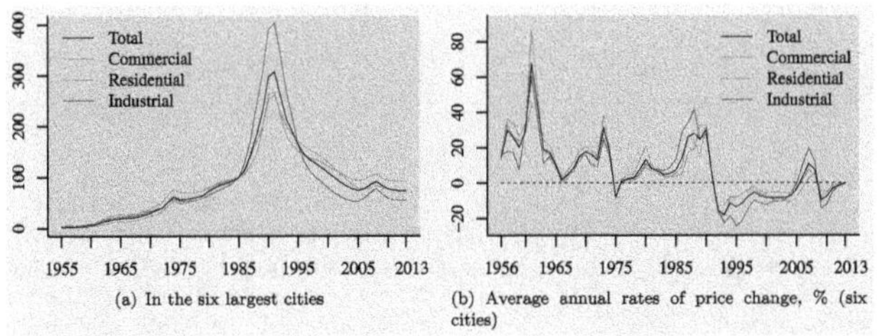

Figure 10. Land price indices for industrial, residential, commercial and all land and annual rates of price change for six largest cities, 1955–2013. Source: Japan real estate institute.

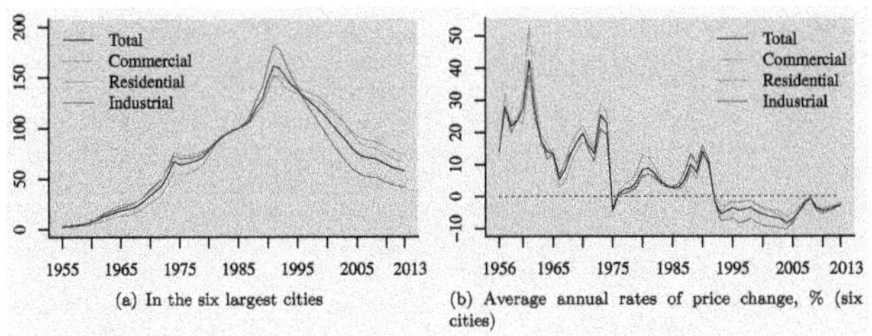

Figure 11. Land price indices for industrial, residential, commercial and all land and annual rates of price change for all land, 1955–2013. Source: Japan real estate institute.

Table 19. Comparison of fundamentals, Japan and the US, 1989.

	Japan	US	Japan as % of US
Population, millions	120	239	50.21
Total area (1000 sq km)	377	9373	4.02
Habitable area (1000 sq km)	80	4786	1.67
Population per habitable area (pop/sq km)	1500	50	3,000.00
GNP per habitable area (million $/sq km)	16.90	0.80	2,122.50
Energy consumption (tone oil equivalent/sq km)	4650	390	1,192.38

Source: Daiwa securities America, Inc.

Table 20. Nikkei-225 from November 2012 to October 2013.

Enter	μ_1	σ	$\|\mu_2/\mu_1\|$ 0.5	1.0	2.0	5.0
$\alpha = 0.0$						
01.02.13	0.00512	0.01206	30.05.13 (87.0%)	30.05.13 (87.0%)	23.05.13 (92.7%)	23.05.13 (92.7%)
01.03.13	0.00383	0.01527	13.06.13 (79.6%)	03.06.13 (84.9%)	30.05.13 (87.0%)	23.05.13 (92.7%)
01.04.13	0.00269	0.01596	22.08.13 (85.5%)	13.06.13 (79.6%)	03.06.13 (84.9%)	30.05.13 (87.0%)
$\alpha = -0.5$						
01.02.13	0.00512	0.01206	30.05.13 (87.0%)	27.05.13 (90.5%)	23.05.13 (92.7%)	23.05.13 (92.7%)
01.03.13	0.00383	0.01527	13.06.13 (79.6%)	03.06.13 (84.9%)	30.05.13 (87.0%)	23.05.13 (92.7%)
01.04.13	0.00269	0.01596	20.08.13 (85.7%)	07.06.13 (82.4%)	03.06.13 (84.9%)	30.05.13 (87.0%)
$\alpha = -1.0$						
01.02.13	0.00512	0.01206	30.05.13 (87.0%)	27.05.13 (90.5%)	23.05.13 (92.7%)	23.05.13 (92.7%)
01.03.13	0.00383	0.01527	06.06.13 (82.6%)	03.06.13 (84.9%)	30.05.13 (87.0%)	23.05.13 (92.7%)
01.04.13	0.00269	0.01596	20.08.13 (85.7%)	06.06.13 (82.6%)	03.06.13 (84.9%)	30.05.13 (87.0%)

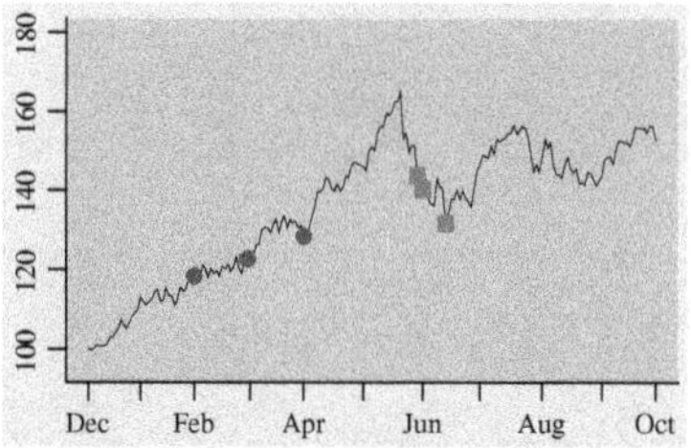

Figure 12. Nikkei225 from November 2012 to October 2013.

9. Conclusion

This paper studies the Nikkei stock average and golf course membership prices around 1990 in Japan. Both of these asset markets were in bubble type markets and had huge rises up and then dramatic falls. High interest rates relative to stock earnings seems to be the main cause of both crashes. The bond stock earnings yield difference model predicted the stock market crash. In time sequence, the stock market fell first, then the golf course membership market and finally, the land markets. We use a changepoint detection model designed to exit bubble-type markets and apply it successfully to the Nikkei stock average and the golf course membership markets in various areas of Japan.

Data from 1990 to 2013 indicate that both the stock and land markets have never recovered to their circa 1990 prices. The Nikkei had a big rise in 2013 fueled by a weak yen policy and this market peaked in mid 2013 and the changepoint detection model suggested an exit then. In virtually all entry cases the stopping rule model has good exits as they were close to the global price peaks and produce profits.

Acknowledgements

This paper was written during visits to the Hausdorff Research Institute for Mathematics at the University of Bonn in the framework of the Trimester Program Stochastic Dynamics in Economics and Finance and at the Systematic Risk Centre, London School of Economics. The work of W. T. Ziemba was also partially supported by the University of Manchester Economics Department and its Hallsworth Lecture series fund. Helpful comments from seminar participants at the University of Bonn, the Swiss Banking Institute, the University of Zurich, the University of Bordeaux and the London School of Economics are gratefully acknowledged.

References

Anderson, K., Brooks, C. and Katsaris, A., Testing for speculative bubbles in asset prices. In *Handbook of Research Methods and Applications in Empirical Finance*, edited by A.R. Bell, C. Brooks and M. Prokopczuk, pp. 73–93, 2013 (Edward Elgar: Cheltenham).

Berge, K., Consigli, G. and Ziemba, W.T., The predictive ability of the bond stock earnings yield differential. *J. Portfolio Manage.* 2008, Spring, 63–80.

Boone, P., High land values in Japan: Is the archipelago worth eleven trillion dollars? Technical Report, Department of Economics, Harvard University, 1989.

Breiman, L., Optimal gambling systems for favorable games. In *Proceedings of the Fourth Berkeley Symposium on Mathematical Statistics and Probability*. Vol. I, pp. 65–78, 1961 (University of California Press: Berkeley, CA).

Buffett, W.B., Warren Buffett on the stock market. Fortune, 10 December, 2001.

Camerer, C., Bubbles and fads in asset prices. *J. Econ. Surv.*, 1989, **3**(1), 3–14.

Canaway, H., Land prices in Japan: No cause for alarm. Baring Securities, May, 1990.

Chopra, V.K. and Ziemba, W.T., The effect of errors in mean, variance and co-variance estimates on optimal portfolio choice. *J. Portfolio Manage.*, 1993, **19**, 6–11.

Comolli, L.R. and Ziemba, W.T., Japanese security market regularities, 1990–1994. In *Security Market Imperfections in World Wide Equity Markets*, edited by D.B. Keim and W.T. Ziemba, pp. 458–491, 2000 (Cambridge University Press: Cambridge, UK).

Corcos, A., Eckmann, J.-P., Malaspinas, A. and Malevergne, Y., Imitation and contrarian behaviour: Hyperbolic bubbles, craches and chaos. *Quant. Finance*, 2002, **2**, 264–281.

Evanoff, D. D, Kaufman, G. and Malliaris, A.G., *New Perspectives on Asset Price Bubbles*, 2012 (Oxford University Press: Oxford, UK).

French, K.R. and Poterba, J., Were Japanese stock prices too high? *J. Financ. Econ.*, 1991, **29**(2), 337–363.

Gapeev, P.V., Two switching multiple disorder problems for Brownian motions, 2010. arXiv:1011.0174.

Jarrow, R., Kohia, Y. and Protter, P., How to detect an asset bubble. *SIAM J. Financ. Math.*, 2011, **2**, 839–865.

Kelly, J. Jr, A new interpretation of the information rate. *Bell Syst. Tech. J.*, 1956, **35**, 917–926.

Kindleberger, C. and Aliber, R., *Mainias, Panics and Crashes*. 6th ed., 2011 (Palgrave Macmillan: Hampshire).

Lleo, S. and Ziemba, W.T., Does the bond-stock earning yield differential model predict equity market corrections better than high P/E models? 2013. Available online at: SSRN:http://ssrn.com/abstract=2296836.

Lleo, S. and Ziemba, W.T., Some historical perspectives on the bond-stock earnings yield model for crash prediction around the world. *Int. J. Forecast.*, in press.

MacLean, L.C., Thorp, E.O. and Ziemba, W.T., *The Kelly Capital Growth Criterion: Theory and Practice*, 2010 (World Scientific: Singapore).

Peskir, G. and Shiryaev, A., *Optimal Stopping and Free-boundary Problems*, 2006 (Birkhäuser: Basel).

Phillips, P.C.B., Shi, S.P. and Yu, J., Testing for multiple bubbles 1: Historical episodes of exuberance and collapse in the S&P500. New Economics Papers (October), 2013.

Poor, H. and Hadjiljadis, O., *Quickest Detection*, 2009 (Cambridge University Press: Cambridge, UK).

Poterba, J. and Summers, L., Mean reversion in stock prices: Evidence and implications. *J. Financ. Econ.*, 1985, **22**(1), 27–59.

Rachev, S. and Ziemba, W.T., The distribution of golf course membership prices in Japan. Presentation at ORSA-TIMS Meeting in San Francisco, November, 1992.

Reinhart, C.M. and Rogoff, K.S., *This Time is Different: Eight Centuries of Financial Folly*, 2009 (Princeton University Press: Princeton, NJ).

Robbins, H., Sigmund, D. and Chow, Y., *Great Expectations: The Theory of Optimal Stopping*, 1971 (Houghton Mifflin: Boston, MA).

Scheinkman, J. and Xing, W., Overconfidence and speculative bubbles. *J. Political Econ.*, 2003, **111**(6), 1183–1219.

Schwartz, S.L. and Ziemba, W.T., Predicting returns on the tokyo stock exchange. In *Security Market Imperfections in World Wide Equity Markets*, edited by D.B. Keim and W.T. Ziemba, pp. 492–511, 2000 (Cambridge University Press: Cambridge, UK).

Shewhart, W., The application of statistics as an aid in maintaining quality of a manufactured product. *J. Am. Stat. Assoc.*, 1925, **20**(152), 546–548.

Shiller, R., *Irrational Exuberance*. 2nd ed., 2009 (Princeton University Press: Princeton, NJ).

Shiryaev, A.N. and Zhitlukhin, M.V., Optimal stopping problems for a Brownian motion with a disorder on a finite interval. Working Paper, 2012.

Sornette, D., Critical market crashes. *Phys. Rep.*, 2003, **378**(1), 1–98.

Sornette, D., *Why Stock Markets Crash: Critical Events in Complex Financial Systems*, 2004 (Princeton University Press: Princeton, NJ).

Sornette, D. and Zhou, W.-X., The US 2000–2002 market descent: How much longer and deeper? *Quant. Finance*, 2002, **2**, 468–481.

Stiglitz, J. E. (Ed.), Symposium on bubbles. *J. Econ. Perspect.*, 1990, **4**(2), 13–18.

Stone, D. and Ziemba, W.T., Land and stock prices in Japan. *J. Econ. Persp.* 1993, **7**(3), 149–165.

Weigand, R.A. and Irons, R., The market p/e ratio, earnings trends, and stock return forecasts. *J. Portfolio Manage.*, 2007, **33**(4), 87–101.

Yan, W., Woodard, R. and Sornette, D., Detection of crashes and rebounds in major equity markets. *Int. J. Portfolio Anal. Manage.*, 2012a, **1**(1), 59–79.

Yan, W., Woodard, R. and Sornette, D., Role of diversification risk in financial bubbles. *J. Invest. Strategies*, 2012b, **1**(4), 63–83.

Yardeni, E., Feds stock market model finds overvaluation.Technical report. US Equity Research, Deutsche Morgan Grenfell, 1997.

Zhitlukhin, M., Stochastic dynamics of financial markets. PhD Thesis, The University of Manchester, 2013.

Ziemba, W.T., The chicken or the egg: Land and stock prices in Japan. *Japanese Financ. Market Res.*, edited by W.T. Ziemba, W. Bailey and Y. Hamao, pp. 45–68, 1991 (North Holland: Amsterdam).

Ziemba, W.T., *The Stochastic Programming Approach to Asset Liability and Wealth Management*, 2003 (AIMR: Charlottesville, VA).

Ziemba, W.T., *Calendar Anomalies and Arbitrage*, 2012 (World Scientific: Singapore).

Ziemba, W.T. and Schwartz, S.L., *Invest Japan*, 1991 (Probus: Chicago, IL).

Appendix: Publications of William T. Ziemba

B — Selected Books, Published and in Progress

B1 Ziemba, W. T., Vickson, R. G. (Eds.) (1975 July) *Stochastic Optimization Models in Finance*. Academic Press, p. 744 (388 pages reprinted and 356 pages new). 2nd edition with new preface, World Scientific, Singapore, 2006.

B2 Ziemba, W. T., Akatay, A., Schwartz, S. L. (1979) *Turkish Flat Weaves*. Scorpion Publications Ltd., London, p. 144.

B3 Ziemba, W. T., Schwartz, S. L., Koenigsberg, E. (Eds.) (1980 April) *Energy Policy Modeling: United States and Canadian Experiences; Vol. I: Specialized Energy Policy Models*, Martinus Nijhoff Publishing, Boston, p. 396.

B4 Ziemba, W. T., Schwartz S. L. (Eds.) (1980 May) *Energy Policy Modeling; United States and Canadian Experiences: Vol. II: Integrative Energy Policy Models*, Martinus Nijhoff Publishing, Boston, p. 378.

B5 Schaible, S., Ziemba, W. T. (Eds.) (1981 November) *Generalized Concavity in Optimization and Economics*, Academic Press, p. 780.

B6 Hausch, D. B., Ziemba, W. T. (1984) *Beat the Racetrack*. Harcourt, Brace and Jovanovich, p. 432; revised and expanded 2nd edition titled *Dr. Z's Beat the Racetrack*, William Morrow, 1987, p. 524. Both re-issued in hardback and paperback in 2018, 2019 by Echo Books.

B7 Ziemba, W. T., Hausch, D. B. (1985 November) *Betting at the Racetrack*. Dr. Z Investments, Los Angeles, p. 176; 2nd edition, Norris Strauss, New York, November 1986, p. 140.

B8 Ziemba, W. T., Brumelle, S. L., Gautier, A., Schwartz, S. L. (1986 June) *Dr. Z's 6/49 Lotto Guidebook*. Dr. Z Investments, Los Angeles, p. 124.

B9 Amershi, A., Feltham, J., Ziemba, W. T. (Eds.) (1988 July) *Economic Analysis of Information and Contracts: Essays in Honour of John E. Butterworth*. Kluwer Academic Publishers, Boston, p. 415.

B10 Ziemba, W. T., Schwartz, S. L. (1991 November) *Invest Japan: The Structure, Performance and Opportunities of Japan's Stock, Bond and Fund Markets*. Probus Publishing, Chicago, p. 596.

B11 Ziemba, W. T., Bailey, W., Hamao, Y. (Eds.) (1991 December) *Japanese Financial Market Research.* North Holland Publishers, Amsterdam, p. 616.

B12 Ziemba, W. T., Schwartz, S. L. (1992 August) *Power Japan: How and Why the Japanese Economy Works.* Probus Publishing, Chicago, p. 385.

B13 Hausch, D. B., Lo, V., Ziemba, W. T. (Eds.) (1994) *Efficiency of Racetrack Betting Markets.* Academic Press, p. 648. (Reprinted in 2008 by World Scientific with a new preface).

B14 Jarrow, R. A., Maksimovic, V., Ziemba, W. T. (Eds.) (1995 December) *Finance*, North Holland Handbook Series, p. 1165. Reprinted in Japanese, 1998, and in Chinese, 2002.

B15 Keim, D. B., Ziemba, W. T. (Eds.) (2000) *Security Market Imperfections in World Wide Equity Markets.* Cambridge University Press, p. 531. (Reprinted in Chinese, 2003).

B16 Ziemba, W. T., Mulvey, J. M. (Eds.) (1998) *Asset and Liability Management from a Global Perspective*, Cambridge University Press, p. 665, and in Chinese, 2003. [A review by Ton Vorst is in the *Journal of Finance*].

B17 Wets, R. J. B., Ziemba, W. T. (Eds.) (1999 March) *Stochastic Programming — State of the Art 1998*, (main lectures VIII International Conference on Stochastic Programming), Baltzer Science Publishers BV (Special Issue Annals of Operations Research), p. 285.

B18 Birge, J. B., Edirishinghe, N. C. P., Ziemba, W. T. (Eds.) (2001 June) *Research in Stochastic Programming* (Selected, refereed papers from the VIII International Conference on Stochastic Programming), Baltzer Science Publishers BV (Special Issue Annals of Operations Research), p. 306.

B19 Ziemba, W. T. (2003 December) *The Stochastic Programming Approach to Asset Liability and Wealth Management.* AIMR, p. 192 plus 72-page appendix. [A review by Alan King is in *Interfaces* April 2006].

B20 Wallace, S. W., Ziemba, W. T. (Eds.) (2005). *Applications of Stochastic Programming.* SIAM — Mathematical Programming Society Series on Optimization, p. 707.

B21 Zenios, S. A., Ziemba, W. T. (Eds.) (2006) *Handbook of Asset and Liability Modeling.* North Holland *Volume 1: Theory and Methodology*, pp. 1–487. *Volume 2: Applicaitons and Case Studies*, June 2007, pp. 489–1147.

B22 Ziemba, R. E. S., Ziemba, W. T. (2007) *Scenarios for Risk Management and Global Investment Strategies.* Wiley, p. 315 (November, in UK and January 2008 in US).

B23 Hausch, D. B., Ziemba, W. T. (Eds.) (2008 September) *Handbook of Sports and Lottery Markets*. North Holland Handbooks in Finance Series, p. 536.

B24 MacLean, L. C., Thorp, E. O., Ziemba, W. T. (Eds.) (2011) *The Kelly Capital Growth Criterion: Theory and Practice*. World Scientific, Singapore, p. 853 (hardback) 2012 (paperback).

B25 Bertocchi, M., Schwartz, S. L., Ziemba, W. T. (Eds.) (2010 February) *Optimizing the Aging, Retirement and Pensions Dilemma*. Wiley, p. 411; 2nd edition 2015.

B26 Ziemba, W. T. (2012) *Calendar Anomalies and Arbitrage*. World Scientific, Singapore, p. 586.

B27 Gassman, H. I., Ziemba, W. T. (Eds.) (2012) *Stochastic Programming Applications in Finance, Energy and Production*. World Scientific, Singapore, p. 518.

B28 MacLean, L. C., Ziemba, W. T. (Eds.) (2013) *Handbook of the Fundamentals of Financial Decision Making* (2 volumes). World Scientific, Singapore, p. 891.

B29 Ziemba, R. E. S., Ziemba, W. T. (2013) *Investing in the Modern Age*, (Some Wilmott columns revised and expanded, 2007–2012). World Scientific, Singapore, p. 563 (hardback and paperback).

B30 Mallarias, A. G., Ziemba, W. T. (Eds.) (2015) *Handbook of Futures Markets*. World Scientific, Singapore.

B31 Ziemba, W. T. *Collected Works* (5 volumes) to include volumes on *Portfolio Theory and Applications*, *Asset Liability Management*, and *Stochastic Programming: Theory and Applications*. World Scientific, Singapore (in preparation).

B32 Ziemba, W. T. (Ed.) (2016) *Great Investment Ideas*. World Scientific, Singapore.

B33 Ziemba, W. T. (2017) *The Adventures of a Modern Renaissance Academic in Gambling and Investment*. World Scientific, Singapore.

B34 MacLean, L. C., Ziemba, W. T. (Eds.) (2017) *Problems in the Theory of Financial Decision Making and Stochastic Optimization Models in Finance*. World Scientific, Singapore.

B35 Ziemba, W. T., Lleo, S., Zhitlukhin, M. (2017) *Stock Market Crashes: Predictable and Unpredictable and What to Do about Them*. World Scientific, Singapore.

B36 Ziemba, W. T. (2019) *Exotic Betting at the Racetrack*. World Scientific, Singapore.

B37 Ashenfelter, O., Gergaud, O., Storchmann, K., Ziemba, W. T. (Eds.) (2018) *Handbook of the Economics of Wine*. World Scientific, Singapore (2 volumes).

B38 Ziemba, W. T., MacLean, L. C. (2018) *Dr. Z's NFL Guidebook.* World Scientific, Singapore.

B39 D'Eclessia, R., Zenios, S., Ziemba, T. (2019) *Memorial Volume to Honor Marida Bertocchi.* World Scientific, Singapore.

B40 Guerard, J., Ziemba, W. T. (2020) *Handbook of Applied Investment Research.* World Scientific, Singapore.

B41 Ziemba, W. T. (2020a) *Handbook of Portfolio Theory and Practice.*

B42 Ziemba, W. T. (2020b) *Investing and Gambling in Sports and Financial Markets.*

J — Selected Published Journal Articles

J1 Ziemba, W. T. (1969) A myopic capital budgeting model. *Journal of Financial and Quantitative Analysis* IV: 305–328.

J2 Ziemba, W. T. (1970a) Computational algorithms for convex stochastic programmes with simple recourse. *Operations Research* XVIII: 414–431.

J3 Ziemba, W. T. (1970b) Stochastic programming models of dynamic planning problems. *Economic Computation and Economic Cybernetics (Studies and Research)* 3: 67–85.

J4 Ziemba, W. T. (1971a) Transforming stochastic dynamic programming problems into nonlinear programmes. *Management Science* XVIII: 450–462.

J5 Ziemba, W. T. (1971b) Duality relations, certainty equivalents and bounds for convex stochastic programmes with simple recourse. *Cahiers du Centre d'Etudes de Recherche Operationnelle* XIII: 85–97.

J6 Ziemba, W. T. (1971c) A note on economic policy under uncertainty. *Socio Economic Planning Sciences* V: 407–410.

J7 Forbes, J. D., Ziemba, W. T. (1971) Estimation of super market drawing power: An extension of location theory and practice. *Annals of Regional Science* V: 112–125.

J8 Warburton, A., Ziemba, W. T. (1971) Convex inversion. *Journal of Mathematical Analysis and Application* XXXIV: 58–66.

J9 Ziemba, W. T. (1972a) Solving nonlinear programming problems with stochastic objective functions. *Journal of Financial and Quantitative Analysis* VII: 1809–1827.

J10 Ziemba, W. T. (1972b) Note on 'optimal growth portfolios when returns are serially correlated'. *Journal of Financial and Quantitative Analysis* VII: 1995–2000.

J11 Ziemba, W. T., Parkan, C., Brooks-Hill, F. J. (1974) Calculation of investment portfolios with risk free borrowing and lending. *Management Science* XXI: 209–222.

J12 Ziemba, W. T., Butterworth, J. E. (1974) Bounds on the value of information in uncertain decision problems. *Stochastics* IV: 1–18.

J13 Ziemba, W. T. (1974) Note on the behavior of a firm subject to stochastic regulatory review. *Bell Journal of Economics and Management Sciences* 710–712.

J14 Ohlson, J. A., Ziemba, W. T. (1976) Optimal portfolio policies for an investor with a power utility function facing a log normal securities market. *Journal of Financial and Quantitative Analysis* XI: 57–71.

J15 Huang, C. C., Wehrung, D. A., Ziemba, W. T. (1976) A homogeneous distribution problem with applications to finance. *Management Science* XXIII: 297–304.

J16 Ziemba, W. T. (1977) Multiperiod consumption-investment decisions: Further comments. *American Economic Review* LXVII: 766–767.

J17 Huang, C. C., Vertinsky, I., Ziemba, W. T. (1977a) Sharp bounds on the value of perfect information. *Operations Research* XXV: 128–139.

J18 Huang, C. C., Ziemba, W. T., Ben-Tal, A. (1977b) Bounds on the expectation of a convex function of a random variable: With applications to stochastic programming. *Operations Research* XXV: 315–325.

J19 Huang, C. C., Vertinsky, I., Ziemba, W. T. (1978) On multiperiod stochastic dominance. *Journal of Financial and Quantitative Analysis* XIII: 1–13.

J20 Kira, D., Ziemba, W. T. (1980) The demand for a risky asset. *Management Science* XXVI: 1158–1165.

J21 Kallberg, J. G., Ziemba, W. T. (1979) On the robustness of the arrow-Pratt risk aversion index. *Economic Letters* II: 21–26.

J22 Hausch, D. G., Ziemba, W. T., Rubinstein, M. E. (1981) Efficiency of the market for racetrack betting. *Management Science* XXVII: 1435–1452.

J23 Kallberg, J. G., White, R., Ziemba, W. T. (1982) Short term financial planning under uncertainty. *Management Science* XXVIII: 670–682.

J24 Hausch, D. B., Ziemba, W. T. (1983) Bounds on the value of information in uncertain decision problems, II. *Stochastics* X: 181–217.

J25 Kallberg, J. G., Ziemba, W. T. (1983) Comparison of alternative utility functions in portfolio selection problems. *Management Science* XXIX: 1257–1276.

J26 Judah, S., Ziemba, W. T. (1983) Three person baccarat. *Operations Research Letters* II: 187–192.

J27 Schwartz, S. L., Fuller, D., Ziemba, W. T. (1985) Long run effects of the national energy agreements. *Energy Journal* VI: 63–77.

J28 Hausch, D. B., Ziemba, W. T. (1985) Transactions costs, entries and extent of inefficiencies in a racetrack betting model, *Management Science* XXXI: 381–394.

J29 Schaible, S., Ziemba, W. T. (1986) On the concavity of the sum of lognormals in lognormal approximation in portfolio theory. *Zeitschriff fur Operations Research* XXIX: 161–186.

J30 Gassmann, H., Ziemba, W. T. (1986) A tight upper bound for the expectation of a convex function of a multivariate random variable. *Mathematical Programming Study, Recent Advances in Stochastic Programming* XXVII: 39–53.

J31 Kusy, M. I., Ziemba, W. T. (1986) A bank asset and liability management model. *Operations Research* XXXIV: 356–376.

J32 Sick G., Ziemba, W. T. (1986) Review of 'Arbitrage theory: Introductory lectures on arbitrage based financial asset pricing' by J. E. M. Wilhelm. *European Journal of Operations Research* XXVII: 255–256.

J33 Ziemba, W. T., Canfield, B., Fauman, B. (1987) Efficient market adjustment of odds prices to reflect track biases. *Management Science* XXXIII: 1428–1439.

J34 Ziemba, W. T. (1988) Synopsis of 'playing the turn of the year effect with index futures'. *OR/MS Today* XV: 37–38.

J35 Clark, R., Ziemba, W. T. (1988) Playing the turn-of-the-year effect with index futures. *Operations Research* XXXV: 799–813.

J36 Thaler, R. H., Ziemba, W. T. (1988) Parimutuel betting markets: Racetracks and lotteries. *Journal of Economic Perspectives* II: 161–174.

J37 Ziemba, W. T. (1988) Discussion of 'The buying and selling behavior of individual investors at the turn of the year' by Jay R. Ritter. *Journal of Finance* XLIII: 717–719.

J38 Li, Y., Ziemba, W. T. (1989) Characterizations of optimal portfolios by univariate and multivariate risk aversion. *Management Science* XXXV: 259–269.

J39 Hausch, D. B., Ziemba, W. T. (1990a) Arbitrage strategies for cross track betting on major horseraces. *Journal of Business* LXIII: 61–78.

J40 Hausch, D. B., Ziemba, W. T. (1990b May-June) Locks in racetrack minus pools. *Interfaces* 41–48.

J41 Li, Y., Ziemba, W. T. (1990) Rules for diversification by all risk averters. *Journal of Economics and Business* (Fall special issue): 165–170.

J42 Ziemba, W. T., Schwartz, S. L. (1991) The growth in the Japanese stock market, 1949–1990 and prospects for the future. *Managerial and Decision Economics* 12: 183–195.

J43 Ziemba, W. T (1991) Fundamental factors in Japanese stock returns, 1979 to 1989. *Investing* (Winter): 73–79.

J44 MacLean, L. C., Ziemba, W. T (1991) Growth-security profiles in capital accumulation under risk. *Annals of Operations Research*, 31: 501–510.

J45 Ziemba, W. T. (1991) Japanese security market regularities: Monthly, turn of the month and year, holiday and golden week effects. *Japan and the World Economy* 3: 119–146.

J46 Edirishinghe, N. C. P., Ziemba, W. T. (1992) Bounds for stochastic programmes with recourse. *Operations Research* 40: 660–677.

J47 Markowitz, H. M., Schaible, S., Ziemba, W. T. (1992) An algorithm for portfolio selection in a lognormal market. *International Journal of Financial Analysis* 1(2): 109–113.

J48 MacLean, L. C., Ziemba, W. T., Blazenko, G. (1992). Growth versus security in dynamic investment analysis. *Management Science* 38: 1562–1585.

J49 Ziemba, W. T. (1993) Comment on 'why a weekend effect?' *Journal of Portfolio Management* (Winter): 93–99.

J50 Chopra, V., Ziemba, W. T. (1993) The effect of errors in mean and co-variance estimates on optimal portfolio choice. *Journal of Portfolio Management* (Winter): 6–11.

J51 Stone, D., Ziemba, W. T. (1993) Land and stock prices in Japan. *Journal of Economic Perspectives* (Summer): 149–165.

J52 Ziemba, W. T. (1994) Worldwide security market regularities. *European Journal of Operational Research* 74: 198–229.

J53 Li, Y., Ziemba, W. T. (1993) Univariate and multivariate measures of risk aversion and risk premiums. *Financial Engineering* (Special issue of Annals of Operations Research), 45: 265–296.

J54 Edirishinghe, N. C. P., Ziemba, W. T (1994) Bounds for two-stage stochastic programs with fixed recourse. *Mathematics of Operations Research* 19: 292–313.

J55 Cariño, D. *et al.*, Ziemba, W. T. (1994 January–February) The Russell-Yasuda Kasai model: An asset/liability model for a Japanese insurance company using multistage stochastic programming. *Interfaces* (Edelman Prize issue): 29–49. (A story about this paper is in the March 31, 1991 issue of the *New York Times*.)

J56 Ziemba, W. T. (1994) Investing in the turn-of-the-year effect in US futures markets. *Interfaces* 24(3): 46–61.

J57 Hensel, C. R., Ziemba, W. T. (1995 March/April) US small and large capitalized stocks, bonds and cash returns during democratic and republican administrations, 1928–1993. *Financial Analysts Journal* 51(2): 61–69.

J58 Hensel, C. R., Ziemba, W. T. (1995) The January barometer: Swiss, European and global results. *Finanzmarket and Portfolio Management* 9(2): 187–196.

J59 Shaw, J., Thorp, E. O., Ziemba, W. T. (1995) Convergence to efficiency of the Nikkei Put Warrant market of 1989–1990. *Applied Mathematical Finance* 2: 243–271.

J60 Hensel, C. R., Sick, G., Ziemba, W. T. (1996) Investment results from exploiting turn-of-the month-effects. *The Journal of Portfolio Management* (Spring): 17–23. (A story about this paper is in the November 7, the *Wall Street Journal*.)

J61 Cariño, D., Ziemba, W. T. (1998 July/August) Formulation of the Russell-Yasuda Kasai financial planning model. *Operations Research* 46(4): 433–449.

J62 Cariño, D., Myers, D., Ziemba, W. T. (1998 July/August) Concepts, technical issues and uses of the Russell-Yasuda Kasai financial planning model. *Operations Research* 46(4): 450462.

J63 MacLean, L. C., W. T. Ziemba (1999) Growth versus security tradeoffs in dynamic investment analysis. In R. J.-B. Wets, W. T. Ziemba (Eds.), *Stochastic Programming: State of the Art 1998, Annals of Operations.* Research Balzer Science Publishers, pp. 193–226.

J64 Zhao, Y., Ziemba, W. T. (2000) A dynamic asset allocation model with downside risk control. *The Journal of Risk* 3(Fall): 91–113.

J65 Zhao, Y., Ziemba, W. T. (2001) A stochastic programming model using an endogeneously determined worst case risk measure in a risk-return framework for dynamic asset allocation. *Mathematical Programming, Series B* 89(2): 293–309.

J66 Zhao, Y., Haussmann, U., Ziemba, W. T. (2003 October) A dynamic investment model with a minimum attainable wealth requirement. *Mathematical Finance* 13: 481–501.

J67 Board, J. L. C., Sutcliffe, C. M. S., Ziemba, W. T. (2003 March–April) Applying operations research techniques to financial markets. *Interfaces* 32(2): 12–34.

J68 MacLean, L. C., Sanegre, R., Zhao, Y., Ziemba, W. T. (2004) Capital growth with security. *Journal of Economic Dynamics and Control* 28(4): 937–954.

J69 Rudolf, M., Ziemba, W. T. (2004) Intertemporal asset-liability management. *Journal of Economic Dynamics and Control* 28(4): 975–990.

J70 Lane, D., Ziemba, W. T. (2004) Jai-Alai Hedging strategies. *European Journal of Finance* 353–369.

J71 Douglass, J., Wu, O., Ziemba, W. T. (2004) Stock ownership decisions in defined contribution pension plans. *Journal of Portfolio Management* (Summer): 92–100.

J72 Ziemba, W. T. (2005) The symmetric downside risk Sharpe ratio and the evaluation of great investors and speculators. *Journal of Portfolio Management* (Fall): 108–122.

J73 MacLean, L., Ziemba, W. T., Li, Y. (2005) Time to wealth goals in capital accumulation and the optimal trade-off of growth versus security. *Quantitative Finance* 5(4): 343–357.

J74 Koivu, M., Pennanen, T., Ziemba, W. T. (2005) Co-integration analysis of the FED model. *Finance Research Letters* 2: 248–259.

J75 MacLean, L. C., Zhao, Y., Ziemba, W. T. (2006) Dynamic portfolio selection with process control. *Journal of Banking and Finance* 30(2): 317–339.

J76 Hausch, D. B., Bain, R., Ziemba, W. T. (2006) An application of expert information to win betting on the Kentucky Derby, 1981–2001. *European Journal of Finance* 12: 283–301. (Featured on BCTV, May 1999 and in *Louisville Times*, June 2001).

J77 Zhao, Y., Ziemba, W. T. (2007) On Leland's option pricing and hedging strategy with transactions costs. *Finance Research Letters* 4: 49–58.

J78 Kouwenberg, R., Ziemba, W. T. (2007) Incentives and risk taking in hedge funds. *Journal of Banking and Finance* 31: 3291–3310.

J79 MacLean, L. C., Foster, M., Ziemba, W. T. (2007) Empirical Bayes estimation with dynamic portfolio models. *Journal of Banking and Finance* 31: 3503–3523.

J80 Kallio, M., Ziemba, W. T. (2007) Using Tucker's theorem of the alternative to simplify, review and expand discrete arbitrage theory. *Journal of Banking and Finance* 31: 2281–2302.

J81 Rendon, J., Ziemba, W. T. (2007) Is the January effect still alive in the futures markets? *Finanzmarket and Portfolio Management* 21: 381–396.

J82 Zhao, Y., Ziemba, W. T. (2007) Comments on and corrigendum to "Hedging errors with Leland's option model in the presence of transaction costs" [*Finance Research Letters* 4(2007): 49–58] *Finance Research Letters* 4: 196–199.

J83 Zhao, Y., Ziemba, W. T. (2008) Calculating risk neutral probabilities and optimal portfolio policy in a dynamic investment model with downside risk control. *European Journal of Operational Research* 185: 1525–1540.

J84 Geyer, A., Ziemba, W. T. (2008) The Innovest Austrian pension fund planning model InnoALM. *Operations Research* 56(4): 797–810.

J85 Berge, K., Consigli, G., Ziemba, W. T. (2008) The predictive ability of the bond stock earnings yield differential. *Journal of Portfolio Management* (Spring): 63–80.

J86 Rodriguez, J., Ziemba, W. T. (2008) Duality relations of hedge fund managers' incentive fee optimization problems. *Mathematical Programming* 113: 95–131.

J87 Ziemba, W. T. (2008 October) Use of stochastic and mathematical programming in portfolio theory and practice: Keynote address. *Annals of Operations Research* 166: 5–22.

J88 Consigli, G., MacLean, L. C., Zhao, Y., Ziemba, W. T. (2009) The bond-stock yield differential as a risk indicator in financial markets. *Journal of Risk* 11(3): 3–24.

J89 Dzhabarov, C., Ziemba, W. T. (2010) Do seasonal anomalies still work? *Journal of Portfolio Management* 36(3): 93–104.

J90 MacLean, L. C., Thorp, E. O., Ziemba, W. T. (2010) Long term capital growth: The good and bad properties of the Kelly and fractional Kelly capital growth criterion. *Quantitative Finance* 681–687.

J91 MacLean, L. C., Consigli, G., Zhao, Y., Ziemba, W. T. (2011) Risk indicators in equity markets. *Mathematical Methods in Economics and Finance* 3(2): 101–118.

J92 MacLean, L. C., Zhao, Y., Ziemba, W. T. (2011) Intertemporal mean variance efficiency with Markovian state price density. *Journal of Banking and Finance* 27.

J93 MacLean, L. C., Thorp, E. O., Zhao, Y., Ziemba, W. T. (2011) How does the Fortune's Formula-Kelly capital growth model perform? *Journal of Portfolio Management* 37(4): 96–111.

J94 Ziemba, W. T. (2011) Investing in the turn-of-the-year effect. *Finanzmarket und Portfolio Management* 25(4): 455–472.

J95 MacLean, L. C., Zhao, Y., Ziemba, W. T. (2011) Mean-variance versus expected utility in dynacmic investment analysis. *Computational Management Science* 8(1): 3–22.

J96 Lleo, S., Ziemba, W. T. (2012) Stock market crashes in 2007–2009: Were we able to predict them? *Quantitative Finance* 12(8): 1161–1187.

J97 Gergaud, O., Ziemba, W. T. (2012) Great investors: Their methods, results and evaluation. *Journal of Portfolio Management* 28(4): 128–147.

J98 MacLean, L. C., Zhao, Y., Ziemba, W. T. (2013) Endogenous volatilities for hedging and pricing option with transaction costs. *Quantitative Finance* 13(5): 699–713.

J99 Ziemba, W. T. (2013) Is the 60–40 stock-bond pension fund rule wise? *Journal of Portfolio Management* 39(2): 63–72.

J100 MacLean, L. C., Zhao, Y., Ziemba, W. T. (2012) Currency returns, market regimes and behavorial biases. *Annals of Finance* 9(2): 249–269.

J101 Ziemba, W. T. (2013) The case for convex risk measures. *Quantitative Finance Letters* 1: 47–54.

J102 Shiryaev, A. N., Zhitlukhin, M. V., Ziemba, W. T. (2014) When to sell Apple and the NASDAQ? Trading bubbles with a stochastic disorder model. *Journal of Portfolio Management* (Winter): 1–10.

J103 Shiryaev, A. N., Zhitukhin, M. V., Ziemba, W. T. (2015) Land and stock bubbles, crashes, entry and exit strategies in Japan,circa 1990 and in 2013. *Quantitative Finance* 30.

J104 Lleo, S., Ziemba, W. T. (2015) Some historical perspectives on the bond-stock yield model for crash prediction around the world. *International Journal of Forecasting* 31: 399–425.

J105 Lleo, S., Ziemba, W. T. (2014) How to lose money in financial markets: Examples from the recent financial crisis. *Alternative Investment Analyst Review* 3(3): 22–35.

J106 Ziemba, W. T. (2015) Response to Paul A Samuelson letters and papers on the Kelly capital growth investment strategy. *Journal of Portfolio Management* 41(1): 153–167.

J107 MacLean, L. C., Zhao, Y., Ziemba, W. T. (2016) Optimal capital growth with convex shortfall penalties. *Quantitative Finance* 16(1): 101–117.

J108 Ziemba, W. T. (2016) Understanding and using the Kelly capital growth. *Alternative Investment Analyst Review* 44–55.

J109 Zhitlukhin, M. V., Ziemba, W. T (2016) Exit strategies in bubble-like models using a change point model. *Quantitative Finance Letters* 4(1): 47–52.

J110 Swetye, J., Ziemba, W. T (2016) Using Zweig's monetary and momentum models in the modern era. *Quantitative Finance Letters* 4(1): 35–39.

J111 Ziemba, W. T (2016a) Non-predictable stock market declines. *Quantitative Finance Letters* 4(1): 5359.

J112 Lleo, S., Ziemba, W. T (2016a) The BSEYD crash prediction model: The basic idea and early applications. *Quantitative Finance Letters* 4(1): 19–25.

J113 Lleo, S., Ziemba, W. T (2016b) The BSEYD crash prediction model: Additional applications and other models for stock market crash prediction. *Quantitative Finance Letters* 4(1): 26–34.

J114 Lleo, S., Ziemba, W. T. (2017) Does the bond stock earnings yield difference model predict equity market corrections better and high PE models? *Financial Markets, Institutions and Instruments* 26(2): 61–123.

J115 Ziemba, W. T. (2016b) An approach to financial planning of retirement pensions with scenario dependent correlation matrices and convex risk measures. *Journal of Retirement* (Summer): 1–13.

J116 Lleo, S., Zhitlukhin, M. V., Ziemba, W. T. (2016) Introduction to bubbles and crashes. *Quantitative Finance Letters* 1–3.

J117 Lleo, S., Ziemba, W. T. (2018) Predicting stock market crashes in China. *Journal of Portfolio Management* 44(5): 25–135.

J118 Edirisinghe, N. C. P., Ziemba, W. T. (2018) A boundary-point LP method and its application to dense linear programs. *International Journal of Mathematics in Operational Research* 1–27.

J119 Dzhabarov, C., Ziegler, A., Ziemba, W. T. (2018) Sell in May: Worldwide evidence. *Quantitative Finance* 18(2): 171–181.

J120 Lleo, S., Ziemba, W. T. (2019a) Can Warren Buffett also predict equity market downturns? *European Journal of Finance* 25(4): 369–393.

J121 Lleo, S., Ziemba, W. T. (2019b) Predicting Chinese stock market crashes. *Financial Markets, Institutions and Instruments*.

J122 MacLean, L. C., Ziemba, W. T., Korgan, A. (2018 November) The expected utility of performance: Dominant betting seasons in baseball. *Wilmott* 40–43.

J123 MacLean, L. C., Ziemba, W. T. (2019 January) Efficiency of NFL betting markets. *Wilmott* 34–38.

J124 Moffitt, S., Ziemba, W. T. (2019a March) A risk arbitrage strategy for lotteries. *Wilmott* 52–62.

J125 Moffitt, S., Ziemba, W. T. (2019b May) Does it pay to buy the pot in the Canadian 6/49 lotto? Implications for lottery design. *Wilmott* 43–52.

K — Selected Articles in Books

K1 MacLean, L. C., Zhao, Y., Ziemba, W. T. (2003) A process control approach to investment risk. *IEEE International Conference on Computational Intelligence for Financial Engineering*, pp. 265–270.

K2 MacLean, L. C., Ziemba, W. T. (2006) Capital growth theory and practice. In *Handbook of Asset and Liability Modeling*, Volume 1: *Theory and Methodology*, S. A. Zenios, W. T. Ziemba (Eds.), *Handbooks in Finance.* North Holland, pp. 429–473.

K3 Ziemba, W. T. (2007) The Russell Yasuda, InnoALM and related models for pensions, insurance companies and high net worth individuals. In *Handbook of Asset and Liability Modeling*, Volume 2: *Applications and Case Studies*, S. A. Zenios, W. T. Ziemba (Eds.), *Handbooks in Finance.* North Holland, pp. 861–962.

K4 Schwartz, S. L., Ziemba, W. T. (2007) ALM in social security, in *Handbook of Asset and Liability Modeling*, Volume 2: *Applications and Case Studies*, S. A. Zenios, W. T. Ziemba (Eds.), *Handbooks in Finance.* North Holland, pp. 1069–1117.

K5 MacLean, L., Zhao, Y., Consigli, G., Ziemba, W. T. (2007). Estimating parameters in a pricing model with state dependent shocks. In P. M. Paradolos, C. Zopounidis (Eds.), *Handbook of Financial Engineering.* Springer, pp. 231–245.

K6 Purnanandam, A., Warachka, M., Zhao, Y., Ziemba, W. T. (2007) Incorporating diversification into risk management. In G. N. Gregoriou (Ed.), *Advances in Risk Management.* Palgrave, p. 2246.

K7 Tompkins, R. G., Ziemba, W. T., Hodges, S. H. (2008) The favorite-longshot bias in S&P500 futures options: The return to bets and the cost of insurance. In *Handbook of Sports and Lottery Markets*, D. B. Hausch, W. T. Ziemba (Eds.), *Handbooks in Finance.* North Holland, pp. 161–180.

K8 Ziemba, W. T. (2008) Efficiency of racetrack betting markets. In *Handbook of Sports and Lottery Markets*, D. B. Hausch, W. T. Ziemba (Eds.), *Handbooks in Finance.* North Holland, pp. 183–221.

K9 Lane, D., Ziemba, W. T. (2008) Arbitrage in team Jai Alai. In *Handbook of Sports and Lottery Markets*, D. B. Hausch, W. T. Ziemba (Eds.), *Handbooks in Finance.* North Holland, pp. 253–271.

K10 Gramm, M., Ziemba, W. T. (2008) The dosage breeding theory for horseracing predictions. In *Handbook of Sports and Lottery Markets*,

D. B. Hausch, W. T. Ziemba (Eds.), *Handbooks in Finance.* North Holland, pp. 307–332.

K11 Ziemba, W. T. (2010) Ideas in asset liability management in the tradition of H. M. Markowitz. In J. Guerard (Ed.), *Essays in Honor of H. M. Markowitz*. Springer, pp. 213–258.

K12 MacLean, L. C., Ziemba, W. T. (2010) The Kelly strategy. In B. Cont (Ed.), *Encyclopedia of Quantitative Finance.* p. 5.

K13 MacLean, L. C., Thorp, E. O., Zhao, Y., Ziemba, W. T. (2010a) Medium term simulations of Kelly and fractional Kelly and proportional betting strategies. In L. C. MacLean, E. O. Thorp, W. T. Ziemba (Eds.), *The Kelly Capital Growth Criterion: Theory and Practice*. World Scientific, pp. 543–561.

K14 MacLean, L. C., Thorp, E. O., Ziemba, W. T. (2010b) Good and bad properties of the Kelly criterion. In L. C. MacLean, E. O. Thorp, W. T. Ziemba (Eds.), *The Kelly Capital Growth Criterion: Theory and Practice*. World Scientific, pp. 563–572.

K15 Ziemba, W. T., Vickson, R. (2010) Models of optimal capital accumulation and portfolio selection. In L. C. MacLean, E. O. Thorp, W. T. Ziemba (Eds.), *The Kelly Capital Growth Criterion: Theory and Practice*. World Scientific, pp. 473–485 (Modified from Ziemba, W. T., Vickson, R. (2006)).

K16 Ziemba, W. T. (2010) Asset-liability management. In R. Cont (Ed.), *Handbook of Quantitative Finance*. Wiley, p. 20.

K17 Board, J. L., Sutcliffe, C. M. S., Ziemba, W. T. (2010a) Portfolio theory mean-variance. In S. I. Gass (Ed.) *Encyclopedia of Operations Research and Management Science* (3rd edn.). Academic Publishers, p. 12.

K18 Board, J. L., Sutcliffe, C. M. S., Ziemba, W. T. (2010b) Financial markets. In S. I. Gass (Ed.), *Encyclopedia of Operations Research and Management Science* (3rd edn.). Academic Publishers, p. 18.

K19 Ziemba, W. T., MacLean, L. C. (2011) Using the Kelly criterion for investment. In M. I. Bertocchi, G. Consigli, M. A. H. Dempster (Eds.), *Stochastic Optimization Methods in Finance and Energy.* Springer, pp. 3–20.

K20 MacLean, L. C., Zhao, Y., Ziemba, W. T. (2011) Growth-security models and stochastic dominance in G. Infanger (Ed.), *Stochastic Programming: The State of the Art in Honor of George B. Dantzig.* Springer, pp. 213–258.

K21 Ziemba, W. T. (2012) Stochastic programming and optimization in horserace betting in Gassman. In H. I. Gassmann, W. T. Ziemba (Eds.),

Stochastic Programming Applications in Finance, Energy and Production. World Scientific, pp. 221–256.

K22 MacLean, L. C., Ziemba, W. T. (2013) The Kelly criterion with games of chance. In L. Vaughn Williams, D. S. Siegal (Eds.), *Oxford Handbook of Economics of Gambling.* Oxford University Press, pp. 402–427.

K23 Ziemba, W. T. (2013) Portfolio optimization. In A. Bell, C. Brooks, M. Protopczuk (Eds.), *Handbook of Research Methods and Applications in Empirical Finance.* Edward Elgar, pp. 45–72.

K24 Ziemba, W. T. (2015) Portfolio optimization: Theory and practice. In K. Zopoundis (Ed.), *Quantitative Financial Risk Management: Theory and Practice*, The Frank Fabozzi Series. Wiley, p. 57.

K25 Ziegler, A., Ziemba, W. T. (2015) Returns from investing in S&P500 futures options, 19852010. In A. G. Mallarias, W. T. Ziemba (Eds.), *Handbook of Futures Markets.* World Scientific, p. 643688.

K26 Lleo, S., Ziemba, W. T. (2015a) The Swiss black swan bad scenario: Is Switzerland another casualty of the eurozone crisis? In J. Guerard (Ed.), *Portfolio Construction, Measurement and Efficiency: Essays in Honor of Jack Treynor.* Springer, pp. 389–420.

K27 Lleo, S., Ziemba, W. T. (2015b) How to lose money in derivatives: Examples from hedge funds and bank trading departments. In A. Malliaris, W. T. Ziemba (Eds.), *Handbook of Futures Markets.* World Scientific, pp. 689–750.

P — Working Papers

P1 MacLean, L. C., Zhao, Y., Ziemba, W. T. Intertemporal mean variance efficiency with Markovian state price density. p. 27.

P2 Ziemba, W. T. What operations research can contribute to your personal financial situation including your retirement. p. 22.

P3 Ghosh, S., Bhalla, G., Ziemba, W. T. The January Barometer, 1926–2005, Technical Report, Sauder School of Business. p. 22.

P4 Berge, K., Ziemba, W. T. The predictive ability of the bond and stock earnings yield differential in US and foreign markets, 1970–2005. Working Paper. p. 40.

P5 Consigli, G., MacLean, L. C., Zhao, Y., Ziemba, W. T. Speculative bubbles: Asset prices with yield dependent market corrections. p. 20.

P6 Lleo, S., Ziemba, W. T. Optimality of rogue traders. p. 20.

P7 Gramm, M., Ziemba, W. T. Market efficiency of America's triple crown races.

P8 Kim, W. C., Lee, Y., Ziemba, W. T. When is 1/N better than the optimal mean variance portfolio? p. 30.

P9 Lleo, S., Markowitz, H., Ziemba, W. T. Is 60–40 on the efficient frontier?

P10 MacLean, L. C., Ziemba, W. T. Measuring batting impact in baseball.

Index

Printed in the USA
CPSIA information can be obtained
at www.ICGtesting.com
LVHW010415130724
785272LV00002B/26